MARKETING RESEARCH

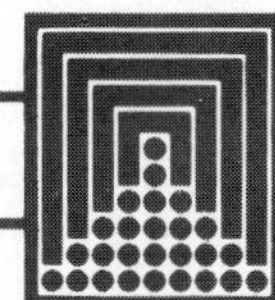

A. PARASURAMAN
Texas A & M University

ADDISON-WESLEY PUBLISHING COMPANY
Reading, Massachusetts • Menlo Park, California
Don Mills, Ontario • Wokingham, England • Amsterdam
Sydney • Singapore • Tokyo • Mexico City • Bogotá
Santiago • San Juan

To my wife Ranga, sons Rohith and Vishnu, and daughter Roopa

Sponsoring Editors: Frank J. Burns; Cindy M. Johnson
Project Editor: Mary Clare McEwing
Packaging Service: Barbara Gracia, Woodstock Publishers' Services
Text Designer: Geri Davis, Quadrata, Inc.
Cover Designer: Marshall Henrichs
Illustrator: Bob Gallison, Textbook Art Associates
Manufacturing Supervisor: Hugh Crawford

Library of Congress Cataloging in Publication Data

Parasuraman, A.
Marketing research.

Includes index.
1. Marketing research. I. Title.
HF5415.2.P37 1986 658.8'3 85-1354
ISBN 0-201-06051-5

Copyright © 1986 by Addison-Wesley Publishing Company, Inc. All rights reserved. No part of this publication may be reproduced, stored in a retrieval system, or transmitted, in any form or by any means, electronic, mechanical, photocopying, recording, or otherwise, without the prior written permission of the publisher. Printed in the United States of America. Published simultaneously in Canada.

ABCDEFGHIJ-DO-898765

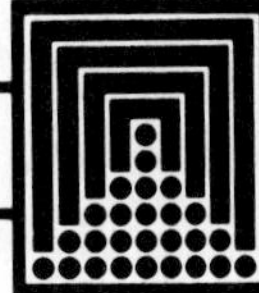

Preface

Studying marketing research can be an enlightening, interesting, and rewarding experience, contrary to what many students believe. The content and the format of *Marketing Research* are designed to aid in offering such an experience, especially to the typical student who approaches the subject apprehensively and reluctantly. This book discusses the various marketing research terms, tools, and concepts in an understandable, lively fashion by using numerous examples in every chapter. A basic objective underlying the entire book is a commitment to presenting a clear and balanced view of the potential applications and limitations of marketing research.

Audience

This book is intended for students who are taking their first course in marketing research. The breadth and the depth of topics included in the book are carefully chosen to benefit those students who will primarily be potential research users as well as those who wish to consider marketing research as a career. To cater to this dual audience, the book stresses the importance of effective communication between research users and researchers and highlights their respective roles and responsibilities at various stages of a research project.

Content and organization

The book contains twenty chapters, organized into seven parts. Part One, consisting of two chapters, discusses the nature and scope of marketing research, the role that it plays in an organization's decision-making activity, and the various parties involved in conducting marketing research. Part Two, also consisting of two chapters, offers an overview of the various research project stages, the interrelationships among the stages, and the basic research approaches and designs available for conducting marketing research.

Part Three contains five chapters. These chapters describe different types of data and discuss alternative methods for obtaining data. Part Four is made up of two chapters that focus on designing data collection forms and instruments.

Four chapters make up Part Five. The first three chapters cover sampling techniques and issues germane to generalizing results obtained from a sample. The fourth chapter discusses sampling and nonsampling errors that enter the data collection process.

Part Six consists of four chapters and deals with data analysis. The first chapter focuses on preparing the raw data for analysis, conducting certain preliminary analyses, and getting a feeling for the types of additional analyses that may be appropriate. The last three chapters in this part discuss a variety of specific analysis techniques.

Part Seven, containing the final chapter of the book, deals with communicating research findings to decision makers. It offers a number of guidelines for preparing written reports and making oral presentations that succinctly describe a research project and effectively convey its findings to the target audience.

Two valuable sources of feedback influenced the content and the organization of this book as a whole, as well as those of each chapter. The first was an extensive mail survey conducted by Addison-Wesley in early 1983 to ascertain the needs and the concerns of college faculty who teach marketing research. The responses of more than three hundred professors who participated in the survey provided a wealth of useful advice about what topics and features to include in the book, how much emphasis to place on them, and how best to present them. I sincerely thank those who participated in the survey. Their collective responses opened my eyes to important issues and ideas from which I benefited a great deal.

As the second source of feedback, the following individuals meticulously reviewed and critiqued parts or all of the book at various stages of its development: O. Ahtola, University of Denver; William O. Bearden, University of South Carolina; James D. Culley, DuPont Company; Raymond P. Fisk, Oklahoma State University; Peter J. Gordon, Southeastern Missouri State University; Glen R. Jarboe, University of Texas at Arlington; Robert E. Krapfel, Jr., University of Maryland; Susan M. Petroshius, Bowling Green State University; A. Coskun Samli, Virginia Polytechnic Institute and State University; William J. Sauer, University of Pittsburgh; Alan G. Sawyer, University of Florida; Ganesan Visvabharathy, Northern Illinois University. I am very grateful to these reviewers for their constructive criticisms, insightful suggestions, and words of encouragement.

Special features

The book has a number of distinct characteristics that should appeal to instructors and students alike.

1. Each of the seven parts in the book begins with an item titled "From the Manager's Desk." This item is a brief essay written by a practitioner on a key

topic germane to the part's content. The viewpoints expressed in each essay should kindle students' interest and could serve as a basis for class discussion.

2. Each part concludes with one or more cases focusing on the facets of marketing research covered in the part. The book includes 23 cases (most of them built around true scenarios) that cover a variety of products, services, and situations.
3. Appendix A at the end of the book contains a real-life data set derived from consumer panel data provided by NPD Research, Inc., of New York. This appendix provides a detailed description of the data set (including labels for and definitions of the variables included) and contains 25 student exercises grouped according to the analysis chapters to which they relate. The data set contains cross-sectional as well as longitudinal data, and it includes variables reflecting metric as well as nonmetric measurement levels. Yet the data set is quite concise, consisting of just 200 70-column records. Instructors can therefore transfer it easily to mainframe or microcomputer memory, and they can use it to run a variety of computer-assisted exercises with the aid of standard analysis packages such as SPSS or SAS.
4. The book provides extensive coverage of the relatively "soft" marketing research procedures that are frequently used in practice but are treated only superficially in many textbooks. For example, this book has a separate chapter on qualitative research (Chapter 7) and one on nonprobability sampling (Chapter 14).
5. Chapter 2 covers, in detail, three topics—namely, research suppliers, marketing research ethics, and careers in marketing research—that are typically covered cursorily or ignored completely in many textbooks.
6. Every chapter in the book has numerous, carefully chosen examples that are well integrated with the textual material. Every key concept, principle, or technique is illustrated with one or more examples.
7. The book has a readable and accessible writing style. The key ideas in each chapter are logically developed and organized to enable students to grasp them clearly and quickly. Charts, diagrams, and other graphical illustrations are used liberally to supplement the textual discussion.
8. The book offers useful frameworks and step-by-step approaches for understanding and applying effectively the more technical aspects of marketing research (e.g., the advanced probability-sampling techniques covered in Chapter 13 and the hypothesis-testing procedures covered in Chapter 17).
9. The questions at the end of chapters discussing some form of data manipulation (e.g., Chapters 12 and 18) include a number of problems that require students to apply the procedures or techniques discussed.
10. The book includes a comprehensive glossary containing definitions of over three hundred key terms.

Flexibility and support for instructors

The content and the organization of this book are designed to offer maximum flexibility for instructors in terms of the teaching approaches they want to use and the relative emphases they wish to place on different topics. The simple writing style and the liberal use of examples should minimize the amount of class time necessary to merely clarify concepts covered in the book. Instructors will therefore have more time for further developing key topics they wish to emphasize and for experiential activities such as case discussions, computer-assisted exercises, and student projects. Suggestions for experiential activities like these, along with complete solutions to the cases, problems, and computer-assisted exercises included in this book, are available in a comprehensive instructor's manual. The instructor's manual also has an objective-test bank and over one hundred transparency masters.

Instructors who wish to place more emphasis on student projects and less on the textual material itself can do so by omitting some or all sections of certain chapters. For example, instructors who do not want to cover experimentation in detail can omit Chapters 8 and 9 (students can still gain insights about the basic ideas underlying experimentation from the material covered in Chapter 4). Similarly, in the area of data analysis, instructors who do not want to go much beyond tabulation procedures and computation of summary statistics can cover Chapter 16 in detail but skip some or all of Chapters 17, 18, and 19. In short, while this book covers a wide range of topics, its content and organization are flexible enough to help instructors choose the breadth and depth of topical coverage they desire.

Acknowledgments

In addition to the survey respondents and reviewers mentioned earlier, a number of other individuals and organizations contributed significantly to the development of this textbook. My sincere appreciation goes to the authors of the "From the Manager's Desk" essays and to the numerous organizations and executives who generously provided material for the cases, exercises, and illustrations in this book. I also thank my graduate assistants—in particular, Lou Lachter, Donna Legg, and Deborah Wright—who successfully tackled the many chores associated with preparing a textbook manuscript. The secretarial staff at Texas A&M's marketing department did a superb job of typing the manuscript and revising it several times; I am especially grateful to Judy Smithwick, Ann Stuenkel, Shelly Yates, and Margaret Young for their ready cooperation and high-quality work. I owe a sincere debt of gratitude to Cindy Johnson and Frank Burns, my sponsoring editors at Addison-Wesley, for their inspiring ideas and continuous support. Several individuals whose expert assistance was crucial in transforming my manuscript into this textbook include Carol Beal, my copyeditor, Geri Davis of Quadrata, Inc., Barbara Gracia of Woodstock Publishers' Services, and Mary Clare McEwing of Addison-Wesley. Finally, words alone are insufficient to thank my wife and children for their generous understanding and support throughout this project.

A. P.
College Station, Texas

Contents

PART THREE Data Collection Procedures 161

5 Secondary Data 165

6 Overview of Primary-Data Collection Methods 202

7 Qualitative Research 240

PART ONE

INTRODUCTION

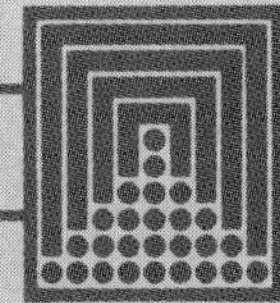

FROM THE MANAGER'S DESK

LEONARD M. FULD is founder and president of Information Data Search, Inc., a Cambridge-based research company pioneering the field of specialized competitor information. Information Data Search has conducted research in most major industries, including electronics, banking, insurance, building materials, and consumer products. Information Data Search's clients include many top industry performers, as well as emerging companies and stable corporations with new products to introduce.

Mr. Fuld has been performing corporate research for almost a decade. He has designed and perfected a series of innovative intelligence-gathering techniques that form the basis for his company. Mr. Fuld presents his methods in a series of seminars, given each year, entitled "Competitor Intelligence: How to Get It—How to Use It." These seminars are well attended by executives of *Fortune 500* and other companies. Mr. Fuld has written a large part of the original material in the field of competitor information. In addition, he is editor of a quarterly newsletter, "Intelligence Update." He was a contributing author to *Business Competitor Intelligence*, a business text published by Ronald Press. In addition, he has authored *Competitor Intelligence: How to Get It—How to Use It*. This text was released in late 1984 and was published by John Wiley & Sons.

Mr. Fuld has appeared on the NBC "Today Show" and CBS radio's "Newsbreak" program. His firm and his methods have been cited in the *Harvard Business Review*, *Fortune*, *Venture Magazine*, *USA Today*, AP, UPI, the *Christian Science Monitor*, and numerous other publications.

Mr. Fuld obtained his undergraduate degree from Yeshiva University, and he attended Boston University for his M.S. in communications.

QUESTION: In your opinion, what impact will the rapid advances in computer and information-processing technology have on the field of marketing research during the next five to ten years?

RESPONSE: Before I offer my views of the benefits and pitfalls of this new technology, let me first say that in spite of all the advances in high tech, basic marketing concepts will not change. I am thinking particularly of marketing's four pillars: product, price, promotion, and place. Technology may allow you to use the four *P*'s more rapidly and more accurately, but it will not eliminate them.

Despite my opening paragraph, I am truly excited about the current technological leaps industry and, in turn, market research are taking. The following list describes some of the ways high technology will probably affect the field of market research in the next decade:

- *More information will be available.* Sounds like a rather naive statement, but as recently as ten years ago, facts about a competitor's activities in the marketplace and data on consumers' attitudes were expensive information to obtain. Often the market researcher had to make decisions on the basis of scanty background information.

  Today more and more data bases are being created and made available to the public. Perhaps as many as 500 data bases are added each year to the 5000 plus already open to any researcher. These on-line libraries—most are accessible through personal computers at low cost—instantly bring census data, Nielsen-type consumer statistics, and complete marketing reports to the market researcher. Whereas ten years ago researchers would have had to generate their own data or spend countless hours hunting for someone else's, in the next five to ten years a cornucopia of knowledge will be open to almost anyone who needs it.
- *Intelligent machines will expedite the research process.* Rapid advances in artificial intelligence and increasingly sophisticated computer hardware will allow the investigator to spend more time making marketing decisions and waste less time both learning computerese and figuring out the data.
- *As consumers feel more at home with high technology, they will naturally provide us with more marketing data.* A case in point: It used to be that only secretaries and college students knew the typewriter keyboard. Today senior executives, stockbrokers, and even five-year-olds are well acquainted with computer keyboards. This familiarity represents only the beginning of high-tech acceptance in the marketplace. Even the most rural communities have begun to employ electronic–bar code checkout counters and electronic-banking machines.

This broad consumer acceptance of high technology will have a tremendous impact on the breadth of data available to the researcher. Whether the consumer be a shipping clerk taking inventory, a mother buying milk for her child, or someone answering a public opinion survey, they will be generating hard data accessible to market researchers sooner and more directly than ever before.

One warning, though: Technology may offer the data gatherer too much of a good thing. In the next decade the researcher may be inundated with data and will have to carefully pick and choose the information he or she uses to make a decision.

1

Nature and Scope of Marketing Research

DEFINITION OF MARKETING RESEARCH

When beginning business students are asked to define marketing research, they usually come up with the following types of answers:

- Marketing research is getting data from your markets.
- Marketing research is a set of quantitative techniques to help you increase your sales and profits.
- Marketing research is determining the needs of your customers.
- Marketing research is gathering sales and market share data of your competitors.
- Marketing research is testing your products in the marketplace.
- Marketing research is estimating the potential sales of your product.

Although these "definitions" describe marketing research, they do not adequately reflect the full scope of it. They are merely examples of potential *applications* of marketing research rather than sound definitions of it. A formal and complete definition of marketing research is given next.

DEFINITION. ***Marketing research*** **is a set of techniques and principles for systematically collecting, recording, analyzing, and interpreting data that can aid decision makers who are involved with marketing goods, services, or ideas.**

One must carefully consider several key aspects that are implied by this definition so as to avoid misconceptions about marketing research and to fully appreciate the nature and scope of it. These aspects are discussed next.

Marketing research involves qualitative principles

Marketing research is more than a set of quantitative techniques. It also involves many *principles,* or *guidelines,* for generating managerially useful information. As we will see in the following example, as well as in other sections of the book, these principles are quite simple and, perhaps, intuitive. They are nevertheless crucial to the proper, and potentially successful, application of marketing research. A key reason for the failure of the Edsel automobile, now considered a collector's item, illustrates this point (Exhibit 1.1 shows four Edsel models).

Exhibit 1.1

Several models of the ill-fated Edsel

Source: Courtesy of News Department, Ford Motor Company, Dearborn, Mich. 48121.

EXAMPLE: The Edsel, introduced by the Ford Motor Company in 1957, is perhaps one of the most publicized and most costly product failures ever. Ford, which had high sales expectations for the Edsel, lost over $200 million before it was finally withdrawn from the market. Why did the Edsel fail? Contrary to what one might think, the Edsel's failure was not due to a lack of marketing research prior to its introduction. Indeed, Ford did extensive marketing research involving several consumer surveys and sophisticated techniques (such as word association tests) in order to (1) determine the images of existing automobiles with which the Edsel would have to compete and (2) select a suitable name for the automobile.

Unfortunately, the decision makers ignored some of the basic principles of marketing research. First, the image studies and consumer surveys were begun almost ten years before the Edsel was introduced. Thus the *timeliness and relevance* of the data generated from those studies were questionable. The managers were apparently unaware of a simple, but important, fact about marketing research: *Marketing research can lead to erroneous decisions if it is not done on a timely basis.*

Second, the image studies generated a lot of data about how consumers perceived the automobiles that were already on the market. However, they did not identify the *physical and style features* that would have to be incorporated in the new automobile to make it uniquely appealing to potential customers. Thus the research conducted was not comprehensive enough, apparently because of inadequate consideration of what the research purpose should be and what data should be gathered. *Careful and clear definition of research objectives is a key requirement for beneficial marketing research outcomes.*

Third, the marketing research that was done to select a name for the automobile did *not* recommend the name Edsel. Apparently, management undertook the research merely to see whether the results would support a decision that had already been made. Management thus violated another simple principle: *Marketing research must not be done when potential research users have already made up their minds.*[1]

The resources invested in conducting marketing research for the Edsel were obviously not very productive—*not* because of a failure to employ sophisticated research techniques but, rather, because of inadequate attention to factors such as the timeliness of data, appropriateness of research objectives, and open-mindedness of decision makers. Principles like the ones just illustrated are as crucial to the effectiveness of marketing research as quantitative tools and techniques are.

[1] Adapted from Robert F. Hartley, "The Edsel: Marketing Planning and Research Gone Awry," *Marketing Mistakes* (Columbus, Ohio: Grid, 1981), pp. 115–127.

Marketing research involves analysis and interpretation

A common misconception about marketing research is that it is merely a set of tools for data collection and recording. Such a misconception seriously underestimates the scope and usefulness of marketing research. *Analysis* and *interpretation* of data are also well within its domain, as the next example shows.

EXAMPLE: The AmEx Company, which issues the well-known American Express card, undertook some research that resulted in substantial increases in the productivity and profitability of its operations. The research consisted of various *analyses* of data that it collected on a routine basis. For example, analysis of data available from past credit card applications revealed that AmEx took an average of 35 days to process applications for personal charge cards. In contrast, an analysis of records of customer inquiries showed that applicants got impatient if they did not obtain a charge card within three weeks after they had made their applications. As a result, AmEx set a deadline of no more than two weeks to process credit card applications.

Similar analysis of data, related to requests from customers for replacement of lost or stolen cards, revealed that AmEx took two or more weeks to send replacement cards. Furthermore, an analysis of the data related to the dollar amounts charged by customers through their American Express cards showed that AmEx was losing about $2.70 in charge volume for every day a customer was without a card. On the basis of these results, AmEx started replacing cards in as little as two days. Speedy issuance of new cards and replacement cards resulted in additional profits of $1.4 million per year for the firm.[2]

As the example illustrates, if marketing research involves no more than the collection and recording of data, it is highly unlikely to be useful for decision-making purposes. After all, AmEx had been routinely gathering and recording the kinds of data mentioned in the example. However, not until the data were analyzed and the analyses interpreted did the firm reap any tangible benefits from the research. Hence a set of data, by itself, cannot be viewed as useful *information*. Analysis and interpretation of data are essential if marketing research is to be truly beneficial to decision makers. The importance of this aspect of marketing research is emphasized by the following statement made by a business executive who responded to a survey about managers' information needs: "Executives have *too much data* and *not enough information*. They have a lot of facts and statistics but need more information relevant to the decisions of the moment"[3] (emphases added).

---

[2] "Boosting Productivity at American Express," *Business Week*, October 5, 1981, p. 62.

[3] "Computers Don't Give Execs Information They Need: Study," *Marketing News*, November 27, 1981, Section 1, p. 8.

Marketing research does not replace decision making

Marketing research, *by itself,* cannot be expected to provide sound marketing decisions. The usefulness of marketing research is affected by the ability of potential research users to determine the nature of the problem, the extent to which marketing research can assist in solving the problem, how much money should be allocated to it, what course of action should be taken after observing the results of the research, and so on. For instance, in the Edsel automobile example certain research-related decisions made by the managers—namely, the timing of the automobile image studies and the decision to ignore the results of the name selection research—contributed to the failure of marketing research. In short, although marketing research can aid and influence decision making, the effectiveness of marketing research is itself affected by the decision makers. There is an interactive, or mutual, relationship between marketing research and decision making; therefore we cannot meaningfully view the former as a *replacement* for the latter.

Another reason marketing research is an aid to decision makers, rather than a replacement for their decision-making process, is that final decisions are influenced not only by research results but also by other factors. A variety of internal factors (e.g., resource constraints, corporate goals) and external factors (e.g., competitors' activities, legal constraints) must be considered in marketing decisions. Therefore decision makers, who should be more knowledgeable about such factors than researchers, have the ultimate responsibility for making decisions and bearing the risk associated with those decisions. The following example illustrates this point.

EXAMPLE: In the early eighties Nissan Motor Company of Japan, marketer of a variety of products under different brand names in 130 countries, including the well-known Datsun automobile in the United States, started replacing its various brand names with the single brand name Nissan. According to marketing research studies conducted in the United States, the Datsun name had an 85% recognition rate among consumers, while the Nissan name had only a 10% to 15% recognition rate. Furthermore, informal surveys of automobile dealers showed only marginal support for the switch in brand names. Was Nissan Motor Company foolish to go ahead with the name change, considering what the marketing research results seemed to suggest? Perhaps so; perhaps not. A major assumption made by the Nissan management in deciding on the name change was that a single "family" brand name for all its products around the world would ultimately strengthen its corporate identity and improve its marketing efficiency.[4]

[4] "A Worldwide Brand for Nissan," *Business Week,* August 24, 1981, p. 80.

This example does not necessarily imply that Nissan ignored the marketing research results. Perhaps the finding that 10% to 15% of the United States consumers were aware of the Nissan name, although not an overwhelming finding, might have encouraged management to view *Nissan* as having good recognition potential in the United States, if it were adequately promoted. Moreover, the results might have been responsible for the company's cautious strategy of introducing the name change gradually by promoting both the Datsun and the Nissan name during the transition period. Though only time can tell whether Nissan's management made a wise decision, the point here is that marketing research is only an input into, rather than a replacement for, managerial decision making. The burden of making decisions and assuming the associated risks must be shouldered by management. This point is illustrated from another perspective by the following example.

EXAMPLE: United States cereal producers, such as Kellogg, General Mills, and General Foods, were faced with some gloomy population trends for the eighties, as far as the cereal market was concerned. Analyses of the data on population characteristics showed that the group of people under 25 years of age—the biggest cereal eaters, with an average annual consumption of 11 pounds per capita—was expected to shrink continuously during the 1980s, while the 25-to-50 age-group—with the smallest per capita consumption of cereals—was expected to be the fastest-growing segment of the population. In response to these projections firms such as General Mills and General Foods started diversifying into other product areas. However, Kellogg decided to stick with the cereal market, and expand its sales in that market, by introducing new brands and broadening the appeal of cereals to a variety of market segments.[5]

What is interesting about this example is that Kellogg and its major competitors made quite *different* strategic decisions from the *same* population trend analyses. These responses are not necessarily inconsistent if one bears in mind that the results of research are no more than an input into the decision-making process. Managers have to consider a host of other factors as well in making their decisions.

Exhibit 1.2 graphically portrays the relationship of marketing research to decision-making activity. Notice the double-headed arrow showing that marketing research influences and *is influenced by* decision-making activity within an organization. Likewise, there is an interactive relationship between an organization's environment and its decision-making activity. The ultimate responsibility for decisions rests with decision makers, not researchers, as signified by the solid arrow leading from the "Decision-making activity" box to the "Final deci-

[5] "Kellogg: Still the Cereal People," *Business Week,* November 26, 1979, p. 80.

Exhibit 1.2
Marketing research's relationship to decision-making activity

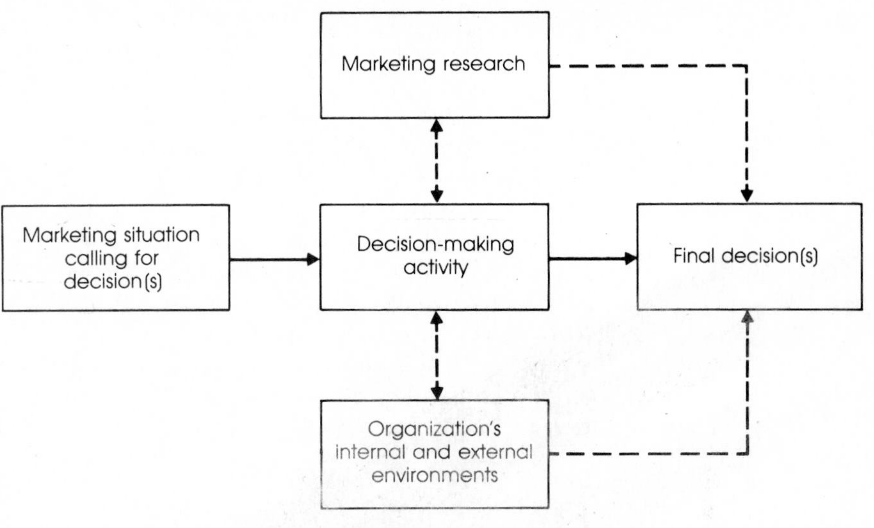

sion(s)" box. Final decisions may be influenced by, but are not *made* by, those responsible for marketing research.

Marketing research applications are not limited to goods and services

Last, but not least, there are many potential applications for marketing research principles and techniques. In addition to being of value in developing strategies for marketing goods (e.g., canned peaches or chemical fertilizers) and services (e.g., carpet-cleaning services or consulting services), marketing research can be of help in successfully marketing *ideas.* The following example illustrates this point.

EXAMPLE: Claritas Corporation is a firm that sells information about the profiles and life-styles of Americans on a zip code–by–zip code basis. Jonathan Robbins, founder of Claritas, developed this information base by meticulously combining demographic data compiled by the U.S. Census Bureau and life-style/attitudinal data generated through various regional surveys. The resulting information base contains descriptive profiles of residents in each of the 36,000 five-digit zip code areas in the United States. This information base, nicknamed PRIZM (Potential Rating Index by Zip Market), has found a variety of applications in effectively marketing products *as well as ideas.* For example, several political organizations are clients of Claritas.

They use the PRIZM information to pinpoint neighborhoods in which their viewpoints (ideas) are likely to be most (or least) well received. In this way they can effectively allocate their campaign resources to maximize popular support for their viewpoints. As another example, labor unions in Missouri used the PRIZM information base in a successful effort to kill an antiunion right-to-work proposal in a popular vote. The labor leaders identified prolabor neighborhoods with the aid of the PRIZM information base and targeted these neighborhoods for serious campaigning and organizing of voter registration drives.[6]

In summary, marketing research is a versatile set of tools, consisting of qualitative and quantitative principles and procedures that can aid decision makers in a variety of settings. It involves more than merely collecting and storing data or statistics, and its applications go beyond traditional marketing situations—that is, situations involving the marketing of goods or services. Nontraditional applications of marketing research are discussed further in a subsequent section of this chapter.

MARKETING RESEARCH'S ROLE IN DECISION MAKING

In any organization a multitude of decisions have to be made; however, our primary focus here will be on the role of marketing research in *marketing* decisions—that is, decisions that are directly related to the marketing of goods, services, or ideas. Specifically, we will examine marketing research's contribution to three major components of marketing decision making: setting marketing goals, developing and implementing marketing plans, and evaluating the effectiveness of marketing plans.[7]

Setting marketing goals

Setting goals is a logical starting point for any decision-making process. In the area of marketing decision making, managers set, or *should* set, goals relating to various aspects of marketing their products. For example, goals should be established for the firm's target markets in terms of the levels of success (e.g., sales or market shares) to be expected. Similarly, in designing advertising campaigns,

[6] Karen Rypka, "Zipping Up America: Computer Matches Mail Codes to Residents' Lifestyles," *Dallas Morning News,* Section C, April 12, 1982, p. 1C.

[7] In the management literature the overall decision making within an organization is usually divided into five distinct phases: planning, organizing, staffing, directing, and controlling; see, for example, Steven L. Mandell, Scott S. Cowen, and Roger Leroy Miller, *Introduction to Business Concepts & Applications* (St. Paul, Minn.: West, 1981), pp. 117–121.

managers should establish goals regarding the specific communication task the campaign should be expected to perform and the time frame in which such a task should be accomplished. There are at least two good reasons for setting marketing goals. First, they are critical for developing marketing plans; goals serve as criteria for determining what should or should not be included in the marketing plans. Second, marketing goals serve as standards, or yardsticks, against which the ultimate results of marketing plans can be judged; they aid in evaluating the effectiveness of marketing plans and their implementation.

Can decision makers set the goals they wish to achieve simply from their subjective judgment? Of course, they can. However, the problem with such an approach is that there is no way of ensuring that the goals will be potentially useful. To be potentially useful in developing plans and evaluating the results of those plans, the goals must be *realistic.* In a marketing context what is realistically achievable will depend on the *opportunities* and *constraints* in the marketplace. Thus if a marketer wants to establish goals that are realistic, he or she should have good information from the marketplace. Marketing research can be valuable here by uncovering marketing opportunities as well as constraints.

The AmEx Company example presented earlier illustrates how marketing research can help in setting goals. Through meaningful analyses and interpretation of data related to credit card applications, customer inquiries, and charge card use patterns, AmEx was able to identify opportunities for providing customer service and hence improving profitability. As a result, AmEx established specific customer service goals (in the form of time deadlines for issuing new cards and replacement cards). These goals led to a significant increase in profits for AmEx. The following example further demonstrates how marketing research can help identify and pursue opportunities in the marketplace.

EXAMPLE: Clairol carefully analyzed the market for nail care products and found that the market was growing fast, but there was no portable manicure device to fill the nail care needs of this market. The company did additional research to pinpoint and understand the market for such a device. This research showed that the potential market for a manicure device was quite large and that customers were eager to try the product. Hence Clairol decided to go after this market with Nail Works, an automatic appliance that can shape fingernails, file toenails, buff nails, and smooth calluses.[8]

Clairol's subsequent success with Nail Works can be at least partly credited to the careful initial research that it conducted to see whether there was a need for such a product and whether the market for such a product was worth pursuing. In contrast, a number of firms have had major new-product failures, mainly owing to their failure to verify, through appropriate marketing research,

[8] "Clairol Does its Marketing by Solving Beauty Problems: Fink," *Marketing News,* June 2, 1978, p. 7.

the *assumption* that opportunities existed for their products in the marketplace. The next example illustrates this point.

EXAMPLE: Levi Strauss & Company, buoyed by the success of its medium-priced jeans business, decided to diversify and put the Levi name on higher-priced, more fashionable apparel, in competition with designer brand names. However, it quickly ran into trouble: In one year alone its earnings dropped by 23%. The company apparently *assumed* (without any verification) that any clothing item under the Levi name would sell well. In the words of Levi's own chief operating officer: "We've realized that just putting the Levi's name on something isn't enough to gain instant market acceptance." After this painful and costly realization, the company decided to refocus attention on its basic jeans business.[9]

As the Clairol and Levi examples demonstrate, studying the market *before* designing a marketing plan is crucial to the plan's ultimate success. The role of marketing research in the goal-setting stage of the decision-making process is steadily increasing as more and more firms embrace the *marketing concept*–the philosophy of customer orientation urging firms to uncover customer needs first and then coordinate all their activities to satisfy those needs.[10] The marketing concept, by emphasizing the need to gain a good understanding of customers, is also stressing the importance of marketing research. Of course, the potential contributions of marketing research are not limited to identifying market opportunities and setting realistic goals. Marketing research can also add to the effectiveness of later stages of the decision-making process, as discussed next.

Developing and implementing marketing plans

A firm that wants to benefit fully from the opportunities that it uncovers in the marketplace must develop an effective "marketing mix"; that is, it must make sound decisions about the nature of its product, the ways of promoting the product, the price it must charge its potential customers, and the means of making the product available to them. Good marketing research will identify whether a firm's marketing mix is effective enough to maximize the benefits (e.g., sales, profits, or market shares) to the firm from available opportunities. Some of the most successful new-product introductions have been preceded by

[9] "It's Back to Basics for Levi's," *Business Week*, March 8, 1982, p. 77.

[10] All modern basic textbooks discuss the marketing concept; for a good discussion, see Philip Kotler, *Marketing Management: Analysis, Planning and Control*, 5th ed. (Englewood Cliffs, N.J.: Prentice-Hall, 1984), pp. 20–28.

extensive marketing research to aid in the development and implementation of one or more elements of their marketing mixes, as the next example illustrates.

EXAMPLE: Panty hose sales, which boomed in the late 1960s and early 1970s, started to drop off in the mid 1970s because of the increasing popularity of slacks among women. About this time the Hanes Company (maker of the well-known L'eggs panty hose) discovered that sales gains could be achieved if panty hose could be promoted to slacks wearers as an "accessory" rather than something to enhance the appearance of their legs. Thus an opportunity had been identified, but no suitable product existed to capitalize on that opportunity. Hanes tested several product concepts, using focus group research (more will be said on this type of research in Chapter 7). From this research the concept of panty hose with built-in underpants was singled out as the one that had the greatest appeal to potential customers.

Hanes then developed prototypes of a built-in underpants garment and tested them in-house among its women employees. The employees, who were skeptical at first, were pleasantly surprised by how much they liked the product. Interviews with the employees revealed two major benefits that they saw in the product: (1) comfort—fewer layers of clothing—and (2) appearance—panty lines disappearing under slacks and dresses. Hanes added two more potential benefits: namely, economy—no need to buy panties—and logic—no need to wear panties. Then they tested all four benefits, or product concepts, among a sample of panty hose wearers to see which one would be most appealing. This research revealed that the "appearance" benefit, or positioning, had the strongest appeal.

Hanes named its product Underalls, introduced it in three test markets, and promoted it as "panties and panty hose all in one" that would eliminate panty lines. The product was a roaring success—within five months it had grabbed 24% of the department store market in the test areas.[11]

Underalls and newer variations of them continue to enjoy sales success, thereby suggesting that it was not merely a faddish product. The successful development and introduction of Underalls was no fluke; it was a result of careful planning based on good marketing research.

While the research conducted by Hanes focused on developing a product and determining how it should be positioned, marketing research has also been used for making effective decisions about other elements of the marketing mix. For instance, Scripto, Inc., successfully employed marketing research to arrive at an appropriate price, as well as develop a promotional slogan, for its Scripto Erasable Pen, as illustrated in the next example.

---

[11] "Underalls' Success Due to 'Flanking Strategy,' Product Idea, Positioning," *Marketing News,* November 14, 1980, p. 11.

EXAMPLE: Scripto, Inc., wanted to introduce an erasable pen that would compete with Eraser Mate, an erasable pen that the Gillette Company had introduced at a retail price of $1.69. Scripto did extensive marketing research to make its product's positioning unique. First, it carefully researched the users of Eraser Mate. Because of Eraser Mate's high price, Scripto expected its users to be older, "affluent" consumers. However, the research showed that 65% of the Eraser Mate users were under 18. From this result Scripto identified students as the primary target market for its Erasable Pen. It then interviewed students in focus groups and found that 98¢ would be perceived as a reasonable price for an erasable pen; students would rather pay 98¢ for an erasable pen than 25¢ for a conventional disposable Bic ballpoint pen.

The focus group research also generated useful ideas for an appropriate promotional theme for the product. From such ideas the following slogan was developed for Scripto's Erasable Pens: "They erase the ink, not the paper." This promotional slogan and a price of 98¢—both derived through sound marketing research—were instrumental in ensuring the sales success that Scripto's Erasable Pen achieved when it was introduced into the market.[12]

Evaluating the effectiveness of marketing plans

Getting feedback from the marketplace and taking needed corrective action—often referred to as *controlling,* or the *control function*—is an important component of the decision-making process. To be successful in the marketplace, a firm must at least periodically monitor market conditions (i.e., obtain feedback) and answer control-related questions like the following: What is the market share of our product? Is its share increasing, decreasing, or staying the same? Who are its users? Are the nature of the users and the volume of their purchases consistent with our expectations (goals)? If not, why not? A firm may want to explore a number of questions like these in order to evaluate its market performance. Accurate answers to such questions can only emerge from marketing research rather than from the intuition of marketers. Thus marketing research plays a vital role in the control stage of the marketing decision-making process. The results of marketing research done at this stage may also lead to revisions in the goals of a firm and/or changes in the firm's marketing mix, as illustrated by the following three examples.

---

[12] "Success of Scripto Erasable Pen Due to Marketing Research: CEO," *Marketing News,* January 23, 1981, p. 8.

EXAMPLE: Ford Motor Company's Granada automobile, which was a very popular car in the United States, ran into sales trouble soon after its introduction in Germany in the early 1970s. Its sales fell from a high of 110,677 cars in 1972 to a mere 40,786 in 1974. Furthermore, while Ford was losing market share and profits in Germany, its rivals such as General Motors were doing quite well there. Ford realized that something must be seriously wrong with its car. Instead of simply guessing about what might be wrong, though, Ford conducted surveys of past and potential buyers of its cars. These surveys revealed that Ford's cars were no longer perceived by consumers to be "authentically" German. Consumers perceived Ford cars to be dominated by American designs and British Ford standards of quality, both of which were held in low esteem by the Germans.

Because of this feedback, the ride of the Granada was hardened (Germans like to experience "the feel of the road"), its power steering was made less sensitive, and its external styling was changed to eliminate its American look. The impact of these design and styling changes on sales was very dramatic—Granada's sales climbed back to about 110,000 units by 1976.[13]

EXAMPLE: The Mirro Company, a well-known producer of aluminum houseware products, introduced a new line of cookware under the Mirro name for use in microwave ovens. The initial sales results of the microwave oven cookware were disappointingly low. When Mirro's salespeople were asked why sales were so low, they indicated that in their judgment the color of the Mirror cookware, which was a cocoa brown (the competitors' was beige), was to blame.

However, instead of *assuming* that the salespeople's perceptions were accurate, Mirro did extensive consumer research (including focus group interviews, shopping mall intercept interviews, and phone calls to registered owners of cookware) to verify those perceptions. This research revealed that the Mirro name was the culprit—consumers associated *Mirro* with aluminum products that could not be safely used in microwave ovens. Contrary to the salesforce's assumption, the color of the product was *not* perceived to be a drawback by consumers. Indeed, consumers were overwhelmingly *in favor* of the cocoa brown color because they perceived it as being stain-resistant and having a quality image.

As a result of this research, Mirro changed the name of its cookware to Koolware (to emphasize that it remained cool when taken out of a microwave oven) but left its color intact. The name change helped boost the cookware's sales.[14]

---

[13] "A Dashing High-Speed U-Turn," *Time,* July 26, 1976, p. 65.

[14] "Mirro Changes the Recipe," *Sales & Marketing Management,* February 8, 1982, p. 13.

Exhibit 1.3

Effectiveness of a firm's marketing decision making

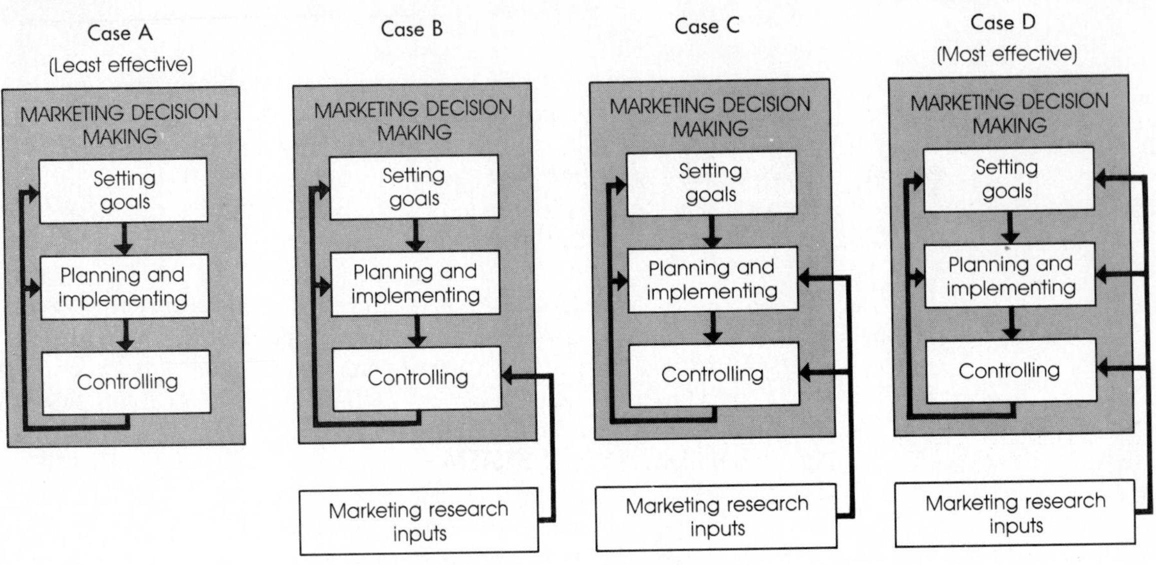

EXAMPLE: In 1975 Airwick Industries, Inc., a one-product company manufacturing room deodorizers, lost $2 million on sales of $35 million. Hoping to bring the firm back to good health, its management commissioned several market and consumer studies. These studies revealed a number of different market opportunities, which led the firm to revise its primary goal—from that of being a one-product firm to one of being a multiproduct firm. The consumer research also led to a number of new-product ideas that the firm was able to use in developing its product and marketing mixes.

As a result of its research and the actions it took, Airwick's sales grew to $154 million with a net profit of $8 million in 1979. Airwick became the market leader, or at least a major competitor, in (1) air deodorizers, with Airwick, Stick-Ups, and Air Wand; (2) carpet care, with Carpet Fresh, Plush, and Glamorene; (3) cleaners, with Chore; and (4) breath fresheners, with Binaca.[15]

In each of these examples marketing research was helpful in properly diagnosing the problem and suggesting appropriate corrective actions—changes in the features of Ford's Granada in Germany, a name change for

[15] "Airwick's Discovery of New Markets Pays Off," *Business Week*, June 16, 1980, p. 139.

Mirro's microwave cookware, and modifications in the corporate goals and product mix of Airwick Industries. These results imply that research done at the control stage will typically also influence decisions at the previous two stages. Therefore in terms of improving decision-making effectiveness, a firm should conduct marketing research *at least* at the control stage.

Marketing decisions are likely to be even better if research is conducted before goals are set and marketing mixes are designed. The overall effectiveness of marketing decisions will vary depending on the stages at which inputs through marketing research are used. This variation is demonstrated graphically in Exhibit 1.3. In case A marketing decisions are made in a vacuum, with no systematic inputs from the marketplace; while such decision making may occasionally produce good results, in the long run it will invariably be ineffective. Decision making will improve with increases in the number of stages at which research inputs are taken into account; case D in Exhibit 1.3 will lead to better decisions in the long run than cases, A, B, or C.

MARKETING INFORMATION SYSTEM

In the preceding section we saw that marketing research can provide valuable inputs at various stages of the marketing decision-making process. A firm that obtains and utilizes such inputs on a regular, systematic basis can be said to have a *marketing information system.* An often-used definition of a marketing information system is given next.

DEFINITION. A *marketing information system* is a continuing and interacting structure of people, equipment, and procedures designed to gather, sort, analyze, evaluate, and distribute pertinent, timely, and accurate information to marketing decision makers.[16]

A firm wishing to be successful in the marketplace in the long run must monitor market conditions and its own marketing performance on an almost continuous basis. Such monitoring is essential if a firm wishes to respond quickly and effectively (through revisions in marketing goals and/or marketing plans) to changes in its marketing environment. It is precisely this type of monitoring that a good marketing information system will be able to offer a firm. Exhibit 1.4 shows a marketing information system, and Table 1.1 briefly describes the key elements included in it.[17]

---

[16] Adapted from Philip Kotler, *Principles of Marketing* (Englewood Cliffs, N.J.: Prentice-Hall, 1983), p. 55.

[17] Design and implementation aspects of marketing information systems are discussed in several books on the subject, such as Van Mayros and D. Michael Werner, *Marketing Information Systems—Design and Applications for Marketers* (Radnor, Pa.: Chilton, 1982).

Table 1.1
Description of Marketing Information System Elements

Data collection system	A set of capabilities for continuously monitoring a firm's internal and external environments and extracting relevant marketing data from them
Data bank	A repository for data collected from within and outside a firm
Data input and retrieval system	A set of capabilities for transferring the collected data to the data bank and for locating and extracting needed data from the data bank
Models/techniques system	A set of frameworks, procedures, and tools for manipulating data so as to obtain useful information
Information dissemination system	A set of capabilities for generating reports from the information obtained and relaying them to appropriate marketing decision makers

Notice in Exhibit 1.4 that data collection, recording, analysis, and interpretation are all implied within a marketing information system. Thus marketing research techniques and principles are relevant and vital for the proper functioning of a marketing information system. But a feature that distinguishes a marketing information system from a marketing research project is that the former is a *regular* or *routine* source of market information relevant for all stages of marketing decision making. A specific marketing research project, in contrast, is intended to meet nonroutine information needs that cannot be met adequately by a firm's marketing information system. To illustrate, a firm that conducts marketing research only when its sales decline cannot be considered to have a marketing information system. While such research may help identify the reasons the firm's sales are declining—and possibly suggest ideas for corrective action—the firm may miss many opportunities during times when its sales are not declining. For instance, opportunities to sell new products that the firm is capable of producing or opportunities to sell the firm's existing products to new market segments will all go unnoticed. The point of this discussion is that conducting marketing research and having a marketing information system are not the same thing, as they are sometimes believed to be.

Many large companies today have sophisticated marketing information systems. Holiday Inns is one such company. The hotel chain continuously collects a variety of data from within (e.g., occupancy rates, extent of guest satisfaction and dissatisfaction) and from outside (e.g., government and industry data on total lodging supply, demand for lodging). The collected data are regularly analyzed to generate information that management uses to make effective decisions in such areas as selecting markets for new hotels, allocating advertising spending

Exhibit 1.4

Elements of a marketing information system

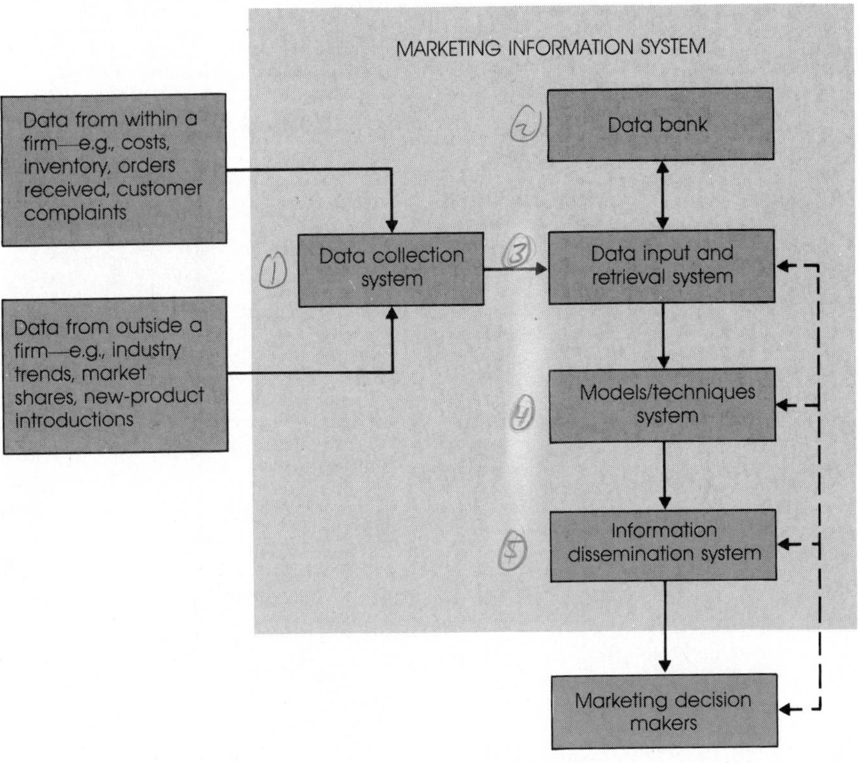

geographically, tracking market shares, and setting prices.[18] An outline of Holiday Inns' marketing information system is shown in Exhibit 1.5.

Marketing decision support system

A good marketing information system, in addition to providing regular reports containing relevant marketing information, should permit managers to request special types of data analyses or reports on an as-needed basis. For example, a product manager may want to know what will happen to sales of brand X if its price is cut by 10%. Of course, if the data, techniques, or models needed to answer such a query are not available within the marketing information system, then a specific marketing research project will have to be conducted. The broken arrows in Exhibit 1.4 show the access that managers should have to key

[18] Thayer C. Taylor, "Computers That Plan," *Sales & Marketing Management,* December 7, 1981, pp. 42–47.

Exhibit 1.5

Marketing information system at Holiday Inns

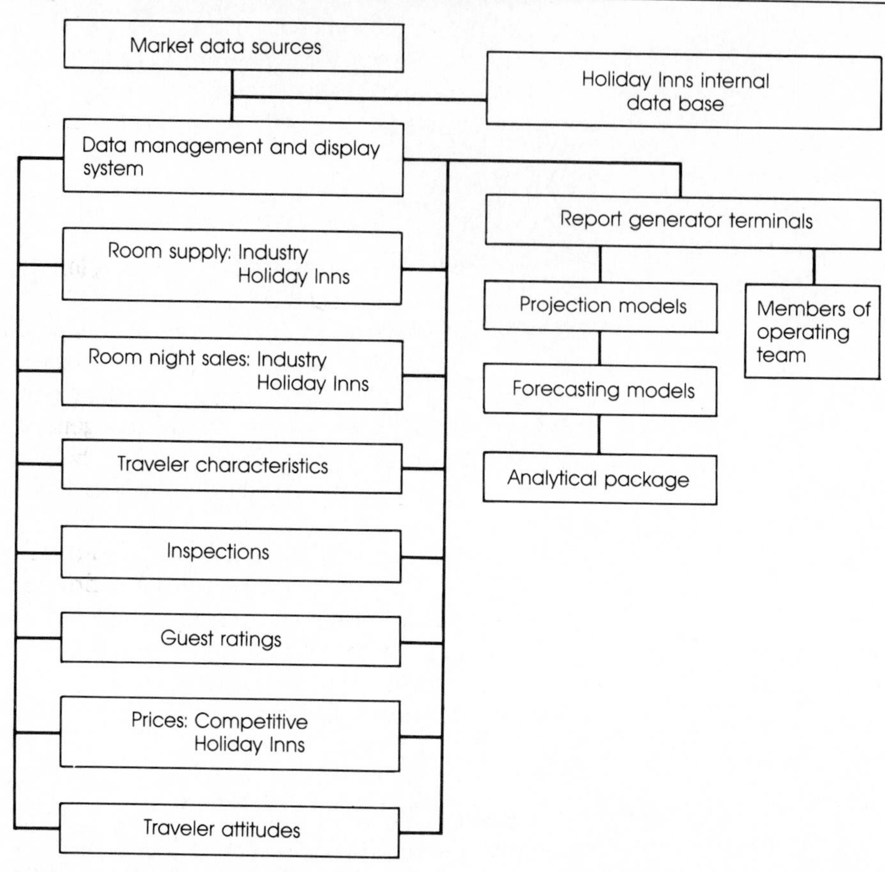

Source: Adapted from Thayer C. Taylor, "Computers That Plan," *Sales & Marketing Management*, Magazine, Copyright December 7, 1981, p. 44.

elements within a marketing information system in order to make such ad hoc requests. A system that allows marketing managers to interact with it is called a *marketing decision support system (MDSS)*.[19]

With rapid advances in computer technology and the proliferation of personal computers and software packages, an increasing number of marketing managers should have access to MDSSs in their offices. A variety of microcompu-

[19] For a good discussion of MDSSs, see John D. C. Little, Lakshmi Mohan, and Antoine Hatoun, "Yanking Knowledge from the Numbers: How Marketing Decision Support Systems Can Work for You," *Industrial Marketing*, March 1982, pp. 46–56; John D. C. Little, "Decision Support Systems for Marketing Managers," *Journal of Marketing*, Summer 1979, pp. 9–26.

ter software programs that are user-friendly—that is, require little or no programming expertise on the part of users and can interact with users in almost conversational terms—are now available. The capabilities of these programs range from simple tabulations to complex statistical analyses of data.[20] Firms currently using MDSSs include American Airlines (for price and route selection decisions), Frito-Lay, Inc. (for price, advertising, and promotion decisions), and Zale Corporation (for evaluating potential store sites).[21]

Marketing information systems and computers

One common misconception about marketing information systems is that a firm cannot have a marketing information system if it does not have access to a computer. Of course, a computer can be useful in efficiently and effectively operating a marketing information system. It can facilitate storage and rapid retrieval of data gathered from a firm's marketing environment, for instance, and it can also aid in the analyses of the data that generate information relevant for decision making. However, a computer is not always necessary for the operation of a marketing information system, as the next example illustrates.

EXAMPLE: Pest Control, Inc. offers year-around pest control services to homeowners in a city. John, the owner of the firm, is responsible for effectively marketing the firm's services. Once every week John contacts the local utility company to obtain a list of the names and addresses of new homeowners moving into the area during the preceding week. He then mails them a brochure detailing the firm's services and listing introductory discount prices. Every evening John also carefully studies the ads run by the firm's competitors in the local newspapers, and he makes note of any changes in their offerings. Furthermore, once every month John randomly picks about twenty of the firm's current customers and talks to them on the telephone to ascertain how satisfied they are with the services offered by Pest Control and whether any improvements can be made. Finally, John routinely contacts homeowners who terminate the services of Pest Control in order to determine the reason(s) for termination.

John makes mental note of the insights gained through these procedures and uses them when making marketing-related decisions. Does Pest Control, Inc. have a marketing information system? It certainly does, although its marketing information system is neither computerized nor very sophisticated.

---

[20] The *Marketing News* publishes a directory of software programs relevant for marketing applications once every four months or so; see, for example, the March 15, 1985, issue, pp. 39–52.

[21] Jack T. Hogue and Hugh J. Watson, "Management's Role in the Approval and Administration of Decision Support Systems," *MIS Quarterly,* June 1983, Table 1, p. 18.

This example illustrates that a firm can be said to have a marketing information system if it has a systematic procedure (not necessarily a computerized procedure) for regularly monitoring its marketing environment and for utilizing the results of such monitoring in its decision-making activities. However, with the current proliferation of rather inexpensive computers, many organizations (including relatively small firms) can afford to use computers to improve the capability and effectiveness of their marketing information systems. Furthermore, the rapid computerization of marketing transactions in several sectors of American business is opening up tremendous opportunities for marketers to establish effective marketing information systems.

The retail grocery sector is a case in point. The advent of the Universal Product Code identification system and the availability of automated checkouts equipped with optical scanners have greatly increased the capability of supermarket operators, as well as manufacturers of grocery products, to monitor and analyze sales trends, changes in brand shares, shifts in consumer preferences, and so on. Several thousand supermarkets have already been equipped with optical scanners, and by the late 1980s a majority of them will be so equipped.

With the aid of computerized optical scanners, retailers can get instant and accurate sales feedback about the relative performance of each brand within a product category.[22] Such continuous feedback can help retailers focus their attention on opportunities as well as problem areas and fine-tune their marketing mixes by responding quickly to changes in their marketing environment. For example, they can improve their profitability through optimally reallocating shelf space, discontinuing losing brands, increasing promotional support, and/or lowering prices for slow-moving products.

Producers of grocery products also have a way of generating information relevant to their products and markets from such a built-in information system. For instance, a firm called Information Resources, Inc., has set up a panel of supermarkets equipped with optical scanners that are hooked up to a central computer. The computer constantly monitors the sales of various brands of grocery products as well as the demographic composition of the types of consumers buying each brand. This system is called BehaviorScan. A producer firm can set up at least a partial marketing information system for its products simply through gaining access to the BehaviorScan system by paying a subscription fee to Information Resources, Inc.[23] The A. C. Nielsen Company has developed a similar system called ScanTrack that is available to subscribers.[24]

---

[22] See "Checkout Scanners Soon Will Revolutionize Market Research, Packaged Goods Marketing," *Marketing News,* December 12, 1980, p. 5.
[23] For details on the BehaviorScan system and its capabilities, see "New 'BehaviorScan' System Ties Sales to TV Ads," *Marketing News,* September 21, 1979, p. 7.
[24] See "Utilizing UPC Scanning Data for New Product Decisions," *Nielsen Researcher,* no. 1, 1981.

MARKETING MANAGER–MARKETING RESEARCHER INTERFACE

The usefulness of marketing research depends not only on how good the research is but also on how potential users perceive the research and apply its results. As we saw earlier, marketing research, *by itself,* cannot be expected to lead to profitable marketing decisions. In other words, marketing researchers and marketing managers (or users of marketing research) must work as a team in order to maximize the benefits derived from research. Does such teamwork exist in practice? Unfortunately, the answer to this question is not an unconditional yes. The relationship between marketing researchers and marketing managers is apparently not as effective as it should be.[25]

What factors are responsible for the less-than-ideal relationship between marketing researchers and marketing managers? An examination of the marketing literature on this issue reveals several general factors that contribute to a lack of effective teamwork between research providers and research users. These factors can be labeled as "complaints" that each party has against the other.

Let us first examine the complaints that managers, in general, have against researchers. A frequent complaint of managers is that *researchers are too technique-oriented;* that is, researchers are more interested in showing their sophisticated techniques than in ensuring and demonstrating the practical utility of their results. The following comments by a senior marketing executive succinctly reflect this concern:

> What we [managers] would like to see them [researchers] do is to define themselves as true staff support, *going beyond their technical specialties* [emphasis added], by using their accumulated knowledge and experience to help us. . . . Any technique or analytical approach we use must contribute to marketing decision making.[26]

A related complaint of managers is that *researchers do not communicate well* with them; researchers do not speak the manager's language. Owing to their obsession with techniques, researchers may tend to use overly technical terminology, thereby annoying managers and essentially shutting them out. Moreover, in their enthusiasm for describing their techniques and methodology, they may fail to adequately recognize and convey the *practical implications*

---

[25] For a discussion of the nature of and reasons for marketing managers' opinions about marketing research, see, for example, Neil Holbert, "How Managers See Marketing Research," *Journal of Advertising Research,* 14 (December 1974), pp. 41–46; Danny Bellenger, "The Marketing Manager's View of Marketing Research," *Business Horizons,* June 1979, pp. 59–65.

[26] "Technique-Obsessed Marketing Researchers Can't Help Managers Make Tough Decisions," *Marketing News,* January 22, 1982, Section 2, p. 1.

of their findings. Here is what a senior vice president of marketing had to say regarding this problem:

> If professional researchers go beyond technique into diplomacy, persuasion, and statesmanship, the communication gap—the weakest link between researcher and management—will be bridged, and they will become a team that makes business succeed.[27]

Managers also believe that *researchers generate information of questionable value* and that *they fail to demonstrate the monetary benefits of their research.* Such a perception obviously jeopardizes managers' trust in marketing researchers and, consequently, widens the rift between them. For instance, a survey of 50 top corporate executives in the United States revealed that while a majority of them acknowledged the critical importance of marketing in strategic planning, only 16% gave an acceptable rating for the work done by marketing researchers.[28] This survey further showed that inefficiency and impractical results of marketing research were the main reasons for the corporate executives' poor opinions about it.

Now let us look at researchers' complaints about managers. One major concern of researchers is that *managers do not provide enough funds for research.* According to one marketing research director:

> In many cases, research costs are held to absurdly low levels despite an extremely high value for the information to be obtained. Although the research conducted might be significantly less reliable or sensitive than a properly funded study, the data often are used in precisely the same manner.[29]

Indeed, several studies have shown that the funds allocated by management to marketing research are quite low in many firms.[30]

Low budget allocations for marketing research can adversely affect the marketing researcher–marketing manager interface in two ways:

1. Researchers may *perceive* the low allocations as demeaning their importance and self-esteem, which, in turn, may aggravate their already rough relationship with managers.
2. If low budget allocations lead to poor-quality research (as alleged by researchers), and if managers use such research results in their decision

---

[27] "Successful Marketing Researchers Have Ability to Communicate, Breathe Meaning into Numbers," *Marketing News,* January 22, 1982, Section 2, p. 1.
[28] "Rabin: Top Execs Have Low Opinion of Marketing Research, Marketers' Role in Strategic Planning," *Marketing News,* October 16, 1981, p. 1.
[29] "Nine Research Mistakes Marketers Should Avoid," *Marketing News,* September 19, 1980, p. 14.
[30] See, for example, A. Parasuraman, "Research's Place in the Marketing Budget," *Business Horizons,* March/April 1983, pp. 25–29.

making, wrong decisions are likely to be made—decisions that managers can blame on the researchers, thereby creating further friction between the two parties.

A second general complaint of researchers is that *managers do not take the research results seriously;* that is, managers ignore marketing research results or, worse still, only use them when they are consistent with their preconceived notions. This complaint is, perhaps, more factual than perceptual, because managers do request marketing research for reasons *other than* aiding their decision making. For instance, a manager may commission a research project simply to use it as a scapegoat in the event a decision (made *before* the research is done) turns out to be a bad decision. Such research has been labeled "pseudoresearch."[31] Obviously, pseudoresearch cannot be expected to foster a healthy, mutually trusting relationship between managers and researchers.

Another complaint of researchers, which is not totally independent of the earlier complaints, is that *managers do not involve them in the decision-making process.* Researchers appear to feel that managers use them merely as data gatherers. Such a feeling, of course, helps neither the self-image of the researchers nor the researchers' opinion of the managers.

Having stated the general complaints of managers and researchers, we can make a couple of observations related to them. First, *both* researchers and managers may be responsible for the less-than-smooth relationship between them that is a result of the perceptions of each group about the other group. For instance, managers may be reluctant to allocate funds for marketing research because they perceive researchers to be more technique-oriented than decision-oriented; however, researchers may *want* to be technique-oriented under the assumption that such an orientation may restore their self-esteem, which they perceive as being denied by managers. To the extent that such perceptual barriers can be removed through the joint and sincere efforts of managers and researchers, the relationship between them can be strengthened and made more productive.

Second, an adversarial relationship certainly does not exist between researchers and managers in *all* firms. Indeed, many firms today have overcome any interface problems and have successfully integrated marketing research with marketing management. For instance, advertising decision making in Sears is closely intertwined with marketing research.[32] Similarly, the strategic decision made by Sears to diversify into consumer financial services was apparently the

[31] For a discussion of this issue, see S. A. Smith, "Research and Pseudo-Research in Marketing," *Harvard Business Review,* 52 (March 1974), pp. 73–76.

[32] "Research Helps Sears Reap Optimum Impact From Ads," *Marketing News,* December 26, 1980, p. 7.

result of the joint efforts of marketing researchers and corporate level executives.[33]

NONBUSINESS APPLICATIONS OF MARKETING RESEARCH TOOLS

Our definition of marketing research clearly indicates that the application of marketing research techniques and principles is not limited to the traditional marketing of goods and services. In fact, we saw earlier that labor unions in Missouri successfully used marketing research information (namely, the PRIZM information base) to swing a public referendum in their favor. There are many other such nonbusiness or nonmarketing applications for marketing research. Organizations such as the United Way, American Red Cross, and Campus Crusade for Christ can and do conduct marketing research to aid them in developing strategies for effectively selling their causes to the public and for maximizing the public's support for their programs.

One of the most extensive applications of marketing research for nonbusiness purposes was made during the 1980 presidential campaign by candidate Ronald Reagan. Reagan's campaign committee spent about $400,000 on consumer opinion surveys during the primaries and an additional $1.4 million before the election on research such as studies dealing with voters' psychographics and attitudes, and periodic surveys tracking voters' awareness of, and preferences for, the various presidential candidates. Reagan's deputy director for strategy and planning, Richard B. Wirthlin, was, before the campaign, a partner in a marketing research company called Decision Making Information. From the various kinds of information generated through research, Wirthlin and his associates developed a 176-page strategy statement including recommendations about geographic areas to focus on and campaign themes to use in them. This strategy document, named the "Black Book," gave shape to a campaign that ultimately resulted in one of the largest victories for a presidential candidate in recent history.[34]

The client lists of large marketing research firms in the United States include many organizations that are nonbusiness. For instance, Yankelovich, Skelly and White, Inc., has conducted research for the American Psychiatric Association, National Board of the YMCA, Federal Trade Commission, Metropolitan Museum of Art, and New York University.[35] Similarly, the client list of Opinion Research

[33] "The New Sears: Unable to Grow in Retailing, It Turns to Financial Services," *Business Week,* November 16, 1981, pp. 140–146.

[34] For an in-depth discussion of the use of marketing research in Reagan's campaign, see J. J. Honomichl, "The Marketing of a Candidate," *Advertising Age,* December 15, 1980, p. 3.

[35] See, "Services Offered by the Firm," a brochure prepared by Yankelovich, Skelly and White, Inc., New York, NY.

Corporation includes the American Economic Foundation, Columbia University, National Education Association, National Society of Professional Engineers, U.S. Department of Transportation, and Veterans Administration.[36]

SUMMARY

The purpose of this chapter was to define marketing research and discuss its role in decision making. Marketing research is more than techniques for gathering data. Its purpose is to generate *information* that can aid decision makers in a variety of business as well as nonbusiness settings.

Marketing research can provide useful inputs at all stages of the decision-making process: goal setting, formulating plans, implementing them, and controlling. The greater the number of stages at which marketing research inputs are used, the more effective the decision making is likely to be. An organization that has a routine system for generating and disseminating information from the marketplace on a regular basis can be said to have a marketing information system. A system that also allows marketing managers to interact with it and make special requests for information is called a marketing decision support system (MDSS).

The benefits realized from marketing research depend on the degree of teamwork between research providers and research users. Unfortunately, there are apparently some barriers to this teamwork, although such barriers (especially perceptual barriers) can be, and have been, successfully overcome through mutually trusting dialogue and cooperation between the two parties.

QUESTIONS

1. Critically evaluate the soundness of the following definition of marketing research: "Marketing research is a set of data collection techniques that can be used by marketers to help them in their decision making."
2. What lessons about marketing research are evident in the Edsel automobile example?
3. Can decision makers in different firms looking at the *same* research information about a market make different decisions? Why or why not?
4. Name a *specific* purpose for which each of the following may be able to use marketing research fruitfully.
   a. A hospital,
   b. A United States congressman,
   c. A gas station,
   d. The Internal Revenue Service.

[36] Names obtained from a client list provided by Opinion Research Corporation, Princeton, N.J.

5. What are the three major components of marketing decision making to which marketing research can contribute?
6. The chief executive officer (CEO) of a firm tells top management: "Our sales have been increasing at a snail's pace over the past five years. Therefore I want our sales to increase by *at least* 15 percent during the next year. Do whatever is necessary to accomplish this." Develop a logical argument that can be used to show the CEO why the stated sales goal may be unrealistic.
7. Briefly discuss a specific example to illustrate the importance of marketing research in determining the corrective action to be taken when results from the marketplace are disappointing.
8. Define *marketing information system,* and briefly describe the key elements involved in it.
9. Is a marketing information system different from marketing research? Why or why not?
10. Define *marketing decision support system.*
11. Discuss the following statement: "Computers are the guts of marketing information systems."
12. State the complaints that managers typically have against marketing researchers.
13. State the complaints that marketing researchers typically have against managers.
14. "The rift between researchers and managers is too wide to be bridged effectively." Discuss this statement.

2

Providers of Marketing Research Services

As we saw in the previous chapter, marketing research is a valuable aid to decision makers in a wide range of organizations. Three basic approaches are available for acquiring marketing research information relevant for decision making:[1]

1. Making marketing research the part-time or full-time responsibility of one or more employees, without setting up a formal marketing research department.
2. Setting up a formal marketing research department with one or more full-time employees.
3. Employing outside suppliers such as commercial marketing research firms and consultants.

While the third approach is external to a firm, the first two approaches are in-house. Furthermore, firms can use the in-house and external approaches simultaneously. In other words, having in-house capabilities to conduct marketing research does not preclude the use of external suppliers.

The purpose of this chapter is to discuss the nature and attributes of various entities that can provide marketing research information, the choice of a suitable approach for obtaining marketing research information in a given situation, and

[1] The three approaches are adapted from Richard D. Crisp, "Organization of the Marketing Research Function," in *Handbook of Marketing Research,* ed. Robert Ferber (New York: McGraw-Hill, 1974), pp. 1–63 to 1–72.

the ethical responsibilities of providers and users of marketing research information toward each other, as well as toward other parties associated with or affected by the conduct of marketing research. Let us now examine the key features of in-house marketing research.

IN-HOUSE MARKETING RESEARCH

Incidence of marketing research departments

In-house marketing research is either contained within a formal marketing research department or merely assigned as a responsibility of some employee(s). What factors determine which approach is used? One would intuitively expect large firms to have separate marketing research departments. Indeed, several research studies have found a strong association between a firm's size and its likelihood of having a separate marketing research department.[2] However, a firm's size is not the sole determinant of whether it should have a separate marketing research department; factors such as the frequency and scope of the firm's information needs may be more crucial. For instance, Lee Adler has identified five conditions as being conducive to upgrading in-house marketing research to a formal research department:[3]

1. When the person responsible for in-house marketing research spends too much of his or her time gathering and analyzing data.
2. When certain research activities become routine and time-consuming.
3. When many critical decisions to be made would benefit from research.
4. When the magnitude of the firm's other expenditures that can be evaluated through research becomes substantial.
5. When the person responsible for in-house marketing research frequently engages the services of outside research suppliers.

In 1983 Dik Warren Twedt conducted a comprehensive survey related to marketing research activities of firms. Over 75% of the firms that responded to Twedt's survey had formal marketing research departments.[4] Exhibit 2.1 illustrates the extent of formalization of in-house marketing research in the surveyed firms.

While the incidence of separate marketing research departments did not vary much across different types of firms, it was highest among firms manufac-

[2] For example, see James R. Krum, "Survey of Marketing Research Directors of Fortune 500 Firms," *Journal of Marketing Research*, 3 (August 1966), pp. 313–317; Dik Warren Twedt, ed., *1983 Survey of Marketing Research* (Chicago: American Marketing Association, 1983).

[3] Lee Adler, "How to Organize a Market Research Department and Why You Should Want To," *Sales & Marketing Management*, 119 (July 11, 1977), pp. 83–85.

[4] Twedt, *1983 Survey*.

Exhibit 2.1

Extent of formalization of in-house marketing research

	Number answering	Percent having formal department	One person	No one assigned
Manufacturers of consumer products	142	83	14	3
Publishing and broadcasting	69	93	7	0
Manufacturers of industrial products	124	69	22	9
Financial services	105	71	26	3
Advertising agencies	60	85	12	3
All others	97	65	32	3
All companies answering this question (excludes marketing research and consulting firms)	597	77	20	3

Source: Dik Warren Twedt, *1983 Survey of Marketing Research* (Chicago: American Marketing Association, 1983), p. 11. Used by permission.

turing consumer products—according to Exhibit 2.1, 83% of such firms reported having separate marketing research departments. Similar findings resulted from a survey of manufacturing firms conducted by James R. Krum.[5] Krum found that over 80% of the firms responding to his survey had separate marketing research departments, with the highest incidence of such departments occurring in consumer product firms (84%).

Although the existence of separate marketing research departments is apparently widespread, the findings of the Twedt and Krum surveys may not apply to all firms in the United States for two reasons:

1. The sample surveyed is likely to have been dominated by relatively large firms. Twedt's sample was restricted to firms that were members of the

[5] Krum, "Survey of Marketing Research Directors."

American Marketing Association, and Krum only surveyed *Fortune 500* firms.

2. Firms with marketing research departments are more likely to have responded to surveys of this nature than firms without marketing research departments. Consequently, the percentage of responding firms with separate marketing research departments is most likely inflated. (Krum has reported that evidence in his study indicated that firms with marketing research departments were more likely to have responded.)

Thus when one considers all business firms in the United States, the percentage of firms with separate marketing research departments may be significantly less than the percentages reported by Twedt and Krum. Nevertheless, over the past couple of decades the number of new marketing research departments formed each year has been steadily growing.[6] Given the increasing importance of marketing research, one can expect this trend to continue.

Organization of marketing research departments

How should an in-house marketing research department be organized? For instance, should it be *centralized*—wherein one corporate department will cater to all the research needs of a firm—or should it be *decentralized*—wherein each "constituency" (e.g., division or group based on product line or market segment) will have its own separate marketing research arm?[7] To whom should the head of marketing research report? Unfortunately, neither the literature on organization design nor the actual practice of marketing research offers any standard or easy answers to questions like these.[8] The best, and perhaps the only meaningful, answer to any such question is, It all depends. Depends on what? On factors too numerous to list here exhaustively. However, the following factors illustrate the types of potential influences that bear on the organization of in-house marketing research.

Variety of information needed. Decentralized marketing research is most appropriate for a diversified firm that has a number of divisions or subsidiaries, selling different product lines to different market segments. R. J. Reynolds Industries, Inc., is an example of such a firm with decentralized marketing research. It has six subsidiaries: Del Monte Corporation (canned foods and beverages), R. J.

---

[6] Twedt, *1983 Survey*.

[7] Most textbooks on organization design discuss different ways of organizing departments and the factors to be considered in doing so; for example, see Richard L. Daft, *Organization Theory and Design* (St. Paul, Minn.: West, 1983).

[8] This result is one of the key conclusions drawn by Crisp, "Organization of the Marketing Research Function."

Reynolds Tobacco Company (cigarettes), R. J. Reynolds Tobacco International, Inc. (cigarettes), Sea-Land Industries Investments, Inc. (containerized shipping), Aminoil U.S.A., Inc. (oil and gas), and R. J. Reynolds Development Corporation (identification and development of consumer markets for the other subsidiaries of R. J. Reynolds Industries).

Role of in-house marketing research. In the previous chapter we saw that marketing research can be of help in three types of decision-making activities: goal setting, developing and implementing plans, and controlling. The nature and scope of the role in-house marketing research is expected to play in each of these activities will have a bearing on how the research function is organized. For example, if the primary role of in-house research is to aid in setting goals or formulating corporate strategies, a centralized marketing research department may be most appropriate. In contrast, decentralizing in-house marketing research (by product group) may be worthwhile when it plays a key role in developing marketing plans and fine-tuning the marketing mixes for a number of products.

Urgency of information needs. The speed with which marketing information is needed for decision-making purposes can affect the organization of in-house marketing research. For example, a firm in a highly volatile industry (e.g., consumer electronics industry) may experience a more urgent and more frequent need to feel the pulse of its marketing environment than does a firm in a less volatile industry (e.g., farm machinery industry). Consequently, a multidivision firm (or even a single-division firm marketing a variety of products) operating in a volatile environment may be better off with a decentralized, rather than centralized, marketing research department.

Economies of scale. In general, the consolidation of any business function in a central location will lead to certain operating efficiencies; marketing research is no exception. For instance, to have a corporate marketing research department, with experts on questionnaire design, sample selection, statistical techniques, and so on, on its staff, may be more efficient than to duplicate such expertise at various decentralized areas. Moreover, when the total marketing research budget is severely constrained, decentralization of marketing research may result in the hiring of unqualified, or only marginally qualified, research personnel. In contrast, with centralization a firm may afford to hire experts who are capable of producing high-quality research information. However, bear in mind that the so-called economies of scale usually exist only up to a certain point. For instance, when a firm's branches, divisions, or product groups become too large, a corporate marketing research department can no longer cope with the diverse demands for information from the various sections of the firm. Excessive demands, in turn, will adversely affect the quality and usefulness of the research information generated. At this time, at least partially decentralizing the marketing research function may be beneficial.

Determining the "best" structure for organizing in-house marketing research is complicated not only by the sheer number of influencing factors, such as the ones we have examined, but also by some of those factors pointing in *different* directions. For instance, while environmental instability may point toward decentralization, economies of scale and budget constraints may suggest centralization. In the absence of any standard procedure for resolving such potential conflicts, top managers often use their best judgment in determining the most appropriate organization for their in-house marketing research activity. Indeed, there are, perhaps, as many different ways of organizing marketing research departments as there are firms with marketing research departments.

Desirable attributes of marketing research departments

Although there apparently is no unique or best way to organize a marketing research department, the experience of a number of executives suggests that every marketing research department must possess certain common characteristics, *irrespective of organizational form.* These characteristics must foster effective teamwork between researchers and research users, which, as we learned in the previous chapter, is the key to ensuring that marketing research is beneficial to a firm. We can conveniently summarize the desirable characteristics of a marketing research department under the following three attribute labels: integration, importance, and independence. These characteristics are described next.

Integration. Integration refers to *coordination and communication* between the marketing research department and other decision-making units within a firm. Effective coordination and communication are essential for ensuring that researchers and research users work as a team rather than as adversaries. Progressive firms place considerable value on achieving such integration, as the following examples show.

EXAMPLE: Heublein, Inc., is a large food and beverage company, with more than one hundred brands and annual sales of over $2 billion. According to Robert W. Pratt, vice president–director of corporate strategic planning, "There is an important role for marketing research in strategic planning. The potential is there, the need is there, the opportunity is there." However, marketing research at Heublein had been unable to achieve that potential, mainly because of an absence of a proper organizational framework and the lack of the right research personnel.

However, Heublein's management made a conscious effort to overcome this barrier. After years of experimenting with different organizational structures, the company finally developed a central marketing services department, with three research directors on its staff: a director of food marketing research, a director of beverage marketing research, and a director of corporate marketing research. While the food and beverage marketing research directors were responsible for researching their respective marketing environments, the corporate research director primarily played an *integrative* role. In addition to drawing from the studies done by the other two directors and conducting his own research, the corporate research director served as the communication link with top management and regularly attended planning staff meetings and planning conferences. According to Pratt, this approach has been very beneficial to Heublein.[9]

EXAMPLE: A prime, and perhaps extreme, example of an organization that is fully committed to integrating marketing research with other departments is General Electric Company's Video Products Division. This division recently started requiring its *engineers* to make personal calls on dealers and customers in order to obtain direct feedback from the marketplace. Although engineers are by no means professional marketing researchers, the point here is that the organization of the marketing research activity at GE's Video Products Division is flexible enough to permit *direct communication* between the designers and customers of its products.[10]

Importance. To function effectively, marketing research must have an adequate degree of *status and prestige* within a firm. A common complaint of researchers is that managers neither provide the necessary resources nor show respect for the researchers' work. Such a complaint is a barrier to effective teamwork between the two parties. The seriousness of this barrier can be reduced if marketing research gets an "important" position within a firm's organizational structure. However, the responsibility for the marketing research department's status does not rest entirely with top management; the marketing research department itself must demonstrate that it is deserving of such status by proving its worth and winning the confidence of those it services. These viewpoints are implied in the following advice given to marketing researchers by Douglas K. Shifflet, vice president of corporate marketing services, Marriott Corporation:

> Acquire the symbols of power and functional access to key decision makers (you'll get the power and access if you [prove that you are valuable]). If

---

[9] "Marketing Research Needs Right Organization, People to Fulfill Its Strategic Planning Potential," *Marketing News,* September 18, 1981, Section 1, pp. 14–15.

[10] "Listening to the Voice of the Marketplace," *Business Week,* February 21, 1983, pp. 90–95.

researchers improve their standing in the corporation, management will be more likely to listen to their insights rather than stifle and reinterpret them.[11]

Independence. The *ability to conduct research objectively,* without facing any explicit or implicit threat from other sections of a firm, is a critical ingredient of a potentially useful marketing research department. A number of practitioners have emphasized the need to grant organizational independence to marketing research departments, as illustrated by the following statement of Douglas K. Shifflet:

> The marketing services department must report *directly* to senior general management. Researchers can't be effective if they are not objective, and they can't be objective if they have to report to another functional area such as planning or finance.[12]

Furthermore, according to John R. Blair, director of marketing research, Quaker Oats Company:

> Good researchers . . . lead research programs rather than develop programs in response to the questions and issues presented to them. Implied here is the notion of independent thinking about priorities and issues, an extremely delicate rope to walk. Research is a staff unit that must service the needs, both real and perceived, of the marketing department. But you must have the independence, both organizationally and in thought, and the courage to identify and work on those additional issues that you believe have a payback to the company in terms of more efficient marketing.[13]

In a nutshell, then, the key to the ultimate effectiveness of in-house marketing research departments is the extent to which their structures and operations are characterized by integration, importance, and independence. For example, the marketing research department in Blue Cross and Blue Shield of Iowa displays all three key attributes. It is under a director of product planning/development who reports directly to senior management, thus indicating its importance and, to a certain degree, its independence (see Exhibit 2.2).

The marketing research department in Blue Cross and Blue Shield of Iowa also uses a Project Proposal Form (shown in Exhibit 2.3) and a Flow Diagram (shown in Exhibit 2.4) for obtaining and processing research requests from other departments. A close examination of Exhibits 2.3 and 2.4 reveals that the marketing research department is effectively integrated with the other departments but, at the same time, has the authority to make independent evaluations.

---

[11] Douglas K. Shifflet, "Six Principles for Repositioning Marketing Research Departments," *Marketing News,* September 17, 1982, Section 2, p. 5.
[12] Shifflet, "Six Principles."
[13] Quoted in "Successful Researchers Influence Marketing Decisions," *Marketing News,* January 21, 1983, Section 1, p. 4.

Exhibit 2.2

Position of marketing research department in Blue Cross and Blue Shield of Iowa

President

Vice president Financial | Vice president External affairs | Vice president Internal affairs

Administrator IPA development | Consultant External affairs | Director Product planning/development | Account consultant IA bankers | Management associate

Manager Marketing research

Marketing research coordinator | Marketing research analyst | Marketing information coordinator

MIS operator

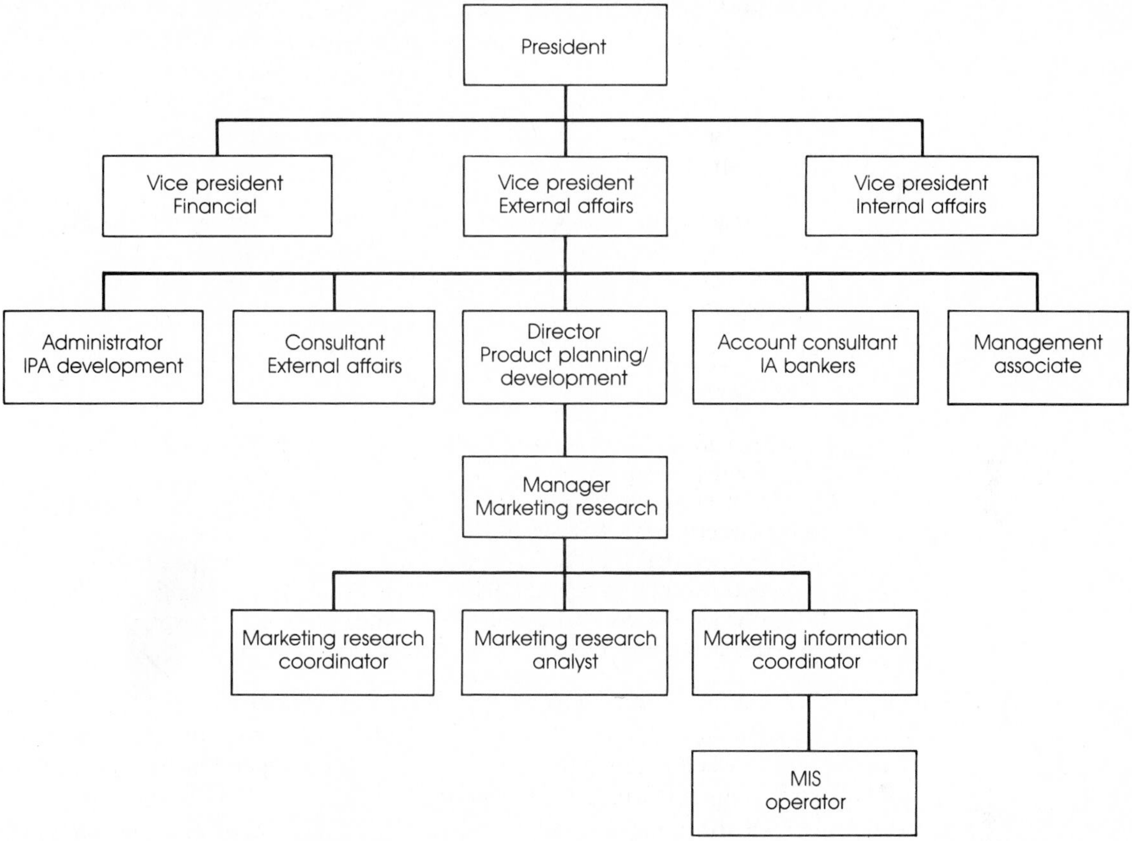

Source: Blue Cross and Blue Shield of Iowa, Des Moines, Iowa." 1983 Organizational Chart." *Note:* Only a partial organization chart is shown here.

For instance, the Project Proposal Form offers the requesting department an opportunity to suggest a suitable method for completing the project (see Exhibit 2.3). The marketing research department itself can revise or even reject a project if it has sound reasons for doing so. However, notice that the research department must explain, in writing, the reasons for revising or rejecting the proposal. It then returns the proposal to the requesting department for whatever further action the requesting department may want to take (see the flow diagram in Exhibit 2.4). The strength of this process is that it permits *true* two-way communication between the marketing research and requesting departments, *without compromising the independence of either department.* Says Thomas C.

Exhibit 2.3

Project Proposal Form

Blue Cross Blue Shield

MARKETING RESEARCH DEPARTMENT PROJECT PROPOSAL FORM

MARKETING RESEARCH PROPOSAL NO. ______

DATE	DIVISION		COST CENTER
DEPARTMENT			PHONE
NAME		TITLE	DATE NEEDED

TITLE OF PROJECT: ______

PURPOSE OF PROJECT: ______

OBJECTIVES:

1) ______

2) ______

3) ______

4) ______

SUGGESTED METHOD FOR COMPLETING PROJECT - CHECK APPROPRIATE BOX

☐ FORECASTING & PREDICTION MODELS

☐ SURVEY RESEARCH TELEPHONE/MAIL

☐ PERSONAL INTERVIEW RESEARCH

☐ INTERNAL AND SECONDARY DATA SEARCH

☐ MARKETING INFORMATION SYSTEM

☐ OTHER - SPECIFY ______

INDICATE IF OTHER DEPARTMENTS ARE INVOLVED - CHECK APPROPRIATE BOX

☐ NO ☐ YES, IF YES, WHICH ONES ______

ADDITIONAL COMMENTS: ______

INDICATE HOW OFTEN PROJECT WILL BE NEEDED - CHECK APPROPRIATE BOX

☐ ONCE ☐ PERIODICALLY SPECIFY ______

DO NOT WRITE BELOW THIS LINE

MARKETING RESEARCH REVIEW COMMITTEE

COMMENTS: ______

☐ PROJECT REJECTED - REASONS ______

☐ PROJECT ACCEPTED - RESEARCH OBJECTIVES & METHODOLOGIES, TIME FRAMES, COST PROJECTIONS WILL BE DEVELOPED FOR REVIEW BY ORIGINATING DEPARTMENT.

ASSIGNED TO ______ PROJECT NO. ______

TITLE ______ DATE PROJECT COMPLETED ______

MARKETING RESEARCH COORDINATOR ______ DATE ______ MANAGER, MARKETING RESEARCH ______ DATE ______

R-1365-T 1/82 DISTRIBUTION: MARKETING RESEARCH, ORGINATOR, FILE

Source: T. C. Benedict, Jr., "Flow Diagram Shows How to Evaluate Research Proposals," *Marketing News,* May 1982, p. 11. Reprinted with permission of the author and the American Marketing Association.

Exhibit 2.4

Flow diagram for obtaining and processing research requests

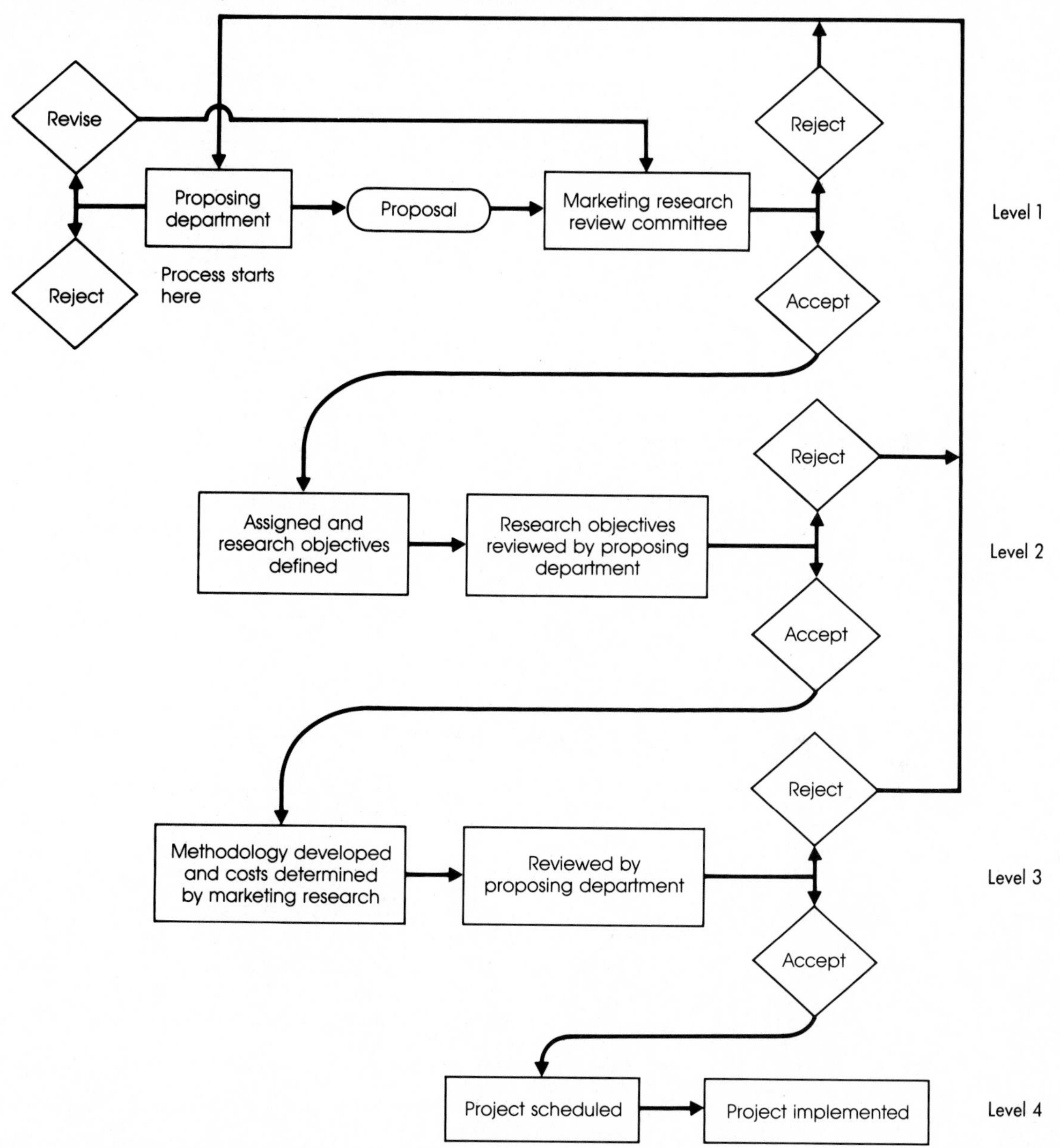

Source: T. C. Benedict, Jr., "Flow Diagram Shows How to Evaluate Research Proposals," *Marketing News,* May 1982, p. 11. Reprinted with permission of the author and the American Marketing Association.

Benedict, Jr., marketing research analyst for Blue Cross and Blue Shield of Iowa, "Keeping communication channels open between the research department and the individual department requesting a study is important. The use of a proposal form such as ours should encourage this interaction."[14]

EXTERNAL SUPPLIERS OF MARKETING RESEARCH

Many organizations—those with and those without their own in-house marketing research capabilities—call upon external research suppliers to meet at least some of their information needs. So let us look at the types of external suppliers.

Types of external suppliers

External suppliers of marketing research services primarily consist of commercial marketing research firms (including one-person consulting firms), academic consultants (i.e., marketing faculty members who offer consulting services on a part-time basis), and other agencies such as trade associations and the U.S. Census Bureau.[15] Of the three types, commercial marketing research firms account for the majority of the total range of services offered by external suppliers. Hence we will discuss such firms in some detail.

According to Richard D. Crisp, commercial marketing research firms

> range from the very large, full-service marketing research agency qualified to handle a major assignment, from planning through delivery of final report and recommendations, to smaller firms that specialize in doing part of the total task. The latter category includes firms specializing in interviewing or other types of fieldwork, in conducting store audit studies as part of test market activities, or new product programs, etc.[16]

Approximately eleven hundred commercial marketing research firms operate in the United States.[17] These firms vary widely in terms of the geographic scope of their operations—ranging from international to local—as well as in

---

[14] Thomas C. Benedict, Jr., "Flow Diagram Shows How to Evaluate Research Proposals," *Marketing News,* May 14, 1982, Section 1, p. 11.

[15] For a discussion of the nature and strengths of a one-person consulting firm, see Margaret R. Roller, "Tight Budget? Hire Independent Research Consultant Instead of Delaying or Weakening Studies," *Marketing News,* September 17, 1982, Section 2, p. 1. The benefits of using academic consultants are discussed in Robert R. Harmon, "Part-Time Consulting Benefits Marketing Educators, Schools, Students, Profession," *Marketing News,* July 23, 1982, Section 1, p. 2.

[16] Crisp, "Organization of the Marketing Research Function," pp. 1–66.

[17] Based on the listings in American Marketing Association, *International Directory of Marketing Research Houses and Services.* (New York: American Marketing Association, 1982).

terms of the range and nature of their services, as the following examples illustrate.

EXAMPLE: Burke Marketing Services, Inc., through its Burke International Research, Inc., and Burke Marketing Research divisions, offers a very wide range of custom-designed research services to client organizations all over the world.[18]

EXAMPLE: A. C. Nielsen Company also operates internationally, but its offerings are dominated by syndicated services rather than custom-designed services (we will see more about syndicated services in Chapter 5 when we talk about secondary data).[19]

EXAMPLE: Namelab is a limited-service firm specializing in developing and testing names for a variety of products and services.[20]

EXAMPLE: Legal Market Research, Inc., is a firm catering exclusively to legal clients. It offers "custom designed and legally oriented marketing research and consulting products for law firms and marketing entities where litigation may be involved. [Its services include] expert witness testimony, trademark and packaging studies, pricing and antitrust situations, advertising studies and others."[21]

EXAMPLE: Associates Interviewing Services operates in a limited geographic area and primarily offers fieldwork services, as the following description indicates: "Philadelphia interviewing service covering entire metro area. High quality work. Personal, telephone, in-store interviewing, product placements, executive and in-depth interviews. Permanent suburban mall location with excellent demographics for group sessions, taste tests, package testing, advertising testing. One-way mirror. Kitchen."[22]

Though there are well over a thousand marketing research firms in the United States, just a handful of them account for a large share of total marketing research industry revenues. In other words, most of the research firms are relatively small. Table 2.1 lists the top 30 research firms, ordered according to their revenues. Notice the wide variation in sizes even within the top 30 firms. While the largest had 1982 revenues of a little over $433 million, the smallest had revenues of only $6.4 million. The skewed size distribution within the marketing research industry results because most firms operate only in a small geographic area and offer only a limited range of research services.

---

[18] American Marketing Association, *International Directory,* pp. 44, 46.

[19] American Marketing Association, *International Directory,* pp. 162–163.

[20] Further details about Namelab are available in a brochure entitled "NAMELAB—Name Development & Testing Laboratory", available from Namelab, 2229 Beach Street, San Francisco, Calif. 94123.

[21] American Marketing Association, *International Directory,* p. 119.

[22] American Marketing Association, *International Directory,* p. 30.

Table 2.1

Leading United States Marketing Research Firms

1982 RANK	1981 RANK	ORGANIZATION	RESEARCH REVENUES (MILLIONS)	PERCENT CHANGE vs. 1981	RESEARCH REVENUES FROM OUTSIDE U.S. (MILLIONS)
1	1	A. C. Nielsen Co.	$433.1	+5.2	$242.1
2	2	IMS International	124.8	+8.3	'81.8
3	3	SAMI	85.0	+17.1	—
4	4	Arbitron Ratings Co.	80.3	+20.9	—
5	5	Burke Marketing Services	52.1	+18.9	1.4
6	6	Market Facts	25.4	0.0	—
7	7	Audits & Surveys	22.5	*	—
8	—	NFO Research	22.0	+14.0	—
9	8	Marketing and Research Counselors	21.9	+21.7	—
10	9	NPD Group	21.5	+20.1	—
11	12	Maritz Market Research	18.5	−2.1	—
12	10	Westat Inc.	17.3	+8.8	—
13	19	Elrick and Lavidge	16.9	+15.8	—
14	13	ASI Market Research	16.3	+9.4	0.7
15	11	Chilton Research Services	16.2	+6.6	—
16	14	Yankelovich, Skelly & White	13.4	+3.9	0.5
17	15	Walker Research	12.6	+7.8	—
18	24	Information Resources	12.3	+109.5	—
19	18	Louis Harris and Associates	12.1	+19.8	3.8
20	16	Ehrhart-Babic Group	11.9	+1.7	0.1
21	17	Data Development Corp.	11.8	+5.4	—
22	25	Winona Research	11.3	+11.9	—
23	20	Opinion Research Corp.	10.2	+24.4	—
24	—	Harte-Hanks Marketing Services Group	9.6	+2.8	—
25	21	Decisions Center	8.4	+21.7	—
26	—	McCollum/Spielman/& Co.	7.1	+16.4	—
27	23	Starch INRA Hooper	7.0	+10.1	1.4
28	28	Market Opinion Research	6.7	+43.4	0.7
29	22	National Analysts	6.6	−1.0	—
30	27	Custom Research	6.4	+36.2	—
			$1,121.2	+10.3%*	$332.5

Source: Reprinted with permission from the May 23, 1983, issue of *Advertising Age*. Copyright © 1983 by Crain Communications, Inc.

*No new input was received from A&S for 1982; therefore it was not included in calculating industry growth from year to year.

Deciding when to use external suppliers

Organizations without in-house marketing research capability invariably have to hire an external supplier when they want information from their marketing environment. Hence for such organizations the question of *when* to use external suppliers has a rather simple answer: "Whenever they have a need to obtain research information." However, this issue is somewhat more complex in the context of firms that have the capacity to conduct marketing research on their own.

Do firms with in-house research capability use external suppliers? Yes. Examples of firms that do so include Coca-Cola, Procter and Gamble, Quaker Oats, and Del Monte Corporation. Moreover, many large firms are establishing ongoing relationships with research suppliers by maintaining them on retainers.[23] A variety of reasons cause a firm to engage the services of an external supplier. In fact, several citations in the marketing literature contain detailed lists of circumstances in which a firm should hire an external supplier.[24] Although some minor discrepancies appear across such lists, they all suggest the same *general* factors to be considered. These factors can be labeled as credibility, competence, cost, and capacity. Each factor is discussed next.

Credibility. *Credibility,* in the context of external suppliers, is akin to the concept of independence that we discussed under in-house research. Even firms with full-fledged in-house marketing research departments hire outside agencies to conduct research in situations where the credibility, and hence usefulness, of the research may depend as much on *who* does the research as on *how well* it is done. For instance, suppose the board of directors of a large corporation wants to know how successful top management has been in building a favorable image for the corporation in the eyes of the public. In this situation the board is likely to find an assessment of corporate image made by an independent research firm more credible than an assessment based on data gathered by in-house marketing research.

In 1980 the Chrysler Corporation ran a series of print ads touting specific Chrysler models as being preferred by consumers over comparable competing models. For example, one of those ads displayed the headline, "The New Chrysler Corporation challenges the Toyota myth: Plymouth TC3 preferred overall to Toyota Corolla 34 to 16." This ad also presented a table showing an attribute-by-attribute comparison of consumer preferences for the two cars.[25] An important feature of each ad in the series was an explicit statement saying that the consumer preference tests were conducted by Nationwide Consumer Testing Institute, Inc. (an independent marketing research firm). Had Chrysler conducted the consumer tests in-house, the credibility of the research results, and hence the credibility of the ads, would have been open to question.

In general, the use of external suppliers is desirable when there is a possibility for conflict of interest (real or perceived) if a research study is conducted in-house—that is, when independence of the source of the research study is crucial in ensuring that the study's findings are credible to their intended audience.

[23] "What Market Research Has to Sell," *Industry Week,* 166 (May 4, 1970), pp. 45–48.

[24] For instance, see R. A. Petersen and R. A. Kerin, "Effective Use of Marketing Research Consultants," *Industrial Marketing Management,* 9 (February 1980), pp. 69–73; R. Paul, "When Does Your Company Need Help From Marketing Research Consultants?" *Industrial Marketing,* 63 (August 1978), p. 48; L. Adler, "How to Tell If You Need the Services of an Outside Research House," *Sales & Marketing Management,* 20 (April 3, 1978), p. 74.

[25] For a look at the ads run by Chrysler, see, for example, *Time,* July 14, 1980, pp. 55–61.

Competence. *Competence* refers to special capabilities or facilities of an external supplier that an in-house marketing research department may not possess. A firm will have to hire an appropriate external supplier for projects requiring special capabilities.

For instance, suppose General Foods wants to obtain a quick assessment of a proposed new type of cereal, *without the knowledge of its competitors.* Here a traditional test-marketing operation, wherein the brand is actually introduced on a trial basis in a limited area, is out of the question (more will be said on test marketing in subsequent chapters). However, General Foods can still obtain the information it wants by using the Laboratory Test Market (LTM) service offered by Yankelovich, Skelley and White, Inc. The LTM

> is a business service which provides management with an economical and effective method of compressing the traditional test marketing of new products into a shorter time span. Time after time, the Laboratory Test Market has proved to be as predictive of the potential share for a new product as the conventional test market . . . *in secret.*[26]

The point here is that without the aid of the *special capabilities*—in this case confidentiality, flexibility, and speed of data collection—of external services like the LTM, General Foods will have difficulty meeting its information objective.

As another illustration of the relevance of the competence factor, consider A. C. Nielsen Company's National ScanTrack Service. This service is based on a nationwide sample of high-volume, scanner-equipped supermarkets, and it provides weekly data on product class, brand and item sales, brand share, selling prices, and so forth, for numerous packaged goods.[27] Nielsen is able to obtain such data readily because of its *wide experience* in store auditing and its *established contacts* with supermarkets. An individual packaged-goods manufacturer, even one with a good in-house marketing research department, will have difficulty gaining access to the kinds of data Nielsen is capable of obtaining.

Cost. With certain types of research projects, for a firm to use an external supplier to do part or all of the work may be more economical than for the firm to do the entire project on its own. External suppliers are especially economical when they specialize in the type of research work to be done. For instance, many in-house marketing research departments may *design* research projects but may hire a field service firm (such as the Associates Interviewing Services mentioned earlier) to perform the *data collection.* For an in-house research department to maintain a full staff of qualified fieldwork professionals such as interviewers and data coders may be prohibitively expensive.

---

[26] "Laboratory Test Market," a brochure prepared by Yankelovich, Skelly and White, Inc., 575 Madison Avenue, New York, N.Y. 10022.

[27] "Nielsen National ScanTrack Service—For Continuous Planning and Evaluation of Promotions," brochure prepared (in 1982) by A. C. Nielsen Company, Nielsen Plaza, Northbrook, Ill. 60062.

As an example, consider the National ScanTrack Service offered by A. C. Nielsen Company. Nielsen's ScanTrack is a syndicated service, that is, one subscribed to by numerous client firms (syndicated services are described in Chapter 5). Consequently, the cost of collecting weekly data on hundreds of packaged products from a national sample of supermarkets is spread over a large number of clients. Thus the cost of ScanTrack data to any one client firm is much lower than if the firm collected the data on its own. A point worth noting here is the *interrelationship* between cost and competence considerations: Hiring an external supplier to perform a research task is likely to be cheaper than doing it in-house *if the supplier has certain special capabilities for performing the task efficiently.*

Capacity. Sometimes, a firm may hire an external supplier to conduct an important research project—one that cannot be delayed—when the firm's in-house research department is fully tied up with ongoing research projects. In other words, external suppliers may be employed to expand the *capacity* of in-house marketing research temporarily to meet urgent research needs. When the timing of a research project is crucial, a firm may be forced to secure the services of an external supplier, even though in-house marketing research might be capable of handling the project *if* it had the time. The critical issue is, "*How soon* can in-house marketing research conduct the project?" rather than, "Is in-house marketing research *qualified* to conduct the project?"

Consider ABC Corporation, consisting of three product divisions (divisions X, Y, and Z), with a corporate in-house marketing research department serving all three divisions. The in-house research department is at present fully occupied with research projects requested by divisions X and Y. Suppose that at this time division Z experiences a sudden and sharp decline in its sales. Understandably, division Z feels an immediate need to conduct marketing research aimed at examining its sales problem and taking corrective action. Under these circumstances ABC Corporation has no choice but to allow division Z to seek the assistance of an external supplier. Given the *urgency* of the need for research information, if ABC waits for the in-house marketing research department to help division Z, it may be too late for the research information to be beneficial.

Selecting external suppliers

What criteria should a firm consider in selecting an external research supplier? Several authorities have offered lists of criteria.[28] Fortunately, the various lists agree to a great extent and lead to a handful of general guidelines—guidelines

[28] For instance, see C. S. Mayer, "Evaluating the Quality of Marketing Research Contractors," *Journal of Marketing Research,* 4 (May 1967), pp. 141–143; J. H. Myers, "Competitive Bidding for Marketing Research Services?" *Journal of Marketing,* 33 (July 1969), pp. 40–45; L. Adler, "How Marketing Research Helps Sales," *Sales & Marketing Management,* 115 (November 3, 1975), pp. 105–107.

related to issues we looked at when we discussed the desirable attributes of in-house research departments and the reasons for hiring external suppliers. Hence rather than examine the lists of suggestions in detail, we will focus on the general guidelines emerging from them.

What criteria would you use if you were in charge of choosing an external research supplier? You would want the chosen supplier to have the desirable attributes of an ideal in-house marketing research department. After all, an external supplier is in many ways an extension of a firm's in-house marketing research capability. You would also want the chosen supplier to be qualified to complete the research assignment effectively and economically. These concerns are reflected in the following set of selection criteria: prestige, past experience, personnel, and price. Each criterion is discussed next.

Prestige. *Prestige* refers to the reputation of a research supplier and is a surrogate indicator of its research quality and capabilities. Like any other profession, the research industry does have charlatans. Hence, a firm should check out the reputation of prospective research suppliers. A simple way of checking their reputation is to ask the suppliers for references or for a list of clients they serve. The reputation of a supplier's clients is a useful measure of the credibility of the supplier's work and the confidence one can have in it. The prestige criterion is *not* meant to imply that only suppliers with lengthy lists of reputable clients should be considered; such an implication would eliminate from consideration competent *new* firms with sophisticated capabilities. Rather, the point here is merely that a client firm should be extra careful in evaluating the capabilities of new suppliers.

Past experience. There is generally an association between a prospective supplier's ability to deal with an assignment adequately and its *past research experience,* especially experience related to the research assignment under consideration. Hence past experience is an important indicator, though not necessarily the *only* indicator, of a supplier's competence. Another facet of past experience is the extent and nature of the working relationship the client firm may have had with the supplier. Rehiring the services of a supplier with whom past experiences have been good may offer certain advantages, such as lower cost and better client-supplier understanding.

Personnel. As we have emphasized numerous times, the worth of any research project depends on effective teamwork or integration between researchers and research users. Consequently, a key consideration in choosing an external supplier is the set of skills possessed by the supplier firm's *personnel,* particularly those employees who will be in direct contact with client personnel. Here the term *skills* is not restricted to *technical* qualifications; quite to the contrary, it includes *nontechnical* skills such as interpersonal skills, communication skills, the ability to understand a client's research problem, and the ability to establish rapport with client personnel. The potential benefits of research conducted by an external supplier will be diminished if there is not enough communication between client and supplier personnel. The importance of maintaining an effective client-supplier interface is underscored by the numerous books that have been written on this subject.[29]

Price. The *price* of a research supplier's services is of obvious concern to any client firm. However, the cheapest buy is not necessarily the best buy. That is, a research supplier with a good reputation and high-quality research capabilities usually can, and most likely will, demand a premium price. Also, competing suppliers may bid different prices for the same research assignment because their perceptions of the nature and scope of the assignment may be different.[30] In fact, a *written proposal,* detailing what will and will not be covered in a research assignment, should be developed and agreed to by both the client and supplier *before* a final research contract is signed.[31] In other words, the price quoted by a supplier, although critical in terms of the client firm's research budget, should *not* be viewed as the *determining factor* in supplier selection.[32]

A recent survey asked marketing executives in client firms to rate the extent to which each of a set of factors influenced their choice of external research suppliers. The survey's findings showed that client executives ranked the price of research services *seventh* in terms of importance. The six factors perceived to be more important than price were (in decreasing order of importance) (1) understanding client's problem, (2) usefulness of research results, (3) quality of research, (4) research firm's reputation, (5) qualifications of key employees, and (6) referral by satisfied clients.[33]

Thus the potential benefits from a research project and the client-supplier relationship crucial to maximizing those benefits are apparently more dominant concerns of research users than the price of the research services. Indeed, the literature on selecting research suppliers urges client firms to attempt to build a long-term relationship with a single reputable research supplier rather than use

---

[29] See, for example, Chip R. Bell and Leonard Nadler, eds., *The Client-Consultant Handbook* (Houston: Gulf, 1979); John J. McGronagle, Jr., *Managing the Consultant—A Corporate Guide* (Radnor, Pa.: Chilton, 1981).

[30] For a detailed discussion of how marketing research suppliers set prices, see J. B. Haynes and P. L. Wilkens, "Pricing of Marketing Research Services," *Business Horizons,* 17 (October 1974), pp. 75–80.

[31] See A. B. Blankenship and R. F. Barker, "The Buyer's Side of Marketing Research," *Business Horizons,* 16 (August 1973), pp. 73–80.

[32] See J. B. Haynes and J. T. Rothe, "Competitive Bidding for Marketing Research Services: Fact or Fiction?" *Journal of Marketing,* 38 (July 1974), pp. 69–71.

[33] A. Parasuraman and Valarie A. Zeithaml, "Differential Perceptions of Suppliers and Clients of Industrial Services," in *Emerging Perspectives on Services Marketing,* Proceedings Series, ed. Leonard L. Berry, G. Lynn Shostack, and Gregory D. Upah (Chicago: American Marketing Association, 1983), pp. 35–39.

Exhibit 2.5
Criteria for evaluating external research sources

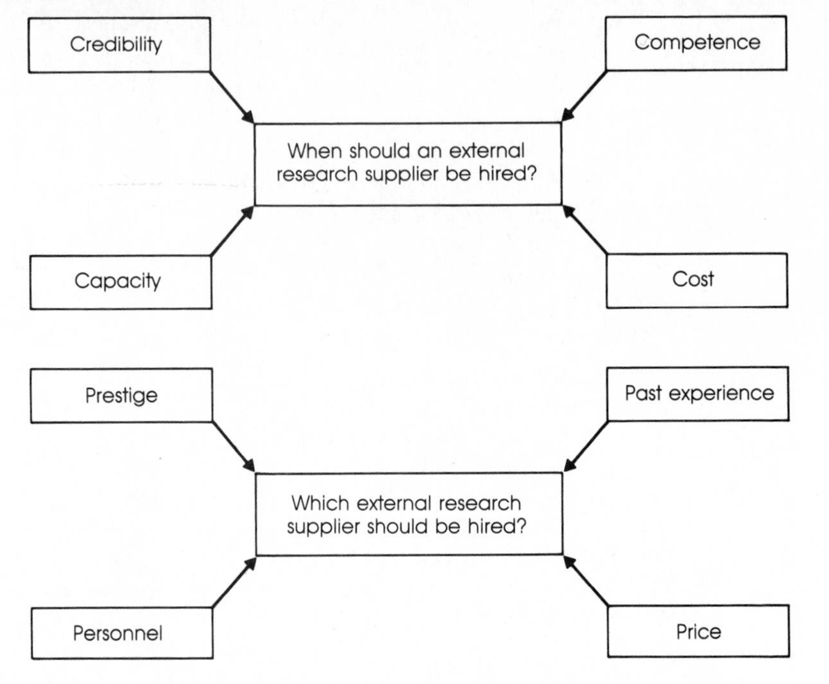

a different supplier for each research assignment because of factors such as price.[34]

The four general considerations discussed in this section—prestige, past experience, personnel, and price—do not constitute an exhaustive set of guidelines to be used in selecting research suppliers. Nevertheless, they do concisely capture the essence of the more detailed lists of evaluation criteria found in the literature. Exhibit 2.5 summarizes the criteria for evaluating the worth of external suppliers.

ETHICS IN MARKETING RESEARCH

The purpose of this section is to expose you to certain key issues relating to the rights and obligations of all those involved in and affected by marketing re-

[34] Two sources that make this recommendation are "What's the Yardstick for Research? A Symposium," *Printer's Ink,* 284 (August 2, 1963), pp. 45–49; J. Pope, "Tips for Research Clients," *Advertising Age,* 51 (November 24, 1980), p. 42.

search. Marketing research ethics seldom receive as much attention as other aspects of research. Nevertheless, ethical considerations pervade the practice of marketing research, often very subtly. In fact, the main reason for discussing research ethics early in this book is to encourage you to ponder the ethical questions implicit in many topics to be covered later.

Code of ethics

The *American Heritage Dictionary* defines ethics as "the rules or standards governing the conduct of the members of a profession."[35] From this definition marketing research ethics may simply be viewed as the ***rules and standards that govern the marketing research profession.*** In fact, several professional marketing organizations have their own written codes of marketing research ethics. For instance, Exhibit 2.6 contains the code of marketing research ethics drawn up by the American Marketing Association, whose members are professionals from academic and business organizations as well as a variety of nonbusiness organizations such as government agencies.

Codes of ethics can serve as useful general guidelines, and perhaps a genuine need for them exists in every profession.[36] However, resolving ethical questions in specific research situations is not as simple as a written code may lead you to believe. The president of Creative Research Group Ltd. (Toronto), Richard Crosby, had this to say about codes of ethics:

> Various marketing research associations have codes of ethics, which implies that ethical matters have been nipped, cauterized even before the bud. The problem is that circumstances are so variable and individualized that they defy generalization. Debate over the need for a code of ethics is as old as the research profession and [my remarks] won't settle the matter. However, the case against a uniform ethical code is a strong one, based on the nature of the marketing research industry.[37]

Furthermore, few, if any, existing ethical codes can be considered comprehensive in their coverage of even the broadest topics concerning ethics in their respective professions. For instance, the following criticism has been leveled against the American Marketing Association's code of marketing research ethics: "This code focuses on the researcher-client relationship and is most relevant to survey techniques. . . . The code neglects issues that emerge in researcher-subject relationships which are particularly salient in experiments."[38]

---

[35] *American Heritage Dictionary of the English Language* (New York: American Heritage, 1973).

[36] See Dik Warren Twedt, "Why a Marketing Research Code of Ethics," *Journal of Marketing,* 27 (July 1963), pp. 45–50.

[37] Richard Crosby, "Uniform Ethical Code Is Impractical Due to Shifting Marketing Research Circumstances," *Marketing News,* September 18, 1981, Section 2, p. 16.

[38] Alice M. Tybout and Gerald Zaltman, "Ethics in Marketing Research: Their Practical Relevance," *Journal of Marketing Research,* 11 (November 1974), p. 357.

Exhibit 2.6

Marketing research code of ethics of the American Marketing Association

The American Marketing Association, in furtherance of its central objective of the advancement of science in marketing and in recognition of its obligation to the public, has established these principles of ethical practice of marketing research for the guidance of its members. In an increasingly complex society, marketing management is more and more dependent upon marketing information intelligently and systematically obtained. The consumer is the source of much of this information. Seeking the cooperation of the consumer in the development of information, marketing management must acknowledge its obligation to protect the public from misrepresentation and exploitation under the guise of research.

Similarly the research practitioner has an obligation to the discipline he practices and to those who provide support for his practice—an obligation to adhere to basic and commonly accepted standards of scientific investigation as they apply to the domain of marketing research.

It is the intent of this code to define ethical standards required of marketing research in satisfying these obligations.

Adherence to this code will assure the users of marketing research that the research was done in accordance with acceptable ethical practices. Those engaged in research will find in this code an affirmation of sound and honest basic principles which have developed over the years as the profession has grown. The field interviewers who are the point of contact between the profession and the consumer will also find guidance in fulfilling their vitally important role.

For Research Users, Practitioners and Interviewers

1. No individual or organization will undertake any activity which is directly or indirectly represented to be marketing research, but which has as its real purpose the attempted sale of merchandise or services to some or all of the respondents interviewed in the course of the research.
2. If a respondent has been led to believe, directly or indirectly, that he is participating in a marketing research survey and that his anonymity will be protected, his name shall not be made known to anyone outside the research organization or research department, or used for other than research purposes.

For Research Practitioners

1. There will be no intentional or deliberate misrepresentation of research methods or results. An adequate description of methods employed will be made available upon request to the sponsor of the research. Evidence that fieldwork has been completed according to specifications will, upon request be made available to buyers of research.
2. The identity of the survey sponsor and/or the ultimate client for whom a survey is being done will be held in confidence at all times, unless this identity is to be revealed as part of the research design. Research information shall be held in confidence by the research organization or department and not used for personal gain or made available to any outside party unless the client specifically authorizes such release.
3. A research organization shall not undertake marketing studies for competitive clients when such studies would jeopardize the confidential nature of client-agency relationships.

For Users of Marketing Research

1. A user of research shall not knowingly disseminate conclusions from a given research project or service that are inconsistent with or not warranted by the data.
2. To the extent that there is involved in a research project a unique design involving techniques, approaches or concepts not commonly available to research practitioners, the prospective user of research shall not solicit such a design from one practitioner and deliver it to another for execution without the approval of the design originator.

For Field Interviewers

1. Research assignments and materials received, as well as information obtained from respondents, shall be held in confidence by the interviewer and revealed to no one except the research organization conducting the marketing study.
2. No information gained through a marketing research activity shall be used directly or indirectly, for the personal gain or advantage of the interviewer.
3. Interviews shall be conducted in strict accordance with specifications and instructions received.
4. An interviewer shall not carry out two or more interviewing assignments simultaneously unless authorized by all contractors or employers concerned.

Members of the American Marketing Association will be expected to conduct themselves in accordance with the provisions of this Code in all of their marketing research activities.

Source: Marketing Research Standards Committee, *Marketing Research Code of Ethics* (Chicago: American Marketing Association, 1972). Used by permission.

As another illustration of the inadequacy of codes of ethics, consider the plight of the Ethics Committee of the American Marketing Association's New York Chapter, which attempted to choose a code of ethics that would best address the chapter members' requests for ethical guidance on research issues: "Committee members produced 15 codes, none of which was suitable. The standards were either too broad and vague, too focused on a particular function of research, or too limited to the interest of a given organization."[39]

An additional drawback of a code of ethics is that any so-called standard in an ethical code is in reality subject to different interpretations stemming from the values and priorities of the individuals seeking guidance from the code. Research ethics "are guidelines and principles that help us uphold *our values*—to decide which goals of research are most important and to reconcile values and goals that are in conflict"[40] (emphasis added).

C. Merle Crawford conducted an interesting study that found evidence of how individuals' value systems and interpretations can influence their perceptions about what is ethical and what is not.[41] Crawford presented, to a sample of marketing managers and researchers, several hypothetical research scenarios, each involving an action that was potentially questionable on ethical grounds. The survey respondents were asked to state whether they approved or disapproved of the action taken in each scenario and to give reasons for their answers. One of the scenarios was the following:

> One product of the X Company is brassieres, and the firm has recently been having difficulty making some decisions on a new line. Information was critically needed concerning the manner in which women put on their brassieres. So the Marketing Research Director designed a study in which two local stores cooperated in putting one-way mirrors in their foundations dressing rooms. Observers behind these mirrors successfully gathered the necessary information.[42]

About 80% of the managers and researchers disapproved of the use of one-way mirrors in this situation. As one might expect, the predominant reason for their disapproval was their perception of the action as a serious invasion of privacy. However, 20% of the respondents *approved* the action since they apparently assumed that the observers were female and hence felt that the need for information was much more critical than the issue of moral infractions. One of these respondents is reported to have said, "The women don't know they've been observed, and thus can suffer no mental anguish." How do you feel about the appropriateness of using one-way mirrors in this scenario?

---

[39] Marilyn Landis (Hauser), "Why It Took Three Years for Ethics Panel to Polish Pledge," *Marketing News,* September 19, 1980, p. 1.
[40] Edward Diener and Rick Crandall, *Ethics in Social and Behavioral Research* (Chicago: University of Chicago Press, 1978), p. 3.
[41] C. Merle Crawford, "Attitudes of Marketing Executives Toward Ethics in Marketing Research," *Journal of Marketing,* 34 (April 1970), pp. 46–52.
[42] Crawford, "Attitudes of Marketing Executives," p. 47.

In sum, perceptions about what is ethical clearly depend on one's value system and subjective judgment.

Ethical issues concerning various parties

Several different parties are directly or indirectly associated with marketing research. We can classify them into five groups:

1. Research firms that directly deal with client organizations; these firms are traditionally known as *research suppliers.*
2. Data-gathering firms that cater to research suppliers as well as in-house marketing research departments; these firms are typically referred to as *field service firms.*
3. *Research subjects* or respondents who provide the data collected.
4. *Clients* who are the users of marketing research information.
5. The *general public* that may be affected by the dissemination of research results.

Each of the five groups has certain *rights,* which implies that each also has certain *obligations* toward the others. Examples of the rights of each party are discussed next.

Research suppliers. Research suppliers have a right to be treated fairly by clients and by field service firms, the two groups they most frequently deal with. Alternatively, clients and field service firms have an obligation to treat research suppliers fairly. What does *fair treatment* mean? It can refer to a variety of ethical issues depending on the nature of the situation and values of the individuals involved. Let us look at an example.

EXAMPLE: Client, Inc., hires Research, Inc., to conduct a study to determine the extent of use of Client's brand (say, brand X) versus the use of competing brands. Research, Inc., conducts a study and presents the following conclusion to Client, Inc.: "Of the 2000 respondents surveyed 1000 refused to disclose the brand used; of the remaining 1000 respondents 500 used brand X, 300 used brand Y, and 200 used a variety of other brands." From this conclusion Client, Inc., develops the following ad campaign: "One out of every two consumers uses brand X, according to a study conducted by Research, Inc."

What are the ethical issues involved in this example? Client has conveniently ignored the half of the sample that refused to disclose the brand used. Hence the ad claim is certainly questionable, unless Client has additional evidence suggesting that respondents to the study did not significantly differ from nonrespondents or that the 1000 respondents were similar to target market consumers. In the absence of such evidence the ad may also tarnish Research's reputation since it explicitly identifies Research as the source of the claim. Other knowledgeable industry sources, such as Client's major competitors, which may be aware that Client's ad claim is not true, are likely to think poorly of Research's methodology and hence its image. And what about the rights of the general public that will be exposed to the ad campaign? We will discuss more on this issue later.

Although the situation depicted in the example is fictitious, similar happenings are apparently not uncommon in real life. For instance, according to Nancy Finn, group marketing manager for Clairol, many marketers deliberately distort research findings. Finn labels them "data manipulators," who "have little respect for the contribution of an individual researcher or the discipline of marketing research."[43]

Field service firms also have certain obligations to research suppliers. For instance, a field service firm that deviates from the data collection procedures laid down by a research supplier, *without the consent of the latter,* is not being ethical. Yet such violations apparently occur frequently. As an executive of Data Development Corporation (a research supplier in New York), calling for greater professionalism, honesty, and accuracy on the part of field services, says: "We don't get the quality product we would like. . . . We trust field supervisors, yet it is in this area that my expectations suffer the most."[44]

Field service firms. One of the rights of field service firms is to receive adequate respect and compensation for their fieldwork. This statement almost sounds like a truism. However, in practice, adequate compensation is not always received.[45] Consider the following scenario, which is claimed as being typical of the experiences of many field service firms:

> A field service firm on the West Coast receives a rush order for a long-distance telephone study from a client firm on the East Coast. Since time is short, a *verbal contract* is agreed to over the telephone, with the understanding that the field service will be reimbursed for all the study expenses, as long as the study is completed on time. The field service firm completes the job on time and mails the findings to the client along with a bill for the study's costs. However, the client questions certain charges on the bill, such as certain long-distance telephone charges and the charge for a field supervisor's time, and refuses to pay the bill in full. Instead, the client only pays what it feels is fair.

---

[43] Quoted in "Marketers Are Information Lovers, Expediters, or Manipulators When Interfacing with Researchers," *Marketing News,* January 22, 1982, Section 2, p. 12.

[44] Quoted in "Marketing Research Clients, Suppliers, Field Services Tell Expectations of One Another," *Marketing News,* September 18, 1981, Section 2, p. 3.

[45] "Marketing Research Clients, Suppliers, Field Services." See also "Marketing Research Suppliers, Clients Should Respect the Professionalism of Data Collectors," *Marketing News,* January 22, 1982, Section 2, p. 2.

The field service firm feels cheated and is frustrated at being unable to collect from an out-of-state firm.[46]

Is the client firm being ethical? The field service firm would definitely not think so. Since there was no written contract, however, the ethical question is very hard to resolve objectively. Possibly, the conflicting viewpoints of the two parties arose owing to a genuine misunderstanding about what was covered by the verbal contract. This scenario is illustrative of the many gray areas in marketing research ethics; only the expectations, value systems, and sense of fairness of the particular parties involved can adequately resolve such issues.[47]

Research subjects. Many modern-day forces such as the consumer movement and the increasing importance of individualism are placing the rights of research subjects in the limelight. Of particular interest to marketing research practice are the following rights of research subjects: the *right to privacy,* the *right to be informed,* the *right to decline to participate* in a study, the *right to physical and psychological safety,* and the *right to confidentiality* of responses. Although the American Marketing Association's code of ethics (Exhibit 2.6) does not explicitly address these rights, the codes of other associations, like the American Psychological Association, do so.[48] These rights are self-explanatory, and any concerned researcher should be aware of them and be willing to respect them. However, looking beyond the mere definitions of these rights, one will see numerous ethical gray areas in which a researcher will have to make judgment calls.

Take a survey respondent's right to privacy, for instance. All of us will probably agree that telephoning a respondent in the middle of the night as part of a survey is a serious violation of the respondent's right to privacy. What about calling the respondent about 7 P.M? You will probably say, "That's okay." But see if you still think so after reading the next scenario.

EXAMPLE: It is 7 P.M. and John Hagen is right in the middle of what he considers to be a very important dinner with others. The phone rings, and the caller is conducting a survey. Says the caller: "Mr. Hagen, you are one of a scientifically chosen few to participate in this *extremely important* study dealing with . . . . It is critical that you take just a few minutes *now* to

---

[46] Adapted from "How Unethical Firms 'Prey' on Marketing Research Suppliers," *Marketing News,* September 18, 1981, Section 2, p. 16.

[47] Other illustrations of ethical conflicts in client-researcher dealings can be found in Sidney Hollander, Jr., "Ethics in Marketing Research," in *Handbook of Marketing Research,* ed. Robert Ferber (New York: McGraw-Hill, 1974), pp. 1–107 to 1–127.

[48] *Ethical Principles in the Conduct of Research with Human Participants* (Washington, D.C.: American Psychological Association, 1973).

respond to my survey. Your refusal to participate now will seriously affect the usefulness of the study. Won't you *please* help us by participating?"

Should John agree to participate? If he does, his important dinner is going to be further interrupted; moreover, depending on the nature of the survey questions, his mood may be affected. The result can be viewed as an unfair invasion of John's privacy. What if John simply exercises his right to decline to participate and hangs up? This action will prevent any further violation of his privacy; but will it also make him feel guilty and cause him psychological pain? If it does, his right to safety will be violated to a certain degree.

Does the researcher have any ethical responsibility here? Should, or could, the researcher have anticipated a situation like this and taken precautions to prevent it from happening?

Although the situation in this example is hypothetical, and perhaps even somewhat extreme, it is illustrative of real ethical issues researchers wrestle with frequently. A *broad* ethical question underlying scenarios such as the one presented is, Where does one draw the line between a researcher's need (or right) for information and the rights of research subjects? There are no easy solutions to such questions.[49]

Clients. Client organizations have a right to expect fair treatment from the other parties in the marketing research arena. For instance, they have a right to get an accurate, honest estimate of the cost of a study to be done by a research supplier. This right appears to be straightforward. However, consider this situation: A research supplier estimates that a study will cost $10,000, and the client agrees that this price is reasonable. But when the study is completed, the research supplier submits a bill for $15,000, claiming that the cost increased because of changes the client wanted made during the course of the study. The client, while acknowledging that certain unplanned changes were made, argues that such changes should have cost no more than an additional $2000. Who is to be blamed here? This question, too, is an ethical issue with no easy answer.

Clients also have a right to expect research suppliers to be honest and accurate in meeting the clients' information needs. Research practice indicates again that this right is not easily achieved. The nature of the research industry is such that research suppliers may be tempted, or even forced, to compromise their integrity in their quest for business survival. For instance, here is what Harry Heller, president of Harry Heller Research Corporation, a research supplier, had to say about his industry: "The proliferation of research suppliers has led to the basic, underlying problem in our field. Suppliers are over-promising.

[49] For a related discussion, see Leo Bogart, "The Researcher's Dilemma," *Journal of Marketing,* 26 (January 1962), pp. 6–11.

As a result, clients are over-demanding. . . . There are more than enough companies that will promise anything."[50]

General public. The rights of the general public are not very different from those of research subjects. The only major difference between the two sets of rights is that while the rights of the research subjects become relevant *during data collection,* the rights of the general public become relevant *if and when any research information is disseminated.*

Recall the scenario involving Client, Inc., and Research, Inc., that we looked at while discussing the rights to research suppliers. In that scenario Client made a questionable ad claim, which we said was unfair to the reputation of Research. By using the claim in a national ad campaign, Client would also violate the right of the general public to be informed accurately. This action is a clear case of unethical behavior on the part of Client. Unfortunately, ethical matters concerning the rights of the general public are not always as clear-cut, as the next example indicates.

EXAMPLE: During the 1980 presidential election on November 4, NBC, ABC, and CBS interviewed numerous voters so as to be able to predict the winner. On the basis of its interviews NBC was the first to predict that Ronald Reagan would be the winner. NBC made its prediction public before its competitors and *before the polls closed on the West Coast.*[51] NBC certainly had the right to inform the public and the right to stay ahead of its competition. But were any of the general public's rights violated? Specifically, did NBC violate the rights of any West Coast voters by announcing a predicted winner *before* they had a chance to vote?

The area of ethics in marketing research is extremely important and concerns the rights of a variety of parties. Nevertheless, the resolution of real-life ethical conflicts is not always easy. Potential ethical conflicts can perhaps be minimized, but not necessarily eliminated, if the three parties in the research industry—research suppliers, field service firms, and client organizations—make a conscious effort to be aware of and respect the rights of one another as well as those of the research subjects and the general public. This section presented a number of situations involving ethical questions but, by necessity, left many of those questions unanswered. However, the objective of this section can be considered to be accomplished if it has sensitized you to be concerned about marketing research ethics.

---

[50] Quoted in "Honesty, Better Quality Needed from Research Suppliers, Field Services," *Marketing News,* September 18, 1981, Section 2, p. 4.
[51] "Peacock's Night to Crow," *Newsweek,* November 17, 1980, p. 82.

SUMMARY

The purpose of this chapter was to present an overview of the providers of marketing research services, including their key attributes and tasks. Marketing research can be conducted *in-house* or through an *external supplier.* In-house marketing research ranges from a part-time responsibility of an employee to a separate department. Large firms are more likely than small firms to have formal marketing research departments. However, the nature of a firm's information requirements, rather than its size, is the critical determinant of whether the firm should have a formal marketing research department.

A number of factors play a role in deciding the organizational structure for in-house marketing research. Illustrative of such factors are (1) the *variety* of information needed by a firm, (2) the *role* in-house marketing research is expected to play in decision making, (3) the *urgency* of the firm's information needs, and (4) *economies of scale.* Since trade-offs are involved in considering the various factors, the best organizational structure for in-house marketing research is difficult to determine objectively. Irrespective of organizational form, in-house marketing research must be effectively *integrated* with research users and given adequate *importance* and *independence.*

External suppliers consist of commercial marketing research firms, academic consultants, and other associations or agencies. Of these, commercial marketing research firms are most frequently used by client organizations. *Credibility, competence, cost,* and *capacity* considerations are crucial in deciding *when* to hire an external supplier. The selection of specific suppliers from an available pool of suppliers must be based on the *prestige, past experience,* and *personnel* of the suppliers as well as on the *price* of the services (although the cheapest is not necessarily the best).

Ethical questions pervade the field of marketing research and concern five different parties: *research suppliers, field service firms, research respondents, clients,* and the *general public.* A number of marketing organizations have codes of ethics. Unfortunately, a code of research ethics is merely a set of *general* guidelines. What is considered ethical in any given situation depends on the value systems and subjective judgment of the parties involved. Nevertheless, in view of the importance of ethics, the research industry should be cognizant of the rights of the various parties and make a conscious effort to respect those rights.

The appendix to this chapter discusses career opportunities in marketing research.

QUESTIONS

1. State the three alternative approaches that a firm can use to acquire marketing research information.

2. "Firms that are large must have formal marketing research departments." Discuss this statement.
3. Give two examples of the types of factors that should be considered in determining whether an in-house marketing research department should be centralized or decentralized.
4. Determining the proper organizational structure for marketing research departments is more objective than subjective. True or false? Briefly explain your answer.
5. State, and describe in a sentence or two, the three attributes that marketing research departments should ideally have.
6. Write a brief paragraph supporting the following statement: "The three desirable attributes of marketing research departments are crucial in minimizing, if not avoiding, friction between managers and researchers."
7. Would you consider each of the following a full-service research firm or a limited-service research firm? For each firm, indicate your reason in a sentence or two.
   a. Burke Marketing Services, Inc.,
   b. Legal Market Research, Inc.,
   c. Associates Interviewing Services.
8. State, and briefly describe, the four factors that form the basis for deciding when or whether to hire an external supplier.
9. State, and briefly describe, the four selection criteria useful in evaluating external research suppliers.
10. "When a firm obtains bids from several external research suppliers for the *same* research project, it should hire the lowest bidder." Discuss this statement.
11. Briefly discuss why a written code of ethics is not a panacea for resolving ethical questions in marketing research. (*Hint:* There are three basic reasons.)
12. List the various parties that can be potentially involved in or affected by ethical issues in marketing research.
13. Are there any ethical issues implicit in the Edsel automobile example we discussed in Chapter 1? If so, briefly discuss them.
14. Which two parties are most closely and frequently associated with research suppliers? Give examples to illustrate the obligations of these two parties toward research suppliers.

APPENDIX TO CHAPTER 2

Careers in Marketing Research

The first chapter and the material covered in this chapter presented an overview of what marketing research practice is all about. If this overview has generated some interest in marketing research, you may ask, What are the job opportunities in the marketing research field? However, even if some students get excited about a marketing research *course,* they seldom get interested in thinking about a *career* in marketing research. Unfortunately, the lack of interest in exploring job opportunities in the marketing research field may stem from certain erroneous assumptions on the part of students. The following are typical of such assumptions:

> "I have never seen a recruiter visit campus to fill a marketing research job—there must not be any job opportunities out there for me in marketing research."
>
> "I don't get turned on by statistics. I would rather work with people than numbers. So why should I take a job that will keep me busy crunching numbers?"
>
> "If I take a marketing research job, I will be entering a dead-end street—I cannot hope to move on to senior management positions."

The purpose of this appendix is to dispel the myths about marketing research jobs and to present a balanced picture of the opportunities and constraints in a career in marketing research.

MARKETING RESEARCH JOBS ARE AVAILABLE

It is true that few, if any, firms recruit on campus for marketing research positions.[1] However, this fact does not imply that job openings in the marketing research field are scarce. According to research industry sources, the demand for marketing researchers is quite high.[2] Indeed, a recent survey of research firms—research suppliers and field services—found that 74% hire college graduates *fresh from college.*[3] Marketing research positions are also available in numerous client firms with in-house marketing research departments. In addition, a variety of organizations that may not necessarily have formal marketing research departments—such as TV stations, newspaper publishers, banks, nonprofit agencies, or retail institutions—do have exciting research positions.

THE NATURE OF MARKETING RESEARCH JOBS

The jobs available in the marketing research field cover a wide range of tasks. The following jobs are examples (with key tasks involved in each):

- Fieldworker (interviewing).
- Clerical supervisor (overseeing fieldwork).
- Research analyst (designing projects, constructing questionnaires, analyzing results, preparing reports).
- Statisticians (setting up complex sampling plans and analysis procedures).
- Project director (overseeing research projects and research personnel).
- Manager or director of marketing research (overall management of research-related resources and activities).

The positions of fieldworker and clerical supervisor normally require only a high school diploma; the rest usually require at least a bachelor's degree. Salaries for the positions vary, depending on the nature of the position as well as on the qualifications and prior experience of the research personnel. A recent study

[1] A recent study found that on-campus recruiting was *least used* by firms recruiting for marketing research positions; see A. Parasuraman and Deborah G. Wright, "A Study of Marketing Research Jobs for College Graduates: Implications for Educators," *Proceedings of the American Marketing Association's Educator's Conference, Dearborn, Michigan, 1983,* pp. 181–185.

[2] Jack Honomichl, "Professional Staff Needs Detailed," *Advertising Age,* 52 (October 26, 1981), p. S–34; also see B. C. Vovovich, "Researchers Are Much in Demand," *Advertising Age,* 50 (October 15, 1979), pp. S–1.

[3] A. Parasuraman, "Commercial Marketing Researchers' Evaluations of Academic Journals and Marketing Research Education," *Journal of Marketing Education,* Fall 1981, pp. 52–58.

found that typical starting salaries for positions that usually require a college degree were as follows:

Research analyst	$15,000 to $20,000
Statistician	$20,000 to $25,000
Project director	$25,000 to $30,000
Director of marketing research	$30,000 to $40,000[4]

Of course, as you might expect, entry into some of the high-salary positions (e.g., project director) requires several years of prior experience in the research field.

Taking a marketing research job is not synonymous with signing a contract to live in a world of numbers and techniques. As the illustrative positions outlined earlier imply, working with numbers is only a minor component of many marketing research jobs. Alan R. Cox, group brand research manager for R. J. Reynolds Tobacco Company, had this to say about the nature of marketing research assignments in his company:

> From our viewpoint, research techniques are secondary for marketing researchers who want to do well at R. J. Reynolds. More important is that they have a solid marketing background and are, in fact, marketing generalists with research expertise. . . . I do not mean to downplay techniques, but we think a technique is a means to an end (that "end" is solving tough marketing questions) and not the end itself.[5]

Exhibit A.2.1 describes in further detail the nature and scope of marketing research assignments at Reynolds Tobacco. Note especially the types of traits a good marketing research analyst at Reynolds Tobacco is expected to have. Clearly, a marketing research job involves more than, and is likely to be more exciting than, mere number crunching. Indeed, many practitioners feel a major weakness of college graduates who enter the marketing research field is that they are too technique-oriented and lack other critical skills, such as communication skills and interpersonal skills.[6]

ADVANCEMENT OPPORTUNITIES

A marketing research job is apparently no more a dead-end street than other marketing jobs in terms of career advancement. For instance, recognizing the need to make college students aware of the exciting opportunities in the market-

[4] Parasuraman and Wright, "Study of Marketing Research Jobs."
[5] Personal communication to the author, dated November 4, 1982.
[6] Parasuraman and Wright, "Study of Marketing Research Jobs."

Exhibit A.2.1

Nature and scope of marketing research assignments at R. J. Reynolds Tobacco Company

One of the primary reasons for Reynolds Tobacco's continued marketing success has been the company's total commitment to the marketing research process. Marketing research is viewed as the vital link between the consumer and the company's marketing activities. It therefore guides much of our marketing activities.

The Marketing Development Department includes both Established Brands and New Brands Research, Strategic and Functional Research, and Marketing Sciences.

Graduates are hired as Marketing Research Analysts into the Marketing Development Department, and are fully participating members of R. J. Reynold's marketing team.

Marketing researchers have thorough day-to-day involvement with other departments within the company (Brand Marketing, Sales, Research and Development) as well as with outside groups (advertising agencies and research companies). This interaction on key marketing issues provides a broad exposure to, and a solid understanding of, both the marketing process and the company's decision-making process. This experience is invaluable in developing R. J. Reynold's marketing researchers into marketing generalists.

Marketing researchers act as internal marketing consultants and are valued as much for their ability to advise on marketing issues as for their research expertise.

Marketing research analysts are usually assigned to a brand as soon as they begin work. Diverse projects on real issues are used to give broad exposure to, and understanding of, key marketing issues. Some of the following areas would be included:

- Advertising and promotion research
- Consumer attitudes and perceptions of brands
- Market segmentation
- Product development
- Strategic planning
- Test marketing

ing research field, the Chemical Marketing Research Association (CMRA) has prepared a brochure entitled "Careers in Industrial Marketing Research." It says:

> Experience in marketing research is an effective stepping-stone to management. A recent CMRA study showed that the average non-supervisory marketing research analyst stayed in his job for five to six years. With that background, many analysts progressed to supervisory positions in marketing research and other fields. A substantial percentage rose to become general managers. Others entered the consulting arena by working for management or marketing research consulting firms, while many set out on their own as consultants.[7]

The marketing research jobs at Reynolds Tobacco also have potential for leading to senior management positions, as evidenced by the last paragraph in Exhibit A.2.1. In many companies a good marketing researcher can move into

[7] "Careers in Industrial Marketing Research," a brochure prepared by the Chemical Marketing Research Association, 139 Chestnut Avenue, Staten Island, N.Y. 10305.

At some time during their first years in the department, marketing researchers are temporarily assigned to different functional areas to help them gain a broader understanding of specific types of research. Examples of functional areas are product research, forecasting, advertising and promotion testing, and sales analysis. These assignments usually last from six to twelve months.

In addition to this training, company programs and outside seminars are included to accelerate development. Examples of topics are consumer behavior, new product development, advanced analytical techniques, and idea generation as well as management and decision making seminars. Additionally, orientation with the field sales force, Research and Development and advertising agencies are included.

Throughout this program, an analyst is an active member of the brand team and can be a significant contributor to a brand's strategy and tactics.

A good marketing research analyst benefits from certain traits. Some of these are:

- Problem definition and problem solving ability
- Good oral and written communications
- Interpersonal skills and flexibility
- Consulting skills
- Initiative
- Both an analytical ability and a creative thought process

The Marketing Development Department offers exceptional career opportunities by developing marketing generalists with a marketing research background. Career paths generally lead to one of three areas: General Management, Marketing, or Marketing Development. Opportunities exist in Reynolds Tobacco as well as in other Reynolds Industries subsidiaries.

Source: "R. J. Reynolds Tobacco Company: Marketing Opportunities," brochure prepared by the R. J. Reynolds Tobacco Company, Winston-Salem, N.C., pp. 8–10. Permission to reprint granted by the R. J. Reynolds Tobacco Company.

advertising management and product management, and from there into higher levels of marketing management.

THE CONSTRAINTS

There are a few important, but not necessarily insurmountable, constraints facing a student interested in a marketing research career. First, becoming aware of job openings is not as easy in the marketing research field as it is in fields like sales or retailing. Employers seldom use on-campus recruiting for marketing research positions; rather, they use personal referrals (e.g., from colleagues or college professors) and job advertisements in professional publications (e.g., *Marketing News*) to locate prospective candidates.[8] Consequently, a student interested in a marketing research career must be willing to put out a greater-

[8] Parasuraman and Wright, "Study of Marketing Research Jobs."

than-average effort to identify potential employers and to make contact with them.

Second, some real-life experience appears to be a prerequisite for landing a good marketing research job. According to the brochure on marketing research careers prepared by the CMRA:

> Most people enter marketing research only after gaining experience and training in other areas of the company. Sales, marketing, research [and development], production and purchasing are the usual spawning grounds for successful marketing researchers.[9]

Although many marketing research firms (e.g., A. C. Nielsen, Burke Marketing Services) do hire college graduates with no prior experience as trainees, students with some exposure to marketing research are likely to have an advantage over others. The importance of experience is further emphasized by the following types of comments made by potential employers when asked to offer suggestions for students interested in careers in marketing research:

> "Be patient and gain experience—become an excellent listener."
> "Realize that EXPERIENCE is the ultimate teacher."
> "Get as much business experience as you can; volunteer, if necessary."[10]

Hence gaining some experience—for instance, through a business internship sandwiched between blocks of course work—will be a definite advantage.

Third, although marketing research jobs are available to students with only bachelor's degrees, a master's degree is becoming increasingly important, at least in terms of career advancement.[11] An analysis of a sample of ads describing marketing research job openings showed that

> a master's degree was required for over half of all positions that explicitly stated a college degree requirement. Furthermore, a master's degree was preferred for 58% of the positions that required a bachelor's degree. As further evidence of the importance of a master's degree in qualifying for the positions advertised, a master of business administration (MBA) degree was mentioned in over one half of the ads that required some specific major.[12]

In view of the importance of experience and a graduate degree for a successful career in marketing research, a few universities have started offering a graduate program in marketing research that has a built-in business experience component.[13]

---

[9] "Careers in Industrial Marketing Research."

[10] Parasuraman and Wright, "Study of Marketing Research Jobs," p. 184.

[11] B. C. Vovovich, "Researchers Are Much in Demand," *Advertising Age,* 50 (October 15, 1979), pp. S–1.

[12] Parasuraman and Wright, "Study of Marketing Research Jobs," p. 182.

[13] See, for example, "Graduate Program in Marketing Research," a brochure prepared by the University of Georgia, Athens, Ga. 30602.

In conclusion, the marketing research field holds exciting and rewarding career opportunities for interested students, especially those who are willing to expend the extra effort needed to overcome some of the potential constraints we discussed.

SUMMARY

Contrary to the apparent beliefs of many students, the marketing research field does offer exciting job opportunities, involving more than working with numbers and having good career advancement potential. However, for a college student to become aware of job openings is somewhat harder in marketing research than it is in fields such as sales or retailing. Moreover, some business experience and a graduate degree are prerequisites for many marketing research jobs. Nevertheless, these constraints can be overcome by students willing to plan in advance for obtaining employment in the marketing research field.

QUESTIONS

1. Summarize the myths that students typically have about job opportunities in the marketing research field, and indicate why they are not true.
2. Assuming your goal is to start your career in the marketing research field, what specific steps can you take to maximize the chances that your goal will be accomplished?

CASES FOR PART ONE

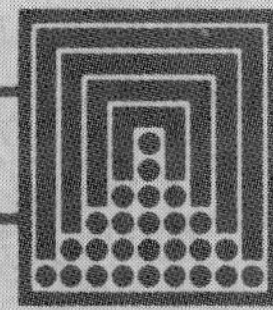

CASE 1.1

Action Market Research Services, Inc.

Action Market Research Services, Inc., is a large national firm offering a variety of marketing research and consulting services to client firms in a number of different industries. Among the services it offers is a two-week marketing research training program for client firms' employees. The program is especially designed for individuals who are likely to conduct marketing research on their own and/or use marketing research information frequently in their decision making.

Action Market Research Services devotes the first day of the training program to giving the program participants a feel for the nature and potential usefulness of marketing research. Topics covered on the first day include ways in which marketing research can be helpful in different decision-making situations, what marketing research can or cannot accomplish, and factors crucial for the overall effectiveness of marketing research. In the very first session of the training program, a number of illustrative situations are briefly described to participants, who are then asked to discuss the role that marketing research can play in each situation. Participants are told that they should focus their discussion on the following three issues:

1. Can marketing research be helpful in the situation?
2. If the answer is yes, in what ways and for what aspects of the situation can it be helpful? What types of marketing research activities are likely to be beneficial in generating information that is pertinent to the situation?
3. If the answer is no, explain. What constraints or limitations are likely to prevent marketing research from being truly beneficial in the situation?

Four of the illustrative situations used by Action Market Research Services in its training programs are presented below.

LIFE INSURANCE FIRM

A major life insurance company is becoming increasingly concerned about the growing lapse rate in the life insurance policies it has been selling to customers. *Lapse rate* is defined as the percentage of policy owners canceling their policies in a given year. For instance, if the average number of policies in force during a year is 50,000, and 5000 policy cancellations occur during that year, the lapse rate is 10%. During the past three years this firm's lapse rate has grown from 6% in the first year, to 7% in the second year, to 10% in the third year.

LOCAL LIQUOR STORE

Mr. Dunham, owner of two liquor stores in a city with a population of about one hundred fifty thousand, is planning to open a third store. While the two existing stores are traditional liquor stores, Mr. Dunham wants to make the third store somewhat sophisticated and unconventional. Specifically, he wants to carry only an exotic product line, consisting of fine and rare liquors, wines, cheeses, and breads from all over the world. He plans to attract a socially upscale group of customers to the store.

ELECTRONIC-COMPONENTS MANUFACTURER

A firm producing a line of electronic components has a customer base of about two thousand electronic-goods manufacturers. This firm's research and development (R&D) department has just developed a new design for the component. This newly designed component is expected to greatly increase the reliability of the products into which it is installed. However, the improved version of the component will cost about 30% more than the current version being sold.

PACKAGED-GOODS FIRM

Top management of a firm producing a variety of consumer packaged goods is wondering whether the firm should build another plant to increase its production capacity. The firm's existing plant is operating at 90% capacity, and the firm's sales growth rate has been better than the industry's growth rate during the past three years. Top management feels that the need for increased production capacity depends directly on consumer demand. It therefore decides to ask the firm's marketing research department to investigate the nature of future consumer demand for its products and decide whether a new plant needs to be built at this time.

QUESTION

1. Assuming that you are participating in Action Market Research Services' training program, what are your reactions to each of the four situations presented? Be sure to address the specific issues that participants in the program are asked to discuss.

CASE 1.2

Modern Silo Systems

Modern Silo Systems, a leading manufacturer of grain silos in the Midwest, has just filed suit against one of its former distributors, Midwest Distributing Company. In its lawsuit Modern Silo Systems contends that Midwest Distributing has illegally copied the design of Silotech, one of Modern Silo Systems' most innovative and lucrative products. According to the lawsuit Midwest Distributing had abruptly severed its relationship with Modern Silo Systems about three years before and had since introduced a silo system of its own called Storesafe, a product very similar to Silotech. Top officials of Modern Silo Systems are in the process of gathering information that they hope will show that Midwest Distributing's recent actions are unfair and have adversely affected their company's sales and market position.

COMPANY BACKGROUND

Modern Silo Systems has been in business for over fifty years. Its products are sold to a large number of farmers and farm cooperative organizations throughout the midwestern section of the United States. The company enjoys a leadership image in the industry because of the many advances it pioneered in the areas of treating, storing, and preserving harvested grain. Technological expertise and manufacturing capability are the firm's major strengths and the reasons for the respect it commands among customers as well as competitors. The company's current sales are a little over $65 million.

Modern Silo Systems introduced Silotech, a sophisticated, energy-efficient system for drying and storing grain, about eight years ago. The year in which Silotech was introduced saw a sharp increase in the company's sales—from about $30 million to $48 million. Virtually all of this sales increase was due to Silotech. This new product continued to do well in succeeding years until about three years ago, when Midwest Distributing cut off relations with Modern Silo Systems.

MARKETING OF SILOTECH

While being a leader in the areas of product development and manufacturing, Modern Silo Systems does not have a strong marketing organization. The company's top-management group has no executive with a marketing title. The responsibility for effectively marketing the company's products is relegated to a handful of distributors who have thorough knowledge of their markets and customers. The distributors are compensated on a sales commission basis.

The marketing of Silotech was almost completely in the hands of Midwest Distributing Company. This distributor had accounted for over 75% of Silotech's sales. Furthermore, Midwest Distributing had played a crucial role in selling other products of Modern Silo Systems. Prior to severing its relationship with Modern Silo Systems, Midwest Distributing had accounted for roughly 50% of the company's total sales.

EVIDENCE GATHERED BY MODERN SILO SYSTEMS

Modern Silo Systems' total sales reached a peak of $80 million during the year in which Midwest Distributing broke off relations. Total sales in the next two years were $72 million and $68 million, respectively. Sales in the past year were just over $65 million.

Modern Silo Systems' top management is convinced that Midwest Distributing's introduction of Storesafe is the primary reason for the company's deteriorating sales performance. The company's engineers are sure that Storesafe's design features are very similar, if not identical, to those of Silotech. Furthermore, investigation of the firm's internal accounting records revealed the following trend in Silotech's unit sales during each of the eight years following its introduction. (*Note:* Midwest Distributing broke off its association with Modern Silo Systems at the end of the fifth year).

Year	Silotech Sales (Units)
1	150
2	180
3	234
4	305
5	400
6	219
7	170
8	160

Modern Silo Systems' managers have heard through several of their current distributors and customers that Storesafe's sales are increasing. They have also found out that Midwest Distributing is selling Storesafe at a price that is about 20% to 30% lower than Silotech's price. According to Modern Silo Systems' accounting department, the gross profit margin (i.e., selling price less total cost) for Silotech is roughly 20% of its selling price.

QUESTIONS

1. Has Modern Silo Systems conducted any marketing research relevant for building its case against Midwest Distributing Company? Why or why not?
2. From the information given, do you feel that Modern Silo Systems has a strong case against Midwest Distributing? Explain your answer.
3. What advice would you give to Modern Silo Systems' top management regarding the extent and the types of marketing research that may be helpful in this situation?

CASE 1.3

Walker Research, Inc.

Walker Research, Inc., headquartered in Indianapolis, Indiana, is one of the top 20 marketing research firms in the United States in terms of sales revenue. It has offices in several cities across the country and conducts hundreds of custom research projects for clients every year. Walker Research's management is strongly committed to following sound ethical principles in its numerous dealings with clients, respondents, and other research suppliers. This commitment to research ethics is evident in the following excerpt from an article titled "Marketing Research Ethics Emphasized at Walker," which appeared in the Fall–Winter 1983 issue of *Marketing Researcher,* a quarterly publication of the firm:

> Are you ethical? Most people and organizations think they are. But in most instances ethics are taken for granted and rarely given top consideration. Not so at Walker Research.
>
> Special meetings were recently held with all marketing professionals and managers in Indianapolis, Cedar Knolls, and Phoenix. As a portion of the program, participants reviewed the results of an ethics quiz that was administered to various Walker Research employees. This quiz involved a simulation of various marketing and research-related situations calling for the exercise of judgment and decision making based on ethical and business-related criteria.
>
> To our knowledge, Walker Research is the only organization that holds sessions on ethics to openly discuss such sensitive subjects. However, we believe ethics are an important and vital undercurrent that must be ever-present in the minds of those people working in marketing research.

THE ETHICS QUESTIONNAIRE

The ethics quiz mentioned in the preceding excerpt had 15 simulated scenarios covering various aspects of marketing research. Five of those scenarios are provided here.

Information for this case was provided by courtesy of Walker Research, Inc., 8000 Knue Road, Indianapolis, IN 46250.

SCENARIO 1: A client company is getting ready for labor negotiations and wants you to do a telephone survey among employees to find out how strongly they support union demands. You are given a list of employee names and telephone numbers. If respondents ask why they were chosen to be interviewed, your interviewers are supposed to say that a computer was used to pick a random sample of community residents. What would you do?

a. If respondents ask how they were chosen, tell them, "At random, by a computer."
b. If respondents ask how they were chosen, say you don't know.
c. Insist on telling respondents the truth if they ask or you will not do the survey.
d. Tell the client that you want to add a few other community citizens chosen at random, so you can say that a computer did it.
e. Other.

SCENARIO 2: You have thoroughly pretested a questionnaire and find that it requires a 45-minute interview. You need a high response rate. The pretest interviewers tell you that if they say in advance that 45 minutes are needed, there are a lot of refusals. But if they say it takes 30 minutes, most respondents will go along and finish the full 45 minutes. What instructions should you give your field interviewers?

a. If respondents ask how long it takes, say 45 minutes.
b. If respondents ask how long it takes, say 30 minutes.
c. If respondents ask how long it takes, say you don't know.
d. Other.

SCENARIO 3: For a mail survey you are doing, your client wants you to use ultraviolet ink to identify the questionnaires for later classification purposes. Because some of the questions are sensitive and private, the survey itself is announced as anonymous, with no way to connect names with answers. What would you do?

a. Approve the use of ultraviolet ink in order to get the information needed.
b. Do not approve the use of ultraviolet ink.
c. Other.

SCENARIO 4: For an in-depth interview study among community leaders, your client wants you to have interviewers use tape recorders hidden in their attaché cases. The tape recorders will ensure that you get a record of everything that is said. The client is concerned that respondents might say different things if they knew they were being taped. The client agrees that only you will have control of the tapes and that as soon as you finish the report, you can destroy the tapes. What would you do?

a. Use the hidden tape recorders, and instruct the interviewers to say nothing.
b. Use the hidden tape recorders, but instruct the interviewers to tell the respondents about them if the respondents become suspicious.
c. Do not use hidden tape recorders.
d. Other.

SCENARIO 5: You have conducted an attitude study for a client. Your data show that the product is not being marketed properly. This finding is not popular with the client's product management, and they request that you omit the data from your formal report on the grounds that the general-overview presentation to management is adequate for management needs. What do you do?

a. Include all data in your formal report.
b. Exclude the marketing data as requested.
c. Other.

For each scenario, the ethics questionnaire also posed the following question to respondents:

Is the above issue mostly a matter of ethics or mostly a matter of research judgment?

a. Ethics.
b. Research judgment.
c. Some of both.
d. Neither.

QUESTIONS

1. What, in your opinion, is the proper thing to do in each of the five scenarios? Why?
2. Is dealing with the issue involved in each scenario simply a matter of research judgment rather than research ethics?

PART TWO

KEY ASPECTS OF THE MARKETING RESEARCH PROCESS

FROM THE MANAGER'S DESK

JANET L. COLLINS has held the positions of sales supervisor, marketing research supervisor, and editor with the higher-education division of Addison Wesley Publishing Company, Reading, Mass. She received her B.S. degree from Cornell University and the M.Ed. from the University of Virginia.

QUESTION: On the basis of your experience, what specific phase or aspect of a marketing research project is most critical for its ultimate effectiveness? Why?

RESPONSE: All phases of the marketing research project are important to the effectiveness of the findings, but the initial meeting between the client and a member of the marketing research department is the most critical aspect. The goal of this meeting is for the researcher to acquire a complete understanding of the needs of the client. This understanding is essential if the researcher is to develop and carry out an effective research study that will be useful in key decision making. In this meeting there must be open and candid communication between the two parties. Rather than being a passive note taker, the researcher should play an active role in this meeting. Thus the researcher should concentrate on the following tasks:

- Identify and understand the problems the client is facing and the issues that need to be addressed in the project. During the initial interview the researcher should investigate and identify key requirements; no question should seem too obvious or trivial.

- Find out what decisions will be made as a result of the research; this information will help determine the direction and the form of the final report. Distinguish between requests for research that indicate the information is clearly for the purpose of decision support and requests that are accompanied by an explanation such as "Because we always do it" or "I've been told to have it done, but I have already made my decisions about this project." If the client appears to be predisposed to a set course of action, the research findings will not likely be properly used, and everyone's time could be better spent elsewhere.
- Determine the budget, the deadlines, and the other expectations the client has so that no misunderstandings occur midway through the work. Surprises by either the researcher or the client in the middle of the project can send everyone into a tailspin.
- Conclude the first meeting by restating the established objectives and needs. This restatement will assure both parties of mutual understanding. Often, to follow up the meeting with a written summary and proposal is helpful.

An initial meeting covering these issues will enable the researcher to develop and implement a research project of benefit to the client in making good decisions. Starting the study in this manner will establish continued communication throughout the project and produce results that match the agreed-upon objectives.

3

Steps in a Marketing Research Project

The first two chapters gave you an indication of the nature and the scope of marketing research as well as the tasks and the responsibilities of research providers and users. This chapter will introduce you to the key steps involved in conducting a marketing research project. The objective of this chapter is to offer a preview of the research process and, at the same time, lay the foundation for succeeding chapters. At appropriate points during our discussion, specific chapters that cover in detail the elements introduced here will be mentioned.

Dividing the marketing research process into a sequence of chronological steps is convenient. However, in reality, the steps are highly *interrelated*—that is, chronologically distant steps may have an impact on steps preceding them. The interrelationships among the steps will become clear as we examine the nature of each. A logical starting point for discussing the marketing research process is the issue of whether a proposed research project should be conducted.

DECIDING WHETHER A MARKETING RESEARCH PROJECT IS WORTH IT

Four considerations influence the worth of a marketing research project: (1) the potential usefulness of the research results, (2) management's attitudes toward the research, (3) the resources available for implementation of the research results, and (4) the cost versus the benefits of the research project. These four considerations are not necessarily independent of one another; however, each is important enough to be discussed separately.

Potential usefulness

The potential usefulness of a research project is the extent to which its findings will be helpful in taking further action in a given situation. Alternatively, it is the extent to which the research findings are likely to reduce a decision maker's uncertainty or provide relevant additional insights in a given situation. Obviously, a proposed project with little potential usefulness should not be undertaken, at least not before appropriate revisions are made. In reality, however, this seemingly simple point is often forgotten. Research projects undertaken hastily, without adequate consideration of their potential usefulness, typically end up generating incomplete information, at best, or totally irrelevant information, at worst.

A major weakness of the consumer survey conducted in the Edsel case (Chapter 1) was that it merely identified the image of a potential customer segment for the new car but failed to uncover specific physical and style features likely to appeal to that segment. The information generated was therefore not complete enough to be beneficial. Had the potential usefulness of the consumer survey been examined more carefully, *before* the survey was conducted, it perhaps would have generated more complete and more relevant data.

What factors are important in evaluating the potential usefulness of research findings in a given situation? The factors we will discuss in subsequent steps of the research process—such as the nature of the research objectives and the types of data to be generated through the research—are the important ones. Thus we see that the steps in the research process are interrelated.

Management attitudes

Management, or research users in general, must view a proposed research project with an open mind if the project is to be beneficial. Research effort will be wasted unless decision makers are inclined to accept the research results. As we saw in Chapter 1, marketing research conducted for reasons other than aiding decision making is pseudoresearch and is of no value to an organization. A case in point is Ford Motor Company's brand name research, in which the findings did not recommend the name Edsel. However, Ford management ignored the research findings since it had apparently already made up its mind to name the new car Edsel. Marketing research is not worthwhile when the potential research users have already decided on a course of action or are unlikely to consider research-generated insights with an open mind.

Resources available for implementation

Suppose a marketing research project produces useful recommendations, and management is willing to pursue those recommendations. Can we say this research project has been worthwhile? Not necessarily. The research will still be wasted if management lacks the resources (e.g., money, personnel, time) needed to implement the research results. This point is especially relevant for situations in which a firm may be considering marketing research for uncovering market opportunities, as the following example illustrates.

EXAMPLE: The XYZ Company is a mass producer and marketer of electric can openers. In an attempt to broaden its product assortment, it is considering a marketing research project to determine the nature and size of consumer demand for electric can sealers. However, XYZ currently has only limited idle-plant capacity and is not sure if it has the money to expand capacity. Moreover, it does not possess the technology to produce electric can sealers on a large scale. Clearly, XYZ would be wise not to spend money on marketing research related to electric can sealers before ensuring the availability of financial and technological resources needed to act on the research results, should the results uncover a market opportunity.

Cost versus benefits

The three factors discussed so far—potential usefulness, management attitudes, and resources available for implementation—do relate, although indirectly, to the cost-versus-benefits issue. After all, each of these factors addresses the question, Is it worthwhile to conduct marketing research? The purpose of this section, however, is to focus directly on the *monetary* costs and benefits associated with marketing research.

Research costs are much easier to quantify than research benefits. When the tasks involved in a particular research project are known, estimating the total cost of accomplishing them should be relatively easy. However, one cannot meaningfully estimate the cost of a project without knowing what is involved in its various stages. This observation emphasizes a point we made earlier—the steps in the research process are *interrelated.* From a research user's standpoint, estimating the cost of research is easiest if a research supplier is to be used, because the research cost is simply the price quoted by the supplier.

How does one quantify research benefits? There is no standard way for quantifying benefits. However, since the basic purpose of any research is to aid decision makers *by reducing their uncertainty,* a useful starting point is to examine the *nature* of the uncertainty facing a decision maker. Consider the following scenarios:

SCENARIO A: Brenda Page, product manager for corporation A, is wondering whether she should conduct marketing research to estimate the likely market share of Natuslim, a new, all-natural, diet soft drink. Specifically, she is wondering if she should test-market Natuslim before deciding whether to introduce it on a full scale.

On the basis of production and marketing cost estimates for Natuslim, its break-even sales translates to a 10% share of the diet-drink market. There are 30 brands of diet drinks currently on the market. Three brands have been leading sellers for a long time and enjoy a market share in excess of 20% each, while each of the other brands has a share of 5% or less.

Ms. Page believes Natuslim is as good as any other brand on the market. However, she is *uncertain* about the market share Natuslim may attract if it is introduced. From her experience and understanding of the diet-drink market, she feels Natuslim's share will be anywhere from 2% to 8%, with an outside chance of being over 8%. Should Ms. Page test-market Natuslim before making a decision about full-scale introduction?

SCENARIO B: Jerry Wilson, advertising manager for corporation B, is *uncertain* about which of two television commercials, X or Y, to use for his company's brand of deodorant. Commercial X employs a fear appeal: In it a man wears a competing brand of deodorant only to be embarrassed later at a party where everyone avoids him, apparently because his deodorant is ineffective. Commercial Y uses a romantic appeal: In it a man wears corporation B's brand of deodorant, goes to a party, and pleasantly discovers that several women are attracted to him, apparently because of the effectiveness of his deodorant.

Mr. Wilson knows commercials using fear appeals have worked extremely well for some products but have adversely affected the sales of others by disgusting potential consumers. He also feels that while romantic commercials like commercial Y have increased the sales of certain products, they can hurt others by lacking believability in the eyes of potential consumers. Should Mr. Wilson conduct marketing research to test the two commercials before deciding which to use for corporation B's deodorant?

Scenarios A and B depict decision makers faced with uncertainty that can be reduced through marketing research. But is marketing research likely to be equally beneficial in both cases? The answer is no, because the *nature* of the uncertainty is different in each scenario.

Let us look at scenario A first. Test-marketing Natuslim will provide a more precise estimate of its potential market share than Brenda Page's current estimate that it will "be anywhere from 2% to 8%." But the *monetary benefit* of reducing this uncertainty will be negligible. The reason is that the break-even share required for Natuslim is 10%, and Ms. Page feels there is only an outside chance its share will be greater than even 8%. In other words, Ms. Page can make a decision *right now* about full-scale introduction of Natuslim. Intuitively, unless corporation A is inclined to take a very heavy risk, Ms. Page may decide not to introduce Natuslim. Regardless of what Ms. Page's decision is, though, it is not likely to change because of any test market outcome.

You are probably wondering, "Won't Ms. Page still benefit by test-marketing Natuslim? For instance, suppose she test-markets Natuslim and finds its share to be over 10% in the test market. Won't this result give her a sound reason to introduce Natuslim on a broader scale?" While this argument has merit, consider this question: How much trust can or *should* Ms. Page place on a test market outcome indicating a greater-than-10% share, *given her prior expectation that there is only an extremely small chance that Natuslim's share will exceed 8%*? There is always room for error in any marketing research project. Consequently, such a test market result may be unusual and not necessarily guarantee a greater-than-10% share after full-scale introduction. In summary, in view of the circumstances in scenario A—especially the *nature* of Ms. Page's uncertainty—the potential benefits of test marketing will be negligible, if not zero. Indeed, even if Ms. Page does decide on full-scale introduction, her decision should be based on other considerations (e.g., corporation A's willingness to take risk) rather than on a favorable test market outcome.

Let us now examine scenario B. The difficulty and the risk of making a decision in the face of Mr. Wilson's uncertainty are much greater than they are for Ms. Page's uncertainty. Choosing the right commercial can ensure the success of corporation B's deodorant, while choosing the wrong one can ensure its failure. More importantly, marketing research is capable of indicating which commercial, X or Y, is most likely to be the right one. Thus the usefulness of marketing research does appear to be greater in scenario B than in scenario A.

Nevertheless, how can Mr. Wilson *quantify* the benefit of marketing research? There is no standard method for quantifying benefits.[1] However, Mr. Wilson may consider the net increase in profits, if the right commercial is chosen, as an indirect estimate of the potential benefits of marketing research. Of course, Mr. Wilson will still have to estimate the net increase in profits, which is not an easy task. On the basis of past experience, as well as the importance of the deodorant to corporation B, Mr. Wilson may be able to make an educated guess about the monetary value of the marketing research information. A comparison of this "guesstimate" with the cost of the research will indicate whether or not the research should be done. A formal mathematical procedure for determining the value of information, along with the assumptions and estimates needed to use the procedure, is described in the appendix to this chapter.

Two important insights emerge from our discussion of scenarios A and B. First, the monetary benefit of marketing research depends heavily on the nature of the uncertainty it is supposed to reduce. Prior to commissioning research, a decision maker should ponder this question: Are the proposed research and the resultant reduction in my uncertainty likely to make any difference in my decision making? The answer to this question was "extremely unlikely" in Brenda Page's case (scenario A) and "extremely likely" in Jerry Wilson's case

[1] Although several conceptual approaches have been suggested in the literature, they all require quantitative inputs that are often difficult to estimate accurately, at least *before* conducting the research project. See James H. Myers and A. Coskun Samli, "Management Control of Marketing Research," *Journal of Marketing Research,* 6 (August 1969), pp. 267–277.

(scenario B). The monetary benefit of research will be *zero* if the reduction in uncertainty is not likely to affect a decision.

Second, even in situations where marketing research intuitively appears to be beneficial, quantifying the benefits *objectively* is not easy. A decision maker's subjective judgment, and even creativity, will play some role in quantifying the benefits of a proposed research project. Hence viewing cost-versus-benefit comparisons as purely objective or scientific just because they involve numbers is erroneous. The following example illustrates this point.

EXAMPLE: A few years ago the author had the opportunity to talk to the president of a large seed company, operating in the Midwest, about his company's use of marketing research. He described an instance when his company wanted to explore the demand for its seeds in the Southwest. He contacted a research supplier, who submitted a proposal bearing a $10,000 price tag. The proposal described a well-thought-out and potentially useful research design aimed at answering the company's questions.

Did the company hire the research supplier to conduct the research? No. According to the president, "The proposal was excellent, but I figured it was worth no more than $6000." When he was asked how he quantified the value of the research project as being no more than $6000, his explanation illustrated the creative and subjective, yet logical, way in which a decision maker can attach a dollar value to a research project.

The president's reasoning ran something like this: "I figured that, instead of commissioning the project proposed by the research supplier, I could hire a full-time salesman for six months—enough time to make several calls on all potential customers in the Southwest. The salesman would cost $1000 a month. At the end of six months I would have a pretty good idea about the demand for our seeds in the Southwest. At worst, the salesman would realize zero sales, in which case we would be short $6000; but then we would also know for sure that there was no demand for our seeds in the Southwest. On the other hand, if the sales calls turned out to be productive, we would know there was some demand there; moreover, the revenue generated by the salesman's calls would at least partly pay for his compensation. If you were me, would you pay more than $6000 for the proposed research project?"

In this example the company president compared the investment in research with the investment in a temporary salesman and felt that the latter would yield a better return per dollar invested. Of course, an implicit assumption in the president's approach was that the quality and the accuracy of the information from the salesman would be just as good as those of the research information. While that assumption may or may not be correct, the example demonstrates that quantification of research benefits, in practice, is often subjective. Other approaches frequently used by managers include comparing the cost of a project with quantities such as a firm's sales, profits, or marketing budget, and then deciding whether the cost seems too high. We see, then, that a variety of subjective but reasonable methods can be, and are, used for quantifying the potential monetary worth of a research project.

In summary, prior to undertaking any research project, decision makers as well as researchers must carefully decide whether the project is worth it: Is the proposed research likely to lead to potentially useful findings? Will the findings be viewed with an open mind? Are adequate resources available to implement the research recommendations effectively? Will the benefits from the research outweigh the costs? Although answering such questions objectively and accurately may be difficult, failure to consider them at the outset will be tantamount to assuming an *unlimited* research budget. And as we saw in Chapter 1, a major concern of researchers is that the budgets allocated to marketing research are extremely limited. Therefore, researchers must use such meager budgets prudently.

DEFINING THE PROJECT'S PURPOSE

Questions crucial to the effectiveness of any research project are, *What* do we want to find out, and *why*? Indeed, our discussion of whether a research project is worth it implicitly assumed that the research purpose was well defined. The costs and potential benefits of research cannot be meaningfully evaluated unless the "what" and "why" aspects of it are clearly established. Consequently, accurate definition of the research problem or research objective is the key to determining whether research should be done and, if so, the nature of the research to be done. According to Robert W. Joselyn, a respected researcher, "Of all the tasks in a marketing research project, none is more vital to the ultimate fulfillment of a client's needs than an accurate and adequate definition of the research problem. . . . All the effort, time, and money spent from this point on will be wasted if the problem is misunderstood and ill-defined."[2] This point is illustrated in the next example.

EXAMPLE: Pac N' Sac, Inc., producer of a variety of paper containers for consumer products, suffered a sales decline of 15% during the past year. Alarmed by this sharp decline, and wondering whether a change in promotional strategy would help boost sales, Pac N' Sac's marketing manager contacted the marketing research department. The research department proposed a well-designed, comprehensive customer study to evaluate promotional strategies, including the one then being used. The marketing manager reviewed the proposed study, found it to be sound, and okayed it.

[2] Robert W. Joselyn, *Designing the Marketing Research Project* (New York: Mason/Charter, 1977), p. 46.

Does anything appear to be wrong with the approach taken by the marketing manager and the research department in attempting to arrest Pac N' Sac's sales decline? Yes, the marketing manager apparently *assumed* the problem was Pac N' Sac's promotional strategy, and the research department went along with that assumption. However, if the assumption is incorrect, the research may be valueless. For instance, what if the cause of the sales decline is really customers' perceptions that Pac N' Sac's products are overpriced or have deteriorated in quality? Under these circumstances the proposed research may be able to identify the best promotional strategy among the alternatives being considered; but employing the best promotional strategy may do little to boost Pac N' Sac's sales if promotion is not the cause of the sales decline in the first place.

Alternatively, what if the total *industry sales* of paper containers had declined by 30% during the past year because of stiff competition from new, nonpaper containers? In this situation the decline in industry sales is the real problem, and Pac N' Sac's sales decline is merely a symptom of it. Furthermore, there is probably not much that marketing research can do to improve Pac N' Sac's sales, since its sales performance is actually much better than the performance of the industry as a whole, despite its 15% sales decline. Therefore any marketing research expenditure will most likely be wasted.

An important lesson emerges from the Pac N' Sac example: At least some time and effort must be expended very early in the research process to identify the correct problem to be researched, *if* there is a problem that marketing research can help tackle. In fact, the firm should usually conduct some exploratory research (a topic discussed at length in the next chapter) simply to define the research problem accurately, before designing a project. *Accurate definition* of a project's purpose requires, first, identifying a number of specific issues pertaining to the situation and, then, deciding which of those issues are worth examining further.

Effective dialogue between decision makers and researchers—the *integration* we emphasized in Chapter 2—is also very critical for properly diagnosing any situation calling for the use of marketing research. In the Pac N' Sac example the marketing manager assumed a certain type of problem existed, and the research department did not challenge that assumption. The chances of the wrong or a nonexistent problem's being researched are greatly increased when there is no healthy discussion between researchers and decision makers during the problem definition stage.

Effective dialogue is especially important when the purpose of a research project is *to explore opportunities* (e.g., What is the market potential for our product?) rather than to solve a specific problem. The absence of a problem may tempt decision makers and researchers to pay no more than lip service to defining the purpose of a research project. However, failure to establish and agree upon clear-cut research objectives will decrease the effectiveness of the research and may lead to unnecessary friction between the two parties after the research is completed.

IDENTIFYING DATA NEEDS

What data should be collected during a research project? The ease with which this question can be answered depends on how clearly the purpose of the research project has been defined in the previous stage. Identifying specific data needs involves scrutinizing the research purpose and listing the kinds of data required to accomplish that purpose. Consider the following example.

EXAMPLE: Consolidated Bakeries, marketer of a national brand of snack food items, is interested in conducting marketing research to evaluate its market position relative to its competitors. Specifically, the purpose of the research is as follows: "To determine our current market share and to ascertain whether our relative market position is likely to improve, stay the same, or deteriorate during the next several years." What kinds of data should Consolidated Bakeries collect through the proposed research project?

The data needed to accomplish the first part of Consolidated Bakeries' research purpose—namely, to determine its current market share—are merely its own sales figures and total industry sales figures. Data requirements for fulfilling the less concrete second part of the research purpose—namely, to assess Consolidated Bakeries' future market position—are not as clear-cut. A variety of data may be able to shed light on what the future looks like for Consolidated Bakeries although none of the data is likely to provide a complete and accurate picture of the future. The following data are examples of the type of data Consolidated Bakeries should collect:

- The *brand loyalty* of consumers toward Consolidated Bakeries' products. Has Consolidated Bakeries been consistently enjoying a loyal clientele up to now? If so, its future market position will probably be as good as its current position.
- The *market shares* of Consolidated Bakeries' *competitors* and the *trends in market shares* during the past several years. Does Consolidated Bakeries have any large, strong competitor(s), or is its competition spread across a number of relatively weak firms? In the past, has Consolidated Bakeries' market share been increasing, holding steady, or declining? What about the shares of its competitors? Answers to these questions can provide some clues about what the future may hold for Consolidated Bakeries.
- The *perceptions of consumers* about Consolidated Bakeries' snack foods and about competing brands on dimensions such as quality, price, and availability.

IDENTIFYING DATA SOURCES

After data needs have been listed, the next logical step is to locate sources capable of providing the data. The relative ease or difficulty in locating data sources will depend on the nature of the data desired. Usually, factual data (such as the number of units of a product sold during the past year) can be obtained through *secondary-data sources,* which we will discuss in Chapter 5. For instance, for Consolidated Bakeries, data on current and past market shares can be readily obtained from commercial research firms such as the A. C. Nielsen Company (offering Nielsen Retail Index[3] and ScanTrack[4] data) and Information Resources, Inc. (offering BehaviorScan[5] data). Data that are readily available from sources like these are called *secondary data.* Systems such as BehaviorScan can also provide data on changes in brand preferences of families over time. Such data can be helpful, for example, in accomplishing Consolidated Bakeries' research purpose by indicating the extent of brand loyalty.

Not all data may be readily available, however. For instance, consumer perceptions, listed as one of Consolidated Bakeries' data needs, can only be obtained by directly contacting consumers. Such data are called *primary data.* More will be said about primary-data collection in Chapters 6 and 7. Suffice it to say here that collecting primary data entails a significant amount of time and effort on the researcher's part.

When the research purpose can be accomplished through secondary data, at least some of the subsequent stages of the research process may not even be relevant. For example, suppose the sole purpose of Consolidated Bakeries' research is to determine its market share and its competitors' market share. This purpose can be accomplished by simply identifying the appropriate secondary sources and obtaining the necessary data from them. The research project will conclude at this stage. An important inference emerging from this observation is that *every project will not necessarily involve all the research stages.*

We have thus far implicitly assumed that researchers will be able to obtain data (either secondary or primary data) to fulfill all the listed data needs. But what if no source is available for the kinds of data needed in a particular project? For instance, suppose the research objective of Consolidated Bakeries is to ascertain consumer tastes and preferences for snack foods five to ten years from now. There probably will not be any good, trustworthy source of data that will be helpful for this objective, since the time frame is too long. Hence the company should abandon the research project at this stage rather than pursue it

[3] "Management with the Nielsen Retail Index Systems," a brochure prepared (in 1978) by the A. C. Nielsen Company, Northbrook, Ill.; see pp. 6–7.

[4] "Nielsen National ScanTrack Service," a brochure prepared (in 1982) by the A. C. Nielsen Company, Northbrook, Ill.; see p. 1.

[5] For details on the BehaviorScan system and its capabilities, see "New 'BehaviorScan' System Ties Sales to TV Ads," *Marketing News,* September 21, 1979, p. 7.

further; the research will undoubtedly not be worth it. This example also reinforces the notion of interrelated stages in the research process: What may occur in subsequent stages can have a bearing on earlier stages.

CHOOSING AN APPROPRIATE RESEARCH DESIGN

Once the research objectives and the nature of the data to be collected have been determined, the researchers must choose an appropriate research design, which, in turn, will influence the tasks involved in the remainder of the project. For instance, an industrial-product firm wishing to generate some ideas for improving its product line can do so through informal discussions with selected customers and distributors. The research design underlying this data collection is an exploratory design. In contrast, a department store wishing to obtain a demographic profile of its customers can do so through a formal and structured survey of its customers. This data collection approach is traditionally called a descriptive research design. The next chapter discusses different research designs, the circumstances under which they are appropriate, and their implications for data collection and analysis.

DEVELOPING DATA COLLECTION FORMS

The stage of developing data collection forms is relevant when a research project involves primary-data collection. Primary data are frequently collected through interviews, but in some instances they are also gathered through observation (these methods are discussed in Chapter 6). Regardless of the data collection method used, some instrument, or form, must be designed to record the data being collected. Although designing a data collection form may appear easy, certain aspects of the form, if not handled carefully, can seriously affect the quality and nature of the data. Chapter 10 focuses on designing data collection forms; certain sections of other chapters (especially Chapters 6 and 15) also address these issues.

DESIGNING THE SAMPLE

Designing a sample to collect primary data involves clearly specifying who, or what units, should provide the needed data. The stage of identifying data sources may offer some *general* guidance for designing the sample. For instance, in a project intended to measure the public's attitudes toward government support for private schools, the source of the primary data may be specified as "individuals over 18 years of age." However, several other issues must be settled before data collection can begin: *How many* individuals over 18 years of age should be chosen for the project? From *what geographic area* should they be chosen? *How* should they be chosen? These issues, as well as other related issues, are discussed at length in Chapters 12 through 14.

COLLECTING THE DATA

Once the data collection form and the sample design are ready, the next logical step is to collect the data. Note that consistent with the interrelationships among the research process stages, designing the data collection form and the sample should have already taken into account the type of data collection method to be used. For example, the wording to be used in a questionnaire depends on whether it is to be used in a personal-interview survey or a mail survey. Chapters 6 and 7, which discuss different data collection methods and the pros and cons of each, will shed more light on such interrelationships. Also, while every chapter in this book directly or indirectly touches upon data collection, the discussions in Chapters 4, 8, and 9 (all dealing with different types of marketing research designs) and in Chapter 15 (dealing with potential errors during data collection) are particularly relevant for choosing the most appropriate data collection method in a given situation.

ANALYZING DATA AND INTERPRETING RESULTS

As we saw in Chapter 1, analysis and interpretation are integral parts of marketing research. The types of analyses permissible in a project depend on the nature of the data, which, in turn, can be affected by factors such as the type of data collection method used. Chapters 16 through 19 discuss a number of ways for analyzing data and interpreting the results. Moreover, given the importance of effectively communicating the research findings to decision makers, an entire chapter (Chapter 20) has been devoted to the presentation of research findings, both in an oral form and in a written form.

In summary, any research project can be broken into a series of logical stages, starting with a determination of the worth of the project and ending with analysis and interpretation of the findings. While viewing the research stages as chronological is convenient, in reality, several stages are not independent of one another. Indeed, a major challenge for researchers and decision makers is to think ahead as they get started with a research project. Planning a potentially valuable research project requires a much broader perspective than focusing solely on one stage at a time.

Exhibit 3.1 shows a flow diagram summarizing the various stages of the research process. The broken arrows to the left in Exhibit 3.1 emphasize the interrelationships among the stages. For instance, even at the very first stage

Exhibit 3.1

Research project stages

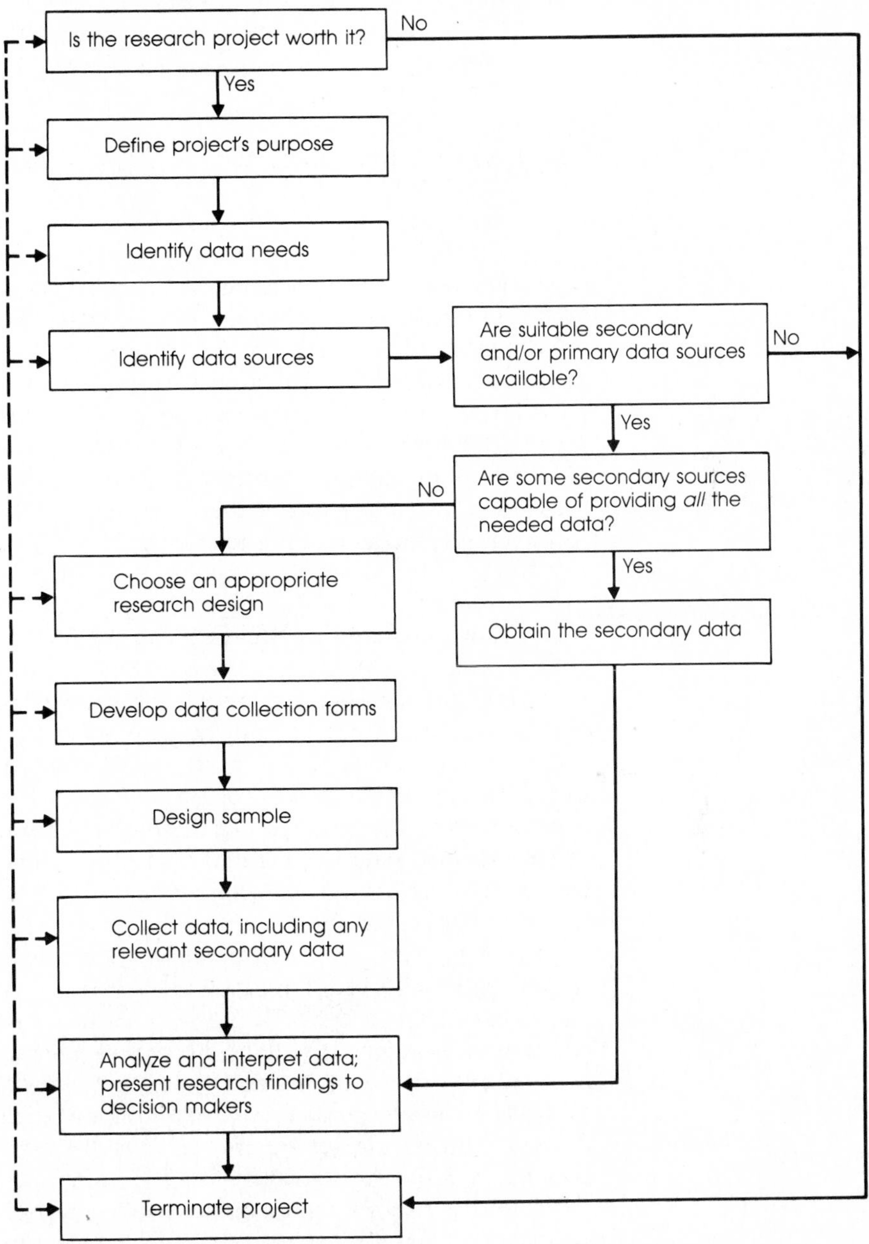

(evaluating a project's worth), the researcher/decision maker must have some idea about what is involved in the remaining stages. Otherwise, making a realistic assessment of whether the project should be undertaken may be difficult.

To give you an idea of how the various research stages fit together in a real-life setting, the next section describes a research project conducted some time ago for the Wayne Engineering Corporation of Cedar Falls, Iowa.

A REAL-LIFE ILLUSTRATION

Background

Wayne Engineering is a manufacturer of garbage collection trucks (commonly known as "garbage packers") used primarily by city/town governments and private garbage collection firms. At the time of this study Wayne Engineering had annual sales of around $4 million and was the smallest of ten garbage packer manufacturers in the United States. Wayne Engineering sold its packers through a national network of dealers. However, it had no sophisticated marketing organization; it had only a few people to coordinate dealer sales activities, plant production, and after-sales service.

Wayne Engineering's sales had remained flat for some time after experiencing rapid growth. According to the company's president, Stan Worthington, the United States market had leveled off for the types of packers produced by the company, which were smaller than the increasingly popular packers produced by competing firms. Consequently, Mr. Worthington wanted to explore the possibility of developing new markets for Wayne's packers. Specifically, he singled out Canada as a new market because of Canada's proximity to the United States (and especially to Iowa, where Wayne's plant was located), the apparent similarities between the United States and Canadian market structures, and the fact that Wayne's United States competitors were already selling a large number of packers in Canada. The author (hereafter referred to as the consultant) worked full-time for Wayne Engineering during the two months when this project was undertaken.

Justification for the project

A primary reason for considering the project was Mr. Worthington's belief that there might be a market in Canada for Wayne's packers. Several years of relatively flat sales in the United States increased the desirability of conducting the research. Mr. Worthington therefore felt that the research would be potentially useful. Moreover, Wayne Engineering had enough production capacity and other necessary resources to tap the Canadian market should the research uncover a demand for Wayne's packers. In short, the proposed research appeared to be worthwhile on the dimensions of potential usefulness, management's open-mindedness, and adequacy of resources to implement the research results.

Comparing accurately the *dollar* costs and benefits of the research project was not possible. However, a rough assessment was made along the following lines: The project cost was estimated to be about $6000 on the basis of compensation for the consultant's time and other data collection expenses (such as travel expenses). Estimating the data collection expenses was neither precise nor easy. What the various stages of the project would involve had to be ascertained right at the start of the process—a difficult, but *necessary,* task.

Potential benefits of the project, although worthwhile in a qualitative sense, were impossible to quantify in monetary terms. Therefore an indirect evaluation was made by looking at the size of the break-even packer sales needed to recover the estimated research cost. When the project was proposed, Wayne's packers were selling at an average price of $25,000, and Wayne's contribution margin was 10%, or about $2500 on every packer sold. Thus if only three packers were sold in Canada, the estimated research cost would be more than recouped. This break-even sales figure was considered reasonable. Also, the estimated cost as a percentage of annual sales was only about 0.15%, a miniscule amount. Hence the research project was deemed to be worthwhile on monetary grounds.

Definition of research purpose

The main objective of the research project was to assess the potential for Wayne Engineering's garbage packers in Canada. Whether this objective was the *most appropriate* research objective warrants some discussion, especially in view of our earlier emphasis on the need to identify the correct research objective.

The motive prompting Mr. Worthington to consider the Canadian market was the flatness of Wayne's sales over a period of time. However, a key question worth raising is whether options *other than exploring the Canadian market* were even considered. For example, could Wayne Engineering have explored the feasibility of boosting sales through more aggressive selling within the United States or through the introduction of new products? Ideally, issues like these must be jointly discussed by the researcher and the decision maker before deciding on the research purpose. However, in Wayne Engineering's case the consultant did not explore such options because Mr. Worthington (who was more knowledgeable about the company and its markets) had already considered them and dismissed them as being infeasible owing to a variety of constraints. For instance, since Wayne Engineering did not have its own sales force, and since its competition was rapidly increasing in the United States, Mr. Worthington had ruled out the option of trying to increase sales through more aggressive selling. The research purpose as defined was considered to be appropriate, at least in Mr. Worthington's judgment.

Identification of data needs

The data requirements for accomplishing the primary research purpose were listed as a set of specific questions:

- What are the main features of the garbage packers used in Canada?
- Are there any similarities or differences between Wayne Engineering's packers and those used in Canada? If so, what are those similarities or differences?
- What type of competition is Wayne Engineering likely to face, from Canadian as well as United States firms, if it decides to enter the Canadian market?
- Are there particular segments in the Canadian market with unique needs capable of being satisfied better by Wayne Engineering's packers than by competing packers? If so, what are the characteristics of those segments?
- What type of Canadian firms or institutions appear to be especially interested in Wayne Engineering's packers? What is the extent of their interest?

Identification of data sources

Most of the data to be collected involved potential customers' perceptions about the fit between the Canadian market's needs and the features of Wayne's packers. As a result, some form of primary-data collection was inevitable. Mr. Worthington and the consultant felt that end users of garbage packers, as well as firms involved in distributing and servicing them, would be able to provide data relevant to the study. Specifically, municipalities (i.e., city/town governments), private garbage collection firms, and truck equipment distributors/manufacturers were identified as sources of primary data. In addition, the library and the Canadian Consulate in Chicago were identified as potential sources of secondary data (such as annual unit sales of garbage packers in Canada) pertaining to the research project.

Designing the questionnaire

Recall that questionnaire design, in addition to considering a research project's objectives and data needs, must also take into account the nature of the respondents and the data collection method to be used (i.e., the stages of designing the sample and collecting the data). Consequently, before designing any questionnaire, Mr. Worthington and the consultant had to think through the procedure to be used in gathering the needed data.

Since Wayne Engineering had little prior data on the Canadian garbage packer market, the project was basically exploratory (more on exploratory research in the next chapter). As is common in many exploratory-research projects, the consultant decided to collect the necessary data through personal interviews of knowledgeable individuals in appropriate Canadian institutions. The personal-interview approach, rather than a telephone or a mail survey, was chosen for the following reason: In order to obtain *meaningful* data, the researcher had to demonstrate the features of Wayne's packers (through pictures and brochures) and to answer any questions the respondents might have. Given the need for such researcher-respondent interaction, telephone and mail surveys were inappropriate (Chapter 6 discusses in greater detail the relative merits and drawbacks of personal interviews vis-à-vis telephone and mail surveys).

The personal interviews were designed to be open-ended and nonstructured because of the exploratory nature of the research; no formal questionnaire was designed and printed. However, the consultant did prepare a set of questions described in the "Identification of Data Needs" section in this chapter. This set of questions was useful in ensuring that all critical topics were discussed during the interviews.

Sample design

The sample for this study was identified earlier as a group of decision makers in municipalities, private garbage collection firms, and truck equipment distributors/manufacturers. From what geographic area(s) of Canada were these institutions to be chosen? How many such institutions should be chosen? What procedure should be used in choosing them? These questions had to be answered before data collection could begin.

The investigation was restricted to the four Canadian states (or provinces as they are called in Canada) closest to Iowa, namely, Ontario, Manitoba, Saskatchewan, and Alberta. Provinces close to Iowa were chosen because the final price of heavy equipment like garbage packers is very sensitive to the distance between potential markets and production facilities. Markets too far away from Iowa were unlikely to be attractive to Wayne Engineering in terms of price competitiveness. Moreover, the limited time available for completing the entire project precluded broader coverage of Canada. Such a practical constraint is not unique to the Wayne Engineering project; many real-life research studies have to make compromises and use less-than-ideal designs because of limited resources (time, money, personnel, etc.).

Within the four Canadian provinces the consultant further decided to restrict the study sample to cities and towns with populations of 50,000 or more. This decision was based partly on the tight time constraint and partly on the assumption that the demand for garbage packers would be strongest in the major population centers. According to the 1971 census reports the four chosen provinces had over 50% of Canada's population. Within these provinces the consultant pinpointed (with the aid of a road atlas) 21 cities and towns that were convenient to get to during the limited time available for the study. The selected cities together accounted for about 25% of the total Canadian population. This population coverage was adequate given the exploratory nature of the project, although the geographic coverage in terms of the actual number of cities included was relatively small.

As part of the sample design, the consultant laid out the travel routes to be taken through the chosen provinces. Exhibit 3.2 shows the consultant's travel route through Ontario; the numbers indicate the sequence in which the major cities in Ontario were to be covered. Similar travel plans were drawn up for the other three provinces.

The final sample included 82 institutions. However, owing to the lack of a readily available list, the consultant could not identify all of them by name *before* starting the data collection. Consequently, the institutions were selected judgmentally after the consultant drove into each city on the travel route. Municipal offices in the various cities were obvious candidates for inclusion in the sample, and they could easily be identified and located. However, the yellow pages of the telephone directory had to be used to get the names and addresses

Exhibit 3.2

Consultant's travel route through Ontario

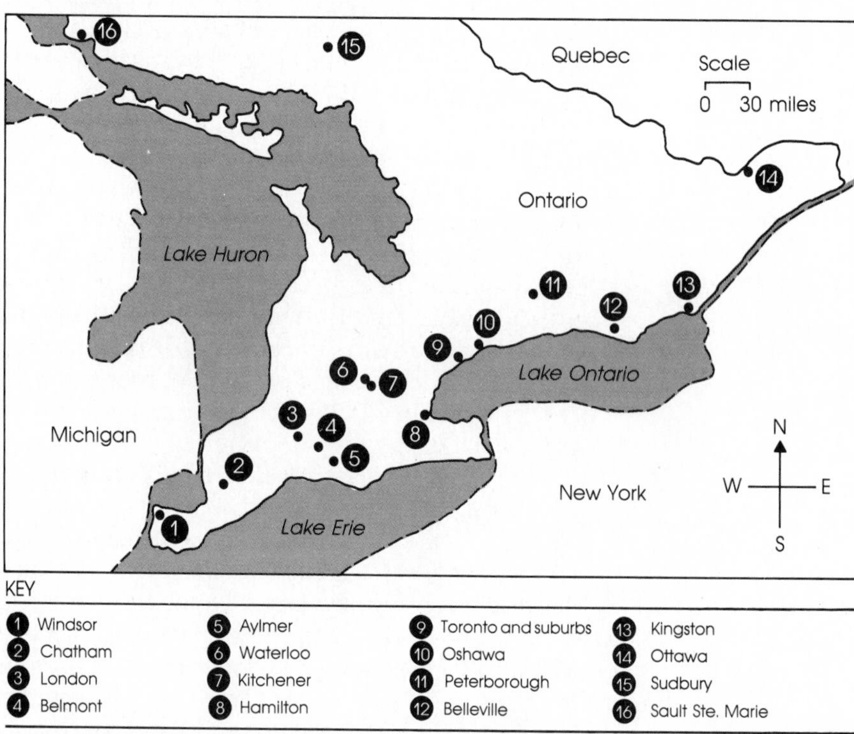

of private garbage collection firms and truck equipment distributors/manufacturers.

The yellow pages in relatively small cities contained only a few such firms; hence all of them could be included in the sample. However, in large cities such as Toronto, Ottawa, and Edmonton, the yellow pages listed numerous private garbage collection firms and truck equipment distributors/manufacturers. Since the consultant could not contact all the listed firms, he used the size of the ads placed by the firms as the basis for selecting a few of them. As a rationale, the consultant assumed that firms placing larger ads were likely to be bigger and hence more inclined to be interested in international trade than other firms. Admittedly, this selection process was not very scientific. However, the use of such judgment sampling is not uncommon, especially when a research project is exploratory. (Chapter 14 discusses judgment sampling as well as other subjective, nonprobability sample selection methods.)

Data collection

Good marketing research practice involves examining potential sources of secondary data before collecting any primary data. Accordingly, the consultant first explored the availability of relevant secondary data in the library and in the Canadian Consulate in Chicago. Unfortunately, neither of these sources had secondary data specific enough to be relevant for the research objectives. However, officials at the Canadian Consulate did offer one important insight: They alerted the consultant to a growing tendency on the part of the Canadian government to restrict the import of foreign goods unless a certain proportion of Canadian content could be added to them. Indeed, this revelation suggested that the study sample should include truck equipment manufacturers, who might be interested in buying garbage packer components or unassembled packers from Wayne Engineering. Moreover, certain types of secondary data were useful at the sample design stage: As we already saw, the Canadian population census data as well as data in a road atlas were helpful in defining the geographic areas to be covered and selecting the specific cities and towns to be studied within those areas.

Primary data were gathered through discussions with decision makers in the selected institutions. At each institution the consultant outlined the purpose of the study and requested a meeting with appropriate personnel. Only 4 of the 82 institutions contacted refused to honor the request for an interview. Most of the respondents interviewed were senior-level decision makers such as purchasing officers, marketing/sales managers, and presidents. Some firms showed a great deal of interest in the survey, and the interviews turned into group discussions with two or more executives participating in them. The length of the interviews ranged from less than 10 minutes to over an hour; on the average, they lasted about 30 minutes.

During each interview, in addition to focusing the discussion on the research questions, the consultant answered any questions the respondents had about Wayne Engineering and also took extensive notes. At the end of each day's round of interviews, the consultant prepared a fairly detailed written report for each institution contacted that day. The interview notes were very useful in preparing these reports. The following details are illustrative of the items included in the reports:

1. Data about the institution, such as its size, nature of operations, and garbage collection products being used or sold.
2. The extent of interest shown by the institution in Wayne Engineering's products and/or in joint ventures with Wayne Engineering.
3. The respondents' perceptions about the Canadian garbage packer market as well as the potential strengths and weaknesses of various garbage packers in the market.
4. The consultant's subjective assessment of the merit of Wayne Engineering's strengthening its association with the institution.

Data analysis and interpretation

Because of the exploratory nature of this project and the nonstructured data collection procedure, the data in the written reports were *qualitative* data. Hence quantitative-analysis procedures were irrelevant and inappropriate. The actual analysis performed consisted of examining the written reports to see whether common patterns of response could be identified regarding issues such as the types of packers likely to have the strongest appeal in the Canadian market and the distinguishing features, if any, of firms showing a keen interest in Wayne Engineering. (More will be said about analysis and interpretation of qualitative research data in Chapter 7.)

Several valuable insights emerged from the examination of the written reports. For example, a technologically revolutionary packer for which Wayne had acquired production rights from a Swedish firm generated virtually no interest in the Canadian institutions, much to the surprise of Mr. Worthington. In contrast, one of Wayne's older products, a small packer capable of holding a relatively light load, got an enthusiastic response from many institutions, especially private garbage collection firms. Moreover, 8 out of 24 truck equipment dealers/manufacturers contacted in Ontario were interested in exploring joint-venture or licensing arrangements with Wayne Engineering for producing and marketing packers of this type. In short, the analysis uncovered unique opportunities and constraints for Wayne Engineering.

The consultant made an oral presentation to Mr. Worthington and other Wayne Engineering executives in addition to giving them a copy of the written reports of the interviews. During the presentation the consultant highlighted the types of packers for which there appeared to be good sales potential in Canada, and pinpointed specific Canadian institutions holding the greatest promise for fruitful future relationships with Wayne Engineering.

Deciding whether the project was worth it

About a year and a half later the consultant contacted Mr. Worthington and asked him whether Wayne Engineering had benefited from the research project. Mr. Worthington felt it had been worthwhile. Several major Canadian cities contacted during the study were in correspondence with Wayne Engineering and frequently requested bids on garbage packers. Moreover, as a result of the study, Wayne Engineering had a list of capable and interested distributors dispersed across the four provinces covered in the study.

Despite these benefits, however, the study had not yet netted any Canadian sales for Wayne Engineering. Mr. Worthington candidly said the study would have been *more beneficial* if they had adequately followed up on the insights and leads generated. But Wayne Engineering had not yet been able to break into the Canadian market aggressively because of personnel and monetary problems. In spite of the earlier effort to weigh the pros and cons of the proposed project, certain potential resource constraints had apparently been glossed over. In retrospect, perhaps Mr. Worthington and the consultant should have more carefully considered questions like the following: What specific action(s) would, or *could*, Wayne Engineering take if the research findings turned out to be such and such?

No doubt the research project offered useful insights about the nature of the Canadian garbage packer market and pointed out several fruitful business contacts in Canada. Nevertheless, had all potential resource constraints been carefully considered at the outset, the research project might have been postponed to a more opportune time when Wayne Engineering could aggressively act on the research findings.

Of course, not all marketing research projects are as unstructured and as informally conducted as the Wayne Engineering study. As mentioned earlier, the nature of the problem and research objectives in a given setting determine the nature of the research design or approach to be used. In subsequent chapters we will see applications of more formal and sophisticated research approaches. Irrespective of the nature of research projects, however, they all involve the same basic interrelated stages, as illustrated by the Wayne Engineering study.

SUMMARY

This chapter introduced you to the various stages involved in planning and conducting a marketing research project. Certain aspects of these stages deserve particular attention. First, although a research project can be viewed as a sequence of chronological stages, the stages are not necessarily independent of one another. Chronologically distant stages may have an impact on preceding stages.

Second, some projects may not involve all the stages shown in Exhibit 3.1. When all the necessary data are available through secondary sources, there is no need to develop a data collection form, design a sample, or collect primary data. At the other extreme, when no trustworthy data source (primary or secondary) capable of adequately meeting a research project's data needs is available, terminating the project is better than proceeding further.

Third, even though the research process is a logical sequence of well-defined stages, it is not totally scientific. The subjective judgment of decision makers and researchers is likely to play a role in at least some of the stages, such as in the evaluation of the worth of a research project. Even mathematically sophisticated approaches for making cost-versus-benefit evaluations (such as the Bayesian analysis approach discussed in the appendix) are based on critical assumptions and require subjective inputs from decision makers. Despite the inevitability of some degree of subjectivity in the research process, marketing research should be conducted in a systematic fashion if it is to be beneficial.

The Wayne Engineering example illustrated the stages of the research process in a real-life setting. Of the several research features implicit in this example, especially noteworthy are the need for subjective inputs at the various stages, the interrelationships among the stages, the systematic way in which marketing research can be done, and the practical constraints researchers often face and must handle in some reasonable way.

QUESTIONS

1. "In conducting a marketing research project, researchers would be unwise to spend time and effort on subsequent stages unless all previous stages have been completed. Discuss this statement.

2. a. State, and briefly describe, the four criteria that are relevant in deciding whether or not a research project should be undertaken.

   b. One of the examples discussed in Chapter 1 dealt with Nissan Motor Company's research concerning relative awareness of the Datsun and Nissan names. Review this example, and state whether each of the four criteria was likely to have been met in this case. Justify your answer.

3. Explain the association between the nature of uncertainty faced by a decision maker and the potential benefit of a research project capable of reducing that uncertainty.

4. State whether you agree or disagree with this statement: "Correct identification and clear definition of the research problem are more crucial to the success of a project than sophisticated research techniques." Explain your answer.

5. Under what circumstances would a project be terminated without completing *all* the research process stages? Give an example of your own to illustrate your answer.
6. Does every marketing research project require a formal questionnaire? Discuss your answer, using one or two examples cited in previous chapters.
7. Considering all the facts given in the Wayne Engineering example, comment on the consultant's decision to restrict the study to cities and towns with populations of 50,000 or more. Specifically, what are the pros and cons of this decision?

APPENDIX TO CHAPTER 3

Bayesian Analysis

This appendix describes a mathematical procedure for estimating the monetary value of a marketing research project. The procedure is commonly referred to as *Bayesian analysis* or the *decision theory approach.*[1] We will use the situation depicted in scenario B presented earlier in the chapter to illustrate this procedure. In scenario B Jerry Wilson, advertising manager for corporation B, is wondering which of two commercials will be more appropriate for promoting his company's deodorant: commercial X, which uses a fear appeal, or commercial Y, which uses a romantic appeal.

WORTH OF PERFECT RESEARCH

Market states

The relative effectiveness of X or Y will hinge on the nature of the market; in particular, factors such as the current attitudes and the personalities of the target customers may determine which of the two commercials is likely to be more effective. For instance, commercial X (fear appeal) may be more effective if most of the target customers have low self-confidence, a personality trait. But if the target customers have high self-confidence, the fear appeal may backfire, while the romantic appeal may be effective. Thus the relative effectiveness of each commercial will depend on the overall disposition, or *state,* of the market. For the sake of simplicity let us assume the market state in scenario B will be either M_1 or M_2, where M_1 and M_2 are defined as follows:

[1] We will be discussing only the very basic elements of the decision theory approach in this appendix. Further details and refinements can be found in several books on the subject, including Joseph W. Newman, *Management Applications of Decision Theory* (New York: Harper & Row, 1971); Robert Schlaifer, *Analysis of Decisions Under Uncertainty* (New York: McGraw-Hill, 1969).

- M_1 is the state in which customer reaction will be favorable to commercial X but not to commercial Y, that is, a state in which the inherent persuasiveness of X is much higher than that of Y.
- M_2 is the state in which customer reaction will be favorable to commercial Y but not to commercial X, that is, a state in which the inherent persuasiveness of Y is much higher than that of X.

Prior probabilities

As we know, Mr. Wilson is *uncertain* about which of the two market states, M_1 or M_2, actually exists. However, suppose Mr. Wilson's intuition tells him M_1 is slightly more likely to exist than M_2. Specifically, suppose he feels there is a 60% chance that M_1 is the true market state and a 40% chance that M_2 is the true market state. On the basis of these subjective feelings, we can specify the probabilities P of the two possible market states as

$$P(M_1) = .6,$$
$$P(M_2) = .4.$$

In decision theory these probabilities are called *prior probabilities.*

Payoff table

Mr. Wilson believes commercial X will result in a net profit to corporation B if market state M_1 exists but will lead to a net loss if M_2 exists. Similarly, he feels commercial Y will be beneficial only if market state M_2 exists. Mr. Wilson's quantified estimates of the net profits (or losses) under the various possible circumstances are summarized in Table A.3.1. A table like A.3.1 is called a *payoff table.* It indicates the payoffs, or monetary returns, associated with each alternative course of action A (A_1 or A_2 in our example) under each possible market state.

Table A.3.1
Payoff table in scenario B

	PAYOFFS UNDER MARKET STATE	
ALTERNATIVE COURSES OF ACTION	M_1	M_2
Use commercial X (alternative A_1)	$800,000	−$20,000
Use commercial Y (alternative A_2)	−$50,000	$900,000

Expected value under uncertainty

Choosing between alternatives A_1 and A_2 *without* conducting marketing research will amount to decision making *under uncertainty*. If Mr. Wilson wants to make his decision under uncertainty, what criterion should he use to choose between A_1 and A_2? The criterion commonly employed under such circumstances is the *expected value* of the alternative, which is its *weighted average payoff*. The expected value EV of A_1 and A_2 can be computed as follows:

$$\begin{aligned}
\text{EV}(A_1) &= (\text{payoff for } A_1 \textit{ if } M_1 \text{ exists}) \times P(M_1) \\
&\quad + (\text{payoff for } A_1 \textit{ if } M_2 \text{ exists}) \times P(M_2) \\
&= (800{,}000) \times (.6) + (-20{,}000) \times (.4) \\
&= 480{,}000 - 8000 = \$472{,}000, \\
\text{EV}(A_2) &= (\text{payoff for } A_2 \textit{ if } M_1 \text{ exists}) \times P(M_1) \\
&\quad + (\text{payoff for } A_2 \textit{ if } M_2 \text{ exists}) \times P(M_2) \\
&= (-50{,}000) \times (.6) + (900{,}000) \times (.4) \\
&= -30{,}000 + 360{,}000 = \$330{,}000.
\end{aligned}$$

As the computations indicate, the expected value of an alternative takes into account not only the payoff associated with it but also the probability of that payoff materializing. Thus an expected value can be interpreted as the overall worth of an alternative. Another way of interpreting the expected value of an alternative is as follows: If one selects this same alternative under each of a large number of similar decision-making circumstances over a period of time, the long-run average payoff per decision will be equal to the expected value. Intuitively, the best alternative under a given set of circumstances is one with the highest expected value. Let us define *expected value under uncertainty* as the *maximum* expected payoff to a decision maker who chooses a course of action under uncertainty. We will use the notation EV(UC) to denote expected value under uncertainty.

In scenario B the expected value under uncertainty is given by

$$\begin{aligned}
\text{EV(UC)} &= \text{maximum } [\text{EV}(A_1), \text{EV}(A_2)] \\
&= \text{EV}(A_1) = \$472{,}000.
\end{aligned}$$

In other words, A_1 is the best alternative Mr. Wilson can choose under uncertainty, and his expected return is $472,000.

Expected value under certainty

Suppose David Cox, a marketing researcher, offers to conduct some *perfect* research to completely eliminate Mr. Wilson's uncertainty. Specifically, Mr. Cox tells Mr. Wilson: "My research will indicate to you for sure whether M_1 or M_2 is the true market state. In other words, if my research indicates customer reaction to be favorable to commercial X (i.e., market state M_1 exists), you can use commercial X and be *certain* your return will be $800,000. But if my research indicates customer reaction to be unfavorable to commercial X (i.e., market state M_2 exists), you can employ commercial Y and be certain about obtaining a return of $900,000." If you were Mr. Wilson, how much would you be willing to pay for Mr. Cox's research?

To answer this question, you must estimate the probability of the potential research outcome, indicating the market state to be M_1 or M_2. In other words, you must estimate the research outcome probabilities, $P(R_1)$ and $P(R_2)$, defined as follows:

$$P(R_1) = P(\text{research outcome showing } M_1 \text{ is the market state}),$$
$$P(R_2) = P(\text{research outcome showing } M_2 \text{ is the market state}).$$

How do we estimate $P(R_1)$ and $P(R_2)$? Bear in mind that Mr. Cox *has not yet* conducted his research; hence at this point you do not know which research outcome (R_1 or R_2) will materialize. You only know that if Mr. Cox's perfect research, when completed, indicates a market state (M_1 or M_2), you can be certain that the indicated state is the true market state. Consequently, your best estimate of the probability of the research outcome indicating a particular market state is merely your *prior probability* estimate for that market state. That is,

$$P(R_1) = P(M_1) = .6,$$
$$P(R_2) = P(M_2) = .4.$$

Which commercial (X or Y) should Mr. Wilson use *if* the outcome of Mr. Cox's perfect research is R_1? Obviously, Mr. Wilson should use X. If R_1 occurs, Mr. Wilson can be sure M_1 exists, because of the perfect nature of the research, and hence using X can guarantee a return of $800,000. Similarly, if R_2 occurs, using Y can guarantee a return of $900,000.

Mr. Wilson will be making his decision *under certainty* if he asks Mr. Cox to conduct the perfect research, observes the research outcome, and then chooses the appropriate course of action. Table A.3.2 summarizes the two possible decision sequences and the corresponding returns when Mr. Wilson makes his decision under certainty.

Table A.3.2
Decision making under certainty

PERFECT RESEARCH OUTCOMES	TRUE MARKET STATE	BEST COURSE OF ACTION	MONETARY RETURN	P (OBTAINING RETURN)
R_1	M_1	A_1	$800,000	$P(R_1) = .6$
R_2	M_2	A_2	$900,000	$P(R_2) = .4$

Using the information in Table A.3.2, we can compute the *expected value under certainty,* EV(C), as follows:

$$\begin{aligned} EV(C) &= (\text{ultimate payoff if } R_1 \text{ occurs}) \times P(R_1) \\ &\quad + (\text{ultimate payoff if } R_2 \text{ occurs}) \times P(R_2) \\ &= (800{,}000) \times (.6) + (900{,}000) \times (.4) \\ &= 480{,}000 + 360{,}000 = \$840{,}000. \end{aligned}$$

The EV(C) can be interpreted as the expected return to a decision maker who commissions a perfect research project, observes the research outcome, and chooses the best course of action corresponding to that outcome.

Expected value of perfect information

Let us now turn our attention to estimating how much Mr. Wilson should be willing to pay for Mr. Cox's perfect research. Our discussion thus far indicates two possible ways for Mr. Wilson to make his decision: *under uncertainty,* by choosing between commercials X and Y without doing any research, or *under certainty,* by observing the outcome of perfect research first and then choosing between X and Y. The worth of perfect research should logically be reflected by how much better off Mr. Wilson would be by making his decision under certainty rather than under uncertainty. We already know the best returns to Mr. Wilson under these two options, namely, EV(C) and EV(UC), respectively. Hence the worth of perfect research, commonly known as the *expected value of perfect information,* EV(PI), is given by

$$EV(PI) = EV(C) - EV(UC) = 840{,}000 - 472{,}000 = \$368{,}000.$$

The EV(PI) can be interpreted as the *maximum* amount a decision maker should be willing to pay for *any* research promising to reduce his or her uncertainty. In other words, EV(PI) provides an upper bound for the worth of marketing research in a given situation. No real-life marketing research is likely to be perfect; there is always room for error. In our example Mr. Cox's promise to conduct perfect research is more hypothetical than real. Consequently, if Mr. Wilson were to commission a real-life research project to aid his decision making, he should pay no more than \$368,000; indeed, realistically speaking, he should only pay some amount *less than* the upper limit of \$368,000. How much less should he pay? The answer depends on how "imperfect" the proposed research is likely to be, or how much room exists for error. We will now discuss a procedure for determining the worth of research that is less than perfect.

WORTH OF IMPERFECT RESEARCH

Conditional probabilities of research outcomes

Suppose Mr. Wilson does not believe Mr. Cox's claim that his research will be perfect. Specifically, on the basis of past experience with research projects of the type proposed by Mr. Cox, Mr. Wilson believes there is only a 70% chance that Mr. Cox's research will identify the existence of M_1 when the true market state is M_1. In other words, when the true market state is that consumer reaction will be favorable to commercial X, there is only a .7 probability that Mr. Cox's research outcome will be R_1; alternatively, there is a .3 probability that the research outcome will be R_2. These probabilities are *conditional probabilities,* which can be represented as follows:

$$P(R_1/M_1) = P(\text{obtaining research outcome } R_1 \textit{ if } \text{the market state is } M_1) = .7,$$
$$P(R_2/M_1) = P(\text{obtaining research outcome } R_2 \textit{ if } \text{the market state is } M_1) = .3.$$

Similarly, suppose Mr. Wilson feels there is only an 80% chance that the research will correctly identify the market state when the true market state is M_2. Then the conditional probabilities of the research outcomes are

$$P(R_1/M_2) = .2 \quad \text{and} \quad P(R_2/M_2) = .8.$$

Posterior probabilities

We know that the prior probability of market state M_1, $P(M_1)$, is .6, on the basis of Mr. Wilson's subjective feelings. Suppose the imperfect research described in the previous section is conducted and outcome R_1 is observed. Would this research information (i.e., outcome R_1) have an impact on Mr. Wilson's assessment of the prior probabilities of market states M_1 and M_2? Yes. Since outcome R_1 has been observed, we would intuitively expect Mr. Wilson to *increase* his estimate of the probability that M_1 is the true market state and *decrease* his estimate of the probability that M_2 is the true market state.

The *revised* probabilities of the market states, upon observation of a particular research outcome, are called *posterior probabilities.* Note that posterior probabilities are contingent on a particular research outcome. Hence each possible research outcome will have a corresponding set of posterior probabilities of the market states. In our example there are two sets of posterior probabilities: (1) the posterior probabilities of M_1 and M_2 when the research outcome is R_1, denoted as $P(M_1/R_1)$ and $P(M_2/R_1)$; and (2) the posterior probabilities of M_1 and M_2 when the research outcome is R_2, denoted as $P(M_1/R_2)$ and $P(M_2/R_2)$.

By what amount should Mr. Wilson revise the prior probabilities in order to obtain the posterior probabilities? The posterior probabilities can be derived from the prior and conditional probabilities by using a principle known as *Bayes's rule.* According to Bayes's rule, for any research outcome R_i and market state M_j,

$$P(M_j/R_i) = \frac{P(R_i/M_j) \times P(M_j)}{P(R_i)}. \tag{A.3.1}$$

In Eq. (A.3.1), $P(M_j/R_i)$ is the posterior probability of market state M_j, given that research outcome R_i is observed; $P(R_i/M_j)$ is the conditional probability of R_i if the market state is M_j; $P(M_j)$ is the prior probability of market state M_j; and $P(R_i)$ is the probability that R_i will be the research outcome. If there are K possible market states ($M_1, M_2, \ldots, M_K$), the probability of research outcome R_i is given by

$$\begin{aligned} P(R_i) = {} & P(\text{research outcome is } R_i \textit{ and } \text{the market state is } M_1) \\ & + P(\text{research outcome is } R_i \textit{ and } \text{the market state is } M_2) + \cdots \\ & + P(\text{research outcome is } R_i \textit{ and } \text{the market state is } M_K). \end{aligned}$$

Each term in this expression is a *joint probability* of research outcome R_i and a particular market state. Thus

$$P(R_i) = \sum_{j=1}^{K} P(R_i \textit{ and } M_j) = \sum_{j=1}^{K} P(R_i/M_j) \times P(M_j).$$

We can rewrite Eq. (A.3.1) as

$$P(M_j/R_i) = \frac{P(R_i/M_j) \times P(M_j)}{\sum_{j=1}^{K} P(R_i/M_j) \times P(M_j)}. \tag{A.3.2}$$

Equation (A.3.2) can be used to calculate the various posterior probabilities.

Table A.3.3 shows the computation of the posterior probabilities of M_1 and M_2 under each of the two possible research outcomes (R_1 and R_2) in our example.

Decision making based on imperfect research

The posterior probabilities computed in Table A.3.3 will be helpful in determining the best alternative course of action (A_1 or A_2) under each of the two possible research outcomes. The criterion for choosing between A_1 and A_2 is the *expected*

Table A.3.3

Computation of posterior probabilities

RESEARCH OUTCOMES	PRIOR PROBABILITIES	CONDITIONAL PROBABILITIES	JOINT PROBABILITIES AND RESEARCH OUTCOME PROBABILITIES	POSTERIOR PROBABILITIES
R_1	$P(M_1) = .6$	$P(R_1/M_1) = .7$	$P(R_1 \text{ and } M_1) = P(R_1/M_1) \times P(M_1)$ $= (.7) \times (.6)$ $= .42$	$P(M_1/R_1) = P(R_1 \text{ and } M_1)/P(R_1)$ $= .42/.50$ $= .84$
	$P(M_2) = .4$	$P(R_1/M_2) = .2$	$P(R_1 \text{ and } M_2) = P(R_1/M_2) \times P(M_2)$ $= (.2) \times (.4)$ $= .08$	$P(M_2/R_1) = P(R_1 \text{ and } M_2)/P(R_1)$ $= .08/.50$ $= .16$
			$P(R_1) = .42 + .08 = .50$	
R_2	$P(M_1) = .6$	$P(R_2/M_1) = .3$	$P(R_2 \text{ and } M_1) = P(R_2/M_1) \times P(M_1)$ $= (.3) \times (.6)$ $= .18$	$P(M_1/R_2) = P(R_2 \text{ and } M_1)/P(R_2)$ $= .18/.50$ $= .36$
	$P(M_2) = .4$	$P(R_2/M_2) = .8$	$P(R_2 \text{ and } M_2) = P(R_2/M_2) \times P(M_2)$ $= (.8) \times (.4)$ $= .32$	$P(M_2/R_2) = P(R_2 \text{ and } M_2)/P(R_2)$ $= .32/.50$ $= .64$
			$P(R_2) = .18 + .32 = .50$	

value of each, *given that a particular research outcome has been observed.* Such contingent expected values can be computed by using a procedure similar to the one presented in the section "Expected Value Under Uncertainty," *with one major difference:* We should use the *posterior* (rather than *prior*) probabilities of the market states in our computation. Table A.3.4 shows how the contingent expected values of A_1 and A_2 are calculated.

From the expected values in Table A.3.4 Mr. Wilson should choose alternative A_1 *if* the research outcome is R_1; he should choose alternative A_2 *if* the research outcome is R_2. The corresponding expected returns are \$668,800 and \$558,000, respectively. But bear in mind that the research project has not yet been conducted; hence we do not know which outcome will emerge if the research is conducted. However, we do know the probabilities of each possible research outcome occurring (see Table A.3.3). Therefore we can compute the *expected value of decision making with imperfect information* as follows:

$$\begin{aligned} \text{EV(DM with II)} &= \text{EV(decision making with imperfect information)} \\ &= (\text{ultimate payoff if } R_1 \text{ occurs}) \times P(R_1) \\ &\quad + (\text{ultimate payoff if } R_2 \text{ occurs}) \times P(R_2) \\ &= (668{,}800) \times (.5) + (558{,}000) \times (.5) \\ &= 334{,}400 + 279{,}000 = \$613{,}400. \end{aligned}$$

Table A.3.4
Contingent expected values

EXPECTED VALUES CONTINGENT UPON RESEARCH OUTCOME R_1	EXPECTED VALUES CONTINGENT UPON RESEARCH OUTCOME R_2
$EV(A_1/R_1)$ = (payoff for A_1 *if* M_1 exists) × $P(M_1/R_1)$ + (payoff for A_1 *if* M_2 exists) × $P(M_2/R_1)$ = (800,000) × (.84) + (−20,000) × (.16) = 672,000 − 3200 = \$668,800	$EV(A_1/R_2)$ = (payoff for A_1 *if* M_1 exists) × $P(M_1/R_2)$ + (payoff for A_1 *if* M_2 exists) × $P(M_2/R_2)$ = (800,000) × (.36) + (−20,000) × (.64) = 288,000 − 12,800 = \$275,200
$EV(A_2/R_1)$ = (payoff for A_2 *if* M_1 exists) × $P(M_1/R_1)$ + (payoff for A_2 *if* M_2 exists) × $P(M_2/R_1)$ = (−50,000) × (.84) + (900,000) × (.16) = −42,000 + 144,000 = \$102,000	$EV(A_2/R_2)$ = (payoff for A_2 *if* M_1 exists) × $P(M_1/R_2)$ + (payoff for A_2 *if* M_2 exists) × $P(M_2/R_2)$ = (−50,000) × (.36) + (900,000) × (.64) = −18,000 + 576,000 = \$558,000

The EV(DM with II) can be interpreted as the expected return to a decision maker who commissions a research project that is less than perfect, observes the research outcome, and chooses the best course of action corresponding to that outcome.

Expected value of imperfect information

How much should Mr. Wilson be willing to pay for the less-than-perfect research project? The answer depends on how much better off Mr. Wilson would be by making a decision on the basis of the research information rather than under complete uncertainty. Specifically, the *expected value of imperfect information* is given by

$$\begin{aligned} \text{EV(II)} &= \text{EV(DM with II)} - \text{EV(UC)} \\ &= 613{,}400 - 472{,}000 = \$141{,}400 \end{aligned}$$

The EV(II) is the monetary estimate of the worth of a research project to a decision maker. In our example, if the cost of the proposed research is less than \$141,400, for Mr. Wilson to undertake the research project will be worthwhile. If the cost is greater than \$141,400, Mr. Wilson will be better off choosing the best alternative *without* doing any research—namely, A_1, as we saw earlier.

DECISION TREES

A *decision tree* is a diagram that presents the following information in a logical sequence:

1. The decision options (or alternative courses of action) available to a decision maker.
2. The intervening events and/or market states that can influence the monetary consequences of choosing each option.

Exhibit A.3.1 is a decision tree summarizing the situation facing Mr. Wilson. Tracing the topmost branch of the tree in Exhibit A.3.1, for instance, we see that *if* Mr. Wilson decides not to conduct any marketing research and chooses alternative A_1, and *if* the market state is M_1, the monetary returns to Mr. Wilson will be $800,000.

Exhibit A.3.2 is a detailed version of Exhibit A.3.1. It is a decision tree showing the expected values of each decision option as well as the appropriate probabilities of the research outcomes and market states. The upper segment of the tree relates to decision making under uncertainty; the lower segment relates to decision making with imperfect information. At any node in the tree from which more than one decision branch emerges, the best branch to take is the one with the ***highest expected value.*** For instance, if Mr. Wilson commissions the research project and outcome R_2 is observed, he should choose alternative A_2.

Constructing a decision tree is not totally different from the computational procedure we discussed earlier for evaluating different decision options and estimating the worth of research information. Indeed, in order to draw a tree with all its branches labeled as shown in Exhibit A.3.2, we would have to go through all the necessary probability and expected value computations. The primary benefit of a decision tree diagram is that it provides a pictorial summary that enables a decision maker to see, at a glance, what the various decision options are and the monetary consequence of choosing each.

LIMITATIONS OF BAYESIAN ANALYSIS

The Bayesian analysis approach to determining the value of research information has several practical limitations that have apparently led to its infrequent use. One limitation of the approach is its complexity. The computations in even the relatively simple example we looked at are overwhelming. A slight increase in the number of decision options, market states, or research outcomes can lead to a sharp increase in the time and effort needed to set up and solve a value-of-information problem. Try setting up a decision tree (like the one in Exhibit A.3.1 or A.3.2) when there are three (rather than two) decision options, market states, and research outcomes. Indeed, one researcher has suggested doing a cost-versus-benefit analysis to see whether using Bayesian analysis to place a dollar value on research information is worthwhile: "Bayesian analysis should be applied to the evaluation of marketing research only if the benefits from its appli-

Exhibit A.3.1
Mr. Wilson's decision tree

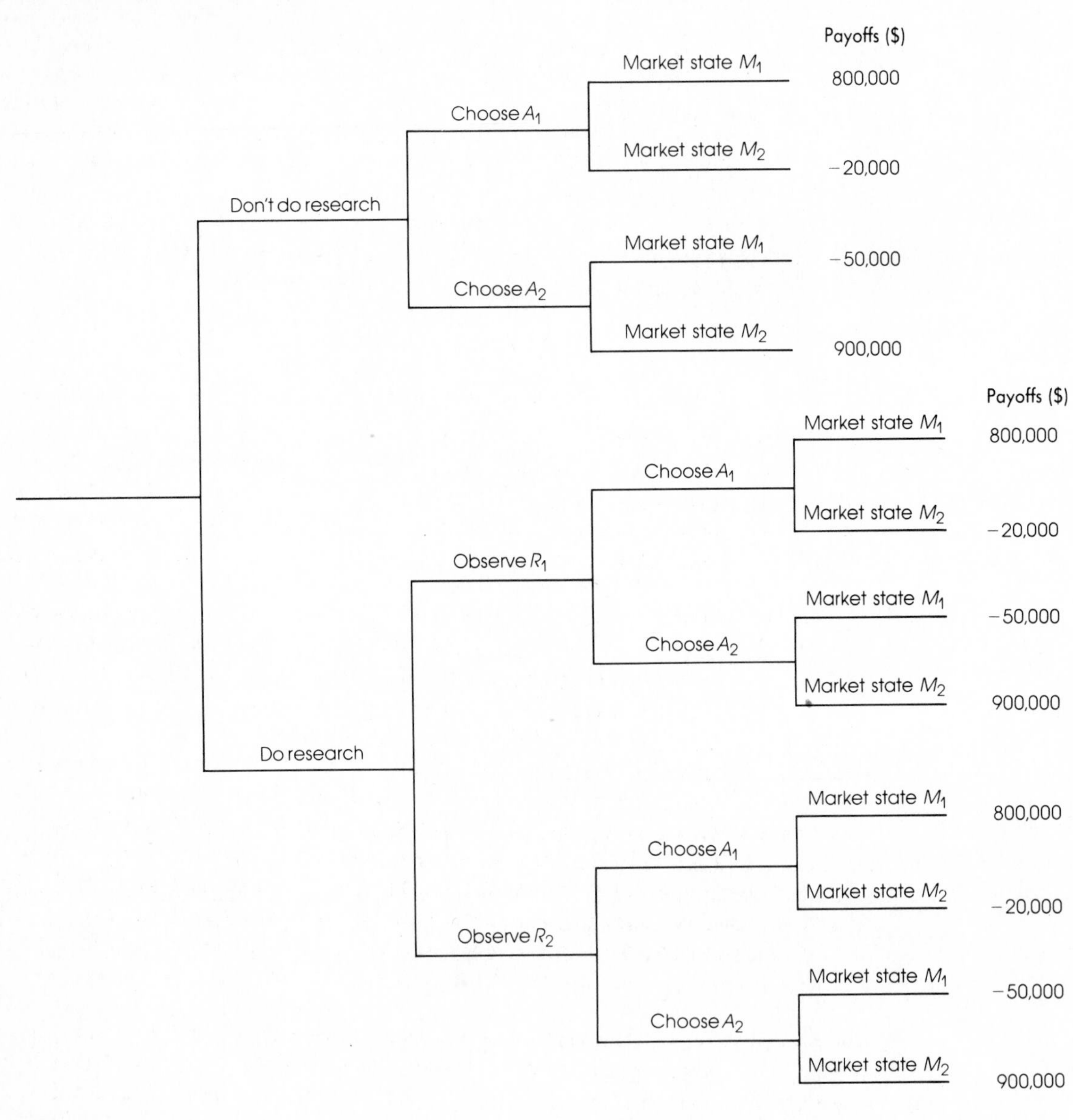

Exhibit A.3.2
Decision tree with probabilities and expected values

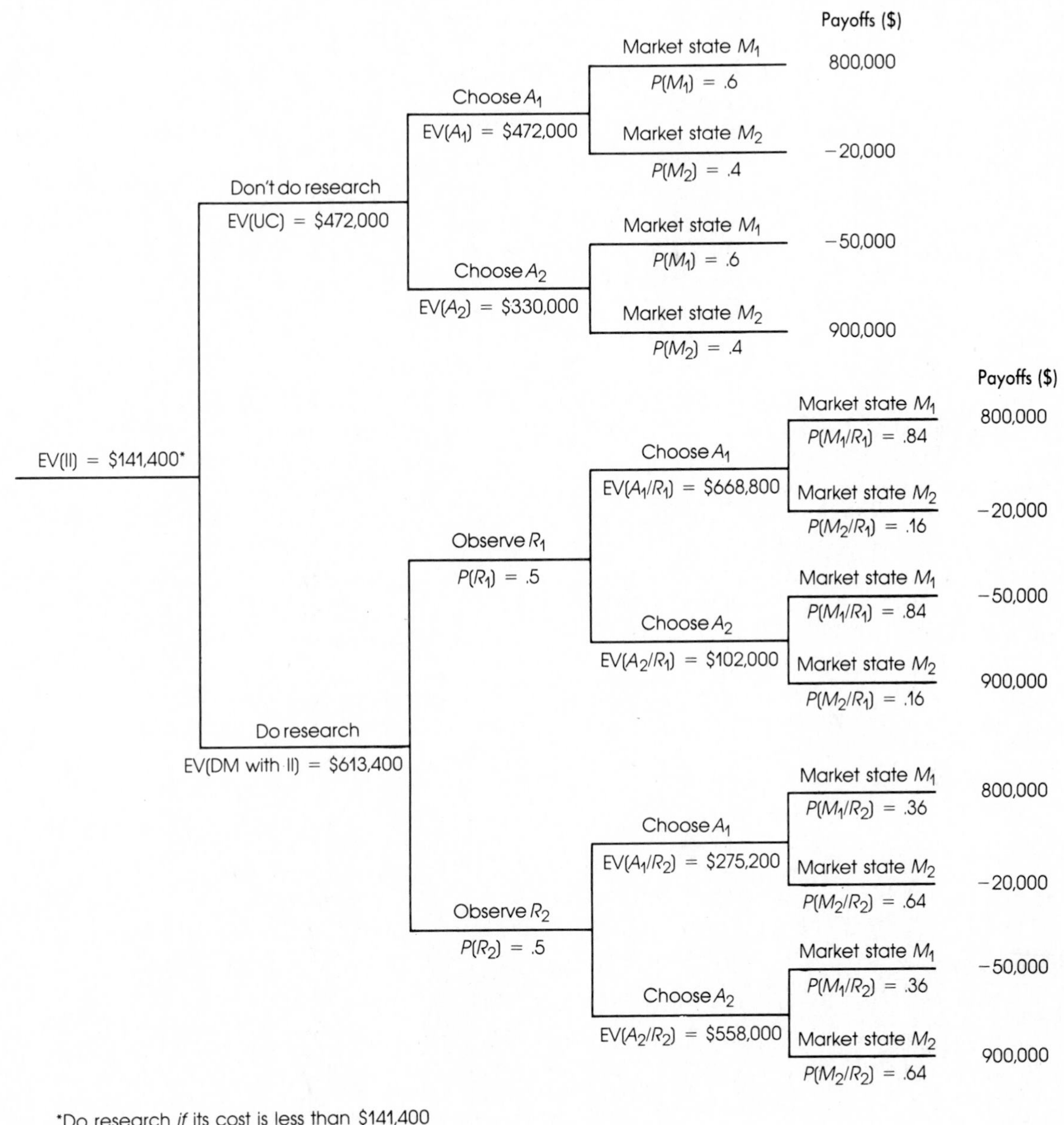

*Do research *if* its cost is less than $141,400

cation are expected to outweigh its costs. These costs are by no means inconsequential."[2]

Another problem with the Bayesian analysis approach relates to the probability estimates. Decision makers may have difficulty in accurately quantifying their subjective feelings about the chances of various market states and research outcomes materializing. And the validity—and hence usefulness—of the expected value of research information computed through Bayesian analysis will be greatly influenced by the accuracy of the probability estimates used in the analysis. Hence if decision makers are unable to provide accurate probability estimates, going through a Bayesian analysis exercise may not be very meaningful. However, a number of guidelines have been suggested in the literature for eliciting meaningful probability estimates from decision makers.[3]

Potential difficulty and inaccuracy in estimating the payoff values is an additional source of concern in using Bayesian analysis to obtain a realistic assessment of the worth of research information. Table A.3.1 shows that in our hypothetical example choosing a particular commercial under a given market state will result in a specific dollar payoff. Realistically, however, what does this payoff represent? How is it arrived at? Is it a short-term or long-term payoff? Questions like these are not easily answered accurately. Naturally, when errors occur in specifying the payoff values, the estimated value of research information will also be erroneous.

Yet another limitation of this approach is that the notion of expected values is most meaningful only when a firm is likely to encounter a series of similar decision-making situations over time. As mentioned earlier, an expected value is a long-run average payoff of making a number of similar decisions. Therefore the actual monetary outcome of any single decision is not likely to coincide with its expected value.

In summary, several potential limitations restrict the use of the Bayesian analysis approach to those situations in which the complexity of the decision problem is not overwhelming; the necessary probabilities and payoffs are easy to estimate with at least a reasonable degree of accuracy; and similar decision-making settings arise frequently. However, in practice, such situations are more an exception than the rule. Nevertheless, some aspects of the approach may still be helpful to decision makers in terms of organizing their thinking in a logical fashion. For instance, constructing a decision tree diagram (even when accurate quantitative estimates of probabilities and payoffs are not available) will force a decision maker to think through the various market states and possible outcomes methodically, prior to making a final choice. Such an exercise may pre-

---

[2] Gert Assmus, "Bayesian Analysis for the Evaluation of Marketing Research Expenditures: A Reassessment," *Journal of Marketing Research*, 14 (November 1977), p. 566.

[3] See, for example, Rakesh Kumar Sarin, "Elicitation of Subjective Probabilities in the Context of Decision-Making," *Decision Sciences*, 9 (January 1978), pp. 37–48; Philip Kotler, "A Guide to Gathering Expert Estimates," *Business Horizons*, 13 (October 1970), pp. 79–87.

vent the decision maker from overlooking any important aspect of the decision problem.[4]

QUESTIONS

1. In the context of the decision theory approach to evaluating the monetary worth of marketing research, clearly state, in a sentence or two, what each of the following terms means: (a) prior probability; (b) payoff table; (c) expected value under uncertainty; (d) expected value under certainty.
2. Since marketing research cannot realistically be perfect, what is the purpose in determining the expected value of perfect information? Discuss your answer.
3. In what ways do posterior probabilities differ from prior probabilities?
4. Briefly discuss the practical limitations of using Bayesian analysis to estimate the value of research information.
5. A marketer has two alternative promotion strategies, A_1 and A_2. The relative success of A_1 and A_2 depends on the attitudinal structure of the target market. From experience the marketer feels that the target market has a 60% chance of having attitudinal structure S_1 and a 40% chance of having attitudinal structure S_2 (assume that S_1 and S_2 are the only possible states of nature). The *incremental returns* from each alternative, depending on each state of nature, are given in the following payoff table:

	S_1	S_2
A_1	\$100,000	−\$50,000
A_2	−\$70,000	\$200,000

The marketer also has the option of doing a research project to reduce her uncertainty about the true states of nature. The research project has two possible outcomes, Z_1 and Z_2. From past experience the potential accuracy of the research results are given in terms of the following conditional probabilities:

$P(Z_1/S_1) = .8,$ $\qquad$ $P(Z_1/S_2) = .2,$

$P(Z_2/S_1) = .2,$ $\qquad$ $P(Z_2/S_2) = .8.$

a. Determine EV(PI) and EV(DM with II).
b. Construct a decision tree for this problem, and represent the appropriate probabilities, expected values, and so on.

6. You are given the following information: The three possible states of nature are S_1, S_2, and S_3. The prior probabilities are $P(S_1) = .4$, $P(S_2) = .4$, and $P(S_3) = .2$. The three decision alternatives are A_1, A_2, and A_3. The three possible outcomes if marketing research is done are Z_1, Z_2, and Z_3. The payoff table (all numbers are in dollars) is as follows:

[4] Paul E. Green offers a concise discussion of the limitations and potential strengths of the Bayesian analysis approach in the concluding section of his article "Bayesian Decision Theory in Pricing Strategy," *Journal of Marketing,* 27 (January 1963), pp. 5–14.

	S_1	S_2	S_3
A_1	−50,000	0	200,000
A_2	0	200,000	−50,000
A_3	100,000	50,000	0

The conditional probability table is as follows:

	S_1	S_2	S_3
Z_1	.6	.2	.1
Z_2	.3	.6	.1
Z_3	.1	.2	.8
	1.0	1.0	1.0

Determine the following information:

a. The best alternative to choose with no research.
b. The EV(PI).
c. The EV(II).
d. The best alternative to choose if the firm cannot afford to lose any money.

7. You are given the accompanying payoff table related to four states of nature and three alternative courses of action. Each state of nature is equally likely; that is, the prior probability for each state of nature is .25. What is the EV(PI), given this payoff table?

	S_1	S_2	S_3	S_4
A_1	50	50	40	80
A_2	60	70	50	100
A_3	30	60	30	90

(*Hint:* This problem can be solved merely by inspection.)

8. A cosmetics manufacturing firm that introduces several new products a year is wondering whether or not to introduce a new hair-coloring product it has developed. From past experience with similar products, management feels that the new product has a 70% chance of success and a 30% chance of failure. If the product is introduced full-scale and it succeeds, the firm stands to make a net profit of $500,000. If the product fails, however, the firm will lose $300,000. Before full-scale introduction the firm has the option of test-marketing the product at a cost of about $85,000. Should it test-market the product? What other recommendation would you make concerning this new product? Explain your answer.

4

Types of Marketing Research

Chapter 3 described the general sequence of steps followed in conducting any marketing research project. However, the nature and type of marketing research varies depending on the unique characteristics of a given situation. Consider the following situations and try to identify similarities and differences among them.

SITUATION A: Modern Office Products, Inc. (MOP), manufactures a broad line of office equipment and supplies. It sells its products to a variety of organizations through its sales force. Despite a healthy growth in industry sales, MOP's sales and profits have declined during the past two years, much to the concern of MOP executives.

SITUATION B: Saver's National Bank (SNB) has grown rapidly since its inception a few years ago. Its growth is apparently due to a unique set of financial services it offers. While SNB management is pleased with the bank's performance thus far, it is worried about growing competition from a variety of financial institutions. To consolidate SNB's current market position, the bank's executives want to ascertain the demographic composition of customers and their perceptions about the bank's strengths and weaknesses.

SITUATION C: Trent Eating Association (TEA) operates a chain of restaurants in eight communities of similar size and population characteristics. The TEA currently has the image of a high-class restaurant chain serving excellent food at premium prices. Its president is wondering whether a 15% reduction in prices of all menu items would hurt, or help, sales revenues and profits.

EXPLORATORY VERSUS CONCLUSIVE RESEARCH

A common feature across situations A, B, and C is the need for marketing research. The managements of MOP, SNB, and TEA are faced with uncertainties capable of being reduced through marketing research. However, if you examine the three situations carefully, you will also notice some differences. For instance, the purpose of any potential marketing research is less clear in the situation facing MOP than in the situations facing SNB and TEA.

The goal of the marketing research conducted in situation A should be to aid MOP's management in arresting the decline in sales and profits. However, some preliminary investigation should be done to identify the right problem to be researched. Correct definition of a research project's purpose is crucial to its effectiveness; this point was emphasized by the Pac N' Sac example discussed in the previous chapter.

Could MOP's poor market performance be a result of deteriorating quality of its products? Could it be due to lack of adequate motivation on the part of MOP's sales force? Could it be due to ineffective promotion and the resultant weak customer awareness of and loyalty toward MOP and its products? The MOP executives must examine such questions to pinpoint the most fruitful avenue for further research. Preliminary investigation of this nature is conventionally labeled exploratory research.

DEFINITION. ***Exploratory research*** **is research intended to develop initial hunches or insights and to provide direction for any further research needed.**

The primary purpose of exploratory research is to shed light on the nature of a situation and identify any specific objectives or data needs to be addressed through additional research. Exploratory research is most useful when a decision maker wishes to better understand a situation and/or identify decision alternatives. In such research the use of large probability samples, formal questionnaires, and the like, are often unnecessary and unwarranted from a cost-versus-benefit perspective. More will be said about exploratory-research methods a little later.

Unlike the situation being faced by MOP, the SNB and TEA scenarios imply a much clearer definition of research purpose and data requirements. The bank is particularly interested in obtaining a demographic profile of its customer base and uncovering customer perceptions of SNB's strengths and weaknesses. Research in this case should therefore focus on obtaining and analyzing demographic and perceptual data from a cross section of SNB's customers. Such research should, in turn, aid SNB in formulating a strategy to consolidate its market position. Trent's president is interested in determining the impact of a price reduction on sales revenues and profits. The situation here is even more clear-cut, and a decision about whether or not to reduce prices can be made after marketing research determines the effect of a price reduction. Therefore in both the SNB and TEA scenarios data requirements are clearer than in the MOP scenario, and the findings are likely to lead to final decisions. Research of this nature is usually termed conclusive research.

DEFINITION. ***Conclusive research*** **is research having clearly defined objectives and data requirements, and it is capable of suggesting a specific course of action to be taken by decision makers.**

The primary purpose of conclusive research is to help decision makers choose the best course of action in a situation. It is hence most useful when a decision maker already has in mind one or more alternatives and is specifically looking for information pertinent to evaluating them. Since data requirements are clearly specified in a situation calling for conclusive research, and since such research is intended as an aid in final stages of the decision-making process, it is typically more formal and rigorous than exploratory research.

In short, the purpose of a research project and the preciseness of its data requirements determine whether the research is exploratory or conclusive. Exploratory research is conducted when decision makers sense a need for marketing research but are unsure of the specific direction the research should take. Conclusive research is conducted when decision makers have a clearer idea about the types of information they want. However, in practice, the distinction and choice between exploratory and conclusive research is not clear-cut for several reasons.

First, many real-life research projects involve *both* exploratory and conclusive research rather than one or the other. Exploratory research often serves as a prelude to, and complements, conclusive research within the same project, as examples later in the chapter will demonstrate.

Second, a well-defined research purpose does not necessarily mean conclusive research is the best research option. The potential usefulness of conclusive research hinges on the extent to which the *specific types* of information generated by the research are likely to be relevant and worth pursuing. If the decision maker and researcher are not confident about the usefulness, they must rethink the research project and design some appropriate exploratory research. To illustrate, in the SNB scenario, while the bank's executives are clear about the need for demographic and perceptual information, they may still be unsure about what specific questions to ask customers concerning their perceptions.

For instance, if a telephone survey of customers is to be conducted, in which case only a limited number of questions can be asked, the executives may be wondering whether questions about the bank's financial stability, physical facili-

Table 4.1
Differences between exploratory and conclusive research

RESEARCH PROJECT COMPONENTS	EXPLORATORY RESEARCH	CONCLUSIVE RESEARCH
Research purpose	General: To generate insights about a situation	Specific: To verify insights and aid in selecting a course of action
Data needs	Vague	Clear
Data sources	Ill-defined	Well-defined
Data collection form	Open-ended, rough	Usually structured
Sample	Relatively small; subjectively selected to maximize generation of useful insights	Relatively large; objectively selected to permit generalization of findings
Data collection	Flexible; no set procedure	Rigid; well-laid-out procedure
Data analysis	Informal; typically nonquantitative	Formal; typically quantitative
Inferences/recommendations	Tentative	Final

ties, appearance, advertising, and other attributes should be asked, and, if so, how detailed they should be. The relevance of measuring customer perceptions of such attributes depends on how meaningful and important the attributes are to customers. If the executives feel they lack sound knowledge about which attributes are likely to be critical to customers, some exploratory research—such as informal discussions with groups of customers (called focus group interviews)—will be necessary before a conclusive-research project is designed. In general, therefore, whether exploratory or conclusive research is the appropriate first step in a given situation depends on the subjective feelings and judgment of those involved in the project. As Robert W. Joselyn aptly observes: "The decision as to whether a particular project is exploratory or conclusive is somewhat arbitrary."[1]

A third reason why the distinction between exploratory and conclusive research is blurred is that both consist of the same research components and differ only in terms of the degree of formalization and flexibility of the components, as illustrated by Table 4.1. The methods used in conclusive-research projects are more formalized and less flexible. This point will become evident later when we discuss specific methods of conducting each form of research.

[1] Robert W. Joselyn, *Designing the Marketing Research Project* (New York: Mason/Charter, 1977), p. 71.

TYPES OF CONCLUSIVE RESEARCH

There are two basic forms of conclusive research: descriptive research and experimental research. The latter is also known as causal research. The distinction between the two is based on the primary purpose of a conclusive-research project and the nature of the inferences that can be drawn from it. The goal of *descriptive research,* as the name implies, is essentially to describe something. Specifically, it is intended to generate data describing the composition and characteristics of relevant groups of units such as customers, salespeople, organizations, and market areas. Data collected through descriptive research can provide valuable insights about the study units along relevant characteristics and also about associations among those characteristics (more on this later).

A drawback of descriptive research is that it generally cannot provide the type of evidence necessary to make *causal inferences* about relationships between variables. Some form of *experimental research* is necessary to make causal inferences with confidence. To be able to say that *X* (e.g., shelf space assigned to a product in a supermarket) has a causal influence on *Y* (e.g., unit sales of the product), one must gather data under controlled conditions—that is, holding constant, or neutralizing the effect of, all variables other than *X* capable of influencing *Y*, and systematically manipulating the levels of *X* to study its impact on *Y*. Manipulation of the presumed causal variable and control of other relevant variables are distinct features of experimental research. Data collected through experimental research therefore can provide much stronger evidence of cause and effect than can data collected through descriptive research.

The preceding discussion does not necessarily mean that analysis of descriptive research data cannot *suggest* possible causal linkages between variables, especially when the effects of uncontrolled variables are filtered through certain analysis techniques available for that purpose. In fact, rather than view descriptive-versus-experimental research as a clear-cut dichotomy, we should think of conclusive projects as falling along a *research continuum,* with "purely descriptive with no control" at one extreme and with "purely experimental with strict control and manipulation" at the other extreme. Virtually all real-life conclusive projects fall somewhere along this continuum, although the point where "descriptive" ends and "experimental" begins is subjective and somewhat arbitrary.

For the sake of highlighting and illustrating key differences between the two types of conclusive research, we will focus for the time being on projects falling toward either end of the research continuum. In other words, in the following discussion we will use the terms *descriptive research* and *experimental research* cautiously, bearing in mind the preceding caveats concerning the descriptive-versus-experimental dichotomy.

Recall situation B presented earlier, pertaining to Saver's National Bank (SNB). The types of data SNB desires—the demographic profile of its customers as well as their perceptions about SNB—are descriptive data. Hence descriptive research is the appropriate form of conclusive research to be used in situation B.

Descriptive research of a relevant group of units can reveal the proportion of units falling into different categories of a variable. For instance, descriptive research using a survey of, say, 1000 SNB customers might provide the following types of information:

- Fifty percent of SNB's customers have annual family incomes of less than $30,000, while the remaining 50% have annual family incomes of $30,000 or more.
- The bank's location is perceived to be convenient (and hence a strength) by 60% of its customers, while it is perceived to be inconvenient (and hence a weakness) by the remaining 40%.

Descriptive research can also point out associations between variables. For instance, in the SNB scenario simultaneous analysis of data pertaining to customer income levels and perceptions about location may reveal that while 90% of the customers with income levels less than $30,000 perceive SNB's location to be convenient, only 30% of the customers with income levels of $30,000 or more perceive SNB as conveniently located. In other words, customer income levels are apparently associated with their perceptions about SNB's location, as illustrated in Table 4.2. Customers with lower income levels are more likely to perceive SNB as being conveniently located. By contrast, higher-income customers are less likely to perceive SNB as being conveniently located.

Descriptive research can provide profile descriptions (e.g., the proportion of high- and low-income customers in SNB's clientele) and point out associations between profile characteristics (e.g., the association between customer income levels and perceptions about locational convenience). But it cannot establish cause and effect between characteristics of interest. The strong association between customers' income levels and perceptions of SNB's locational convenience does not imply that the former is the *cause* of the latter. On the basis of descriptive data, to conclude a causal linkage between higher-income levels and unfavorable perceptions about location will be erroneous—and in

Table 4.2
Association between customers' income levels and perceptions

	NUMBER (%) OF CUSTOMERS PERCEIVING SNB AS		
CUSTOMERS' INCOME LEVEL	Conveniently Located	Not Conveniently Located	TOTAL
Less than $30,000	450 (90%)	50 (10%)	500 (100%)
$30,000 or more	150 (30%)	350 (70%)	500 (100%)

SNB's case even a bit ridiculous. For instance, most of SNB's higher-income customers may reside in areas far away from SNB. If so, the cause of perceptions about SNB's location may be the relative locations of customer residences rather than customer income levels. The analysis of data on income levels and perceptions did not control for the possible influence of the location of customer residences vis-à-vis SNB's location. The dangers of making causal inferences based as cross-tabulations of descriptive data (such as in Table 4.2) are discussed in detail in Chapter 16.

Experimental research is designed to overcome the lack of control suffered by descriptive-research projects. It involves data collection in an environment wherein the hypothesized causal variable is manipulated and the effects of other relevant variables are controlled. To illustrate, consider a consumer goods firm that wants to determine the impact of advertising on sales. To accomplish this objective, it can proceed as follows:

1. Select a group of distinct market areas that have similar demographic, socioeconomic, and competitor characteristics.
2. Vary the level of advertising expenditure from market to market, keeping all other marketing variables, like price and promotion, constant.
3. Monitor sales over a sufficient length of time.
4. Analyze the data to see whether the pattern of variation in sales across markets is consistent with the pattern of variation in advertising expenditures.

These steps constitute an experimental- rather than a descriptive-research approach because factors other than advertising that can influence sales are, by and large, held constant. Assuming that no major differences in external conditions occur within the group of markets during the research period—differences such as a sudden change in the unemployment rate or competitive activity in some markets but not in others—variations in sales can be attributed to those in advertising expenditures.

In contrast, data on advertising and sales gathered through a descriptive-research project—such as a survey of a representative sample of consumer goods firms asking them to indicate their advertising and sales expenditures during some past period—is not capable of providing as strong an indication of cause and effect. A positive correlation between advertising and sales revealed by an analysis of the survey data cannot be interpreted to mean that higher advertising will lead to higher sales for two reasons. First, although high advertising expenditures and high sales apparently occurred together, the latter might be due to other factors such as the larger sizes or more favorable competitive positions of firms reporting higher sales. Second, the sample firms might have allocated a certain portion of their past sales or anticipated sales to advertising, as is frequently done in practice; if so, sales levels determine advertising levels rather than vice versa.

Planned manipulation of the causal variable (e.g., advertising) and explicit control of other variables are preconditions for making causal inferences. Another precondition is that the causal variable (advertising) and effect variable (sales) must occur in the proper time sequence. To ascertain whether advertising causes sales, for instance, one must change advertising levels first, without their being influenced by anticipated sales; any changes in sales must be measured later. These preconditions distinguish experimental research from descriptive research. They will be discussed at length in Chapter 8.

In summary, experimental research is the most appropriate method when the purpose of a research project is to ascertain the impact on another variable when one variable is changed. This purpose is the objective in the TEA example described in situation C. The president of TEA wants to determine the impact on sales revenues and profits when price is manipulated (price is reduced by 15%). An experimental-research study can be set up for situation C as outlined next.

The eight communities having TEA restaurants have similar characteristics. Hence we can arbitrarily divide the eight restaurants into two equivalent groups, say, group X and group Y. Prices are dropped by 15% in the group X restaurants but maintained at current levels in the group Y restaurants. After a few weeks sales revenues and profits are compared for groups X and Y. Any significant differences between the two groups will be an indication of a causal impact of the price reduction on sales revenues and profits. Assuming all other factors capable of influencing sales or profits remained at similar levels in groups X and Y during the research, any significant difference in sales revenues and/or profits between the two groups can be unambiguously attributed to the price reduction.

The preceding design is a two-group experimental design involving an *experimental group* (X) and a *control group* (Y). Since the two groups are equivalent except for the change in the causal variable (e.g., price reduction) in group X, the control group captures all influences on the effect variable (e.g., sales or profits) other than that of the causal variable.

The following alternative approach can be used if dividing the eight restaurants into equivalent experimental and control groups is not feasible: Sales revenues and profits of the eight restaurants are monitored for several weeks. Prices are then dropped by 15% in all eight restaurants, but other marketing variables are left unchanged. Sales revenues and profits of the eight restaurants are again monitored for the same number of weeks as before. Any significant differences between the "before" and "after" measurements will shed light on the causal impact of the price reduction on sales revenue and profits. This approach is known as a one-group, before-after experimental design. This and the preceding design, as well as several other experimental designs, will be covered in detail in Chapter 9.

Let us now examine the data collection procedures typically used in exploratory- and conclusive-research projects.

METHODS OF DOING EXPLORATORY RESEARCH

Interviews with knowledgeable individuals

An effective way of doing exploratory research is to seek out and talk to individuals with expertise in areas related to the situation being investigated. For instance, in situation A described earlier, MOP executives can gain useful insights by informally discussing MOP's deteriorating market performance with a few key salespeople and customers. Discussions with knowledgeable salespeople, for example, may reveal whether lack of sales force motivation is a problem and, if so, whether it is serious enough to warrant further investigation. Conducting exploratory research by interviewing knowledgeable individuals is sometimes called the *key-informant technique.*[2] Some books also refer to it as an *expert-opinion survey.*

The key-informant technique is necessarily a very subjective and flexible procedure with no standard approach. However, proper selection of informants is crucial to obtaining useful information with a minimum of time and effort. In discussing the use of the key-informant technique in industrial-marketing settings, William Cox states: "It is not uncommon to find that less than 1% of the 'knowledgeable' persons associated with an industrial market possess virtually all of the relevant information about the market. . . . [Hence] careful attention [must] be given to the selection of knowledgeable persons, using judgment samples rather than any random sampling method."[3] Indeed, Cox's observation and advice are not limited to industrial marketing settings; they are relevant in almost every context requiring exploratory research.

Users of the key-informant technique must be alert to two potential difficulties:

1. Many individuals claiming to be knowledgeable and eager to be investigated may have little, if any, useful information to convey.
2. Tracking down genuinely knowledgeable individuals and inducing them to cooperate may not be easy, especially when the key informants are outside the organizations for which the research is being done.

[2] Michael J. Houston, "The Key Informant Technique: Marketing Application," in *Conceptual and Methodological Foundations of Marketing,* ed. Thomas V. Greer (Chicago: American Marketing Association, 1974), pp. 305–308, contains a good discussion of the use of this technique in marketing contexts.

[3] William E. Cox, Jr., *Industrial Marketing Research* (New York: Wiley, 1979), pp. 22–23. Claire Selltiz, Lawrence S. Wrightsman, and Stuart W. Cook, *Research Methods in Social Relations* (New York: Holt, Rinehart and Winston, 1976), also emphasizes the importance of carefully selecting key informants.

Being aware of these constraints and planning in advance to overcome them will minimize wasted resources and maximize the generation of useful insights.

The key-informant technique, if properly used, can be very productive in situations where a decision maker senses the need for research but does not have well-defined research objectives. Table 4.3 presents several such situations, along with examples of knowledgeable individuals capable of providing valuable insights in each situation.

Focus group interviews

Talking to experts or knowledgeable individuals is not the only way of gaining a better understanding of a situation calling for research. Another frequently used informal-interviewing method is the *focus group interview,* which is sometimes simply called focus group. In a focus group interview respondents (typically about 8 to 12) discuss a given topic in a fairly informal fashion. The discussion is led by a well-trained researcher, called a moderator. The moderator's primary tasks are to ensure that key aspects of the topic get discussed and to observe/record the reactions of the participants. Focus groups are used in a variety of situations, such as for gaining insights about consumer acceptance of a new product idea, about potential reactions to an advertising theme, or about types of questions to include in a consumer survey and how to word them. Since a major portion of Chapter 7 is devoted to focus group interviews, we will not discuss them further here.

Table 4.3
Examples of knowledgeable individuals

SITUATION CALLING FOR EXPLORATORY RESEARCH	KNOWLEDGEABLE INDIVIDUALS WITH USEFUL INSIGHTS
A company's brand X detergent, a leader in the detergent market, is suddenly losing market share	Key managers in wholesale and retail firms through which the company distributes brand X
A newly formed nonprofit organization to aid people with serious physical handicaps is wondering about the charitable programs it should develop and the strategies it should use to seek donations from the public	Officers in well-established public service organizations, such as the United Way, the American Red Cross, and the Muscular Dystrophy Association
A farm equipment manufacturer is thinking about developing a new line of completely automatic, programmable, seed planters	Farm equipment dealers, farmers with huge farms, and farmers currently using sophisticated farm equipment
A United States presidential candidate is wondering how to allocate campaign resources efficiently across various regions of the country	State and local party officials with knowledge about public sentiment and attitudes in their respective areas

Analysis of secondary data

Secondary data, as we saw in the previous chapter, are data that have already been collected. Examining appropriate secondary data is a fast and inexpensive way of doing exploratory research. Analysis of secondary data relating to situations requiring marketing research can generate valuable insights. Such insights, in turn, will provide a proper focus for conclusive research. Sometimes, the insights revealed by secondary-data analysis may even eliminate the need for conclusive research, as illustrated by the following example.

EXAMPLE: In 1975 Blue Cross and Blue Shield of Iowa introduced a new program, the School Delta Dental Accident Program, offering dental-injury coverage to students, faculties, and staffs of schools.[4] The program attracted an initial enrollment of 73 schools with 11,143 participants and grew to a peak enrollment of 262 schools with 20,457 participants by December 1977. However, by the end of the 1981–1982 school year, enrollment in the program had dropped to 150 schools with only 5638 participants.

The marketing research division of Blue Cross and Blue Shield analyzed a variety of secondary data in order to determine possible reasons for the decline in enrollment. Several enlightening revelations emerged from this analysis:

- Because of increases in taxes and inflation, the average American worker experienced a decline in real pay in the late 1970s. This observation emerged from data published in the *U.S. News and World Report* (November 9, 1981) and suggested that consumers were limiting their expenditures to perceived necessities. Hence the marketing research division hypothesized that consumers might be viewing the school dental program as an additional, unnecessary expense.
- School enrollment in Iowa was declining, and the trend was expected to continue for several years, according to statistics and projections published by the Iowa Department of Public Instruction. Thus enrollment in the School Delta Dental Accident Program was likely to decline further.
- Employers were increasingly offering comprehensive health coverage (including dental coverage) to their employees through group medical insurance programs, according to U.S. Department of Commerce publications and insurance industry publications. Furthermore, many Blue Cross and Blue Shield group insurance contracts already included dental coverage for accidental injuries, according to internal company records. Therefore the demand for a separate dental-coverage program was bound to be weak.

[4] This example is based on "Product Analysis of the School Delta Dental Accident Program," a report prepared (in 1982) by the Marketing Research Division of Blue Cross and Blue Shield of Iowa, 636 Grand Avenue, Des Moines, Iowa 50307.

- Mutual of Omaha, a leading firm in the insurance field, was offering a similar dental program at slightly lower cost, as indicated in their literature and brochures. Thus the dental program offered by Blue Cross and Blue Shield did not appear to have any unique competitive advantage.
- The School Delta Dental Accident Program was barely profitable, and even a slight increase in administrative costs would result in the program incurring a loss, according to cost and revenue data from internal company records.

All these insights, which emerged from a variety of secondary-data sources, were clearly unfavorable to the School Delta Dental Accident Program. Moreover, an informal investigation of key officials in ten schools suggested that any change in the marketing strategy for the program was unlikely to arrest the decline in enrollment. Rather than conduct additional research, the marketing research division came to the following conclusion: "Based on the results . . . it appears that the School Dental Program is faced with a changing market. While alternative marketing strategies such as offering a reduced price for two or more children enrolling per family, . . . or consideration of new packaging strategies may be viable alternatives, it is unlikely that they will be successful."[5] The company phased out the school dental program shortly after the marketing research division submitted its report.

The Blue Cross and Blue Shield example clearly demonstrates that internal company records as well as external data sources can be helpful in understanding a situation well enough to determine what specific additional research, if any, is needed. Valuable time and money would have been wasted if the marketing research division had decided to formally research the market for the School Delta Dental Accident Program (e.g., through a comprehensive survey of schools and program participants) *without first performing the secondary-data analysis.* We will present more details about various types of secondary data and ways of locating such data in Chapter 5.

Case study method

A *case study* is an in-depth examination of a unit of interest. The unit can be a customer, store, salesperson, firm, market area, and so on. Julian Simon succinctly describes the purpose and nature of a case study as follows:

> It is the method of choice when you want to obtain a wealth of detail about your subject. You are likely to want such detail when you do not know exactly what you are looking for. The case study is therefore appropriate when you are trying to find clues and ideas for further research; in this respect, it serves a purpose similar to the clue-providing function of expert opinion [or the key-informant technique].

[5] Blue Cross and Blue Shield of Iowa, "Product Analysis," p. 12.

> The specific method of the case study depends upon the mother wit, common sense, and imagination of the person doing the case study. The investigator makes up his procedure as he goes along, because he purposely refuses to work within any set categories or classifications; if he did so, he would not be obtaining the benefits of the case study.[6]

The case study method, by virtue of its insight-generating potential, is a useful form of exploratory research. Let us look at a hypothetical example to illustrate the use of case studies in a marketing context.

EXAMPLE: Allied Associates Company (AAC) is a national chain of discount stores, with over 500 retail outlets spread across the country. During the past several years the company's sales have grown rapidly, and its profitability has remained above the industry average. Top management wants to identify the key elements crucial to the company's success and capitalize on these elements. Where and how should one start looking to accomplish top management's objectives?

The AAC scenario fits a research setting likely to benefit from the case study method; that is, it is a setting in which the company has a general research objective but is unsure of exactly what it is looking for. Moreover, each AAC retail outlet can be viewed as a case. Valuable insights can be gained by thoroughly examining certain selected retail outlets. For instance, the three best-performing and the three worst-performing stores can be studied in depth on numerous dimensions. Store size and layout, product lines carried, employee morale, and trade area characteristics are but a few of the factors for which data can be collected. In a case study only the investigator's time and imagination limit the number and types of factors to examine.

Insights about factors critical to AAC's success can be gained by looking for similarities and differences between the two types of cases, namely, the best and the worst stores. For instance, if employee morale is higher in all three best stores than in any of the worst stores, employee morale is likely to be critical to AAC's success. In contrast, a factor such as product lines carried is likely to be less important, although not necessarily unimportant, to AAC's success if both types of stores carry the same product lines. Insights like these can help researchers single out key determinants of performance variations across AAC stores. Before devoting attention and resources to the critical factors identified by the case analysis, top management may want to verify the association between the factors and store performance through a focused examination of a larger number of AAC stores; this study would, of course, constitute conclusive research.

As the AAC example illustrates, the analysis of case data is nonquantitative and primarily involves numerous comparisons and contrasts of the data. It

[6] Julian L. Simon, *Basic Research Methods in Social Science* (New York: Random House, 1969), p. 276.

requires an alert investigator capable of recognizing even subtle differences across cases as well as possible relationships among factors within a case.

Conducting exploratory research is not limited to using one of the four methods described—talking with knowledgeable individuals, focus group interviews, analysis of secondary data, and case studies—although these are the most frequently used methods. Variations or combinations of these methods can also be employed in an exploratory-research project.

METHODS OF DOING CONCLUSIVE RESEARCH

Methods of doing conclusive research differ from exploratory research methods more in terms of degree than in terms of kind. As we saw earlier, the distinction between exploratory and conclusive research is not sharp and primarily depends on how one perceives the nature of the situation requiring research. The more clear-cut a situation, the more formal, less flexible, and more conclusive the research will be.[7] The same basic methods (e.g., surveys) can be used in both types of research, although the methods are less formal and more flexible under exploratory research.

Let us look at a couple of real-life examples to illustrate the nature of the differences between exploratory- and conclusive-research methods.

EXAMPLE: The American Telephone and Telegraph Company (AT&T) undertook a study several years ago to investigate the communication needs of nonprofit organizations.[8] The study was conducted by a New York marketing research firm and had an exploratory as well as a conclusive phase.

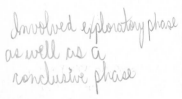

The exploratory phase involved four focus group interviews. They were held in cities with heavy concentrations of nonprofit association headquarters: New York, Washington, Chicago, and Los Angeles. An average of eight association officers, with titles like executive director, managing director, and executive assistant, were subjectively selected for each focus group session. The duration of each session was about two hours.

According to the marketing research firm:

> The results of these qualitative [focus group] sessions enabled us to design the research questionnaire with a keener awareness of the true areas that re-

[7] Strictly speaking, no single research classification system has an unambiguous label for every research project. In fact, while some authors—such as Harper W. Boyd, Jr., Ralph Westfall, and Stanley F. Stasch, *Marketing Research: Text and Cases* (Homewood, Ill.: Irwin, 1981), Chap. 2—have employed the exploratory-versus-conclusive classification scheme, other authors have suggested different classification schemes. A good discussion of this point is presented by C. William Emory, *Business Research Methods* (Homewood, Ill.: Irwin, 1980), pp. 82–88.

[8] This example is based on "Survey of Communication Needs of Nonprofit Organizations," a research report prepared (in 1979) for AT&T, by Barbini, Pesce & Gaines, 633 Third Avenue, New York, N.Y. 10017.

quired quantitative input and to structure questions so they would provoke maximum response. Additionally, the open dialogue that evolved from the panelists provided observers with an in-depth reflection of customers' feelings regarding their telephone needs.[9]

The conclusive phase involved the mailing of 12,500 questionnaires (more on mail surveys in Chapter 6) to a carefully and objectively selected list of business and trade organizations, chambers of commerce, and nonprofit professional organizations. Data from approximately 2000 completed questionnaires were analyzed in this phase.

The focus group sessions revealed several valuable insights. For example, the focus group participants viewed telephones/communications as critical factors for the success of nonprofit organizations and indicated certain special communication needs. They were very interested in new telephone products but appeared to be cost-conscious and extremely conservative in their buying decisions.

The mail survey findings (conclusive research) strongly supported the insights gained through the focus group sessions. The following findings are a few of the key findings emerging from the conclusive phase of the study:

> The survey findings confirm the importance of cost in explaining the dichotomy between the associations not having a product or service and their considering the product or service useful. . . . Cost of equipment and cost of maintenance and repair were rated very important or somewhat important factors in planning for new telephone equipment and services by nearly 90% of the associations. . . . Many associations are interested in considering the use of new products and services. For example, at a monthly rate of $1 per station, nearly 70% would consider using Push Button Dialing.[10]

On the basis of the study's findings, AT&T established sales action plans to better serve the nonprofit marketplace.

The objective of the exploratory and conclusive phases of the AT&T study were clearly different: While *generating* insights about nonprofit associations' communication needs was the objective of the former, *confirming* those insights was the objective of the latter. However, the procedures in the two phases had some basic similarities (they differed mainly in their degree of formality and flexibility). For instance, both involved primary-data collection, although the focus group sessions were more informal and in-depth than the mail survey; and both used samples of respondents, although the focus group samples were much smaller and more subjectively chosen.

To further illustrate that exploratory and conclusive research differ more in terms of research purpose than in terms of basic methods used, consider sec-

[9] "Survey of Communication Needs," p. 2.
[10] "Survey of Communication Needs," p. 7.

ondary-data analysis. Although secondary-data analysis is traditionally regarded as an exploratory-research method, it is used in certain contexts as the basis for making *final* decisions. The Communications Satellite General Corporation (COMSAT General) is a case in point. According to Leslie Sherman, market analyst for COMSAT General:

> Researchers in the telecommunications industry are fortunate to have a wealth of published information on competitors. The Federal Communications Commission (FCC) requires companies to file detailed information for many service offerings and tariff filings for regulated services. In addition to FCC data, there is an abundance of literature and financial data available on major competitors in this industry.
>
> Data is compiled and analyzed to determine strengths and weaknesses in organizational structure, services and products offered, financial status, and pricing structure. The objective is to determine how and where our company can position services to compete effectively. Strategies and tactics are then formulated using these recommendations.[11]

Thus COMSAT General apparently uses secondary-data analysis as the primary basis for *designing competitive strategies and tactics* rather than for gaining insights about competitors' activities. Of course, secondary-data availability and quality may not always be high enough to warrant their use as the basis of conclusive recommendations. However, the point this example makes is that labeling any basic method as a purely exploratory or a purely conclusive research method is incorrect.[12]

Thus far we have focused on conclusive-research methods in general, without distinguishing between descriptive- and experimental-research methods. Is there any difference between these two subclasses of methods? The differences show up only in the *conditions* under which data are collected. Experimental data are collected from an environment deliberately manipulated or controlled by the researcher by using research designs such as the ones mentioned in our discussion of the TEA scenario. In contrast, descriptive data are collected from an environment with little or no researcher-imposed control. Of course, consistent with the idea of a research continuum introduced earlier, the degree of control over the data collection environment in many real-life projects varies between the two extremes. At what degree of control a descriptive-research project becomes an experimental research project is arbitrary. We will postpone further discussion of experimental-research methods to Chapters 8 and 9.

---

[11] Personal communication to the author, December 17, 1983.

[12] In fact, while we have viewed the purpose of so-called exploratory-research methods as insight or hypothesis generation, several authors have suggested another purpose for them: the drawing of *final* inferences in situations where resources are too limited to permit formal conclusive-research studies. For example, see Cox, *Industrial Marketing Research,* pp. 17–18; Joselyn, *Designing the Marketing Research Project,* pp. 70–71; and Houston, "Key Informant Technique," p. 306.

Descriptive research, or research falling closer to the descriptive end than to the experimental end of the research continuum, is by far the most frequently used form of conclusive research. Data in descriptive research are generally collected through questionnaires (administered by mail, over the telephone, or in person) or through observation (more on these procedures in Chapter 6). Descriptive-research studies are of two basic types: cross-sectional studies and longitudinal studies. We turn to these topics now.

CROSS-SECTIONAL VERSUS LONGITUDINAL STUDIES

Cross-sectional studies are onetime studies involving data collection at a single period in time. *Longitudinal studies* are repeated-measurement studies involving data collection at several periods in time. While a cross-sectional study yields a "snapshot" of a situation being researched, a longitudinal study produces a "motion picture" (or a series of snapshots) of a situation over time. In general, longitudinal studies are more informative than cross-sectional studies, just as motion pictures are more revealing than still pictures. But longitudinal studies are also more expensive. Further, the choice between the two depends on the objectives of the research.

A cross-sectional study makes use of a *cross-sectional sample,* or group of units (e.g., consumers, stores, organizations) selected specifically and solely for the onetime data collection. The sample is disbanded after the data are collected. A longitudinal study typically employs a *panel,* or group of units recruited to provide measurements over a period of time. At the conclusion of each measurement phase, a panel is maintained intact for future use.

Thus there is a clear distinction between a cross-sectional sample and a panel. However, this distinction is blurred in practice. Sometimes, cross-sectional samples are used in longitudinal studies, and panels (or certain segments of panels) are used in cross-sectional studies.

For example, suppose the U.S. Department of Defense wants to ascertain peoples' attitudes toward nuclear weapons and nuclear warfare and to monitor changes in those attitudes over time. Specifically, suppose the Defense Department wants to measure the public's attitudes on a quarterly basis. The appropriate research design is clearly a longitudinal study. However, one need not necessarily set up a panel of respondents for this purpose. Rather, one can select a separate cross-sectional sample of people for each quarterly measurement. In fact, using cross-sectional samples instead of a panel of respondents may have advantages, as will be discussed later. The point is that a cross-sectional study and the use of a cross-sectional sample (or a longitudinal study and the use of a panel) are not paired in all situations.

Cross-sectional studies

We saw earlier that descriptive research is the most frequently used form of conclusive research. The most popular method within the domain of descriptive research is the cross-sectional study. Also, cross-sectional studies account for the majority of formal research projects involving primary-data collection.

By definition, a cross-sectional study involves data collection at only one period in time. However, data pertaining to different periods in time can be obtained through such a study. In other words, the *scope* of the data collected is not necessarily limited to the time at which a cross-sectional study is conducted. The following example clarifies this point.

EXAMPLE: Capital Cola Company (CCC) wants to obtain a descriptive profile of consumers who drink only caffeine-free soft drinks. Specifically, CCC wants to know the demographic composition and use characteristics (e.g., brands consumed, volume consumed, frequency of consumption) of such consumers. The company is considering a cross-sectional study involving a random sample of consumers.

Can CCC obtain data other than current demographic and use characteristics through the cross-sectional study? Yes, it can. For instance, the study respondents can be asked about their *past* consumption of soft drinks: What brand(s) did they consume during the past year? Was their past consumption more than, about the same as, or less than their consumption at the present time? Similarly, data can also be obtained about *future* consumption: Do the respondents intend to continue buying their present brand(s) of soft drinks? Do they plan to change their volume of consumption during the coming year? Answers to questions like these can be valuable to CCC in understanding the dynamics of soft-drink consumption patterns.

The CCC example implies that a cross-sectional study is capable of yielding longitudinal data of sorts, that is, data pertaining to an interval of time rather than a single point in time. Indeed, many cross-sectional studies collect longitudinal data of this nature. However, a rather serious limitation of such data is that their accuracy depends heavily on the mental capabilities (memory of past events and intentions about future behavior) of the study respondents. For the most part, consumers' memories are unreliable, particularly with respect to remembering things that occurred very far in the past. Hans Zeisel makes this point clearly:

> The memory of a minor expenditure, or a fleeting observation will disappear within days. Moreover, to rely on memory is always a treacherous undertaking, because of unconscious and even conscious forces that tend to distort it.

> The question, for instance, "For whom did you vote?" asked one day after election day, will always elicit too many votes for the victorious candidate.[13]

Likewise, consumer intentions may be a poor indicator of future behavior.[14] This problem becomes increasingly severe as the time frame extends farther into the future. A longitudinal study is much more reliable than a cross-sectional study for monitoring changes over time. A longitudinal study is more reliable because it relies less on consumers' mental capabilities through more frequent monitoring of events as close to their time of occurrence as feasible.

The sample used in a cross-sectional study is typically selected solely for the onetime data collection and disbanded after the data collection. However, several firms, especially certain commercial marketing research firms, maintain *omnibus panels* as a source of samples for cross-sectional studies. Firms maintaining omnibus panels have the capability to custom-design cross-sectional samples to meet specific research requirements. Such samples are composed of panel members who are returned to the panel after participating in a cross-sectional study.

One firm that maintains an omnibus panel is National Family Opinion, Inc. (NFO). The NFO panel consists of 130,000 households in the United States and represents the population on a variety of characteristics. According to NFO:

> Fifty demographics on each household, ranging from income, education and occupation to ownership of such things as video cassettes, are on file to provide easy computer selection. . . . From this background we can economically produce cross-sectional samples of most segments of the consumer market (e.g., farmers, large-city dwellers, homeowners, high income households, racial minorities, singles, pet owners, etc.).[15]

The NFO print advertisement shown in Exhibit 4.1 illustrates how a custom-designed cross-sectional sample can be chosen from an omnibus panel.

The Home Testing Institute (HTI) is another firm specializing in omnibus panels. The HTI maintains several unique panels, such as the HTI baby panel. Exhibit 4.2 describes this panel and lists the types of cross-sectional samples that can be chosen.

---

[13] Hans Zeisel, *Say It with Figures* (New York: Harper & Row, 1968), p. 202; see also Yoram Wind and David Lerner, "On the Measurement of Purchase Data: Surveys Versus Purchase Diaries," *Journal of Marketing Research,* 16 (February 1979), pp. 39–47, for a study that emphasizes the pitfalls of surveys relying on respondents' memories.

[14] Studies have shown that many consumer purchase decisions are made on impulse. For instance, Kenneth E. Runyon, *Consumer Behavior and the Practice of Marketing* (Columbus, Ohio: Merrill, 1977), p. 324, has reported that about half of all buying decisions in supermarkets are impulse decisions made on the spot. The point is that inferring behavior from intentions is very dangerous.

[15] "Creative Use of the NFO Household Panel," a brochure prepared by National Family Opinion, Inc., 660 Madison Avenue, New York, N.Y. 10021.

Exhibit 4.1

Selecting a special cross-sectional sample from an omnibus panel

Catching people catching cold is one of our routine tricks.

What do you do when . . .

You need a sample of people with colds to test your new cold relief medicine?

Call NFO.

A proprietary medicine manufacturer with a promising new cold relief product wanted to conduct an in-home test among people suffering colds. It's the cold season, but how do you put together a meaningful sample of people currently suffering colds?

Identifying people with ailments is a routine assignment for NFO. In this case, we mailed a post card to several thousand panel households in the "frost belt" states and asked the cooperation over a 2-week period of all members of the household 16 years and over. The minute a cold struck, the panel member was to report it on one of NFO's in-bound WATS lines. At that time we shipped the cold relief medicine with instructions to begin exclusive use immediately. One week later NFO phone interviewers directly contacted the cold sufferer to determine satisfaction with the product.

NFO Household Panels — the creative solution to most data gathering problems.

With nearly 700,000 individuals represented in our 230,000 households, it's no problem to locate and build samples of people with all kinds of physical problems . . . young people with acne, old people with arthritis, people who suffer headaches, toothaches, psoriasis, oily hair, acid stomach – even spavined horses and dogs suffering from heartworm. Such work is usually done for follow-up concept tests, product tests and attitude and usage research.

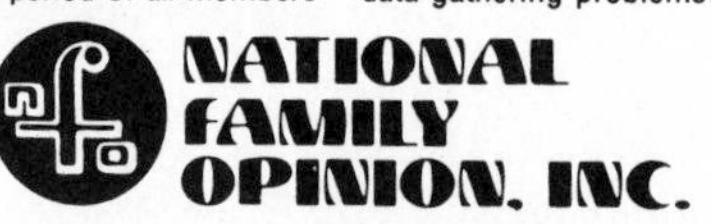

P. O. Box 315 Toledo, Oh 43691 (419) 666-8800

New York Chicago St. Louis Houston Beverly Hills San Francisco

Source: "Creative Use of the NFO Household Panel," a brochure prepared by National Family Opinion, Inc., 660 Madison Avenue, New York, N.Y. 10021, Reprinted by permission.

Exhibit 4.2

Description of the HTI baby panel

HTI's innovative Baby Panel consists of 35,000 cooperating families with children 5 years of age and younger, and 1000 expectant mothers. Among this group 10,000 are nationally balanced. The Panel is updated demographically every quarter to ensure the proper proportion of children 5 years of age and younger.

HTI's nationally balanced panel of 10,000 families includes:

Families with children 3 years and under:

- 1000 with children 1 year and younger
- 2000 with children 18 months and younger
- 3500 with children 24 months and younger
- 6000 with children 36 months and younger

Families with children 3 to 5 years of age:

- 1500 with children 3.1 to 4 years
- 1250 with children 4.1 to 5 years
- 1250 with children 5.1 to 5.11 years

The remaining 25,000 families with children 5 years of age and younger include:

- 11,500 with children 3 years and under
- 13,500 with children 3.1 years to 5.11 years

HTI can also provide a data base of 1000 expectant mothers.

The HTI Baby Panel permits you to select a sample based on any of the following criteria:

- A Nationally Representative Sample
- First-time Mothers
- Multiple Children Families
- Age of Mother
- Number of Children in Family
- Census Region
- Market Size
- Family Income
- Education of Mother and Father
- Occupation of Mother and Father

HTI can interview all these samples by self-administered questionnaires through the mail, by telephone, or by a combination of these survey techniques.

Source: "The HTI Baby Panel" brochure. Used with the permission of Home Testing Institute, Inc., one of the NPD Group of Marketing & Research Companies, 900 West Shore Road, Port Washington, N.Y. 11050.

Longitudinal studies

The primary purpose of longitudinal studies is to monitor changes over time. The following examples illustrate situations calling for longitudinal studies:

- A firm manufacturing frozen orange juice is interested in keeping track of consumers' use of brands and types of orange juice.
- A social service organization wishes to monitor the well-being of an urban community.
- A public health institution wants to ascertain whether and how people's eating and drinking habits vary from season to season.

Successive measurements in longitudinal studies can be obtained from a physically different, but representative, sample of units or from the same sample of units each time. Although both sample options will yield longitudinal data, the nature of the findings and the implications can differ, as demonstrated in the next example.

EXAMPLE: The marketer of brand X of a product wishes to monitor X's share versus competing brands. For the sake of simplicity, let us assume there are only two other brands competing with brand X, say, brand Y and brand Z. At the end of each suitable period (e.g., month or quarter), the marketer can survey a different cross section of users of the product and ascertain the brands they use. Alternatively, the marketer can form a panel of users and ask the panel members to periodically report the brands they use; in this case the *same* respondents will provide data during the course of the study.

Suppose the marketer surveys a different, but representative, sample of 100 users for each measurement and obtains the results shown in Table 4.4. Two insights pertaining to the marketer's research objective emerge from Table 4.4. First, brand X is the leader with about a 40% brand share (since the sample size is 100, the number of users of a brand can be interpreted as the brand's percentage share of the market). Second, the overall percentage shares of the three brands seem to remain stable over time.

Table 4.4
Results of longitudinal brand use study

	NUMBER OF CONSUMERS USING BRAND AT THE END OF		
USE OF	Period 1	Period 2	Period 3
Brand X	40	42	42
Brand Y	30	29	28
Brand Z	30	29	30
Total	100	100	100

The type of information provided by the longitudinal study would have been somewhat different if the marketer had used the *same* sample of users for each measurement. Such a panel study, in addition to indicating overall brand shares, would have permitted the firm to monitor brands used by *individual* users from period to period. Tracking brand use at the individual-user level will shed light on how the brands achieved their overall shares at the end of each period. This additional information will be available only if the same sample of users is surveyed at each data collection phase.

Exhibits 4.3 and 4.4 demonstrate this point by providing two sets of hypothetical results. In the exhibits the numbers within the boxes under each period are the numbers of buyers of each brand during that period. The solid arrows show how buyers of brand X in one period divided their purchases among the three brands in the next period. For example, in Exhibit 4.3, of the 40 who bought brand X in period 1, 17 bought brand X again in period 2, 21 switched to brand Y, and 2 switched to brand Z. Similarly, the dashed and dotted arrows indicate period-to-period changes in the brand choices of brand Y and brand Z buyers, respectively.

In both exhibits the overall brand shares are identical to the brand shares presented in Table 4.4. Hence the inferences we made earlier about the overall shares of brands X, Y, and Z still hold. However, Exhibits 4.3 and 4.4 contain additional data about how each brand obtained its overall share. Specifically,

Exhibit 4.3

Changes in brand shares: Case 1

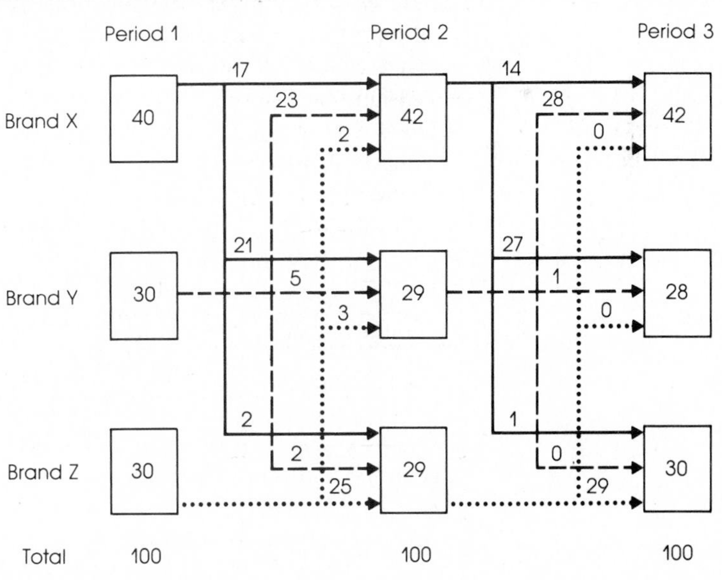

Exhibit 4.4

Changes in brand shares: Case 2

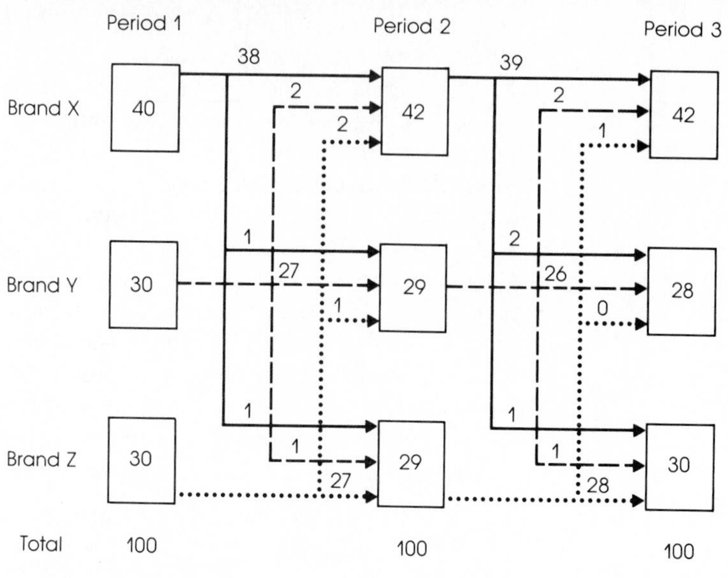

according to Exhibit 4.3 (case 1), while all three brands have stable shares, only brand Z appears to enjoy *brand loyalty;* a majority of brand X and brand Y users switched brands during each period. In contrast, Exhibit 4.4 (case 2) shows all three brands' having stable shares and enjoying high brand loyalty. Clearly, the marketing implications for brand X emerging from case 1 are quite different than those emerging from case 2.

The point of this discussion is that a longitudinal study using the same sample of respondents will provide richer information than one using a series of different samples. Indeed, the dynamics of changes between measurements can only be captured by using the same panel of respondents. Such a panel has been labeled a *true panel,* to distinguish it from omnibus panels used to generate different cross-sectional samples at various periods in time.[16]

A true-panel study, compared with a longitudinal study using different samples for the various measurements, is also capable of generating more data directly pertaining to the research purpose, for the following reasons:

1. A true panel is a captive sample of willing respondents who are likely to tolerate extended interviews or fill out lengthy questionnaires.

[16] Gilbert A. Churchill, Jr., *Marketing Research: Methodological Foundations* (Chicago: Dryden Press, 1983), pp. 68–74, provides an excellent discussion of the additional capabilities of a true panel over those of an omnibus panel.

2. Background data such as demographic and life-style data need not be collected from panel respondents during each measurement. Therefore for a given interview or questionnaire length, more data of primary research interest can be collected.[17]

Consumer panels are not without drawbacks. A major difficulty in setting up a panel is identifying a *representative* sample of respondents who are willing to cooperate over a long period of time. Certain types of consumer groups are especially hard to recruit for panels. Examples of such groups include nonwhites, housewives under 25, employed housewives, and illiterates.[18] Even if a researcher initially succeeds in putting together a representative panel, there will be some attrition of panel members during a longitudinal study. As a result, the panel may no longer be representative unless the departing members are replaced with similar new members—an expensive and time-consuming task. Another potential problem with consumer panels is that the multiple-survey participation by panel members may, over a period of time, induce them to alter their natural or usual behavior. Sudman and Ferber label this difficulty *panel conditioning* and illustrate it as follows:

> A homemaker who keeps a weekly purchase diary with a separate section for canned goods may feel guilty about not having made any such purchases recently and may deliberately purchase some canned goods to be able to record it in the diary. In a similar fashion, a family asked month after month about ownership of savings accounts may decide to open a savings account, even though they originally had no such intention.[19]

Most commercial marketing research firms operating consumer panels take steps to ensure that the behavior of panel members is normal and that the reporting of such behavior is accurate. For instance, the National Purchase Diary Panel, Inc. (NPD), which maintains a panel of families, states:

> Families are dropped from the panel at their request or if they fail to return three of their last five diaries. In addition NPD has instituted the policy of eliminating family members after 4–5 years of reporting since buying behavior may change after detailed reporting of purchases over this period of time.[20]

Obviously, precautionary procedures like the ones used by NPD add to the expense of maintaining and operating a panel. Nevertheless, they are necessary if panel data are to be trusted.

---

[17] For a complete discussion of the advantages and the limitations of panels, see Seymour Sudman and Robert Ferber, *Consumer Panels* (Chicago: American Marketing Association, 1979); see also Simon, *Basic Research Methods,* Chap. 19, and Zeisel, *Say It with Figures,* Chap. 13.

[18] "Sharpening Marketing Decisions with Diary Panels," a brochure prepared (in 1975) by National Purchase Diary Panel, Inc., 900 West Shore Road, Port Washington, N.Y. 11050, p. 20.

[19] Sudman and Ferber, *Consumer Panels,* p. 6.

[20] "Sharpening Marketing Decisions," p. 20.

Because of the potential limitations of true panels, researchers may be wise to restrict their use to situations where periodic monitoring of the same respondents is essential. The unique capabilities of a true panel will not be needed when the purpose of a longitudinal study is merely to track variables at a macro, or aggregate, level. Under those circumstances choosing several cross-sectional samples from the general population—or from a suitable omnibus panel if a special type of sample is required—may be better than using a true panel.

Exhibit 4.5

Flow diagram for selecting the appropriate research type

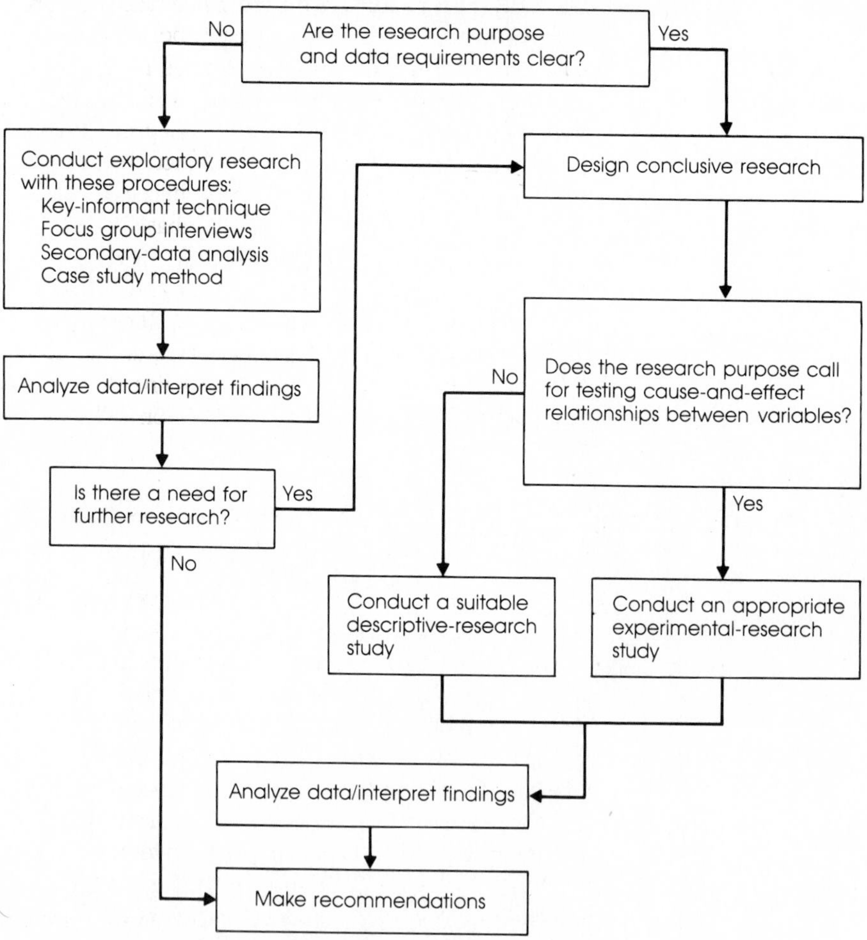

Are the research purpose and data requirements clear?

No → Conduct exploratory research with these procedures:
- Key-informant technique
- Focus group interviews
- Secondary-data analysis
- Case study method

→ Analyze data/interpret findings → Is there a need for further research? (Yes → Design conclusive research; No → Make recommendations)

Yes → Design conclusive research → Does the research purpose call for testing cause-and-effect relationships between variables?

No → Conduct a suitable descriptive-research study

Yes → Conduct an appropriate experimental-research study

→ Analyze data/interpret findings → Make recommendations

DETERMINING WHICH TYPE OF RESEARCH TO CONDUCT

Choosing the most appropriate type of research—exploratory or conclusive—in a situation is somewhat subjective. The choice depends not only on the nature of the situation but also on how the decision maker and researcher perceive it. In general, exploratory research is most appropriate in situations where the research objectives and data requirements are unclear. Some form of conclusive research is appropriate in other situations. Insights gained through exploratory research typically form the foundation for more formal conclusive research. Occasionally, however, exploratory-research results may strongly suggest that further research of a conclusive nature may be unnecessary or unproductive.

In situations calling for conclusive research, the choice of the type of conclusive research—descriptive or experimental—depends on whether testing causal relationships between variables is the primary research purpose. If so, some form of experimental research is appropriate; if not, descriptive research will suffice. Of course, as implied in preceding sections of this chapter, the descriptive-versus-experimental distinction exists more along a research continuum than as a clear-cut dichotomy. Therefore one may at times be able to make tentative causal statements on the basis of data from a well-designed and -conducted descriptive-research study. By the same token, one can rarely conduct a pure experimental-research study. As we will see in Chapters 8 and 9, many experimental-research studies suffer from varying degrees of lack of control owing to resource, environmental, and other constraints. Exhibit 4.5 is a flow diagram that offers general guidelines for identifying the most appropriate research type(s) to employ in a situation calling for research.

SUMMARY

Marketing research can be broadly divided into exploratory research and conclusive research. Exploratory research is useful for gaining initial insights when research objectives or data requirements are vague. Conclusive research is appropriate when specific, clear-cut research objectives and data requirements have been identified. The choice between exploratory and conclusive research in a situation is somewhat subjective. In practice, many research projects involve aspects of both exploratory and conclusive research.

Two forms of conclusive research are descriptive research and experimental research. The purpose of descriptive research, as the name implies, is to generate data describing units of interest and to enable researchers to identify associations between variables or factors of interest. However, descriptive research cannot unambiguously establish causal linkages. Experimental research, by generating data under controlled conditions, is capable of establishing cause and effect between variables with a greater degree of certainty.

Frequently used approaches for conducting exploratory research include talking with knowledgeable individuals (the key-informant technique), focus group interviews, analysis of secondary data, and the case study method. These approaches are quite flexible from the researcher's standpoint. The effectiveness of exploratory research depends to a large degree on the researcher's resourcefulness and skills. Conclusive-research methods differ from exploratory-research methods more in degree than in kind. Specifically, both types have the same basic research components, but conclusive-research methodology is more formalized and structured.

A majority of descriptive-research projects involve cross-sectional studies. However, longitudinal studies are used when the research objective calls for data on the same variables at different points in time. Since a cross-sectional study involves merely a onetime measurement, the study sample is usually chosen on an *ad hoc* basis and disbanded after data collection. In contrast, longitudinal studies typically use permanent samples, called panels, from which data are collected on a periodic basis.

The differences between cross-sectional and longitudinal studies are not as clear in practice as they may seem in theory. Many cross-sectional studies of consumers collect data relating to past and future behavior, although the accuracy of such data is questionable. Moreover, the samples for some cross-sectional studies are chosen from omnibus panels. Likewise, some longitudinal studies employ a series of cross-sectional samples rather than a true panel (i.e., fixed sample) of respondents. A true panel, while capable of generating more data and data of a more revealing nature, has certain serious potential limitations. Chief among them are lack of panel representativeness, attrition of panel members and the costs involved in replacing them, and panel conditioning leading to atypical behavior on the part of panel members.

QUESTIONS

1. What is the basic difference between exploratory and conclusive research?
2. Give examples of your own to illustrate when descriptive research should be conducted and when experimental research should be conducted.
3. "Exploratory and conclusive research are not substitutes for each other." Discuss this statement.
4. Briefly discuss the types of information that descriptive research can and cannot provide.
5. What is the key-informant technique? What precautions should a researcher take to make it effective?
6. When is the case study approach likely to be appropriate? What are its distinct features?

7. How do the nature and the purpose of a cross-sectional study differ from those of a longitudinal study?
8. "A cross-sectional study can only generate data about a single point in time." Do you agree or disagree with this statement? Explain your answer.
9. What are the advantages and the limitations of using true panels?
10. Four different scenarios calling for some form of research are outlined below. For each scenario, indicate whether the most appropriate research design should be exploratory or conclusive; descriptive or experimental; cross-sectional or longitudinal. Explain your answers, and briefly describe what specific research method(s) you would use under each scenario.
    a. An industrial-goods firm is expecting a recession within the next two years. It wants to know what changes, if any, it should make in its current marketing strategy so as to minimize any adverse effect on its performance because of a recession.
    b. A firm marketing an established brand of home computer is concerned about a new brand just introduced by a competitor. It wishes to monitor how the new brand will affect the market shares of its own brand and those of its competitors during the next 12 months.
    c. A packaged-foods firm has developed a new frozen dinner that it feels is superior to other frozen dinners already on the market. It wants to develop a unique promotional theme for the new dinner so as to set it apart from competing brands and to appeal to a broad cross section of consumers.
    d. A large bank currently has over twenty thousand loan customers. It is concerned about the increasing number of customers who are defaulting on their loans. It therefore wants to know whether customers with good payment records differ from those who defaulted recently. Specifically, the bank wants information on each of the following characteristics: age, sex, income, occupation, marital status, and past credit record.

CASES FOR PART TWO

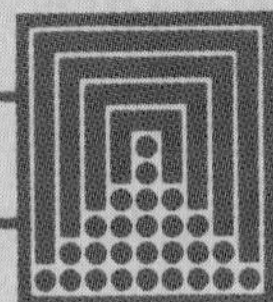

CASE 2.1

Bettcher Industries, Inc.

Dan Buttner, marketing research manager for Bettcher Industries, Inc., was wondering how he should respond to a letter he had just received from a marketing professor. In that letter the professor had asked Mr. Buttner if he could provide, from his experience, examples of real-life applications of marketing research for possible use in marketing research classes. Here are some excerpts from the professor's letter:

> One of the greatest challenges that I continue to face as an instructor of marketing research is to make students appreciate the reality of marketing research. Surveys of professionals like you have consistently shown that fresh college graduates are too idealistic and technique-oriented; that is, they are not fully aware of the *practical* limitations of the techniques and tools that they learn in the classroom.
>
> I am sure you would agree with me that a fruitful way of attempting to remedy this weakness in students is to expose them to *real-life* applications of marketing research. Unfortunately, unlike examples of different types of advertising or packaging, examples of actual applications of marketing research are hard to come by.
>
> Can you please send me any material(s), of a nonconfidential nature, that can help students gain an understanding of marketing research practice?

COMPANY BACKGROUND

Bettcher Industries, Inc., located in Birmingham, Ohio, was founded in 1944 and incorporated in 1955. Bettcher designs and manufactures processing and portion control equipment for meat, fish, and poultry. The company's major product line is a wide range of machines for pressing, forming, tenderizing, slicing, and portioning meats and related products. Markets for these machines include meat-processing plants, restaurants, hotels, supermarkets, caterers, and all major food service organizations and food processors.

Bettcher holds a position of leadership in the meat industry and has a reputation for introducing highly innovative products. Such products include a line of hand-held

Information for this case was provided by courtesy of Bettcher Industries, Inc., State Route 60 and Ohio Turnpike, Birmingham, OH 44089.

Whizard brand trimmers. These air- and electric-powered devices can replace straight knives used in meat plants throughout the United States and foreign nations. The company is also noted for its Whizard brand protective wear, a line of accessories, such as safety gloves and arm protectors, of cut-resistant fabric for use by meat processors, food stores, and general industrial/commercial food processors. According to a company brochure, these gloves are made of a "space-age, seamless, knitted fabric," which consists of a stainless steel core encased in soft but high-strength textile. Bettcher has sold Whizard Protective Wear to several hundred organizational customers in a variety of industries. These customers include institutions such as John Deere, Levi Strauss, GE, GM, Coors, IBM, Exxon, Safeway, RCA, Rath, Land O Lakes, the U.S. Postal Service, the Texas Department of Corrections, Firestone, and J. C. Penney.

When Mr. Buttner received the professor's request, Bettcher Industries had just signed an agreement to acquire Sam Stein Associates of Sandusky, Ohio. Stein designs and manufactures batter and breading equipment for preportioned meat, fish, and poultry. It also makes fryers, cooking ovens, and snack-food-processing equipment. The product lines of the two companies were believed to complement each other and appeal to similar markets. While Bettcher equipment is used from the point of slaughter through portion control, Stein's is an extension past that point, with coating, breading, and cooking. According to officials at both companies: "Our mutual technical facilities and complementary processing equipment greatly expands our ability to give customers a total package of quality products and service expertise—all from the same corporate source." The combined sales of the two firms after the acquisition were estimated to be in the range of $25 to $30 million.

MR. BUTTNER'S RESPONSE

While Mr. Buttner had conducted several research projects in the recent past, he did not have any formal reports he could send to the professor. Therefore he decided to summarize the general research procedure he employed rather than describe any one research project in detail. After reflecting a while about the types of projects he most frequently conducted, he wrote the following letter to the professor.

> Dear Professor:
>
> The market research I do for Bettcher Industries is basic industrial research and rarely involves a structured format, such as the highly statistically oriented consumer products market research. As you suggest, it is somewhat difficult to provide documented research case histories that would explain a research project from its inception to conclusion.
>
> In brief, the type of research I do typically starts with the question: "Dan, how big is the market for an X type of machine?" No formalized, step-by-step research procedure is drawn up; there is no proposal or cost justification. I start by gathering some statistical data to quantify the market, such as pounds of ham produced yearly, number of firms producing turkey, head of cattle slaughtered yearly. These data give me a feel for the upper limit. I then rely on various contacts in the government, trade associations, trade magazines, and industry to further limit and quantify the market. The information I am looking for includes who uses machines of this type, what they do with them, how many they use.

This step is probably the most important part of industrial market research. Knowing who to call and where to get information usually takes a long time—years. Developing the ability to get the information after you have found the right person is also somewhat difficult. You get a lot of no answers before you develop the right technique. I do most of this search by phone and some of it in person.

After I understand the market limitations, I contact potential end users and ask them specific questions, such as, Would you purchase a machine of this type? How would you use it? Who else would have a need for this machine? How are you doing the job now?

Finally, I summarize these data, including companies and names of people contacted, and present an estimate of market size to management, including all pluses and minuses I have discovered, such as impending technological changes, competition, economic barriers.

Feel free to call me if you think I can be of more help.

Very truly yours,

Daniel A. Buttner
Marketing Research Manager

QUESTIONS

1. Compare the research steps used by Mr. Buttner with the components of the research project we discussed.
2. Would you classify the research process described in Mr. Buttner's letter as exploratory or conclusive? Discuss your answer.
3. Critically evaluate the type of marketing research conducted by Bettcher Industries. What are its pluses and minuses?
4. Could Bettcher benefit from using different research procedures or from conducting research other than the type described in Mr. Buttner's letter? If so, what are they?

CASE 2.2

Fast-Test: To Use or Not to Use?

Nancy Diamond was recently hired as the marketing manager for the Beauty Aids Division of General Products Corporation. During the past week she has been wondering about the cost-effectiveness of using Fast-Test, a new-product evaluation service. Fast-Test is offered by Innovations Research, Inc., a well-known marketing research firm specializing in evaluating new products and estimating the sales potential for them.

Nancy is particularly interested in the Fast-Test service because the Beauty Aids Division has just developed a new hair spray for which she has complete marketing responsibility. In fact, one of the first challenges of her new job is to decide fairly quickly whether or not the new hair spray should be introduced.

COMPANY BACKGROUND

General Products Corporation is a leading marketer of health care, personal-hygiene, and beauty aid products, with annual sales in excess of $100 million. The company is divided into three divisions, one corresponding to each of its three product groups. The Beauty Aids Division is the largest of the three and accounts for over half of total sales revenue.

Products marketed by the Beauty Aids Division include a variety of hair sprays, hair-coloring products, hair conditioners, shampoos, facial creams, and makeup products. The division has about thirty different brands of these products on the market. Competition for market share is extremely fierce for all the products marketed by the Beauty Aids Division. As a result, new-product introductions, as well as the exit of unsuccessful products, are numerous and frequent in the division's markets. Over the past several years the division has introduced an average of about six new products a year. Fortunately, many of these new-product introductions have fared much better than those introduced by the division's competitors. According to company sources, at least part of the above-average performance of the division's new-product entries can be attributed to the Fast-Test service, which Nancy's predecessor had routinely used to screen all new products prior to market introduction.

FAST-TEST

Innovations Research, Inc., describes its Fast-Test service as a very reliable method of quickly predicting what the market share for a new product will be at the end of the first year after introduction. An attractive feature of this service is that it does not involve any actual test marketing. Thus Fast-Test can predict the likely market performance of a new consumer product without incurring the enormous expense, time delay, and competitive risk associated with a traditional test-marketing operation.

Fast-Test is apparently based on sophisticated data collection and analysis procedures. While technical details about these procedures are confidential, Innovations Research releases a brochure describing the key elements of generating Fast-Test market share predictions for new products. Briefly, once a client firm has developed samples of a new product and drawn up a tentative marketing plan for it, the Fast-Test process consists of the following sequence of steps

1. Selecting a representative sample of target customers.
2. Exposing the potential customers to promotional materials about the new product.
3. Measuring customers' level of interest in and preference for the new product.
4. Providing customers pricing information on the new product and measuring their intentions to buy the product.
5. "Selling" samples of the new product to customers interested in buying it at a price somewhat lower than the proposed introductory market price.
6. After a few weeks, measuring the reactions of those who bought the product, including their likelihood of buying the product again.
7. Feeding all the data collected in the previous steps (along with data about market characteristics, consumer demographics, and competing products already on the market) into a computer simulation model to predict year-end market share for the product.

Past users of Fast-Test on Innovations Research's client list include over a hundred consumer product marketers, several of which are *Fortune 500* companies.

FAST-TEST'S TRACK RECORD

The Beauty Aids Division has used Fast-Test to evaluate 20 new products over the past three years. Fifteen of these products were introduced into the market, while the rest were dropped on the basis of Fast-Test's predictions. Specifically, Nancy's predecessor had used a cutoff market share of 4% in deciding whether to introduce a new product. In other words, any new product whose estimated market share at the end of the first year (as predicted by Fast-Test) was below 4% was not introduced.

Upon questioning her colleagues about the rationale for the 4% cutoff share, Nancy discovered two reasons:

1. Top management was very reluctant to continue to support, or even tolerate, new products that did not achieve a "respectable" market share by the end of the first year after introduction.
2. Historically, new products that did not gain at least a 4% market share by the end of the first year had tended to lose rather than make money.

Nancy felt these reasons made sense, especially since she had been told that a key criterion used by top management in conducting annual reviews of the marketing manager's performance was the profitability of new products introduced during the year.

Wondering just how good Fast-Test had been in predicting the market performance of her division's new products, Nancy compiled all the data she could find on products considered for introduction during the past three years. Compiling the data took her a while because she had to go over numerous sales records and related documents. But her effort was well worth it because she was able to uncover the following information:

1. Fast-Test's market share predictions for each of the 20 new products evaluated over the past three years.
2. Actual year-end market shares for 15 of those products that were introduced.
3. Profits (or losses) generated by each of them during their first year on the market.

Table 1

Comparison of Fast-Test's predictions with actual results

NEW PRODUCT NUMBER	PREDICTED MARKET SHARE (%)	ACTUAL MARKET SHARE (%)	PREDICTION ERROR: ACTUAL MARKET SHARE − PREDICTED MARKET SHARE
1	9	8	−1
2	8	8	0
3	5	6	+1
4	6	3	−3
5	7	5	−2
6	8	9	+1
7	4	6	+2
8	5	6	+1
9	5	3	−2
10	6	7	+1
11	4	2	−2
12	5	7	+2
13	7	8	+1
14	6	7	+1
15	5	5	0
16	1	—	—
17	3	—	—
18	0	—	—
19	2	—	—
20	2	—	—
Average*	6	6	0

Note: All percentages have been rounded to nearest integers.
*Average is based only on products 1 through 15.

From an analysis of the data Nancy was able to compute the prediction errors made by Fast-Test. She defined *prediction error* as the difference between the actual and the predicted market shares. The results of her analysis are summarized in Table 1. Prediction errors could not be computed for products 16 through 20 in Table 1 because they were not introduced into the market; Fast-Test had predicted a market share of less than 4% for each of them.

During her investigation Nancy also discovered that products 4, 9, and 11 had been withdrawn from the market a year after introduction. These three products, in addition to failing to achieve the critical 4% market share, had each lost money. On the average they had resulted in a net loss of about $400,000 apiece. Hence these products were considered to be market failures, although Fast-Test had predicted their market shares to be 4% or better. The remaining 12 products were all considered to be market successes—indeed, all of them were still on the market. Moreover, Nancy's analysis of profitability data showed that the average net profit contribution during their first year on the market was about $500,000.

NANCY'S DILEMMA

Nancy felt she had assembled some interesting data about Fast-Test's predictions. But she felt somewhat frustrated because she did not know what the data meant for the *specific problem she faced,* namely, whether to use Fast-Test for the Beauty Aids Division's newest hair spray. On the one hand, she felt like simply continuing her predecessor's routine practice of using Fast-Test for all new products, especially since she believed the new hair spray would face market conditions similar to those faced by many new products recently considered by her division. On the other hand, she was not sure whether the benefit of using Fast-Test would outweigh the service's hefty price of $80,000. In fact, Innovations Research had just raised the price for conducting a Fast-Test from $75,000 to $80,000.

Prior to joining the Beauty Aids Division of General Products Corporation, Nancy had worked for about five years as an assistant marketing manager for a packaged-goods firm. Her previous employer did not spend much money on marketing research and only infrequently used the services of marketing research firms. During Nancy's association with that firm, she had never seen the marketing manager approve any marketing research project costing over $10,000. Indeed, Nancy believed that the general perception of the firm's top management concerning marketing research was: "Why pay someone to tell you what you already know?" Having gained experience in that kind of environment, Nancy found it particularly difficult to accept Fast-Test.

However, Nancy did not want her previous employer's skepticism to unduly influence her decision making, especially since her intuition—from what she had heard and learned about Fast-Test so far—seemed to indicate that the service was probably worth its price. She was particularly impressed by the computations that showed relatively small prediction errors, which also averaged to an error of 0%. Thus she even wondered whether Fast-Test was not error-free, or perfect, on the average. Could she somehow *verify* her intuition?

In pondering this question, Nancy remembered that in a marketing research course she had been exposed to something called a Bayesian analysis approach to determining the monetary worth of a research project. So she pulled her marketing research textbook out of her bookshelf and started going through its table of contents.

QUESTIONS

1. Is Fast-Test "perfect" on the average, as Nancy believes it may be? Why or why not?
2. Can the Bayesian analysis approach be used to evaluate the worth of using Fast-Test to predict market share for the Beauty Aids Division's new hair spray? What assumptions would you have to make in order to use it? How realistic will each of those assumptions be?
3. Should Nancy use Fast-Test for predicting the new hair spray's market share? Develop a qualitative as well as quantitative rationale for your answer.

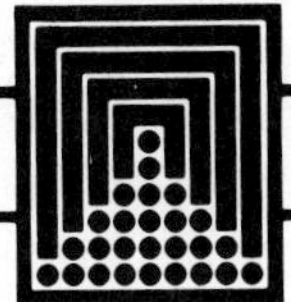

CASE 2.3

Superior Landscape Company

THE COMPANY

Superior Landscape Company (SLC) is a firm selling a variety of lawn products (e.g., fertilizers, weed killers, privacy fences, decks, sprinklers) as well as landscaping and lawn maintenance services (e.g., landscape design and installation, lawn mowing, fertilizing). The SLC is five years old and is owned by John Norwood, who also holds the title of president. In addition to Mr. Norwood, SLC has four other employees: a salesperson in the retail store operated by SLC, a landscape specialist who designs landscapes and offers landscaping advice to customers, and two servicepeople who provide on-site services such as lawn mowing, fertilizing, and planting trees and shrubs.

THE LOCAL ECONOMY

The SLC is located in a city with a population of 125,000 in the southwestern United States. The local economy is supported by a number of small, but rapidly growing, high-technology firms. The local economy is expected to expand at a fast pace in the coming years. The city's population is expected to grow to 150,000 by the end of the next five years.

SALES AND PROFITS

Mr. Norwood is pleased with the sales growth of his firm. Its total sales in the past year were $335,000, up from $266,000 during the first year the firm opened for business. Additional data about changes in total sales and changes in the contributions made by lawn products and landscaping/lawn maintenance services to total sales are shown in Table 1.

Mr. Norwood is also pleased with the profit performance of SLC. Profits before taxes, as a percentage of sales, have averaged about 20% during the past five years. During the past year SLC's profits before taxes were about $75,000.

COMPETITOR'S MARKETING RESEARCH STUDY

Mr. Norwood recently discovered that a major competitor of SLC had just completed a personal-interview survey of 200 customers in the area. The survey was conducted by a local marketing research firm. Mr. Norwood estimated that the survey cost the competitor about $4000.

Mr. Norwood did not know the details of the survey—particularly, what the findings of the survey were. However, one of SLC's customers who had participated in the survey volunteered some information about the personal interview. The interview lasted about 30 minutes and dealt with a variety of issues, such as the types of lawn-related products and services used by the respondent, annual expenditures on lawn care, and the respondent's perceptions about various lawn care/landscaping firms in the area.

MR. NORWOOD'S DECISION

The idea of conducting a consumer survey intrigued Mr. Norwood. He believed that a survey similar to the one conducted by SLC's competitor could provide valuable information about customer needs and preferences regarding lawn-related products and services. He also felt that such a survey could uncover customer perceptions about SLC's products and services versus those offered by key competitors. In Mr. Norwood's opinion information from a survey of this nature would be of great help in formulating SLC's future marketing strategy and strengthening its market position in the coming years. He therefore made a note to call the local marketing research firm and make plans for conducting a survey similar to the one conducted by SLC's competitor.

Table 1

Summary of SLC's sales

YEAR	SALES OF LAWN PRODUCTS	SALES OF LANDSCAPING AND LAWN MAINTENANCE SERVICES	TOTAL SALES
1	$213,000	$53,000	$266,000
2	$212,000	$60,000	$272,000
3	$220,000	$73,000	$293,000
4	$228,000	$88,000	$316,000
5	$235,000	$100,000	$335,000

QUESTIONS

1. Should Mr. Norwood commission a survey similar to the one conducted by SLC's competitor? Why or why not?
2. What kinds of information are likely to be most helpful in planning SLC's future marketing strategy? How should such information be obtained? Justify your answer with specific reasons.
3. Is there any ethical issue involved in Mr. Norwood contacting the marketing research firm that conducted the survey for SLC's competitor? Should the marketing research firm agree to conduct a survey for SLC if Mr. Norwood requests one?

PART THREE

DATA COLLECTION PROCEDURES

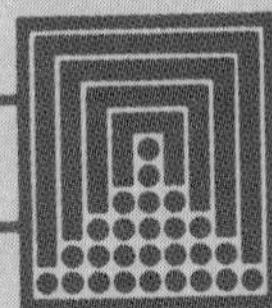

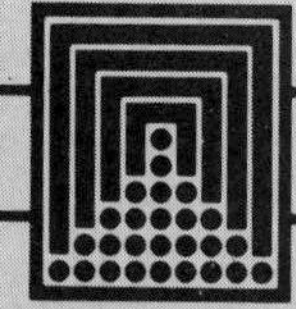

FROM THE MANAGER'S DESK

DR. R. E. PIFER is a manager in the Hershey Chocolate Company's Marketing Research Department. In this capacity he directs all consumer-oriented survey and experimental marketing research activities dealing with advertising, promotions, packaging, and the products themselves. Prior to holding this position, Dr. Pifer worked for Market Facts, Inc., and Leo Burnett Advertising.

QUESTION: What problems, if any, do you see in using marketing research to predict the true impact of marketing expenditures on such items as advertising and promotion? To what extent and in what ways can such problems be overcome?

RESPONSE: Historically, predicting the impact of advertising and promotions has been one of the most important questions encountered in marketing research. Although recent technological advances allow for more precise estimates, definitive answers generally will continue to elude us.

To understand this issue, let's consider it in more detail.

- The objective of any such expenditure is to maintain or increase retail sales of the brands being promoted or advertised. Brand sales at retail, therefore, constitute the generally most meaningful and actionable measure of these expenditures. Knowing how much is to be gained in dollars compared with how much is spent permits one to evaluate whether the advertising or promotion will be profitable.
- The "true" impact of these expenditures is best estimated by way of an experiment—research involving random assignment of experimental units to systematically manipulated causal conditions. Until a history of experimental results is accrued and our theory of marketing becomes more mature, these experiments must be conducted by way of unobtrusive observation in the field and not under laboratory conditions. Laboratory conditions are suspected of exert-

ing strong reactive effects, since the respondents know they are participating in an experiment.

- Synergy is likely to exist between advertising and promotions. Thus manipulating both variables jointly is important so that the interactive effects of the two on sales can be estimated.
- Advertising and promotions for one brand can affect the sales performance of other brands the manufacturer markets. These spillover effects are not always detrimental to the other brands, and their sales as well as sales and marketing conditions of directly competitive brands should be monitored.

These conditions for our field experiment can be met by using one of the better split-cable, mini-test-marketing services to collect the relevant data. Answers coming from this use can be very good, although, clearly, the study could suffer from a lack of complete control over the people and the conditions involved. For example, nothing could stop a household assigned to a low level of advertising from visiting friends assigned to a high level and thereby becoming subjected to more exposures than intended. A potentially more serious problem involves purchasing at nonmonitored retail outlets. To the extent that activities like these occur, the true impact of the marketing expenditures will be underestimated. For many applications this underestimation will be small.

In practice, however, certain things related to the true impact cannot be learned definitively. First, because anticipating and simulating competitive activity is difficult, we can only monitor existing competitive conditions and perhaps incorporate this information into our analyses of the data. If a competitor responds to our advertising or promotion with a compensating expenditure higher than monitored in the experiment, our original estimate of the true impact will be faulty. Second, information needs and research costs can constrain us to perform our test in a period of one year or less. Part of the true impact of the marketing expenditures may take place over a longer time frame, however. Consequently, these cumulative effects, especially as related to such issues as brand versus price loyalty, will not be estimated.

5

Secondary Data

The notion of secondary data was introduced in previous chapters, especially Chapters 3 and 4. For instance, we discussed the role of secondary data in the data source identification stage of a research project (Chapter 3) and in the different types of marketing research designs (Chapter 4). *Secondary data* are data collected for some purpose other than the research situation at hand. They are usually readily available. The following are all examples of secondary data:

- Data on warranty cards (e.g., date, place, and purpose of purchase) mailed to an appliance manufacturer by recent buyers of the firm's appliances.
- Nielsen television ratings indicating the relative popularity of various TV programs in a certain week.
- Unemployment rates in different sections of the country, estimated and released by the U.S. Department of Labor.
- Data made available by an automobile dealers' association to its members regarding the volume and models of used cars sold in a certain part of the country during a given period.
- Data reported by Ronald Milliman in an article published in the *Journal of Marketing* (a professional journal of the American Marketing Association) indicating a relationship between the tempo of background music played in a supermarket and the amount of purchases made by supermarket customers.[1]

[1] Ronald E. Milliman, "Using Background Music to Affect the Behavior of Supermarket Shoppers," *Journal of Marketing,* 46 (Summer 1982), pp. 86–91.

As the examples illustrate, a wide variety of secondary data is available for possible use by a researcher. However, the purpose for which secondary data were originally gathered will normally differ from the objective of the specific project the researcher is contemplating. After all, secondary data, by definition, are data collected for purposes other than specific research objectives. Thus a marketing researcher faces the twofold challenge of identifying the various secondary data that may be useful and evaluating such data vis-à-vis the requirements of the research study. The purpose of this chapter is to present details concerning this challenge and to offer guidelines for dealing with it.

Let us first examine the pros and cons of secondary data in order to highlight why a researcher must seek out such data and, at the same time, exercise caution in using them.

BENEFITS OF SECONDARY DATA

Secondary data obviously have cost and time advantages over *primary data*, which are data collected specifically for a project. A research study will invariably be less expensive and easier to complete if it utilizes secondary data rather than primary data. As an illustration, consider the following hypothetical situation:

EXAMPLE: The American Lung Association (ALA) has just developed an antismoking campaign, consisting of television and radio commercials warning the public about the hazards of cigarette smoking. Although the ALA would like to launch the campaign nationally, it faces a serious budget constraint at the present time. However, rather than delay the campaign launch until its financial position improves, the association wants to introduce the campaign selectively in states where it is likely to do the most good. For this purpose, the association must identify states with relatively high per capita consumption of cigarettes. How can the ALA identify such states?

One option available to the ALA is to conduct surveys of, say, 1000 people in each state to collect the data needed to estimate per capita consumption. As you might imagine, such a primary-data collection approach will be expensive and time-consuming. For instance, even if the ALA spends only about $500 per state for collecting and analyzing data—which is a conservative cost estimate—it will have to spend a total of $25,000. Given its tight financial situation, the ALA would be unwise to spend that kind of money on primary-data collection, especially since useful secondary data are likely to be available at much lower cost.

Several potentially productive secondary-data collection approaches are available for estimating per capita cigarette consumption on a state-by-state basis. For instance, data on state cigarette tax revenues (available through published state government documents) can be used to estimate total consumption of cigarettes in a state. Per capita cigarette consumption in the state can then be determined by dividing total consumption into the number of people in the state (available through U.S. Census Bureau data). Alternatively, perhaps someone else—such as an academic researcher, a commercial marketing research firm, a governmental agency, or a trade association—has already collected data about cigarette consumption in various states. The availability of such data can be ascertained by a trip or a telephone call to a library.

Invariably, plunging into primary-data collection without first looking into the availability of secondary data is a cardinal mistake. Researchers making this mistake will be squandering valuable resources—money and time. Using secondary data to ascertain such things as demographic compositions of markets, retail sales of a product category, changes in brand shares over time, and market potentials for industrial products can be particularly cost- and time-efficient because a variety of rich secondary-data sources are available for these purposes.

In addition to their obvious cost and time benefits over primary data, secondary data have a more subtle advantage. Certain kinds of data a firm may find difficult to collect on its own as primary data may be available as secondary data. For example, the Census of Retail Trade (published by the U.S. Census Bureau) contains data on the sales of retail establishments, classified according to numerous categories of outlets. This census may be the only source of accurate data available to a manufacturing firm selling its products to retailers and wishing to ascertain the size of its markets as measured by the sales of different categories of retail outlets. Given the sensitive nature of the data, the manufacturing firm may find that gathering accurate and comprehensive data on its own is difficult. However, the U.S. Census Bureau, by virtue of its legal authority, can collect and disseminate such data. Another federal agency that has similar authority is the Securities and Exchange Commission (SEC). A variety of publicly held business firms in the United States are required by law to file certain financial data with the SEC, which, in turn, makes them public.

While some forms of secondary data are available free (e.g., data contained in most government publications and in research studies published in books and journals), those made available by commercial marketing research firms are not. Secondary data sold by research firms are usually called *syndicated data,* or *syndicated services.* The cost of collecting syndicated data is spread over a number of client firms; the cost to any one firm is invariably lower than the cost the firm would incur were it to collect the data on its own. Indeed, firms with tight budgets and other resource constraints simply cannot afford to gather primary data about their markets and the performance of their products in those markets.

As an illustration, consider a small firm manufacturing a line of canned vegetables and distributing its brands to supermarkets across the country through food brokers. The firm has no direct contact with the supermarkets or the customers who buy its brands. Therefore it may be unable to learn much about who buys its brands, what its brands' shares are in various regional markets, and so on, if syndicated services—such as the National Purchase Diary Panel and the Nielsen National ScanTrack Service[2]—are not available.

The point of the preceding discussion is to emphasize an important, although somewhat subtle, benefit of secondary data: Such data, especially those available through government documents and syndicated services, can shed light on certain aspects of markets, products, consumers, and so on, that may be extremely difficult, if not impossible, for a firm to study on its own.

LIMITATIONS OF SECONDARY DATA

Relevance

Secondary data are not without drawbacks. One major drawback relates to the relevance of the data for the specific research purpose. Available secondary data may not match the data needs of a given project on one or more of the following factors: (1) the *units* in which the data are measured, (2) the *category breakdowns or definitions* of variables for which the data are reported, and (3) the *time period* during which the data are measured.[3]

Data on many variables of interest can be gathered by using a number of alternative units of measurement. Sales of a product can be measured in dollars or in physical units; product shipments can be measured in terms of volume, weight, dollar value, or truckloads; a consumer's education level can be measured in terms of the highest degree held or the number of years of formal education completed. A particular choice of measurement units by the source of secondary data may render the data useless for certain research purposes, as the following example illustrates.

EXAMPLE: Carpets Unlimited and Sentinel Corporation are two newly started firms. Carpets Unlimited manufactures a variety of carpets, and Sentinel Corporation produces a line of smoke detectors. Both firms are eager to estimate the total residential-market potential for their products in different sections of the country.

One surrogate estimate of potential for their products in a region is the total size of residential-housing units in that region. However, size of residential housing can be measured in at least two alternative ways: number of

[2] The data made available through these syndicated services are described in the following brochures: "Sharpening Marketing Decisions with Diary Panels," prepared (in 1975) by NPD Research, 900 West Shore Road, Port Washington, N.Y.; and "Nielsen National ScanTrack Service," prepared (in 1982) by the A. C. Nielsen Company, Nielsen Plaza, Northbrook, Ill. 60062.

[3] These three factors are outlined in a number of marketing research textbooks; see, for example, Harper W. Boyd, Ralph Westfall, and Stanley F. Stasch, *Marketing Research—Text and Cases* (Homewood, Ill.: Irwin, 1981), p. 139.

rooms and square feet of area. Residential-housing size expressed in number of rooms may be adequate and appropriate for the data needs of Sentinel Corporation but not for the data needs of Carpets Unlimited. A meaningful estimate of market potential for carpeting requires size data expressed in square feet.

The U.S. Census of Population and Housing contains a variety of data on residential housing that may be quite useful to Sentinel Corporation in estimating market potential for smoke detectors. Data are available on total number of rooms, number of bedrooms, year in which a unit was built, and number of stories in the unit. However, these data do not yield meaningful estimates of market potential for residential carpeting.

Thus, in general, while data on a variable of interest (e.g., size of residential housing) may be readily available, the relevance of data for a particular application depends on the measurement units used. However, one must not hastily dismiss secondary data as being irrelevant just because the measurement units do not exactly match the requirements of a project. In certain situations converting the reported data into the specific units of interest may be possible. For example, a trucking company interested in the *volume* of industrial chemicals transported may find secondary data reported in *weight* units. But the secondary data here are useful since they can be easily modified to meet the trucking company's needs by using appropriate weight-to-volume conversion factors. Similarly, total *unit* sales of some product, say television sets, can be derived from total *dollar* sales data if a meaningful estimate of the average price per television set is available. Of course, such conversions may not always be possible. Data on total television set sales reported in dollars will be useless if one is interested in unit sales of different sizes of television sets rather than total unit sales.

Secondary data may also be irrelevant if the categories for which data are summarized are not consistent with the categories of interest to a researcher. Consider a marketer of products and services primarily aimed at senior citizens. This marketer is interested in obtaining data about the life-styles and activities of different age-groups of senior citizens. Suppose a comprehensive study of life-styles and activities of adults classified by different age-groups is readily available. The life-style and activity data are summarized in the study according to the following five age-groups:

18 to 25   26 to 35   36 to 45   46 to 55   over 55

This study is not useful to the marketer because even though the study contains data on relevant variables, the categories chosen for the age variable are not consistent with the marketer's specific needs. The highest age-group for which data are summarized in the study is "over 55"—a category too broad to be relevant to the marketer.

The mismatch between categories as defined by a secondary-data source and as desired by a decision maker may not always be as obvious as in this illustration. The difference may be quite subtle and, if a secondary-data user fails to recognize it, can lead to erroneous inferences. This point is forcefully made by a situation reported in *American Demographics* magazine:

> Are metropolitan areas markets? Consider the case of Brownsville, Texas. A chain store whose products are geared to an upscale clientele argued that Brownsville deserved a high priority for a new store because retail sales per household there were much higher than the national average.
>
> Brownsville is a border town; and the standard metropolitan statistical area [SMSA] of which it is a part, Brownsville–Harlingen–San Benito, consists of Cameron County. According to the 1980 census, the SMSA's median household income is only $11,700—well below the $16,800 national average.
>
> With income so low, how could retail sales be so high? The answer is that Mexicans routinely cross the border to shop. Thus, dividing total retail sales by the number of county households inflates the real spending attributed to the average Brownsville household. For this chain to open a new store in the area would be a mistake, because few upscale residents live there.[4]

The inflated per-household retail sales figure resulted from the chain store's failure to recognize the distinction between the market, or *trading area,* of retail outlets in Brownsville and the Census Bureau's definition of the area—namely, Cameron County—for which data on retail sales and number of households were readily available.

Researchers using census data for studying the nature of geographic markets must be especially cautious. Well-defined geographic areas (e.g., counties or states) for which census data are summarized typically do not coincide with trading areas surrounding core cities or SMSAs. From an analysis of secondary data on variables most likely to be associated with consumer's shopping behavior—such as place of residence and work, commuting patterns, and newspapers read—the U.S. Bureau of Economic Affairs has divided the United States into 183 economic areas, whose boundaries are very different from traditional SMSA, county, or state boundaries.[5] Exhibit 5.1 shows the United States segmented into fifteen major consumer product market regions by aggregating the 183 core economic areas. Notice that the boundaries of these regions are markedly different from those of the ten Census Bureau divisions for which census data at the regional level are published.[6]

---

[4] Thomas I. Rubel, "Metros, Markets . . . and More," *American Demographics,* © July 1983, p. 22, excerpted with permission from *American Demographics,* Ithaca, N.Y.

[5] For a discussion of the procedure used in creating the economic areas, see Rubel, "Metros, Markets . . . and More," pp. 22–25, 44.

[6] The possible lack of relevance of census division boundaries for marketing applications is further supported by a theory proposed by Joel Garreau in his book *The Nine Nations of North America* (Boston: Houghton Mifflin, 1981). From economic, social, cultural, political, topographical, and natural-resource factors, Garreau claims that North America can be divided into nine distinct "nations."

Exhibit 5.1

Discrepancies between economic regions and census divisions

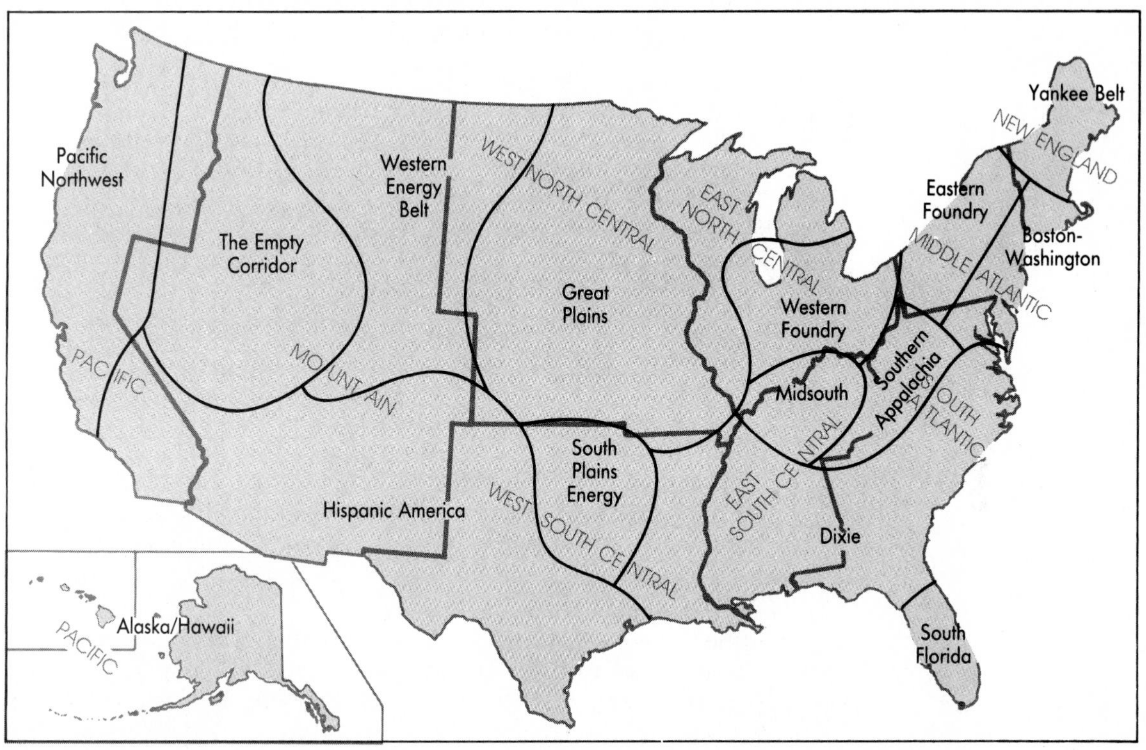

Source: Reproduced from Thomas I. Rubel, "Metros, Markets . . . and More," *American Demogaphics,* July 1983, p. 25. Used by permission.

Another facet of the category problem of which secondary-data users must be aware relates to *changes* in category definition that may occur from one time period to the next. For instance, in the 1970 census Hispanics were classified as whites, while in the 1980 census they were assigned a separate race category. Before drawing inferences from secondary data obtained from multiple time periods, one must ensure that no changes occurred in the definitions of variables or their categories. Table 5.1 summarizes the definition changes for certain variables between the 1970 and 1980 censuses of population. Obviously, researchers interested in studying the changes in variables between 1970 and 1980 must first determine whether they can meaningfully compare the data over time.[7]

The time period during which secondary data were collected is the third

[7] An interesting discussion of faulty inferences stemming from failure to recognize definition changes is given in "10 'Shortcuts' to Evaluating Demographics Statistics," *Marketing News,* September 17, 1982, Section 1, pp. 9–10.

Table 5.1

Changes in variable definitions between the 1970 and 1980 censuses

Farm definition	Old definition can be reconstructed
Householder	Replaces household head concept
Industry	Many code changes; classification system changed somewhat
Occupation	Classification system substantially changed
Poverty definition	Some adjustments, but old definition can be reconstructed
Race	Several categories added; revised coding rules affect "White" and "Other"
Residence in 1975/ place of work	Broad categories in 1970, but coded to county group in 1980
Telephone in unit	Narrower than telephone availability in 1970
Work disability	Not counted if it has lasted less than six months

Source: Adapted from Paul T. Zeisset, *Public-Use Microdata Samples from the 1980 Census,* U.S. Department of Commerce, Bureau of the Census, Data User Services Division (Washington, D.C.: U.S. Government Printing Office, 1983), p. 9.

factor affecting the data's relevance for a specific application. Using data that are too old can be more dangerous than using no data at all, especially in making decisions relating to rapidly changing or highly volatile markets. Consider, for instance, the market for personal computers. Given the state of turmoil in this market—with rapidly changing competitors, computer models, prices, and applications—secondary data on, say, the demographics of personal-computer owners will most likely become useless shortly after they are collected.

Data published by the U.S. Census Bureau are particularly prone to being out of date. To illustrate, the Census of Population and Housing is conducted only once every ten years. Moreover, there is a lag of about two years between collection and publication of the data. Fortunately, difficulties stemming from the recency of secondary data are somewhat mitigated by two factors: Secondary-data sources usually provide periodic updates for their data, and rapid advances in computer and communication technology continue to reduce the lag between data collection and dissemination. The U.S. Census Bureau, for example, issues *Current Population Reports,* which update population data on an annual basis for major market areas. Similarly, some marketing research firms as well as state and local agencies periodically update census data on the basis of their own research.[8] Certain syndicated services (e.g., Chase Econometrics and DRI, Inc.) allow clients' computers direct access to their own computer files containing the most current demographic data.[9]

[8] See William J. Klocke, "Don't Overlook Secondary Data When Researching Retail Markets," *Marketing News,* May 14, 1982, Section 1, p. 17.

[9] See Doris L. Walsh, "Giving Demographics More Byte," *American Demographics,* April 1983, pp. 18–23, 47–48.

In summary, the relevance of secondary data depends on three factors: (1) measurement units; (2) variable and category definitions; and (3) data recency. A mismatch between any of these and the specific needs of a research study will reduce the data's relevance. Under such circumstances, however, a researcher must not be hasty in concluding that the data are useless. The researcher should explore whether the data can be modified in some way—for example, converted to different units, recast into different categories, or updated—so as to render them useful. While making such modifications (assuming they are feasible) will require some effort, it is still likely to be cheaper and less time-consuming than collecting primary data.

Accuracy

Secondary-data users, in addition to ensuring the relevance of such data, must verify their accuracy. The concepts of relevance and accuracy do overlap somewhat because they jointly determine the potential usefulness of a particular set of secondary data. However, the two terms refer to distinct facets of usefulness. While relevance focuses on the *suitability* of the data (i.e., the form and recency of the data), accuracy focuses on the *trustworthiness* of the data. Obviously, the usefulness of secondary data will be diminished if they lack *either* of these two traits.

The key to assessing the accuracy of secondary data lies in learning as much as possible about the process involved in collecting the data. This task may not always be easy and may require some effort on the part of researchers planning to use secondary data. Indeed, in many cases a major limitation of secondary data is the lack of information necessary to evaluate the data's accuracy rather than their degree of accuracy per se. After all, a researcher's decision about whether to use a particular set of secondary data will be relatively simple *if* adequate information is available to ascertain the data's trustworthiness. Unfortunately, the proliferation of easily accessible secondary data, on the one hand, and the scarcity of readily available information to evaluate them, on the other, may tempt some researchers to downplay the issue of accuracy. This temptation should be avoided; with a little effort researchers can usually get at least some feel for the trustworthiness of secondary data.

The following set of interrelated questions plays a central role in evaluating secondary-data accuracy: *Who* collected the data? *Why* were the data collected? *How* were the data collected? Answers to the who, why, and how questions can provide valuable insights about the trustworthiness of the data. Let us now examine each of these questions.

Who collected the data? The reputation of the sources of secondary data is an indicator of data accuracy. Well-known governmental sources like the U.S. Bureau of Census and many commercial marketing research firms, especially those established in the profession for a long time, have a reputation for setting and maintaining high data quality standards. Secondary data from such sources require far less scrutiny than data offered by organizations not well-established within the research profession or by sources whose credibility and competence are unknown.

Why were the data collected? An examination of the explicit, or even implicit, reason for the data collection can sometimes indicate the accuracy of the data. To illustrate, suppose a firm publishing a magazine conducts, on its own, a survey of its readers. The survey gathers data on a variety of factors, such as the demographic profiles of the readers and the impact on them of advertisements appearing in the magazine. The purpose of the survey is to generate readership data helpful to potential advertisers in deciding whether to place advertisements in the magazines. Of course, the publisher also hopes that the data will convince many firms to buy advertising space in the magazine.

Now think of yourself as one of the potential advertisers. Assume you have access not only to the secondary data offered by the publisher but also to similar data offered by a marketing research firm specializing in collecting and selling syndicated data about readers of a number of magazines. Which of these two sources—the publishing firm or the marketing research firm—would you trust more?

You are most likely to trust the marketing research firm more, for two good reasons:

1. Being an independent source, with no hidden bias, the marketing research firm is more likely to provide unbiased data.
2. Since the marketing research firm *specializes* in magazine readership surveys, it is more likely to be capable of generating good-quality data. Notice that this reason also relates to the who question discussed earlier.

These factors do not mean you should not use the data provided by the publishing firm—especially since you would have to pay for the research firm's data, while the data provided by the publisher are free. However, they do imply that before making any advertising decision on the basis of the publisher's data, you should carefully review the process involved in collecting the data. We next turn to the role of the data collection methodology in evaluating the accuracy of secondary data.

How were the data collected? Perhaps the most effective way to judge the accuracy of secondary data is to scrutinize the data collection process, *beyond* the who and why aspects already discussed. What specific data collection instruments were used? How large was the sample? What types of sample units provided the data? During what specific time periods (e.g., time of day, day of week) were the data collected? Answers to questions like these are crucial in assessing data accuracy.

Exhibit 5.2

Illustration of a data collection procedure summary

HOW ARE MONITOR DATA COLLECTED?

An annual survey

The social trend and manifestation data covered by Monitor are obtained by means of a survey conducted at the same time each year among a nationally projectable sample of 2,500 adults, 16 years of age and older, including a special subsample of 300 college students living on campus. The sample is based on the most recent Census data. All interviews are conducted in person at the respondent's home, and take approximately $2\frac{1}{2}$ hours to complete.

The size of social trends are determined by compositing scores on item batteries that have undergone extensive pretest and validation procedures. (A comprehensive technical description of Monitor, covering all aspects of its methodology, is available on request. Inspection of the questionnaire employed may also be arranged.)

Ongoing qualitative research

New trends and new manifestations are identified by a continuing program of in-depth research conducted among the general public and "precursor" groups of consumers. This program of original research is supplemented by systematic analyses of publications and custom studies conducted by Yankelovich, Skelly and White, Inc. on a wide variety of business and social problems.

Source: "The Yankelovich Monitor," prepared by Yankelovich, Skelly and White, Inc., 575 Madison Avenue, New York, N.Y. 10016, p. 14.

Secondary-data suppliers with good reputations generally publish at least a brief description of their data collection procedures. Most of them will also furnish additional details if desired by potential data users. For instance, Yankelovich, Skelly and White, Inc., a well-known marketing research firm, offers syndicated services including a brochure entitled "The Yankelovich Monitor." The "Monitor" provides annual statistics on numerous social trends and their association with buying behavior within the general population as well as specific demographic segments.[10] Exhibit 5.2 contains a published summary of the procedures used to collect data for the "Monitor." In the second paragraph of the exhibit, notice the research firm's offer to provide additional details about its methodology.

Good documentation of methodology, including statements about limitations of the data, is itself an indicator of high data quality. A secondary-data source that readily offers such documentation and is willing to submit its proce-

[10] Additional information about this syndicated service is available in "The Yankelovich Monitor," a brochure prepared by Yankelovich, Skelly and White, 575 Madison Avenue, New York, N.Y. 10022.

dures for additional examination will generally have high quality standards. By the same token, organizations unable or unwilling to document their data collection methodologies are suspect. A researcher must be especially cautious in dealing with secondary data coming from such organizations.

One's ability to evaluate the accuracy of secondary data also depends on whether the data are from the original source or a secondhand source. The *original source* is one that actually collects the data. A *secondhand source* is one that uses data collected by the original source to generate its own summaries, interpretations, and the like. For example, a report issued by the Census Bureau on data gathered through the Census of Population and Housing is the original source of such data. However, a report on population characteristics issued by an independent organization, which used data from the Census of Population and Housing as the basis for its report, is a secondhand source of population data.

The original source of secondary data is more likely than a secondhand source to spell out the procedures used in generating the data. Moreover, a secondhand source may unintentionally, or in some cases even deliberately, restate or reinterpret the original source's data in inappropriate ways. Hence, before using secondary data available through a secondhand source, one must identify the original source and examine the procedures used, if possible. As a general rule, one should obtain all the relevant data from the original source, if at all feasible.

SOURCES AND TYPES OF SECONDARY DATA

There are literally thousands of potential sources of secondary data—too numerous to list in a book of this nature. However, from the point of view of a decision maker's organization, a useful technique is to group secondary-data sources broadly into internal sources and external sources. As the terms imply, *internal sources* are sources within the organization, while *external sources* are sources outside the organization. Secondary data are typically labeled internal secondary data or external secondary data, depending on their source.

Internal secondary data

A firm's historical record of sales, a public service association's list of donors, past records of services rendered to patients by a hospital, and public opinion polls conducted in the past by a political candidate's campaign office are all sources of internal secondary data for the respective organizations. We earlier emphasized the usefulness of looking into the availability of secondary data before plunging into primary-data collection. Likewise, when one is seeking secondary data, checking out the availability of internal secondary data before turning to external sources is beneficial. Internal secondary data, if available, may be obtained with less time, effort, and money than external secondary data may be obtained. In addition, they may also be more pertinent to the situation at hand since they are from *within* the organization. These points are illustrated in the following example.

EXAMPLE: The publisher of a Houston newspaper wants to know the "penetration" of the newspaper in the various communities it serves. Specifically, the publisher would like to determine the proportion of households subscribing to the newspaper in each community. A marketing research firm specializing in newspaper audience research has estimates of household penetration for various newspapers in the Houston metropolitan area. These estimates are based on a survey of a representative sample of households in the Houston metro area and are updated every six months. Should the publisher purchase this syndicated service from the marketing research firm?

The penetration estimates provided by the syndicated service, an external secondary-data source, will certainly offer useful insights to the publisher. However, the addresses of current subscribers—internal secondary data that the publisher should have—will be even more beneficial. While the syndicated service is available only for the Houston metropolitan area, addresses of subscribers can pinpoint relative concentrations of subscribers in *all* areas served by the newspaper. These concentration estimates, coupled with readily available census data on total number of households in the corresponding areas, can provide the penetration estimates the publisher desires. Thus the total spread of the geographic area covered by the internal secondary data should be more in line with the publisher's needs. Furthermore, although the syndicated service is updated every six months, the newspaper's subscriber list will be up to date all the time. In short, given the specific objective of the publisher, internal secondary data will be more relevant and less expensive than the syndicated data offered by the research firm.

Of course, internal secondary data may not always be suitable or adequate. For instance, if data are needed on the relative geographic penetrations of the publisher's newspaper and those of competing newspapers, the publisher may have to buy the syndicated data offered by the research firm. In fact, the publisher may even have to collect primary data if it is keen on knowing the competitive penetration rates in communities outside the Houston metro area. But the point of this discussion is that once data needs are identified, a systematic search for data will pay off handsomely. It will ensure the gathering of suitable data without undue expenditures of time, effort, and money.

Exhibit 5.3 shows a flow diagram outlining the sequence of steps in a systematic data search. The logical starting point for any data search should be an examination of internal secondary-data sources. If the data available within the organization are unsuitable or inadequate, the search should be extended to

Exhibit 5.3

Flow diagram for conducting a data search

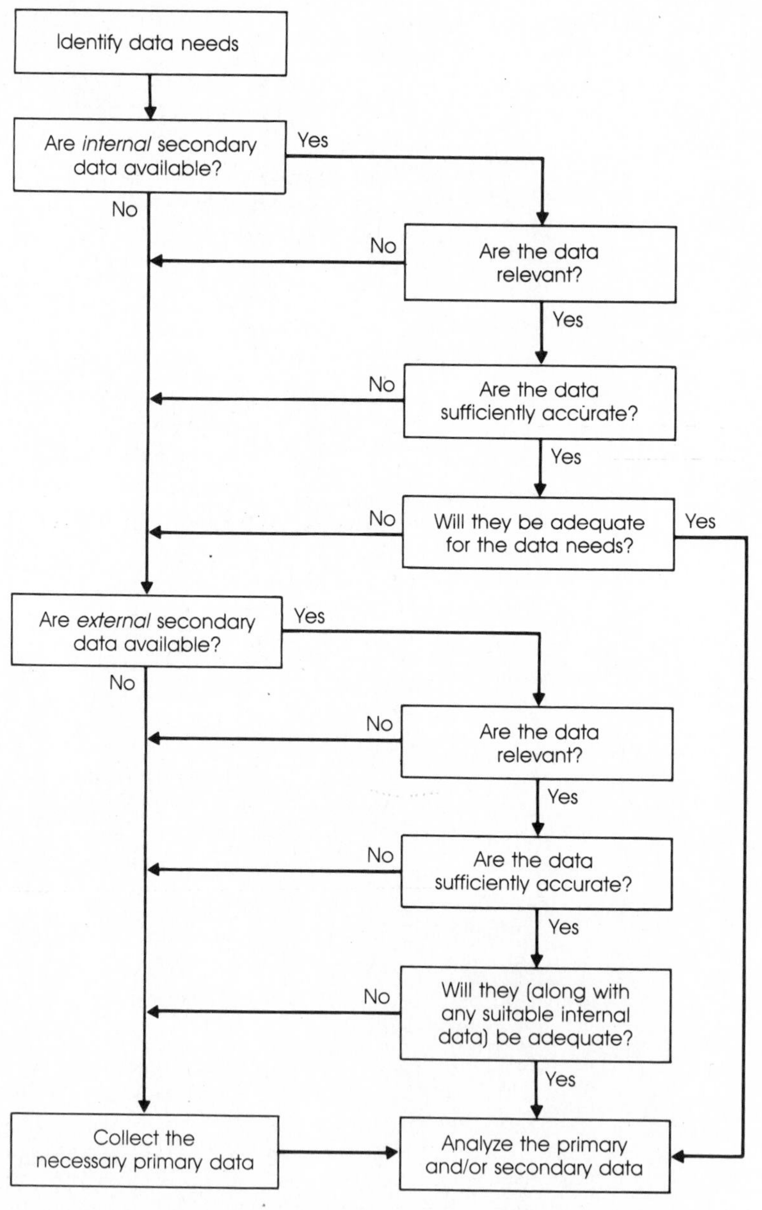

external secondary-data sources. Primary data should be collected only if absolutely essential. Indeed, the rigor with which the relevance and the accuracy criteria are applied in assessing the adequacy of internal and/or external secondary data should be tempered by available resources (time and money) and the purpose of the research. For instance, if resources are tight and the research is basically exploratory, the researcher can, and perhaps should, be somewhat lenient in evaluating available secondary data.

External secondary data

A variety of external sources provide secondary data. Although there is no standard way for classifying them, the following groupings may be helpful in highlighting key distinctions across the various sources: government sources; syndicated sources; trade associations; miscellaneous sources; and abstracts, directories, and indexes. A complete listing of all the sources relevant to marketers under each of these categories is beyond the scope of this book. However, examples of key sources, along with brief descriptions of what they offer, are provided in the appendix at the end of this chapter. Let us now examine the main features of the five broad categories of external sources.

Government sources. Government agencies at federal, state, and local levels collect more data about people, firms, markets, and so on, than any other secondary-data source. They therefore form an extremely rich reservoir of data for researchers. Moreover, much of these data are free. Looking into government sources of secondary data is a must if the information requirements of a project appear to relate to data in the public domain. Depending on the objective of a project, contacting an appropriate government agency or even paying a visit to the government documents section of a library can turn up potentially valuable published data.

Documents published by government sources are typically in the form of summary reports and tabulations based on the raw data collected. However, if additional details or different tabulations are needed, one may be able to obtain some or all of the raw data, usually for a fee. The U.S. Census Bureau, for example, sells computer tapes containing certain types of raw data collected through the variety of censuses it conducts. A case in point is Public-Use Microdata Files, containing data from the Census of Population and Housing.

Public-Use Microdata Files are raw data records, stored on computer tape, for a representative sample of housing units in the United States. These records provide data on the characteristics of each unit and the people living in it. However, to protect the confidentiality of respondents, the Census Bureau excludes all identifying information from the records. For the same reason microdata records do not identify geographic areas with less than 100,000 people. When census data users have unique needs not met by published documents, microdata files offer them the flexibility to analyze the raw data in whatever manner they desire. Exhibit 5.4 outlines some key capabilities and limitations of microdata files, as described by the Census Bureau.[11]

Syndicated sources. Syndicated sources consist of marketing research firms offering syndicated services. The well-known Nielsen Retail Index is an example of a syndicated secondary-data source. Brief descriptions of several syndicated services are provided in the appendix at the end of the chapter.

Secondary data offered by marketing research firms are not free. However, since such data are syndicated, their cost is spread over a number of client organizations. Therefore if suitable syndicated data are available, they should be more cost-effective than primary data for any individual client. In contrast to secondary data from government sources, syndicated data are likely to directly focus on the needs of decision makers. That is, while government sources cater to a wide variety of constituencies, research firms have a more limited and better-defined clientele. Moreover, syndicated data are typically updated more frequently than government data. Some syndicated data are updated as often as once a week.

In short, while data from government sources are generally less expensive than syndicated data, the latter are more likely to be directly relevant to the needs of decision makers. Of course, the two types of data may not necessarily be substitutes for each other; certain kinds of data may only be available through one type of source. To illustrate, detailed and rich data about the general characteristics of people and markets may only be available through the various government census studies; likewise, specific data on market shares or brand shares may only be available through syndicated sources. Thus a choice between government and syndicated sources may sometimes be influenced more by data availability than by cost-effectiveness or relevance considerations.

Although syndicated sources typically sell the same data to all subscribing clients, some permit a certain degree of customization. Specifically, client firms can submit questions of their own for inclusion in the questionnaire routinely used to gather syndicated data. There is an additional charge for including these custom questions. However, the data generated by these questions, and any analysis of such data, will be revealed only to the firms submitting the questions. Thus, to a certain extent, customization of syndicated services offers benefits of both secondary and primary data.

Roper Reports, prepared by the Roper Organization, is one example of a syndicated service offering customization. This service continuously monitors and reports public opinion and behavior concerning a broad range of social,

[11] Paul T. Zeisset, *Public-Use Microdata Samples from the 1980 Census,* U.S. Department of Commerce, Bureau of the Census, Data User Services Division (Washington, D.C.: U.S. Government Printing Office, 1983).

Exhibit 5.4

Features of public-use microdata files

Uses of microdata files

Public-use microdata files essentially make possible "do-it-yourself" special tabulations. The 1980 files furnish almost the full richness of detail recorded on long-form questionnaires in the census. Subject to the limitations on sample size and geographic identification, it is possible for the user to construct a seemingly infinite variety of tabulations interrelating any desired set of variables. Users have the same freedom to manipulate the data that they would have if they had collected the data in their own sample survey, yet these files offer the precision of census data collection techniques and sample sizes larger than would be feasible in most independent sample surveys.

Microdata samples will be useful to users (1) who are doing research that does not require the identification of specific small geographic areas or detailed cross tabulations for small populations, and (2) who have access to programming and computer time needed to process the samples. Microdata users frequently study relationships among census variables not shown in existing census tabulations, or concentrate on the characteristics of certain specially defined populations, such as unemployed homeowners or families with four or more children.

Subject content

With only minor exceptions, microdata files contain the full range of population and housing information collected in the 1980 census: 503 occupation categories, age by single years up to 90, income by $10 intervals up to $75,000, and so forth. Because the samples provide data for all persons living in a sampled household, users can study how characteristics of household members are interrelated (for example, income and educational attainment of husbands and wives).

Protecting confidential information

Records on public-use microdata samples contain no names or addresses. Also, the Bureau limits the detail on place of residence, place of work, high incomes, and selected other items to further protect the confidentiality of the records. Microdata records identify no geographic area with fewer than 100,000 inhabitants. Microdata samples include only a small fraction of the population, drastically limiting the chance that the record of a given individual is even contained in a microdata file, much less identifiable.

Source: Paul T. Zeisset, *Public-Use Microdata Samples from the 1980 Census,* U.S. Department of Commerce, Bureau of the Census, Data User Services Division. (Washington, D.C.: U.S. Government Printing Office, 1983), p. 3–4.

economic, and political issues, as well as various kinds of goods, services, and life-styles. Data are gathered every five weeks through personal interviews with a national sample of 2000 adults 18 years of age or older. In addition to the standard or regularly asked questions, a tack-on custom-question service is available to *Roper Reports* subscribers and nonsubscribers. The cost of the custom-question service depends on question complexity, the number of questions used in a given survey, the number of surveys in which the same questions are repeated, and whether the firm submitting questions is a *Roper Reports* subscriber. According to the Roper Organization: "This service offers a unique combination of frequency, speed of report delivery, quality, low cost, large sample size and extensive demographic breaks."[12]

One interesting syndicated service that is "fully customized" is AIM (abbreviation of Association-Identification-Measure), offered by R. H. Bruskin Associates.[13] The AIM service is conducted monthly and is based on personal interviews with a national probability sample of 2500 homes. A female adult is interviewed in half of the homes, and a male adult is interviewed in the other half. Each AIM interview consists of two parts:

1. The respondent is asked to examine a standard-size deck of 52 cards, each card containing a product name, slogan, trademark, symbol, or the like, submitted by a client firm. The purpose of this part is to measure consumer awareness and recognition of whatever is printed on each card.
2. The respondent is asked a set of custom questions—again, submitted by individual client firms—dealing with subjects such as product use, interest in products and services, and advertising or media exposure.

Exhibit 5.5 describes the two parts in greater detail, and Exhibit 5.6 contains examples of cards used in an AIM survey.

Responses to the card messages and/or questions submitted by each client are separately tabulated (by sex, age, income, and region) and made available only to that client. As in the case of the Roper Custom Question Service, the cost of AIM varies from client to client. It depends on the number of cards a client wants to buy (from the 52 cards available per survey), the type of material to be printed on each card, and the number and complexity of custom questions submitted.

Strictly speaking, the data provided by a service such as AIM is primary rather than secondary. Nevertheless, they can still be labeled "syndicated data" because they are collected on a regular basis and the data collection costs are shared by many clients. Moreover, such a service is still not as flexible or versatile as a primary-research project conducted by a client firm on its own. For instance, even in the case of AIM, since it is designed to cater to multiple clients, there are practical limits on the number of cards and/or questions that can be sold to any one client.

Trade associations. There are literally thousands of trade associations, each representing a group of organizations that share a common trade or line of business. Such associations include the National Association of College Stores, Retail Bakers of America, Canadian Roofing Contractors Association, Safety Hel-

---

[12] "Roper Custom Question Service: A Unique Omnibus Research Facility," a brochure prepared (in 1977) by the Roper Organization, Inc., One Park Avenue, New York, N.Y. 10016.

[13] *AIM: A Monthly Omnibus Research Service Designed to Meet the Needs of Participating Clients,* a booklet published by R. H. Bruskin Associates, 303 George Street, New Brunswick, N.J. 08903.

Exhibit 5.5

Description of AIM interviews

The card section

The AIM technique uses actual playing cards with the usual numbers and pictures replaced by the subscriber's test material. A full deck of 52 cards is used.

At the beginning of the interview, the respondent is handed the shuffled deck of cards containing all of the items to be tested. He then sorts these cards into two groups—those he knows or thinks he has seen or heard before, and those he is sure he has never seen or heard before (association). Additional questioning follows to determine the respondent's knowledge and identification of the items (identification).

Extensive testing and experience have revealed that this technique stimulates a great deal of respondent interest. The respondent feels he is "playing a game," which results in a high level of alertness and cooperation during the course of the entire interview. This psychologically favorable climate allows for the highest level of identification and minimizes losses which might otherwise occur.

The omnibus section

Upon completion of this first phase, the interviewer then proceeds with the omnibus section covering the special questions inserted by participating clients. Some clients have purchased as many as three pages of questions, others as little as one question.

In this section the client can insert questions of any type and on any subject. Many techniques have been employed—in-home audits; numerical rating scales; word and statement image listings; self-administered questions; card sorts; as well as the standard question procedures.

Visual aids can be used where appropriate to the objective of the question. The client's questions can follow in sequence or can appear in several positions in this omnibus section if desired.

The omnibus portion of the questionnaire is flexible. It is tailored to the individual needs of *each* participating client.

Source: Reproduced from *AIM: A Monthly Omnibus Research Service Designed to Meet the Needs of Participating Clients,* a booklet published by R. H. Bruskin Associates, 303 George Street, New Brunswick, N.J., pp. 3–4. Used by permission.

met Council of America, Newspaper Advertising Sales Association, Luggage and Leather Goods Salesmen's Association of America, Inc., Roadside Business Association, and American Cultured Dairy Products Institute.[14] These examples, in addition to illustrating the diversity of associations, show that even narrowly defined fields have their own trade groups.

[14] Several directories listing various associations are available; see, for example, Nancy Yakes and Denise Akey, *Encyclopedia of Associations,* vol. 1 (alphabetical index; 1979), vol. 2 (geographic and executive index; 1980) (Detroit: Gale Research).

Exhibit 5.6

Examples from an AIM card deck

PUEBLO COLORADO 81009

A

CHANGING THE WAY
AMERICA COOKS

RP

SHEER ENERGY

RQ

TENDER CHUNKS

RG

SIX FLAGS

B

YOU LOVED IT AS A KID
YOU TRUST IT AS A MOTHER

RT

Source: R. H. Bruskin Associates, 303 George Street, New Brunswick, N.J. Used by permission.

Most trade associations collect background data about their members and markets. They may also collect other types of data of potential interest to their members. Hence they can be valuable sources of secondary data, although a researcher planning to tap such sources may face certain constraints. The data available through associations will usually be quite general, and certain types of data, such as competitively sensitive data about an association's members or trade, may not be available at all. Another potential problem is that some trade associations will release data only to their members; thus whatever data exist will obviously be unavailable to an outsider.

Miscellaneous sources. Miscellaneous sources include sources that do not neatly fit into the three previous categories. Examples are journals, magazines, research monographs, textbooks, and similar published materials. Most libraries, especially those affiliated with academic institutions, have numerous collections of such sources.

A distinguishing feature of sources in this category is that the data they contain is in the form of insights, ideas, suggestions, and so forth, rather than in the form of numbers. Thus their primary purpose is to stimulate the thinking of researchers and decision makers, as opposed to providing them with numbers they can analyze. For example, the *Journal of Marketing* article mentioned at the beginning of this chapter—the article suggesting a relationship between the tempo of background music and supermarket sales—offers supermarket managers food for thought. Similarly, articles dealing with sales force motivation may provide valuable clues to a sales manager who is wondering why his or her sales force's performance is significantly below the performance of competitors' sales forces selling similar products.

Abstracts, directories, and indexes. Abstracts, directories, and indexes, in contrast to the sources discussed earlier, are *guides* or *references* for identifying suitable external secondary-data sources. They are listings of available data sources, classified according to subject matter, topic area, and the like. Several examples of abstracts/directories/indexes are briefly described in the appendix to this chapter. Some of the guides in this category offer more than a mere listing of secondary-data sources; that is, they are annotated and include brief outlines of or data summaries from other sources. Nevertheless, annotated guides are still secondhand sources. A researcher would do well to locate and examine the original source, even when a summary provided by an annotated guide appears to be adequate for the purpose. In short, abstracts, directories, and indexes are good starting points in the search for secondary data, especially when a researcher has little idea about what secondary-data sources exist or what they have to offer.

The rapid technological advances in the computer and communications fields are also revolutionizing the process of searching secondary-data guides to identify suitable data sources. Today many libraries and commercial firms offer *computerized searches* for locating potential sources of secondary data. Traditional, printed abstracts/directories/indexes are being replaced by electronic files. To conduct a computerized search, a researcher merely specifies certain key words relating to the topic area on which data are desired. A computer then searches the electronic files and culls all the sources containing the key words.

An obvious benefit of computerized searches is speed: What would take days or weeks for a traditional, manual search can be completed within minutes or hours by a computerized search. Moreover, the electronic files can be updated almost as soon as a new source of data becomes available, a feature printed guides do not have. Hence computerized searches can uncover the latest available sources.

Commercial firms specializing in computerized searches are reducing the time required for searching yet another way, namely, by providing direct communication links between their computers and their clients' computers. An example is FIND/SVP, a New York–based information and research firm. It recently introduced a service called FINDSEND, which, according to the firm's manager of information resources, "enables us to electronically deliver search results directly to a marketer's terminal, eliminating the need to wait for receipt of printouts by mail."[15]

The availability of fast, efficient, and thorough computerized searches makes it all the more critical that a researcher conduct a search for secondary-data sources before embarking on any form of external data collection. Conducting such a search not only saves time but also eliminates needless expenditures, as one of FIND/SVP's clients apparently discovered:

> A marketing researcher for a high-technology company was about to commission a $20,000 custom research study of the robotics market, a study which would take many months to complete.
>
> At the last minute, he called FIND/SVP to see if a similar study was commercially available. He was told that not one but several such studies were for sale and that virtually all the information wanted could be had immediately for a few thousand dollars.[16]

MANAGING SECONDARY DATA

The proliferation of secondary data (including internal secondary data) presents both an opportunity and a problem to researchers and decision makers. The variety and richness of the available secondary data can often minimize or even eliminate the need for primary data. But just keeping abreast of all the available data, without being overwhelmed, is a challenge. Indeed, two expressions frequently heard in business circles these days are "information explosion" and "drowning in data."

Capitalizing on the so-called information explosion without drowning in data requires effective *secondary-data management*—that is, creating and operating a system for continuously monitoring various data sources and quickly retrieving needed data. Effective secondary-data management is a critical com-

[15] "FINDSEND Service Transmits Results of Data-Base Searches to Marketer's Terminal," *Marketing News,* November 26, 1982, Section 1, p. 14.

[16] Bernie Whalen, "Off-the-Shelf Market Research Studies Save Time and Money," *Marketing News,* September 17, 1982, Section 2, p. 24.

ponent of a sound marketing information system. Many firms have established their own corporate libraries as a means of managing secondary data effectively. A well-equipped corporate library, with computerized data storage and retrieval capabilities, can be a valuable asset.[17]

Recognition of the need to manage secondary data effectively has given birth to a new breed of specialists in the marketing research field, namely, information consultants. Gary Bratton, vice president of Infosource, Inc., describes the role and the capabilities of information consultants as follows:

> Information research and analysis are an information consultant's stock in trade. The information consultant is constantly seeking new sources of information and evaluating their content for decision needs. . . . Most marketing executives have their favorite eight or ten sources of information with which to gather information. But there are literally hundreds that provide a much broader base from which to extract more exact info. . . . An information consultant's strength is knowing the contents of electronic files that are not specifically labeled "marketing." In most instances, sales and marketing people would not know how to identify these files, much less have the expertise to research them.[18]

The potential benefits of good data management are not limited to external secondary data. Systematically monitoring internal secondary data and using them in creative ways can also be very productive. A firm that effectively manages internal secondary data can quickly spot market opportunities and problems. Sears is an example. A well-maintained and -managed customer data base is apparently a major contributor to the firm's rapidly expanding service business. According to *Business Week*:

> By keeping track of the appliance purchases made by each customer, as well as the service plans and maintenance calls for these appliances, Sears has been able to create a powerful marketing tool that is helping it boost service revenue and win customer goodwill. This program is just one of the many ways the retailing giant is mining the wealth of information that it has accumulated on its millions of customers—data that will enable it to develop new products and services.[19]

SUMMARY

Secondary data, although collected for other purposes, may be helpful in a project. In general, secondary data can be obtained more quickly and with less

[17] James R. Fries, "Library Support for Industrial Marketing Research," *Industrial Marketing Management,* 11 (February 1982), pp. 47–51; see also "Putting the Library on a Computer," *Business Week,* March 30, 1981, pp. 104–106.

[18] "Information Specialists Can Tap Computer Data Bases to Provide Market Intelligence," *Marketing News,* November 27, 1981, Section 2, p. 18.

[19] "Business Is Turning Data into a Potent Strategic Weapon," *Business Week,* August 22, 1983, p. 92.

cost than primary data. Secondary data also have a less obvious advantage in that they can sometimes offer insights in situations where a single organization cannot collect primary data.

A potential limitation of secondary data relates to relevance. Available secondary data may lack relevance for a given project for any of the following reasons: the units in which the data are reported may be different from the desired units of measurement; the categories in which the data are grouped may not match the requirements of the project; the data may not be current. However, sometimes a researcher may be able to convert the measurement units, redefine the data categories and rearrange the data, and/or update the data. A researcher should explore these data modification options before dismissing available secondary data as irrelevant.

Another potential drawback of secondary data relates to accuracy, especially the difficulty in verifying the trustworthiness of the data. Answers to the following interrelated questions will shed light on this issue: Who collected the data? Why were the data collected? How were the data collected? The original source of secondary data is more likely to provide the documentation necessary to answer these questions than is a secondhand source. Therefore, if at all possible, the original source should be consulted.

Secondary-data sources can be broadly divided into internal sources (i.e., those within an organization) and external sources (i.e., those outside an organization). The search for secondary data should begin with internal sources since obtaining internal secondary data will require far less time, effort, and money than external secondary data. They may also be more pertinent to the situation being researched.

There is a very wide variety of secondary data sources. One useful way of classifying them is as follows: government sources; syndicated sources; trade associations; miscellaneous sources; and abstracts, directories, and indexes. Each of these categories has distinct features.

Government agencies collect a hugh volume of data, much of which are free and readily accessible. Data offered by syndicated sources are in general more expensive than those offered by government sources, however they may also be more relevant to a research project. Trade associations are good sources of background data about particular trades or professions, although such data may be too general for use by a researcher or unavailable to nonmembers. Miscellaneous sources—journal articles, research monographs, and textbooks—are capable of providing insights, hunches, or ideas pertaining to a research project. Abstracts, directories, and indexes serve as guides in identifying other sources of secondary data; recent technological advances have resulted in computerization of many abstracts, directories, and indexes.

Coping with the variety and abundance of secondary data available today is a major challenge. Effective management of secondary data is essential if maximum benefits are to be derived from them. Systematic procedures for identifying and scanning secondary-data sources and rapidly retrieving required data when needed are the key elements of effective secondary-data management. More and more firms are using information consultants, who specialize in productively utilizing various sources of secondary data.

QUESTIONS

1. "Primary data should be collected only when suitable secondary data are not available." Discuss this statement.
2. What are the three factors that may reduce the relevance of secondary data? Give one example to illustrate each factor.
3. Suppose you have found secondary data that you feel are relevant to a particular problem you are facing. Describe further checks you would make before deciding to use the secondary data.
4. What is the difference between original and secondhand sources of secondary data?
5. "Internal secondary data should only be used when appropriate external secondary data are not available." Do you agree or disagree with this statement? Give reasons for your answer.
6. Discuss the advantages and disadvantages of secondary data obtained from government sources and those obtained from syndicated sources.
7. The inventor of a special type of package material for bread and other baked goods sold through retail outlets wants to estimate the market potential for the material. What specific types of secondary sources should this inventor look into? Why?
8. What does *managing* secondary data mean? Why is it important?
9. Using the appropriate secondary-data source(s), obtain the following information for the standard metropolitan statistical area (SMSA) in which you live or for the SMSA closest to you. For each piece of information, state the source(s) you used and describe any calculations you made.
   a. Number of retail outlets and the annual sales per outlet.
   b. Number of law firms.
   c. Percentage of families with children under 18 years of age.
   d. Identification of the census tracts with the highest and lowest per capita incomes and their geographic locations.
   e. Proportion of the total number of residential housing units that are less than 10 years old.
   f. Proportion of residential housing units with seven or more rooms in (i) the entire SMSA; (ii) the census tract with the highest per capita income; and (iii) the census tract with the lowest per capita income.

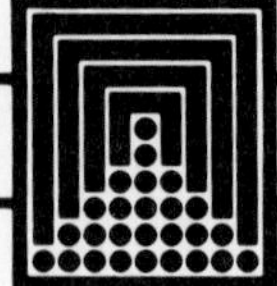

APPENDIX TO CHAPTER 5

External Secondary-Data Sources

As was pointed out in the chapter, listing all potentially valuable external secondary-data sources is impossible. Therefore, this appendix will briefly describe selected sources to illustrate the following categories: government sources; syndicated sources; and abstracts, directories, and indexes. The purpose here is to give you a sense of the nature and the scope of the available sources. The included sources should be of interest to marketing researchers dealing with a variety of situations. However, going through this source list is not a satisfactory substitute for a comprehensive search conducted in a library, preferably with the help of an experienced reference librarian.

GOVERNMENT SOURCES

U.S. Bureau of the Census

Census of Agriculture. This census contains data on farms and farming gathered through censuses taken every five years. Data are reported by state and county and include number and size of farms, farm production and income, farm employment, and characteristics of farm operations.

Census of Government. Conducted every five years, this census contains statistics about state and local governments. Reported data include government operating costs and revenues, number of employees, and size of payroll.

Census of Housing. Conducted every ten years, this census contains a wealth of data about the number and features of households in the United States. Reported data include type of structure, occupancy, number of rooms, and number of appliances. Detailed geographic breakdowns (e.g., by census tracts or city blocks) are provided for standard metropolitan areas. It is updated annually by means of the *Current Housing Report*.

Census of Manufacturers. Conducted every five years, this census provides data for each state under 450 different classes of manufacturing industries. The data include number of establishments in each class, assets, rents, employment, payroll, cost of materials, value of shipments, and capital expenditures. Data are updated by the *Annual Survey of Manufacturers*. Data on some manufactured products are updated more frequently through *Current Industrial Report*. Industry statistics are also arranged by SIC number for convenient referencing.[1]

Census for Mineral Industries. Conducted every five years, this census reports data on about fifty four-digit SIC numeral industries for variables similar to those covered under the Census of Manufacturers.

Census of Population. Conducted every ten years, this census reports population characteristics for states, counties, cities, and towns. More detailed geographic breakdowns are available for standard metropolitan areas. Reported data include age, sex, marital status, race, education level, employment status, family size, income, and occupation. It is updated annually by the *Current Population Report*.

Census of Retail Trade. Conducted every five years, this census reports data by state, standard metropolitan statistical area (SMSA), and areas outside SMSAs for over a hundred types of retail establishments. It includes data on number of outlets, total sales, employment, and payroll. The *Monthly Retail Trade* updates some of these data.

Census of Service Industries. Conducted every five years, this census provides data, similar to those reported by the Census of Retail Trade, for service establishments such as automotive service centers, hotels, and law firms.

Census of Transportation. Conducted every five years, this census provides a variety of travel-related data. It includes three principal types of data: (1) truck inventory and use (e.g., number of vehicles, body type, and major application);

[1] The standard industrial classification (SIC) system was developed by the federal government to classify products, services, and industries. It uses unique code numbers called SIC codes. Many types of data collected by the government and other sources are classified by SIC codes. Details about the SIC system are available in *Standard Industrial Classification Manual* (Washington, D.C.: U.S. Government Printing Office, 1972).

(2) nonlocal passenger travel (e.g., number and characteristics of trips); and (3) commodity shipments (e.g., ton-miles and means of transport).

Census of Wholesale Trade. Conducted every five years, this census contains data on variables such as number of establishments, sales, operating expenses, types of operation, employment, and payroll. Data are reported separately for over one hundred fifty types of wholesaler categories and also are classified by counties and SMSAs. Some of the data are updated by the *Monthly Wholesale Trade.*

County Business Patterns. This census is an annual summary of data on number and types (SIC) of business establishments as well as their employment and taxable payroll. The data are broken down by industry and by county.

Other government sources

Business Statistics. This report is published every other year by the U.S. Department of Commerce. It contains a historical series of data (from the year 1947 to date) on numerous variables monitored monthly by the *Survey of Current Business* (described later) and serves as a supplement to the *Survey of Current Business.*

Economic Indicators. This report is published once a month by the Council of Economic Advisors. It contains the most recent data on economic variables like personal consumption expenses, gross national product, wages, and prices. It is a good source for assessing general economic conditions.

Economic Report of the President. This report is the published version of the speech delivered by the president of the United States to the U.S. Congress regarding the state of the economy. It contains summary tables of economic data gathered by various other agencies.

Statistics of Income. This annual publication of the U.S. Internal Revenue Service consists of a series of three reports: (1) *Corporation Income Tax Returns,* (2) *Business Income Tax Returns,* and (3) *Individual Income Tax Returns.* The three reports contain data derived from tax returns filed by corporations, proprietorships/partnerships, and individuals. The data are broken down by states and SMSAs.

Survey of Current Business. This monthly publication of the Bureau of Economic Affairs of the U.S. Department of Commerce contains data on hundreds of variables related to gross national product, national income, personal income, personal expenditures, government receipts and expenditures, savings and investments, income and employment by industry, and foreign transactions. An annual issue of the *Survey,* called *National Income Issue,* is a valuable source of national income and account statistics.

U.S. Industrial Outlook. This annual publication of the U.S. Department of Commerce presents brief descriptions of and statistics related to recent trends and future projections for more than two hundred different industries. The areas covered include supply and demand, domestic and international developments, employment, and prices.

Government sources of foreign statistics

The U.S. Department of Commerce, the United Nations, and the governments of foreign countries are good sources of international data related to people, markets, and business. Examples of publications from these three types of sources are outlined below.

U.S. Department of Commerce publications. *Foreign Economic Trends and Their Implications for the United States* is a report published semiannually or annually; it is prepared by United States embassies in over a hundred foreign countries. *Overseas Business Reports* is actually a series of reports on individual countries published with varying frequencies by the Domestic and International Business Administration (DIBA) of the Department of Commerce. Many of those reports include data about industry trends, trade regulations, taxes, and the like, and list other sources of economic and commercial data in each country. *International Economic Indicators and Competitive Trends* is published every three months. It provides data on economic trends and indicators for seven leading competitors of the United States: Canada, France, Italy, Japan, the Netherlands, the United Kingdom, and West Germany.

United Nations publications. *World Economic Survey* is published annually and reports data on production and trade in various countries. *Yearbook of International Trade Statistics* reports data on imports and exports of over one hundred countries during the past four years. *World Trade Annual* provides data on international trade, classified according to type of commodity as well as by country. *Statistical Yearbook for Asia and the Pacific* contains statistics related to population characteristics, agriculture, industry, transportation, prices, household expenditures, and other business and social factors. It is organized by country. The United Nations also publishes similar statistical reports for certain other parts of the world, including a compound volume called *Statistical Yearbook* covering all United Nations countries.

Other publications. The Organization of Economic Cooperation and Development publishes a variety of reports, with varying frequency, on 24 member countries. Examples include *Main Economic Indicators, Foreign Trade Statistics*

Bulletins, and *Industrial Production: Historical Statistics*; they are published in Paris. The Statistical Office of the European Communities (EUROSTAT) releases a series of reports (e.g., *General Statistics, Foreign Trade, Monthly Statistics, Industrial Statistics, Yearbook,* and *Social Statistics Annual*) covering nine countries belonging to the European Community. The statistics reported cover a broad range of economic, population, and social variables; the reports are published in Brussels. The government statistical offices of many individual countries (e.g., Canada, Great Britain, and India) collect and publish a variety of statistics on a quarterly, monthly, or weekly basis.

SYNDICATED SOURCES

One useful way of classifying syndicated sources is to group them according to the origin of data reported by them. Marketing research firms typically gather data for their syndicated services from people, retail outlets, wholesalers, or from a combination of units (including various other organizations and publications). Let us label these types of data "consumer data," "retail data," "wholesale data," and "miscellaneous data," respectively. Selected examples of syndicated sources under each of these categories are briefly described below.

Sources of consumer data

National Purchase Diary Panel (NPD). This service is offered by the NPD Research, Inc., of New York. Data are gathered from consumers on some fifty different product categories. The panel contains 13,000 families, representing a broad cross section of the United States. Panel members are asked to keep detailed records about the purchase and use of brands within each of the product categories. A special diary is provided by NPD for this purpose, and panel members mail completed diaries to the firm once a month. Exhibit A.5.1 contains one page from the NPD diary. The richness of the NPD data is evident from the numerous questions asked about each product. Clients subscribing to the NPD service receive tabulations of the diary data, classified by various characteristics of the panel families.

Nielsen Television Index (NTI). Offered by the A. C. Nielsen Company, the NTI provides measures of the relative popularity of television programs. These measures are obtained through an Audimeter, which is an electronic device attached to the television sets of a representative panel of households across the United States. A central computer automatically records the viewing behavior of panel households (e.g., channels viewed and the duration each is viewed). From these measures and the demographic composition of the panel households, the size and the nature of the audience for each television program are reported to clients once every two weeks. Nielsen also has the capability to report audience

Exhibit A.5.1

Sample page from an NPD diary

PAGE 6

CODES FOR SPECIAL OFFERS & PRICES

CODE	COUPON OFFERS	CODE	NON-COUPON OFFERS
01	FROM STORE AD-NEWSPAPER/FLYER	11	CENTS OFF-PRINTED ON PACKAGE
02	FROM MANUFACTURERS NEWSPAPER AD	12	STORE SALE
03	FROM PRIOR PURCHASE OF SAME ITEM	33	BUY ONE GET ONE FREE
04	FROM PURCHASE OF OTHER PRODUCT	13	BONUS SIZE/MORE OF THE SAME FREE
05	RECEIVED IN MAIL	14	GIFT OR PREMIUM ATTACHED TO PACKAGE
06	FROM MAGAZINE	15	DAMAGED OR OPEN CONTAINER
08	DOUBLE/TRIPLE VALUE COUPON	16	OTHER SPECIAL OFFER
09	HANDED OUT AT STORE		
10	SENT FOR COUPON/MAIL-IN OFFER		

NOTE: Free Gifts and Samples on Back Cover.

TOILET TISSUE DIARY TIPS • An individually wrapped roll from the store shelf is **one** package with **one** roll per package. A package containing several rolls is also **one** package. Count and enter the **Number of Rolls per Package.**

TOILET TISSUE

DATE of PURCHASE	BRAND AS SHOWN ON LABEL	HOW MANY OF EACH KIND DID YOU BUY?	SPECIAL OFFER/ SPECIAL PRICE? NO (✓) here	SEE CODES ABOVE. ENTER BELOW ALL CODES THAT APPLY	TOTAL CENTS OFF (if any)	TOTAL CASH PAID (AFTER CENTS OFF) $	¢	WHERE PURCHASED? NAME of STORE or COMPANY	STORE TYPE: GROCERY OR FOOD	OTHER Write in	NUMBER OF ROLLS PER PACKAGE	NUMBER OF SHEETS PER ROLL	NUMBER OF PLIES	COLORS OR PLAIN (✓) One: ALL WHITE	SOLID COLOR	PRINT OR DESIGN	IF NOT ALL WHITE, WRITE IN COLORS: IF SOLID COLOR WHAT COLOR IS IT?	IF PRINT OR DESIGN: WHAT COLOR IS THE DESIGN?	WHAT COLOR IS BACKGROUND?

FACIAL TISSUE

FACIAL TISSUE DIARY TIPS • Include purchases made by family members for use at the office or on business trips or at school.

NUMBER OF SHEETS PER BOX OR PACKET	NUMBER OF PLIES	IF HANKY OR POCKET SIZE, NO. OF PACKETS PER PACKAGE	DESCRIBE HERE WHETHER ITEM IS IN COLORS OR PLAIN (✓) One: ALL WHITE	SOLID COLOR: SINGLE SOLID COLOR IN 1 BOX	MIXED SOLID COLORS IN 1 BOX	PRINT OR DESIGN	IF NOT ALL WHITE, WRITE IN COLORS: IF SOLID COLOR WHAT COLOR IS IT?	IF PRINT OR DESIGN: WHAT COLOR IS BACKGROUND?	WHAT COLOR IS THE DESIGN?	MANUFACTURER'S CODE WRITE IN ALL NUMBERS OF THIS 6 OR 10 DIGIT CODE IF AVAILABLE (Example: 54000 85300)

PAPER TOWELS

Include: Roll Towels, Flat Towels, and All-Purpose Cleaning Cloths

TOWELS AND ALL PURPOSE CLEANING CLOTHS DIARY TIPS • An individually wrapped roll from the store shelf is **one** roll per package. A package containing two or more rolls is also **one** package. Count and enter the **Number of Rolls per package** • The label should tell you the number of towels or sheets, whether a purchase is in rolls or in package or other containers.

• Include purchases made for picnics, trips, etc.

(✓) One: TOWELS	ALL-PURPOSE CLEANING CLOTHS	IF IN ROLLS (Write In): NUMBER ROLLS PER PACKAGE	NUMBER SHEETS PER ROLL	NUMBER OF PLIES	IF NOT IN ROLLS: NUMBER OF TOWELS OR SHEETS	COLORS OR PLAIN (✓) One: ALL WHITE	SOLID COLOR	PRINT OR DESIGN: DESIGN ON BORDER ONLY	DESIGN ON FULL SHEET	IF NOT ALL WHITE, WRITE IN COLORS: IF SOLID COLOR WHAT COLOR IS IT?	IF PRINT OR DESIGN: WHAT COLOR IS BACKGROUND?	WHAT COLOR IS THE DESIGN?

PAPER NAPKINS

PAPER NAPKIN DIARY TIPS • If a label does not say what meal the napkin is for, just write in "Not on label" under the column headed **Type of Napkin.** • Don't forget purchases made for picnics, barbecues, trips,etc.

NUMBER OF NAPKINS PER PACKAGE	TYPE OF NAPKIN (✓) One: LUNCHEON	DINNER	OTHER	NUMBER OF PLIES (✓) One: ONE PLY	TWO PLY	THREE OR MORE PLY	DESCRIBE HERE WHETHER ITEM IS IN COLORS OR PLAIN (✓) One: ALL WHITE	SOLID COLOR: SINGLE SOLID COLOR IN PKG	MIXED SOLID COLORS IN PKG	PRINT OR DESIGN	IF NOT ALL WHITE, WRITE IN COLORS: IF SOLID COLOR WHAT COLOR IS IT?	IF PRINT OR DESIGN: WHAT COLOR IS BACKGROUND?	WHAT COLOR IS THE DESIGN?

Source: NPD Research, Inc., 900 West Shore Road, Port Washington, N.Y. 11050. Used by permission.

measures directly to clients through terminals installed at the clients' locations. These direct reports are available within a day after a particular program is aired.

Arbitron Radio Market Reports. These reports contain measures of radio station audiences in predetermined geographic areas, or markets, across the United States. These markets are surveyed periodically by the Arbitron Company. A representative sample of households in each market is asked to maintain a diary, through which basic listening and demographic data are collected. Listenership data for each radio station are tabulated by 21 different age/sex groups. The Arbitron Company also offers *Arbitron Television Market Reports* for the various geographic markets it covers. The television market reports are based on data obtained through consumer diaries as well as an electronic device (called the Arbitron Television Meter System) attached to television sets in the sample households.

Starch Readership Reports. These reports are a syndicated service offered by Starch INRA Hooper, Inc. The reports provide measures of exposure to print ads in over ninety consumer, business, trade, and professional magazines and newspapers. Each report is based on data obtained from about one hundred people, carefully chosen to represent the readership of the publications being studied. Copies of the publications are shown to the respondents, who are asked to report their degree of exposure to the advertisement being researched. The respondents are grouped into three exposure categories: (1) noted reader, or a person who remembered seeing the ad; (2) associated reader, or a noted reader who also saw or read some part of the ad that clearly indicated the brand or advertiser; and (3) read most reader, or a person who read half or more of the written material in the ad. The reports also provide tabulations of the responses by demographic characteristics such as age, sex, occupation, and income. Each year the *Starch Readership Reports* cover over 75,000 advertisements appearing in about 1000 individual issues.

MRI Mediamarketing Service. Offered by the Mediamark Research, Inc., of New York, this syndicated service provides general audience measures of over two hundred publications as well as certain broadcast media. The MRI data are collected through two waves of personal interviews a year. In each wave a representative sample of 10,000 people are interviewed about their media exposure habits and their use of various products and services. Therefore the MRI reports provide useful information about the personal characteristics of media audiences and their purchase behavior.

Simmons Media/Marketing Service. This service, provided by the Simmons Market Research Bureau, Inc., also provides data on the media and purchase habits of consumers. The data are collected from a national sample of 15,000

METHOD B: At the conclusion of the special promotion, conduct a telephone survey of residents in the store's trading area to ascertain whether they visited the store during the promotional period, and, if so, what their reactions and responses were to the special display.

METHOD C: Same as Method B, except that instead of conducting a telephone survey, mail questionnaires to a sample of residents, along with stamped return envelopes for sending back completed questionnaires.

METHOD D: Hire someone to observe customers and record their reactions as they pass by the special display. Ask the observer to record such things as whether customers stop to look at the display, how long they spend at the display, how interested they appear to be in it, and so on.

METHOD E: Videotape the area where Kwality brand shirts are featured so as to generate a continuous record of customer reactions and behavior as they approach and pass by the special display.

METHOD F: Program the store's electronic cash registers to automatically keep track of the total number of Kwality brand men's shirts sold during the promotional period.

Methods A, B, and C involve questioning customers, while methods D, E, and F involve observing customers or their purchases. *Questioning* and *observation* are the two broad approaches available for collecting primary data. Numerous variations of these approaches are available, some of which are illustrated by methods A through F. Several other forms of questioning and observation will be discussed subsequently. The key distinction between the two basic approaches stems from the role potential respondents play in the data collection process. In the questioning approach respondents play an active role because of their interaction or communication with the researcher. Indeed, some textbooks label the questioning approach as the communication approach, to distinguish it from observation, in which respondents do not directly interact or communicate with the researcher.[1]

The use of the term *questioning approach* rather than *questionnaire approach* in the foregoing discussion is deliberate, because not all questioning or interviewing situations involve the use of formal questionnaires. Stated differently, a questionnaire is simply a tool that is used in many, but not all, research projects employing questioning. For instance, while a large-scale consumer survey invariably requires a formal questionnaire, an informal interview of a few knowledgeable persons does not, despite the fact that both fall under the questioning approach.

The various questioning and observation methods are not necessarily restricted to certain types of research. Chapter 4 described three major research

---

[1] See, for example, Gilbert A. Churchill, Jr., *Marketing Research: Methodological Foundations,* 3rd ed. (New York: Dryden Press, 1983), p. 173.

types: exploratory, descriptive, and experimental, where the latter two are forms of conclusive research. Either of the two data collection methodologies can be used in any of these research types. To illustrate, consider methods A through F for the Kwality Knitware case. Methods similar to each of these can be employed in *any* of the following types of research:

- Exploratory research. Management wants to gain some initial insights about the effectiveness of the special point-of-purchase display. Initial insights can be obtained by gathering data through questioning or observation (in a fairly informal and flexible fashion) from just one or a few stores.
- Descriptive research. Management wants information of a specific nature, such as, What types of customers are attracted to the special display? How do customers who purchase Kwality shirts during the special promotion differ from those who do not? This information can be generated by simply making the data collection process more formal and specific and by collecting data from a larger, more representative sample of stores.
- Experimental research. Management wants to know if the special display *causes* a significant impact on customer perceptions and purchases of Kwality shirts. This research question can be answered by collecting data under more controlled conditions than exist in the previous (descriptive-research) setting. For instance, data on customer reactions and purchases can be gathered from a sufficiently large, representative sample of stores having the special display (i.e., an experimental group) and of stores not having the special display (i.e., a control group).

Thus while the formality/flexibility of the data collection process, the nature of the sample, and the conditions under which data are collected vary from exploratory to descriptive to experimental research, the same basic data collection methods can be used under each. The next section examines the relative advantages and limitations of questioning and observation.

QUESTIONING VERSUS OBSERVATION

To put the discussion in this section into proper perspective, we must mention at the outset a couple of points concerning questioning and observation. First, the two approaches are not necessarily *substitutes*. Each has certain unique capabilities—and, in fact, the two are used as complementary approaches in some research projects. Second, although each approach has certain advantages over the other (as will be discussed shortly), those advantages may not hold true in every situation calling for primary-data collection. In other words, neither approach is likely to be always better than the other along each criterion on which we will be comparing the approaches.

Versatility

A major advantage of the questioning approach is its versatility in terms of the types of data it is capable of generating. The observation approach, by definition, is limited to collecting data about visible characteristics or variables. For example, the amount of time a customer spends looking at the special display for Kwality shirts can be recorded by human observers (method D) or by videotaping equipment (method E). But one cannot observe very well whether the customer is impressed, disappointed, annoyed, or whatever, during the time he or she is looking at the display. In contrast, any of the questioning methods (A, B, or C) can be used to ascertain how the customer felt about the display. In short, observation can provide data only on overt characteristics and behavior. By contrast, direct questioning can shed light on overt variables and also provide data on respondents' feelings, motives, intentions, and other unobservable variables.

Time and cost

The questioning approach usually also has an edge over observation in terms of the time and cost needed for data collection, because a researcher will have much more flexibility in the data collection process when data are collected through questioning. In the Kwality Knitware case the researcher will have some latitude in data collection in each of the three questioning methods—personal interviews (method A), telephone interviews (method B), or mail survey (method C). Therefore these methods can be scheduled in such a way as to generate the needed data efficiently. In contrast, employing a human observer (method D) or using videotaping (method E) is likely to be time-consuming and expensive. The observer and videotaping equipment will not be recording anything relevant when there are no customers in the special-display area. This unproductive observation, in addition to prolonging the duration of data collection, will also have to be paid for.

What about the relative data collection efficiency of method F, namely, programming the electronic cash registers to keep track of Kwality shirt sales during the promotional period? This method is not likely to be more time-consuming and expensive than the various questionnaire methods because the total sales of Kwality brand shirts can simply be read from the cash registers with relatively little effort or expense. An important implication emerges here: *Not all* observation methods may be more expensive and time-consuming than questioning methods in a given situation. Alternatively, the questioning approach is usually, but not always, more efficient in terms of data collection speed and cost.

Method F, however, has one limitation that may nullify its data collection efficiency: The only type of data method F can generate is the sales of Kwality brand shirts. Hence it will be inadequate if Kwality Knitware's management wants richer data—such as the data capable of being generated through observation methods D and E—about customers' reactions and behavior in response to the special display.

Data accuracy

Data accuracy—that is, the extent to which the collected data are error-free and trustworthy—is crucial from a managerial standpoint since it can significantly influence the soundness of decisions based on marketing research. Inaccurate data can be misleading and do more harm than good. How does the questioning approach compare with observation in terms of data accuracy? The answer depends somewhat on the characteristics of a specific research project, including its purpose and data requirements.

To illustrate, suppose Kwality Knitware's management is interested in determining the impact of the special display on sales of Kwality brand shirts. Questioning customers about their reactions to the display and their purchases of Kwality brand shirts may not produce accurate data. For one thing, respondents may be unable to accurately recall their reactions and purchases, especially in the case of a mail survey (method C) owing to the time lag involved. For another, respondents may be unwilling to reveal their true reactions or purchases; if so, they may refuse to answer questions or, worse still, give erroneous answers.

Respondents' inability or unwillingness to provide accurate data will not be a problem, though, if an appropriate observation method is used. For instance, management can accurately assess the sales impact of the special display by programming the cash registers to observe sales (method F) in an experimental group of stores having the special display and in a comparable control group of stores not having the display.

In summary, when the *same type* of data (e.g., sales of Kwality brand shirts or number of customers who saw the special display for those shirts) can be obtained through questioning and through observation, the latter will generally yield more accurate data. Since respondents do not directly interact with researchers in the observation approach, data distortions stemming from respondents are minimized. In other words, to the extent that the observation approach does not involve verbal or written answers from respondents, it is likely to produce more accurate data than the questioning approach.

Bear in mind, however, that the subjectivity or the carelessness of an observer may lead to inaccuracies in observational studies. For instance, in method D the observer may see a customer viewing the display for several minutes and infer that the customer is impressed by the display, when in actuality the customer may be frowning at the display out of annoyance. Just as interviewers may bias data collected through questioning, observers may cause inaccuracies in observational data. Furthermore, as was pointed out earlier, observation cannot provide accurate data on perceptions, motives, attitudes, or other inner feelings of people.

Respondent convenience

By and large, observation studies will be more convenient from the respondent's standpoint and hence are superior in terms of gaining the respondent's cooperation during data collection. This conclusion follows from the fact that respondents do not actively participate in the data collection in observation studies. The few exceptions where observation studies may be somewhat inconvenient to respondents involve situations in which they have to go to a particular place at a particular time to participate in a study (more will be said about such studies later).

In summary, a major limitation of the observation method is its inability to generate data about variables that are not visible. The questioning method is more versatile in this regard and, hence, is more widely used in practice.[2] Another drawback of the observation method is that an observer will typically have to wait for relevant events or behavior to occur. Therefore, it is likely to involve more time and expense. A key strength of observation studies, however, is that they are likely to provide more accurate data since distortions stemming from respondents will be much lower than in studies employing the questioning approach. Moreover, the absence of direct respondent participation in the data collection makes the observation method more convenient to respondents and minimizes the need to secure their cooperation—a significant hurdle in most studies involving questioning of respondents. Therefore observation appears to be the preferable method if the required data can be obtained through either of the two basic methodologies. Exhibit 6.1 lays out a simple framework to help one in choosing between them.

In some research settings, however, a combination of the two methods can be used. For instance, in method D (involving human observation) in the Kwality Knitware case, the observer can first unobtrusively record a customer's reactions to the display. Immediately after the customer leaves the display area, the observer can conduct a personal interview with him or her to obtain additional data and to verify the observer's interpretation of the customer's reactions. Of course, well-trained observer-interviewers, as well as adequate time and monetary resources, will be necessary for such an approach to be beneficial. Resources permitting, the observation-questioning combination may yield more valuable insights than either one used independently.[3]

---

[2] Since questionnaire studies apparently dominate the marketing research field, researchers may not even consider observation as an option. For a discussion highlighting the potential capabilities of observation and emphasizing the overuse of questionnaires, see Michael L. Ray, *Unobtrusive Marketing Research Techniques* (Cambridge, Mass.: Marketing Science Institute, 1973).

[3] For further elaboration of the importance and benefits of using multiple data collection methods see Ray, *Unobtrusive Marketing;* see also Eugene J. Webb, Donald T. Campbell, Richard D. Schwartz, and Lee Sechrest, *Unobtrusive Measures: Nonreactive Research in the Social Sciences.* (Chicago: Rand McNally, 1966), Chap. 7.

Exhibit 6.1

Choosing between the questioning and observation approaches

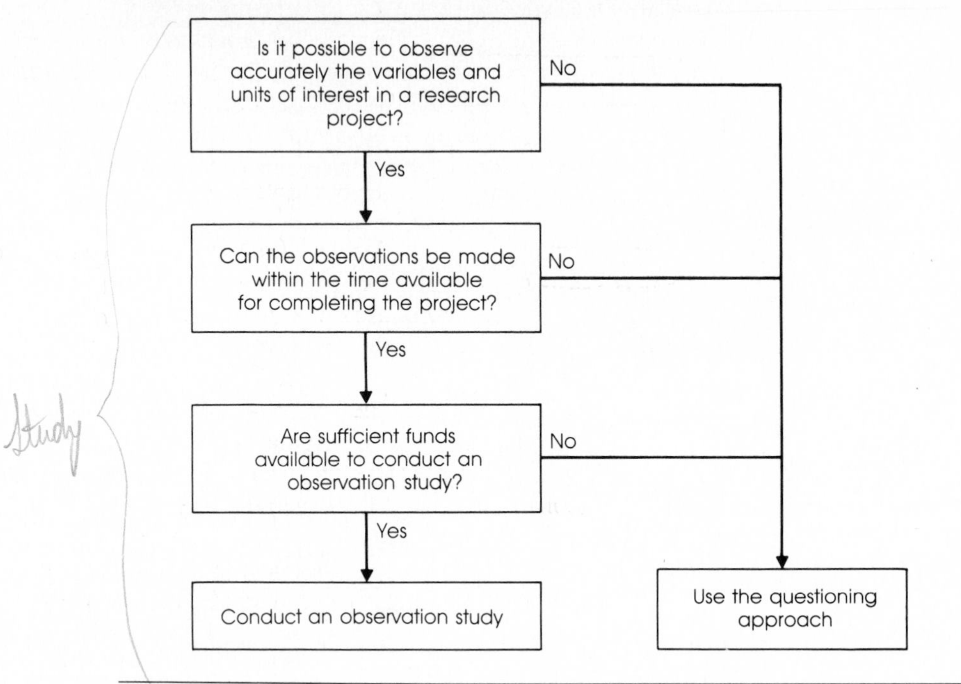

QUESTIONNAIRE FORMAT

Questioning respondents is sometimes done informally, with no questionnaire to guide the interviewing process. In many instances, however, a questionnaire—at least in the form of a checklist of items to be covered during an interview—is used. Our discussion in this section will therefore focus on questionnaires and their variations, although many of the concepts to be covered are germane to questioning in general.

A questionnaire can vary in *format* as well as in terms of *how it is administered.* We will first examine format; in the next section we will examine administration. Questionnaire format is a function of the amount of structure and disguise desired during data collection.

Structure

A question presented verbatim to every respondent and with fixed response categories is a *completely structured question.* The following question is an example:

What are the strengths of Ivory soap in comparison with Dial soap? (Please check as many categories as apply.)

__________Costs less.

__________Lasts longer.

__________Smells better.

__________Produces more lather.

__________Comes in more convenient sizes.

At the other extreme is the *completely nonstructured question,* one that is not necessarily presented in exactly the same wording to every respondent and does not have fixed responses. For instance, instructing an interviewer to "probe a respondent's perceptions of Ivory's strengths relative to Dial" is tantamount to using a completely nonstructured question—one that is very flexible from the standpoint of both the interviewer and the respondent.

Questions characterized by varying degrees of structure between the two extremes are also possible. Thus more flexible versions of the completely structured question presented earlier can be designed as illustrated next.

VERSION 1: Providing one or more open-ended categories, in addition to the fixed response categories already included:

What are the strengths of Ivory soap in comparison with Dial soap? (Please check as many categories as apply.)

__________Costs less.

__________Lasts longer.

__________Smells better.

__________Produces more lather.

__________Comes in more convenient sizes.

__________Other__________ (please specify).

__________Other__________ (please specify).

VERSION 2: Presenting the trunk of the question verbatim to every respondent but allowing a completely open-ended or free response:

What are the strengths of Ivory soap in comparison with Dial soap?________

____

____

____

These two versions are more frequently used than the two extremes in questionnaire studies. Moreover, in practice, a typical structured question is similar to version 1, and a typical nonstructured question (also known as an open-ended question) is similar to version 2.

What are the relative advantages and drawbacks of structuring questions? We can compare structured and nonstructured questions on the same dimensions we used to compare the questioning and observation methods—namely, versatility, time, cost, accuracy, and respondent convenience. Table 6.1 provides such a comparison.

Structured questions have an overall edge over nonstructured questions with respect to speed and cost of data collection and analysis, and convenience to respondents. However, the inflexibility of structured questions makes them inappropriate for studies whose primary purpose is to generate new ideas (i.e.,

Table 6.1

Advantages and disadvantages of structured questions relative to nonstructured questions

EVALUATION CRITERIA	ADVANTAGES OF STRUCTURED QUESTIONS	DISADVANTAGES OF STRUCTURED QUESTIONS
Versatility	Can be used to study diverse populations; literacy levels and communication skills of respondents not as critical as for nonstructured questions More topics/issues can be covered in interview/questionnaire of given length	Not as good in providing new insights/ideas as nonstructured questions Cannot obtain in-depth or detailed responses
Time	Less time to respond as well as to record responses Collected data can be quickly transferred to computer memory for analysis; in some studies recording coded responses directly into computer terminals as interview is taking place may be possible	May take more time to design, unless researcher has clear idea of what to ask and what specific responses to expect
Cost	Cheaper since interviewer time and skill levels required to record and interpret data are usually lower than for nonstructured questions	
Accuracy	Less chance of interviewer and respondent errors in recording answers	No guarantee that checked responses fully and/or truly reflect respondents' intended answers
Respondent convenience	More convenient to respondents in terms of time needed to respond and ease of responding	

exploratory research). Moreover, the accuracy or objectivity of data collected through structured questions will not be high unless all potential answers to a question are unambiguously implied by the precoded response categories.

The limitations of structured questions offer a clue about the circumstances in which they will be appropriate. Structured questions are likely to be most suitable in a situation where (1) uncovering new ideas is *not* the main objective and (2) the researcher has a good feel for the range and types of responses so that meaningful and valid response categories can be constructed. A research setting likely to possess these two features is one where the research purpose and data requirements are clear, from preliminary research results or relevant past experience, and hence the need is for research of a conclusive nature. This inference is also consistent with our discussion in Chapter 4 concerning differences in the nature of data collection in exploratory- and conclusive-research projects (see Table 4.2 in Chapter 4).

In short, the degree of finality of a research project will have a direct bearing on the extent of questionnaire structure. The more conclusive the research, the more structured the questionnaire can be. Likewise, the more exploratory the research, the more nonstructured the questionnaire can, or perhaps should, be. Nonstructured questionnaires are ideal for exploratory-research projects not only because they have insight-generating potential but also because the time and cost drawbacks are mitigated somewhat by the small sample sizes and, hence, the low volume of collected data.

We now turn to the second determinant of questionnaire format, namely, disguise.

Disguise

A *disguised question* is an indirect question whose true purpose is not obvious to respondents. Disguised questions are used to examine issues for which direct questions may not elicit truthful answers. Using direct questions to investigate sensitive topics or topics that may be embarrassing to respondents will most likely yield data of questionable accuracy. Consider the following direct, or nondisguised, question:

> Would you buy a cheap brand of liquor and serve it from a bottle from an expensive brand to impress your guests?
>
> ________Yes ________No

As you might expect, respondents who practice the deception described by this question will prefer not to answer it.[4] But since refusing to answer may be interpreted as a yes response, they will invariably be tempted to answer no.

[4] Further discussion of this topic can be found, for example, in Claire Selltiz, Lawrence S. Wrightsman, and Stuart W. Cook, *Research Methods in Social Relations* (New York: Holt, Rinehart and Winston, 1976).

Indeed, to obtain valid data about the number of respondents who engage in the practice described in the question may be impossible.

However, a useful surrogate measure of respondents' feelings toward the practice can be obtained by asking a disguised question like the following one:

> Would people you associate with buy a cheap brand of liquor and serve it from a bottle from an expensive brand to impress their guests?
>
> __________Yes __________No

This question may be more acceptable to respondents than the direct question, and answers to it may provide a more accurate measure of respondents' own inclinations toward serving cheap liquor out of bottles from expensive brands.

In general, disguised questions are preferable when respondent resistance to direct questions is likely to be high. However, constructing suitable disguised questions and properly interpreting the responses require special skills and training in such areas as psychology and psychoanalysis. Therefore, using disguised questions can become quite expensive if it is to be done correctly.

Types of questionnaires

The degree of finality of a research project and the amount of expected respondent resistance to direct questions about the issues to be examined determine the types of questions to be used. From these two characteristics, four broad categories of questionnaire formats can be identified, as shown in Table 6.2. They are structured, nondisguised; nonstructured, nondisguised; nonstructured, disguised; and structured, disguised. Each type is discussed next.

Structured, nondisguised questionnaires. Structured, nondisguised questionnaires are widely used in marketing research studies, especially those involving large sample sizes. Structured, nondisguised questionnaires have all the advantages of structuring we saw earlier. They are especially appropriate for

Table 6.2
Determinants of questionnaire format

DEGREE OF FINALITY OF RESEARCH	EXPECTED RESPONDENT RESISTANCE TO DIRECT QUESTIONS	
	Low	High
High	Structured, nondisguised questionnaire	Structured, disguised questionnaire
Low	Nonstructured, nondisguised questionnaire	Nonstructured, disguised questionnaire

descriptive-research studies where the issues to be examined are clear-cut and there is no need for any disguise.[5]

Exhibit 6.2 contains two sample pages from a structured, nondisguised questionnaire used by the Bankers Life and Casualty Company in a mail survey of new buyers of auto, homeowners', and renters' insurance. Several aspects of the partial questionnaire in Exhibit 6.2 illustrate key points made earlier. First, the questions have prespecified response categories. However, notice that question 4 and the "Other" category in questions 2 and 7 are open-ended; but since they can be answered with very few words, the questionnaire is essentially structured. In fact, it is not unusual for a typical structured questionnaire to have a few open-ended items. Second, since the questions and the response categories are straightforward, the questionnaire is likely to be quite convenient and easy to answer for a wide variety of respondents. Third, preparing the collected data for analysis will also be quite easy and fast. Notice the numbers printed beside each response category. These numbers facilitate rapid coding of the responses after the questionnaires are returned. Numbers within parentheses refer to the computer record positions in which responses to the corresponding questions are to be stored; numbers without parentheses are the code numbers corresponding to the various responses. For instance, if a respondent answered no to question 6, position 15 of his or her computer record would be assigned a 2.

Nonstructured, nondisguised questionnaires. The flexibility and the directness of nonstructured, nondisguised questionnaires make them ideally suited for situations in which a researcher wants to give respondents a free hand in providing information. Hence the nonstructured, nondisguised format is very popular in exploratory-research projects involving personal interviews. In many such instances the questionnaire merely consists of a checklist of relevant issues to be covered, and the interviewer is free to change the wording as well as sequencing of the issues so as to make the interview flow smoothly and naturally. The main idea is to let respondents provide as much information, in as unrestricted a fashion, as possible. Interviews of this nature are appropriately called *depth* (or sometimes *in-depth*) *interviews.*

Depth interviews are much more common than structured interviews in industrial marketing research surveys.[6] According to J. M. Smith, in these surveys,

> the respondents, unlike those in consumer market research, are usually experts holding senior managerial posts in business or industry. Such people do not react at all favorably to the rigidity of a formal, structured interview. It has been found from experience that most expert respondents have a story to

[5] For an elaboration on the pros and cons of structured, nondisguised questionnaires, see Selltiz, Wrightsman, and Cook, *Research Methods in Social Relations.*

[6] William E. Cox, Jr., *Industrial Marketing Research* (New York: Wiley, 1979), p. 245.

Exhibit 6.2

Structured, nondisguised questionnaire

BANKERS MULTIPLE LINE/BANKERS LIFE AND CASUALTY
NEW POLICYOWNER ATTITUDE SURVEY QUESTIONNAIRE

(1-4)
(5)

Throughout this questionnaire you will see questions asking about "Bankers". These questions are about *both* Bankers Life and Casualty *and* Bankers Multiple Line.

1. **How long have you been a Bankers policyowner?**

	(6)	
I am a new policyowner	☐	1
Less than one year	☐	2
One year or more, but less than five	☐	3
Five years or more	☐	4

2. **The following question asks about the types of insurance coverage you now own.**
   A. In Column A please check the type(s) of policy (or policies) you just purchased from Bankers.
   B. In Column B please check each type of policy you already owned from Bankers.
   C. In Column C please check each type of group coverage you have (at work, or elsewhere).
   D. In Column D please check each type of policy you own with other companies. (Aside from group coverage).

	A. New Policy	B. Other Bankers Policies	C. Group Coverage	D. Other Policies	
	(7)	(8)	(9)	(10)	
Life	☐	☐	☐	☐	1
Health	☐	☐	☐	☐	2
Annuity	☐	☐	☐	☐	3
Auto	☐	☐	☐	☐	4
Homeowner/Renters	☐	☐	☐	☐	5
Disability Income	☐	☐	☐	☐	6
Other? ________	☐	☐	☐	☐	7

unfold about some aspect of the subject of the survey. This "story" is usually very valuable and it should not be suppressed because of the limits imposed by the precoded question.[7]

For example, recall the industrial marketing research project conducted for the Wayne Engineering Corporation (the garbage packer manufacturer) that was

[7] Joan Macfarlane Smith, *Interviewing in Market and Social Research* (London: Routledge & Kegan Paul, 1972), p. 142.

3. **Did your new Bankers policy replace a policy you had before?** (11)

Yes ☐ 1   No ☐ 2

4. **From what company did you purchase your old policy?** ______________ (12-13)

I did not have this coverage before. ☐ 99

5. **How long ago did you purchase your old policy?** (14)

Within the last two years	☐ 1
Two to five years ago	☐ 2
Over five years ago	☐ 3
I did not have this coverage before	☐ 4

6. **Had you heard of Bankers before buying your new policy?**

	(15)
Yes	☐ 1
No	☐ 2
Don't Recall	☐ 3

7. **Based on your knowledge of Bankers, by reputation or personal experience, how would you rate it in each of these areas:**

	Above Average 1	Average 2	Below Average 3	Don't Know 4	
Financially sound	☐	☐	☐	☐	(16)
A large, well known company	☐	☐	☐	☐	(17)
Offers good policies at reasonable cost	☐	☐	☐	☐	(18)
Has competent, well trained agents	☐	☐	☐	☐	(19)
Answers inquiries promptly and fully	☐	☐	☐	☐	(20)
Pays claims promptly and fairly	☐	☐	☐	☐	(21)
Serves the needs of senior citizens	☐	☐	☐	☐	(22)
Serves the needs of families	☐	☐	☐	☐	(23)
Other__________	☐	☐	☐	☐	(24)

Source: Marketing Research Department, Bankers Life and Casualty Company, 1000 Sunset Ridge Road, Northbrook, Ill. 60062. Used by permission.

described in Chapter 3. Personal interviews in this project were conducted without the aid of a formal questionnaire; the consultant only had a list of issues to be discussed during each interview. After raising a particular issue, the consultant simply listened and took notes while the respondent did most of the talking.

A variation of the depth interview is the focus group interview, involving the simultaneous interviewing of a group of respondents. Several examples of research projects using focus group interviews were presented in earlier chapters.

For instance, in Chapter 4 we saw how AT&T employed focus group interviews to gain insights about the communication needs of nonprofit organizations. Focus group interviewing is so widely used that a detailed discussion of it is presented in the next chapter. We will therefore not elaborate on it here.

Nonstructured, disguised questionnaires. Nonstructured, disguised questionnaires are primarily used in so-called motivation research studies. "Motivation research is a phase of marketing research which attempts to answer the question, 'Why?' . . . Motivation research seeks to relate behavior to underlying processes such as people's desires, emotions, and intentions."[8] Consumers are at times unable or unwilling to reveal their true reasons for buying a particular product or reacting in a certain way to a marketing stimulus. That is, consumers may consciously or unconsciously try to suppress their motives.

For instance, a socially upscale man who is motivated to buy his clothes from a discount store because of cost considerations will be very reluctant to discuss his purchases. A woman who does all her cooking from scratch because she feels "good" women should do so may be unwilling to reveal her true motives for fear of being labeled "old-fashioned." In situations like these a direct-questioning approach is likely to lead to either no responses or less-than-truthful responses. What is needed is a procedure in which a person can feel uninhibited enough to describe freely (i.e., in a nonstructured fashion) his or her inner feelings, by projecting them onto a setting that supposedly is unrelated to the respondent (i.e., disguised). Such nonstructured, disguised questioning procedures are called *projective techniques.*

Although different types of projective techniques are available, they all share two common features: (1) A fairly ambiguous stimulus is presented to respondents, and (2) in reacting to or describing the stimulus, the respondents will indirectly reveal their own inner feelings.[9] Examples of projective techniques used in marketing research include the word association test, the sentence completion test, the thematic apperception test (commonly referred to as TAT), and the cartoon test. We will briefly examine each of these.

The stimulus in *word association tests* is a list containing anywhere from just a few to over a hundred words of interest mixed in with somewhat irrelevant or neutral words designed to preserve the disguised nature of the study. For instance, a list in a study dealing with home computers may include relevant words such as prestige, bookkeeping, and video games as well as neutral words such as cooking, exercise, furniture, and newspapers. Word association tests can be especially useful in uncovering people's feelings about new products or services, brand names (recall from Chapter 1 that Ford Motor Company used

---

[8] George Horsley Smith, *Motivation Research in Advertising and Marketing* (New York: McGraw-Hill, 1954), p. 3.

[9] The concept of projection, which is the key to any projective technique, is actually quite complex and has been given differing shades of meanings in the psychology literature; for a discussion of this issue, see Boris Semeonoff, *Projective Techniques* (New York: Wiley, 1976), Chap. 2.

word association tests in evaluating the name Edsel), and key words being considered for use in advertising copy or other promotional materials.

In a typical word association test the words are read aloud, one at a time, to each respondent. The respondent is asked to say the first word that comes to mind as soon as each stimulus word is presented. Interpretation of the responses is not easy. It is based on several factors and includes analyzing the meanings of the response words, the overall nature of responses given by each respondent, the patterns of responses across respondents, the time taken to respond to each stimulus word, and the physical reactions of respondents.[10]

A *sentence completion test* involves asking respondents to finish a set of incomplete sentences. Each incomplete sentence consists of a few words related to or neutral to the topic being researched, followed by a blank space for the response. To illustrate, a study dealing with people's inner feelings toward labor unions may contain the following sentences:

The American worker______________________________.

Belonging to a labor union__________________________.

Labor costs in the United States______________________.

Management and labor______________________________.

Production efficiency______________________________.

Sentence completion tests are typically given to groups of respondents who are asked to finish the sentences in writing. Neither the time taken to respond to each item nor the respondents' physical reactions are monitored, as they are in word association tests. Hence sentence completion tests are easier to administer.[11] Moreover, they allow researchers greater flexibility to give direction to the stimuli so that the responses obtained are more likely to be associated with the subject matter under study. In contrast, word association tests, by pressuring respondents to react quickly to single words, may lead to answers that are hard to interpret. However, there is a price for the greater flexibility and ease of administration of sentence completion tests: The respondents can think through their answers, and therefore the information obtained is limited to what each respondent is *willing* to divulge.

The *thematic apperception test* (TAT) was first developed by Henry A. Murray to measure personality.[12] The original TAT consisted of a set of 20 cards with

[10] Detailed discussion of the analysis and the interpretation of responses to word association tests, as well as to other projective techniques, is beyond the scope of this textbook. However, several books on motivation research that treat this topic in detail are available; see, for example, Smith, *Motivation Research*.

[11] For further details about the comparison between administration of word association tests and administration of sentence completion tests, see Paul G. Datson, "Word Associations and Sentence Completion Techniques," in *Projective Techniques in Personality Assessment,* ed. A. I. Rabin (New York: Springer, 1968), pp. 264–289.

[12] Henry A. Murray, *Explorations in Personality* (New York: Oxford University Press, 1938).

pictures printed on them. However, adaptations of the TAT have since been developed for special groups such as children.[13] In a typical administration of the TAT, the respondent is shown each picture for a short period (about 20 seconds) and is asked to write a story about it in 20 minutes or so. The respondent is specifically asked to describe such things as what is happening in the picture, why it is happening, and what the feelings of the characters in the picture are. These stories are interpreted by specially trained analysts to ascertain the respondent's personality. The TAT can be administered individually or in groups.[14]

Adaptations of the TAT have been employed in marketing research by using pictures specifically designed for the research topic. To illustrate, in a study of attitudes toward magazine reading, "a picture was included which showed a family sitting in a living room reading. In making up stories for this picture, respondents revealed many of their views about magazines, the family and home, what the husband reads, what the wife reads, and so on."[15] Other possible applications of TAT techniques in marketing research include the evaluation of pictures being considered for use in advertisements, in promotional brochures, and in product packaging.

A *cartoon test* (sometimes also known as a *balloon test*) is another pictorial technique like the TAT. The stimuli in cartoon tests are line drawings such as the one shown in Exhibit 6.3. The cartoon in Exhibit 6.3 can, for instance, be used to gain insight into housewives' attitudes toward home computers.

The respondent in a cartoon test is asked to examine the stimulus picture and fill in the empty "balloons" with words reflecting thoughts or verbal statements of the characters involved. Unlike the stories required in a TAT, responses to a cartoon test are limited and specific. Therefore the time needed to respond as well as the volume of responses to be analyzed should be less. Cartoon tests have been used in a number of marketing research projects, including one conducted by State Farm to determine customer perceptions about automobile insurance promoted with a price appeal.[16]

The tests described so far by no means exhaust the variety of projective techniques that can be, and are being, used in marketing research. For instance, Child Research Services (CRS), a division of McCollum/Spielman Associates, Inc., employs a number of projective techniques in researching children. According to CRS:

> A variety of projective children's games are used in service of a particular client's needs. These include charades, sentence completions and word asso-

[13] Charles Neuringer, "A Variety of Thematic Methods," in *Projective Techniques in Personality Assessment,* ed. A. I. Rabin (New York: Springer, 1968), pp. 222–261.
[14] For further details concerning TAT administration, see, for example, Smith, *Motivation Research,* pp. 126–130.
[15] Smith, *Motivation Research,* pp. 142–143.
[16] Joseph W. Newman, *Motivation Research and Marketing Management* (Boston: Harvard University, Division of Research, 1957), pp. 80–81.

Exhibit 6.3

Cartoon test

ciations, drawing or completing pictures, creating dialogue for "bubbles" above characters in cartoon-style pictures. There's also the whispering of "secret votes" to the group leader, and children are frequently asked to "pretend telephone," projecting themselves into the role of parents describing a recent purchase.

Youngsters may also be asked to "act out" commercials in a wide variety of shopping and domestic situations. Out of these creative play sessions, many a commercial has been re-structured for more effective communication to children; prototypes for many new products have been designed based on children's uses and needs; and many products have been revitalized to enhance their appeal to children.[17]

A researcher's imagination is the only limit on the uniqueness of a projective technique to be used in a situation. Indeed, one of the first applications of motivation research in a marketing context—one that is cited as a classic exam-

[17] "The Child Research Services," a brochure prepared by Child Research Services, a division of McCollum/Spielman Associates, Inc., 235 Great Neck Road, Great Neck, N.Y. 11021.

ple in many textbooks—involved the use of a very creative and interesting projective technique. The study was conducted in response to unexpected customer resistance to Nescafe instant coffee when it was first introduced some thirty-five years ago.[18] When women were questioned directly about why they did not like instant coffee, the typical answer was that they did not like its flavor. However, suspecting that consumers were merely using flavor as an excuse, the researchers devised a unique projective technique to get at the real reason(s) for the resistance to instant coffee.

The researchers selected two comparable samples of 50 housewives each. They also drew up the following two shopping lists:

List 1	List 2
Pound and a half of hamburger	Pound and a half of hamburger
2 loaves of Wonder Bread	2 loaves of Wonder Bread
Bunch of carrots	Bunch of carrots
1 can Rumford's baking powder	1 can Rumford's baking powder
Nescafe instant coffee	Maxwell House coffee (drip ground)
2 cans Del Monte peaches	2 cans Del Monte peaches
5 lb potatoes	5 lb potatoes

The women in one sample were shown list 1, and those in the other sample were shown list 2. Each respondent was asked to examine the shopping list and then write a description of the type of woman who could have made out the list.

The descriptions of the hypothetical shopper which emerged from the two samples were remarkably different. The sample that saw list 1 tended to describe the woman as a lazy person, a poor planner, and a spendthrift. In contrast, the descriptions provided by the respondents who saw list 2 were much more favorable to the hypothetical shopper: Many of them perceived her as a good housewife who was thrifty. These findings implied that the convenience feature of instant coffee, which was being used as a unique selling point for Nescafe, was apparently backfiring owing to its incongruence with society's expectations from homemakers. As a result of this study, the promotional theme for Nescafe was modified by toning down the emphasis on convenience.

In short, the nonstructured, disguised, or projective, method of data collection is flexible enough to be tailored to fit any research setting calling for an examination of people's inner feelings. Projective techniques can be valuable if properly used. Unfortunately, designing valid projective tests and correctly interpreting the results of these tests are not easy. They require very special skills and training. Researchers who are fascinated by projective techniques but are not qualified to use them can end up misusing them. Thus, after being widely used in the 1950s to solve marketing problems, projective techniques have been gradually losing their popularity, primarily because of inappropriate use by unqualified researchers who could not deliver on their promises to decision

[18] Mason Haire, "Projective Techniques in Marketing Research," *Journal of Marketing*, 14 (April 1950), pp. 649–652.

makers. Today there is considerable skepticism, especially among practitioners, about the whole area of motivation research. Even the validity of the shopping list study just described has been challenged. A senior research psychologist working for du Pont has presented evidence showing that items in the lists other than coffee could have biased respondents' perceptions about the hypothetical shopper.[19]

Structured, disguised questionnaires. Structured, disguised questionnaires are generally used to uncover people's attitudes toward sensitive issues of concern to society, like abortion, pollution, or deregulation. A structured, disguised questionnaire consists of a number of factual items to which respondents provide structured answers such as yes or no and true or false. A wide variety of items—ranging in degree of favorableness toward the issues being investigated—are included in the questionnaire. The items themselves can be real or fictitious.

The rationale behind a structured, disguised test is the following assumption: What and how much people *claim they know* about an issue can shed light on their attitudes toward the issue. For instance, a person who favors deregulation would tend to agree with, or label as correct, many more supposedly factual statements that are proderegulation than those that are antideregulation. So that respondents indirectly expose their inner feelings, they are deliberately told that each item has a correct and an incorrect response: "In contrast with most projective tests, in which the individual is encouraged to believe that there are no objectively 'correct' answers, the subject [in a structured, disguised test] is led to believe that there are 'right' and 'wrong' responses, and the attempt is made to motivate him to do as well as possible on the test."[20]

Structured, disguised tests, while somewhat more convenient to answer and code than nonstructured, disguised tests, are not any easier to design and interpret. For this reason, and perhaps also because these tests are typically designed to gauge people's attitudes toward fairly broad issues, they are not widely used in marketing research.

Thus far we have examined a variety of questionnaire methods classified according to their format. Let us now look at different methods of administering questionnaires.

QUESTIONNAIRE ADMINISTRATION METHODS

In the Kwality Knitware example the first three methods (A, B, and C) describe the basic approaches for collecting data through questionnaires: *personal inter-*

[19] James C. Anderson, "The Validity of Haire's Shopping List Projective Technique," *Journal of Marketing Research,* 15 (November 1978), pp. 644–649.

[20] Claire Selltiz, Marie Jahoda, Morton Deutsch, and Stuart W. Cook, *Research Methods in Social Relations,* rev. ed., 1 vol. (New York: Henry Holt, 1959), p. 300.

views (method A), *telephone surveys* (method B), and *mail surveys* (method C). As demonstrated by the Kwality Knitware illustration, any of these three basic questionnaire administration methods can generally be used in a research project requiring primary-data collection. But not all of them may be equally appropriate in a given situation. While each method has certain advantages and limitations, the strength of the advantages and the seriousness of the limitations depend on the specific features of the situation. Keep this point in mind throughout the following discussion of the advantages and disadvantages of the three methods on the dimensions of versatility, time, cost, accuracy, and respondent convenience.

Versatility

A number of factors affect the versatility of questionnaire administration methods. Examples include the amount of data that can be collected, the types of questions that can be asked, and the kind of stimuli that can be presented to respondents during data collection. As you might expect, personal interviews are much more flexible and allow for the collection of a greater variety of data than telephone or mail surveys. Thus personal interviews are better than the other approaches for obtaining customer reactions to the appearance of a package, the taste of alternative formulations of a food product, and so on. Telephone and mail surveys are somewhat deficient in terms of presenting stimuli to respondents, although modern technological advances are improving the versatility of these methods. For instance, one can present visual stimuli (including the questionnaires themselves) through respondents' television sets (via video cable) and obtain responses over the telephone or through other means of electronic feedback.[21]

The personal-interview method is also better when the research involves lengthy nonstructured questionnaires, since respondent resistance is likely to be especially high to such questionnaires if administered through telephone or mail surveys. In a face-to-face interview, once a respondent initially agrees to cooperate, it may be psychologically difficult for him or her to terminate the interview.

Telephone surveys are more flexible than mail surveys in the sense that there is at least verbal contact between the interviewer and respondent. This added flexibility of telephone interviews allows the interviewer to ask some open-ended questions and to probe a respondent as needed during the interview. Although mail questionnaires can generally have a larger number of questions than questionnaires administered over the telephone, they typically will

[21] One such interactive video data collection system, called QUBE, is already in place in Columbus, Ohio. For a description of this system, see "QUBE: The Ultimate Testing Device," *Marketing News,* May 2, 1980, p. 7.

have to be quite structured to encourage respondent cooperation, which, in turn, reduces flexibility.

In summary, with respect to overall versatility, personal interviews are perhaps the best, followed by telephone and mail surveys, in that order.

Time

Telephone interviewing is usually the best form of questionnaire administration when information is needed in a hurry. Telephone surveys avoid the time-consuming travel involved in personal-interview surveys. They also do not suffer from the postal delays and respondent tardiness generally present in mail surveys.

Certain *computerized* telephone-interviewing systems, in addition to cutting down data collection time, can also reduce the time required for data analysis. Market Facts, Inc., is a commercial marketing research firm having such a system. Exhibit 6.4 presents a schematic description of Market Facts' National Telephone Center in Chicago. Respondents in any geographic area of the United States can be interviewed through the 70 WATS (wide area telephone service) interviewing stations at Market Facts' National Telephone Center. The questionnaires used in conducting interviews from this center appear on computer terminals (called cathode ray tubes, or CRTs) in front of the interviewers. The responses are entered directly into these terminals as the interviews take place. Therefore the collected data are immediately transferred to computer memory and can be readily processed at any time. For example, the firm can conduct interviews one evening and have the responses analyzed and ready for presentation the next day.[22]

Personal interviews can normally generate data faster than mail surveys, especially when adequate resources are available to hire as many interviewers as needed to collect the desired data within a specified time period. In contrast, the time needed to obtain data through mail surveys is essentially out of the hands of the researcher once the questionnaires are mailed out.

Thus on the time dimension the typical rank ordering of questionnaire administration methods is as follows: (1) telephone surveys, (2) personal interviews, and (3) mail surveys.

Cost

While mail surveys are generally the slowest for obtaining data, they are also the least expensive. They are the least expensive mainly because mail surveys have

[22] Additional details about this telephone-interviewing system are presented in "Data Collection and Analysis for Reducing Business Decision Risks," a brochure prepared by Market Facts, Inc., 676 North St. Clair Street, Chicago, Ill. 60611.

Exhibit 6.4

Market Facts' national telephone center

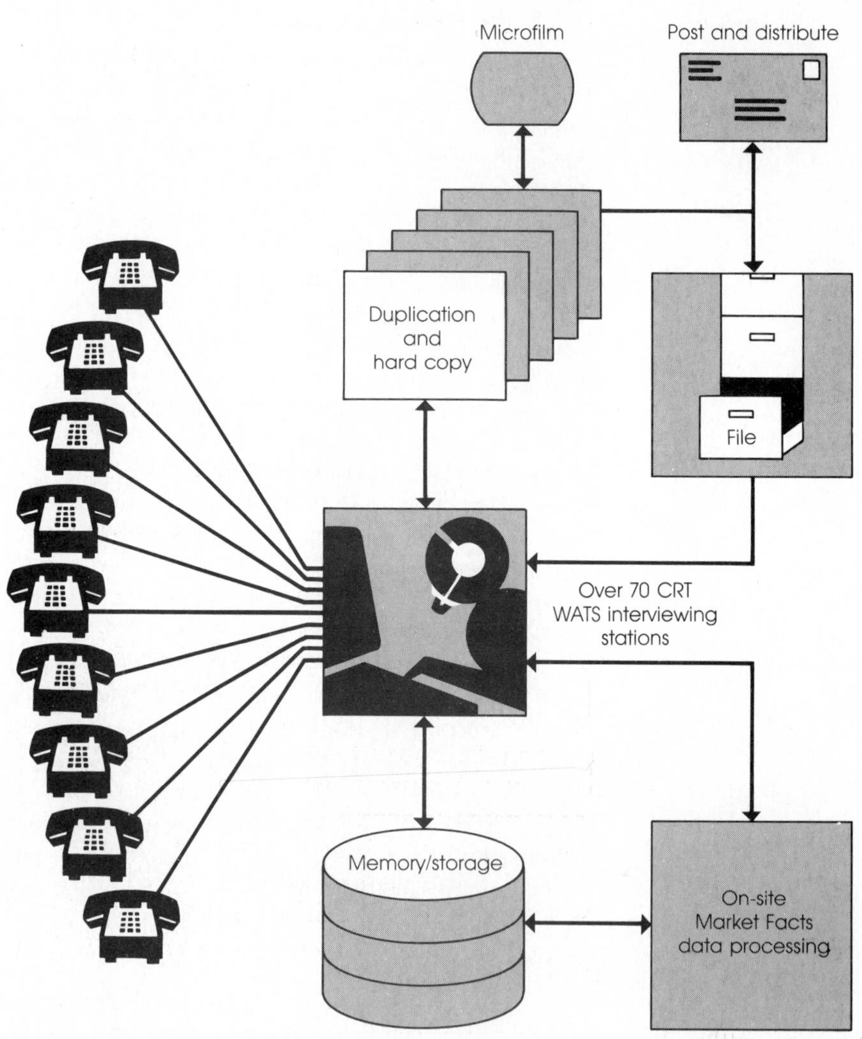

Source: "Data Collection and Analysis for Reducing Business Decision Risks," a brochure prepared by Market Facts, Inc., 676 North St. Clair Street, Chicago, Ill. 60611, p. 12.

no interviewers, who usually account for a large share of the data collection costs in surveys using personal or telephone interviewing. Personal interviews are typically more expensive than telephone surveys because of travel expenses involved. Of course, telephone interviewing can also become quite expensive if lengthy long-distance calls are needed. Nevertheless, even under those circumstances personal interviews may be more expensive on a per-completed-interview basis, especially if one or several callbacks are necessary before contact is made with designated respondents (callbacks are discussed further in Chapter 15 dealing with potential errors in fieldwork).

The implied ranking of the three questionnaire administration methods on the basis of cost—personal interviews (most expensive), then telephone interviews, then mail surveys—is not universal. Exceptions can, and do, occur under certain conditions. For instance, suppose a one-page structured questionnaire is to be administered to a sample of residents within a town. The cost per completed questionnaire in this case may well be lower for telephone interviewing than for a mail survey.[23]

Accuracy

A variety of factors, such as the format of a questionnaire, the content and the wording of questions, and the moods of respondents while answering the questions, can influence data accuracy, irrespective of the questionnaire administration method used. However, the administration methods differ on three key determinants of data accuracy: degree of control over the sample (sampling control), degree of control over the questioning process (supervisory control), and the ability to sense and overcome any respondent difficulty in understanding or answering questions (opportunity for clarification). We will therefore focus our comparison of the questionnaire administration methods along these three dimensions.

Sampling control refers to the ability to collect data from a sample that adequately represents relevant segments of the population of interest. Inferences based on nonrepresentative data cannot be generalized and hence are not trustworthy. The degree to which data can be obtained from a representative sample in a questionnaire administration method depends on two attributes of the method: (1) the ability to *identify and reach* an appropriate sample of respondents, and (2) the ability to *secure cooperation* from each respondent contacted.

The personal-interview method, given its versatility, is most capable of reaching the right respondents and securing cooperation. Any desired set of respondents (even those without a telephone or a mailing address) can poten-

[23] Seymour Sudman, *Reducing the Cost of Surveys* (Chicago: Aldine, 1967), provides a discussion of various facets of evaluating survey costs, including cost versus data quality comparisons.

tially be reached by well-trained interviewers. Moreover, refusing to participate is likely to be more difficult for a respondent when face-to-face with an interviewer than when contacted by telephone or mail. Therefore cooperation rates are normally higher when personal interviews are used.

Telephone surveys face two potential hurdles in attempting to reach a representative sample of households within the general population: (1) households with unlisted telephones and (2) households without telephones. Of the two, unlisted telephones present the more serious problem, at least in the United States. While over 95% of all households in the United States now have telephones, on the average about 20% of the households in any given area have unlisted telephones.[24] Moreover, households with unlisted telephones differ in significant ways from those with listed telephones.[25] Therefore a sample of households chosen from an area's phone book will invariably be an inadequate representation of the entire area.

Telephone numbers can be chosen by using random-dialing procedures instead of a phone book in order to properly represent households with unlisted telephones. Techniques such as random-digit dialing and plus-one dialing (see Chapter 15) are available for this purpose. However, even if contact is made with respondents having unlisted telephones, a significant number of them may refuse to be interviewed.[26] Hence respondent cooperation may not be as high as in a typical personal-interview survey, although it is still likely to be better than in most mail surveys. One review of published studies using telephone surveys found the percentage of telephone calls resulting in completed interviews to range between 45% and 95%, implying a typical completion rate of about 70%.[27]

Mail surveys are generally the worst in terms of the percentage of contacts resulting in completed questionnaires. Getting back over 50% of the questionnaires initially mailed is an exception. Moreover, studies have shown that people who fill out and return questionnaires may be significantly different from nonrespondents. For instance, people with higher incomes and education levels are more likely to respond to mail surveys than others.[28]

As you might expect, researchers have tried numerous respondent inducements to improve mail survey response rates, not all of which have been effec-

---

[24] Tyzoon T. Tybjee, "Telephone Survey Methods: The State of the Art," *Journal of Marketing,* 43 (Summer 1979), pp. 68–78.

[25] Patricia E. Moberg, "Biases in Unlisted Phone Numbers," *Journal of Advertising Research,* 22 (August/September 1982), pp. 54–55; Gerald J. Glasser and Gale D. Metzger, "National Estimates of Nonlisted Telephone Households and Their Characteristics," *Journal of Marketing Research,* 12 (August 1975), pp. 359–361.

[26] Moberg, "Biases in Unlisted Phone Numbers."

[27] Tybjee, "Telephone Survey Methods."

[28] Two review articles that present comprehensive discussions of mail survey response rates are Leslie Kanuk and Conrad Berenson, "Mail Surveys and Response Rates: A Literature Review," *Journal of Marketing Research,* 12 (November 1975), pp. 440–453; Arnold S. Linsky, "Stimulating Responses to Mailed Questionnaires: A Review," *Public Opinion Quarterly,* Spring 1975, pp. 82–101.

tive.[29] The more successful inducement techniques include mailing questionnaires by first-class mail, sending follow-up questionnaires, and enclosing incentives—monetary or nonmonetary—with the questionnaires. Using incentives has been found to be particularly effective in improving response rates, apparently since people receiving them may feel obligated to cooperate.[30]

Incentives offered to respondents, however, may increase the number of returned questionnaires without necessarily improving sample representativeness. That is, people who respond because of an incentive may differ on critical characteristics from those who do not respond at all. Therefore, although a mail survey can reach virtually any and every potential respondent, it is generally less likely to provide a representative final sample, and hence has less sampling control, than personal interviews or telephone surveys.

We do not mean to imply that the problem of nonrepresentative samples is limited to mail surveys. As we will see in Chapter 15, lack of responses from particular types of respondents that result in biased samples can occur in personal and telephone surveys as well. But this problem is generally more severe in mail surveys.

The issue of supervisory control refers to the ability to minimize interviewer errors such as failure to follow instructions, mistakes in recording answers, and cheating.[31] In this regard mail surveys, since they involve no interviewers, have an edge over personal and telephone interviews (assuming, of course, that the mail questionnaire is well designed with clear instructions so that errors by the respondents when they interview themselves are avoided). The personal-interview method is especially prone to problems stemming from interviewer errors. Supervising the work of face-to-face interviewers is hard, since they typically work alone in the field, although certain validity checks can be made *after* the data collection (see Chapter 15). Even rigorous interviewer training cannot guarantee that fieldworkers will not make mistakes. Indeed, according to studies conducted by the U.S. Census Bureau: "The evidence is compelling that, even with very structured training programs, interviewers exhibit considerable variability in their data collection for certain items."[32]

---

[29] For a discussion of these inducement techniques and studies using them, see Kanuk and Berenson, "Mail Surveys and Response Rates"; Linsky, "Stimulating Responses"; Don A. Dillman, *Mail and Telephone Surveys* (New York: Wiley, 1978).

[30] One study involving a mail survey of respondents in a sample of firms found that in terms of improving response rates, the *size* of the incentive really may not matter as much as that *some* incentive is included; see Milton M. Pressley and William L. Tullar, "A Factor Interactive Investigation of Mail Survey Response Rates from a Commercial Population," *Journal of Marketing Research,* 14 (February 1977), pp. 108–111.

[31] A good discussion of interviewer-induced errors in survey research is available in Charles F. Cannell, Kent H. Marquis, and Andre Laurent, *A Summary of Studies of Interviewing Methodology,* U.S. Department of Health, Education, and Welfare, Publication no. (HRA) 77–1343, (Washington D.C.: U.S. Government Printing Office, 1977).

[32] Barbara Bailar, Leroy Bailey, and Joyce Stevens, "Measures of Interviewer Bias and Variance," *Journal of Marketing Research,* 14 (August 1977), p. 343.

Telephone interviews conducted from central locations (like Market Facts' National Telephone Center in Chicago discussed earlier) are better than personal interviews in terms of supervisory control over the data collection. Most such centers have special CRTs and audio equipment that supervisors can use to monitor any interviewer's work as the interviewing is taking place. Therefore interviewer mistakes can be quickly spotted and corrected. Moreover, the interviewers themselves are likely to be extra careful because they know that a supervisor can monitor their work at any time.

On the dimension of opportunity for clarification—that is, the ability to detect and overcome problems respondents may experience in answering certain questions—mail surveys are the worst since there is no direct interaction with the respondent. Hence errors are bound to occur in mail survey data if respondents misunderstand certain questions or are unsure of how to answer them. In contrast, personal and telephone interviews can reduce such errors by allowing respondents to seek clarification and enabling interviewers to provide the necessary clarification. Personal interviews are perhaps the best in this regard because face-to-face contact allows interviewers to visually detect any respondent confusion or difficulty that may occur even when respondents do not explicitly seek clarification.

In terms of overall accuracy—that is, taking into account sampling control, supervisory control, and opportunity for clarification—generalizing about which method is best and which is worst is difficult, since each has strengths and weaknesses along different dimensions pertaining to data accuracy. Therefore, which questionnaire administration method (or methods) will provide the most accurate data depends on the specific characteristics of a research setting.

Respondent convenience

The mail survey method, which is least disruptive and most flexible from a participant's perspective, is naturally the best in terms of respondent convenience. Personal interviews are perhaps the worst, especially since respondents may find it difficult to say no when confronted by a persistent interviewer. Telephone surveys generally fall between the other two methods with respect to respondent convenience.

Deciding on which questionnaire administration method to use

As with other decisions, the decision about questionnaire administration method depends on the research project. Table 6.3 provides a comparative summary of the three methods on the various criteria. As has been pointed out earlier, however, the rankings implied by this table will not necessarily hold in every research setting. But even if they did, no method can claim to be the best on *all* criteria. According to Joselyn: "It is rare to encounter a research situation

Table 6.3
Comparison of questionnaire administration methods

CRITERIA	RANKING OF METHODS		
	Best	Second Best	Third Best
VERSATILITY			
Number of questions	Personal	Mail	Telephone
Amount/variety of information	Personal	Telephone	Mail
Presentation of stimuli	Personal	Telephone	Mail
TIME	Telephone	Personal	Mail
COST	Mail	Telephone	Personal
ACCURACY			
Sampling control	Personal	Telephone	Mail
Supervisory control	Mail	Telephone (central location)	Personal
Opportunity for clarification	Personal	Telephone	Mail
RESPONDENT CONVENIENCE	Mail	Telephone	Personal

Note: The comparative rankings of the personal, telephone, and mail survey techniques implied by this table are not universal; exceptions to these rankings can and do occur, depending on specific circumstances surrounding a research situation.

in which all considerations point to a single survey technique."[33] Or as Dillman correctly observes:

> Although each method has certain strengths and weaknesses, they do not apply equally, or sometimes not at all, to every survey situation. Thus, until the attributes of each method are considered in relation to the study topic, the population to be surveyed, and the precise survey objectives, the question of which is best cannot be answered.[34]

The purpose of our lengthy discussion concerning the relative merits and limitations of the three survey approaches was not so much to pinpoint the best approach; rather, it was to emphasize and illustrate the variety of factors to be considered in selecting the most suitable approach in a research project. Situation-specific considerations are particularly crucial in collecting primary data from countries other than the United States. Exhibit 6.5 offers a few interesting facts that illustrate unique research constraints that may have a significant bear-

[33] Robert W. Joselyn, *Designing the Marketing Research Project* (New York: Mason/Charter, 1977), p. 92.
[34] Dillman, *Mail and Telephone Surveys,* excerpted with permission from the publisher.

Exhibit 6.5

Examples of potential research constraints in foreign countries

- Door-to-door interviews in Japan are conducted just inside or outside the home, rather than in a comfortable living room or den.
- In Japan each personal-interview participant expects to receive a gift, usually costing about $1.50 to $2.50.
- While virtually every household in the United States has a telephone, less than 50% of households in France have telephones.
- A questionnaire to be administered in Singapore must have an English version as well as equivalent Malay, Hokkien, Mandarin, Tamil, and Cantonese versions.
- Business executives and government officials in West Germany resist telephone interviews but are willing to be interviewed face to face.
- Several developed countries in Europe have no comprehensive lists of business establishments.

Source: The first two items are adapted from Andrew Watt, "A Day in the Working Life of a Japanese Interviewer Shows Some Similarities to U.S. and Some Differences," *Marketing News,* May 15, 1981, Section 2, p. 12; the other items are adapted from David C. Pring," Filling the Overseas Gaps," *Advertising Age,* October 26, 1981, p. 5.

ing on the choice of an appropriate survey method and on the type of data that can be collected.

Nowadays, researchers are able to use hybrid or modified survey techniques that possess desirable features of the basic approaches and, at the same time, do not suffer seriously from their weaknesses. To illustrate, consider *shopping mall intercept interviewing,* which, according to several sources, is becoming increasingly popular.[35] This technique is a variation of the traditional in-home personal interview; respondents are intercepted in shopping centers and interviewed face to face. Shopping mall intercept interviews can be conducted at a faster rate than in-home interviews since interviewer travel is considerably reduced. They are also significantly less expensive.[36] Yet they can be conducted in such a way as to generate representative samples that are comparable to samples attainable through in-home or door-to-door interviewing.[37] Shopping mall interviews are also likely to be less intrusive and hence more convenient to respondents than in-home interviews.

Several commercial marketing research firms now have well equipped and sophisticated interviewing facilities in shopping malls. In such facilities, after potential respondents are intercepted and screened for eligibility by an inter-

[35] Roger Gates and Paul J. Solomon, "Research Using the Mall Intercept: State of the Art," *Journal of Advertising Research,* 22 (August/September 1982), pp. 43–49.

[36] See, for example, Howard N. Gundee, "MULTI-MALL Surveys Reduce Personal Interviewing Costs," *Marketing Today* (published by Elrick and Lavidge, Inc.), 21 (1) (1983); MULTI-MALL is a registered trademark of Elrick and Lavidge, Inc.

[37] Guidelines for carefully selecting shopping mall samples and adjusting for errors that may occur are discussed by Seymour Sudman, "Improving the Quality of Shopping Center Sampling," *Journal of Marketing Research,* 17 (November 1980), pp. 423–431.

Exhibit 6.6

Sophisticated shopping mall interviewing

A major food manufacturer wishes to evaluate a new package design for one of its cereal products.

The research consultant has recommended the use of a shopping mall intercept technique where shoppers will be interviewed in the mall to find out their perceptions of and reactions to the new package design.

The marketing research firm has eight full-time shopping center facilities geographically dispersed across the United States. Each of the eight centers has a microprocessor unit with a video display and keyboard. To get a valid attitude measurement of the new package design, 400 interviews are needed. A total of 50 interviews will be completed in each of the eight facilities.

A questionnaire is designed in the headquarters office and programmed into the central computer. The eight shopping center facilities are then telephoned via a data-link line, and the questionnaire program is loaded into each microprocessor using a floppy disk. Different programs can be placed on a floppy disk and this allows program manipulation. The microprocessor is now ready for interviewing use.

Qualified consumers are intercepted in the mall, shown variations of the package design, and asked to self-administer the questionnaire. The individual actually sits at the terminal, reads the questionnaire as it appears on the video screen, and punches in responses. The data are automatically stored and tabulated in the microprocessor.

Once interviewing is completed, the central computer polls the results from the microprocessor at each shopping mall location, and data are read back to the central computer. Tabulated data are delivered to the client within three days, as compared to the two-week turnaround time that would probably have been required with less sophisticated methods.

Source: Reprinted by permission from *Business* magazine. "The New Technology for Market Researchers," by John T. Rougeou, July-September 1982, pp. 49–50.

viewer, they can self-administer the survey questionnaire at a CRT terminal; as each question appears on the CRT screen, the respondent can directly type in his or her answer. To a certain degree, this technique offers respondents the privacy and flexibility of a mail questionnaire. It also offers researchers the speed, efficiency, and control of a computerized, central-location telephone survey. The example presented in Exhibit 6.6 illustrates the capabilities of sophisticated shopping mall research facilities.

TYPES OF OBSERVATION TECHNIQUES

We earlier looked at a few illustrations of using observation to collect data, before we discussed the various questionnaire techniques. The purpose of this section is to show the ways that observation studies can vary, depending on *how* the observations are made and *what* exactly is observed. The three observation methods presented in the Kwality Knitware case (methods D, E, and F) serve to illustrate some of these differences. Recall that method D involves employing human observers, method E uses videotaping, and method F involves programming the cash registers to keep track of sales of Kwality brand shirts. The similarities and the differences across methods D, E, and F are discussed in the following subsections.

Natural versus contrived observation

One feature common to methods D, E, and F is that they all involve making observations in a *natural setting*; that is, customer reactions and behavior are observed as they occur naturally in a real-life situation. Observations can also be made in a *contrived setting,* which is an environment artificially set up by the researcher.

An example involving contrived observation is the Laboratory Test Market (LTM) service offered by Yankelovich, Skelley and White, Inc., to predict how well a new product is likely to perform in the marketplace. A key feature of the LTM is a simulated, or contrived, store. The procedure used in LTM research is as follows: A sample of potential customers first self-administers a background questionnaire dealing with demographics and buying habits. The respondents then view an actual TV program containing commercials for the test product as well as for other products. Next, they are led in small groups to the store, where they are given a fixed amount of money to spend as they wish or not spend at all. Sales of the test product and other products in the same product category are observed. These sales data, along with additional feedback obtained from the respondents after they finish their shopping trip, are used to predict the market performance of the new product.[38]

An important advantage of contrived observation over natural observation is the greater degree of control the former offers. Such control permits researchers to collect relevant data in a speedy, efficient, and less expensive fashion. A potential drawback of contrived observation is the question of whether the collected data would result from a real-life setting. This limitation may be especially serious when respondents know they are being observed—which brings up another dimension on which observation methods can differ, namely, whether they are disguised or nondisguised.

Disguised versus nondisguised observation

An observation is *disguised* when respondents are unaware they are being observed; it is *nondisguised* when respondents are aware they are being ob-

[38] Additional details about the LTM are given in "Laboratory Test Market," a brochure prepared by Yankelovich, Skelly and White, Inc., 575 Madison Avenue, New York, N.Y. 10022; also see Exhibit 8.2 in Chapter 8.

served. Monitoring sales at the cash register (method F) in the Kwality Knitware case is an illustration of disguised observation. Methods D and E can also be viewed as disguised observation if the researcher ensures that the human observers or videotaping equipment are not visible to the store's customers.

The main strength of disguised observation is that it allows for monitoring of the true reactions of individuals. Alternatively, data gathered through nondisguised observation may be contaminated by respondent-induced errors, just as in any questionnaire method. As Michael Ray points out: "Observation measures lose their advantage over interviews if the observation becomes apparent to respondents. This can happen with simple observation if the observer appears to be unusual, carries a clipboard, etc."[39] Since disguised observation is nonintrusive, it is also more convenient from the respondent's standpoint.

Serious ethical questions can arise, however, if disguised observation involves monitoring aspects of respondents' behaviors that are normally private or that they may not voluntarily reveal to researchers (recall our discussion of marketing research ethics in Chapter 2). Moreover, data gathered through a study using disguised observation may not be as rich as those obtained from a study involving nondisguised observation. Data from a nondisguised observation are richer because observation that is not hidden from respondents is generally done with their cooperation. Consequently, the respondents can be questioned before or after the observation to obtain additional data about their characteristics that cannot be observed (e.g., data on demographics and buying habits collected in the LTM procedure discussed earlier).

Human versus mechanical observation

Data collection in observation studies can be done by people or by *mechanical devices.* Method D in the Kwality Knitware example involves human observers; methods E and F use mechanical observation or, perhaps more appropriately, electronic observation. With the advent of increasingly sophisticated technological gadgets, mechanical observation is rapidly replacing human observation. Of course, irrespective of how observations are made, *interpretation* of those observations is very much a human responsibility.

A key strength of mechanical observation is that it can be used to monitor, in a more precise fashion, virtually anything a human observer is capable of monitoring. For instance videotaping customers in the special display area for Kwality brand shirts (method E) is likely to generate more complete and accurate observations than using human observers (method D). Moreover, method E is also likely to be less conspicuous to customers than method D—an important consideration if disguised observation is crucial.

Numerous mechanical and electronic devices are now available to observe things human observers may find very difficult, if not impossible, to study. A

[39] Ray, *Unobtrusive Marketing,* p. 15.

comprehensive discussion of such devices is beyond the scope of this text. However, several illustrations are provided next.

Eye-tracking equipment. This equipment is used to ascertain precisely which sections of an ad, product packaging, or promotional display attract customers' attention, and how much time they spend looking at those sections.[40]

Devices to measure response latency. *Response latency* is the speed with which a respondent provides an answer. Response latency measures are being increasingly employed to determine the effectiveness of ads in influencing the strength of consumers' brand preferences. The rationale underlying the use of response latency measures is that the *quicker* a respondent expresses preference for a brand, the *stronger* the preference is. For instance, when two customers are asked whether they prefer 7-Up or Sprite, they may both say 7-Up; however, the one that responds faster, even by a fraction of a second, presumably has a lower degree of doubt in his or her mind and hence a stronger preference for 7-Up. Only electronic devices can accurately monitor and detect differences in response latency.[41]

Instruments to conduct voice pitch analysis (VOPAN). *Voice pitch analysis,* not unlike response latency measures, is used to determine how strongly a respondent feels about an answer or how much emotional commitment is attached to it. The VOPAN involves measuring the voice pitch of verbal responses during an interview. This voice pitch is then compared with the respondent's normal voice pitch used during routine conversation about neutral topics such as the weather. The extent to which the voice pitch of responses to a survey question deviates from normal voice pitch is considered a measure of the respondents' emotional commitment to the answer.[42]

Television Audimeter. As we saw in Chapter 5, the Audimeter is a device used by the A. C. Nielsen Company to monitor television-viewing behavior—what channels are watched, when they are watched, and for how long they are watched. In an attempt to further refine its TV audience measurements, Nielsen

---

[40] For further details about the capabilities of eye-tracking equipment, see, for example, Bernie Whalen, "Eye Tracking Technology to Replace Day-After-Recall by '84," *Marketing News,* November 27, 1981, Section 1, p. 18; Elliot Young, "Use Eye Tracking Technology to Create Clutter-Breaking Ads," *Marketing News,* November 27, 1981, Section 1, p. 19.

[41] Several recent articles discuss response latency measures and their use in marketing research; see James MacLachlan and John G. Myers, "Using Response Latency to Identify Commercials That Motivate," *Journal of Advertising Research,* 23 (October/November 1983), pp. 51–57; David A. Aaker, Richard P. Bagozzi, James M. Carman, and James M. MacLachlan, "On Using Response Latency to Measure Preference," *Journal of Marketing Research,* 17 (May 1980), pp. 237–244.

[42] For further discussions of VOPAN and its use, see, for example, Ronald Nelson and David Schwartz, "Voice Pitch Gives Marketer Access to Consumer's Unaware Body Responses," *Marketing News,* January 28, 1977, p. 21; Nancy J. Nighswonger and Claude R. Martin, Jr., "On Using Voice Analysis in Marketing Research," *Journal of Marketing Research,* 18 (August 1981), pp. 350–355.

Exhibit 6.7

Nielsen's audience composition push button meter

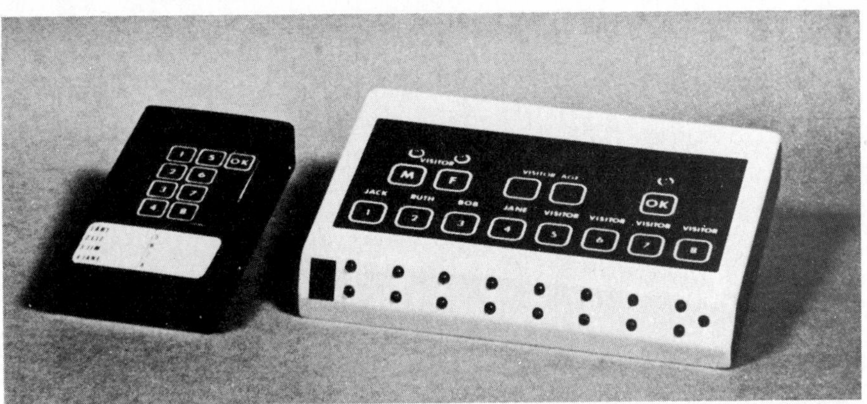

Source: A. C. Nielsen Company, Nielsen Plaza, Northbrook, Ill. 60062. Courtesy of A. C. Nielsen Company.

has recently devised an audience composition push button (ACPB) meter; it is shown in Exhibit 6.7. The ACPB is designed to monitor *who* is watching TV when it is turned on. It uses the latest electronic technology and has separate buttons for all family members as well as for visitors. The individual viewers simply press their corresponding buttons on the ACPB when they start or stop watching TV. This detailed information is automatically transmitted to Nielsen's computers.[43]

Direct versus indirect observation

Suppose Mr. Smith, owner of a gift shop, wants to know how much customer traffic his store attracts during the last quarter of a year relative to the first three quarters. One option available to Mr. Smith is to use human observers or mechanical/electronic monitors to count the number of people entering his store during each quarter. This procedure is *direct observation* since the actual behavior or phenomenon of interest is observed. Another option for Mr. Smith is to use some form of *indirect observation,* which consists of examining the results or consequences of the phenomenon. For instance, Mr. Smith could install, just inside the store entrance, a temporary patch of floor covering specially designed to wear out easily and show the extent of wear. Replacing the patch every quarter and comparing the wear on the fourth-quarter patch with

[43] Additional details about the ACPB are given in "NTI—Leading the Way: Summary of 1982 Client Meetings," a brochure prepared (in 1983) by A. C. Nielsen Company, Nielsen Plaza, Northbrook, Ill. 60062, pp. 17–18.

the wear on patches used in previous quarters can help answer Mr. Smith's question.

Indirect observation, when compared with direct observation, can give only relatively crude or imprecise indications of a phenomenon. Nevertheless, it does have a couple of attractive features. It will generally be more efficient than direct observation from a time and a cost perspective, especially if the behavior to be observed is stretched out over a long period of time and is likely to occur infrequently during that time. As we saw earlier, monitoring sales of Kwality brand shirts at the cash register (method F)—an indirect-observation method—will be less time-consuming and expensive than methods D and E, both of which involve direct observation. Other examples of efficient indirect observation include examining the wear and tear on magazines to estimate their readership and analyzing the accumulation of fingerprints on advertisements to ascertain the amount of consumer exposure to them.[44]

Another advantage of indirect observation is that it may be the only way of getting relevant data from situations that are impractical to observe directly. To illustrate, Information Data Search, Inc., (IDS), a competitive intelligence firm, uses a number of creative indirect-observation techniques, one of which is cardboard box analysis. Leonard M. Fuld, managing director of IDS, describes this technique as follows:

> You can learn a great deal about a company just by looking at the boxes it uses to ship its products to retailers. The bottom of the box has a seal, and numbers, and the name of the cardboard manufacturer. . . . So all you do is call up the suppliers and talk to them. Usually they'll tell you how many they produced for a company in a certain period. That information can be used to generate pretty reliable estimates of production runs, unit shipments, sales—you name it.[45]

Structured versus nonstructured observation

Whether an observation is structured or nonstructured depends on the nature and type of data recorded. Observation is *structured observation* when a study's data requirements are well-established and can be broken into a set of discrete, clearly defined categories—much like the precoded response categories in structured questions.

Consider a restaurant manager who wants to know the number of single customers and the number of parties of two or more customers who eat at the restaurant. This setting is eminently suited for structured observation since the data requirements are clearly defined. For instance, waiters and waitresses can

[44] For an excellent discussion of these and other indirect-observation techniques, see Webb, Campbell, Schwartz, and Sechrest, *Unobtrusive Measures,* Chapter. 2.
[45] Bernie Whalen, "Marketing 'Detective' Reveals Competitive-Intelligence Secrets," *Marketing News,* September 16, 1983, Section 1, p. 1.

be used as observers and asked to keep a tally of the number of single customers and the number of groups of customers they serve.

Suppose, however, that the manager wants to observe the moods and behaviors of single customers and of customer groups. Given the vagueness of the manager's objective, some form of *nonstructured observation* will be required in this situation. For instance, the manager may use inconspicuous videotaping equipment or human observers to monitor "everything of relevance" concerning the restaurant's customers.

While structured observation is generally easier to record and analyze than nonstructured observation, it is limited in terms of the depth and richness of data it can provide. These pros and cons of structured observation are similar to those of structured questionnaires discussed earlier. Along the same lines, structured observation is more suitable for conclusive-research projects than for exploratory-research projects.

A final note on the observation method: What we have discussed so far under "Types of Observation Techniques" are really five dimensions along which observation methods can vary. Numerous types of observation methods are possible from unique combinations of these dimensions. Differences between observation methods, and the extent of those differences, depend on how the methods vary along the five dimensions. For example, method D in the Kwality Knitware case can be labeled as natural, disguised (if the observer is not conspicuous), human, direct, nonstructured observation. In contrast, method F is natural, disguised, mechanical, indirect, structured observation.

SUMMARY

This chapter described a number of primary-data collection techniques that can broadly be classified into questioning and observation methods. In general, the questioning method is more versatile than the observation method, mainly because the latter can only be used to study what is visible. The questioning method is also typically, but not always, faster and cheaper. However, the observation method, since it is less likely to suffer from respondent-induced errors, is capable of generating more accurate data. The observation method is also more convenient from the respondent's perspective. In some studies one may be able to use a combination of the two methods in such a way as to capitalize on the advantages of both.

The format of questionnaires can vary along two dimensions, structure and disguise. The more conclusive, or final, a research project, the more appropriate and advantageous structured questionnaires are. The need to use disguised questionnaires increases with anticipated respondent resistance to direct questions.

On the basis of structure and disguise, questionnaires can be roughly classified into four broad categories. First are structured, nondisguised questionnaires, which are frequently used, especially in descriptive-research projects. Second are nonstructured, nondisguised questionnaires, which are particularly appropriate for exploratory-research projects and for interviewing executives or officers in businesses and other institutions. Third are nonstructured, disguised questionnaires, which usually employ projective techniques and are used in motivation research studies to explore consumers' inner feelings and motives. Fourth are structured, disguised questionnaires, whose typical purpose is to uncover people's attitudes toward broad social issues; because of their purpose, they are not frequently used in traditional marketing research studies.

Questionnaires can also be classified into three categories according to the method used to administer them: personal interviews, telephone surveys, and mail surveys. These questionnaire administration methods differ in terms of their versatility, speed, cost, accuracy, and convenience from the respondent's standpoint. That any one method will be the best on *all* criteria in a given situation is highly unlikely. Therefore the researcher must carefully consider situation-specific characteristics and ascertain which criteria are most critical before selecting a questionnaire administration method. At times, the researcher may wish to improvise a hybrid questionnaire administration method possessing key strengths of all the basic methods.

A variety of techniques are available for collecting data through observation. Specifically, an observation study can be (1) conducted in a natural or a contrived setting; (2) disguised or nondisguised from respondents; (3) conducted by human observers or by mechanical/electronic means (the latter are becoming increasingly popular because of technological advances); (4) direct or indirect, depending on whether an actual occurrence or its consequences are observed; and (5) structured or nonstructured. As in the selection of a questionnaire method, the choice of an appropriate observation technique must be based on a careful examination of factors such as the nature of the research, the type of data required, and the resources available.

QUESTIONS

1. Can observation methods be used in exploratory research? Why or why not?
2. In what ways is the questionnaire method more versatile than the observation method?
3. The manager of a large independent supermarket in a city wants to estimate the proportion of households in the city that make a purchase in the supermarket at least once a month. What method(s) should the manager use to generate this estimate? Explain your answer.
4. A suburban shopping mall is planning to exhibit antiques and various types of art in its lobby area so as to generate more customers for the mall. Describe a *combination* of the questionnaire and observation methods that can be used to ascertain the effectiveness of the antique and art exhibit.

5. What are *depth interviews*? In what situations are they likely to be most useful? Explain your answer.
6. Describe the distinct features that all projective techniques have. Pick any one of the several projective techniques discussed in the chapter, and give an example of your own to illustrate a real-life situation in which the technique will be useful.
7. Discuss the accuracy of the following statement: "Nondisguised questionnaires are much more widely used in marketing research today than disguised questionnaires."
8. What advantages do telephone surveys have over personal interviews and mail surveys?
9. A state university wants to do a study of graduate students' attitudes about its summer school calendar. What survey method would you recommend? Why?
10. What is *shopping mall intercept interviewing*? What are its advantages over the more traditional questionnaire administration methods?
11. Recall the Trent Eating Association (TEA) situation presented in Chapter 4 (situation C at the beginning of Chapter 4). Assume that an experimental study is to be conducted in this situation and that the necessary data are to be gathered through observation. Describe what this observation method would look like along each of the five observation dimensions discussed in this chapter.

7

Qualitative Research

WHAT IS QUALITATIVE RESEARCH?

Qualitative research involves collecting, analyzing, and interpreting data that cannot be meaningfully quantified, that is, summarized in the form of numbers. For this reason qualitative research is sometimes referred to as *soft* research. This term is somewhat unfortunate, because as subsequent sections of this chapter will show, soft research is no less valuable than so-called hard, or quantitative, research.

Any study using *nonstructured*-questioning or -observation techniques can be labeled as qualitative research, but another distinguishing feature of qualitative research is that it typically involves only a relatively small number of respondents or units. In other words, a study involving a large representative sample would normally not be called qualitative research even if it used some nonstructured questions or observations.

The nonstructured and small-sample features of qualitative-research techniques have an important implication concerning their application: Such techniques are intended to provide initial insights, ideas, or understanding about a problem; they are *not* meant to recommend a final course of action. Therefore qualitative-research techniques are most appropriate in situations calling for exploratory research. Several techniques covered in previous chapters—for example, the key-informant technique, the case study method, the focus group interview, the in-depth interview, the word association test, and nonstructured observation—are qualitative-research techniques that are often used in exploratory research.

QUALITATIVE VERSUS QUANTITATIVE RESEARCH

Quantitative research, in contrast to qualitative research, is characterized by more structure and by larger, more representative respondent samples. Consequently, the logical place for quantitative-research techniques (usually in the form of large-scale questionnaire surveys or structured observations) is in conclusive-research projects.

Table 7.1 outlines several illustrative situations to highlight the distinction between qualitative- and quantitative-research applications. A common thread running through the research settings under "Qualitative Research" in Table 7.1 is the need for developing an initial understanding of something. In contrast, each of the situations under "Quantitative Research" calls for very specific data,

Table 7.1
Applications of qualitative and quantitative research

	EXAMPLES OF RESEARCH SETTINGS BEST FOR	
TOPIC AREA	Qualitative Research	Quantitative Research
Advertising	The marketer of Shine detergent wants to come up with ideas for creatively communicating the detergent's benefits through a television commercial	Two different commercials for Shine detergent have been developed; management wants to know which of the two will be more effective in favorably influencing target customers' preferences for Shine
Product planning and promotion	The brand manager in charge of Rise baking soda wishes to develop an understanding of how, when, where, and why consumers use Rise	The brand manager wants to know whether distributing a 20-cents-off coupon for Rise will significantly increase its unit sales
Personal selling	The sales of a firm employing a large sales force have been dropping steadily; the sales manager wants to identify possible reasons for this decline	From discussions with several salespeople the sales manager suspects that the sales force's morale is low and wants to confirm it by using a standard employee morale questionnaire
Services marketing	The administrators of a hospital want to develop a feel for the nature and the extent of apprehension experienced by patients when they are in the hospital	The administrators want to ascertain patients' ratings of specific attributes of such things as room service, food service, and medical treatment
Politics	A candidate running for a U.S. Senate seat from Alaska wants to understand the social, economic, and environmental concerns of Alaskans	The candidate wants to determine the percentage of registered Alaskans that favor him over opponents vying for the same Senate seat

capable of suggesting a final course of action. Thus differences in methodology (e.g., sample selection, data collection, data analysis) between qualitative- and quantitative-research studies parallel methodological differences between exploratory and conclusive research discussed in Chapter 4 (see Table 4.1).

IMPORTANCE OF QUALITATIVE RESEARCH

We saw in Chapter 1 that there is a lot more to marketing research than numbers and statistics. This point needs to be reemphasized since it is tempting to believe (and some *do* believe) that qualitative research is somehow inferior to quantitative research and hence is truly not marketing research. However, quantification by itself does not make research any more accurate or valuable than soft research. One marketing research practitioner had the following reaction to those who refuse to recognize the importance of anything but quantitative research:

> The line between qualitative and quantitative research is not nearly as distinct as the numbers people would have us believe, consistent with a discipline which is more art than science. Both types of research have drawbacks which we must account for in deriving maximum value from their use. . . . Quantitative research is subjective, sometimes highly so, though admittedly generally less so than qualitative. If this is true, where then do we draw the line between marketing research and "something else"? . . . Numbers don't speak; analysts do. Figures lie and liars figure.[1]

Similar sentiments have been expressed by other practitioners. For instance, according to a director of marketing research for the Pillsbury Company:

> While these two terms [qualitative and quantitative] distinguish between two different forms of research, the dichotomy isn't quite as clearcut as some would think. . . . All data are "soft" and any way of gathering data is a series of compromises. What's key in commercial research is transforming data into information, insights, and knowledge.[2]

And in the words of Ernest Dichter, a pioneer in the area of applying motivation research techniques to marketing: "Too much [quantitative] attitude research is oversimplified. It counts noses instead of trying to explore the complexity of the human soul."[3] Some researchers have even suggested that qualitative research is needed to verify the accuracy of quantitative research results and to interpret

---

[1] "Qualitative *Is* Marketing Research Because It Aids Decision Makers, Helps Reduce Risk," *Marketing News,* January 22, 1982, Section 2, p. 8.

[2] Roger E. Bengston, "Despite Controversy, Focus Groups Are Used To Examine Wide Range of Marketing Questions," *Marketing News,* September 19, 1980, p. 18.

[3] "Try These 10 Research Techniques To Uncover *Real* Attitudes", *Marketing News,* May 13, 1983, Section 2, p. 6.

them properly.[4] "Frequently, statistical results from survey data analysis can be validated by recourse to qualitative observations and informant interviews."[5]

In fairness to the critics of qualitative research, however, we must mention that qualitative research has been misused by careless, and at times unscrupulous, researchers.[6] The most frequent misuse is making generalizations from research that is primarily intended to provide preliminary insights about a given research setting.

The proper position to take in a qualitative-versus-quantitative debate is to view *both* types of research as playing a legitimate and important role in marketing research. Just as exploratory research is a necessary prelude to conclusive research in most situations, qualitative research can be viewed as generating just the right type of raw material needed to produce a finished product in the form of a relevant quantitative-research project. Carrying this product analogy further, to view the raw material as the finished product is inappropriate and ridiculous. Similarly, without suitable raw material the finished product is likely to be unsatisfactory and even dangerous. The point is that in a properly conceived study qualitative- and quantitative-research techniques must *complement,* rather than *compete with,* each other.

We now turn to focus group interviews, which are perhaps the most widely and frequently used form of qualitative research.

FOCUS GROUP INTERVIEWS

As stated earlier, we have already covered several qualitative-research techniques. One technique mentioned in previous chapters but not discussed in detail is the *focus group interview,* often simply called focus group. This technique is such a popular type of qualitative research that many marketing research practitioners consider it synonymous with qualitative research. (As evidence of this practice, most articles on the topic appearing in *Marketing News* use the two terms interchangeably.)

A survey of business firms conducted in the midseventies revealed that about 50% used focus groups in their marketing research.[7] Also, a 1981 study of a sample of the largest consumer product companies in the United States showed that 95% used focus groups, up from 87% in a similar study conducted

[4] F. D. Reynolds and D. K. Johnson, "Validity of Focus Group Findings," *Journal of Advertising Research,* (June 1978), pp. 21–24.

[5] Rohit Deshpande, "'Paradigms Lost': On Theory and Method in Research in Marketing," *Journal of Marketing,* 47 (Fall 1983), p. 108.

[6] See, for example, "Qualitative Research Isn't Marketing Research; New Name May Promote Proper Use of Tools," *Marketing News,* January 22, 1982, Section 2, p. 9.

[7] Barnett A. Greenberg, Jac L. Goldstucker, and Danny N. Bellenger, "What Techniques Are Used by Marketing Researchers in Business?" *Journal of Marketing,* 41 (April 1977), pp. 62–68.

in 1978.[8] Finally, according to a 1981 survey of commercial marketing research firms in the United States, approximately 60% of them frequently conducted focus group interviews for their clients.[9] Clearly, there is a prevalence of focus groups in marketing research practice.

A significant portion of the remainder of this chapter is devoted to focus groups—not only because of their popularity but also because certain methodological issues related to focus groups may be relevant to other qualitative-research techniques as well.

Definition

A good way to get a feel for what goes on in focus group interviews is to examine the actual procedure followed by a firm that conducts a large number of them. The following description provided by Burke Marketing Research, Inc. serves as a useful introduction to focus group interviews.

> The respondents are requested to come to the Burke studios at a specified time. There the discussion is conducted in a relaxed atmosphere, with the environment approximating that found in a home, rather than those of an office or institution. Placing the respondents in a normal, relaxed situation is an important factor in gaining the prompt cooperation of the individuals in the group as the discussion begins. Interviewing is done during the day, if only non-working housewives are required, or at night if working women or men are needed.
>
> Burke discussions usually begin with the session leader explaining to the respondents the general purpose of group interviewing and the importance of their candid opinions. The discussion leader will normally have a written outline, which has been prepared to make sure that all subjects relevant to the objectives of the research will be covered. This outline proceeds from the general to the specific. Very often the leader, having brought up the broad general subject, will need to do very little guiding to see that all subject areas are covered. Usually these will be covered in any order brought up by respondents rather than following the written outline. This promotes normal conversation and the discussion leader only needs to probe into details within each area and to keep bringing out those respondents who are reluctant to voice their feelings. The discussion leader's own attitudes, of course, must never influence the discussion.[10]

---

[8] "Consumer Market Research Technique Usage Patterns and Attitudes in 1981," a report prepared (April 22, 1981) by Market Facts, Inc., 676 North St. Clair Street, Chicago, Ill. 60611.

[9] A. Parasuraman, "A Study of Techniques Used and Clients Served by Marketing Research Firms," *European Research,* 10 (October 1982), pp. 177–185.

[10] "Group Interviewing," an internal manual (out of print) prepared by Burke Marketing Research Inc., 800 Broadway, Cincinnati, Ohio 45202 (undated), p. 7.

This procedure is not unique to focus group interviews conducted by Burke; rather, it is a fair description of focus groups in general. It also suggests the following concise definition:

DEFINITION. **A *focus group interview* involves an objective discussion leader or moderator who introduces a topic to a group of respondents and directs their discussion of it in a nonstructured and natural fashion.**

The apparent air of informality implied in this definition does not mean that focus group interviews are easy to conduct. Quite to the contrary, focus groups as well as other qualitative-research techniques must be conceived and conducted with the utmost care if they are to be useful. As Bobby Calder correctly observes, "Qualitative marketing research is more complex than any simple notion that quantitative research permits objective numerical analysis which qualitative research sacrifices for intensive analysis and fast turnaround."[11]

The potential worth of focus group interviews depends highly on factors such as group composition, moderator characteristics, and the interview atmosphere itself. Unfortunately, there is no unanimous agreement among researchers about how one should select or manipulate these factors in order to reap maximum benefits from focus group interviews. According to the authors of a comprehensive monograph on qualitative research: "The interviews conducted with researchers and the readings examined in the preparation of this monograph revealed a number of disagreements concerning the use and methods involved in conducting research using focus group interviews."[12] Therefore, remember that any general inferences about focus groups made in the following sections, while reflecting the opinions of a majority of researchers, are not absolute.

Group composition

The effectiveness of a focus group depends very much on the number of participants and their characteristics. There is no scientific basis for determining the optimum focus group size. However, virtually all focus groups conducted by marketing research practitioners involve between 8 and 12 participants. Since focus groups have been in use for many years, and since practitioners are likely to continue to follow a guideline only if they find it useful, we can infer that the 8-to-12 group size is a rule of thumb. Groups with less than 8 participants are

[11] Bobby J. Calder, "Focus Groups and the Nature of Qualitative Marketing Research," *Journal of Marketing Research,* (August 1977), p. 360.

[12] Danny N. Bellenger, Kenneth L. Bernhardt, and Jac L. Goldstucker, *Qualitative Research in Marketing* (Chicago: American Marketing Association, 1976), p. 7. This monograph provides an excellent discussion of qualitative-research techniques; several of the ideas developed in this section stem from it.

apparently not likely to generate the momentum and group dynamics necessary for a truly beneficial focus group session (benefits unique to well-conducted focus groups will be discussed later). Similarly, a group with more than 12 participants may be too crowded to be conducive to a cohesive and natural discussion.[13]

Regarding the characteristics of participants, there is considerable agreement among published articles discussing this issue that a focus group must be as *homogeneous* as possible with respect to demographic and socioeconomic characteristics. "It is essential to get as much commonality in a group as possible so that the numerous interacting demographic variables do not confuse the issues; to be most productive, all the participants must be on the same wave length."[14]

Conducting focus groups using similar respondents has important implications concerning the generalizability and truthfulness of the collected data. An example will help clarify these implications.

EXAMPLE: Beauty Products, Inc. (BPI), is a firm marketing a variety of women's cosmetics. BPI is currently seeking ideas or concepts for developing a new cosmetic line with products appealing to a wide cross section of women. One logical starting point for BPI is to conduct focus group interviews with women to get them to talk freely about their makeup needs, use of cosmetics, satisfaction and dissatisfaction with existing products, suggestions for improvements, and so on. BPI decides to conduct a focus group interview of working women between the ages of 20 and 30.

Clearly, whatever inferences BPI draws from the focus group information cannot be generalized. There is no guarantee that ideas for new cosmetic products stemming from this group will appeal to other groups of women. This limitation is present in virtually all focus groups since they typically involve the use of small homogeneous samples. This limitation does not mean that focus groups are useless, though. The purpose of a focus group—as a matter of fact, the purpose of *any* qualitative-research technique—is to generate preliminary insights rather than to make generalizations.

The researchers for BPI would do well to conduct a *series* of focus groups, each internally homogeneous but different from the others in terms of age and employment status of the participants. Such a series of focus group interviews is likely to generate a range of new-product ideas appealing to a wide cross section of women. Indeed, judging from what is done in practice, very seldom is just

[13] That rules of thumb are just that and not universal laws is emphasized in at least one controlled study (as opposed to studies involving focus groups conducted in practice), which found that two four-member groups are better than one eight-member group; see Edward F. Fern, "The Use of Focus Groups for Idea Generation: The Effects of Group Size, Acquaintanceship, and Moderator on Response Quantity and Quality," *Journal of Marketing Research,* 19 (February 1982), pp. 1–13.

[14] Bellenger, Bernhardt, and Goldstucker, *Qualitative Research in Marketing,* p. 9.

one focus group conducted for a research project. A rule of thumb is to conduct at least two focus groups aimed at a single research issue so as to generate a meaningful, interpretable set of insights. Ideally, resources permitting, additional focus groups should be conducted as long as new information continues to emerge from them.

Though conducting several focus groups may yield a rich reservoir of data, the fact still remains that it is dangerous to draw any definitive conclusions from such data. This point is important because making generalizations on the basis of focus group interviews is perhaps the most frequent misuse of the technique. As one practitioner recently observed:

> [An] abuse [related to focus groups] is accumulating a large sample by a series of groups and trying to quantify the data. The need for qualitative or quantitative data should be determined before commitment to the technique. . . . Information from 100 respondents in 10 focus groups still isn't representative, because of the strong sampling and group dynamics biases. Information from 100 respondents interviewed individually might well be representative.[15]

Let us now examine the issue of the extent to which responses generated in a focus group are truthful or trustworthy. As we saw in the previous chapter, data obtained through questioning respondents can be biased owing to a variety of factors, such as respondent untruthfulness and interviewer errors. Focus group interviews are no exception to this bias, especially since participants in a group interview may be tempted to provide biased responses to impress others, to appear socially responsible, and so on. Moreover, a group that does not look "natural" from the participants' perspective may lead to forced or contrived responses, thereby aggravating the problem of response inaccuracies.

Intuitively, a homogeneous group in which participants can identify and feel comfortable with one another is likely to be more natural and relaxed than a heterogeneous group. Therefore contrived responses or responses intended merely to impress others are less likely to arise in a homogeneous group. To illustrate this point, let us once again look at the BPI case.

What would you expect to happen if BPI used heterogeneous rather than homogeneous focus groups in its quest for new-product ideas? Specifically, suppose a focus group interview is to be conducted with working and nonworking women, drawn from a wide range of age-groups. Since working status and age can strongly influence perceptions about the use of cosmetics, the participants in this group will most likely hold widely varying, and perhaps conflicting, opinions. Furthermore, differences in working status and age may lead to undesirable consequences; for instance, some women may become reticent, some may provide socially acceptable responses, and others may attempt to show off. The result is likely to be an unproductive focus group session, in terms of both

[15] Martin M. Buncher, "Focus Groups Seem Easy to Do and Use, but They're Easier to Misuse and Abuse," *Marketing News,* September 17, 1982, Section 2, p. 14.

the number of relevant insights generated and the validity of those insights. Thus homogeneous focus groups, although not capable of guaranteeing completely valid responses, are less likely to suffer from response inaccuracies than heterogeneous groups are.

The preceding discussion emphasizes the need to use proper screening procedures to ensure suitable group composition. Demographic similarity among participants in a group is desirable from the standpoint of generating useful, trustworthy data. An easy way of accomplishing this similarity is to recruit respondents from organizations such as church groups, clubs, and professional associations whose members are likely to be similar. A potential problem here, however, is whether this selection procedure will lead to any detrimental group behavior. According to Bellinger, Bernhardt, and Goldstucker: "Many researchers believe that an individual should not be allowed to participate in a group containing a friend, neighbor, or relative; they will tend to talk to each other and not to the group as a whole."[16]

However, controlled studies have not demonstrated any definite problem associated with having acquaintances and friends in the same group.[17] Moreover, several well-known commercial marketing research firms apparently do recruit focus group participants from organizations like churches and schools.[18] Such recruiting can be justified, since a well-qualified moderator can usually overcome difficulties such as participants talking to each other and not the group as a whole.

A problem more serious than participants who know one another beforehand is the problem of so-called *professional respondents,* people who have participated in numerous focus groups before. Professional respondents are atypical consumers, and their responses during a group session can lead to serious validity problems.[19] While one is screening respondents for focus groups, a good practice is to exclude those who have participated in a focus group within the previous six months or so.

Last, but not least, recruited participants must have had some experience related to the product or the issue to be discussed.[20] The reason should be obvious: Respondents lacking relevant experience are not likely to make any valuable contribution to the group discussion. To the contrary, they may adversely affect the discussion by making meaningless remarks just for the sake of participating. Therefore the screening procedure should query potential respondents about their past experience with or exposure to the focus group topic.

---

[16] Bellenger, Bernhardt, and Goldstucker, *Qualitative Research in Marketing,* p. 10.
[17] See Fern, "The Use of Focus Groups for Idea Generation."
[18] Burke Marketing Research Inc. is one such group; see "Group Interviewing," p. 5.
[19] For an interesting and insightful discussion of problems stemming from professional respondents, see Hazel Kahan, "'Professional' Respondents Say They're Better for Research than 'Virgins,' but They're Not," *Marketing News,* May 14, 1982, Section 1, p. 22.
[20] Bellenger, Bernhardt, and Goldstucker, *Qualitative Research in Marketing,* p. 10.

Exhibit 7.1 shows a screening questionnaire used by a research firm to recruit female respondents via telephone for a focus group dealing with appliance repair services. The first question is intended to ensure that potential respondents have had relevant experience. The second and third questions reflect client-imposed restrictions regarding participant characteristics. The last two questions are meant to screen out atypical and professional respondents. Only individuals who pass all five questions are recruited to participate in the focus group.

Moderator characteristics

Of all the factors influencing the effectiveness and usefulness of a focus group, the discussion leader or moderator is perhaps the most crucial. The moderator's role, in addition to being crucial, is an extremely delicate one. It involves stimulating natural discussion among all the participants while at the same time ensuring that the focus of the discussion does not stray too far from the topic.

Having a relatively homogeneous group can help to a certain extent in maintaining group cohesiveness and getting everybody to participate. Nevertheless, a group in which the personalities of all participants are mutually compatible is more of an exception than the rule. Focus groups usually have one or two people who strive to dominate the discussion and one or two shy individuals who are reluctant to participate. Therefore a moderator must have good *observation, interpersonal,* and *communication skills* to recognize and overcome threats to a healthy group discussion. Exhibit 7.2 describes several skills a good moderator should have. As the descriptions of the skill dimensions indicate, a moderator should maintain a delicate balance on each; swinging too far toward an extreme on any of them is likely to be detrimental.

In addition to the skills just described, moderators should have *interpretative skills.* Good moderators must be able to go beyond what the participants are saying by making note of such things as tone of voice, facial expressions, and other nonverbal behaviors of the group members. Such additional information will be valuable in interpreting the content of a focus group interview.[21] The importance of interpretative skills is evidenced in the following claim made by a research firm concerning its discussion leaders: "Leaders who have the knack of stimulating active participation in the discussions. Who benefit clients with insightful interpretations of what is said. *What is not said. What is meant*"[22] (emphasis added). Indeed, some have even suggested that a focus group is as much an observation technique as it is an interviewing technique.[23]

---

[21] See, for example, "Focus Group Moderators Should Be Well Versed in Interpretative Skills," *Marketing News,* February 18, 1981, p. 23.
[22] "Marketing Research," a brochure describing the services offered by Elrick and Lavidge, Inc., 10 South Riverside Plaza, Chicago, Ill. 60606.
[23] Robert W. Joselyn, *Designing the Marketing Research Project* (New York: Petrocelli/Charter, 1977), p. 90.

Exhibit 7.1

Screening questionnaire to recruit focus group participants

NAME:________________ DATE:____________

ADDRESS:______________ PHONE:___________

CITY & STATE:___________ INTERVIEWER:________

Hello, this is ________ from Chicagoland Field Service. We are planning a group discussion on the topic of appliance repair and service. Would you be interested in participating in such a session on ________ at ________? (IF "NO" terminate and tally)

1. Have you had an appliance (such as a television, washer, dryer, toaster, etc.) serviced or repaired within the last year?

   YES. . . . . 1 CONTINUE
   NO. . . . . 2 TERMINATE AND TALLY

2. Are you between the ages of 30 and 64?

   YES. . . . . 1 CONTINUE
   NO. . . . . 2 TERMINATE AND TALLY

3. Do you live in zipcodes, 60646, 60202, 60076 or 60077?

   YES. . . . . 1 CONTINUE
   NO. . . . . 2 TERMINATE AND TALLY

4. Do you or any member of your family work for an advertising agency, a market research firm or a company which makes, sells or distributes appliances?

   YES. . . . . 1 TERMINATE AND TALLY
   NO. . . . . 2 CONTINUE

5. When, if ever, did you last attend a market research group?

   ____

   (IF LESS THAN 6 MONTHS AGO—TERMINATE AND TALLY)

Source: Chicagoland Field Service, 6200 N. Hiawatha, Chicago, Ill. 60646. Used by permission.

There are apparently no clear-cut guidelines regarding the physical or demographic characteristics of the moderator vis-à-vis those of the focus group participants. For instance, there is no agreement among researchers about whether the moderator should be of the same sex as the participants.[24] The ability to quickly establish rapport with the participants and make them feel at ease within the group seems to be more critical than the moderator's physical characteristics.

To summarize, not every individual, even one who may be good at one-on-one interviewing, may be an effective focus group moderator. Being able to conduct a focus group interview productively requires certain inherent personal skills as well as extensive training. Several commercial marketing research firms have ongoing, real-life training programs for their moderators. These programs involve conducting real-life focus groups—not for any particular client but purely for the sake of training moderators.[25]

Conducting Focus Groups

Focus group sessions typically last between one and a half to two hours. To use this relatively short period of time productively, the moderator must make the participants feel relaxed and comfortable with one another as quickly as possible. A skilled moderator can aid in creating an atmosphere conducive to a congenial and effective group discussion. Other means of attempting to generate a relaxed atmosphere include making the focus group room and its furnishings informal, and serving some light refreshments before the session starts and making them available throughout the session.

Focus group interviews are invariably recorded at least on audiocassettes for subsequent replay, transcription, and analysis. They can also be recorded on videotapes, especially if conducted in a well-equipped focus group facility rather than in an improvised setting such as a hotel room. Videotaping a focus group interview in the latter case can sharply increase costs.

Recording focus group interviews, in addition to increasing costs, has another potential drawback: The recording equipment, especially if it is perceived by participants as intrusive and threatening, can make creating a relaxed atmosphere difficult. A similar limitation is also associated with the presence of one-way mirrors, which most focus group rooms have. These mirrors enable client personnel to observe the group session without themselves being observed.

One way to minimize the detrimental effects of electronic devices or other means of observing focus groups is to make the equipment as inconspicuous as possible. Indeed, one research firm boasts: "Our mirrors are decorative

---

[24] Bellenger, Bernhardt, and Goldstucker, *Qualitative Research in Marketing,* p. 16.

[25] For one such example, see Peggy Lang, "Women Executives Discuss Dressing the Part in Focus Group Sessions" *Marketing Today* (published by Elrick and Lavidge Inc.), 19 (1) (1981), p. 1.

Exhibit 7.2

Desirable focus group moderator skills

- **Kind but firm.** In order to elicit necessary interaction, the moderator must combine a disciplined detachment with understanding empathy. To achieve this, he must simultaneously display a kindly, permissive attitude toward the participants, encouraging them to feel at ease in the group interview environment, while insisting that the discussion remain germane to the problem at hand. Only with experience can the moderator achieve an appropriate blending of these two apparently antithetical roles.

  It is also the moderator's responsibility to encourage the emergence of leadership from within the group, while at the same time avoiding tendencies of domination of the group by a single member. The kindly but firm moderator must be sensitive to bids for attention and must maintain his leadership without threatening or destroying the interactional process.
- **Permissiveness.** While an atmosphere of permissiveness is desirable, the moderator must be at all times alert to indications that the group atmosphere of cordiality is disintegrating. Before permissiveness leads to chaos, the moderator must reestablish the group purpose and maintain its orientation to the subject.

  The moderator must be ready and willing to pursue clues to information that may at first appear tangential to the subject for it may open new areas of exploration. He must also be prepared to cope with expressions of unusual opinions and eruptions of personality clashes within the group. The manner in which these are handled may well be the difference between a productive and an unproductive group session.
- **Involvement.** Since a principal reason for the group interview is to expose feelings and to obtain reactions indicative of deeper feelings, the moderator must encourage and stimulate intensive personal involvement. If the moderator is unable to immerse himself completely in the topic being discussed, the group will sense his detachment, and the depth contribution of the interview will be lost.
- **Incomplete understanding.** A most useful skill of the group moderator is his ability to convey lack of complete understanding of the information being presented. Although he may understand what the participant is trying to express, by carefully inserting noncommittal remarks, phrased in questioning tones, the respondent is encouraged to delve more deeply into the sources of his opinion. He is, by this process, able to reveal and elaborate on the kinds of information for which the group interview is designed. The goal is to encourage respondents to be more specific about generalized comments made by group members.

  The usefulness of this technique can be endangered if its application is inappropriate. If the "incomplete understanding" is a superficially assumed role, the group will soon detect this artificiality, and will feel that the moderator is playing some sort of cryptic game with the group. The group interview will then deteriorate into a sterile collection of mutual suspicions. Incomplete understanding on the part of the moderator must be a genuine curiosity about the deeper sources of the participant's understanding.

- **Encouragement.** Although the dynamics of the group situation facilitate the participation of all members in the interaction, there may be individuals who resist contributing. The skillful moderator should be aware of unresponsive members and try to break down their reserve and encourage their involvement.

  The unresponsive member offers a real challenge to the group moderator. There are numerous ways in which a resistant or bashful member can be encouraged to participate, such as by assigning him a task to perform, or by providing an opening for his remarks. If this is inappropriately attempted, it may only reinforce a reluctance to participate in a verbal fashion. The ability to interpret nonverbal clues may provide a means of discovering a tactic to broaden the scope of the group's active participation.
- **Flexibility.** The moderator should be equipped prior to the session with a topic outline of the subject matter to be covered. By committing the topics to memory before the interview, the moderator may use the outline only as a reminder of content areas omitted or covered incompletely.

  If a topic outline is followed minutely, the progress of the interview will be uneven and artificial, jumping from topic to topic without careful transitions. This procedure communicates a lack of concern to the participants, for its mechanical nature makes the moderator appear to lack genuine interest in the responses.

  At the same time, the interview cannot be allowed to wander aimlessly. Under such conditions, control of the situation soon passes from the moderator to a self-appointed group leader.

  The group interview should be conducted the way one walks across a rope bridge. The handrails are gripped firmly and the objective is kept in mind constantly. If the bottom foot rope should break, the walk is continued hand over hand until the destination is reached. This requires an ability to improvise and alter predetermined plans amid the distractions of the group process.
- **Sensitivity.** The moderator must be able to identify, as the group interview progresses, the informational level on which it is being conducted, and determine if it is appropriate for the subject under discussion. Sensitive areas will frequently produce superficial rather than depth responses. Depth is achieved when there is a substantial amount of emotional responses, as opposed to intellectual information. Indications of depth are provided when participants begin to indicate how they feel about the subject, rather than what they think about it.

Source: Reprinted from Danny N. Bellenger, Kenneth L. Bernhardt, and Jac L. Goldstucker, *Qualitative Research in Marketing* (Chicago: American Marketing Association, 1976), pp. 12–16; as adapted by the authors from Donald A. Chase, "The Intensive Group Interview in Marketing," *MRA Viewpoints* (1973). Used by permission.

walls . . . not tell-tale windows."[26] However, such measures may still not guarantee the absence of any ill effects. This point is emphatically made by two practitioners who have conducted numerous focus groups:

> Researchers who conduct [focus] groups today often bring respondents into unfamiliar surroundings. And then they hope the "guinea pigs" won't be aware of, or inhibited by, the "laboratory" aspects of the facility. These aspects include corporate marketers lurking behind a giant one-way mirror; microphones carefully displayed to avoid distraction; and wires and cables running behind dropped ceilings to avoid detection. . . . Our tests and observations have shown that most group respondents are *not* fooled in the slightest by the mirror. In fact, many instantly were inhibited, apprehensive, or suspicious.[27]

We do not mean to say that the use of recording devices and observation of focus groups by anyone other than the moderator must be avoided. In fact, a primary strength of a focus group interview is that it offers decision makers a direct report of what consumers say and how they feel about products, services, and the like. Furthermore, with current technology client personnel who are geographically dispersed may observe a group session in progress at a central location[28]—a valuable benefit that would be lost by a self-imposed ban on the use of equipment by which outsiders can watch a focus group session.

How, then, can one reconcile the need for a natural, relaxed atmosphere on the one hand and the decision makers' need to get the most out of a focus group on the other? A good compromise is to use whatever devices are essential to obtain maximum benefits from a group session but to be open with participants about them. One should inform the participants about any recordings or observations that will take place during the session and explain the reasons for them. From the author's own experience with several focus groups, such candor, coupled with assurances from a well-trained moderator that no ulterior motives are involved, can put respondents at ease rapidly. In some instances it may be feasible and desirable to introduce client observers to the participants and even seat them in the focus group room.[29]

Advantages of focus groups

A number of articles have discussed many specific advantages of focus groups.[30] Rather than repeat any lengthy list here, we provide a synthesis in the form of

---

[26] "Answers to your Questions About Winona, Inc.," a brochure prepared by Winona, Inc., 8200 Humboldt Avenue So., Minneapolis, Minn. 55431, p. 12.

[27] John O. Davies III and Jay F. Wilson, "Focus Groups Need New Focus, Changes in Their Facilities, Moderator Strategy, Marketing," *Marketing News,* May 13, 1983, Section 2, p. 19.

[28] For an illustration of this capability, see F. George du Pont, "Use Telephone to 'Attend' Distant Qualitative Research Sessions," *Marketing News,* May 13, 1983, Section 2, p. 19.

[29] The use of such an approach is reported by Davies and Wilson, "Focus Groups Need New Focus."

[30] See, for example, Bellenger, Bernhardt, and Goldstucker, *Qualitative Research in Marketing,* pp. 17–28; John M. Hess, "Group Interviewing," in *New Science of Planning,* ed R. L. King (Chicago: American Marketing Association, 1968), pp. 193–196; Alfred E. Goldman, "The Group Depth Interview," *Journal of Marketing,* 26 (July 1962), pp. 61–68.

general advantages, each of which encompasses several specific advantages cited in the literature.

Richness of data. A well-conducted focus group interview can provide numerous important insights that a series of one-on-one depth interviews may be unable to generate.[31] Respondents are generally less likely to feel inhibited in the company of others similar to them than they are when alone with an interviewer. They are also likely to be more creative in terms of offering insights about the topic being discussed. A comment made by one participant may trigger a stream of new ideas from the others; this reaction obviously cannot occur in a series of individual interviews.

Versatility. Focus groups can be used to gain insight into a great variety of problems (examples of common applications of focus groups will be described in a subsequent section). Almost any product, service, concept, issue, or the like, can be productively discussed in a focus group setting. Focus groups are also versatile in another respect: A number of different techniques (e.g., a projective question or a TAT type of picture) and stimuli (e.g., a product or an ad) can be used in conjunction with or during a focus group in order to increase the productivity of the discussion.[32] As one research firm puts it: "Consumers [in our focus groups] have turned knobs, opened doors, used pots and pans, eaten foods, ripped and pulled at materials, laughed and frowned at greeting cards, and in hundreds of other ways have acted naturally, as consumers normally do when confronted with a new idea or a new product designed for their consumption."[33]

Ability to study special respondents. Focus groups may be the only feasible method of gathering data in certain situations where conducting one-on-one interviews is unproductive or impossible. Such situations involve special types of respondents such as children, especially very young children. Interviewing children on a one-on-one basis is often difficult and frustrating. A researcher using focus group interviews for research with children is likely to be more successful in generating useful information. According to Child Research Services (CRS), a division of McCollum/Spielman specializing in studying children: "While there may be major impediments to talking candidly with children, this does not mean that they are uncommunicative. In fact, children communicate very well through play, which has become the linchpin of CRS's methodology

---

[31] Although this view is held by a majority of researchers, it is not unanimously believed; for some differing viewpoints, see, for example, Fern, "The Use of Focus Groups for Idea Generation"; Melanie S. Payne, "Individual In-Depth Interviews Can Provide More Details Than Groups," *Marketing Today,* 20 (1) (1982), pp. 1–3.

[32] Goldman, in "The Group Depth Interview," discusses the use of several techniques and stimuli during focus group sessions.

[33] "Group Interviewing," Burke Marketing Research Inc., p. 1.

for extracting information from small children in *focus groups*"[34] (emphasis added).

Other groups of hard-to-interview respondents include professionals such as doctors and lawyers who frequently refuse to be interviewed individually. However, these professionals may be receptive to a group interview, which gives them an opportunity to be with their colleagues and compare notes with them on topics of mutual professional interest.[35]

Impact on managers. As has been pointed out in previous chapters, one of the pet peeves of managers (i.e., users of marketing research) is that researchers overemphasize sophisticated techniques and statistical results. Consequently, quantitative-research reports often do no more than collect dust on managers' shelves. However, qualitative-research studies, in general, and focus group studies, in particular, stand a much better chance of making an impression on managers (i.e., of being acted upon). Why? Because managers have the opportunity to get actively involved in and observe a focus group study instead of merely reading a research report. Moreover, key ideas emerging from a focus group, and a few crucial statements made by the participants, can sometimes have a greater impact on decision makers than a report full of impressive tables and statistics. Relevant quotes from a focus group interview may be worth a thousand numbers, so to speak. The following example is a case in point from the author's personal experience.

EXAMPLE: A securities brokerage firm commissioned a series of focus groups to understand customers' perceptions of and satisfaction with brokers who handled their transactions. One respondent in a male focus group made the following statement, indirectly describing his own frustration with brokers: "Sometimes, consumers tend to go along with what the broker says because they don't want to sound like 'morons'!" All the other participants nodded in agreement. Just as if designed to reinforce this feeling, another male respondent in a *different* focus group held in a *different* city described an ideal broker this way: "I like to be able to ask dumb questions. How he [the broker] reacts to the dumb question is very important to me." The two statements, emerging from two different focus groups, conveyed the same powerful message: Brokers tend to talk over customers' heads and make them feel stupid and uncomfortable. Needless to say, these customer remarks and others like them made a deep impression on the firm's executives.

---

[34] "The Child Research Services," a brochure published by McCollum/Spielman Associates, Inc., 18 East 48th Street, New York, N.Y. 10017.

[35] Lee Adler, "To Learn What's on the Consumer's Mind, Try Some Focused Group Interviews," *Sales & Marketing Management,* 122 (April 9, 1979), pp. 76–77.

The point here is that "colorful" and natural customer statements, capable of having a significant impact on decision makers, can only emerge from a focus group setting.

Disadvantages of focus groups

As in the case of advantages, a concise set of general or global disadvantages—synthesizing numerous specific drawbacks cited in the literature—is presented here.

Lack of generalizability. To emphasize what we have already seen, *focus group results cannot be viewed as conclusive.* The small sample sizes and homogeneous group compositions, while crucial to conducting focus groups effectively, make any insights gained from them highly tentative. Moreover, a person who agrees to participate in a focus group interview is typically more outgoing than the average consumer. This bias, coupled with the possible presence of professional respondents who routinely participate in numerous group interviews, can further erode the representativeness of a focus group.

Opportunity for misuse. Some of the very strengths of focus groups—richness of data and impact on managers, for example—can turn into serious drawbacks when the technique is employed by careless researchers and managers. One potential misuse of focus groups occurs when managers yield to a temptation to generalize a few key remarks made by participants, especially when similar remarks are made in several focus groups. Generalization is a serious mistake, since the primary purpose of focus groups is simply to generate insights or hypotheses, which must be verified through more formal research using representative samples.

Another potential misuse stems from the opportunity for moderators and managers to interpret focus group data any way they want to. Although this problem can occur with the use of any qualitative-research technique, it is particularly serious in focus group interviews. Since focus groups are informal, and since the data they generate are typically varied and rich, moderators and managers with preconceived notions about an issue may be able to find support for their positions by interpreting the data selectively—that is, by hearing and emphasizing only those remarks that do not dispute their opinions. If such selective perceptions occur, the focus group results will be questionable. Objective moderators and open-minded managers are essential to ensure proper use of focus groups. The former is especially critical: A moderator who is not objective can misinterpret the focus group data and also lead the discussion in a direction consistent with his or her personal viewpoints.

Cost. A focus group interview that is professionally conducted in a research firm's facility can easily run up a total bill of around $2000. If this figure sounds high, consider the following variety of expensive items essential for a well-conducted focus group: Numerous telephone calls are usually needed to recruit even a handful of qualified participants—several research firms charge around $15 to $20 just to recruit *each* respondent (this cost will be even higher if rare or hard-to-reach respondents are to be recruited). And, normally, the firm must recruit a few extra respondents because of the possibility of no-shows at the time of the interview. An incentive of around $30 is usually paid to each recruit who shows up (even to those who have to be turned away if everybody recruited shows up). A qualified moderator's fee for conducting a focus group may run around $300. Adding to the above items such things as renting the focus group facility, transcribing and interpreting the interview, and videotaping (each of these usually cost several hundred dollars apiece) shows why a single focus group can cost $2000.

Some managers, though, may perceive the total cost of even a series of focus groups as low because a typical quantitative project conducted by a research firm can carry a price tag of $15,000 to $20,000. However, this perception is fallacious since focus groups are a prelude to, and *not* a replacement for, quantitative research. Furthermore, on a *cost-per-respondent* basis, focus groups are extremely expensive.[36] Therefore focus groups that are conducted without the managers' establishing a need for them, and without thinking through what they can and cannot deliver, will be an unnecessary drain on a firm's resources. Managers who rely on focus group research, believing that the technique is a quick substitute for formal research, run the risk of making bad decisions in addition to wasting valuable resources.

Focus group applications

Focus groups can be used in almost any situation requiring some preliminary insights. However, specific applications of focus groups are too numerous to discuss here. Therefore this section simply presents three broad application categories that include the most frequent applications of the technique: understanding consumers, product planning, and advertising.

Understanding consumers. Focus groups can be helpful in attempting to get a feeling for consumers' perceptions, opinions, and behavior concerning products or services. For example, a manufacturer of cake mixes may be interested in questions such as these: What do consumers like about baking? What do they dislike? Why do they bake? How do they bake? What words/terms do they use in describing baking products and their use? Insights about these issues can be useful in a variety of situations, such as when the firm wants to identify marketing problems or opportunities worthy of further investigation, or when it is

[36] These points are emphasized by Adler, "To Learn What's on the Consumer's Mind."

planning a formal consumer survey and wants to know what questions are worth including in it and how they should be worded.

Product planning. Focus groups are useful in generating ideas for new products. For instance, consider the case of Glass*Plus, an all-purpose, light-duty spray cleaner marketed by Texize Chemicals. Before conception of the idea for Glass*Plus, Texize had conducted a survey of consumers concerning their use of its products, one of which was Fantastik, a heavy-duty cleaner. This survey showed that many consumers were using Fantastik to clean glass despite the product's not being recommended for cleaning glass. Texize therefore conducted a series of focus group interviews to understand why consumers were using Fantastik to clean glass when products like Windex were specifically available for that purpose. Insights from these focus groups pointed out the need for an intermediate-strength product that could be used for cleaning glass as well as for other household-cleaning chores. The idea for Glass*Plus was thus born.[37] Focus group interviews can also be used to suggest ideas for modifying existing products so as to improve their market performance.

Advertising. Perhaps the most frequent application of focus groups is in developing creative concepts and copy material for advertisements. Advertising agencies almost constantly face the challenge of changing advertisements to give them a new look and to increase their impact on consumers. They are heavy users of focus groups since a major strength of the technique is its ability to generate new ideas. Focus groups can suggest appropriate words, slogans, copy themes, pictures, and product benefits for use in advertisements. They can even offer hints on acting for television commercial models, as the following example demonstrates.

EXAMPLE: A marketer of a painkiller specifically intended for people with a certain type of disease wanted to develop an effective television commercial for it. A group of people afflicted by the disease was assembled, and each person was asked to describe and discuss the pain resulting from the disease. The group discussion was videotaped. "By closely examining the videotapes, [it was] found that there were a series of some 45 nonverbal facial and body expressions people used when they spoke about pain and its relief—gestures which were incorporated into the commercials used to advertise the product."[38]

To further demonstrate the application of focus groups and to emphasize their proper use, we provide a real-life illustration in Exhibit 7.3. In this illustra-

[37] Bellenger, Bernhardt, and Goldstucker, *Qualitative Research in Marketing,* p. 22, discuss this and other examples in greater detail.

[38] Lisa Gubernick, "Are Market Research Groups Out of Focus?" *Adweek,* September 5, 1983, p. 22.

Exhibit 7.3

Focus group application: Johnson car air-conditioning filter

The Johnson company developed a new filter to be used in car air conditioning systems. Management wanted to find out the feasibility of the new product and develop a workable marketing plan. A two-stage research process was followed. Focus group interviews were used in stage 1 to help develop hypotheses to identify potential markets, to determine advantages and disadvantages of the product from the consumer viewpoint, and to identify specific points for questionnaire design.

The focus group interviews indicated that families in which one or more members had allergy or respiratory problems might be the best prospects for the new product. Persons seriously concerned about air pollution were also identified as good potential buyers. The major disadvantages of the product were the performance capability of the filter and the cost of replacement cartridges. Some individuals feared that the filter would cause their car's air conditioning system to malfunction. Nonallergic consumers expressed doubt about their need for the product. An unexpected resistance occurred when consumers were informed that the filter would need to be changed periodically.

After hearing the results of the focus group, the client wanted to proceed immediately with market introduction as a result of the findings that seemed favorable. On the advice of the research firm, the quantitative study in stage 2 of the research process was conducted. An analysis of 1500 respondents in five cities showed that the original marketing strategy for introducing the new product was not economically feasible. This led to the development of an alternative marketing plan.

Source: Reprinted from Keith K. Cox, James B. Higginbotham, and John Burton, "Applications of Focus Group Interviews in Marketing," *Journal of Marketing,* 40 (January 1976), pp. 78–79. Used by permission of the publisher, the American Marketing Association, Chicago, Ill.

tion, note especially that the focus groups were helpful in gaining an initial understanding of the target market and in developing an appropriate questionnaire for the quantitative study; that the company executives were eager to take final action simply on the basis of *some* of the focus group results (this temptation is not uncommon); and that had such final action been taken, the consequences could have been very unfavorable.

OTHER QUALITATIVE-RESEARCH TECHNIQUES

The traditional focus group interview as described in the preceding sections is the most frequently used, but not the *only,* form of qualitative research. Several techniques presented in the previous chapter as illustrations of nonstructured data collection (e.g., in-depth interviews and projective techniques) are also types of qualitative research, but they will not be discussed again here. Rather, techniques we have not seen thus far, several of which are variations of the traditional focus group interview, will be presented to illustrate the wide variety of choices available in qualitative research.

Dual-moderator group

The *dual-moderator group,* as its name implies, is a focus group interview conducted by two moderators. Dual-moderating can be particularly useful in focus groups involving discussion of a highly technical topic.[39] An example is a group of electronic engineers discussing new concepts for computer memory chips. If dual-moderating is used in such a group, the two moderators will have distinct roles: One will be responsible for the smooth flow of the session, and the other will be responsible for ensuring discussion of specific technical issues that might otherwise be overlooked. The former is a sort of social moderator, while the latter is a technical moderator. To be truly beneficial, dual-moderating requires effective coordination between the two moderators as well as good rapport between each moderator and the respondents. This coordination may not always be easy to accomplish.

An interesting variation of the dual-moderator group is the *dueling-moderator group* in which the two moderators deliberately take opposite positions on the issue to be discussed. The moderators get together before the focus group session starts and agree to a plan outlining what positions each will support, as well as how often and when they will do so during the session. Dueling-moderator groups are appropriate for examining and understanding people's perceptions about controversial social or political issues.[40] Properly conducted dueling-moderator focus groups can offer valuable suggestions for correcting misperceptions and changing opinions. As you might expect, however, such focus groups conducted by ill-qualified and inexperienced moderators run the risk of resulting in pandemonium rather than providing useful insights.

Other extensions of the dual-moderator group include the following:

- Respondent-moderator groups in which the real moderator may ask selected participants to temporarily play the role of moderator so as to improve group dynamics and productivity.
- Client-participant groups in which client personnel are introduced to respondents and made part of the group. The client-participant's primary role (in addition to gaining firsthand knowledge about the session) is to offer clarifications and other relevant inputs that can improve the efficiency and effectiveness of the discussion.[41]

---

[39] J. Pope, "Six Ways to Improve Today's Focus Group Research," *Advertising Age,* 48 (July 11, 1978), p. 150.

[40] Buncher, "Focus Groups Seem Easy," elaborates on these points.

[41] Further discussion of these two and other focus group variations are found in Buncher, "Focus Groups Seem Easy,"; Pope, "Six Ways to Improve."

Groups receiving instant feedback about participants' collective opinions

Some research firms are now using electronic technology to cut down on unproductive discussion time and hence increase the value of focus groups. The electronic gadgetry used for this purpose is called the *consensor,* and it provides each participant with a hand-held terminal. All terminals are connected to a common video-display screen visible to the entire group. Each hand-held terminal has two dials: an opinion dial, which is used to anonymously express an opinion about an issue on a scale of 0 (no) to 10 (yes), and a weighting dial, which is used to express strength of an opinion on a 0%–100% scale.

The consensor is a valuable timesaver when the moderator wants to poll the participants on some issue germane to the group discussion. Participants simply express their feelings using their hand-held terminals, and the results are instantly tabulated and displayed in the form of a histogram on the video screen.

According to one practitioner who has used this technology: "The Consensor allows a group leader to focus more on the issue of *why* people feel the way they do, and not *how* they feel."[42] The consensor provides a tangible stimulus (i.e., the video display) to guide the discussion, and, apparently, it also stimulates greater participant interest and involvement than a traditional focus group does. Using the consensor does involve a potentially serious risk: The histograms and numbers may tempt clients to believe that the results are *generalizable.* Such a belief constitutes a misuse of focus groups.

Crowded one-on-one interview

A *crowded one-on-one interview* is actually a variation of the in-depth interview. In a crowded one-on-one interview up to three client personnel are present in the room and observe a depth interview, as it is conducted by a professional interviewer in a conventional fashion. After the interview is over, the client personnel can ask additional questions or seek clarifications of responses already given. According to one marketing researcher: "Crowded one-on-ones are particularly effective when new concepts, designs, advertising, promotional messages, etc. are in the formulation stage."[43]

Shopper study

In a *shopper study* a professional interviewer plays the role of a customer and gathers relevant data (through questioning as well as observation) on issues of

[42] Lynn M. Moss, "Consumer's 'Visual Feedback' of Opinions Could Revolutionize Focus Group Research," *Marketing News,* November 26, 1982, Section 2, p. 6.

[43] Richard E. Matheson, "Qualitative Research Methods (Other than Focus Groups) Can Provide Valuable Information," *Marketing News,* May 13, 1983, Section 1, p. 14. This reference discusses crowded one-on-ones as well as other variations of in-depth interviews; it also mentions several potential applications of the shopper studies described next in this text.

interest. Shopper studies that generate data in an unobtrusive or disguised fashion (so as to ensure data validity) can provide valuable insights. For instance, a retail establishment whose sales depend heavily on its floor salespeople can hire interviewer-shoppers to gather data about the selling techniques used by the salespeople. Interviewer-shoppers can also be hired to generate information about such things as competitors' prices, product assortments, and product display effectiveness. Shopper studies have very many such applications.

The preceding list of qualitative-research techniques is by no means exhaustive. A researcher's imagination is the limit on the specific form qualitative research takes in a given situation, as demonstrated by the variations of traditional techniques illustrated in this section. Such flexibility and opportunity to improvise is a major strength of qualitative research. Unfortunately, this very strength is also an invitation for ill-qualified and/or unscrupulous researchers to misuse and abuse qualitative research.

A high degree of subjectivity is involved in every stage of the qualitative-research process, including the critical stages of sample selection, data collection, analysis, and interpretation, which has a major bearing on the validity of the results. Therefore using qualitative research carelessly and irresponsibly can give a very misleading picture of reality, on top of wasting a firm's resources. The three limitations discussed in connection with focus groups—unprojectable results, opportunity for misuse, and high cost per respondent—apply to other qualitative techniques as well and must be kept in mind by all qualitative researchers and potential users of the research results.

SUMMARY

Qualitative research involves generating information that cannot be summarized in the form of numbers. It is characterized by nonstructured, flexible data collection from relatively small respondent samples. The primary purpose of qualitative research is to generate insights and ideas. Therefore the proper place for qualitative techniques is in exploratory-research projects. In contrast, quantitative techniques are more appropriate for conclusive-research projects.

Qualitative research is no less important or valuable than quantitative research. The two types of research should be viewed as complementing each other—qualitative research can be a valuable, and many times necessary, prelude to quantitative research.

The most widely used qualitative-research technique is the focus group interview. Three major determinants of focus group effectiveness are (1) group composition, (2) moderator characteristics, and (3) the manner in which the focus group is conducted (i.e., group atmosphere). Although there are no absolute guidelines for these factors, several rules of thumb have emerged through experience.

Focus groups typically have 8 to 12 participants. Homogeneity of group members, especially on characteristics such as sex and age, is crucial. Focus group participants must also have had some experience with or exposure to the discussion topic, and they should not be professional respondents. A generally accepted practice is to conduct at least two focus groups on a given topic.

To be effective, a focus group moderator should have good observation, interpersonal, communication, and interpretative skills. The physical or demographic characteristics of the moderator are apparently not as critical as his or her ability to establish rapport with respondents and guide the discussion in a natural, yet focused, fashion.

To be of maximum benefit, focus groups should be conducted in a relaxed, comfortable atmosphere. Having the appropriate physical setting and amenities can be helpful. Focus groups are invariably recorded by electronic means and are often observed unobtrusively by client personnel. An important factor here is to ensure that the means used for recording and observing do not adversely affect group atmosphere and hence the quality of the discussion.

The major advantages of focus groups include the richness of the data they can generate, their versatility—in terms of their wide application potential as well as their flexibility to be used in conjunction with other techniques—their usefulness in gathering data from otherwise hard-to-interview respondents, and their ability to make a lasting impression on managers. A limitation of focus groups is that their results are not generalizable. Moreover, the subjectivity involved in conducting and interpreting focus groups is an invitation for irresponsible users to abuse the technique. Focus groups are also expensive, especially on a cost-per-respondent basis.

A general application of focus groups is to develop an understanding of consumers and their perceptions. Focus groups can reveal signs of potential problems, suggest reasons for existing problems, and point out possible marketing opportunities. They can also be helpful in designing formal-research studies of consumers. More specific applications of focus groups occur in the area of product planning and advertising.

Qualitative-research techniques other than the traditional focus group interview include some techniques that were discussed in previous chapters (e.g., case studies, in-depth interviews, and projective techniques); variations of focus group interviews (e.g., dual-moderator and dueling-moderator groups); and variations of in-depth interviews such as crowded one-on-ones and shopper studies. While these techniques can provide valuable insights, they also suffer from the potential limitations of focus groups.

QUESTIONS

1. Summarize the key differences between qualitative and quantitative research.
2. "Qualitative research must not be conducted in situations where obtaining quantitative data is the ultimate objective." Discuss this statement.

3. Discuss the reasons why a focus group should consist of similar participants.

4. How many focus groups should be conducted on any given topic? Explain your answer.

5. Who are professional respondents? In what ways can they affect a focus group?

6. Briefly describe the skills that an effective focus group moderator should have.

7. "It is not advisable to record a focus group interview through electronic means." Discuss the pros and cons of this statement, indicate what *your* position is, and defend your position.

8. State the general advantages and disadvantages of focus groups, and describe each in a sentence or two.

9. Why are focus groups widely used in advertising?

10. What are the differences between dual-moderator and dueling-moderator focus groups?

11. State and briefly describe two variations of the traditional in-depth interview.

12. For each of the following scenarios, indicate whether qualitative or quantitative research is more appropriate. Also recommend a specific technique for each, and justify your answer.

a. A manufacturer of food coloring wants to know how often and for what purposes or occasions consumers use food-coloring products.

b. A firm marketing chewing gum has two alternative wrapper designs for the product and is wondering which one is likely to result in higher sales.

c. A medical products company is in the final stages of perfecting a new method of contraception. It wants to guage the reactions of men and women to the new method and their potential acceptance of the method.

d. A national charitable organization wants to identify ways of sharply increasing the amount of contributions from the public.

8

Introduction to Experimentation in Marketing

Questions like the following are frequently faced by decision makers in a variety of organizations:

- Question facing the advertising manager of a firm marketing canned soups: "Will replacing commercial A with commercial B for our canned soups lead to a marked increase in consumer preference for our brand?"
- Question facing the marketing vice president of a retail store chain selling a line of fashion clothing: "Can we improve the profitability of our fashion clothing line by increasing its price by 10%?"
- Question facing the sales manager of an industrial marketing firm selling components to electronic-goods manufacturers: "Will an increase in the average number of sales calls per customer from six to eight per year significantly improve sales?"
- Question facing the fund-raising chairman of a charitable organization: "Will it be worthwhile to mail to last year's donors an attractive (but expensive) brochure describing our organization's activities and soliciting higher contributions for this year?"

Decision makers typically answer questions like these on the basis of results from limited exploratory or descriptive research (see Chapter 4 for a discussion of these types of research) or, sometimes, solely on their intuitions. Yet each of these illustrative questions implies that an accurate answer can only be ascertained through some form of *controlled* research. That is, each question involves investigating the nature of a *causal association* between two things: the impact of type of commercial on consumer preference in the first case, the impact of a price increase on profitability in the second, the impact of a greater number of sales calls per customer on sales in the third, and the impact of using a brochure on the volume of contributions in the last case. As we saw in Chapter 4, given data pertaining to two variables, the assurance with which one can estimate the impact of one variable on the other critically depends on the conditions under which the data are gathered. Of all the various types of research that may suggest causality between two variables, the greatest assurance that a causal inference is sound will stem from experimental research.

DEFINITION. An *experiment* is a procedure in which one (or sometimes more than one) causal variable is systematically manipulated and data on the effect variable are gathered, while controlling for other variables that may influence the effect variable.

This chapter will provide an overview of experiments in the field of marketing research, including the major approaches to conducting marketing experiments and potential biases that can limit the degree of researcher control in such experiments. The next chapter will cover certain standard experimental designs useful for marketers and discuss the advantages and disadvantages of each. To place marketing experiments in their proper perspective, we will first review the distinction between experimental and descriptive research and the general conditions that must be met for making conclusive statements about the nature of causality between variables. The next two sections provide this review.

DESCRIPTIVE VERSUS EXPERIMENTAL RESEARCH

Keith Cox and Ben Enis succinctly describe the distinguishing features of experimental research as follows (in the quotation "independent variable" and "experimental variable" are what we referred to earlier as "causal variable," and "dependent variable" is what we referred to as "effect variable"):

> Experimentation differs from alternative methods of marketing research in that in experimentation the researcher manipulates the independent variable or variables before measuring the effect upon the dependent variable. For example, the effect of price changes on sales volume of a particular product can be examined by actually varying the price of the product. A nonexperimental approach would be to ask consumers whether they would buy more of the product if [its price were lowered]. The manipulation of independent variables, together with procedures of controlling extraneous variation . . . forms the basis of the power of experimental research relative to other research techniques. The better the researcher's control over the experimental

variables and extraneous variation, the more confident the researcher can be that he is in fact determining cause and effect relationships.[1]

The distinction between descriptive and experimental research is more a matter of degree than of kind. While descriptive-survey data will merely suggest causation, data generated through experimental research will increase the degree of confidence one can have in any suggested cause. Although, theoretically, a completely controlled experiment can indicate for sure whether something is caused by something else, in marketing practice complete control is rarely possible. Therefore seldom can causation be conclusively established in practical settings. This point is especially noteworthy because the term *marketing experiment* does not necessarily imply that evidence of association between variables based on experimental data is *proof* that the association is a causal one. The following illustrations provided by a noted scholar highlight the strength of experimental research and yet underline the fact that such research cannot establish causality with 100% certainty:

> When an experimenter paints the skins of rats with carcinogenic substances (x), adequately controls other variables, and the rats ultimately develop carcinoma (y), the argument [favoring a causal link between x and y] is compelling because x (and other possible x's, theoretically) is controlled and y is predicted. But when an investigator finds cases of lung cancer (y) and then goes back among the multiplicity of causes ($x_1, x_2, \ldots, x_n$) and picks cigarette-smoking (say x_3) as the culprit, he is in a more difficult and ambiguous situation. Neither situation is sure, of course; both are probabilistic. But in the experimental case the investigator is *more* sure.[2]

The discussion in the next section should further reinforce our contention that experimental research is not necessarily infallible.

CONDITIONS FOR INFERRING CAUSALITY

When can one confidently conclude that some variable (say X) has a causal influence on another variable (say Y)? The literature on experimental research suggests three rather intuitive conditions that must be satisfied for making a statement such as "If X, then Y":[3]

1. Temporal ordering of variables. The variable X (or a change in X) must occur before the variable Y (or a change in Y) is observed.

---

[1] Keith K. Cox and Ben M. Enis, *Experimentation for Marketing Decisions* (Scranton, Pa.: International Textbook, 1969), p. 5.

[2] Fred N. Kerlinger, *Foundations of Behavioral Research* (New York: Holt, Rinehart and Winston, 1973), p. 380.

[3] See, for example, Claire Selltiz, Marie Jahoda, Morton Deutsch, and Stuart W. Cook, *Research Methods in Social Relations* (New York: Holt, Rinehart and Winston, 1959), pp. 83–88.

2. Evidence of association. The data on variables *X* and *Y* must suggest that the two are related in some fashion. In Chapter 4 we saw briefly how evidence of association (or lack thereof) between variables can be ascertained through cross-tabulation. This technique and other analysis procedures for examining associations will be covered in detail in Chapters 16 and 18.

3. Control of other causal factors. Unless all potential causal factors other than *X* are satisfactorily controlled or accounted for, the statement "If *X*, then *Y*" may be false *even when* *X* precedes *Y* and evidence of association between the two exists.

All three conditions must be met before causality between *X* and *Y* can be inferred. Of the three, the third condition is most critical and perhaps also the most difficult to satisfy in practical research projects. Proper temporal ordering of variables and evidence of association can usually be inferred from observational and/or questionnaire data collected through descriptive research. But some form of experimental research is invariably required to account for other causal factors.[4]

Even in experimental settings, however, one cannot always be sure that *all* extraneous factors have been accounted for. Sometimes experimental researchers may not even be aware of some potential causal factors. As Charles Ramond correctly observes:

> Designing a conclusive marketing experiment requires a thorough knowledge of the specific situation and the ability to control, observe, or even foresee enough of the possible causes of the effect under study to permit observation of the undiluted influence of some of them. This ability can sometimes be learned from a thorough analysis of the sales and marketing history of the product involved. . . . In other cases there may be no way of knowing until some experiments have been done.[5]

Fortunately, most real-life situations call for *reasonable* (rather than *complete*) assurance of control, which sound experimental studies are capable of providing. Nevertheless, one must be cautious in making causal inferences simply because the first two conditions are satisfied.

To highlight the fallacy of such inferences, consider the well-known fact that roosters crow every morning before the sun rises. In this case roosters' crows certainly precede sunrises, and there is evidence of strong association between the two. Yet it is obviously ridiculous to infer that the sun rises *because* roosters crow. Although that one would make such an inference is unthinkable, the moral of this example is often subtly ignored by those who make causal infer-

[4] Several real-life studies leading to incorrect causal inferences owing to inadequate control of extraneous factors are described by Charles Ramond, *The Art of Using Science in Marketing* (New York: Harper & Row, 1974), pp. 180–184.

[5] Ramond, *Art of Using Science,* pp. 187–188.

ences solely on the basis of proper temporal sequencing and evidence of association. The following example illustrates this point.

EXAMPLE: In a *Time* magazine article examining the MTV cable channel devoted to music videos, an executive associated with MTV is quoted as saying: "I think Duran Duran (a British rock music band) owes its life to MTV." In apparent support of this executive's inference, the article states:

> Even the record industry . . . noticed that the Duran Duran album, *Rio,* was being sold out at half the record stores in Dallas and was gathering dust in the other half. A check of the local television listings showed that parts of the city that were wired for cable and carrying MTV were the very same parts where the album was flourishing.[6]

The implication here is that availability of the MTV channel *caused* a sharp increase in sales of the Duran Duran album. The former certainly preceded the latter, and there is no question that the two were strongly associated. Yet, borrowing some terminology from the criminal justice system, the evidence here is mainly "circumstantial" and does not show "beyond a reasonable doubt" that MTV was responsible for the sales success of Duran Duran's album in some parts of Dallas. Other uncontrolled factors might have been responsible for what was observed. For instance, availability of the MTV channel and high sales of the album may *both* have been caused independently by unobserved factors such as the socioeconomic status and interests of residents in various parts of Dallas. If so, the observed association between availability of the MTV channels and the record album's sales is spurious.

Exhibit 8.1 provides illustrations of how lack of control of extraneous factors can lead to erroneous causal inferences. In this figure X is the causal, or independent, variable; Y is the effect, or dependent, variable; and Z represents one or more extraneous causal factors. The solid boxes and arrows represent the observations and inferences that are actually made; the dotted boxes and arrows represent factors and relationships that exist but are neither controlled nor observed. The $+$, $-$, and 0 notations along the arrows refer to positive, negative, and no association, respectively. The temporal sequence of variables and observations in the exhibit is from left to right.

Case A in Exhibit 8.1 illustrates an observed causal relationship between X and Y that is spurious because changes in both X and Y are independently caused by the uncontrolled factor Z. Case B represents a spurious *absence* of an observed relationship between X and Y. This case is particularly noteworthy because it is a classic illustration of why the third condition for inferring causality (i.e., control of all extraneous causal factors) is even more critical than the first two conditions. Case B demonstrates that lack of evidence of association

[6] "Sing a Song of Seeing," *Time,* December 26, 1983, p. 56.

Exhibit 8.1

Three instances of erroneous inferences owing to lack of control of extraneous factors

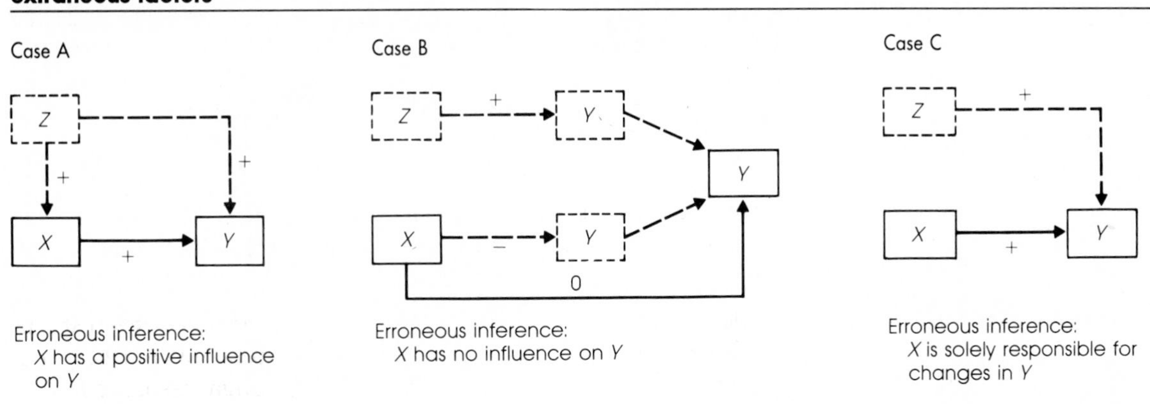

between variables does not necessarily mean a lack of causal relationship between them, *unless all other relevant factors have been accounted for.* Proper control of Z in case B will reveal the true negative influence of X on Y. In case C, while X has a causal influence on Y, the true nature and strength of this influence may not be revealed by the observed relationship since the uncontrolled factor Z also has a causal influence on Y. Changes in Y are only partly due to X. The three cases in Exhibit 8.1 are but a few of the ways in which errors can occur in causal inferences made without adequately accounting for variations in the effect variable caused by uncontrolled factors.

LABORATORY VERSUS FIELD EXPERIMENTS

Consider the following scenario, which we will use to illustrate our discussion in this and subsequent sections of the chapter: The advertising agency for Gourmet Food Products Company (GFPC) has developed two quite different television commercials (say A and B) for the company's line of frozen pizzas. The final decision about which commercial to use in an upcoming national campaign rests with GFPC's advertising manager, Mr. Thompson. Before choosing one of the two commercials, Mr. Thompson wants to get a feeling for the potential impact of each on consumer preference for GFPC's frozen pizzas. He therefore asks the ad agency to conduct an appropriate marketing experiment to assess the differential impact of one commercial over the other. As summarized next, the ad agency can use one of two general experimental approaches for generating the information requested by Mr. Thompson.

APPROACH 1: Invite a group of, say, 100 consumers to the agency's marketing research facility. Divide the group randomly into two similar groups of 50 consumers and take each to a different television-viewing room. Show each group an hour-long episode of a current television program with a normal number and variety of commercials inserted into it at appropriate time slots. Manipulate the set of commercials to be seen by the two groups such that one group will see test commercial A twice during the program and the other group will see test commercial B. In other words, both groups will see the same program and set of commercials except for the differences in the test commercials. To prevent participant knowledge of the experimental manipulation, and to evoke normal reactions to the test commercials, disguise the purpose of the study by telling consumers that the study's purpose is to get their reactions to the television program. After the consumers have seen the program, administer a questionnaire to obtain their reactions to the program and to the various products advertised during the program, including GFPC's frozen pizzas. Compare the mean preferences for GFPC's frozen pizzas for the two groups to assess the impacts of commercial A and commercial B.

APPROACH 2: Select two test cities that are as similar as possible in terms of consumer demographics and food purchase characteristics. Select an appropriate television program that will be shown simultaneously in both cities but one that allows for airing different local television spots in the two cities during the program. Arrange to show, twice, commercial A in one city and commercial B in the other. After the program has been aired, conduct random telephone surveys in the two cities to measure viewer reactions. Specifically, in each city, measure preference for GFPC's frozen pizzas among a sample of 50 consumers who saw the program. Compare the mean consumer preference for GFPC's frozen pizzas for the samples in the two cities to assess the impacts of commercial A and commercial B.

What similarities and differences do you see between approaches 1 and 2?

Both are experimental in that they involve manipulating a causal variable (namely, the type of test commercial shown) and measuring its impact on an effect variable (namely, consumer preference for GFPC's frozen pizzas). A major difference between the two approaches, however, is the degree of control available during the manipulation and measurement process. Approach 1 clearly offers better control than approach 2 with respect to extraneous factors capable of influencing consumer preferences toward GFPC's frozen pizzas. Approach 1 is a form of laboratory experiment, while approach 2 is a form of field experiment.

DEFINITION. **A *laboratory experiment* is a research study conducted in a contrived setting in which the effect of all, or nearly all, possible influential**

independent variables not pertinent to the immediate problem is kept to a minimum.

DEFINITION. A *field experiment* is a research study conducted in a natural setting in which one or more independent variables are manipulated by the experimenter under as carefully controlled conditions as the situation will permit.[7]

The key procedural difference between the two types of experiments, in terms of the research setting and hence the degree of control over extraneous factors, has an important bearing on the validity of the experimental results. The validity of experimental results is usually evaluated on two dimensions: external validity and internal validity.[8] Campbell and Stanley describe these two forms of validity as follows:

> *Internal validity* is the basic minimum without which any experiment is uninterpretable: Did in fact the experimental treatments make a difference in this specific experimental instance? *External validity* asks the question of *generalizability*: To what populations, settings, treatment [independent] variables, and measurement [dependent] variables can this effect be generalized?[9]

Internal validity is the extent to which observed results are solely due to the experimental manipulation; external validity is the extent to which observed results are likely to hold beyond the experimental setting. An ideal experiment is one whose results will have high internal as well as external validity. Unfortunately, there is usually a trade-off between these two forms of validity. That is, control of all extraneous factors—that is, holding constant other causal variables, or at least estimating and filtering out the influence of such variables on the effect variable—is typically only possible in a contrived setting, which may cast doubt on whether the results apply to realistic settings. Thus laboratory experiments generally have an advantage over field experiments in terms of internal validity but not external validity. The opposite is true for field experiments.

Let us reexamine the two alternative experimental approaches described in the GFPC scenario in light of our discussion of laboratory versus field experi-

---

[7] The two definitions are adapted from those given in Kerlinger, *Foundations of Behavioral Research,* pp. 398, 401.

[8] Although these forms are the two most commonly used forms of validity in experimental research, they are by no means the only forms; for definitions and a comparative discussion of other forms of validity, see Thomas D. Cook and Donald T. Campbell, *Quasi-Experimentation: Design & Analysis Issues for Field Settings* (Chicago: Rand McNally, 1979), pp. 80–91.

[9] Donald T. Campbell and Julian C. Stanley, *Experimental and Quasi-Experimental Designs for Research* (Chicago: Rand McNally, 1963), p. 5.

ments and internal versus external validity. Suppose *both* approaches were used and the following results were observed:

- Approach 1 (laboratory experiment). In the group exposed to commercial A, 60% preferred GFPC's frozen pizzas over competing brands. Consumer preference for GFPC's frozen pizzas in the group exposed to commercial B was 40%.
- Approach 2 (field experiment). Consumer preference for GFPC's frozen pizzas was 25% among those exposed to commercial A and 30% among those exposed to commercial B.

The results from the two experiments are obviously at odds with each other. Can such inconsistent results occur in this scenario? They certainly can, since neither experiment can claim high internal *and* external validity.

The 20-point difference in preference between the two groups in the laboratory experiment can be attributed confidently to the two different test commercials because virtually everything else remained strictly controlled. The results therefore have high internal validity. There is some question, however, about whether commercial A would be so much more effective than commercial B in a real-life setting, given the artificial environment in the laboratory experiment. For instance, consumers watching television under normal circumstances may not pay as keen attention to the program and the commercials in it, and, as a result, consumer preferences may not differ to as great an extent as in a laboratory experiment.[10] Thus the 20-point difference in consumer preference cannot be generalized confidently.

The results of the field experiment, giving commercial B a slight edge over commercial A, may suffer from a different type of problem. While the experimental setting itself was quite realistic, uncontrolled factors (in addition to the test commercial) may have influenced consumer preferences in different ways in the two cities. For instance, competing brands of frozen pizza may have been heavily promoted on the day of the experiment in the city in which commercial A was shown but not in the city in which commercial B was shown. If so, the finding that commercial B is somewhat more effective than commercial A will lack internal validity and cannot be fully trusted.

Which of the two approaches should the advertising agency use? Or, more generally, are laboratory experiments likely to be better than field experiments, or vice versa, in terms of overall usefulness of the results? There are no clear-cut answers. As we will see in the next section, a variety of situational factors play a

[10] Indeed, several research studies have shown that laboratory experiments have a tendency to overestimate the effect of experimental manipulations. For an example of such a study involving price manipulations in a laboratory setting, see John R. Nevin, "Laboratory Experiments for Estimating Consumer Demand: A Validation Study," *Journal of Marketing Research,* 11 (August 1974), pp. 261–268.

role in the choice of an appropriate experimental approach. Nevertheless, the preceding discussion and illustrations have an important message to all researchers using marketing experiments: No matter how much control and realism you *think* you have incorporated into your experiment (be it a laboratory or a field experiment), unanticipated or uncontrolled conditions may influence the results, and therefore you should temper your inferences accordingly when such conditions do crop up.

DECIDING ON WHICH TYPE OF EXPERIMENT TO USE

So far we have considered only validity issues relating to laboratory versus field experiments. Other practical considerations relevant in choosing between the two types of experiments include time, cost, exposure to competition, and nature of the manipulation. These issues are addressed in the following subsections.

Time

As you might suspect, conducting an experiment in a real-life setting will generally be more time-consuming than conducting it in a contrived setting. A field experiment will usually require additional time for such activities as identifying appropriate field locations and introducing the experimental manipulations into those locations. For instance, consider approach 2 in the GFPC scenario. Selecting two similar test cities, identifying an appropriate television program to be aired simultaneously in both cities, purchasing commercial airtime on that program, and so on, are quite likely to be time-consuming tasks.

Cost

With cost, again, laboratory experiments generally have an advantage over field experiments. The larger scale on which manipulations have to be introduced and results monitored in field experiments can sharply increase their cost. For instance, in the GFPC scenario, buying commercial airtime on television programs in the two test cities is likely to make approach 2 significantly more expensive than approach 1. Given a situation requiring experimental research, a laboratory experiment can usually be conducted for a fraction of the cost of running a field experiment.

Exposure to competition

A potential drawback of any marketing field experiment is the danger of exposing it to competitors. Exposure may invite competitors to monitor the experiment and gain valuable insights virtually for free. It may also prompt competitors to change the experimental environment (e.g., by drastically changing their own promotional or pricing levels) and hence invalidate the experimental results. Clearly, competitive monitoring and interference in an experiment are highly undesirable from the experimenter's perspective.

The threat of competitive interference is especially great in *test marketing*, which is a form of field experiment for assessing the market's reactions to a new product and its associated marketing mix. Test marketing is a formal step prior to full-scale introduction in the new-product-planning processes of many consumer goods firms.[11] But the risk of competitive interference does not necessarily mean that laboratory experiments must be used instead of field experiments for gaining insight into the potential market impact of new products. Consumer response to new products, especially major innovations (e.g., videocassette recorders and videodisc players), simply cannot be gauged accurately in a laboratory environment. Because of consumers' lack of familiarity with new products, their reactions to conceptual descriptions or even prototypes of the product in a laboratory setting may be no better than wild guesses, which are unlikely to have external validity.[12] Furthermore, laboratory experiments cannot adequately duplicate important phenomena like diffusion of advertising messages through various groups of consumers and the effect of manufacturer's advertising on the inventory decisions of wholesalers and retailers, which, in turn, can influence sales.[13] The point of this discussion is that test marketing, despite the risk of exposure to competition, may still be the most meaningful approach in certain situations. A key to avoiding drawing erroneous inferences from test market results is to take into account any unusual competitive activity when one is interpreting the results.[14]

Accurate assessment and interpretation of competitive activity during a test-marketing operation may not always be easy, however. The following example illustrates this point.

EXAMPLE: When Procter and Gamble test-marketed its Wondra brand hand-and-body lotion, a leading competitor, Cheseborough Ponds, ran a buy-one-get-one-free promotion for its Vaseline Intensive Care Lotion in the test

---

[11] For a succinct discussion of test marketing, see Philip Kotler, *Marketing Management: Analysis, Planning and Control* (Englewood Cliffs, N.J.: Prentice-Hall, 1980), pp. 336–339; another excellent reference concerning test marketing is N. D. Cadbury, "When, Where, and How to Test Market," *Harvard Business Review,* May/June 1975, pp. 96–105.

[12] A thought-provoking article that makes this point forcefully, with several excellent examples, is "Marketing Researchers: Investigate Why New Products Succeed, Not Why They Fail," *Marketing News,* September 18, 1981, Section 1, p. 13; see also Edward M. Tauber, "Forecasting Sales Prior to Test Market," *Journal of Marketing,* 41 (January 1977), p. 82.

[13] Paul W. Farris and David J. Reibstein, "Overcontrol in Advertising Experiments," *Journal of Advertising Research,* 24 (June/July 1984), pp. 37–42.

[14] Several useful precautions to take when one is conducting test-marketing experiments are discussed in Thomas D. DuPont, "How to Avoid Test-Marketing 'Traps'", *Marketing News,* May 13, 1983, Section 2, pp. 16–18.

cities. Needless to say, the sales performance of Wondra was quite poor. Nevertheless, Procter and Gamble apparently felt that Ponds could not afford to run such a promotion on a national basis. It therefore went ahead with full-scale introduction of Wondra, despite its disappointing test market performance. Procter and Gamble's assessment of Ponds' promotional capability turned out to be inaccurate; Ponds ran a buy-one-get-one-free promotion wherever Wondra was introduced. Consumers stocked up on Vaseline Intensive Care Lotion, which seriously hurt Wondra's chances of establishing a strong foothold in the hand-and-body-lotion market. Eight years after national introduction of Wondra, the brand still had only a 4% market share, while Vaseline Intensive Care had 22%.[15]

The point of this example is that proper interpretation of test market results requires good knowledge of not only how competitors react during the test-marketing operation but also what they are capable of doing in the future.

Nature of the manipulation

The type of independent variable used and how it is to be manipulated also have a bearing on which experimental approach will be most appropriate. Laboratory experiments will be more appropriate than field experiments—especially given the time, cost, and secrecy advantages of the former—*as long as the manipulations are likely to be meaningful in a contrived setting.* For example, laboratory experiments may be quite appropriate for assessing consumer reactions to different types of package designs for a soft drink, different levels of flavoring added to an ice cream, and so on.

Field experiments are better when the manipulation is likely to be meaningless or difficult to implement in a laboratory setting. We have already seen that the potential market impact of major innovations cannot be adequately assessed through laboratory experiments because of the difficulty in evoking meaningful reactions from respondents. Lodish and Pekelman offer additional examples of situations where the nature of the manipulations will make laboratory experiments inappropriate:

> Though laboratory experiments may be useful in some situations, certain types of changes in the system can be investigated only by means of field experimentation. These changes are very difficult to duplicate realistically in the laboratory. Common examples are changes in salesmen's compensation, in the organization of the salesforce, in promotional methods used by salesmen, in the structure of the distribution system, and in pricing policies or credit terms. The most common experimental approach is to implement the change in some subset of the present territories, and then to compare the

[15] "How to Improve Your Chances for Test-Market Success," *Marketing News,* January 6, 1984, Section 1, pp. 12–13.

performance of these territories with that of the ones not receiving the treatment.[16]

To summarize our discussion of the pros and cons of laboratory versus field experiments: Laboratory experiments are strong in terms of internal validity (ability to determine the sole impact of a causal variable), time, cost, and negligible risk of exposure to competition. Field experiments are strong in terms of external validity (generalizability of inferences) and meaningfulness of the manipulations. To capitalize on the strengths of both types of experiments, and to circumvent the difficulty of making a strictly either-or decision, researchers have developed hybrid experimental approaches. These hybrid approaches are essentially laboratory experiments that imitate real market conditions as much as possible. They are therefore often called *simulated test markets*. Several commercial marketing research firms have facilities especially designed for conducting experiments under conditions closely resembling actual market conditions. A description of one such facility (called the Laboratory Test Market) and how it is used is given in Exhibit 8.2.

Simulated test markets are by no means completely devoid of artificiality. However, a few studies comparing results obtained from simulated and actual market experiments have shown a moderate degree of consistency between the two sets of results.[17] Experiments conducted in simulated test markets are likely to be more frequently used in the future because they are becoming increasingly sophisticated and also because they bring together the complementary strengths of laboratory and field experiments.[18] In the GFPC scenario, for instance, testing the relative impacts of commercials A and B in a simulated market (such as the one described in Exhibit 8.2) may be better than either of the two proposed approaches. The simulated test market results will yield estimates of the immediate as well as the longer-term impacts of the commercials on *sales* (rather than on *preference* alone). Thus the information generated is likely to be richer and managerially more useful than that generated in a traditional laboratory experiment.

---

[16] Leonard Lodish and Dov Pekelman, "Increasing Precision of Marketing Sales Areas," *Journal of Marketing Research,* 15 (August 1978), p. 449.

[17] See, for example, Glen L. Urban and Gerald M. Katz, "Pre-Test-Market Models: Validation and Managerial Implications," *Journal of Marketing Research,* 20 (August 1983), pp. 221–234; Andre Gabor, Clive W. J. Granger, and Anthony P. Sowter, "Real and Hypothetical Shop Situations in Market Research," *Journal of Marketing Research,* 7 (August 1970), pp. 355–359.

[18] Given the ability of laboratory experiments to detect even minute differences in the impact of various manipulation levels, some authors have suggested the following alternative approach for taking advantage of the complementary strengths of laboratory and field experiments: Use laboratory experiments as a *prelude* to field experiments. Specifically, when the effects of several independent variables have to be studied, the ones that are not likely to make much difference can be identified through laboratory experiments and eliminated from further consideration. The effects of the remaining independent variable(s) can be studied in a field experiment, which will be much less complex and cumbersome than it would have been had all the original independent variables had to be manipulated in a field setting. See Alan G. Sawyer, Parker M. Worthing, and Paul E. Sendak, "The Role of Laboratory Experiments to Test Marketing Strategies," *Journal of Marketing,* 43 (Summer 1979), pp. 60–67.

We have so far seen specific illustrations of biases (primarily in the context of the GFPC scenario) that can lower the validity of experimental results. In the next two sections of the chapter we will examine certain standard threats to the internal and the external validity of experiments in general. As you examine those threats, keep in mind that not all of them may be present in every experiment. The type of experiment (laboratory or field) and the type of units from which data are gathered (whether they are human respondents or nonhuman entities such as stores) will have a bearing on which threats are likely to be serious. Furthermore, as we will see in the next chapter, some of the threats, even if they cannot be completely removed from an experimental setting, can be neutralized or accounted for by choosing an appropriate experimental design.

THREATS TO INTERNAL VALIDITY

Internal validity, as we saw earlier, refers to the extent to which one can be confident that the manipulated independent variable is solely responsible for observed changes in the dependent variable. Therefore the presence of any condition or occurrence (other than the independent-variable manipulation) that can offer a competing explanation for the experimental results is a threat to internal validity. We will discuss the following effects (i.e., conditions or occurrences) that can lower the internal validity of experiments: history, maturation, pretesting, instrument variation, selection, and mortality.[19]

History effect

History effect refers to *specific* external events or occurrences during an experiment that are likely to affect the dependent variable. The history effect is not a frequent problem in laboratory experiments. Because of the controlled environments in which such experiments are conducted, the researcher is in a good position to prevent, or at least monitor and account for, any extraneous event or occurrence other than the planned manipulation. The history effect is potentially a more serious problem in field experiments. Unusual shifts in competitors' marketing mix variables when a field experiment is in progress are the most likely form of the history effect.

Suppose the producer of Dole canned fruits wishes to study the impact of a special store display on the brand's sales. A representative group of stores in a test area is selected, and sales of Dole canned fruits are monitored in these stores for a one-month period. The special display is then introduced, and sales

[19] This list is not an exhaustive list of threats to internal validity. Rather, it represents threats that are most likely to be present in experimental designs used in marketing, particularly those designs to be discussed in the next chapter. The book by Campbell and Stanley, *Experimental and Quasi-Experimental Designs,* and the one by Cook and Campbell, *Quasi-Experimentation,* provide a more comprehensive coverage of threats to internal validity.

Exhibit 8.2

Laboratory test market

The original Laboratory Test Market facility was located in New Jersey; now facilities are available throughout the United States. These facilities contain an experimental supermarket where products are sold to consumers under controlled conditions, a theater-auditorium where advertisements and other promotional materials can be exposed to consumers, rooms for interviewing consumers after they have made their purchases, and facilities for interviewing consumers, by telephone, after they have used the products purchased.

The techniques used in the Laboratory Test Market are basically the same if sales prediction of one option is desired or if choosing between options is the objective. The variance occurs in the number of cells that will be used in the design—as many cells as there are alternate options.

Considering any cell, the following step-by-step procedure is followed in a Laboratory Test Market, designed to produce a sales level prediction. A representative sample of consumers (the size and characteristics of the sample are contingent upon the product category under investigation) participate in a series of experiments, as follows:

- Consumers, in groups of 30 to 35, are led into a theater where they fill in a self-administering questionnaire with the aid of a moderator. This form furnishes data on: age, family composition, living standard level (occupation of head of household, family income, etc.); practices and purchase behavior vis-à-vis the product category; and other pertinent background facts.
- After consumers have completed the questionnaire, an actual TV program is shown containing a number of communications for different existing brands in the product category as well as the brand/option being tested, along with communications for other product categories. (If finished commercials are not available, rougher presentations, in one form or another, can be used to communicate the product message for each brand.)

  —It is not essential to the design that a commercial for every brand stocked in the "store" be included in the vehicle. In the "real" world, there are cases of products being marketed that are not supported by advertising. At the same time, it is desirable to include commercials for the leading, heavily advertised brands on the market.

- After consumers have seen the film, they are led in small groups to the "store." The store is stocked with the brands that have been shown in the commercials and others that enjoy an important share of market in the testing area. Upon entering the "store," consumers are provided with a fixed amount of money to stimulate purchase. This step has been found useful for maximizing the number of purchases.

  —It has been our experience that an amount equivalent to about one-fourth the average purchase

are monitored for another month. Ideally, the impact of the special display should be revealed by the difference between the second and first month's sales of Dole canned fruits in the test stores. But what happens if the prices or promotional strategy for Del Monte canned fruits change significantly during the two-month experimental period? Or if Del Monte experiences distribution problems during that period and stocks out in several of the test stores? Occurrences like these are history effects and may be responsible, at least partly, for any difference between sales of Dole canned fruits with and without the special display. Consequently, the experimental findings cannot be taken at face value.

The history effect is not limited to changes in competitors' marketing mixes price for the product class is a sufficient stimulus to encourage purchase at the time of the "store" visit.

- Having been given the money, consumers are then asked to make a purchase or not, as they wish, knowing full well that the difference between the money they are given and the price of the product requires that they use their own money to make the purchase.

  —We have found that the use of one's own money is an important factor in the experiment; only consumers who are interested in a particular product's benefit will spend their own money; and further, the assessment of the product after usage is more realistic if one's own money is invested.

- After respondents have made their purchases, they are led into small meeting rooms where focused group discussions are conducted to determine the reasons for purchase or nonpurchase in the "store."
- Once these attitudinal data have been collected, the respondents will, of course, go home to use their various products as they normally would.

  —They are not told, however, that they will be contacted for further interviewing.

- After a certain time period has elapsed (timing is contingent upon product type), consumers are reinterviewed by telephone to determine:

  Reactions to the product.

  Reactions of other family members.

  Degree of satisfaction or dissatisfaction.

  Reasons for satisfaction or dissatisfaction.

  Comparisons with previous products/brands used.

  Usage data.

  Repurchase data.

- If a sales wave/extended usage test is to be incorporated in the research design, consumers are given the opportunity to repurchase the product, which is then delivered to them. After a certain time period has elapsed, a follow-up interview takes place to obtain further product usage and assessment data.

The above data are collected and analyzed for *all* brands sold in the "store." In this way, the data on the test product/option can be studied in relation to the other brands in order to establish the test product's relative strengths and weaknesses vis-à-vis leading competitive products.

Source: Reprinted from "Laboratory Test Market", a brochure prepared (in 1976) by Yankelovich, Skelly and White, Inc., 575 Madison Avenue, New York, N.Y. 10022, pp. 11–15. Used by permission.

or strategies. It can also occur because of major changes in external factors like the weather or general economic conditions in the area where a field experiment is being conducted. Examples are a prolonged heat wave in an area where the effect of a price reduction on sales of a brand of soft drink is being tested, and a series of plant closings and layoffs in an industrialized area where the effect of a promotional campaign on sales of a brand of microwave ovens is being tested.

The type of units (human or nonhuman) from which data are gathered during an experiment does not really have a bearing on the extent of the history effect. The history effect stems from the experimental environment rather than the experimental units. To illustrate, compare the field experiment in the GFPC scenario to test the impact of commercials A and B on consumer preferences with the field experiment to test the impact of the special store display on sales of Dole canned fruits. In the GFPC experiment preference data are obtained from consumers, while in the Dole experiment brand sales data are gathered from stores. Despite this difference in type of units, however, any history effect—for example, a change in a leading competitor's advertising campaign—can be expected to affect the dependent variable in both experiments (consumer preference in the former and brand sales in the latter).

Maturation effect

Unlike the history effect, which stems from the external experimental environment, the *maturation effect* stems from the experimental units. The term *maturation* refers to physiological or physical changes in the units that occur with the passage of time. Any impact such changes may have on the dependent variable being measured constitutes a maturation effect.

Consider a laboratory experiment to ascertain the impact of a new Toyota commercial on consumer opinions about Toyota cars. A representative group of consumers is brought to a laboratory setting, and their current opinions about Toyota cars are measured through an appropriate questionnaire. They are then asked to watch an hour-long television program in which the test commercial is inserted. Next, their opinions about Toyota cars are measured once again. Could any physiological changes have occurred in the respondents during this experiment? Yes, since some of them may have started feeling hungry toward the end of the experiment, others may have become tired, and so on. If such changes prompted the respondents to "just get the whole thing over with," their opinions as measured through the second questionnaire would be inaccurate and the maturation effect would be present. In other words, the difference between the pretest and posttest measures of opinions cannot be completely attributed to the test commercial; part of the difference may be due to maturation.

Maturation is not limited to changes in the hunger and fatigue levels of respondents. It also involves changes that naturally occur with the passage of time, such as changes in respondents' ages and their ability to react quickly to stimuli. However, such changes occur so gradually that they are unlikely to pose a problem in marketing experiments, which are invariably of relatively short duration. In contrast, physical conditions like the respondents' fatigue and hunger levels can change rapidly, especially when respondents are placed in an unusual environment. This point highlights the possibility of the maturation effect's occurring in the contrived settings that characterize laboratory experiments. The longer the duration of a laboratory experiment and the more unusual the respondents' experiences during the experiment, the greater is the risk of reduced internal validity owing to some form of maturation effect.

The maturation effect can also occur when the units participating in an experiment are nonhuman (e.g., stores, as in the field experiment for sales of Dole canned fruits). For instance, the layout or other physical features of test stores can change over time, which in turn can influence sales. Or the overall sales in the test stores may be following a certain general trend (upward or downward), which, if not recognized and controlled for during an experiment, may be mistakenly viewed as an effect on the experimental manipulation.

Pretesting effect

The pretesting effect is a problem unique to experiments involving human participants in which the same respondents are measured more than once. Specifically, the *pretesting effect* is said to occur when responses given during a later measurement are influenced by those given during a previous measurement, regardless of what happens between the measurements. When the pretesting effect occurs, the difference between the pretest and posttest measures of the dependent variable will not accurately reflect the impact of the experimental manipulation, thereby lowering internal validity.

Recall the laboratory experiment to measure the impact of a new Toyota television commercial. In this experiment, suppose consumers' opinions before and after exposure to the commercial are measured through a series of 10-point rating scales relating to various attributes of Toyota (rating scales and their development are discussed in Chapter 11). While responding to the second measurement, the respondents may remember how they rated Toyota on each scale during the first measurement. Furthermore, some of these respondents may provide the same ratings they gave in the previous measurement, perhaps through a desire to appear consistent. If so, the difference between the two measurements will reveal nothing about the true impact the Toyota commercial may have had on these respondents. Alternatively, some respondents may provide a different set of ratings during the second measurement, not because their opinions about Toyota cars had changed but because they did not want to give the same set of ratings twice. In either case the result is a lowering of internal validity: The difference, or lack thereof, between the pretest and posttest opinions about Toyota cars cannot be attributed solely to the Toyota commercial.

The pretesting effect stems from the tendency (for whatever underlying reasons) to remain consistent or to reveal differences between the pretest and posttest measurements. Since this tendency is purely a human phenomenon, the pretesting effect is rarely a threat to the internal validity of experiments in which measurements are obtained from nonhuman units. Thus, for example, the pretesting effect is unlikely in the experiment for measuring the impact of a special store display on sales of Dole canned fruits, even though this experiment involves both a pretest and a posttest measurement.

Instrument variation effect

Instrument variation effect is a bias that relates to differences between pretest and posttest measurements owing to changes in the instruments (questionnaires) and/or procedures used to measure the dependent variable. It is a potential internal-validity threat only in experiments involving more than one measurement of the same dependent variable. However, it is unlikely to be a problem when the units from which measurements are obtained are nonhuman (e.g., stores). That is, dependent variables on which data are obtained from nonhuman units are typically straightforward (e.g., sales, inventory turnover, brand share), with little room for variation in how they are measured. Of course, if the definitions of these variables or the ways in which they are measured change during the experiment, the instrument variation effect will be a problem. But to the extent that such changes can be prevented by the researcher in measuring nonhuman units, the threat of the instrument variation effect is unlikely to be serious.

The instrument variation effect is a much more serious threat to the internal validity of experiments involving the measurement of human respondents. Dependent variables in such experiments are invariably nebulous constructs like attitudes, opinions, preferences, or purchase intentions. Measuring such variables typically requires a questionnaire and calls for some form of interaction between respondents and the interviewer. Any changes in the questionnaire or the interviewer between pre- and post-measurements can, in and of itself, produce a difference between the results obtained.[20]

Ideally, the experimenter should use identical data collection procedures for pre- and post-measurements so as to avoid the problem of instrument variation effect. Unfortunately, in some situations changes in data collection procedures between measurements may be inevitable. For example, changes in wording may be necessary in the postmeasurement questionnaire because respondents had difficulty understanding some questions in the premeasurement questionnaire. (A good way to minimize the need for such changes is to thoroughly pretest the questionnaire before finalizing it. We will discuss the topic of questionnaire pretesting—not to be confused with the pretesting effect—in Chapter 10.) Such changes will obviously increase the chances of obtaining an instrument variation effect. Sometimes, a different interviewer might be needed to conduct the posttest measurement because the original interviewer quit or was incompetent. For instance, consider an in-home product-testing experiment, in which respondents are initially interviewed in their homes concerning their views about a product; then samples of the product are left with respondents for their use over a period of time; at the end of this period

[20] As we will see in Chapter 10, even slight changes in a questionnaire can lead to big differences in responses. For a discussion of the extent to which responses can be influenced by the characteristics of the interviewer, see M. Venkatesan, "Laboratory Experiments in Marketing: The Experimenter Effect," *Journal of Marketing Research,* 4 (May 1967), pp. 142–146.

the respondents are reinterviewed to ascertain whether and to what extent their opinions have changed. Instrument variation effect can be a problem here if the person conducting the second interview is different from the person who conducted the initial interview.

In summary, an experimenter should use the same measurement procedures if at all possible. If some changes are inevitable, the experimenter must be especially alert to the possibility of instrument variation effect and take it into account in interpreting the results.

Selection effect

Selection effect is a potential problem in experiments involving more than one group of units. This bias is present when multiple groups participating in an experiment differ on characteristics that have a bearing on the dependent variable. For instance, the laboratory as well as the field experiment approaches proposed in the GFPC scenario to test the relative effectiveness of commercials A and B involved two groups of respondents. Suppose the group exposed to commercial A was dominated by heavy users of frozen dinners, while the group exposed to commercial B was dominated by consumers who typically ate only home-cooked meals. Also, suppose 40% of those who saw commercial A indicated a preference for GFPC's frozen pizzas while only 5% of those who saw commercial B did so. These results cannot necessarily be interpreted as showing commercial A to be more effective than commercial B. All or part of the observed difference in preferences may be due to the critical difference between the general food preferences of the two groups rather than to the experimental manipulation (i.e., the difference between the two commercials). The internal validity of the experiment under these circumstances is likely to be quite low because of the presence of selection effect.

Selection effect is not limited to only those experiments involving human participants. To illustrate, recall the example we discussed earlier concerning sales of the Duran Duran album *Rio* in various sections of Dallas. The implied inference in this example was that the availability of MTV was responsible for the sales success of the album. We have already seen that this inference is likely to be erroneous owing to the lack of control of extraneous factors. But let us reexamine this situation from a somewhat different perspective to illustrate the concept of selection effect. This experiment used two groups of nonhuman units: Sections of Dallas that had MTV made up one group, and those that did not have MTV made up the other group. The sales results showed that the album was a big success in the former group but not in the latter. However, this difference cannot be attributed with assurance to the MTV–no-MTV distinction because the two areas could have differed significantly on characteristics like socioeconomic status and interests of residents. Stated differently, no attempt was made to ensure that the two areas were equivalent on attributes (other than availability of MTV) likely to affect the album's sale. The possibility of selection effect is a primary reason why the inference implied in this situation cannot be fully trusted.

Mortality effect

Mortality effect occurs when certain participating units drop out of an experiment, and, as a result, the set of units completing the experiment significantly differs from the original set of units. To illustrate the mortality effect, we will use the in-home product-testing experiment mentioned earlier (under "Instrument Variation Effect"). Suppose the product is a new and improved bathtub and tile cleaner, and the initial set of participants consists of 100 users of the current version of the product. In the pretest interview these participants are asked to state their overall opinion of the old version of the bathtub and tile cleaner on a scale of 1 to 10 (the higher the number, the more favorable is the opinion). Assume that the mean rating across all 100 participants turns out to be 6. The participants are then given samples of the new and improved version and asked to use it over a two-month period. At the end of this period, suppose only 70 participants are reinterviewed because the rest simply refuse to be interviewed. Assume that the mean rating across the 70 participants is 8 on the same 10-point scale. The key question now is, Can the two-point improvement in the mean opinion rating be attributed to the new and improved version?

The answer to this question critically depends on the *composition* of the 30 dropouts vis-à-vis the composition of the original set of participants. For instance, if the 30 that dropped out were people with negative reactions to the product, the postmeasured mean rating of 8 could be inflated. In other words, the difference in mean opinion ratings is not a true reflection of the effectiveness of the new and improved version because the composition of participants changed critically between measurements. Thus mortality effect is present.

Since 30 participants dropped out, why not simply recalculate the initial mean opinion rating over just the 70 participants that completed the experiment and compare it with the mean rating from the postinterviews? Will this procedure solve the mortality effect problem? Unfortunately it will not; while this procedure will ensure that the pretest and posttest mean ratings are based on the same group of participants, inferences stemming from such a comparison cannot be generalized to the original group or to the larger body of product users the original group represents. In short, the inference will lack external validity. Thus while the mortality effect is typically viewed as a threat to internal validity, it can become a threat to external validity if the experimenter attempts to circumvent the problem by making inferences on the basis of data from only those units that completed all phases of the experiment.

Of course, if the 30 people that dropped out were random dropouts—that is, if the characteristics of those dropping out had no systematic connection to the dependent variable—the pre- and postinterview groups would differ in size but not in composition. Hence there would be little or no mortality effect. This last point is important because the mortality effect is not necessarily present whenever a loss of participants occurs; it is a problem only when such a loss results in a group that critically differs from the original group. Therefore an experimenter should collect data on critical participant characteristics (e.g., demographics, extent and frequency of product use) during both the pre- and postinterviews. In the event of loss of participants during an experiment, such data can be valuable in ascertaining whether and in what ways group composition has changed. This information will lower the risk of making erroneous inferences.

Mortality effect can occur in experiments involving human as well as nonhuman participants. For instance, mortality effect can be a threat in the field experiment involving the store display for Dole canned fruits if certain test stores, all belonging to the same supermarket chain, refuse to feature the store display midway through the experiment. The mortality effect is also more likely to be a problem in field experiments than in laboratory experiments because a participant's role in most laboratory experiments is confined to a relatively short duration, with usually no opportunity for dropping out.

THREATS TO EXTERNAL VALIDITY

External validity of experimental results relates to their generalizability. The various internal-validity threats we have discussed also indirectly affect external validity since it would be meaningless to generalize experimental findings that are not even internally valid. In other words, internal validity can be viewed as a necessary but not sufficient condition for external validity. Our discussion in this section will focus on conditions that must be met beyond those needed for internal validity in order for one to conclude that experimental findings have external validity. We will examine biases that stand in the way of generalizing experimental results even when they have high internal validity. Specifically, we will discuss the following three biases: reactive bias, pretest-manipulation interaction bias, and nonrepresentative-sample bias.[21]

Reactive bias

Reactive bias is the problem of participants' exhibiting abnormal or unusual behavior simply because they are participating in an experiment. This bias is limited to experiments involving human units and is likely to occur only when

[21] As in the case of internal-validity threats discussed in this chapter, these three biases are not the only external-validity threats, although virtually all other external-validity threats are related to these biases. For further details, consult Campbell and Stanley, *Experimental and Quasi-Experimental Designs*; Cook and Campbell, *Quasi-Experimentation*. One point worthy of note concerning the *names* given to the validity threats: External-validity threats are labeled *biases* rather than *effects* merely to distinguish them from internal-validity threats.

the units know they are participating in an experiment. Reactive bias can be quite severe in laboratory experiments because the artificial environment and the attention paid to participants by the experimenter are especially conducive to this type of bias. As Kerlinger observes, "Almost any change, any extra attention, any experimental manipulation, or even the absence of manipulation but the knowledge that a study is being done, is enough to cause subjects to change. In short, if we pay attention to people, they respond."[22]

Reactive bias typically prompts participants to overreact and to look for minute features or differences in experimental stimuli that they normally would not even notice. This reaction may lead to an internally valid inference (assuming all other internal-validity threats have been controlled) that the experimental manipulation had a significant impact. Such an inference cannot be confidently generalized beyond the experimental setting, however.

Although reactive bias is more likely to occur in laboratory experiments, field experiments involving human subjects are by no means immune to it. In Chapter 4 we discussed consumer panels, which are permanent samples of respondents that are repeatedly measured over time. Many field experiments use data obtained from consumer panels. For example, the impact of a campaign using a 50-cents-off coupon for a brand of detergent can be estimated by comparing purchases of the detergent made by panel members before and after the campaign. A potential problem with this approach is that panel members, *because they know their purchases are being monitored,* may behave differently from normal consumers. In other words, the external validity of inferences based on consumer panel data may be questionable owing to the possibility of reactive bias.

Pretest-manipulation interaction bias

Pretest-manipulation interaction bias is simply a special form of reactive bias that is unique to experiments involving premeasurement of human participants before exposing them to the experimental manipulation. While reactive bias stems from the influence of the experiment as a whole, pretest-manipulation interaction bias stems from the influence of the premeasurement. Specifically, pretest-manipulation interaction bias will arise when the premeasurement increases or decreases respondents' sensitivity to the experimental manipulation.

To illustrate this bias, and to contrast it with *pretesting effect,* let us reexamine the laboratory experiment to measure the impact of a new Toyota commercial on consumer opinions about Toyota cars. The premeasurement in this experiment will undoubtedly contain questions about Toyota cars. In answering these questions, respondents are quite likely to think a lot about Toyota cars—so much so that they may be entering the next phase of the experiment (i.e.,

[22] Kerlinger, *Foundations of Behavioral Research,* p. 345.

exposure to the TV program containing the Toyota commercial) with a heightened level of sensitivity toward Toyota cars. Alternatively, they may have become so tired of thinking about Toyota cars that they may be entering the exposure phase with a decreased level of sensitivity toward Toyota cars. In either case, because of their altered mental state and sensitivity, their reactions to the Toyota commercial will most likely be different from those of normal consumers who are not premeasured. In particular, the respondents in the experiment may pay abnormally high or abnormally low attention when the Toyota commercial is shown.

The opinion changes (or lack thereof) induced by these abnormal reactions will be reflected by the postmeasurement. Nevertheless, since these reactions still basically stem from the experimental manipulation, the difference between the pre- and postmeasured opinions is attributed to the Toyota commercial *within the experimental context.* In other words, the results will be *internally valid* (assuming that there were no other internal-validity threats). However, they cannot be generalized beyond the experimental setting because the impact of the same commercial on consumers who are not premeasured cannot be expected to be the same.

What is the difference between pretesting effect and pretest-manipulation interaction effect? Very simply, pretesting effect is a *direct* effect that the premeasurement introduces on the postmeasurement, *irrespective of the manipulation.* It is therefore a threat to internal validity. Pretest-manipulation interaction bias, in contrast, is more subtle and occurs because the premeasurement interferes with the mental sensitivity and hence reactions of respondents to the experimental manipulation. This bias ultimately contaminates the postmeasurement, of course. However, since it occurs through an interaction between the premeasurement and the manipulation, rather than because of the premeasurement per se, it is typically considered an effect of the manipulation on the dependent variable. It is therefore regarded as a threat to external validity rather than to internal validity.

Nonrepresentative-sample bias

Nonrepresentative-sample bias occurs when the units participating in an experiment are not representative of the larger body of units to which the experimental results are to be generalized. This bias stems from improper or inadequate recruiting of units and is a sampling problem (problems associated with sampling are presented in Chapters 12 through 15). When the composition of units participating in an experiment critically differs from that of the total collection of units, the experimental results will lack external validity, no matter how internally valid they are.

Nonrepresentative-sample bias can be a potential threat to external validity in all types of experiments, laboratory as well as field, and those involving human and nonhuman participants. It is particularly likely to be present in laboratory experiments and experiments involving consumer panels. There is always the risk that participants willing to expend the effort to take part in a laboratory experiment, or to respond to the repeated measurements to which panel members are subjected, may differ in significant ways from the population at large.[23]

CONCLUDING REMARKS ON VALIDITY THREATS

The preceding two sections covered a number of problems that can lower the internal or external validity of experimental results. These problems, though not exhaustive, are the ones that underlie the practical constraints most frequently encountered in conducting experimental research in marketing.[24] An additional complication concerning these problems is that there are often trade-offs between them; that is, minimizing one problem may aggravate another. For example, an attempt to reduce the pretesting effect by using different questionnaires (i.e., questionnaires with the same content but different formats) for the pre- and postmeasurements is likely to lead to the instrument variation effect. An attempt to circumvent the mortality effect by analyzing data from only those units completing all phases of an experiment may result in nonrepresentative-sample bias. The point is that an experimenter, in striving to avoid certain threats to validity, should not lose sight of the possible increased risk of other threats.

If the number and the variety of potential problems give you the hopeless feeling that experimental research in marketing is useless, do not despair. First, not all problems are likely to be severe in every marketing experiment. As was discussed earlier, the *seriousness* of problems likely to be encountered in a situation depends on the nature of the experiment (laboratory or field) and the nature of the participating units (human or nonhuman). Table 8.1 provides a summary of the circumstances in which each validity threat is likely to be serious.

Second, although a researcher may not be able to eliminate certain threats in a situation, he or she may still be able to account for them by filtering out their influences from the experimental results. In fact, the primary focus of the next chapter is on experimental designs that adequately consider extraneous influences on the dependent-variable measure in assessing the true impact of the causal variable(s).

Third, recall from our discussion at the beginning of the chapter that to conclusively establish causality between variables is virtually impossible. There-

[23] Urban and Katz, "Pre-Test-Market Models," and Gabor, Granger, and Sowter, "Real and Hypothetical Shop Situations," offer several examples illustrating nonrepresentative-sample bias and reactive bias associated with consumer panels.

[24] For a clear and concise review of practical limitations of marketing experiments, see Cox and Enis, *Experimentation for Marketing Decisions,* pp. 108–109.

Table 8.1

Circumstances under which various validity threats may be serious

	THREAT MAY BE SERIOUS FOR	
TYPE OF THREAT	Experiment	Participants
History effect	Field experiment	Human or nonhuman units
Maturation effect	Laboratory or field experiment	Human or nonhuman units
Pretesting effect	Laboratory or field experiment	Human units
Instrument variation effect	Laboratory or field experiment	Human units
Selection effect	Laboratory or field experiment	Human or nonhuman units
Mortality effect	Field experiment	Human or nonhuman units
Reactive bias	Laboratory experiment	Human units
Pretest-manipulation interaction bias	Laboratory or field experiment	Human units
Nonrepresentative-sample bias	Laboratory or field experiment	Human or nonhuman units

fore the realistic role of experimentation in marketing is not so much to *prove* causality as to increase one's confidence in making causal inferences. Viewed from this perspective, carefully conducted experimental research, even if less-than-perfect, can provide more meaningful and accurate causal insights than descriptive research can. Stated differently, experimental research in marketing can serve a useful purpose as long as the experimenter recognizes the validity threats that may arise, takes steps to eliminate or control as many of them as possible, and interprets the findings with caution.

SUMMARY

Experimentation is research conducted under controlled conditions to shed light on causal associations between variables. However, the distinction between experimental research and descriptive research is more a matter of degree than of kind. In fact, both types of research typically involve collecting and analyzing similar kinds of data to understand relationships between variables.[25] The distinguishing feature of experimental research is that it can greatly increase one's confidence in making causal inferences.

Three conditions must be satisfied in order to infer that one variable is the cause of another: (1) temporal ordering of variables—that is, the variables (or

[25] Hans Zeisel, in *Say It with Figures* (New York: Harper & Row, 1968), p. 108, demonstrates with examples that *tabulated results* from both types of research will be virtually indistinguishable.

changes in them) must occur in a time sequence consistent with the causal inference; (2) evidence of association—that is, data on the two variables must show a definite relationship; and (3) control of other causal factors—that is, all extraneous influences on the two variables and their relationships must be adequately accounted for.

Two approaches are available for conducting experimental research: laboratory experiments and field experiments. A laboratory experiment is conducted in an artificial setting under tightly controlled conditions. It therefore generally offers better internal validity (i.e., assurance that the results obtained are solely due to the experimental manipulation) than a field experiment, which is conducted in a natural setting with as much control as possible. A key drawback of laboratory experiments is that the results obtained may not be generalizable beyond the experimental setting, thereby lowering external validity.

The choice between laboratory and field experiments is not always easy because of the trade-off involved between internal and external validity. Furthermore, issues such as time, cost, risk of exposure to competition, and nature of the manipulation must also be considered in choosing an appropriate experimental approach. In some instances a researcher may be able to use a hybrid approach that pools the complementary strengths of laboratory and field experiments. Several commercial marketing research firms have facilities, called simulated test markets, especially designed for conducting hybrid experiments. An experiment conducted in a simulated test market is a laboratory experiment in which the environment and the procedures used imitate real-life market features as much as possible.

There are six standard threats that can jeopardize the internal validity of experiments: history, maturation, pretesting, instrument variation, selection, and mortality effects. These threats also indirectly affect external validity because generalizing results that lack internal validity is meaningless. Direct threats to external validity include reactive bias, pretest-manipulation interaction bias, and nonrepresentative-sample bias.

Not all threats to internal and external validity may be present in every experiment. Whether an experiment is a laboratory or a field experiment, and whether the participants are human or nonhuman units, play a role in determining which threats are serious. Specific experimental designs capable of either eliminating or accounting for the various threats are discussed in the next chapter.

QUESTIONS

1. Are descriptive and experimental research totally different? Why or why not? Explain your answer with an example of your own.
2. Toys & Games is a children's toy store located in a shopping mall. Toys & Games ran a major in-store promotion (consisting of special displays and price reductions)

during the last quarter (October to December) of each of the past five years. Every year, without fail, its sales in the last quarter were at least 25% higher than sales in any of the previous quarters. Thus the store manager is seriously thinking about expanding the in-store promotion to at least one other quarter each year. What advice would you give the store manager? Discuss your answer from the perspective of the three conditions for inferring causality.

3. Distinguish between laboratory and field experiments, pointing out the relative strengths and weaknesses of each.
4. A food products company has designed a new and improved container for its brand of peanut butter that will reduce waste and maintain freshness over a longer period of time. However, this container will increase the product's price by 30%. The company wants to ascertain whether and to what extent the new and improved container will affect sales of its peanut butter. Propose an appropriate experimental approach that can provide the information desired. Defend your answer.
5. Apart from validity considerations, what factors play a role in the choice between laboratory and field experiments?
6. Briefly describe simulated test markets and their strengths.
7. In what ways does the history effect differ from the maturation effect?
8. "Instrument variation effect will not be a problem as long as the researcher is very careful and consistent." Discuss the extent to which this statement is likely to be true.
9. Can the mortality effect lower *external validity* in any way? Why or why not?
10. Why is the maturation effect more likely to be a problem in laboratory experiments than in field experiments?
11. Refer to the situation described in Question 2, and assume that the research conducted by Toys & Games is an experiment. Is this experiment a laboratory or a field experiment? Does it involve human or nonhuman participants? Go through the list of internal- and external-validity threats we discussed and indicate which are and which are not likely to be serious in this experiment.
12. In what way does reactive bias differ from pretest-manipulation interaction bias?
13. Describe, with an example of your own, the distinction between pretesting effect and pretest-manipulation interaction effect.

9

Selected Experimental Designs

The previous chapter presented an overview of experimental research, with emphasis on the conditions to be met for making causal inferences, the laboratory versus field approaches for conducting marketing experiments, and the various internal- and external-validity threats to experimental findings. In this chapter we will discuss several standard experimental designs that frequently serve as the basis for causal inferences in marketing. Before we examine those designs, a few points concerning them are in order.

First, most of the standard designs can be employed in laboratory or field settings and can involve human or nonhuman participants. Therefore although each design has certain inherent weaknesses, whether and to what extent those weaknesses are likely to be serious may depend on the particular context in which the design is employed. (Recall that the seriousness of several of the validity threats depends on these features; see Table 8.1.) Second, the experimental designs we will look at are not the only ones available.[1] Third, depending on the unique feature of a given situation and the experimenter's ingenuity, the experimenter may be able to create an *ad hoc* design to fit the situation by modifying one of the standard designs or borrowing ideas from several of them. In other words, a *standard design* does not necessarily mean that the design should be used without modification.

The designs we will examine in this chapter are classified into three groups: preexperimental designs, true experimental designs, and quasi-experimental designs. We will use the following symbolic notation to depict these designs

[1] For a comprehensive treatment of experimental designs, see, for example, Donald T. Campbell and Julian C. Stanley, *Experimental and Quasi-Experimental Designs for Research* (Chicago: Rand McNally, 1979); Seymour Banks, *Experimentation in Marketing* (New York: McGraw-Hill, 1965).

parsimoniously and to aid in easy comparisons across designs (this notational scheme is very similar to the schemes followed in several standard books):

O Any formal observation or measurement of the dependent (or effect) variable that is made as part of the experimental study (symbols O_1, O_2, etc., will be used when two or more measurements are involved during the experiment)

Note: In many experiments one must also make formal measurements of the *independent* (or causal) variables to make sure that the experimental manipulations worked as planned. Such measurements, called *manipulation checks,* will not be explicitly shown in the designs we will look at so as to keep the designs simple.

X Exposure of units participating in the study to the experimental manipulation or treatment (symbols X_1, X_2, etc., will be used when two or more experimental treatments are involved)

Note: The ordering of *O*'s and *X*'s from left to right will represent the time sequence in which they occur.

EG An *experimental group* of units that gets exposed to the experimental treatment (symbols EG_1, EG_2, etc., will be used when the experiment has more than one experimental group)

CG A *control group* of units participating in the experiment but not exposed to the experimental treatment (symbols CG_1, CG_2, etc., will be used when there are multiple control groups)

(R) Used in some designs in conjunction with the notations for experimental and control groups to indicate that units participating in the study have been *randomly assigned* to the groups (more on random assignment later)

PREEXPERIMENTAL DESIGNS

Studies using *preexperimental designs* are, strictly speaking, not experimental studies at all. They have little or no control over the influence of extraneous factors and hence are not much better than descriptive studies when it comes to making causal inferences. While preexperimental studies can certainly lead to hypotheses about causal relationships, one cannot have much confidence in the existence of such relationships without additional research. The label *pre*experimental emphasizes the fact that these studies are more exploratory than conclusive as far as causal inferences are concerned.

Why should we even bother to discuss preexperimental designs when they are not really experiments? There are two good reasons for doing so. First, studies employing preexperimental designs often form the basis for causal inferences in the real world, and one needs to be aware of their pitfalls so as to avoid interpreting their findings at face value. Second, comparisons with preexperimental designs can be helpful in highlighting the merits of true experimental and quasi-experimental designs. The preexperimental design we will look at first is the one-group, after-only design. Then we will examine the one-group, before-after design and the two-group, *ex post facto* design.

One-group, after-only design

Before we examine the basic features of the one-group, after-only design, let us consider the following two situations:

SITUATION A: A company introduces a new brand of margarine in four test market areas and employs a very unique and revolutionary promotional campaign for it. The brand captures at least a 10% share in each market within two months after introduction. The company's management concludes that the revolutionary promotional campaign played a major role in the market share achieved by the brand.

SITUATION B: The president of the United States makes a television speech soliciting public support for legislation favoring prayer in public schools. A telephone survey of those who viewed the presidential speech indicates that 70% favor such legislation. The president's speech is therefore considered to have had a significant impact on the American public.

A causal inference is implied in each of these situations. However, while the inferences seem to be sound from an intuitive standpoint, they cannot be trusted to any extent. To see why, let us first depict the experimental design underlying the two situations in terms of the symbols defined earlier. Both situations involve the following *one-group, after-only design*:

EG X O

One group of units (EG)—the four test markets in situation A and the television audience for the president's speech in situation B—was exposed to a manipulation (X)—the new brand's promotional campaign in situation A and the presidential speech in situation B. Then a single measurement (O) was made—the brand's market share in situation A and support for school prayer legislation in situation B. A readily apparent problem with this design is the total lack of control of extraneous influences. Stated differently, factors other than X may well be partly or fully responsible for the observed results (O). Another obvious limitation is the absence of any objective standard against which the results can be compared in ascertaining whether and to what extent X influenced O.

In situation A the inference that the promotional campaign was responsible for the brand's market share was quite subjective; it was based on an *assumption* that the brand's market share would have been significantly less than 10% without the promotional campaign. Similarly, in situation B the inferred effectiveness of the president's speech stemmed from a subjective notion that the percentage of respondents favoring the legislation would have been substantially less than 70% had the president's speech not been aired. The potential fallacy of such causal inferences based on data from one-group, after-only designs is emphasized by the following statement made by a marketing research director:

> I find it difficult, if not impossible, to interpret any consumer research number in a vacuum. Knowing, for example, that 61% of a sample of homemakers rated my new furniture polish "excellent" doesn't mean much to me without knowing how many gave my *old* product, or my competitor's product, a similar rating.[2]

One-group, before-after design

The *one-group, before-after design* is an improvement over the previous design because it includes a premeasurement. The symbolic representation of this design is as follows:

$$\text{EG} \quad O_1 \quad X \quad O_2$$

The premeasurement serves as an objective benchmark against which the postmeasurement is compared to determine the impact of the experimental manipulation. Nevertheless, the design is still plagued by potential validity problems. Several experiments described in the preceding chapter to illustrate validity threats—the laboratory experiment to assess the impact of a new Toyota commercial on consumers' opinions about Toyota cars; the field experiment to study the impact of a special store display for Dole canned fruits on the brand's sales; the in-home test to determine the effect of a new and improved bathtub and tile cleaner on consumer preference for the product—used this design. Each of these experiments had serious internal-validity, and possibly some external-validity, problems, as was demonstrated by our discussion in the previous

---

[2] "Don't Commit Product Testing's '7 Deadly Sins,'" *Marketing News,* January 6, 1984, Section 2, p. 20.

chapter. Potential validity threats that can become serious in studies employing the one-group, before-after design are summarized next.

- In laboratory experiments, which invariably involve measurement of human participants, such as the one for assessing the impact of the new Toyota commercial: maturation effect, pretesting effect, instrument variation effect, reactive bias, and pretest-manipulation interaction bias. (See Chapter 8 for definitions and illustrations of these validity threats.)
- In field experiments involving measurements of nonhuman units, such as the one for studying the effect of the special store display for Dole canned fruits: history effect, maturation effect, and mortality effect.
- In field experiments involving measurement of human respondents, such as the in-home test of the new and improved bathtub and tile cleaner: history effect, pretesting effect, instrument variation effect, mortality effect, reactive bias, and pretest-manipulation interaction bias.

Each of these experiments can also suffer from nonrepresentative-sample bias if the units chosen for the experimental study do not adequately represent the total body of units. Of course, nonrepresentative-sample bias stems from inadequate sampling and can occur in any experimental design.

In short, although the one-group, before-after design is a shade better than the one-group, after-only design, its potential validity problems make it no more than a preexperimental design.

Two-group, *ex post facto* design

The *two-group, ex post facto design* has two groups of units: one exposed and the other unexposed to the experimental manipulation. There is no premeasurement, and both groups are postmeasured after the manipulation has been introduced. The symbolic representation of this design is as follows:

EG	X	O_1
CG		O_2

Recall situation B, the study to evaluate the effectiveness of the president's speech on school prayer. A major weakness of this study was the absence of a benchmark against which to compare the finding that 70% of those who viewed the television speech favored the school prayer legislation. Suppose the telephone survey conducted in this study covered a random sample of the public, including those who did not view the speech, instead of being limited to those who viewed the speech. In other words, let us assume the survey sought the opinions of those who said they viewed the speech as well as those who said they did not. Also, suppose 20% of the latter group of respondents (i.e., nonviewers) favored the school prayer legislation, in contrast to the 70% of the viewers who favored it.

Do these results imply that the president's speech was effective in swaying public opinion in favor of the school prayer legislation? It is tempting to think so since the experimental group of respondents seems to be much more favorable toward the legislation than the control group. Yielding to such a temptation can be a serious mistake, however. Although opinions were sought and compared from an exposed and unexposed group, the catch here is that the groups were *self-selected.* That is, determination of who belonged to the experimental group and who belonged to the control group was made solely on the basis of what the respondents said in the survey following the speech. The researcher had no control over the composition of the two groups and hence no way of ensuring that they had similar feelings about school prayer before the president's speech. For instance, respondents who watched the speech by and large may have shared the president's viewpoints to begin with, including those relating to school prayer. By the same token, the majority of people who did not watch the speech may have been individuals whose opinions were at odds with those of the president. Such a sharp discrepancy between the groups with respect to their prior opinions about school prayer is bound to result in serious selection effect, a major internal-validity threat.

The very term *ex post facto* (meaning "after the fact") in the label for this design underlines its inherent weakness—namely, that the compositions of EG and CG are determined *after* the manipulation has been introduced, with no way of ensuring prior similarity between the groups. An additional problem associated with self-selection when human participants are involved is that some respondents, either intentionally or unintentionally, might state that they were exposed to the manipulation when they really had not been, or vice versa. Hence there is no guarantee that all units in EG got exposed to *X* and all units in CG did not get exposed to *X*.

Why the two-group, *ex post facto* design is a preexperimental design should be clear by now. The results of a study using this design are no better than cross-tabulations or correlations of data obtained through descriptive-research studies. Since the researcher has no control over group compositions or over exposure or nonexposure to the manipulation, any causal inference is based solely on the postmeasurement survey. Specifically, the survey data on the dependent variable are cross-tabulated according to units that happened to be exposed to the manipulation and those that happened not to be. As we have seen several times earlier (especially in Chapter 4), cross-tabulations of descriptive-survey data can only point out associations between variables. To make causal inferences merely from evidence of associations is risky. Yet it is not uncommon to find causal inferences being made on the basis of studies using a two-group, *ex post facto* design. A case in point is the example we discussed in Chapter 8 concerning the impact of MTV on sales of a Duran Duran album in the Dallas area. Researchers and managers must be wary of such causal inferences.

TRUE EXPERIMENTAL DESIGNS

In sharp contrast to preexperimental designs, *true experimental designs* have built-in safeguards for controlling all, or almost all, threats to internal and external validity. As we will see later, the effectiveness with which various threats are neutralized by true experimental designs may still depend to some extent on the context in which they are applied. Nevertheless, these designs are generally far superior to preexperimental designs in terms of making causal inferences with confidence.

True experimental designs have two key features that enable them to exercise tight control over extraneous influences: the presence of one or more control groups and, more importantly, the *random assignment* of units to various experimental and control groups. Random assignment involves distributing the sample units chosen for a study to various groups on a strictly random, objective basis so that the group compositions can be considered to be equivalent before one starts the experiment. As Kidder observes:

> Random assignment controls for the influence of all the extraneous subject [sample unit] variables that you do not want to study but also do not want to hold constant because holding them constant limits the generalizability of your study. It is the defining feature of a true experiment.[3]

Since random assignment is a critical characteristic of true experiments, we should examine how it differs from an alternative approach for ensuring group equivalence, called *matching,* which is often used. Matching involves forming groups in such a way that the composition of units is similar across groups with respect to some specific characteristic(s). To illustrate, suppose a sample of respondents is to be divided into two groups in a laboratory experiment for testing the relative effectiveness of two different commercials for a new car. Assuming that respondents' income levels, for instance, may have a bearing on how they react to the commercials, forming two matched groups involves ensuring that the two groups have similar income distributions. Any differences in reactions to the two commercials that can be attributed to income levels will then cancel out between the two groups.

A potential limitation of matching, however, is that the groups can differ on key characteristics on which they are not explicitly matched. For example, the two groups with matched income distributions may differ significantly on characteristics such as their interests and driving habits, which, in turn, may result in differential impact of the commercials, thereby lowering internal validity. Another practical limitation of matching is that data on the matching characteristics must be readily available in order to form the groups. Matching obviously will not be possible when such data are not available.

[3] Louise H. Kidder, *Selltiz Wrightsman and Cook's Research Methods in Social Relations* (New York: Holt, Rinehart and Winston, 1981), p. 18.

Random assignment, in contrast to matching, equalizes groups on all relevant characteristics with no special emphasis on one or a few characteristics. Furthermore, random assignment does not require any data on characteristics of the initial sample of units. Between matching and random assignment, the latter is therefore the generally recommended approach for forming equivalent groups.[4] According to Kerlinger:

> Theoretically, randomization is the only method of controlling *all* possible extraneous variables. Another way to phrase it is: if randomization has been thoroughly accomplished, then the experimental groups can be considered equal in all possible ways. . . . All other methods leave many possibilities of unequality. If we match for intelligence, we may successfully achieve statistical equality in intelligence (at least in those aspects of intelligence measured), but we may suffer from inequality in other significantly influential independent variables like aptitude, motivation, and social class.[5]

Before we look at specific true experimental designs, three additional points concerning random assignment are noteworthy. First, *random assignment* is not synonymous with the term *random sampling,* which we will cover in detail in Chapters 12 and 13. Kidder nicely points out the distinction between the two:

> *Random assignment* is a procedure you use after you have a sample of subjects and before you expose them to a treatment. It is a way of assigning subjects to treatments so that the groups do not differ before the treatment begins. . . . *Random sampling* is the procedure you use to *select* the subjects you will study. Random sampling serves not to equate two or more experimental groups but to make whatever subject group you study representative of a larger population. . . . Random sampling allows you to say that what you have found in [a] sample is true of [units] in the larger [body of interest]. It maximizes the external validity of research. Random assignment, on the other hand, enables you to say, "*X* caused *Y*" with some degree of certainty. It maximizes the internal validity of research.[6]

Thus random sampling is a means of controlling *nonrepresentative-sample bias,* an external-validity threat. Random assignment, by contrast, minimizes *selection effect,* an internal-validity threat.

Second, *strict* random assignment may not always be desirable. Specifically, forming matched sets of units first and then randomly assigning units within each set to the various groups may be better when the number of units available for an experimental study is small. For instance, consider a field experiment to

[4] For a discussion of a few other related approaches for controlling extraneous influences, see M. Venkatesan and Robert J. Holloway, *An Introduction to Marketing Experimentation: Methods, Applications and Problems* (New York: Free Press, 1971), pp. 35–37.

[5] Fred N. Kerlinger, *Foundations of Behavioral Research* (New York: Holt, Rinehart and Winston, 1973), p. 310.

[6] Kidder, *Selltiz Wrightsman and Cook's Research Methods,* p. 19.

test the effectiveness of a point-of-purchase material for a brand of cookies. Let us say that eight supermarkets in a test area have agreed to participate in the experiment. Four of the eight stores are to be in an experimental group in which the point-of-purchase material will be displayed, and the rest are to form a control group. Assigning four stores each to the experimental and control groups on a *completely* random basis may be risky in this case. For instance, what if the four stores in one group turn out to be the largest of the eight? Or what if all four stores happen to be located in neighborhoods that are wealthier than those in which the other stores are located? The obvious danger here is that the skewed group compositions will lead to selection effect. Therefore a better procedure is to first form pairs of stores subjectively so that the stores within each paired set are similar on critical characteristics like size and location. This pairing results in four pairs of stores. One store from each pair is now *randomly* selected and assigned to one group (experimental or control), and the remaining store is assigned to the other group.

Random assignment is not a panacea; it is merely a procedure for minimizing the odds of systematic differences between groups at the start of an experiment.[7] However, the ability of random assignment to lower those odds depends on the number of units available for assignment: The larger the initial sample size, the more successful random assignment will be in achieving equivalence across groups. Hence when the initial sample size is quite small, some suitable matching procedure followed by random assignment from within matched sets of units is better than strict or complete random assignment.

Third, in many marketing field experiments, especially those involving units such as stores or sales territories, practical constraints may make random assignments infeasible. For example, consider a firm selling industrial chemicals through two independent sales divisions in two regions of the country. The firm has a sales force of 80, divided about evenly between the two divisions. The firm's sales vice president wants to conduct a field experiment to ascertain the impact on sales of a 5% increase in the salespeople's commission rate. An ideal procedure for the field experiment is to divide the sales force of 80 *randomly* into two groups of 40 each, increase the commission rate by 5% for one group of salespeople, make no change in commission rate for the other group, and observe the sales results. Random assignment of salespeople to the experimental and control groups may not be feasible in this case, however, because of the friction and morale problems it may create within each division's sales force. A more practical and sensible thing to do is to treat salespeople in one division as the experimental group and those in the other division as the control group, especially since the two divisions are autonomous. Which of the two divisions gets to be the experimental group can still be determined randomly by, for instance, the toss of a coin. The main point of this example is that complete

[7] Charles Ramond, *The Art of Using Science in Marketing* (New York: Harper & Row, 1974), pp. 181–182, further discusses this point and offers several examples.

random assignment may not always be practical, even if a sufficiently large sample of units is available. Studies conducted under these circumstances cannot employ experimental designs that are strictly true, and hence their findings must be interpreted with caution.

We will now discuss three specific true experimental designs: two-group, before-after design, two-group, after-only design and four-group, six-study design.

Two-group, before-after design

The symbolic representation of the *two-group, before-after design* is as follows:

EG(R)	O_1	X	O_2
CG(R)	O_3		O_4

We will first examine the general features of this design and then discuss specific applications of it. Since the study units in this design are randomly assigned to EG and CG, the two groups can be considered equivalent. That is, they will be influenced by the same extraneous factors and are likely to go through similar experiences, *except* for the exposure to the experimental manipulation (X), which will occur in EG but not in CG. Therefore the difference between the pre- and postmeasurements of CG (that is, $O_4 - O_3$) should give a good indication of all extraneous influences experienced by EG. The difference between the pre- and postmeasurements of EG (that is, $O_2 - O_1$) reflects the impact of X as well as any extraneous influences. Hence the true impact of X is given by

$$(O_2 - O_1) - (O_4 - O_3).$$

This expression completely accounts for and neutralizes all validity threats *except* the following (if they happen to be present):

1. Mortality effect. Recall that the mortality effect will occur only if certain units fail to complete the entire study *and* if the units dropping out differ systematically from the ones that remain. Since EG and CG are equivalent to begin with, the experimental results may have internal validity if similar units drop out of both EG and CG; that is, if the composition of the two groups is similar at the postmeasurement stage. But if this composition is different from that of the total body of relevant units, the findings will lack external validity.

2. Reactive bias. Reactive bias occurs when study participants behave abnormally because they know they are participating in an experiment. To the extent that EG and CG will go through similar experiences, any reactive bias should influence both groups equally. Therefore the net difference between the EG and CG measurements—that is, $(O_2 - O_1) - (O_4 - O_3)$—should still provide a broad indication of whether X had any impact. However, the external validity of the findings may be questionable if reactive bias is present. Although the typical purpose of marketing experiments is to assess the *relative* effectiveness of experimental treatments—for example, Is X better than no X? Is X_1 more effective than X_2?—rather than to accurately predict the absolute impact of a treatment,[8] one should be careful in generalizing the results of laboratory experiments that are prone to reactive bias.

3. Pretest-manipulation interaction bias. As we saw in Chapter 8, pretest-manipulation interaction bias is a potential external-validity threat. It may occur in situations where human participants are premeasured concerning a topic and then are exposed to a manipulation that closely relates to the *same* topic. When the two-group, before-after design involves human participants, a premeasurement followed by a manipulation that is linked to the subject matter of the premeasurement will occur *only in EG and not in CG.* In other words, the contaminating influence of pretest-manipulation interaction will be present in the $(O_2 - O_1)$ difference but *not* in the $(O_4 - O_3)$ difference. The CG therefore does not really control for pretest-manipulation interaction bias (although it does control for *pretesting effect*). In short, the external validity of this design may be questionable when human participants are involved.

4. Nonrepresentative-sample bias. Nonrepresentative-sample bias stems from a discrepancy between the composition of the entire sample of units participating in a study and the composition of the total collection of units. Since this bias depends on the sample selection procedures rather than the nature of a particular design, it is bound to be present in *any* experiment that starts out with a nonrepresentative sample. Hence this bias, if present, is *not* due to any inherent weakness of the two-group, before-after design.

We will now look at three illustrative applications of the two-group, before-after design and identify the validity threats that will be, and those that will not be, neutralized by this design under each application.

EXPERIMENT 1: A field experiment is conducted to study the impact of a price reduction on the sales of a brand of paper towels. A sample of 50 supermarkets in a certain region is divided into EG and CG, each containing 25 stores, through random assignment. Unit sales of the paper towel brand are monitored for a four-week period in EG and CG and constitute the O_1 and O_3 measurements. Then the price of the brand is reduced 10% (that is, X is introduced) in EG but is left unchanged in CG for a four-week period. Unit sales are once again monitored during this period to yield the O_2 and O_4 measurements.

[8] Banks, *Experimentation in Marketing,* pp. 1–3, offers a good discussion of this point.

EXPERIMENT 2: A field experiment is conducted to measure the impact of a two-page brochure describing the harmful effects of sugar on consumption of sugar-free soft drinks. A sample of 200 households is chosen from an area. One-half of the sample is randomly assigned to EG and the other half to CG. A questionnaire about general food consumption behavior is completed by all households. A part of this questionnaire deals with current consumption levels of sugar-free soft drinks in the various households and provides the O_1 and O_3 measurements. A booklet on general nutrition and good eating habits is left behind in all households, with one key difference: The booklets given to households in EG contain the two-page brochure on the ill effects of sugar, but those given to households in CG do not. The heads of households in both groups are requested to read the booklets at their leisure. After an interval of three months the households are recontacted and requested to fill out the same questionnaire once again. The O_2 and O_4 measurements are obtained through this questionnaire.

EXPERIMENT 3: A laboratory experiment is conducted to determine the impact of a personal-computer commercial (demonstrating how easy it is to use the product) on consumer perceptions about its ease of use. One hundred consumers are recruited for this experiment and randomly divided into two groups (EG and CG). Both groups are administered a questionnaire dealing with a variety of home appliances. Through this questionnaire current perceptions about the personal computer are measured (O_1 and O_3). The EG and the CG are then shown the same hour-long television program (in different viewing rooms) containing commercials for a variety of products. The test commercial (X) is inserted in the version of the program seen by EG but not by CG. Then the relevant O_2 and O_4 measurements are obtained through the same questionnaire.

The type of validity threats present and their degree of seriousness vary somewhat across experiments 1, 2, and 3, even though they all employ the same experimental design. Table 9.1 contains a list of the validity threats and, for each experiment, indicates which threats are controlled by the design and which are not.

As demonstrated by Table 9.1, the two-group, before-after design suffers from just one serious problem *stemming from the nature of the design itself,* namely, the problem of pretest-manipulation interaction bias in experiments 2 and 3, both involving human participants. The next design eliminates this problem.

Two-group, after-only design

As its name implies, the *two-group, after-only design* has two groups but does not involve any premeasurements. The two groups are formed by random

Table 9.1

Validity threats in experiments 1, 2, and 3

TYPE OF THREAT	EXPERIMENT 1	EXPERIMENT 2	EXPERIMENT 3
History effect	May occur but is controlled	May occur but is controlled	Unlikely to occur
Maturation effect	May occur but is controlled	May occur but is controlled	May occur but is controlled
Pretesting effect	Unlikely to occur	May occur but is controlled	May occur but is controlled
Instrument variation effect	Unlikely to occur	May occur but is controlled	May occur but is controlled
Selection effect	Unlikely to occur	Unlikely to occur	Unlikely to occur
Mortality effect	May occur; whether it does depends on the nature of the units dropping out	May occur; whether it does depends on the nature of the units dropping out	Unlikely to occur
Reactive bias	Unlikely to occur	May occur; if so, the EG and CG equivalence should still preserve internal validity, although external validity may be lowered	May occur; if so, the EG and CG equivalence should still preserve internal validity, although external validity may be lowered
Pretest-manipulation interaction bias	Unlikely to occur	May occur; if so, it is *not* controlled	May occur; if so, it is *not* controlled

Note: Nonrepresentative-sample bias is not listed because it stems from inadequacies in initial sample selection and is not unique to any particular experimental design.

assignment, following which the experimental group is exposed to the manipulation while the control group is not. The two groups are then postmeasured. Hence this design looks like the two-group, before-after design except for the absence of premeasurements, as shown next (the subscripts 2 and 4 are used for the postmeasurements merely to be consistent with the previous design and to facilitate easy comparison):

$$\begin{array}{lll} EG(R) & X & O_2 \\ CG(R) & & O_4 \end{array}$$

The potentially troublesome bias in the two-group, before-after design—that is, the pretest-manipulation interaction bias—is absent in this design because there are no premeasurements. Furthermore, since EG and CG are considered equivalent, the two groups should go through similar experiences, except for the presence of X in EG but not in CG. The O_4 measurement therefore includes all extraneous influences, while the O_2 measurement represents the impact of X and includes the same extraneous influences. Hence the true impact of X is given by the difference $O_2 - O_4$.

Consider the three illustrative experiments described in the preceding section. They would each employ the two-group, after-only design if they did not involve any premeasurements. In such a case, what would Table 9.1 (which summarizes the validity threats under each experiment when the two-group, before-after design is used) look like? It would look the same except for the following changes: Because of the absence of formal premeasurements, the pretesting effect, the instrument variation effect, and the pretest-manipulation interaction bias would be unlikely to occur in *any* of the three experiments. Consequently, experiments 2 and 3, both involving human participants, would no longer face the threat of pretest-manipulation interaction bias. Eliminating the threat of this bias is perhaps the single most important advantage of the two-group, after-only design over the two-group, before-after design. Another obvious strength of the design is that it requires two fewer measurements than the previous design.

You are probably wondering how the true impact of X can be obtained from just two measurements (O_2 and O_4), when the previous design required four measurements and yet could not guarantee the absence of pretest-manipulation interaction bias. Stated differently, does the two-group, after-only design have any catch? Before we answer this question, let us reexamine the expression for the impact of X derived under the previous design, namely,

$$(O_2 - O_1) - (O_4 - O_3).$$

Rearranging terms, we can write this expression as

$$(O_2 - O_4) - (O_1 - O_3).$$

When the premeasurements O_1 and O_3 are the same, or when they differ by a negligible amount, this expression reduces to $O_2 - O_4$. As we saw earlier, $O_2 - O_4$ represents the impact of X in the two-group, after-only design.

The derivation of the $O_2 - O_4$ difference from the expression for the impact of X in the two-group, before-after design highlights a distinct feature of the two-group, after-only design: *It implicitly treats the premeasurements as being equal (or almost equal)*. In other words, a basic assumption of the design is that EG and CG would have yielded extremely similar, if not identical, premeasurements had such measurements been made.

The answer to our earlier question of whether this design has any catch depends on the validity of this basic assumption. Of course, verifying this assumption is impossible since there are no premeasurements of the groups. Nevertheless, to the extent that random assignment is supposed to create equivalent groups, this assumption is likely to be quite sound. As Campbell and Stanley point out:

> While the pretest is a concept deeply embedded in the thinking of [researchers] . . . it is not actually essential in true experimental designs. For psychological reasons it is difficult to give up "knowing for sure" that the experimental and control groups were "equal" before the differential experimental treatment. Nonetheless, the most adequate all-purpose assurance of lack of initial biases between groups is randomization.[9]

One critical caveat concerning random assignment is worth bearing in mind, however. As we saw earlier, the ability of random assignment to achieve prior equality of groups depends on the initial sample size: The larger the pool of units available for assignment, the more successful random assignment will be in creating equivalent groups. Alternatively, the smaller the initial pool of units, the greater are the chances of obtaining dissimilar groups through random assignment. Of course, appropriate matching followed by random assignment will lower the severity of this problem. Nevertheless, the basic assumption of prior equality underlying the two-group, after-only design may still be shaky when the number of units available for participation in an experiment is relatively small. Under such circumstances, using the two-group, before-after design will at least provide an opportunity (through the O_1 and O_3 measurements) to verify whether the groups are similar to start with. But then the premeasurements will introduce the possibility of pretest-manipulation interaction bias.

Fortunately, however, marketing contexts characterized by small initial sample sizes typically involve *nonhuman* units (stores, test market areas, etc.). Since pretest-manipulation interaction bias is not a concern in experiments involving nonhuman units, the two-group, before-after design can be used in such situations. As a general rule, the two-group, before-after design is better for field experiments involving nonhuman units (e.g., experiment 1 described earlier), while the two-group, after-only design is better for field or laboratory experiments involving human respondents (e.g., experiments 2 and 3 described earlier) in which sample sizes can usually be increased sufficiently without much difficulty.[10]

[9] Campbell and Stanley, *Experimental and Quasi-Experimental Designs,* p. 25.

[10] Many experimental studies involving human subjects and published in the marketing literature have used the two-group, after-only design (or variations of the design, such as designs involving more than two groups to study the relative effectiveness of multiple experimental treatments). For example, one interesting after-only study involving 12 experimental-treatment groups and 1 control group was recently reported: Marjorie J. Caballero and William M. Pride, "Selected Effects of Salesperson Sex and Attractiveness in Direct Mail Advertisement," *Journal of Marketing,* 48 (Winter 1984), pp. 94–100.

Four-group, six-study design

The *four-group, six-study design* has four randomly assigned groups—two experimental and two control—and involves six measurements.[11] It is simply a combination of the two preceding designs:

$EG_1(R)$	O_1	X	O_2
$CG_1(R)$	O_3		O_4
$EG_2(R)$		X	O_5
$CG_2(R)$			O_6

As an illustration of how this design is employed, recall experiment 2 presented earlier, namely, the field experiment to assess the impact of an informational brochure on the consumption of sugar-free soft drinks. The following revised procedure will be employed in that experiment if the four-group, six-study design is used instead of the two-group, before-after design. The initial sample of 200 households will be randomly assigned to EG_1, CG_1, EG_2, and CG_2, each containing 50 households. Current consumption levels of sugar-free soft drinks in the EG_1 and CG_1 households will be measured through the food consumption questionnaire. The households in all four groups will then receive the booklet on general nutrition and good eating habits, but only the booklets received by households in EG_1 and EG_2 will contain the two-page brochure on the harmful effects of sugar. Three months later the consumption of sugar-free soft drinks by households in each of the four groups will be measured, using the same questionnaire as before.

This experiment will provide a wealth of data to measure not only the impact of the brochure (i.e., the experimental manipulation X) but also the individual magnitudes of the pretesting effect and the pretest-manipulation interaction bias. Since the four groups are formed through random assignment, premeasurements of EG_2 and CG_2, had such measurements been made, should be similar to O_1 and O_3. Hence a logical estimate of the premeasurement corresponding to EG_2 and CG_2 is the average of O_1 and O_3, that is, $(O_1 + O_3)/2$. Let D_1, D_2, D_3, and D_4 represent the differences between the premeasurement (*estimated* premeasurement for EG_2 and CG_2) and the postmeasurement for EG_1, CG_1, EG_2, and CG_2, respectively. These differences have the following interpretations:

$D_1 = O_2 - O_1$ Represents the impact of X plus all extraneous influences

[11] This design was first proposed by R. L. Soloman in his article "An Extension of Control Group Design," *Psychological Bulletin,* 46 (1949), pp. 137–150; hence it is also known as the Solomon four-group design.

$D_2 = O_4 - O_3$ Represents the impact of all extraneous influences except pretest-manipulation interaction bias

$D_3 = O_5 - \frac{O_1 + O_3}{2}$ Represents the impact of X plus all extraneous influences except the pretesting effect and the pretest-manipulation interaction bias

$D_4 = O_6 - \frac{O_1 + O_3}{2}$ Represents the impact of all extraneous influences except the pretesting effect and the pretest-manipulation interaction bias

The differences D_1, D_2, D_3, and D_4, given these interpretations, can be used to estimate the true impact of X, the magnitude of the pretesting effect, and the magnitude of the pretest-manipulation interaction bias. Specifically,

$D_3 - D_4$ = true impact of X,

$D_2 - D_4$ = magnitude of the pretesting effect,

$D_1 - D_3$ = combined magnitude of the pretest-manipulation interaction bias and the pretesting effect,

$D_1 - D_3 - (D_2 - D_4)$ = magnitude of the pretest-manipulation interaction bias.

This design is seldom employed in marketing experiments because it is so complex and, more importantly, because marketing researchers are typically interested only in *controlling,* rather than measuring the magnitudes of, such extraneous influences as the pretesting effect and the pretest-manipulation interaction bias.[12] After all, simpler designs like the two-group, after-only design are quite capable of measuring the true impact of an experimental manipulation. Nevertheless, the four-group, six-study design is perhaps the most rigorous of true experimental designs because it offers multiple indications of a manipulation's effectiveness and increases one's ability to make causal inferences with assurance. As Campbell and Stanley state:

> The effect of X is replicated in four different fashions: $O_2 > O_1$, $O_2 > O_4$, $O_5 > O_6$, and $O_5 > O_3$. The actual instabilities of experimentation are such that if these comparisons are in agreement, the strength of the inferences is greatly

[12] One exception is the following study using the four-group, six-study design to examine the effectiveness of corrective advertising for Listerine antiseptic: Richard W. Mizerski, Neil K. Allison, and Stephen Calvert, "A Controlled Field Study of Corrective Advertising Using Multiple Exposures and a Commercial Medium," *Journal of Marketing Research,* 17 (August 1980), pp. 341–348.

> increased. Another indirect contribution to the generalizability of experimental findings is also made, in that through experience with [the four-group, six study design] in any given research area one learns the general likelihood of [pretest-manipulation] interactions, and thus is better able to interpret past and future [two-group, before-after designs].[13]

In short, while the four-group, six-study design may not always be practical or necessary, it is an ideal design. Experimenters may benefit by incorporating at least some of its features into any *ad hoc* designs they create to suit specific situations.

QUASI-EXPERIMENTAL DESIGNS

Quasi-experimental designs are those that do not offer as much control as true experimental designs but usually provide more measurements and more information than a typical preexperimental design. Several quasi-experimental designs are available. However, we will focus only on one such design, called the time series experiment or panel design, which is the most frequently used quasi-experimental design in the marketing field.

As its name suggests, the *panel design* makes use of data routinely gathered from a consumer panel or other types of panels such as a panel of supermarkets. (See Chapter 4 for a discussion of panels and their capabilities and limitations.) The panel essentially acts as the experimental group, and the periodic measurements it provides become the observations (O_1, O_2, etc.). The panel design can be shown symbolically as follows:

$$\text{EG} \quad O_1 \quad O_2 \quad O_3 \quad O_4 \quad X_1 \quad O_5 \quad O_6 \quad O_7 \quad X_2 \quad O_8 \quad O_9 \quad \cdots$$

To illustrate, suppose EG is a panel of grocery stores in which sales of various brands of food products are monitored at the end of every month. Let O_1, O_2, and so on, be monthly unit sales of Oatmeal brand cereal, and let X_1, X_2, and so on, represent specific changes in Oatmeal's marketing mix that are introduced into the market area where the panel is located. Suppose X_1 is a 50-cents-off coupon good on a package of Oatmeal purchased during month 5. Exhibit 9.1 shows four hypothetical patterns of Oatmeal's sales in the panel stores during months 1 through 7 (that is, measurements O_1 through O_7).

The advantage of the panel design over preexperimental designs stems from the *pattern,* or *trend,* of measurements on the dependent variable. The trend established before introduction of the experimental manipulation—Oatmeal's sales trend during months 2, 3, and 4 in our example—serves as a sort of control in this design. A comparison of the trend after introducing the manipula-

[13] Campbell and Stanley, *Experimental and Quasi-Experimental Designs,* p. 25.

Exhibit 9.1

Four hypothetical patterns of measurements in an experiment using the panel design

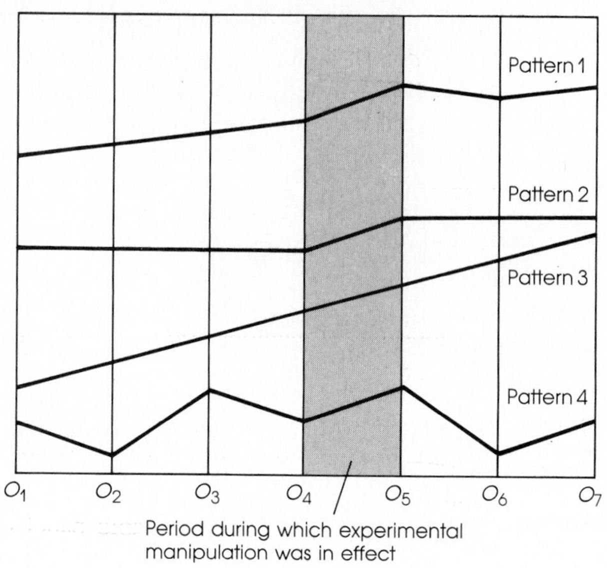

tion with the previously established trend can offer valuable insights that a simple one-group, before-after preexperimental design cannot.

The shaded section of the panel design shown in Exhibit 9.1—namely, O_4 X_1 O_5—is in essence a one-group, before-after design. Assume for a moment that no measurements were made before O_4 or after O_5; that is, only a one-group, before-after design was used to measure the impact of the 50-cents-off coupon on Oatmeal's sales. What would our conclusion be about the effectiveness of the coupon campaign under each of the four situations depicted in Exhibit 9.1? Looking solely at the shaded portion of the figure, we would infer that the 50-cent coupon was *equally effective* in each situation because the $O_5 - O_4$ difference is identical in all four patterns. Yet such an inference would be clearly erroneous, as discussed next.

Pattern 1 suggests that X_1 had an impact on sales but only a short-term impact; the sales trend after removal of X_1 appears to have returned to the original trend. Pattern 2 suggests that X_1 had a longer-term impact on sales, as reflected by the upward shift in the trend line even after removal of X_1. Patterns 3 and 4, in contrast, suggest that X_1 had *no* impact on sales; in each case the manipulation produced no noticeable deviation from the traditional sales pattern. These assessments of the coupon's effectiveness are much different from and *more accurate* than inferences based on the $O_5 - O_4$ difference alone.

Panel designs:
• advantages

• Drawback

In summary, panel designs can lead to more trustworthy causal inferences than preexperimental designs. In addition to providing a benchmark pattern of measurements, experiments employing panels that are well designed and well run can minimize extraneous influences such as the pretesting effect, which can be serious threats in simple one-group, before-after designs.[14] However, a potentially serious drawback of panel designs is the threat of the history effect. Since panel designs are invariably used as part of field experiments, they offer virtually no control over environmental forces such as competitor's strategies. Therefore anyone employing a panel experimental design must be particularly alert to any environmental change in addition to, or instead of, the experimental manipulation that may influence the pattern of measurements. One option for minimizing the influence of the history effect in panel designs is to have a control panel (CG). Although one can seldom create experimental and control panels through random assignment and selectively expose the former to an experimental manipulation, a *matched* control panel can sometimes be established.[15]

In summary, marketers who have access to data from panels can conduct quasi-experiments by manipulating their marketing mixes and examining the panel measurement patterns to detect any significant shifts. Indeed, quasi-experiments are conducted quite frequently by marketers, perhaps because of ready access to commercially available panel data. Typically, all that an individual marketer has to do to employ a panel design is to introduce the experimental manipulation into a market area and purchase the relevant panel data from one of several marketing research firms that specialize in maintaining panels and measuring them periodically. Nevertheless, the relative ease of conducting an experimental study by using panel data should not blind one to the pitfalls of panel data, especially their susceptibility to the history effect. While quasi-experimental designs like the panel design are better than preexperimental designs, they do not possess the rigor of true experimental designs.[16]

OTHER EXPERIMENTAL DESIGNS

As was stated at the beginning of this chapter, the standard experimental designs we have examined are not the only ones available for studying causal associa-

[14] In Chapter 4 we saw examples of well-run panels such as the National Purchase Diary Panel (NPD). Several studies have shown that sales predictions based on consumer panel data are fairly consistent with actual market results; for example, see J. H. Parfitt and B. J. K. Collins, "Use of Consumer Panels for Brand Share Prediction," *Journal of Marketing Research*, 7 (May 1970), pp. 160–167; Yoram Wind and David Lerner, "On the Measurement of Purchase Data: Surveys Versus Purchase Diaries," *Journal of Marketing Research*, 16 (February 1979), pp. 39–47.

[15] For a discussion of the use of matched panels in testing the effectiveness of promotional strategies, see Jeffrey K. McElnea, "Save Time, Money With 5-Phase Promotion Pretesting Model," *Marketing News*, May 25, 1984, Section 2, p. 2.

[16] Kidder, *Selltiz Wrightsman and Cook's Research Methods*, pp. 56–57, offers a good comparative discussion of the validity of preexperiments, true experiments, and quasi-experiments.

tions between variables. One can modify standard designs to fit a given situation by incorporating specific features and controls germane to the situation. For instance, consider the following design, which is a modified version of the two-group, before-after design:[17]

EG_1(R)	O_1	X	
EG_2(R)		X	O_2

This design was used by an outdoor-advertising firm in the Midwest to test the effectiveness of a billboard campaign to promote awareness about metric conversions. Specifically, ten billboards with the message "One ounce = 28.3 grams" painted on them were to be erected at various locations within a metropolitan area. The firm wanted to know whether over a three-month period the billboard messages would have any significant impact on the public's awareness of this particular metric conversion.

A major difficulty in this situation was the firm's inability to control the public's exposure to the billboards. The firm could not selectively expose an experimental group of people to the billboards and compare them with an unexposed control group. The firm therefore decided to use the modified design and implemented it in the following way: Before the billboard messages went up, a random sample of 500 adult respondents (EG_1) was selected from odd-numbered pages of the area's phone book. As part of a brief telephone survey, the percentage of respondents aware of the ounce-to-grams conversion was determined (O_1). The billboard messages were then put up (X). After three months a fresh sample of 500 respondents (EG_2) was selected from even-numbered pages of the area's phone book. This sample was interviewed, using the same telephone survey procedure as before, and the percentage of respondents aware of the metric conversion was obtained (O_2).

Since the pre- and postmeasurements came from statistically equivalent groups, the difference between them (that is, $O_2 - O_1$) indicated the impact of the billboard campaign. [In case you are wondering about the actual results, O_1 was somewhat less than 1% and O_2 was 2%. The difference between the two was not statistically significant (tests of statistical significance are discussed in Chapter 17). The billboard campaign was therefore considered ineffective.]

Note that both EG_1 and EG_2 had an opportunity for exposure to X, and EG_1 could have reacted to X with greater sensitivity than EG_2 owing to the premeasurement. However, the threat of pretest-manipulation interaction bias in EG_1 was of no concern in this study since that group's sole purpose was to provide the premeasurement that served as a benchmark.

Modified designs like the one used in the billboard campaign experiment are frequently employed by marketing researchers. Some of those modified

[17] Campbell and Stanley, *Experimental and Quasi-Experimental Designs,* call this design the separate-sample pretest-posttest design.

designs are quite sophisticated and are capable of measuring the relative effectiveness of multiple treatments within the same study (e.g., four versions of a television commercial for a product) or the influence of different levels of more than one independent variable (e.g., three different price levels in combination with two types of promotion). Such designs are sometimes called *statistical designs* because they require somewhat complex data analysis procedures for sorting out the separate effects of multiple independent variables and/or treatment levels. Let us now look at brief descriptions of certain commonly employed statistical designs. Chapter 19 further discusses these designs under "Analysis of Variance," which is the most frequently used procedure for analyzing data from such designs.

Completely randomized design

The various examples used in discussing the standard designs involved one experimental (causal) variable at just two levels, such as price reduction–no price reduction; commercial–no commerical; educational brochure–no brochure. We can extend the basic designs discussed earlier to include more than two levels of the experimental variable. The term *completely randomized design* is typically used for representing the simplest of such extended designs.

Strictly speaking, the use of the term *completely randomized design* is not limited to designs with more than two levels of the causal variable; it can also be used in situations involving just two levels. However, the analysis procedure for two levels (it is a *t*-test procedure, discussed in Chapter 17) is somewhat simpler than the procedure for more than two levels. The appropriate procedure in the latter case is ANOVA (discussed in Chapter 19), with which the term *completely randomized design* is usually associated. Therefore *completely randomized design* is typically used to label an experiment with more than two treatment levels.

To illustrate the design, we will consider a supermarket chain that wants to conduct a field experiment to test the relative effectiveness of three levels of point-of-purchase promotion for a certain product. The three levels are as follows:

1. No special point-of-purchase promotion (let X_1 represent this treatment level).
2. Special display of the product at its usual shelf location (X_2).
3. Special display at a high-traffic, end-of-aisle location (X_3).

The chain has selected a representative sample of 90 of its stores for the experimental study.

The use of a completely randomized design in this situation involves the following steps:

1. Randomly divide the 90 stores into three groups of 30 each.
2. Randomly assign the three treatments (X_1, X_2, X_3) to the three groups.
3. Monitor and compare product sales (O_1, O_2, O_3) in the three groups, over an appropriate period of time, to ascertain the relative effectiveness of the three promotional levels.

Using our symbolic notation, we can represent the completely randomized design in this example as follows:

$$\begin{array}{lll} EG_1(R) & X_1 & O_1 \\ EG_2(R) & X_2 & O_2 \\ EG_3(R) & X_3 & O_3 \end{array}$$

Notice that in this example EG_1 is actually a control group since X_1 represents "*no* special point-of-purchase promotion." An explicit control group is not always necessary, however. Specifically, when the research objective is to evaluate the relative effectiveness of various experimental-treatment levels (e.g., four different commercials), rather than to compare the effectiveness of each against a no-treatment condition (e.g., no commercial), there is no need for a separate control group. Each experimental group will act as a control group for the others.

Randomized-block design

The *randomized-block design* is basically a refined version of the completely randomized design. The main difference between the two designs is in terms of how the total sample of units is allocated to the various experimental groups. In a completely randomized design the allocation procedure is purely random. In a randomized-block design the groups are formed by using a matching-followed-by-randomization procedure, which is similar to the procedure we saw earlier in the discussion of the limitation of complete random assignment when the total sample size is small.

Using a randomized-block design in our supermarket chain example involves forming matched sets of 3 stores each on the basis of a relevant characteristic—called the *blocking factor*—which, in addition to the experimental manipulation (that is, the three promotional levels), is likely to influence the dependent variable (that is, product sales in our example). For instance, the size of the sample stores (as measured by total sales or floor space) could have a bearing on the sales of the product, irrespective of the type of point-of-purchase promotion used. Store size is therefore a suitable blocking factor. Matched sets of stores are formed by ranking the 90 sample stores from largest to smallest (or vice versa). The first 3 stores form one set, the second 3 stores form another set, and so on. There will thus be 30 sets, or blocks, of matched stores. The stores within each block are randomly assigned to the three groups (EG_1, EG_2, EG_3).

The three groups will therefore have equal representation from each of the 30 blocks.

After the three groups are formed, the remaining steps in conducting the experiment are the same as in the case of a completely randomized design. The symbolic representation of the randomized-block design is also similar to that of the completely randomized design, except for the fact that the EGs are formed through matching followed by randomization. In forming blocks of matched units, we include as many units in each block as there are treatment levels (three in our example).

The randomized-block design increases the ability, or power, of the experiment to detect differences between the impacts of the various treatment levels by accounting for, or blocking, the influence of a key extraneous factor, such as store size in our example. Analysis of the data collected will reveal the separate effects on product sales from the treatment levels and from the blocking factor.

Latin-square design

The basic principle underlying a *Latin-square design* is the same as that of the randomized-block design—namely, to block the effect of extraneous influences so as to get a sharper picture of the relative effects of the experimental treatments. But the Latin-square design permits us to block the influences of two extraneous factors rather than just one.

To illustrate this design, suppose the following two extraneous factors can influence the sales of the product in our supermarket chain example: store size and variety of products carried. One important requirement of the Latin-square design is that the number of blocks, or categories, of each extraneous factor must be the same as the number of levels of the independent variable. Therefore we cannot have 30 blocks of stores based on store size, as we had in the previous design. We can only have *three* blocks since there are three independent-variable levels (X_1, X_2, X_3). We can, for instance, divide the 90 stores into 30 large-size, 30 medium-size, and 30 small-size stores. Next, stores in each of these size categories are further divided into three subcategories on the basis of variety of products carried—for example, 10 wide-variety, 10 medium-variety, and 10 narrow-variety stores. This allocation process results in nine subgroups of stores, as shown by the following matrix:

	Product Variety		
Size	Wide	Medium	Narrow
Large	EG_1	EG_2	EG_3
Medium	EG_4	EG_5	EG_6
Small	EG_7	EG_8	EG_9

The three treatment levels (X_1, X_2, X_3) are assigned to the nine groups at random, subject to the condition that each treatment level is assigned once, *and only once,* to each block of the two extraneous factors. The following symbolic representation is one of several possible configurations for the resulting group assignments and measurements (the symbol R denotes random assignment of treatments to the groups, subject to the condition stated):

$EG_1(R)$	X_1	O_1
$EG_2(R)$	X_2	O_2
$EG_3(R)$	X_3	O_3
$EG_4(R)$	X_2	O_4
$EG_5(R)$	X_3	O_5
$EG_6(R)$	X_1	O_6
$EG_7(R)$	X_3	O_7
$EG_8(R)$	X_1	O_8
$EG_9(R)$	X_2	O_9

Analysis of sales results (the *O*'s) will not only indicate the relative effectiveness of the three point-of-purchase promotion levels but also reveal the effects of the two blocking factors on sales of the product.

Factorial design

A *factorial design* involves the simultaneous manipulation of two or more independent (causal) variables. For instance, suppose the supermarket chain in our example wants to study the impact of a price reduction for the product in addition to the relative sales effectiveness of the three point-of-purchase promotion levels (X_1, X_2, X_3). For the sake of simplicity, let us assume that price has just two treatment levels: regular price (Y_1) and reduced price (Y_2).

Conceptually, the basic factorial design is like a completely randomized design with as many groups (treatment levels) as there are *combinations* of independent-variable levels. In our example, since there are three levels of point-of-purchase promotion and two levels of price, there are six combinations of independent-variable levels: X_1Y_1, X_1Y_2, X_2Y_1, X_2Y_2, X_3Y_1, and X_3Y_2. We therefore randomly divide the total sample of 90 stores into six groups of 15 stores and then randomly assign the six treatment combinations to those groups. We can depict this design symbolically as follows:

$EG_1(R)$	X_1 Y_1	O_1
$EG_2(R)$	X_1 Y_2	O_2

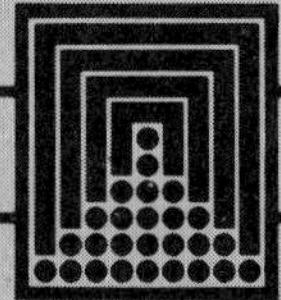

PART FOUR

DESIGNING FORMS AND SCALES FOR COLLECTING DATA

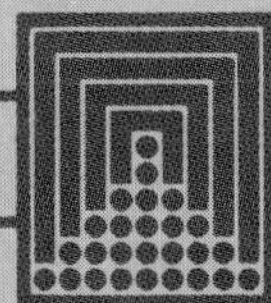

FROM THE MANAGER'S DESK

A. DAWN LESH is vice president and director of marketing research for Bank of America. Ms. Lesh coordinates and supervises all marketing research conducted for Bank of America. Dawn's previous work experience includes research positions with a variety of product and service industries. Prior to joining Bank of America, Dawn worked as a consultant conducting packaged-goods, political, and financial research, and she has also held key positions at Shaklee Corporation (senior project manager of marketing research) and Wells Fargo Bank (director of marketing research). Dawn also worked at the Medical Care Foundation of Sacramento and Doremus (Advertising Agency).

Dawn Lesh received her B.A. from the University of California at Davis and her M.A. from California State University at Sacramento. Ms. Lesh has been a member of the American Marketing Association, San Francisco chapter, since 1974 (board of directors, 1983). Dawn is cochair of A.R.F. Workshop for the Financial Advertising Council, is a member of the Financial Women's Association, New York, and is also one of the founders of W. C. Fields (Women in Communication Fields).

QUESTION: What specific approach or method have you found to be most useful in measuring consumer attitudes toward a product or a service? Can you describe an application of this approach that you are familiar with?

RESPONSE: Marketing research in the financial services industries provides researchers with many opportunities to use a wide array of attitude measurement techniques, including not only the traditional ones but also some of the innovative techniques that have come along in recent years. Generally speaking, however, I find that the techniques that have been around for years are still the best for most applications.

The attitude research I most commonly become involved in includes product/service development and market assessment studies, including tracking studies, advertising research, and quality-of-service research. The quantitative-survey techniques most frequently used include telephone surveys, mail surveys, and central-location intercept interviews. The types of attitude rating scales used include dichotomous agree/disagree scales, three-to-seven-point verbal scales, ten-point numeric scales, paired comparisons, and, occasionally, semantic-differential scales. Recent studies have employed conjoint analysis using a computer-assisted-interviewing technique where respondents answer questions on personal computers.

The type of attitude scale used is determined by the objective to be achieved, the survey vehicle (i.e., mail, telephone), the type of statistics to be applied, a good dose of intuition, and the ease with which the results can be presented. Research findings that people with limited research backgrounds have difficulty understanding are self-defeating. My department often has to take research findings and reduce them to the simplest of terms in order to clearly communicate the results. By clearly communicating the research results, we increase the likelihood that we will obtain our goal of making the research as actionable as possible.

Telephone surveys are frequently used in quantitative studies where we are measuring consumer attitudes about new products for financial institutions, because they are easily communicated over the telephone. The rating scales most frequently used are typically of the five-point variety, such as agree/disagree ratings or importance ratings. These scales usually have two positive choices (i.e., strongly agree, generally agree), two negative choices (i.e., strongly disagree, generally disagree), and a neutral midpoint (neither agree nor disagree). However, a neutral midpoint is not always appropriate, again depending on the objective of the question. The ten-point scale is extensively used in our image research. The broader the scale, the better the discrimination is. However, a high level of discrimination is not always needed.

Mail surveys are used frequently to obtain customer opinions on quality of service. Survey response levels vary from as low as 25% to over 50% if incentives and follow-up mailings are employed. Since mail surveys are self-administered, I generally lean toward smaller attitudinal scales of either three or four points. The excellent-good-fair-poor scale is one most respondents readily understand and is useful in many applications.

The ultimate selection of the proper methodology for attitude measurement stems from experience, both personal and that shared by professional marketing researchers, as a function of which questions do the best job of obtaining the desired information from consumers. Once a scale is selected for a survey, especially a tracking survey, then the same methodology for the rating scales should be used so that answers to questions can be compared from wave to wave.

10

Designing Data Collection Instruments

As we saw in Chapter 6, questioning and observation methods are the two basic approaches available for gathering primary data. Of the two, the former is used much more frequently in research projects involving primary-data collection. Furthermore, although data collection instruments are needed in both methods, designing an instrument for a questionnaire study is far more difficult than designing one for an observation study. Researchers as well as users of marketing research must develop an appreciation for the difficulties in constructing a good questionnaire and the potential dangers of using a poorly designed one. The primary focus of this chapter will therefore be on designing questionnaires. Constructing observation forms will be discussed briefly at the end of the chapter.

QUESTIONNAIRE DESIGN

A *questionnaire* is simply a set of questions designed to generate the data necessary for accomplishing a research project's objectives. As was demonstrated in earlier chapters, primary data may be needed in exploratory- as well as conclusive-research projects. A key difference in data collection in these two types of projects centers around the formality and flexibility of the methods used. Primary-data collection in exploratory-research projects is accomplished in an informal, flexible fashion. Indeed, seldom is a standard questionnaire needed in such projects; rather, all that is normally required is a checklist of items to be investigated. Therefore, questionnaire design considerations are not as germane to exploratory-research projects as they are to conclusive-research projects. The bulk of the material to be covered here relates to constructing standard questionnaires (i.e., those to be used in conclusive-research projects), although some of the guidelines discussed may be relevant for exploratory questioning as well.

COMPLEXITY OF QUESTIONNAIRE DESIGN

Designing questionnaires may appear to be simple, especially to those who have not designed one before. After all, you may think, once you have a clear notion of the information desired, it should be easy to formulate appropriate questions and arrange them in the form of an instrument. But experienced researchers will quickly point out that nothing is farther from the truth. Indeed, even the age-old adage "Practice makes perfect" is debatable when it comes to designing questionnaires. Perhaps "Practice makes *almost* perfect" is the best a researcher can hope for in questionnaire construction.

There are no rules that if faithfully followed can guarantee a flawless questionnaire. As numerous illustrations in this chapter will demonstrate, even questionnaires constructed by skilled researchers may have drawbacks. For example, consider the following question, which appeared in a mail questionnaire the author recently received from an apparently experienced researcher:

> Do you consider the many marketing research texts adequate for most of your business majors at the *undergraduate* level?
>
> ________Yes ________No
>
> If no, briefly, why not?________________________

At first glance there appears to be nothing wrong with this question. However, a closer examination reveals potential problems. It is subject to varying interpretations by different respondents and may be difficult to answer meaningfully. For instance, what exactly do the words *many, adequate,* and *most* refer to in this question? Will one respondent's interpretation of *many* (or *adequate* or *most*) be the same as that of another? If Jane Smith feels there are three "adequate" texts, should she answer yes or no? What if she feels there are six "adequate" texts? Several issues like these can be raised concerning the meaningfulness of this question.

One positive feature of the question is the inclusion of "If no, briefly, why not?" This part at least offers the respondents an opportunity for an open-ended answer if they are unsure of their response. However, open-ended answers, in addition to creating potential coding problems, may just point out the difficulty the respondents had in answering the question rather than provide data directly pertaining to the purpose of the research.

The intent of this illustration is not to criticize the researcher who wrote the question but to emphasize the complexity of designing questionnaires. Generally, an outsider can easily find some fault with even the most carefully thought-out question. Yet the same outsider may be at a loss to construct a *flawless* question to replace the one being criticized. Even seasoned researchers may discover questionnaire flaws only *after* data collection occurs. This point is highlighted by the following statement made by Al Blankenship, a well-respected researcher, concerning one key question in a study that he himself conducted: "Hindsight suggests that it might have been wiser to have phrased the question in such a manner as to discriminate between characteristics necessary for success in almost any business endeavor and those crucial to marketing research."[1]

In summary, even carefully designed questionnaires are not immune to questionnaire errors. So a research project in which questionnaire design is taken lightly will most likely be worthless. As the next section shows, the questionnaire is a critical determinant of data accuracy—that is, the extent to which the collected data are error-free and trustworthy.

QUESTIONNAIRE'S IMPACT ON DATA ACCURACY

The questionnaire is the main channel through which data are obtained from respondents and transferred to researchers in conclusive-research projects employing personal interviews, mail surveys, or telephone surveys. This channel has a dual communication role: (1) It must communicate to the respondent what the researcher is asking for, and (2) it must communicate to the researcher what the respondent has to say. The accuracy of data gathered through questionnaires will be greatly influenced by the amount of distortion, or "noise," that occurs in the two types of communication. Unless a set of questions faithfully reflects a researcher's data requirements, and unless those questions are interpreted and answered correctly by respondents, the accuracy of the collected data will suffer. A sloppy questionnaire can lead to a great deal of distortion in the communication from researcher to respondents and vice versa.

An additional source of potential distortion in questionnaire studies using face-to-face or telephone interviews is the entry of an intermediary—namely, the interviewer—into the communication channel between researcher and respondent. A poorly designed questionnaire, such as one that confuses an interviewer or is subject to varying interpretations by different interviewers, is an open invitation for the interviewer to bias the data being collected.

Exhibit 10.1 shows the vital position occupied by the questionnaire in the link between researcher and respondent. The communication flows represented by the arrows in this figure are of major concern when one is construct-

[1] A. B. Blankenship, "What Marketing Research Managers Want In Trainees," *Journal of Advertising Research,* 1 (February 1975), p. 13.

Exhibit 10.1

Questionnaire—link between researcher and respondent

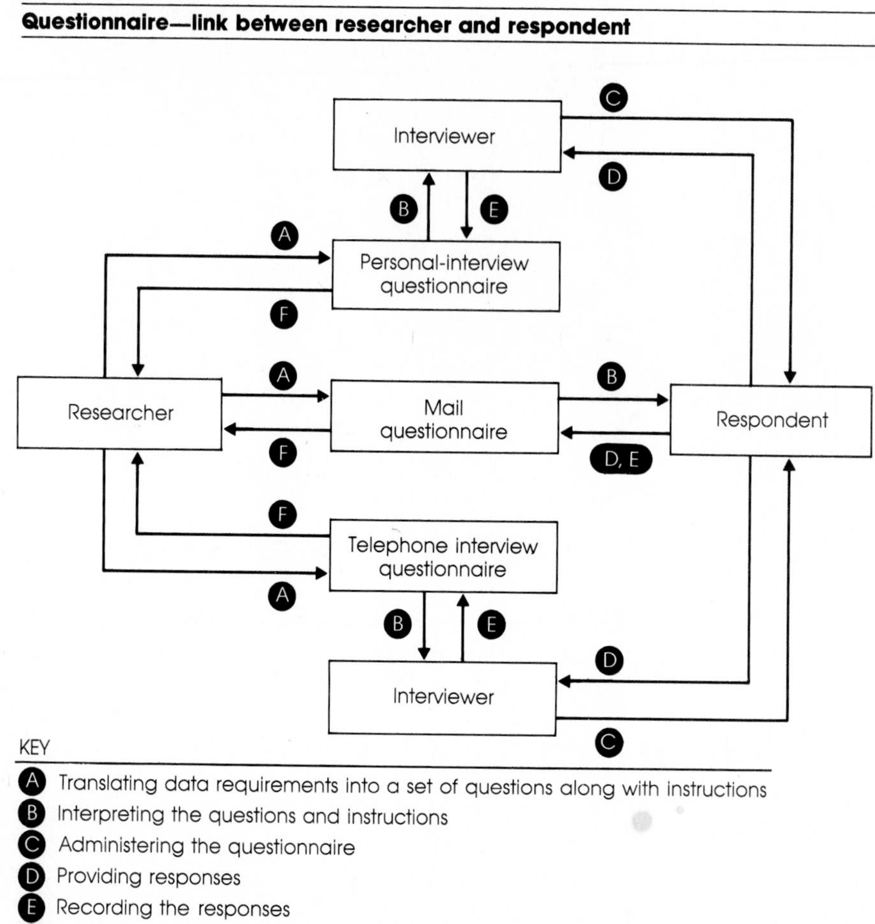

ing questionnaires. Lack of adequate attention to questionnaire design will lead to distortions in these communication flows, thereby generating data of doubtful accuracy.

Although there are no rules for developing a flawless questionnaire, the collective experience of numerous researchers offers a broad set of guidelines for minimizing the likelihood and the severity of data validity problems. Several excellent books have been written on the subject of questionnaire design.[2]

[2] One of the classic books on questionnaire design is Stanley L. Payne, *The Art of Asking Questions* (Princeton, N.J.: Princeton University Press, 1951); a more recent book on the subject is Seymour Sudman and Norman M. Bradburn, *Asking Questions* (San Francisco: Jossey-Bass, 1982).

Therefore, we need not and cannot cover all the issues of questionnaire design in a mere chapter. Rather, the focus here will be on discussing, with several illustrations, the key tasks a researcher must perform in order to design a good questionnaire.

QUESTIONNAIRE DESIGN ELEMENTS

The process of drawing up a questionnaire is a sequence of interrelated tasks. This section will provide an overview of the process; subsequent sections will describe each task in detail. Exhibit 10.2 shows the key questionnaire design tasks and the relationships among them.

The logical starting point for constructing a questionnaire is to translate the data requirements of a project into a set of rough questions. Of course, as pointed out in earlier chapters, an important prerequisite for being able to identify the appropriate types of data to be collected is a clear and correct definition of the research problem, objectives, or hypotheses. Next, certain critical checks of the rough draft have to be made: Does each question have the most appropriate *form* (e.g., *structured* versus *nonstructured*)? Is each question *relevant* and *properly worded* to obtain meaningful, valid responses? Is the *sequencing* of the questions likely to introduce any bias? Are the *layout* and *appearance* of the questionnaire conducive to accurate and easy data collection?

Each of these checks will invariably suggest changes in the rough draft. Moreover, the questionnaire features involved in these checks are interrelated in that changes in one may call for corresponding changes in others. For instance, a change in question sequencing may also require changes in the form and the wording of questions. The point is that questionnaire design is an *iterative* process: Numerous loops through the various checks may be needed before a suitable draft of the questionnaire is available for *pretesting,* which is another critical task. Depending on the number and the magnitude of changes resulting from pretesting, one may also have to repeat this task—in some cases several times—before a final draft of the questionnaire is ready.

The general process outlined in Exhibit 10.2 is relevant for designing questionnaires to be used in face-to-face, telephone, or mail surveys. Nevertheless, the type of questionnaire administration method will normally have unique requirements concerning certain questionnaire features. These requirements will be pointed out where appropriate in the following sections.

QUESTION FORM

There are basically two forms of questions: *nonstructured* (open-ended) *questions* and *structured* (fixed-response) *questions.* The relative advantages and disadvantages of these two question forms were covered in Chapter 6 (see Table

Exhibit 10.2

Components of the questionnaire design process

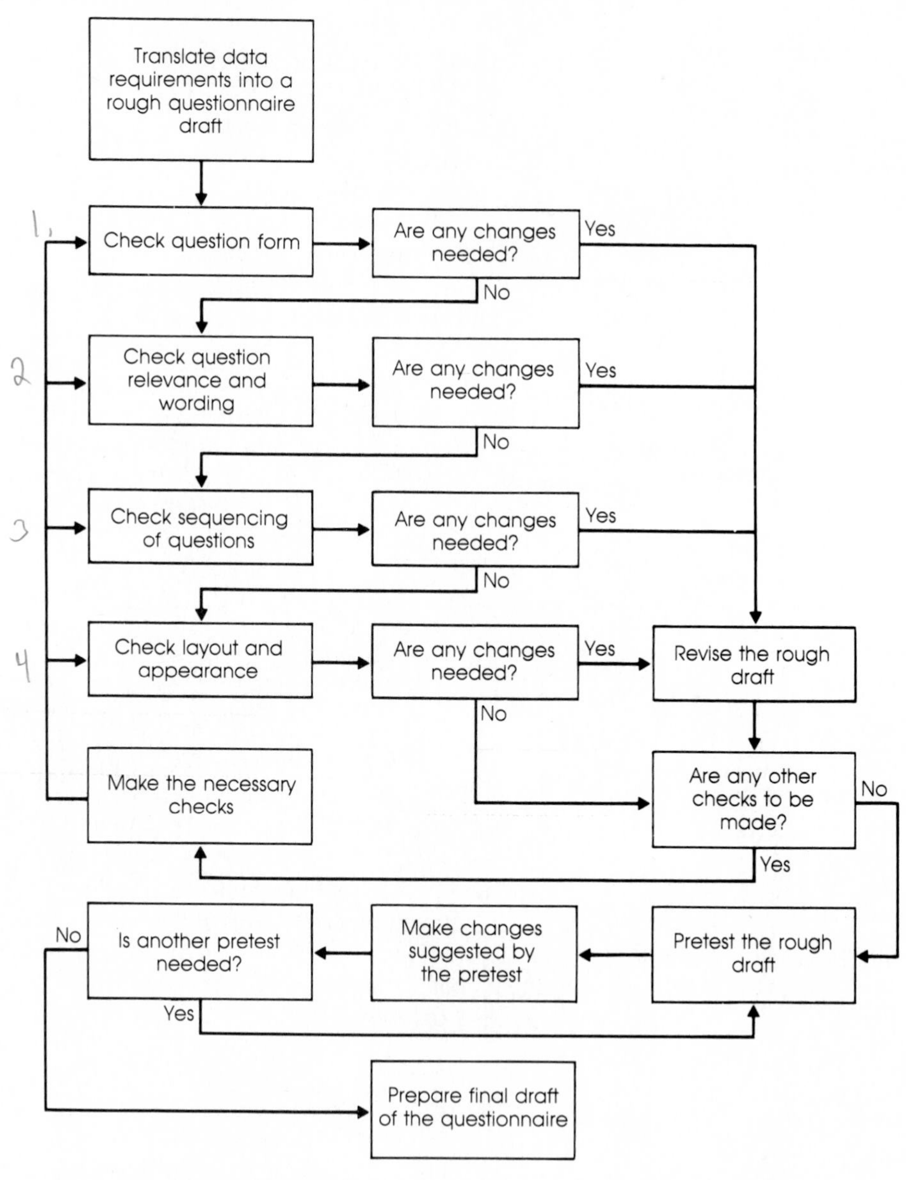

6.1). They will not be re-covered in this chapter. The emphasis here will be on looking at *variations* of the two basic forms and discussing when and how they can be most effectively used in a questionnaire.

Nonstructured questions

While nonstructured questions permit free responses, not all of them may require lengthy or wordy responses. Consider the following illustrative questions:

How old are you?__________

What do you like *most* about owning your own home?__________

Will you please describe your thoughts about a person who shoplifts items from a grocery store to keep from going hungry?__________

____

All three questions are nonstructured. However, the effort, time, and space required to answer them obviously vary considerably. Questions like the last one (i.e., the one dealing with shoplifting) may be inappropriate for questionnaires to be used in conclusive-research projects; the large samples typically required in such projects will make data collection, coding, and analysis particularly difficult. But open-ended questions such as the first two, especially the age question, can be effectively used even in large-scale studies since responses to them will be relatively short. Hence not *all* open-ended questions must be avoided in a standard questionnaire intended for a large sample of respondents.

Depending on the types of information desired from a conclusive-research project, one may at times need to leave certain questions open-ended, provided that the expected responses are likely to be brief. For example, compare the data to be obtained by asking the open-ended age question we just saw with data to be obtained through a structured question like this one:

In which of the following categories does your age fall?

__________Less than 18

__________18 to 30

__________31 to 45

__________46 to 60

__________Over 60

The open-ended question will generate refined data (i.e., the exact ages of respondents), while the structured question will only give a rough indication of respondents' ages. Depending on the types of analyses needed to provide the information desired in a project, refined data and hence appropriate open-ended questions may be necessary. More will be said in the next chapter and in Chapters 16–19 about different types of data and their impact on the choice of analysis procedures.

Some researchers also recommend starting a face-to-face or telephone interview with a *general* open-ended question in order to put the respondent at ease and kindle interest in the study. For example, an interview dealing with home computers might begin with a question like "What are your feelings about how the numerous electronic products available today are affecting people's life-styles?" After whatever answer is given, the respondent can be introduced to the main questionnaire with a statement such as "That is very interesting. Our interview deals with home computers. . . ."

Beginning an interview with an open-ended question is worthwhile if it will be easy to answer and aid in smooth completion of the rest of the interview. Sometimes, a general open-ended question may also be helpful during an interview to ensure smooth transition from one major topic to another (e.g., from purchase to use of a product). For such open-ended questions to accomplish their intended purpose, they must be chosen carefully, ensuring that they are unlikely to be difficult for or embarrassing to the respondent. Assuming a suitable nonstructured question is available for starting an interview, one can use it without worrying about constraints that would normally preclude its use in a large-scale survey. That is, neither coding nor analyzing of the responses to the question is necessary.

Structured questions

Structured questions are of two basic forms: dichotomous and multiple-category. A *dichotomous question* offers just two answer choices, typically in a yes/no format:

Do you smoke cigarettes?

__________Yes __________No

Have you ever watched the *Tonight Show*?

__________Yes __________No

Questions with more than two answer choices are *multiple-category questions.* A number of variations of the multiple-category question are possible.[3]

[3] An especially good discussion of multiple-category questions is provided by Don A. Dillman, *Mail and Telephone Surveys: The Total Design Method* (New York: Wiley, 1978), pp. 86–95.

Consider the following illustrative questions:

Approximately how many long-distance telephone calls do you make per week?

__________0 to 1 call

__________2 to 3 calls

__________4 to 5 calls

__________6 to 7 calls

__________More than 7 calls

In your opinion, which division of General Motors makes the most attractive automobiles?

__________Buick Division

__________Cadillac Division

__________Chevrolet Division

__________Pontiac Division

__________Oldsmobile Division

What do you like about First City Bank's automatic-teller machines?

__________24-hour service

__________Privacy during transaction

__________Convenient location

__________No long lines

__________Other____
(Please specify)

Although these questions are all multiple-category questions, they differ in distinct ways that have important implications for response quality. We will discuss the differences and their implications under the following headings: response category sequence, response category content, and number of response categories.

Response category sequence. The response categories in the question about long-distance telephone calls follow a *natural sequence.* In fact, no alternative sequence, other than presenting the categories in reverse order, will be meaningful. However, for the other two questions the specific response categories under each can be presented in any order. This distinction is important because the sequence of presentation, by itself, can influence a respondent's choice, especially when the respondent is not quite sure how to answer the question. Researchers have found, for instance, that categories in the middle have greater drawing power than the ones at the extremes if the categories involve numbers (e.g., the question on long-distance telephone calls). When the categories are in the form of words, phrases, or statements, the categories at the extremes have greater drawing power.[4]

To eliminate entirely the biases stemming from response category sequence may not be possible. However, some precaution can be taken to minimize such biases. An approach frequently followed is to rotate the sequence of categories from one questionnaire to the next. Through systematic rotation of the order of presentation of response choices, each of them will occupy various positions within the sequence. The assumption underlying this procedure is that any possible response bias arising from using a particular sequence will be neutralized across all respondents. The appropriateness of this assumption has been challenged, however.[5]

The ease and effectiveness with which sequence rotation can be accomplished depends on the nature of the response choices. As we just saw, the only sequence rotation possible when response categories follow a natural order is a complete reversal of the sequence. Unfortunately, even reversing the response sequence in one-half of the questionnaires—an approach known as the *split-ballot technique*—may not effectively neutralize potential response position bias.[6]

Response category rotation is also somewhat more difficult in a mail survey than in face-to-face or telephone interviews. When an interviewer is asking a multiple-category question, he or she can simply be instructed to start with a different response category in each interview and follow the listed sequence until the starting category is reached. For instance, in the question dealing with General Motors, the interviewer can be instructed to start with Buick and end with Oldsmobile in one interview, start with Cadillac and end with Buick in the next interview, and so on.[7] Response category rotation in mail questionnaires will require printing and mailing different versions of the same question-

---

[4] Stanley L. Payne, *The Art of Asking Questions,* p. 134.

[5] For further details, see Niels J. Blunch, "Position Bias in Multiple-Choice Questions," *Journal of Marketing Research,* 21 (May 1984), pp. 216–220.

[6] For instance, a study by William B. Locander and John P. Burton, "The Effect of Question Form on Gathering Income Data by Telephone," *Journal of Marketing Research,* 13 (May 1976), pp. 189–192, suggests that one type of ordering of numerical-response categories to a question might lead to more valid data than a reverse ordering of the same categories.

[7] When questionnaires are administered through CRT terminals (as we saw in Chapter 6), one may be able to program the central computer to rotate the response categories automatically from interview to interview; see, for example, James F. O'Hara, "CRT Interviewing: People Still Make the Difference," *The Marketing Researcher* (Walker Research), Winter 1982, p. 2.

naire, which may not always be feasible owing to the additional expenses involved.

Clearly, even as subtle a feature as the sequence in which response categories are presented can result in biased data. Nevertheless, depending on the nature of the response categories and the type of questionnaire administration method to be used, one may be able to reduce potential biases. Certainly a prudent procedure is to take as many precautions as feasible.

Response category content. What should be included in the response choices to a multiple-category question? The nature of the variable the question is attempting to investigate, as well as the type of data desired, will have a bearing on category content. However, as a general rule, the response choices must be *collectively exhaustive* (i.e., taken together, they should provide for every possible answer a respondent might give) and *mutually exclusive* (i.e., they should not overlap).

For questions dealing with a respondent's attributes (e.g., age) or behavior (e.g., number of long-distance calls made per week), one can easily construct response categories that are collectively exhaustive and mutually exclusive. All one needs to do is to determine the total range of possible answers (which will usually be in the form of numbers) and divide the range into as many suitable categories as the researcher's data requirements dictate (the number of categories is discussed in the next subsection). A case in point is the question on long-distance telephone calls presented earlier.

Not quite so easy is constructing structured-response categories for questions dealing with respondents' attitudes, beliefs, opinions, and motives (i.e., *reasons* for behavior). The range of possible answers to such questions will usually not be clear-cut. Wording the categories in such a way as to reflect potential responses accurately may also be difficult. For example, questions like "What do you think of our president's foreign policy?" or "Why do consumers fail to use manufacturer's coupons when buying products?" will be more difficult to cast into a structured format than a question like "How many years of formal education have you completed?"

Converting open-ended questions about attitudes, beliefs, and the like into structured questions may require some exploratory research just to get a feeling for the range and the content of responses.[8] Even if such preliminary research is conducted, however, one should usually include an "other" category, just in case the structured responses listed are not collectively exhaustive. Inclusion of an "other" category, like the one in the question dealing with automatic-teller machines, will make a question partially nonstructured. But using a partially

[8] This point is discussed further in A. N. Oppenheim, *Questionnaire Design and Attitude Measurement* (New York: Basic Books, 1966), pp. 25–30; see also Donald P. Warwick and Charles A. Liniger, *The Sample Survey: Theory and Practice* (New York: McGraw-Hill, 1975), pp. 136–137.

nonstructured question is better than using a fully structured question when one is not certain that the response choices provided are collectively exhaustive. Otherwise, a respondent whose intended answer does not fit into any of the listed alternatives will be forced to give an invalid response or no response at all. In either case the quality of the data collected will be adversely affected.

Another potential reason that response choices to a multiple-category question may not be collectively exhaustive is failure to include a "don't know" or "no opinion" category. When there is a possibility that some respondents may have no basis for answering a question, failure to provide a "don't know" or "no opinion" response choice will most likely lower data accuracy. As evidence for this statement, a controlled study involving two different groups of respondents led the researchers to conclude: "Clearly, respondents will express an opinion about issues of which they have no knowledge. Such a response occurred even in a situation involving relatively limited pressure to respond".[9] These researchers also found that inclusion of a "don't know" category reduced the occurrence of uninformed, and hence invalid, responses. Look again at the question dealing with General Motors' divisions and decide for yourself whether a "don't know" response choice should be added. Also, reexamine the other two examples of multiple-category questions. Would you recommend any modifications in them?

In addition to being collectively exhaustive, response choices must be mutually exclusive. That is, a respondent's answer must fit one, and only one, response category. In the following question, for instance, the response choices are collectively exhaustive but not mutually exclusive:

On the average, how many cans of beer do you drink per week?

__________0 to 3 cans

__________3 to 6 cans

__________More than 6 cans

Changing the 3 in the second category to a 4 will make the response choices mutually exclusive.

Now refer to the question "What do you like about First City Bank's automatic-teller machines?" and its response choices presented earlier. The meanings of the response choices are distinct and nonoverlapping. However, they overlap in another sense: Respondents' answers to the question may fall into more than one of the listed alternatives. From the way the question is currently set up, whether the researcher expects each respondent to check only one category is not clear. Consequently, while some respondents will just check one response, others will check several, even if *all* of them like more than one attribute of First City's automatic-teller machines.

[9] Del I. Hawkins and Kenneth A. Coney, "Uninformed Response Error in Survey Research," *Journal of Marketing Research,* 18 (August 1981), p. 373.

Two options are available to ensure that the question is interpreted in the same way by all respondents:

1. Modify the question to read, "Which one of the following do you like *most* about First City Bank's automatic-teller machines?" With this revision each respondent would, or should, check only one response category.
2. Augment the question to read, "What do you like about First City Bank's automatic-teller machines? (Please check as many categories as apply.)" This revision explicitly indicates that multiple answers are allowed.

A researcher choosing the second option must realize, however, that coding and analyzing multiple responses may be somewhat cumbersome. Which of the two revisions should be made depends on the nature of the researcher's data requirements.

Number of response categories. Multiple-category questions fall between dichotomous questions and open-ended questions in terms of the variety of responses they permit. Consider a question dealing with income, for instance. If the researcher just wants to know whether a respondent's income is above a certain amount, a dichotomous question will suffice. At the other extreme, if a respondent's exact income is to be ascertained, an open-ended question will be necessary. Frequently however, a project's data requirements will be between the two extremes, and the researcher has to decide on the number of response categories to provide. Although no rules exist for determining the optimum number of categories, the following considerations are worth taking into account.

One useful approach for deciding on the number, as well as content, of response categories is to examine past studies similar to the one being contemplated. This approach can be especially beneficial if a purpose of the research is to compare the data to be generated with available secondary data. To illustrate, suppose a study of videocassette recorder owners is to be conducted to see how their demographic characteristics compare with those of the general public. Data on the general public's demographic characteristics are readily available through publications of the U.S. Census Bureau. Therefore a beneficial procedure is to make the form of the study questions (including the number of response choices) consistent with the census classifications.

Another important consideration is the type of questionnaire administration method to be used. Having too many response choices to each of numerous multiple-category questions can cause problems in a mail questionnaire. The increased questionnaire length may not only increase mailing costs but also discourage potential respondents from filling out and returning the questionnaires. The best solution under these circumstances is to list only the most likely responses (perhaps determined through exploratory research) along with an "other" category.

Multiple-category questions may pose a somewhat different set of problems in personal and telephone interviews, especially when the categories have to be read out loud to the respondents. One obvious drawback of having too many response choices when the interviewer has to read them aloud is increased interview time, which, in turn, may irritate the respondent. Another drawback is the very real possibility that the respondent may not remember all the alternatives by the time the interviewer gets to the end of the list. As a result, the answer may be biased in favor of alternatives mentioned at the very beginning or at the very end. One option for tackling these problems is to not read response categories at all—that is, to ask an open-ended question but have a collectively exhaustive list of response choices printed on the questionnaire so that coding will be easy and fast.

Unfortunately, the option of not reading aloud the response choices may not always be feasible. For example, in studies dealing with advertisements researchers may wish to measure ***aided recall*** of ads by respondents. Aided recall requires that all alternatives (e.g., all ads appearing in a certain issue of a magazine) be mentioned to the respondent. Aided recall can be accomplished adequately and efficiently in a personal interview by, for instance, handing the respondent a card listing all the alternatives and asking him or her to respond after looking through the list. This technique will obviously not be possible in a telephone interview. Thus the nature of the questions to be asked may dictate the type of questionnaire administration method to be used. For instance, a complex magazine readership and advertising recall study may leave the researcher no choice other than personal interviewing, which, as we saw in Chapter 6, is the most versatile questionnaire administration method.

QUESTION RELEVANCE AND WORDING

One of the most critical tasks after drawing up a rough questionnaire draft is to ensure the relevance of every question on it. Each question must be carefully examined to see whether the data to be generated will be pertinent to the purpose of the research. While this piece of advice seems obvious (after all, who would want to ask a question if it is irrelevant?), it is frequently overlooked, especially by inexperienced questionnaire designers. Sudman and Bradburn describe this problem:

> The process of writing questions is fun and quickly engages the interest of the participants. Competition develops among the question writers to see who can come up with the cleverest and most interesting questions. A game of "Wouldn't it be nice to know . . . ?" emerges, and soon there are many more questions than the budget can afford or the respondents' patience will endure. Too often questionnaire writers are so caught up in the excitement of question writing that they jump rapidly into writing questions before they

have adequately formulated the goals of the research and thoroughly understood the research questions.[10]

A worthwhile issue to raise concerning each question on the rough draft is: "Can the research objective(s) be fulfilled *without* asking this question?" If the answer is yes, the question should be deleted. The only exceptions are general open-ended questions that may be asked at the start of an interview to kindle the respondents' interest or put the respondent at ease or asked during the interview to aid transition from one topic to another. If the answer is anything other than a yes (e.g., no, maybe, don't know), the question may *still* be a candidate for revision or deletion and must be further examined with respect to criteria like the ones discussed next.

Can the respondent answer the question?

Even when a question is apparently relevant, it will be useless if respondents are unlikely to have a meaningful basis for answering it. For instance, consider the following question taken from a mail questionnaire the author received from someone conducting a study of professors' perceptions about marketing education and marketing students:

> In your opinion, how many students in your marketing courses are potentially successful marketing managers?
>
> Ten percent_________
>
> Twenty percent_________
>
> Thirty percent_________
>
> _________percent_________

This question deals with professors' perceptions of their students and is therefore relevant for the study. But many respondents, like the author, will be at a loss to answer it meaningfully. In other words, the data sought is likely to be beyond the realm of experience of many respondents. By the way, see if this question has any other drawbacks.

Another frequent reason for respondents' inability to answer a question, even when the information it seeks is within their realm of experience, is lack of memory. Most people can readily recall the number of traffic accidents they were involved in during the past year or even the past several years. However, most people will have difficulty remembering the number of times they have been to a McDonald's within the past year—within the previous week perhaps,

[10] Sudman and Bradburn, *Asking Questions,* p. 13.

but not within the past year. Ability to remember a past event depends on the time elapsed since its occurrence as well as the importance of the event to the respondent. The latter factor is crucial, because what may be extremely important to the researcher may be trivial to the respondent.

For instance, consider the following question taken from a questionnaire used by a marketing research firm in conducting a face-to-face survey of female household heads:

> How much has your family spent in the last 12 months on cookware? $__________

No doubt this question was important to the research firm and its client. But how many respondents would have been able to remember the amount they spent on cookware during the previous 12 months? My guess is very few, if any. Yet many of them would have come up with *some* amount, whose accuracy, of course, would have been highly questionable.

The point is that good question writers, rather than become blinded by what is important to the researcher or research user, must put themselves in the respondent's shoes when evaluating a question's potential value. Questions that seem meaningless or difficult from the respondent's standpoint must be modified or deleted.

Will the respondent answer the question?

When a question deals with a sensitive issue or is embarrassing, respondents may refuse to answer it, even if they have sufficient information to respond accurately. Worse still, they may actually provide less-than-truthful responses. Questions about personal financial matters or sexual behavior are examples of sensitive questions. Such questions also run the risk of irritating the respondents. Therefore, unless they are absolutely essential, they should not be included in the questionnaire. In studies where data on sensitive issues are crucial, the researcher may have to use disguised techniques (such as the ones discussed in Chapter 6) or some other special types of questioning.[11]

The relevance of a question, the respondents' ability to answer it, and their willingness to answer it can all be affected by its *wording*. Writing questions capable of generating relevant and valid data is perhaps the most critical and most difficult part of designing a questionnaire. Unfortunately, there is no magic

---

[11] Such special types of questioning are not needed frequently in marketing research studies and are beyond the scope of this textbook. A good source of further information is Sudman and Bradburn, *Asking Questions,* Chap. 3; see also Ed Blair, Seymour Sudman, Norman M. Bradburn, and Carol Stocking, "How to Ask Questions About Drinking and Sex," *Journal of Marketing Research,* 14 (August 1977), pp. 316–321; James E. Reinmuth and Michael D. Geurts, "The Collection of Sensitive Information Using a Two-Stage Randomized Response Model," *Journal of Marketing Research,* 12 (November 1975), pp. 402–407.

wand one can wave to produce the *best* question(s) to fit each research objective. Most books on questionnaire design devote numerous pages to the dos and don'ts of proper wording.[12] Yet as Dillman observes:

> Writing questions for a particular questionnaire means doing them for (1) a particular population, (2) a particular purpose, and (3) placement next to other questions in the questionnaire. Words that are too difficult for use with some populations may be perfectly acceptable for others. . . . A question that makes little sense by itself may be quite clear when asked after the ones which precede it in the questionnaire. . . . A list of admonitions, no matter how well intended, therefore cannot be considered as absolute principles that must be adhered to without exception.[13]

In short, the wording of a question and its influence on responses may be so situation-specific and complex as to defy any universal set of guidelines. For this reason, and also because of space limitations, we will not cover all the issues of question wording here; books dealing specifically with questionnaire design offer excellent discussions. Rather, in the following sections we will examine several examples to highlight some of the most frequent errors stemming from question wording and the ways such errors can be minimized.

Double-barreled questions

Suppose the following question is to be used in conducting a survey of the general public:

> Do you feel firms today are concerned about their employees and customers?
>
> _________Yes _________No _________No opinion

This question is a classic example of a *double-barreled question*, one that raises several *separate* issues but only provides one set of responses.

Answers to double-barreled questions are very difficult to interpret. For instance, suppose a respondent answers no to this question. A "no" response can be interpreted three different ways:

- The respondent feels firms are concerned about neither employees nor customers.
- The respondent feels firms are concerned about employees but not customers.

[12] For example, see Payne, *Art of Asking Questions;* Sudman and Bradburn, *Asking Questions.*

[13] Dillman, *Mail and Telephone Surveys,* pp. 96–97, excerpted with permission from John Wiley & Sons, Inc. Several controlled studies have found that the *context* in which a question is asked will affect the nature of the response; see, for example, Howard Schuman, Stanley Presser, and Jacob Ludwig, "Context Effects on Survey Responses to Questions About Abortion," *Public Opinion Quarterly,* 45 (Summer 1981), pp. 216–223.

- The respondent feels firms are not concerned about employees although they are concerned about customers.

Which of these interpretations is accurate? Only the respondent will know for sure. A "yes" or a "no opinion" response to this question may be equally difficult to interpret.

If meaningful, easy-to-interpret data are to be obtained, a double-barreled question must be reworded to focus on one specific issue at a time and must provide an unambiguous set of response choices. This revision is usually accomplished by breaking it up into several questions. Thus our illustrative question can be reworded as two separate questions:

1. Do you feel firms today are concerned about their employees?

   ________Yes ________No ________No opinion

2. Do you feel firms today are concerned about their customers?

   ________Yes ________No ________No opinion

Leading questions

A *leading question,* also known as a *loaded question,* is one that may steer respondents toward a certain answer, irrespective of what their true answers are. The following questions illustrate:

Don't you think offshore drilling for oil is environmentally unsound?

________Yes ________No ________No opinion

Do you think the quality of products on the market today is as high as it used to be ten years ago?

________Yes ________No ________No opinion

Of course, not all respondents may be led to a certain answer by questions like these. Respondents who have very definite feelings about the environmental impact of offshore drilling or about the quality of products currently on the market are unlikely to be swayed by the way the questions are worded. However, other respondents, including those who really have no opinion, are likely to be tempted to answer yes to the first question and no to the second. Invalid data will result if those respondents yield to the temptation.

The risk of asking leading questions is especially great when the focus of research is on people's attitudes, beliefs, or opinions. A researcher may end up designing leading questions, often unknowingly, by failing to maintain an objective posture during the questionnaire design process—that is, by wording questions in such a way as to bias potential responses in favor of his or her own preconceived notions about the issues being studied. A conscious effort to construct questions in as neutral a fashion as possible is a prerequisite for obtaining unbiased data.

The two leading questions we saw earlier can be modified for neutrality as follows:

What is your feeling about the environmental impact of offshore drilling for oil?

_________Offshore drilling is environmentally sound.

_________Offshore drilling is environmentally unsound.

_________No opinion.

How do you feel about the quality of products on the market today compared with the quality of products on the market ten years ago?

_________Product quality is better now than ten years ago.

_________Product quality is worse now than ten years ago.

_________Product quality is the same now as ten years ago.

_________No opinion.

One-sided questions

As their name implies, *one-sided questions* present only one aspect of an issue for which respondents' reactions are being sought. One-sidedness can bias the response, often very subtly. Consider the following questions (notice that the first question is one of the two we came up with in modifying the double-barreled question presented earlier):

Do you feel firms today are concerned about their employees?

_________Yes _________No _________No opinion

Would you agree or disagree that deregulation of the airline industry has benefited consumers?

_________Agree _________Disagree

_________No opinion

To appreciate why these questions are one-sided, and hence may lead to biased responses, look at the following rewordings of the same questions:

Do you feel that firms today are concerned about their employees or that they are unconcerned about their employees?

_________Concerned _________Unconcerned

_________No opinion

Do you feel deregulation of the airline industry has benefited consumers, has had no impact on consumers, or has hurt consumers?

__________Has benefited consumers.

__________Has had no impact on consumers.

__________Has hurt consumers.

__________No opinion.

The reworded questions are more neutral in that they make explicit all sides of the issues involved. Intuitively, they should be better than their one-sided counterparts, which may nudge the respondents toward the side presented. One-sided questions are, in a way, leading questions, although they may lead respondents in a more subtle fashion.

Several studies have shown that respondents, especially those with low levels of education, have a tendency to agree with whatever side is presented by one-sided questions.[14] This phenomenon is referred to as *yea-saying*, and the resulting bias is known as *acquiescence bias*. The rationale behind presenting all sides of an issue is that the respondent will at least have something to think about instead of blindly answering yes or agreeing with whatever the question says. Presenting all sides of an issue should reduce erroneous responses.

The *split-ballot technique*, mentioned in our earlier discussion about rotating response choices in a multiple-category question, has also been suggested as a means of neutralizing possible acquiescence bias.[15] In using this technique to nullify acquiescence bias, two versions of the questionnaire are prepared: one version with questions presenting one side of the issues being researched and the second version with questions presenting the other side. (While the split-ballot technique usually involves only two versions of the same questionnaire, as many versions as there are alternatives to be presented can be created.) The respondent sample is also randomly split into two comparable halves, and each half is administered one version of the questionnaire. The data obtained from the two halves are merged with the hope that any acquiescence biases will cancel out.

Although the split-ballot technique appears elegant, it has a couple of limitations. First, preparing different versions of the questionnaire can become complicated and quite expensive if several different versions are needed. Second, if responses to the same question vary widely across the different versions, combining the responses to yield an average response may not be meaningful, in

---

[14] See, for example, George F. Bishop, Robert W. Aldendick, and Alfred J. Tuchfarber, "Effects of Presenting One Versus Two Sides of an Issue in Survey Questions," *Public Opinion Quarterly*, 46 (Spring 1982), pp. 66–85; Alfred M. Falthzik and Marvin A. Jolson, "Statement Polarity in Attitude Studies," *Journal of Marketing Research*, 11 (February 1974), pp. 102–105; Warwick and Liniger, *The Sample Survey*, p. 146.

[15] See, for example, Falthzik and Jolson, "Statement Polarity in Attitude Studies."

which case the question will be essentially useless. Therefore the split-ballot technique is not recommended, unless stating all sides of an issue within the same question is likely to make the question too complex or awkward.

A variation of one-sidedness can occur in multiple-category questions when the alternatives presented are loaded toward one side, as in the following example:

> How important is price to you in buying a new car?
>
> __________More important than any other factor.
>
> __________Extremely important.
>
> __________Important.
>
> __________Somewhat important.
>
> __________Unimportant.

The alternatives listed are *unbalanced*: Four out of the five suggest price is an important criterion.[16]

To understand the potential bias that unbalanced alternatives may subtly introduce, consider the following version of the same question:

> How important is price to you in buying a new car?
>
> __________Very important.
>
> __________Relatively important.
>
> __________Neither important nor unimportant.
>
> __________Relatively unimportant.
>
> __________Very unimportant.

The balanced alternatives in this version offer a wider choice to respondents who do not consider price to be a critical factor. Stated differently, respondents who feel that price is relatively unimportant or is neither important nor unimportant, may be *forced* to check "somewhat important" in the unbalanced version of the question for lack of a more suitable category. This response can lead to erroneous interpretations: The researcher has no way of knowing whether respondents who indicated "somewhat important" really meant to give that response. Clearly, a prudent procedure is to provide respondents with as balanced a set of alternatives as possible—and thereby reduce the chances of drawing invalid inferences from the data collected.

[16] Payne, *The Art of Asking Questions,* pp. 90–92, contains a more detailed discussion and additional examples of questions with unbalanced alternatives.

Questions with implicit assumptions

The responses to some questions can be greatly influenced by what respondents assume in answering them. *Questions with implicit assumptions* do not provide, or imply, the same frame of reference to all respondents. Thus the question should state explicitly what respondents should assume, rather than let them make their own assumptions. Suppose the following question is part of a questionnaire to be mailed to a city's residents:

> Are you favorable, indifferent, or unfavorable toward a 10% increase in city taxes?
>
> __________Favorable __________Indifferent
>
> __________Unfavorable

A respondent's answer to this question will differ depending on whether he or she has accurate information, inaccurate information, or no information about why the 10% tax increase is needed. The researcher must provide a common frame of reference to all respondents in order to obtain meaningful responses and draw valid inferences from them: To assume that all respondents have the same accurate background information pertaining to the question is dangerous. The question on city taxes can be improved as follows:

> Are you favorable, indifferent, or unfavorable toward a 10% increase in city taxes to repair potholes in the city's streets?
>
> __________Favorable __________Indifferent
>
> __________Unfavorable

Implicit assumptions may be embedded in a question in more ways than one. Consider the following question:

> Do you drink beer while watching football, baseball, and so on?
>
> __________Yes __________No

This question makes several implicit assumptions. First, from the respondent's standpoint it is not clear whether "watching football, baseball" applies to doing so at home (i.e., on TV), outside the home, or both. Therefore the answer is likely to vary depending on what a respondent assumes. Second, what exactly "and so on" includes is unclear. Does it, for example, include or exclude sporting events other than ball games? Again, the question is subject to varying interpretations by different respondents. Third, the question apparently assumes that the respondent *is* a beer drinker. Whether this implicit assumption is a problem depends on what questions were asked before this particular one.

The first two problems, concerning vagueness of the question, may be remedied by rewording the question as follows:

During which of the following activities do you drink beer? (Check as many as apply.)

__________Attending ball games.

__________Attending sporting events other than ball games.

__________Watching ball games on TV.

__________Watching sporting events other than ball games on TV.

The number and types of response categories included in this question depend on the researcher's specific objectives. But the important point is that the reworded format has much less room for varying assumptions across respondents.

Let us now turn to the apparent assumption that the respondent is a beer drinker. The question will obviously be irrelevant to respondents who do not drink beer at all. One way to avoid asking this question of such respondents is to use a filter question. A *filter question* is meant to qualify respondents for a subsequent question or to ensure that the question is within their realm of experience. A possible filter question in our example is: "Do you ever drink beer?" Only those who answer yes will be asked the question about activities during which they drink beer.

One note of caution concerning filter questions is that too many of them can sharply increase questionnaire length and interview time. They should therefore be used sparingly—perhaps only when they are needed to qualify respondents for the entire interview or to avoid asking a question of an ineligible respondent that can be ridiculous or embarrassing (e.g., asking a respondent how many children he or she has before ascertaining whether he or she has ever been married). Under other circumstances any potential problem of lack of question relevance can be overcome by simply adding a special response category (in lieu of a separate filter question) to be checked by respondents if the question does not apply. For instance, in the multiple-category version of the question on beer drinking, the following response choice can be provided at the *top* of the list:

__________I do not drink beer. (Go on to the next question.)

The following question is yet another illustration of a question that is vague as a result of the question writer's failure to make explicit what exactly certain key words include or refer to:

How often do you eat eggs for breakfast?

__________Frequently

__________Occasionally

__________Rarely

__________Never

The problem with this question is that different respondents may attach different meanings to the first three response choices. For instance, one respondent's notion of "occasionally" may be what another respondent may term "rarely." When such varying interpretations are possible, the meaningfulness of the data collected will be questionable. One way of guarding against errors due to misinterpretations is to revise the question as follows:

On the average, how many days per week do you eat eggs for breakfast?

__________Every day.

__________5 or 6 days.

__________3 or 4 days.

__________1 or 2 days.

__________Less than 1 day per week.

__________Never eat eggs for breakfast.

Of course, the question writer may not always be able to come up with categories that are as clearly spelled out as in this instance. But the point is that to the extent possible the question writer must choose words and categories that will be interpreted the same way by all respondents.

Complex questions

Words that a question writer may understand perfectly may be unfamiliar or sound complicated to the respondent. Using such words in a question will make it *complex,* as the following example shows:

In which of the following do you typically invest your liquid assets?

__________Insured accounts

__________Stock market

__________Insured accounts and stock market

__________Other accounts

If this question is posed to respondents drawn from the general public, many of them may not know what "liquid assets" mean, and some of them may even be unfamiliar with terms like "stock market." Nevertheless, most of them will probably give some response so as not to reveal their ignorance. One obviously cannot have much trust in data obtained from respondents who answer a question without understanding it. The moral is, Use simple words, when possible, in writing questions and make sure respondents can easily understand them. However, this guideline cannot be used rigidly. As Dillman correctly points out: "Substituting simple for complex words often has the paradoxical effect of turning simple sentences into complex ones."[17]

In trying to cast a question in the simplest possible terms, the writer must also ensure that it does not get complicated because of increased length. Stated differently, in the interest of keeping questions relatively short, one may use complex words as long as potential respondents are likely to be familiar with them. A sample of business executives, for example, should have no difficulty understanding the terms *liquid assets* and *stock market.* In fact, when the respondents are knowledgeable, spelling out such terms in simple words may be viewed as an insult.

In short, whether a question is perceived as simple or complex depends not only on its wording but also on the type of respondent sample to which it will be posed. A good question writer must be sensitive to respondents' capabilities and design questions that neither go over their heads nor talk down to them.

Another type of complex question is one that demands too much effort from the respondents. An example of such a question is as follows:

> Of the total number of miles you drove during the past month, approximately what percentage was for driving to and from work?
>
> _________percent

This question is complex not because it is difficult to understand but because it is hard to answer. A respondent has to expend a lot of mental effort to answer it. An approach to simplifying it somewhat is to break it into two questions: one focusing on the total number of miles driven and the other focusing on the number of miles driven to and from work. The desired percentage figure can then be computed by the researcher during the data analysis stage. Whenever feasible, one should ask several simple questions rather than one complex question. The less work the respondents have to do, the greater is their willingness to answer a question and the lower is their chance of making errors in responding.

In summary, despite our lengthy treatment of question wording, we have merely scratched the surface of this topic. However, our discussion of the various types of faulty questions—double-barreled questions, leading questions, one-sided questions, questions with implicit assumptions, and complex questions—does illustrate the most common wording problems and highlights the dangers of not remedying them. Some of these same problems, or variations of them, are bound to be present in most rough questionnaire drafts.

---

[17] Dillman, *Mail and Telephone Surveys,* p. 97.

SEQUENCING OF QUESTIONS

Questions must be arranged in a logical sequence in order to minimize data errors and to facilitate easy and smooth administration of the questionnaire. The ordering of specific questions in a given situation, of course, depends on characteristics unique to that situation. However, the broad guidelines presented in this section should be helpful in virtually all situations.

Position of demographic and sensitive questions

Place questions about respondents' personal or demographic characteristics (e.g., age, education level, and income) at the end of a questionnaire. These questions are included in virtually all questionnaires since they provide *classification data* useful in obtaining a profile of the respondent sample and in cross-classifying responses to other questions that pertain more directly to the study objectives. However, asking these questions at the beginning may irritate some respondents and affect their willingness to complete the rest of the survey. The only situation in which demographic questions should be asked at the beginning is when they are to serve as filter questions to qualify respondents for the survey. This situation will arise when respondents are chosen through quota sampling (discussed in Chapter 14).

Sensitive questions likely to embarrass respondents or put them in an awkward position should also be placed near the end of the questionnaire. This placement is especially critical if the questionnaires are to be administered through face-to-face or telephone interviews. Good rapport between interviewer and respondent is essential for obtaining truthful responses to sensitive or threatening questions. So a delay in asking sensitive questions will offer the interviewer additional time to build rapport with the respondent. Placing sensitive questions toward the end of a questionnaire has another advantage: Even if the respondent refuses to answer such questions, data gathered through earlier questions may still be useful. But asking sensitive questions at the beginning may cause the entire interview to be lost.

Ask simple questions as early as possible. This guideline is a corollary of sorts to the preceding guidelines. Easy-to-answer questions can get the questionnaire administration process off to a smooth start (even in the case of mail questionnaires, which are self-administered). They also help pave the way for more difficult questions.

Arrangement of related questions

When a questionnaire addresses a variety of topics, clustering questions that focus on the same topic is advisable. Skipping from topic to topic in a haphazard fashion may confuse respondents, break their train of thought, and cause errors in the data. In other words, grouping questions into meaningful clusters can increase respondents' ease in answering the questions and reduce the chance of response errors. For instance, in a survey of business executives' views on the economy, competition, and employee turnover, a prudent approach is to divide the questionnaire into three parts, with questions in each linked to a single topic.

Funnel and inverted-funnel sequences

Move from general to specific questions within a topic. This approach is also known as using a *funnel sequence.*[18] It involves beginning with a very general question on a topic and gradually leading up to a narrowly focused question on the same topic. Employing a funnel sequence is advisable in virtually all situations (with one exception, which we will consider a little later). But it is *essential* in situations where asking specific questions first can bias the answers to later questions.

To illustrate, consider the following sequence of multiple-category questions. (*Note:* Only illustrative answer categories have been shown for each question to conserve space.)

1. Which of the following types of TV shows do you watch? (Check as many categories as apply.)

   ________News shows ________Quiz shows

   ________Game shows

2. Which of the following types of TV shows do you *like the most?* (Check as many categories as apply.)

   ________News shows ________Quiz shows

   ________Game shows

3. Which of the following specific shows did you watch during the past seven days? (Check "yes" or "no" for each show listed.)

   "All in the Family" ________Yes ________No

   "The Price Is Right" ________Yes ________No

   "CBS Evening News" ________Yes ________No

These three questions follow a funnel sequence. Reversing this sequence (i.e., asking first about the specific shows watched during the past seven days) may

[18] Sudman and Bradburn, *Asking Questions,* pp. 219–221, contains a good discussion of the funnel sequence and its pros and cons.

bias responses to the questions on the *types* of shows watched and liked most. That is, respondents may intentionally or unintentionally give more weight to the types of shows similar to the specific ones they recalled watching during the past seven days.[19]

Although a funnel sequence is the generally recommended format for ordering questions pertaining to the same topic, it may not always be appropriate. An *inverted-funnel sequence* may be better when respondents do not have clearly formulated views about a topic or when they need to have a common frame of reference in responding to general questions on the topic.[20]

For example, consider a survey of consumers to measure the image they have of XYZ Company, one of numerous other companies of similar size within the same industry. Given the proliferation of companies, many respondents may be at a loss to readily express what they feel about any particular company, including XYZ. Furthermore, if they are first asked a general-image question (e.g., "What is your overall impression of XYZ Company?"), they may not all use the same frame of reference in answering it. For instance, some may base their responses on XYZ's ads; others may base their responses on XYZ's products. Therefore, it may be preferable to ask the respondents what they think of specific attributes of XYZ (e.g., ads, products, employees) *before* asking them for their overall opinions. This inverted-funnel sequence may help jog the respondents' memories and may provide them with a common set of criteria on which to base their overall opinions.

Skip patterns

Ensure that question sequencing is conducive to clear and simple skip patterns. In many questionnaires not all questions may apply to all respondents. Questions that are not relevant to certain respondents must be skipped. Consequently, the number of questions asked and the sequence in which they are asked may vary across respondents and give rise to different skip patterns. Proper sequencing of questionnaire items is essential to avoid complicated skip patterns that may confuse interviewers and respondents.

To illustrate this guideline examine Exhibit 10.3, which contains part of a mail questionnaire. The five questions appear straightforward at first glance. Notice, however, that questions 13 and 14 require the respondent to first determine whether they should even be answered. Making respondents screen themselves for a question by using *if* statements has two undesirable features: (1) The respondents have to do extra work to decide whether or not to answer the

[19] Studies have shown that responses to questions dealing with people's attitudes and opinions are especially likely to be influenced by the location of the questions within a questionnaire; see, for example, Lee Sigelman, "Question-Order Effects on Presidential Popularity," *Public Opinion Quarterly,* 45 (Summer 1981), pp. 199–207; Schuman, Presser, and Ludwig, "Context Effects on Survey Responses."

[20] See Sudman and Bradburn, *Asking Questions,* pp. 219–221.

Exhibit 10.3

Question sequence needing improvement

11. Do you own or rent your current place of residence?

    ________ Own ________ Rent

12. How long have you lived in this state?

    ________ Less than one year

    ________ One year to less than 5 years

    ________ 5 years or more

13. If you have lived outside this state, in which state did you live immediately before moving here?

    ____

14. If you have lived in this state for 5 years or more and if you currently rent your residence, do you intend to buy a home within the next two years?

    ________ Yes ________ No ________ Don't know

15. How long have you lived in your current place of residence?

    ________ Less than one year

    ________ One year to less than 5 years

    ________ 5 years or more

question, and (2) too many *if*s in the filter part of the question (e.g., as in question 14) may confuse respondents and cause errors. While question *wording* is crucial in preventing these potential problems, question *sequencing* is equally important, as discussed next.

Exhibit 10.4 presents a modified version of the partial questionnaire in Exhibit 10.3. The revised question sequencing and the corresponding wording changes have simplified the questionnaire. The *if* filters requiring a certain amount of effort from respondents to screen themselves have been replaced with simpler *go to* instructions at appropriate places. Furthermore, the question sequencing appears more logical than in the original version. Moving question 11 in the original version to the position of question 13 in the revised version offers a major benefit: Questions dealing with the same issue are now closer together. While all the questions deal with respondents' places of residence, questions 11, 11a, and 12 deal with the state of the residence, and questions 13, 14, and 15 deal with the building of the residence. The questions also follow a funnel sequence: state questions first, followed by building questions.

The preceding observations about Exhibit 10.4 have an important message to questionnaire designers: Just following the various question-wording and -sequencing guidelines outlined earlier (e.g., ask simple questions, cluster simi-

Exhibit 10.4

Improved question sequence

11. Have you always lived in this state?

_________Yes (Go to Question 12) _________No (Go to Question 11a)

11a. In which state did you live immediately before moving into this state?

____

12. How long have you lived in this state?

_________Less than one year

_________One year to less than 5 years

_________5 years or more

13. Do you own or rent the place where you live?

_________Own (Go to Question 15) _________Rent (Go to Question 14)

14. Do you intend to buy a home within the next two years?

_________Yes _________No _________Don't know

15. How long have you lived in your current place of residence?

_________Less than one year

_________One year to less than 5 years

_________5 years or more

lar questions) can be very helpful in devising skip patterns that are clear and simple.

You probably have noticed that the skip patterns in Exhibits 10.3 and 10.4 are not equivalent. Specifically, in the original version only respondents who currently rent *and* have lived in the state for 5 years or more are required to answer question 14. In the revised version, however, *all* respondents who currently rent are required to answer question 14. Is this revision a problem? It is not really a problem, for three reasons. First, question 14 is appropriate and meaningful to all respondents who currently rent. Second, and perhaps more importantly, introducing an additional filter to qualify current renters on the basis of length of residence within the state will unduly complicate the questionnaire. Third, the researcher can still selectively ascertain the home-buying intentions of only those renters who have lived in the state for 5 years or more by cross-tabulating the responses to questions 12 and 14 (more on cross-tabulation in Chapter 16).

The point is that in the interest of keeping a questionnaire simple and minimizing potential confusion, filters are best used only when a subsequent question is likely to be meaningless or embarrassing to certain respondents. Alternatively, keeping the number of filter questions to a minimum, through appropriate wording and sequencing of questions, can facilitate questionnaire administration and reduce the chances of errors.

QUESTIONNAIRE APPEARANCE AND LAYOUT

How a questionnaire looks and how questions are laid out within it can influence the degree of respondent cooperation as well as the quality of the data collected. Appearance and layout are especially critical in mail surveys, because the questionnaire has to sell itself. A professionally done, attractive mail questionnaire can increase the chances of respondent cooperation. Furthermore, an uncluttered questionnaire—one with clear instructions, adequate separation between questions, properly located answer spaces, and so on—will significantly lower the chances of errors.[21]

To illustrate, consider the following two versions of the same question:

VERSION 1:

How old are you?

_____Less than 18 _____18 to 25 _____26 to 40 _____Over 40

VERSION 2:

How old are you?

__________Less than 18

__________18 to 25

__________26 to 40

__________Over 40

Version 2 is laid out better than version 1. Also, it is less likely to lead to the error of inadvertently checking the wrong category (e.g., a respondent who is thirty years old checking the "over 40" category—a serious error, but one that cannot be detected by the researcher). Clearly, paying careful attention to questionnaire layout before data collection begins is worthwhile. Yet layout considerations are often overlooked, especially by those new to questionnaire design.

A detailed discussion of questionnaire features such as type of paper, type of printing, and paper size is beyond the scope of this text, but it can be found

[21] An interesting example of how a seemingly unimportant layout consideration led to significant response errors is described by Charles S. Mayer and Cindy Piper, "A Note on the Importance of Layout in Self-Administered Questionnaires," *Journal of Marketing Research*, 19 (August 1982), pp. 390–391.

elsewhere.[22] In general, a questionnaire must appear attractive, neat, and uncluttered. It must also be convenient to handle, easy to read, and simple to fill out.

An important consideration in deciding how a questionnaire should look is *cost*. As you might expect, making a questionnaire look professional and eye-catching can be expensive. However, cost is usually more of a constraint on appearance (e.g., quality of paper and printing) than on layout (e.g., arrangement of questions and answer categories). Therefore a limited budget is *not* an excuse for a cluttered and confusing questionnaire.

We next turn to pretesting, which can point out potential problems with questionnaire layout and with question wording and sequencing.

PRETESTING

Pretesting involves administering a questionnaire to a limited number of potential respondents and other individuals capable of pointing out design flaws. It is indispensable because even the most diligent questionnaire designer may make mistakes that can only be detected through an external evaluation. While most researchers recognize the importance of pretesting, it is often improperly conducted, or even misused, as discussed next.

A common misuse of pretesting stems from viewing it as a *substitute* for careful thought and attention in the earlier stages of questionnaire design. This view can lead to a false sense of security about the soundness of a questionnaire. As Payne aptly puts it:

> The value of [pre]testing lies first in knowing the points for which to test. Knowledge of considerations that go into the original wording is essential to good testing. . . . Wording and testing necessarily go hand in glove. To shift all the responsibility from one to the other would, like taking off the glove, let both hand and glove go cold.[23]

Pretesting must be viewed as a tool for shedding light on specific features or issues in a questionnaire that the researcher is particularly concerned about. For example, are the answer categories to question XX collectively exhaustive? Is such and such a word likely to be understood in the same way by all respondents? Are instructions to skip such and such a question clear? It must not be viewed solely as a general "fishing expedition" capable of catching whatever flaws the questionnaire may have.

To assume that pretest respondents will be able to uncover all the potential limitations of a questionnaire is incorrect. In fact, one study found that pretest respondents failed to detect even glaring errors, especially those concerning

---

[22] See, for example, Dillman, *Mail and Telephone Surveys;* Paul L. Erdos, *Professional Mail Surveys* (New York: McGraw-Hill, 1970).

[23] Payne, *The Art of Asking Questions,* pp. 13–14.

questions with loaded and ambiguous terms. According to the authors of this study: "In case of ambiguity, a respondent may not realize that more than one meaning can be associated with a particular term. Because the error arises from different meanings being used by different respondents, a single respondent would be unlikely to bring this error to the attention of the interviewer."[24] Thus all errors stemming from differences in interpretation across respondents will go undetected in a pretest unless the researcher scrutinizes the questionnaire beforehand, identifies potential trouble spots, and specifically probes the pretest respondents about those trouble spots. Stated differently, a researcher who considers a questionnaire to be sound simply because pretest respondents filled it out completely without any apparent difficulty is making a big mistake.

There are no standard specifications for the number and the nature of pretests to conduct in a given situation. However, generally, one pretest should be conducted by using personal interviews, irrespective of the administration method to be used ultimately, because being face to face with respondents may suggest problem areas or points of confusion that may otherwise go unnoticed.[25] Also normally recommended is that a second pretest be conducted using the proposed questionnaire administration method. The purpose of this pretest is to detect problems that may be unique to the way in which the questionnaire is to be administered. Finally, when a questionnaire draft is substantially modified from the results of any pretest, one or more additional pretests may be necessary before the questionnaire is finalized.

How many respondents should be included in the pretest sample? Pretest sample size is a subjective decision that depends on a variety of factors, such as how confident the researcher is that the questionnaire is sound and the time and money available. In general, however, it is better to pretest the questionnaire systematically (i.e., by having specific objectives in mind and by extensive probing of respondents) on a relatively small sample than to pretest it on a relatively large sample by simply asking the respondents to fill it out. In other words, the potential usefulness of pretesting will depend more on quality than on quantity.

Regarding the composition of pretest respondents, they should be similar to respondents who will ultimately participate in the study. However, pretesting need not be limited to such respondents. Other individuals capable of providing valuable insights include the researcher's colleagues as well as potential users of the data to be gathered.[26] Pretesting the questionnaire on them can be extremely valuable since they are likely to look at the questionnaire more critically than the typical survey respondent. In fact, a worthwhile approach is to first obtain feed-

---

[24] Shelby D. Hunt, Richard D. Sparkman, Jr., and James B. Wilcox, "The Pretest in Survey Research: Issues and Preliminary Findings," *Journal of Marketing Research,* 19 (May 1982), pp. 269–273; the quotation is from p. 272.

[25] Ironically, however, the study by Hunt, Sparkman, and Wilcox, "The Pretest in Survey Research," found that under certain circumstances telephone pretests were able to detect more errors than face-to-face pretests.

[26] Dillman, *Mail and Telephone Surveys.*

back from such expert respondents and modify the questionnaire draft as necessary *before* pretesting it on survey respondents.

QUESTIONNAIRES FOR COMPUTERIZED INTERVIEWING

As we saw in Chapter 6, recent technological advances are leading to increased use of computerized interviewing such as centralized telephone interviewing with the aid of CRT terminals and questionnaires filled out by respondents sitting at computer keyboards in shopping malls. Although questionnaires used in computerized interviewing are stored in computer memory, they still have to be designed first, bearing in mind the guidelines and caveats discussed thus far. Also, properly programming the questionnaire into computer memory requires additional time and expense. Nevertheless, computerized interviewing, in addition to eliminating the need for printed questionnaires and enabling instant analysis of the collected data, offers several attractive questionnaire features not possible in the past. The following list illustrates these features.

- Randomizing response choices. For multiple-category questions in which category sequence may influence response choice, the computer can be programmed to randomize the order of presentation of the categories *separately* for each respondent. Randomization provides neutralization of any response bias stemming from the way response categories are ordered.
- Checking for response consistency. The computer can be programmed to check for consistency between the response given to a question at hand and responses given to certain key questions asked earlier. As soon as any inconsistency is detected, the CRT screen can bring it to the respondent's attention and give him or her an opportunity to correct the inconsistency. In this way the accuracy of the collected data can be improved.
- Incorporating complex skip patterns. Earlier in the chapter we saw that complex skip patterns—such as "If the answer to question 5 is "yes" and the answer to question 7 is "no," skip to question 10; otherwise, go to question 9"—can confuse respondents and/or interviewers and hence should be avoided. However, computerized interviewing can handle even very complex skip patterns. The computer can easily check as many *if* statements and previous responses as necessary, decide which question should be asked next, and pose that question on the CRT screen almost instantaneously.
- Personalizing. Once a respondent's name is entered into the computer keyboard at the start of an interview, that name can be automatically inserted into key questions and instructions throughout the questionnaire to provide a degree of personalization that would be very time-consuming to

achieve in noncomputerized interviewing. Personalization can add greatly to the rapport established with the respondent.

- Adding "new" response categories. Consider a multiple-category question with an "other" category. In computerized interviewing, when a prespecified number of respondents provide the same open-ended response to the "other" category, that response can be automatically converted into an explicit checkoff category by adding it to the set of prespecified categories. The addition of such new categories may help reduce the time required for subsequent interviews.

The preceding features are by no means an exhaustive list of the increased capabilities offered by computerized interviewing. The questionnaire designer's and computer programmer's ingenuity is the only limit on the creative ways in which computerized interviewing can be used to overcome some of the limitations of traditional interviewing. One must remember, however, that the computer cannot *design* a questionnaire; design is still a human responsibility. Computerized interviewing is therefore not a panacea for questionnaire design.

DESIGNING COVER LETTERS FOR MAIL QUESTIONNAIRES

Among the factors likely to have a major impact on whether a mail questionnaire is filled out and returned is the cover letter accompanying it. The primary purpose of a *cover letter* is to win the cooperation of respondents. Studies have shown that what the cover letter says and how it says it can affect the response rate to a mail survey.[27] Therefore a researcher planning to use a mail questionnaire must spend some time and effort on designing an effective cover letter.

A comprehensive discussion of how to construct a good cover letter is beyond the scope of this text.[28] In a nutshell, the cover letter should tell potential respondents what the study is about and, more critically, convince them of the importance of participating in it. The cover letter should also be concise and objective (i.e., it should not bias the respondent in any way). Several of the guidelines mentioned in connection with wording, appearance, and layout of questionnaires are relevant to designing cover letters as well.

Exhibit 10.5 presents an illustrative cover letter and a list of its key features. The numbers identifying different sections of the cover letter correspond to the numbers accompanying the features listed. Notice that virtually all the features either directly or indirectly attempt to impress upon respondents the need to

27 See, for example, Michael J. Houston and John R. Nevin, "The Effects of Source and Appeal on Mail Survey Response Patterns," *Journal of Marketing Research,* 14 (August 1977), pp. 374–378.

28 For a detailed treatment of cover letter design, see Erdos, *Professional Mail Surveys,* Chap. 12.

Exhibit 10.5

Illustrative cover letter and key features

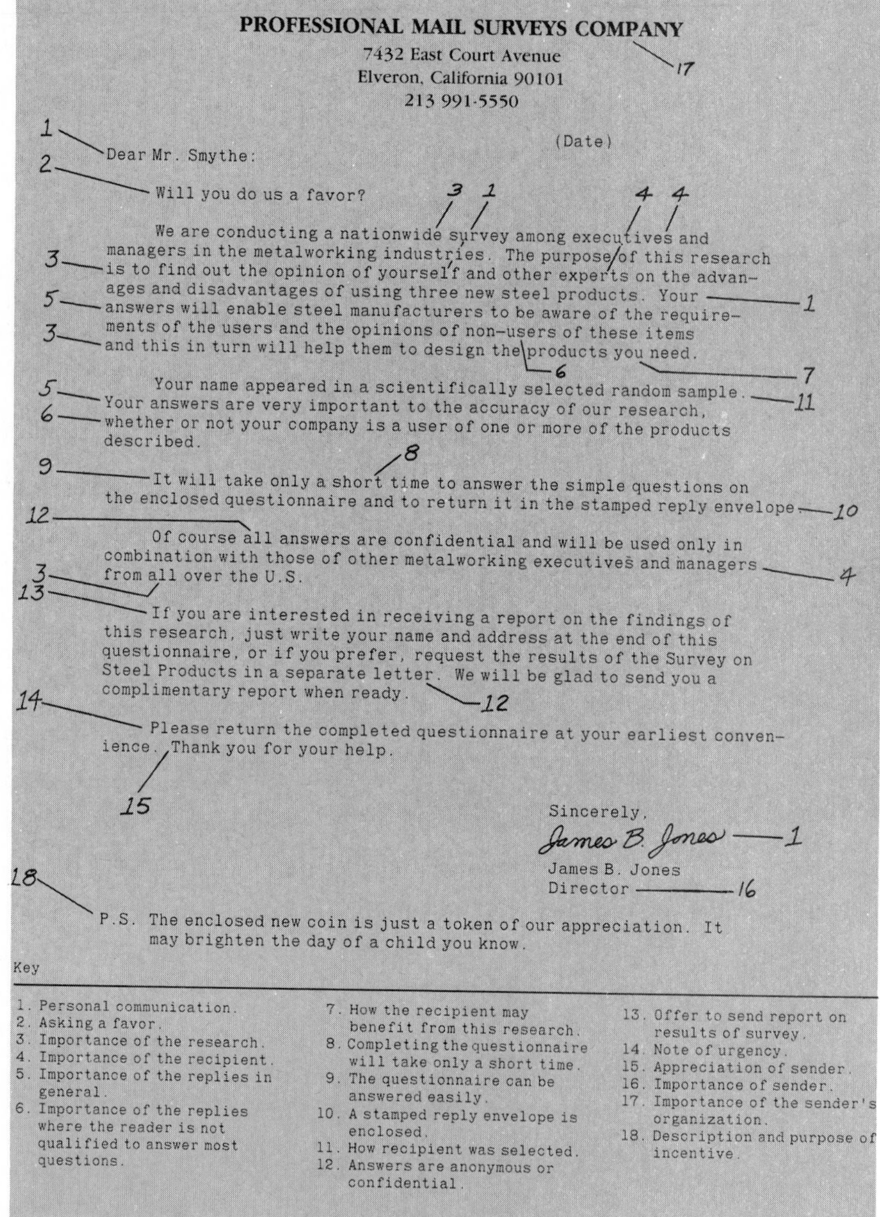

PROFESSIONAL MAIL SURVEYS COMPANY
7432 East Court Avenue
Elveron, California 90101
213 991-5550

(Date)

Dear Mr. Smythe:

Will you do us a favor?

We are conducting a nationwide survey among executives and managers in the metalworking industries. The purpose of this research is to find out the opinion of yourself and other experts on the advantages and disadvantages of using three new steel products. Your answers will enable steel manufacturers to be aware of the requirements of the users and the opinions of non-users of these items and this in turn will help them to design the products you need.

Your name appeared in a scientifically selected random sample. Your answers are very important to the accuracy of our research, whether or not your company is a user of one or more of the products described.

It will take only a short time to answer the simple questions on the enclosed questionnaire and to return it in the stamped reply envelope.

Of course all answers are confidential and will be used only in combination with those of other metalworking executives and managers from all over the U.S.

If you are interested in receiving a report on the findings of this research, just write your name and address at the end of this questionnaire, or if you prefer, request the results of the Survey on Steel Products in a separate letter. We will be glad to send you a complimentary report when ready.

Please return the completed questionnaire at your earliest convenience. Thank you for your help.

Sincerely,

James B. Jones

James B. Jones
Director

P.S. The enclosed new coin is just a token of our appreciation. It may brighten the day of a child you know.

Key

1. Personal communication.
2. Asking a favor.
3. Importance of the research.
4. Importance of the recipient.
5. Importance of the replies in general.
6. Importance of the replies where the reader is not qualified to answer most questions.
7. How the recipient may benefit from this research.
8. Completing the questionnaire will take only a short time.
9. The questionnaire can be answered easily.
10. A stamped reply envelope is enclosed.
11. How recipient was selected.
12. Answers are anonymous or confidential.
13. Offer to send report on results of survey.
14. Note of urgency.
15. Appreciation of sender.
16. Importance of sender.
17. Importance of the sender's organization.
18. Description and purpose of incentive.

Source: Reproduced from Paul L. Erdos, *Professional Mail Surveys,* rev. ed. (Melbourne, Fla.: Krieger Publishing, 1983), pp. 102–103. Used by permission.

cooperate. However, not *all* these features need to be incorporated in every cover letter. In fact, a cover letter containing every listed feature can at times be self-defeating; it may become, or at least appear to be, so lengthy that some respondents may not even be interested in reading it. The purpose of Exhibit 10.5 is merely to show the variety of ways respondents can be encouraged to participate in a survey. An effective cover letter must possess at least several, but not necessarily all, of the illustrated attributes.

OPENERS FOR PERSONAL AND TELEPHONE INTERVIEWS

What are good openers?

Just as cover letters are important in mail surveys, good openers (i.e., introductory statements) are essential in securing respondent cooperation in personal and telephone interviews. Openers in these interviews need not, and perhaps should not, be as lengthy as a typical cover letter. But they should usually include the following features:

- An appropriate salutation, such as "Good morning! I am Ralph Johnston with Marketing Research Associates Company."
- A brief statement about the project and its purpose, such as "We are conducting a survey of heads of household regarding their feelings about modern home appliances."
- An indication of how long the interview might last, such as "This survey should take no more than ten minutes."
- A polite request for permission to conduct the interview, such as "May I please talk to the male or female head of your household for a few minutes?"

Openers for personal and telephone interviews should be carefully constructed and be an integral part of the questionnaire so as to ensure consistency across interviews and across interviewers. Lack of consistency in openers can result in unnecessary distortions and biases in the data to be collected. And just as a suitable opener is important for getting the interview off to a good start, common courtesy demands that the questionnaire end with an appropriate "thank you" statement.

DESIGNING OBSERVATION FORMS

As mentioned at the beginning of the chapter, designing observation forms is somewhat easier than constructing questionnaires. Nevertheless, the quality of data gathered through observation depends on the clarity of the instructions

Exhibit 10.6

Observation form for recording characteristics and behavior of customers stopping at a special display

Structured Observation Form

Observation number ________

AS SOON AS YOU OBSERVE ANY ADULT CUSTOMER (ANY CUSTOMER WHO APPEARS TO BE 18 YEARS OF AGE OR MORE) STOPPING AT THE DISPLAY, START YOUR STOPWATCH, AND RECORD THE FOLLOWING:

1. Sex of the customer: Male ________ Female ________
2. Approximate age of the customer: 18–30 ________
   31–50 ________
   Over 50 ________
3. Number of individuals accompanying the customer: ________
   (IF NONE, GO ON TO ITEM 4.)
   a. How many of the accompanying individuals are adults? ________
   b. How many are children? ________
4. Does the customer touch or handle the product?
   Yes ________ No ________
5. Do any of the accompanying *adults* touch or handle the product?
   Yes ________ No ________ No accompanying adult ________
6. Do the customer or accompanying adults, if any, leave the display with one or more units of the displayed product?
   Yes ________ No ________
   ↓
   How many *total* units? ________

STOP YOUR STOPWATCH WHEN THE CUSTOMER *AND* ACCOMPANYING ADULTS, IF ANY, LEAVE THE DISPLAY AREA. RECORD BELOW THE TOTAL TIME SPENT AT THE DISPLAY:

________Minutes ________Seconds

GO TO A NEW OBSERVATION FORM AND RECORD INFORMATION FOR THE NEXT ADULT WHO STOPS AT THE DISPLAY.

given and the tasks assigned to the observers. A standard form is not necessary when a study involves nonstructured observation; the observer simply makes mental and/or written notes about whatever is being observed. In these studies the training and the skills of the observer are critical for generating relevant and objective information.

When structured observation is involved, however, a standard form that clearly states the specific observations to be made and provides for efficient recording of those observations is desirable. Several of the guidelines concerning such aspects as wording, sequencing, and layout, which we discussed under questionnaire design, are germane to constructing observation forms as well. After all, a structured-observation form is basically a questionnaire that the observer fills out. A cluttered or confusing observation form can cause problems for the observer and result in erroneous data.

Exhibit 10.6 illustrates a form that can be used in a structured-observation study to ascertain the impact on customers of a special in-store display (such as the one in the Kwality Knitware scenario described in Chapter 6). The primary purpose of Exhibit 10.6 is to show what a structured-observation form might look like. It is not to be viewed as an exhaustive list of items to be observed in order to evaluate the special display's impact. As in the case of a questionnaire, the content of an observation form—that is, the various observation tasks and items included in it—should be based on well-defined objectives and specific information requirements in a given setting.

SUMMARY

Constructing questionnaires is not an easy undertaking. Even seasoned researchers at times inadvertently overlook design flaws. Devoting adequate time and effort to questionnaire design is therefore a must. The quality and the ultimate usefulness of data to be gathered through a survey are vitally dependent on how good the questionnaire is.

No standard methodology exists for designing questionnaires; however, we can regard the design as a sequential process consisting of *interrelated* steps. Once the data requirements of a project are clearly defined, they can be transformed into a corresponding set of rough questions. The rough draft must then go through one or more iterations involving a variety of checks.

A key decision to be made concerning each question is whether it should be open-ended or structured. Open-ended questions are generally not recommended for surveys of large samples. However, they can be used as warm-up questions or as transition questions to aid the smooth flow of the interview. Structured questions can be dichotomous or multiple-category. The categories in a multiple-category question must be collectively exhaustive and mutually exclusive. One should also rotate the categories, if feasible. The number of response categories to include depends on the nature of the research objectives and the data requirements, and the type of questionnaire administration method to be used.

The relevance of each question must be carefully examined, and irrelevant questions must be dropped. This guideline is especially important since there is a normal tendency to include more questions than are really needed. Also, questions that a respondent cannot answer meaningfully or will not answer truthfully should be eliminated if they cannot be suitably rephrased.

Question wording is perhaps the most critical determinant of data accuracy. Unfortunately, the essentials for wording questions properly cannot be reduced to a neat, concise set of rules. However, even unseasoned researchers can spot wording problems by putting themselves in the respondents' shoes and critically examining each question. Particular attention must be focused on identifying problem questions such as double-barreled, leading, one-sided, and complex questions, as well as questions with implicit assumptions.

The sequencing of questions is another determinant of data accuracy. Questions must be arranged in a logical sequence. The following principles should generally be heeded, unless certain exceptional situations demand otherwise: Questions that are personal, sensitive, or difficult to answer should be placed as far into the questionnaire as possible. Questions related to the same topic should appear together. Questions within a topic should go from general to specific (i.e., follow a funnel sequence). And question skip patterns should be simple and kept to a minimum. Questionnaire appearance and layout, if ignored, can lead to confusion and coding errors. In mail surveys they can also have a significant impact on respondents' willingness to cooperate.

Pretesting involves administering a questionnaire to a limited number of respondents so as to uncover and correct any faults before the final draft is prepared. A researcher's colleagues and potential users of the data to be generated are valuable critics at this stage. Resources permitting, a questionnaire should be pretested on survey respondents at least twice: once through personal interviews involving in-depth probing, and a second time using an administration procedure similar to the one proposed for the study. For pretesting to be most effective, the researcher should have already identified specific items likely to be potential trouble spots in the questionnaire and should probe for information capable of shedding light on those items.

An element unique to mail surveys, and critical for obtaining high response rates, is the cover letter. Above all else, a good cover letter should convince respondents to cooperate and should do so in a concise and objective fashion. Personal and telephone interviews require some appropriate, concise openers, as well.

Studies involving structured observation typically use standard data collection forms. Although these forms are somewhat easier to construct than questionnaires, they must be designed with care. Several of the guidelines presented for designing questionnaires are also relevant for designing observation forms.

QUESTIONS

1. "Designing a questionnaire for a conclusive-research project is more difficult than designing one for an exploratory-research project." Discuss this statement.
2. Using Exhibit 10.1 as a guide, briefly discuss the major ways in which a questionnaire may result in inaccurate data.
3. Give two examples to illustrate why the steps involved in questionnaire design are interrelated.
4. Under what circumstances could you use nonstructured questions in a conclusive-research study?
5. Suppose you want to ascertain the extent to which students in your class are paying for their educational expenses through their own earnings. Assuming you want to ask just one question, how would you phrase it in each of the following forms: open-ended, dichotomous, and multiple-category? In what ways would the type of data obtained through each form differ?
6. Why must responses to multiple-category questions be collectively exhaustive and mutually exclusive?
7. What is the split-ballot technique? For what purpose(s) can it be used? What are its potential drawbacks?
8. What factors should be considered in deciding on the number of categories to include in a multiple-category question?
9. Do you agree or disagree with this statement? "As long as a question pertains to at least one of the research objectives, it must be included in the questionnaire." Explain your answer.
10. Make up an example of your own to illustrate each of the following: (a) a double-barreled question; (b) a leading question; (c) a question with an implicit assumption. In each case, suggest a revised question that will reduce potential bias.
11. What is a filter question? When are such questions most appropriate?
12. What is meant by a funnel sequence? Is it always beneficial in a questionnaire? Why or why not?
13. What guidelines should one keep in mind to make pretesting as beneficial as possible?
14. In what ways does the design and the use of a mail questionnaire differ from those of other types of questionnaires?

11

Types of Scales and Attitude Measurement

A variety of question formats and their advantages and disadvantages were presented in the previous chapter. This chapter's focus is on measuring or quantifying responses to different types of questions, with particular emphasis on questions dealing with people's feelings, opinions, and the like. A typical definition of *measurement* is "the assignment of numbers to observations [or responses] according to some set of rules."[1] We will use this definition, although the term *measurement* has also been given somewhat different interpretations.[2]

Assigning numbers to responses has two potential benefits. First, quantified responses from a large sample can be summarized more efficiently and parsimoniously than nonquantified responses. Second, quantified responses can be manipulated by using a variety of mathematical techniques. The results of the data analyses can provide rich insights that may go undiscovered by merely examining unquantified responses.[3] Despite these attractive advantages, however, assigning numbers to survey responses in a meaningful fashion is no easy task. As will be shown in the next section, depending on the nature of the questions and the responses being quantified, the numbers assigned may not possess all the mathematical properties commonly attributed to the number system. Therefore a thorough understanding of what the scaled responses represent is essential for determining the types of analyses that can be legitimately performed by using the collected data. The next section describes four types of

[1] Gene F. Summers, ed., *Attitude Measurement* (Chicago: Rand McNally, 1970), p. 1.
[2] Alternative definitions and interpretations of the term *measurement* are presented in Warren S. Torgerson, *Theory and Methods of Scaling* (New York: Wiley, 1958), pp. 13–14.
[3] These benefits are reflected in the remarks of Summers, *Attitude Measurement,* p. 11.

scales representing different levels of quantified responses and the numerical properties of each.

TYPES OF SCALES

Let us briefly review the nature of the number system. Any given set of numbers—say 3, 6, 9, 12, 24, and 36—has certain basic properties. First, the numbers follow a *rank order;* thus 9 is greater than 3, 12 is less than 24, and so on. Second, the differences, or *intervals,* between pairs of numbers can be compared. Thus the interval between 6 and 3 is the same as the interval between 9 and 6; the interval between 36 and 24 is twice the interval between 12 and 6; and so on. This property stems from the fact that the interval separating a pair of adjacent numbers in the number system is, by definition, equal to the interval between any other such pair. Third, we can divide one number by another and interpret the resulting *ratio* as being indicative of the relative magnitudes of the two numbers. Thus 6 is twice as large as 3, 12 is one-third as large as 36, and so on. We can compute and interpret ratios of numbers because the number system has a *unique zero point.* In other words, all elements within the number system are measured from the *same* starting point—namely, zero.

Although the three properties of the number system are obvious and invariably taken for granted, they are of special significance in the context of quantifying survey responses. That is, to interpret quantified responses as if they were numbers is not always appropriate. Quantified responses fall into one of four scale types: nominal, ordinal, interval, or ratio, with varying properties. We will examine each type next.

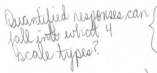

Nominal-scaled responses

Numbers forming a *nominal scale* are no more than labels and are used solely to identify different categories of responses. The following examples illustrate:

What is your sex?
1 Male
2 Female

Which one of the following media influences your purchasing decisions the most?
1 Television
2 Radio
3 Newspapers
4 Magazines

The numbers accompanying the response categories in these questions have none of the three properties described earlier. They do not imply any particular rank ordering of the responses. Moreover, the intervals between, as well as ratios of, pairs of these numbers reveal nothing about the nature of the responses. That these numbers form no more than a nominal scale is easily demonstrated by the fact that *any* set of numbers can be used to represent the response categories. For example, the following numbers would serve to describe the responses just as well as the numbers previously used:

265	Male	600	Television
575	Female	755	Radio
		523	Newspapers
		129	Magazines

The only permissible mathematical operation with nominal-scaled responses is counting the number of responses falling within each category. From counting, one can report, for instance, that 75% of the respondents checked category 600 in answering the media question, and hence 600 is the *modal* (i.e., most frequently checked) response category. Determining any measure of central tendency other than the *mode* is inappropriate when response categories form only a nominal scale.

Ordinal-scaled responses

An *ordinal scale* is more powerful than a nominal scale in that the numbers possess the property of *rank order*. Consider the following question:

How long do you spend reading newspapers on a typical weekday?
1 Less than 5 minutes.
2 5 minutes to less than 15 minutes.
3 15 minutes to less than 30 minutes.
4 30 minutes or more.

The scale values of 1, 2, 3, and 4 assigned to the response categories, in addition to serving as labels, provide an indication of the extent of newspaper reading. For instance, a respondent checking category 4 spends more time reading newspapers than one checking category 3; however, the numbers do not indicate *how much more time* the former spends than the latter. A respondent who spends 15 minutes per day and another who spends 25 minutes per day will both check category 3. Since the exact reading times cannot be inferred from the scale values, the intervals between them have no meaningful interpretation. Stated differently, given the nature of the response categories, any set of four numbers can be used as scale values, as long as they go from lowest to highest. For example, a set of scale values such as 10, 15, 25, 40 is equivalent in this case to the set 1, 2, 3, 4.

Two measures of central tendency are meaningful for ordinal-scaled responses: their mode as well as their *median*—that is, the category in which the 50th percentile response falls when all responses are arranged from lowest to highest (or vice versa). To illustrate, consider the following distribution of responses to the question about reading newspapers:

Response Category	Percent of Respondents Checking Category
1	40%
2	25%
3	25%
4	10%

In this case the mode is category 1 and the median is category 2.

For numbers forming an ordinal scale we can determine percentile values other than the median—for example, the 25th and 75th percentile values—so as to get a feeling for how widely or narrowly dispersed the data are on either side of the median.

Interval-scaled responses

Interval-scaled responses are more powerful than ordinal-scaled responses because an *interval scale* has all the properties of an ordinal scale and, in addition, the *differences* between scale values can be meaningfully interpreted. Strictly speaking, variables such as attitudes, opinions, and preferences cannot be quantified to yield exact interval scales. Nevertheless, responses to questions like the following are frequently assumed to form an interval scale:

> How likely are you to buy a new automobile within the next six months? (Please check the most appropriate category.)
>
> Will definitely not buy ________ (1)
>
> Extremely unlikely ________ (2)
>
> Unlikely ________ (3)
>
> Likely ________ (4)
>
> Extremely likely ________ (5)
>
> Will definitely buy ________ (6)

The values assigned to this set of responses run from 1 through 6 (these numbers could also be in reverse order) and, strictly speaking, form only an ordinal scale. But they are considered to be interval-scaled under the assumption that respondents will treat the differences between adjacent response categories to be equal, especially since the categories are physically separated by equal distances.

Unfortunately, verifying whether respondents' *mental* or *psychological* perceptions of the differences between adjacent response categories are equal is very difficult, if not impossible. Some authorities have argued that scales like the one just illustrated are no more than ordinal.[4] However, others have demonstrated that such scales are robust enough to be treated as interval scales for analysis purposes.[5] There is still considerable debate in academic circles about whether so-called interval-scaled responses are really so. Nevertheless, such scales are more often than not treated as having interval properties in marketing research practice.

Numbers forming an interval scale, in addition to possessing ordinal-scale attributes, permit one to compute their *mean* (their simple average) and their *standard deviation,* which is a measure of dispersion (i.e., degree of deviation of the numbers from their mean). Suppose the question about likelihood of buying a new automobile is posed to a sample of 200 respondents and the following response distribution is obtained:

Response Category	Number (Percent) of Respondents Checking Category
1	10 (5%)
2	10 (5%)
3	70 (35%)
4	60 (30%)
5	20 (10%)
6	30 (15%)
	200 (100%)

The mode and the median for the distribution are 3 and 4, respectively. The mean response turns out to be 3.8, computed as follows:

$$\begin{aligned} &1 \times .05 + 2 \times .05 + 3 \times .35 + 4 \times .3 + 5 \times .1 + 6 \times .15 \\ &= .05 + .10 + 1.05 + 1.20 + .50 + .90 \\ &= 3.80 \end{aligned}$$

[4] See, for example, James H. Myers and W. Gregory Warner, "Semantic Properties of Selected Evaluation Adjectives," *Journal of Marketing Research,* 5 (November 1968), pp. 409–412; John A. Martilla and Davis W. Carvey, "Four Subtle Sins in Marketing Research," *Journal of Marketing,* 39 (January 1975), pp. 8–15; Gary M. Mullet, "Itemized Rating Scales: Ordinal or Interval?" *European Research,* April 1983, pp. 49–52.

[5] See, for example, Sanford Labovitz, "The Assignment of Numbers to Rank Order Categories," *American Sociological Review,* 35 (1970), pp. 515–524; Mark Traylor, "Ordinal and Interval Scaling," *Journal of the Market Research Society,* 25 (4), pp. 297–303; William D. Perreault, Jr., and Forrest W. Young, "Alternating Least Squares Optimal Scaling: Analysis of Nonmetric Data in Marketing Research," *Journal of Marketing Research,* 17 (February 1980), pp. 1–13.

Thus the mean likelihood of purchase for the total sample is precisely at the 3.8 mark on the 1-to-6 scale. The computation and the interpretation of the mean are legitimate because of the assumption that the unit of measurement remains constant throughout the scale.

Now suppose the same question is administered to a *different* sample of 200—say, a sample of respondents with lower income levels than in the earlier sample—and these responses are obtained:

Response Category	Number (Percent) of Respondents Checking Category
1	120 (60%)
2	40 (20%)
3	10 (5%)
4	10 (5%)
5	10 (5%)
6	10 (5%)
	200 (100%)

In contrast to the first sample's mean of 3.8 on the 6-point scale, the mean for the second sample is only 1.9:

$$\begin{aligned} &1 \times .60 + 2 \times .20 + 3 \times .05 + 4 \times .05 + 5 \times .05 + 6 \times .05 \\ &\quad = .60 + .40 + .15 + .20 + .25 + .30 \\ &\quad = 1.90 \end{aligned}$$

Although 3.8 is twice as large as 1.9, we cannot say that the first sample is twice as likely to buy a new automobile within the next six months as the second sample. Even though the unit of measurement remains constant throughout an interval scale, its starting, or zero, point is *arbitrary*.

The ratio of two values on an interval scale is also arbitrary and has no meaningful interpretation, since it depends on the scale's starting point. To illustrate, suppose we number the six response categories 0 through 5, instead of 1 through 6. We still have an interval scale, but it has a different starting point. Exhibit 11.1 shows the impact of this change on the mean responses of the two samples. From the exhibit we see that the ratio of sample mean values on scale A is 3.8/1.9 = 2.0. The ratio of sample mean values on scale B, though, is 2.8/.9 = 3.1.

As demonstrated by Exhibit 11.1, with the new starting point for the interval scale, the first sample on the average is now over three times as likely to buy a new automobile as the second. This conclusion is obviously ludicrous, since the answers obtained from the two samples and the relative positions of their mean responses on the scale have not changed. Although this point is subtle, it is extremely important, because there is usually a strong temptation to compute and interpret ratios of quantified responses that are no more than interval-scaled. For instance, you have probably heard claims like "Users of our brand are twice as satisfied as users of competitors' brands," and "Homeowners are four times as strongly opposed to a property tax increase as renters." Such

Exhibit 11.1

Impact of arbitrariness of an interval scale's starting point

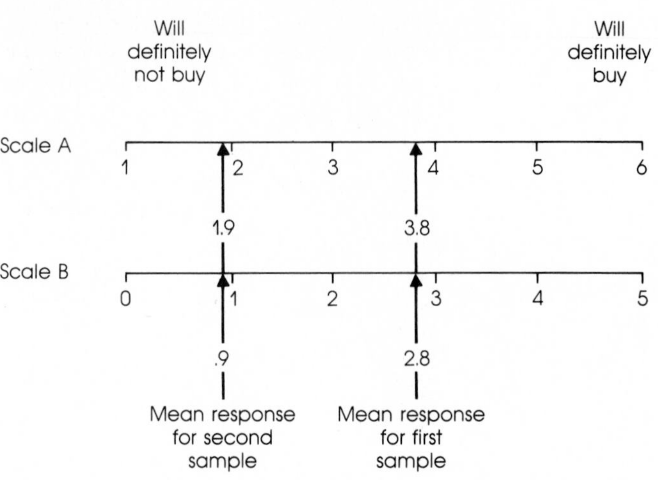

claims, even when based on data from well-conducted surveys, are suspect because scales used to measure respondents' feelings, opinions, and other internal variables are invariably only interval scales.

Ratio-scaled responses

Quantified responses forming a *ratio scale* are analytically the most versatile. They possess all the properties of the scales discussed thus far. In addition, ratios of numbers on these scales have meaningful interpretations. Data on attributes of respondents such as attitudes and opinions typically will not satisfy the stringent requirements of a ratio scale. However, data on certain demographic or descriptive attributes, if they are obtained through open-ended questions, will have ratio-scale properties. Consider the following questions:

What is your annual income before taxes? $__________

How far is your workplace from your home? __________ miles

Answers to these questions have a natural, unambiguous starting point, namely zero. Since the starting point is not chosen arbitrarily, as in the case of an interval scale, computing and interpreting ratios make sense. For instance, we can say that a respondent with an annual income of $40,000 earns twice as much as one with an annual income of $20,000.

In summary, quantified responses fall into one of four scale types: nominal, ordinal, interval, or ratio. Each scale possesses the attributes of the scales below it. That is, ratio scales have the properties of interval scales, which, in turn, have the properties of ordinal scales, and so on. The permissible data analyses and inferences depend on the scale level of the data. (Data analysis procedures are discussed in Chapter 16; see Table 16.4 for a summary of the permissible statistics associated with each scale.)

One final point before we examine the classes of variables typically encountered in marketing research and the levels of measurement appropriate for them: Data with only nominal or ordinal properties are classified as *nonmetric data*, while data with interval or ratio properties are classified as *metric data*. The feature differentiating these two types of data is that the differences between numbers have precise meaning for metric data but not for nonmetric data.

CLASSES OF VARIABLES

The nature of a variable plays a key role in determining the most powerful scale on which it can be measured meaningfully. To demonstrate the influence of the nature of variables on levels of measurement, we will consider a classification scheme for variables proposed by Don Dillman. According to Dillman, virtually all variables encountered in survey research can be classified under one of four categories: attributes, behavior, beliefs, and attitudes.[6] *Attributes* are personal or demographic characteristics, such as education level, age, size of household, and number of children. *Behavioral variables* relate to such things as frequency of visits to a store and extent of magazine readership. *Beliefs* relate to knowledge and are what respondents consider to be true (correctly or incorrectly); for example, do respondents believe banning print advertisements for cigarettes will lower lung cancer deaths? *Attitudes* are similar to beliefs, except that they also involve respondents' evaluative judgments; for instance, do respondents feel print advertisements for cigarettes should be banned?

In this classification scheme attributes and behavioral variables are similar in that they are less ambiguous and more readily measurable than the other two types of variables. Therefore, ascertaining the most appropriate levels of measurement for them, from the degree of detail desired by the researcher, is somewhat easier. For instance, consider income level, an attribute of respondents. If the researcher desires metric data on income, a ratio scale of measurement can be used; that is, an open-ended income question can be asked. However, if the researcher is merely interested in nonmetric data (i.e., the relative income levels of respondents), the scale of measurement can be ordinal and consist of a multiple-category income question. Similarly, consider people's

[6] The four classes of variables and their description are from Don A. Dillman, *Mail and Telephone Surveys: The Total Design Method* (New York: Wiley, 1978), pp. 80–86.

smoking habits, a behavioral variable. Depending on how much detail the researcher desires, data on smoking can be obtained on a nominal scale (by asking a dichotomous question about whether or not a respondent smokes), an ordinal scale (by asking a suitable multiple-category question), or a ratio scale (by asking an open-ended question to ascertain the number of cigarettes smoked per day).

Measurement of beliefs and attitudes, however, is not quite as simple. Since beliefs and attitudes are more cognitive than factual, they are more nebulous than attributes or behavior. Therefore, defining them, let alone measuring them precisely, is difficult. To understand this difficulty, let us look briefly at two types of definitions of constructs, or variables, that cannot be directly observed: constitutive, or conceptual, definitions and operational definitions.

A *constitutive definition* of a construct describes it in terms of other constructs. For instance, a constitutive definition of *attitude* may be a predisposition to respond favorably or unfavorably to a stimulus object." This definition makes use of the constructs "predisposition to respond" and "stimulus object" to define *attitude.* An *operational definition* of a construct describes how the construct is to be measured. It lays out the steps or procedures to be completed in order to assign a value to the construct. For instance, an operational definition of a person's attitude toward a particular retail store may be as follows: It is the total of the person's expressed degree of agreement—on a 5-point, "strongly agree" to "strongly disagree" scale—with each of a set of 20 evaluative statements about various aspects of the retail store.

The operational definition of a construct is guided by its constitutive definition. In the illustrative operational definition the terms "set of 20 evaluative statements" and "expressed degree of agreement" with each of those statements are, in effect, operationalizations of the constructs "stimulus object" and "predisposition to respond" in the constitutive definition. Intuitively, the accuracy of the measured attitude will depend on the degree of correspondence between the constitutive and the operational definitions—that is, the extent to which constructs in the constitutive definition are *truly* captured by the steps in the operational definition. Obviously, the more ambiguous the constructs in the constitutive definition of a variable, the more difficult it is to measure the variable precisely. For this reason obtaining accurate, unambiguous measures of unobservable variables such as beliefs and attitudes is generally difficult. Interestingly, from a measurement standpoint these variables are typically neither nominal nor ratio. They usually have ordinal or interval properties and fall in the gray area between nonmetric and metric measurements.

Consider consumers' consumption of frozen TV dinners, a behavioral variable. This variable can be measured on a nominal scale at one extreme (e.g., Have you eaten a frozen TV dinner anytime during the past month?) or on a ratio scale at the other extreme (e.g., How many frozen TV dinners have you eaten during the past month?). In terms of measuring consumers' *attitudes* toward frozen TV dinners, however, a nominal scale does not make much sense. Of course, asking a consumer "Do you have an attitude toward frozen TV dinners?"

will yield a yes or no, nominal-scale response. But this question does not really measure the consumer's attitude. What it does measure is an attribute rather than an attitude. Moreover, given that everyone is likely to have *some* attitude (even if it is neutral) toward frozen TV dinners, the question is meaningless. Similarly, since there is no unambiguous, fixed zero level of attitude toward frozen TV dinners, a ratio scale of measurement is also out of the question. Therefore any meaningful measure of attitudes must be either ordinal or interval.

Debate still rages, however, about whether metric measurements of attitudes are possible. This chapter cannot settle the debate and will not attempt to do so. Rather, the remainder of this chapter will provide an overview of the methods and scales usually employed to measure attitudes. The complexity of attitude measurement and the resultant need for its separate treatment are succinctly described by Dillman:

> People's attitudes on a specific subject are often complex and intertwined with other attitudes and beliefs they hold. Further, attitudes are held in varying degrees and are subject to considerable fluctuation. Thus when people are asked to express their attitudes on a given subject, they are likely to engage in considerable contemplation that involves carefully considering how well the particular wording of the question reflects the degree to which they hold the attitude under investigation. . . . When a question seems likely to be sensitive to wording variations, it is advisable to ask another or perhaps several questions. Thus people interested in attitudes, and to a certain extent beliefs, often ask a number of similar questions from which they try to construct attitude scales by combining the responses in certain ways. At the other extreme, it is seldom necessary to ask for information on attributes in more than one way.[7]

You probably noticed that the focus of the preceding paragraphs has been on measuring attitudes, almost to the exclusion of beliefs. This focus is intentional, for two reasons. First, beliefs and attitudes—for that matter, all inner or cognitive variables—are interrelated, despite shades of differences in their conceptual definitions. Second, even assuming attitudes are completely distinct from other cognitive variables such as beliefs, the general attitude measurement techniques can be used for measuring the other variables as well. Therefore applications of the measurement procedures to be discussed in the remainder of this chapter go beyond attitude assessment alone.

ATTITUDE SCALING

The term *attitude* has been defined in a number of different ways.[8] The purpose here is not to present the various definitions and discuss their diversity. Rather,

[7] Dillman, *Mail and Telephone Surveys,* pp. 85–86, excerpted with permission from John Wiley & Sons, Inc.

[8] Several of these definitions are presented in Summers, *Attitude Measurement,* pp. 1–2.

it is primarily to review scaling techniques suitable for measuring attitudes and, more generally, any internal disposition of people that can affect their behavior. Fortunately, even the seemingly different definitions of attitudes share certain common threads. They all depict *attitudes* as underlying mental states capable of influencing a person's choice of actions and maintaining consistency across those actions.[9] These common threads imply that attitudes can be interpreted quite broadly. Therefore the general principles underlying attitude-scaling techniques should also be useful in measuring other internal variables such as beliefs, opinions, preferences, motives, and purchase intentions. Indeed, virtually all consumer behavior textbooks portray attitudes as being multifaceted and consisting of three components: *cognitive* (knowledge, beliefs), *affective* (liking, preference), and *behavioral* (action tendency, purchase intentions).[10] Thus measuring attitudes actually involves measuring several internal variables making up the three components.

Attitudes are widely believed to be a key determinant of behavior, although some authors suggest that behavior can also lead changes in attitudes. For instance, when a person with a mildly positive attitude toward Apple computers buys an Apple computer, his or her attitude may become much more positive following the purchase, perhaps to mentally justify the purchase. In any event, firms and institutions are constantly interested in the attitudes of various constituencies that are of interest to them. For example, General Motors may be interested in the attitudes of consumers toward its automobiles, the attitudes of employees toward its working environment, and the attitudes of shareholders toward its business performance. The United Way may be interested in the public's attitude toward charitable organizations in general and toward itself in particular. How can General Motors, the United Way, and other organizations measure the attitudes of relevant constituencies? A variety of methods are available for this purpose. Before we discuss the methods, however, we point out that attitude measurement as a whole is *indirect*. In other words, attitudes can only be inferred and cannot be directly ascertained.

Several measurable responses can offer clues about people's attitudes. Cook and Selltiz have classified them into five broad categories:

(a) Measures in which the material from which inferences are drawn consists of self-reports of beliefs, feelings, behavior, etc., toward an object or class of objects.
(b) Measures in which inferences are drawn from observed overt behavior toward the object.
(c) Measures in which inferences are drawn from the individual's reactions to, or interpretations of, partially structured material relevant to the object.

---

[9] For further discussion of the commonalities, see Summers, *Attitude Measurement,* pp. 1–2.
[10] See, for example, Carl E. Block and Kenneth J. Roering, *Essentials of Consumer Behavior* (Hinsdale, Ill.: Dryden Press, 1976), pp. 220–222.

(d) Measures in which inferences are drawn from performance on objective tasks where functioning may be influenced by disposition toward the object.

(e) Measures in which inferences are drawn from physiological reactions to the object.[11]

The major focus of this chapter will be on self-report, or so-called paper-and-pencil, methods—category (a) in the list—because they are by far the most widely used in attitude-scaling studies. However, we will first briefly review the other four types of methods.[12]

Observing overt behavior

We commonly assume that a person's behavior concerning an object will be consistent with his or her attitudes toward it. This assumption has found empirical support, although there has been debate about whether attitudes are trustworthy *predictors* of behavior.[13] Nevertheless, the notion of consistency between attitudes and behavior seems almost intuitive. For instance, a consumer with an unfavorable attitude toward a certain brand of automobile is more likely than not to buy a competing brand. A television viewer with a strong negative image of a particular firm may frown visibly upon seeing a commercial touting the firm's products. The assumed link between attitude and behavior is the rationale behind inferring the former from observing the latter.

Observation of overt behavior is useful when other attitude measurement methods are inconvenient or infeasible. For instance, an observation study can be used to ascertain the attitudes of very young children toward a variety of toys. Children in groups, or individually, can be left in a room containing the stimulus set of toys, and their behavior—how long and how enthusiastically they play with each toy—can be observed. Inferences about the children's attitudes toward each toy can be made from those observations. The use of one-way mirrors to observe focus groups (as we saw in Chapter 7) is another example of this approach to gaining insight into people's attitudes.

As you might suspect, observation of behavior can only yield rough estimates of attitudes, at best. A number of factors, other than attitudes, can influence behavior. To illustrate, a housewife may buy a cheap brand of detergent, despite an unfavorable attitude toward it, because she cannot afford a more expensive brand that she really likes. A teenager who hates cigarettes may still

[11] Stuart W. Cook and Claire Selltiz, "A Multiple-Indicator Approach to Attitude Measurement," *Psychological Bulletin,* 62 (1964), p. 38.

[12] More detailed discussions of these methods are given in Cook and Selltiz, "Multiple-Indicator Approach."

[13] See, for example, William L. Wilkie and Edgar A. Pessemier, "Issues in Marketing's Use of Multiattribute Attitude Models," *Journal of Marketing Research,* 10 (November 1973), pp. 428–441.

smoke them because of peer pressure. Thus the validity of attitudes inferred solely from overt behavior may be questionable (validity of attitude measures is discussed later). Furthermore, this approach can become quite expensive, because it requires the services of highly skilled and qualified observers.

Analyzing reactions to partially structured stimuli

As its name implies, the approach of analyzing reactions to partially structured stimuli involves asking respondents to react to, or describe in some fashion, an incomplete, vague stimulus. The responses obtained are analyzed by trained professionals to reveal the respondents' attitudes. The underlying rationale here is that a person's response to an object or situation depicted by a vague stimulus will necessarily be shaped by his or her attitudes. This approach to measuring attitudes is similar to the projective techniques discussed in Chapter 6. The various projective techniques we examined—word association test, sentence completion test, TAT, cartoon test—are examples of methods employing partially structured stimuli. Therefore these techniques can be used to infer attitudes. The advantages and disadvantages of projective techniques, as well as several illustrative applications, are given in Chapter 6 and hence will not be repeated here.

Evaluating performance on objective tasks

In the approach of evaluating performance on objective tasks, respondents are asked to complete an ostensibly objective, well-defined task. The nature of their performance is then analyzed to infer their attitudes. To illustrate, consider the attitudes of a rural community toward attracting manufacturing firms to locate within the community. One way of using the performance-on-objective-tasks approach to gauge the community's attitudes toward industrialization is as follows: A representative sample of residents is asked to read carefully (or even memorize) an essay containing numerous facts and figures and presenting a balanced view of the pros and cons of industrializing rural communities. After a period of time the respondents are quizzed on the essay's content. The specific parts of the essay they remember and how well they remember them will offer clues about the community's attitudes concerning industrialization. For instance, sound memory of a disproportionately large amount of unfavorable information about industrialization will signal a negative attitude toward increased industrialization.

Methods we discussed under structured, disguised questionnaires in Chapter 6 are also illustrations of the performance-on-objective-tasks approach. As implied in Chapter 6, a major drawback of this approach is the difficulty in constructing appropriate objective tasks and meaningfully interpreting performance on those tasks.

Monitoring physiological responses

The approach of monitoring physiological responses is based on the premise that a person's emotional reactions to a stimulus will be accompanied by corresponding involuntary physiological changes. For example, a feeling of fear or anxiety can induce physiological reactions such as shivering, perspiration, and increased heartbeat. Mechanical and electronic gadgets like the galvanic skin response (GSR) meter (to measure changes in the electrical resistance of the skin caused by changes in the amount of perspiration) and pupillometer (to measure the extent of pupil dilation in response to a visual stimulus) are available to measure physiological reactions from which internal emotions can be inferred. Other illustrations involving the use of physiological measurements include eye-tracking equipment and response latency measures (e.g., VOPAN) that we discussed under mechanical-observation techniques in Chapter 6.

Physiological measurements, however, have a serious drawback, because they merely measure *emotional arousal* rather than *attitudes*. They cannot, by themselves, reveal whether the source of the arousal is a positive or a negative emotion. For instance, a respondent who is annoyed by a test advertisement and one who is favorably impressed by it may both be equally *interested* in it and hence display identical pupil dilations as measured by a pupillometer. Consequently, physiological responses may serve as no more than measures of the attention-getting power or excitement-generating potential of marketing stimuli such as product advertisements and packages.

One marketing research firm specializing in physiological measurements based on eye-tracking technology is Perception Research Services, Inc. The following excerpt from a brochure describing the firm's services emphasizes the inappropriateness of inferring attitudes solely on the basis of physiological measures:

> Eye tracking is an addition to, not a substitute for, the data provided by traditional question and answer procedures. Eye tracking provides an indication of two stages in the communications process:
>
> - Attention
> - Involvement
>
> To examine the remaining dimensions, it is necessary to uncover opinions, attitudes, and inclinations which reflect if the material generates a favorable impression of the brand and encourages trial and/or usage.[14]

[14] "Multidimensional Communications Research," a brochure prepared by Perception Research Services, Inc., 560 Sylvan Avenue, Englewood Cliffs, N.J. 07632, p. 1.

SELF-REPORT MEASUREMENTS OF ATTITUDES

As mentioned earlier, attitudes can only be inferred and cannot be directly observed or measured. Nevertheless, self-report measures are somewhat more straightforward than the other four categories of methods. They involve asking respondents relatively direct questions concerning attitudes toward whatever is of interest to the researcher. The questions are typically in the form of rating scales on which respondents check off appropriate positions that best reflect their feelings.

Rating scales can take on a variety of physical forms. To illustrate, suppose the management of Safeway stores in a town wants to measure overall consumer attitudes toward Safeway. Exhibit 11.2 presents a number of alternative rating scales that Safeway's management can use. Although the questions in the table do not include all possible rating scale formats, they demonstrate the wide variety of ways in which ratings indicative of consumer attitudes can be obtained.

Differences among the eight alternative formats presented in Exhibit 11.2 illustrate several key dimensions on which rating scales and the nature of the data they yield can vary: graphic versus itemized formats; comparative versus noncomparative assessments; forced versus nonforced response choices; balanced versus unbalanced response choices; labeled versus unlabeled response choices; number of scale positions; and measurement level of data obtained. We will now briefly discuss each of these dimensions.

Graphic versus itemized formats

A *graphic rating scale* presents a continuum, in the form of a straight line, along which a theoretically infinite number of ratings are possible. The implicit rationale for using a graphic rating scale is that it enables one to detect fine shades of differences in attitudes. A true, or pure, graphic rating scale resembles question 1 in Exhibit 11.2. To quantify responses to question 1, one measures the physical distance between the left extreme position and the response position on the line; the greater the distance, the more favorable is the attitude toward Safeway. Even less refined rating scales, however, are typically labeled "graphic" rating scales as long as they contain a straight line signifying an underlying continuum (e.g., question 2 in Exhibit 11.2).[15]

A potential difficulty in using a graphic rating scale is that coding and analysis will require a substantial amount of time since one has to first measure

[15] For a discussion of other variations and properties of graphic rating scales, see, for example, Chem L. Narayana, "Graphic Positioning Scale: An Economical Instrument for Surveys," *Journal of Marketing Research,* 14 (February 1977), pp. 118–122.

Exhibit 11.2

Different types of rating scales

1. Indicate your overall opinion about Safeway by placing a √ mark at an appropriate position on the line below:

Very bad	Very good

2. Indicate your overall opinion about Safeway by placing a √ mark in the category that best summarizes your feelings.

Very bad																			Very good
1	2	3	4	5	6	7	8	9	10	11	12	13	14	15	16	17	18	19	20

3. Indicate your overall opinion about Safeway by checking one of the following categories:

Very bad		Bad		Neither bad nor good		Good		Very good
[ ]	[ ]	[ ]	[ ]	[ ]	[ ]	[ ]	[ ]	[ ]
1	2	3	4	5	6	7	8	9

4. Which of the following best describes your overall opinion of Safeway?

Terrible	Poor	Fair	Good	Very good	Excellent
[ ]	[ ]	[ ]	[ ]	[ ]	[ ]

5. What is your overall rating of Safeway in comparison with other supermarkets in your area?

Much worse	Worse	About the same	Better	Much better
[ ]	[ ]	[ ]	[ ]	[ ]

6. Rank the following by placing a 1 beside the store you think is best overall, a 2 beside the store you think is second best, and so on:

Kroger ______
Piggly Wiggly ______
Safeway ______
Tom Thumb ______
Winn-Dixie ______

7. In each of the following pairs, which store do you think is better? (Please check one store within each pair.)

______ Kroger or ______ Safeway
______ Safeway or ______ Piggly Wiggly
______ Tom Thumb or ______ Safeway
______ Safeway or ______ Winn-Dixie

8. Allocate a total of 100 points among the following stores, depending on how favorable you feel toward each; the more highly you think of each store, the more points you should allocate to it. (Please check that the allocated points add to 100.)

Kroger ______ points
Piggly Wiggly ______ points
Safeway ______ points
Tom Thumb ______ points
Winn-Dixie ______ points

100

physical distances on the scale for each respondent. An even more serious drawback is that respondents may be incapable of even mentally perceiving fine shades of differences in attitudes, let alone accurately translating their perceptions into measurable physical distances. In other words, while graphic rating scales are capable of facilitating precise attitude measurements *in theory,* whether they can be meaningfully used *in practice* is arguable. Consequently, graphic rating scales (at least the pure variety) are not widely used in marketing research surveys.

Itemized rating scales have a set of distinct response categories; any suggestion of an attitude continuum underlying the categories is implicit. They essentially take the form of the multiple-category questions discussed in Chapter 10. Typical itemized rating scale formats are illustrated by questions 3, 4, and 5 in Exhibit 11.2. While less refined than a graphic rating scale, an itemized rating scale should be easier to respond to—and more meaningful from the respondent's perspective. Also, coding and analysis of the raw data should be somewhat less laborious. As you may expect, itemized rating scales are much more widely used than the graphic type.

Comparative versus noncomparative assessments

Contrast the set of the first four questions in Exhibit 11.2 with the set of the last four. A key difference between the two sets is that questions in the latter set *explicitly* ask respondents to compare Safeway with other stores. While the first four questions seek absolute or noncomparative ratings, the last four seek relative or comparative ratings. Which type of rating scale is better? This question has no clear-cut answer other than "It depends."

A *comparative rating scale* provides all respondents with a common frame of reference. In contrast, a *noncomparative rating scale* implicitly permits respondents to use any, or even no, frame of reference. A comparative rating scale, by virtue of its common frame of reference, allows the researcher to be confident that all respondents are answering the same question (recall our discussion of questions with implicit assumptions in Chapter 10). However, in the context of measuring attitudes, a standard frame of reference imposed by the researcher may not necessarily be meaningful to all respondents (e.g., some respondents may have had no exposure to or experience with the stated comparison norm). Under such circumstances the validity of the comparative ratings may be questionable.

The choice between the comparative and noncomparative formats must, therefore, be situation-specific. Depending on the nature of potential respondents and their realms of experience with the attitude objects about which ratings are desired, the researcher must decide which format is likely to be most appropriate.

Forced versus nonforced response choices

A *forced-choice scale* does not give respondents the option of expressing a neutral, or middle-ground, attitude. A *nonforced-choice scale* does give respondents the option of expressing a neutral attitude. Questions 3 and 5 in Exhibit 11.2 provide a neutral-attitude option (question 1, which is a pure graphic rating scale, also does so implicitly). In general, an itemized rating scale with an odd number of response categories will have a neutral position, represented by the category falling exactly in the middle (one possible exception is a scale with unbalanced response choices, which is discussed later). By the same token, a scale with an even number of categories will typically force respondents to take a definite position on either the positive or the negative side of the scale (e.g., questions 2, 4, and 7 in Exhibit 11.2).

The issue of whether scales with forced response choices are better than those with nonforced response choices (or vice versa) has no unambiguous answer. Intuitively, a prudent choice is to include a neutral position (i.e., have an odd number of response choices) to accommodate respondents with no definite attitudes toward the subject matter.[16] In the author's experience scales with an odd number of categories appear to be more widely used than those with an even number of categories. But provision of a neutral position may tempt certain respondents, especially those who for some reason are reluctant to reveal their true positions, to select it as a sort of fake response. Therefore scales with an even number of categories deserve serious consideration when the topic to be studied is such that few respondents are likely to have a strictly neutral attitude toward it. Just as in comparative versus noncomparative rating scales, the choice between a forced or nonforced format must be made after carefully considering the characteristics unique to the situation.

Balanced versus unbalanced response choices

The balanced-versus-unbalanced dimension is relevant in constructing itemized rating scales and relates to our discussion of one-sided questions in Chapter 10. A *balanced scale* is one that has an equal number of positive/favorable and negative/unfavorable response choices (e.g., questions 3 and 5 in Exhibit 11.2). Consistent with what was recommended in Chapter 10, itemized rating scales, in general, should be balanced in order to reduce response biases.

One exception to this recommendation is a situation when the true attitudes

[16] In fact, some researchers argue that even provision of an odd number of categories, with a neutral category in the middle, may not guarantee that a scale does not force respondents; they further suggest that a truly nonforced-choice scale should have a separate "not applicable" or "no opinion" category. See, for example, G. David Hughes, "Some Confounding Effects of Forced-Choice Scales," *Journal of Marketing Research*, 6 (May 1969), pp. 223–226.

When should an unbalanced scale be used?

of respondents are likely to be predominantly one-sided, either positive or negative. When this situation is anticipated, one should use an *unbalanced scale,* with a larger number of response choices on the side of the scale where the overall attitude of the respondent sample is likely to fall. Using a balanced scale under these circumstances would lead to a phenomenon called *end piling,* wherein most responses fall into just a few categories at one end of the scale. A scale on which end piling occurs will not be very sensitive (sensitivity of scales is described later). Question 4 in Exhibit 11.2 illustrates an unbalanced rating scale.

Define

Labeled versus unlabeled response choices

Rating scales will usually have a pair of *anchor labels* that define their two extremes. For instance, the rating scales in questions 1 through 5 in Exhibit 11.2 all have anchor labels. However, notice the wide variations in these questions with respect to the labeling of intermediate scale categories: No intermediate category is labeled in questions 1 and 2; some intermediate categories are labeled in question 3; and all intermediate categories are labeled in questions 4 and 5. Furthermore, while the scale categories in questions 2 and 3 have numerical labels, the categories in the other questions do not. Thus a researcher has considerable latitude in deciding whether to include one or more intermediate labels and whether those labels should be in the form of words, numbers, or both.

No rules exist for determining the number and the types of labels to include in a scale. Intuitively, however, when generating a simple and appropriate label for an intermediate category is difficult, leaving the category unlabeled is better than making up an ill-fitting label for it. To illustrate, consider questions 2 and 3 in Exhibit 11.2. To come up with meaningful verbal labels for the unlabeled categories in these two questions is likely to be very difficult, if not impossible; hence the best approach is not to have verbal labels for those categories. Moreover, when the researcher plans to treat the response categories as being interval-scaled (as is presumably the case in questions 2 and 3), the use of inappropriate verbal labels can cast doubt on the assumption of interval data. According to one study that examined the impact of category labels, even labels such as "reasonably poor" and "reasonably good," or "pleasant" and "unpleasant," were not perceived by respondents to be equidistant from the middle "neutral" position.[17] Another study found that the types of labels used as well as their locations had an impact on responses.[18] Thus verbal labels should be used cautiously and sparingly when the quantified ratings are to have interval-scale properties.

[17] Myers and Warner, "Semantic Properties," pp. 409–412.

[18] Albert R. Wildt and Michael B. Mazis, "Determinants of Scale Response: Label versus Position," *Journal of Marketing Research,* 15 (May 1978), pp. 261–267.

Numerical labels, while easier to generate than verbal labels, must also be used and interpreted cautiously. Placing numbers on a rating scale can be helpful in suggesting to respondents the notion of equal distances between adjacent response categories. Herein lies a hidden danger, however, when the scale categories already have verbal labels that suggest no more than an ordinal scale. Sequentially numbering the categories on such a scale can result in the researcher's erroneously interpreting as interval data what is really only ordinal data.

An example is question 4 in Exhibit 11.2. The six scale categories in this question already have verbal labels. Suppose we also number the categories 1 through 6, with terrible = 1 and excellent = 6. Can we now treat the coded responses as having interval-scale properties? We cannot although it is tempting to do so. But whether the psychological distance between "excellent" and "very good" is equal to that between "very good" and "good," or between "good" and "fair," is moot. In the author's judgment, given the meanings of the verbal labels in question 4, the resulting data will have no more than ordinal-scale properties. An interval-scale assumption may be tenable if the scale has just the anchor labels "terrible" and "excellent" (with no intermediate verbal labels), and if the categories are numbered 1 through 6.

One final point concerning category labels: Although our discussion has focused on verbal and numerical labels, other types of labels (e.g., picture labels) are also used to help respondents understand the categories and distinguish between them. Picture labels can be especially useful in surveying samples of children or illiterates, for instance. Exhibit 11.3 gives examples of scales with picture labels used by one marketing research firm to measure children's reactions to commercials.

Number of scale positions

The number of points or categories to include in a rating scale is another area with no rigid rules. However, rating scales used in most surveys typically have between five and nine categories. Logically, more precise measurements should result as the number of scale positions increase.[19] Of course, a scale with a large number of positions will not be meaningful if respondents are unable to make fine mental distinctions with respect to whatever is being measured. Therefore the nature of the variable as well as the capabilities of potential respondents must be taken into account when one is deciding on the number of scale positions to use.

Another factor to be considered is whether the variable will be measured by

[19] This intuition is supported by empirical studies examining the impact of the number of scale positions on the nature of the information obtained; see, for example, Warren S. Martin, "Effects of Scaling on the Correlation Coefficient: Additional Considerations," *Journal of Marketing Research,* 15 (May 1978), pp. 304–308.

Exhibit 11.3

Rating scales with picture labels

How much did you like what you just saw?
(Cross out one answer.)

Source: Adapted from "The Child Research Services," a brochure prepared by McCollum/Spielman Associates, Inc., 18 East 48th Street, New York, N.Y. 10017. Used by permission.

a single-item scale represented by just one question (such as those in Exhibit 11.2) or by summing response values obtained from a number of questions, that is, by using a multiple-item scale (we will discuss multiple-item scales in a subsequent section). The literature suggests that for accurate measurements a larger number of scale positions are needed when a single-item scale is used than when a multiple-item scale is used.[20]

Measurement level of data obtained

Measurement level refers to how powerful the data are—whether they are nominal, ordinal, interval, or ratio. The type of question and the type of rating scale used have a major bearing on the measurement level of the data generated. This point is illustrated by the questions and rating scales in Exhibit 11.2. Consider question 8, asking respondents to allocate 100 points among the five stores. The scale implied in this question is commonly known as a *constant-sum*

[20] A discussion of this issue is in Jum C. Nunnally, *Psychometric Theory* (New York: McGraw-Hill, 1967), Chap. 14.

scale, and it has a natural starting point (namely, zero). In question 8 the lowest possible rating for each store is zero, which is nonarbitrary and remains the same across all respondents. Constant-sum scales, by virtue of their fixed starting point, have ratio-scale properties. Thus a respondent's opinion of Safeway can be said to be twice as favorable as his or her opinion of Kroger if he or she allocates, say, 50 points to Safeway and 25 points to Kroger. The graphic rating scale in question 1 also has ratio-scale properties, since responses on it are quantified as physical distances (e.g., inches), which necessarily have a fixed zero point.

Now examine question 7, asking respondents to select one store from each of several pairs of stores. What measurement level is achieved in this case? For each pair of stores a respondent can be classified as either one who "prefers Safeway" or one who "does not prefer Safeway." At first glance this classification resembles a nominal scale. However, the two categories are actually ordinal; the "prefers Safeway" category connotes a more favorable attitude toward Safeway than the "does not prefer Safeway" category.

Items seeking comparative evaluations of two objects at a time are sometimes called *paired-comparison rating scales.* These scales are frequently used in marketing research, especially in studies involving consumer evaluations of physical products or product concepts.[21] While a respondent's task in comparing two objects at a time is seemingly simple, using paired-comparison rating scales to assess attitudes toward each of several objects has a serious drawback: Even when the number of objects to be evaluated is modest, a disproportionately large number of pairs have to be compared. For example, assessment of 6 objects requires 15 paired comparisons. And the number of paired comparisons rises sharply even with a slight increase in the number of objects. [When the number of objects to be evaluated is n, the number of possible paired comparisons is given by $n(n - 1)/2$.] Therefore the paired-comparison approach can quickly become laborious and time-consuming when the number of objects to be rated increases.

Let us now examine the measurement levels implied by the remaining questions (2 through 6) in Exhibit 11.2. Data to be generated by question 6 will clearly be ordinal since the numerical responses in this case, by definition, are no more than ranks. The measurement levels implied by questions 2 through 5 are not quite as clear-cut. They fall in the gray area between ordinal and interval scales—an area still subject to considerable debate, as pointed out earlier in this chapter. The safest approach is to treat them all as ordinal, although in practice they are almost always assumed to have interval properties.

---

[21] Paired-comparison ratings are also used as input for an analysis technique called multidimensional scaling. This technique is capable of inferring metric distances between objects from an analysis of ordinal ratings. It is discussed briefly in Chapter 19. Further details of it are available in Paul E. Green, "Marketing Applications of MDS: Assessment and Outlook," *Journal of Marketing,* 39 (January 1975), pp. 24–31; Paul E. Green and M. G. Greenberg, "Ordinal Methods in Multidimensional Scaling and Data Analysis," in *Handbook of Marketing Research,* ed. Robert Ferber (New York: McGraw-Hill, 1974), pp. 3.44–3.61.

Researchers' preference for interval data over ordinal data—or, more generally, metric over nonmetric data—stems from the possibility of conducting richer, more sophisticated analyses with interval data. Unfortunately, attitude scales capable of generating truly metric data are hard to construct and are difficult for respondents to comprehend and respond to meaningfully. Thus researchers often face a dilemma that is succinctly described by Garner and Creelman:

> The more powerful scale has greater utility once it has been established, but the scaler has much less freedom in establishing the scale values of the more powerful scale in the first place. In effect, the scaler is always in a certain amount of conflict. He wants to establish as powerful a scale as possible, but he is much less sure that he has done so correctly than if he had attempted to establish a weaker scale. Often the scale produced is a compromise between a scale with maximum power and a scale with minimum restriction on the scaler.[22]

In summary, the foregoing discussion, while describing the number of ways rating scale formats can vary, does not recommend any particular format as being the most desirable. Indeed, there is no such thing as *the* ideal scale format. On the basis of a controlled study examining the appropriateness of several different rating scales, one researcher concluded: "No one scale is best for all products or all types of studies."[23] Thus the choice of a rating scale should be made after one carefully considers the characteristics and requirements unique to the research setting—the nature of the variable to be measured, the extent to which potential respondents are capable of making refined mental judgments concerning the variable, and the types of analyses the researcher intends to perform on the data to be collected.

SINGLE-ITEM VERSUS MULTIPLE-ITEM SCALES

A *single-item scale,* as its name implies, attempts to measure feelings through just one rating scale. For example, the rating scales in questions 1 through 5 in Exhibit 11.2 are single-item scales. In contrast, a *multiple-item scale* is one that contains a number of statements pertaining to the attitude object, each with a rating scale attached to it; the *combined rating,* usually obtained by summing the ratings on the individual items, is treated as a measure of attitude toward the object.

A single-item scale, while capable of offering clues about respondents' overall feelings toward an object, is a rather crude measure. To understand why, we

[22] W. R. Garner and C. D. Creelman, "Problems and Methods of Psychological Scaling," in *Attitude Measurement,* ed. Gene F. Summers (Chicago: Rand McNally, 1970), p. 47.
[23] Jack Abrams, "An Evaluation of Alternative Rating Devices for Consumer Research," *Journal of Marketing Research,* 3 (May 1966), p. 191.

must consider three criteria on which the adequacy of attitude scales should be judged: validity, reliability, and sensitivity. We will now define and discuss each criterion as it relates to attitude scales.

Validity

The *validity* of a scale is the extent to which it is a true reflection of the underlying variable it is attempting to measure. Alternatively, it is the extent to which the scale fully captures all aspects of the construct to be measured. Single-item attitude scales are typically deficient on this criterion because, as we have already seen, attitudes are multifaceted; a number of different factors concerning an object or issue can contribute to how a person feels about it. For instance, one's attitude toward Safeway is likely to be shaped by what one knows and feels about Safeway's appearance, physical layout, product assortment, employees, and other such factors. When a researcher attempts to ascertain respondents' attitudes solely through a single-item rating scale, there is invariably doubt about whether the scale is trustworthy. Therefore a carefully designed multiple-item scale containing numerous items, each intended to tap the respondent's position on a key facet of the attitude object, is likely to be a more valid measure.

Assessing the validity of attitude scales is a complex task, and a comprehensive discussion of it is beyond the scope of this textbook.[24] Nevertheless, you should be aware that it includes examining several different types of validity, as outlined next.

Content validity. Also known as *face validity,* the criterion of *content validity* represents the extent to which the content of a measurement scale seems to tap all relevant facets of an issue that can influence respondents' attitudes. To illustrate, consider a scale intended for measuring the job satisfaction of industrial salespeople that is made up of multiple items dealing with pay, promotional opportunities, and the quality of supervision. This scale lacks content validity because it lacks items dealing with certain key aspects of a salesperson's job, such as traveling and visiting with customers. Content validity of an attitude scale is a sort of global criterion, but it can only be assessed through a researcher's subjective judgment.

Construct validity. *Construct validity* relates to the question "What is the nature of the underlying variable or construct measured by the scale?" Construct validity of an attitude measure can be assessed quantitatively by computing its correlations with measures of other constructs that one would expect to be

[24] Several excellent books on research methods provide comprehensive discussions of validity assessment. See, for example, Claire Selltiz, Lawrence L. Wrightsman, and Stuart W. Cook, *Research Methods in Social Relations* (New York: Holt, Rinehart and Winston, 1976); and Nunnally, *Psychometric Theory.* See also Donald T. Campbell and Donald W. Fiske, "Convergent and Discriminant Validation by the Multitrait-Multimethod Matrix," *Psychological Bulletin,* 56 (1959), pp. 81–105.

strongly associated with the attitude, and measures of constructs that one would *not* expect to be closely tied to the attitude. Strong correlations in the former case are indicative of what is commonly labeled *convergent validity,* and weak correlations in the latter case are indicative of *discriminant validity.* For a scale to have high construct validity, it must possess both convergent and discriminant validity. A scale purporting to measure attitudes toward abortion can be said to have high construct validity if, for instance, it has relatively strong correlations with measures of attitudes toward respect for life in general (reflecting high convergent validity) and relatively weak correlations with attitudes toward civil rights (reflecting high discriminant validity).

Predictive validity. As its name implies, *predictive validity* deals with the question "How well does the attitude measure provided by the scale predict some other variable or characteristic it is supposed to influence?" For example, a scale measuring attitudes toward Safeway will have high predictive validity if respondents with relatively high scores on it are found to patronize Safeway more frequently than respondents with relatively low scores on it.

Reliability

The *reliability* of an attitude scale refers to how consistent or stable the ratings generated by the scale are likely to be. While validity focuses on whether a scale truly measures the construct (and not something else), reliability focuses on whether the scale consistently measures "something" (whatever that "something" may be). Clearly, a good attitude scale must be both valid and reliable. Indeed, unless a scale is reasonably consistent, it cannot be viewed as a true, trustworthy measure of whatever it purports to measure. In this sense, reliability is a necessary, although not sufficient, condition for validity.

Scale reliability can be measured through several different criteria. Two popular criteria are test-retest reliability and split-half reliability.[25]

Test-retest reliability. *Test-retest reliability* measures the stability of ratings over time and involves administering the scale to the same group of respondents at two different times. The scale can be considered to have high test-retest reliability if the ratings generated through the two measurements correlate strongly and hence are consistent. The time interval between the two measurements is crucial for test-retest reliability to be a meaningful indicator of a scale's stability. The interval must be long enough so that respondents' ratings during the second measurement are not influenced by their remembering what ratings they gave on the first measurement. But the interval must not be so long that the

[25] Selltiz, Wrightsman, and Cook, *Research Methods in Social Relations,* and Nunnally, *Psychometric Theory,* give excellent, detailed discussions of reliability assessment.

underlying attitudes change between measurements. Unfortunately, no clear guideline exists for determining an optimum time interval that is sufficiently long yet not too long. A rule of thumb, however, is to allow an interval of about two to four weeks between measurements; attitudes, which are often viewed as being deep-rooted, are unlikely to change during such a short interval.

Split-half reliability. *Split-half reliability* measures the degree of consistency across items within a scale and can only be assessed for multiple-item scales. It involves splitting the scale items randomly into two sets, with an equal number of items in each set, and examining the correlation between respondents' total scores derived from the two sets of items.

For example, consider a 20-item scale designed to measure customer attitudes toward electronic-banking services. Suppose each item in this scale has five response categories, numbered 1 through 5. After this scale has been administered to a sample of customers, the 20 scale items can be randomly divided into two sets of 10 items. For each respondent the total score in each set will be between 10 (i.e., 10 scale items times the lowest scale value of 1) and 50 (i.e., 10 scale items times the highest scale value of 5). If the 20 scale items are measuring the same underlying construct—namely, customer attitude toward electronic-banking services—a respondent whose total score for the first set of items is, for instance, 38 should have a total score close to 38 for the second set also. Likewise, comparison of the total score for the two sets across respondents should show a consistent pattern of association; the stronger the association, the higher is the split-half reliability of the scale.[26]

Note that the two illustrative methods of assessing a scale's reliability actually focus on two separate dimensions of reliability. Test-retest reliability is a measure of *stability* of the scale items (i.e., the degree to which scores obtained through the scale remain the same *from measurement to measurement over time*), while split-half reliability is a measure of their *equivalency* or *internal consistency* (i.e., the degree to which scores obtained through randomly split halves of the scale correlate with each other *within the same measurement*). Both dimensions are important for a scale's overall reliability.

Ratings on a single-item scale are more susceptible to erratic or random fluctuations (thereby lowering reliability) than summated ratings obtained from a multiple-item scale. Summing the ratings across a number of items has the effect of neutralizing random fluctuations; positive errors in a respondent's

[26] A more rigorous measure of internal consistency among scale items is called Cronbach's alpha, or coefficient alpha; for details about the procedure involved in computing this measure of reliability, see L. J. Cronbach, "Coefficient Alpha and the Internal Structure of Tests," *Psychometrika,* 16 (1951), pp. 297–334. Also see the review article on various aspects of reliability by J. Paul Peter, "Reliability: A Review of Psychometric Basics and Recent Marketing Practices," *Journal of Marketing Research,* 16 (February 1979), pp. 6–17.

ratings on certain items may be offset by negative errors in his or her ratings on other items.[27] Therefore multiple-item scales are generally more reliable than single-item scales.

Sensitivity

The *sensitivity* of an attitude scale is closely tied to its reliability, and focuses specifically on its ability to detect subtle differences in the attitudes being measured. A highly sensitive attitude scale should be able to discriminate between respondents who differ even slightly in terms of their attitudes toward something. Alternatively, it should be capable of uncovering minute changes in the same respondent's attitude over time.

This description of sensitivity implies that reliability is a prerequisite for it. When an attitude scale is unreliable, one cannot be sure whether differences in attitude scores reflect real differences in attitudes or merely random fluctuations. Therefore for a scale to be sensitive, it must also be reliable.

Another requirement for a sensitive scale is that it should have a sufficient range of numbers to facilitate detection of fine variations in attitudes (we touched on this point earlier in the chapter). While a single-item scale can theoretically have a large number of rating positions (e.g., questions 1 and 2 in Exhibit 11.2), respondents may not be capable of making such fine judgments. In this regard multiple-item scales have a definite advantage. Even when individual items only have a limited number of response categories, the total scores obtained by summing responses across all items will span a wide range. For example, suppose a multiple-item attitude scale consists of 10 items, each with seven response categories, numbered 1 through 7. Respondents' *total* scores on this 10-item scale can range from 10 to 70. From these total scores respondents can be classified into categories reflecting more subtle variations in attitude than would be reflected if only a single-item, seven-point scale is used.

Our discussion has shown why a multiple-item scale is far superior to a single-item scale when it comes to measuring attitudes. The former is likely to be more valid, reliable, and sensitive than the latter. The next section discusses three types of multiple-item scales that are popular in marketing research practice.

COMMONLY USED MULTIPLE-ITEM SCALES

Developing a multiple-item scale capable of providing valid, reliable, and sensitive measures of attitudes toward something is no simple task. Pioneering

[27] Gilbert A. Churchill, Jr., "A Paradigm for Developing Better Measures of Marketing Constructs," *Journal of Marketing Research*, 16 (February 1979), pp. 64–73.

work in establishing a rigorous procedure for constructing multiple-item attitude scales was done by L. L. Thurstone, and the general format of the resulting scale has been named after him—the Thurstone equal-appearing intervals scale, or simply the Thurstone scale, as it is often called. The procedure involved in developing a Thurstone scale is quite complex and will not be discussed here.[28] Furthermore, some questions have been raised about interpreting the data generated through a Thurstone scale, and respondents have been known to experience difficulty in meaningfully expressing their views on such a scale.[29] Perhaps as a result of these limitations, the Thurstone scale is only very rarely used these days.[30] Nevertheless, we must point out that several of the ideas involved in constructing and using the more popular attitude scales—three of which will be discussed in this section—have their roots in the original Thurstone-scaling procedure.

Likert scale

Based on a format originally developed by Rensis Likert,[31] the ***Likert scale*** consists of a series of evaluative statements (or items) concerning an attitude object. Each statement has a five-point agree-disagree scale. The number of statements included in the scale may vary from study to study, depending on how many relevant characteristics the attitude object has. However, a typical Likert scale has about twenty to thirty statements.

Exhibit 11.4 presents six illustrative statements from a Likert scale that a supermarket like Safeway can use to measure customer attitudes toward itself and its competitors. Two points concerning the statements in Exhibit 11.4 are worthy of special note. First, the response categories have verbal labels but no numerical labels; this format is the usual format in which Likert scale statements are presented to respondents. After the scale is administered, however, numbers are assigned to the responses in order to generate a quantified measure of attitudes. The numbers 1 through 5 are normally employed for this purpose, although other sets of numbers (e.g., +2, +1, 0, −1, −2) can also be used.

Second, while statements 1, 3, and 4 are favorable toward the store, the others are unfavorable—another typical feature of statements making up a Likert scale. A good Likert scale must have a balanced set of statements, containing approximately the same number of favorable and unfavorable statements. Such

---

[28] The method is discussed in detail in L. L. Thurstone and E. J. Chave, *The Measurement of Attitude* (Chicago: University of Chicago Press, 1929).

[29] G. David Hughes, "Selecting Scales to Measure Attitude Change," *Journal of Marketing Research,* (February 1967), pp. 85–87.

[30] According to one survey of marketing research departments in business firms, only about 7% reported using Thurstone scales. See Barnett A. Greenberg, Jac L. Goldstucker, and Danny N. Bellenger, "What Techniques Are Used by Marketing Researchers in Business?" *Journal of Marketing,* 41 (April 1977), pp. 62–68.

[31] Rensis Likert, "A Technique for the Measurement of Attitudes," in *Attitude Measurement,* ed. Gene F. Summers (Chicago: Rand McNally, 1970), pp. 149–158.

Exhibit 11.4
Likert scale items

	Strongly disagree	Disagree	Neither agree nor disagree	Agree	Strongly agree
1. Clerks at the store's checkouts are friendly	____	____	____	____	____
2. Lines at the store's checkouts move slowly	____	____	____	____	____
3. Prices in the store are reasonable	____	____	____	____	____
4. The store has a wide variety of products to choose from	____	____	____	____	____
5. The store's operating hours are inconvenient	____	____	____	____	____
6. The store has a rather confusing layout	____	____	____	____	____

a mix of statements will reduce the chances of acquiescence bias (discussed in Chapter 10), which can occur if all statements are in the same direction.

A respondent's overall attitude is measured by summing his or her numerical ratings on the statements making up the scale. However, since some statements will be favorable and others unfavorable, there is one important task to be performed before summing the ratings; namely, numbers must be assigned to the scale categories in such a way that a high (or low) numerical rating on each statement always represents the *same* attitude direction. In other words, the "strongly agree" category attached to favorable statements and the "strongly disagree" category attached to unfavorable statements must both be assigned the same number (e.g., the number 5, if a 1-through-5 numbering scheme is used).

The overall usefulness (validity, reliability, and sensitivity) of a Likert scale depends on how carefully the statements making up the final scale are chosen. The statements must be sufficiently varied to capture all relevant aspects of the attitude object. In addition, they must be unambiguous so as to minimize erratic fluctuations in the responses. Last, but by no means least, each statement must be sensitive enough to discriminate between respondents with differing attitudes. For instance, consider the following statement: "Safeway is a very large supermarket chain in the United States." Customers with favorable attitudes toward Safeway, as well as those with unfavorable attitudes, are bound to agree strongly with this statement. Consequently, such statements must be eliminated from the final scale, since they will contribute little toward the measurement of true attitudes. Indeed, such statements will detract from the overall sensitivity of the scale.

As implied by the foregoing discussion, designing a good Likert scale involves first generating a large pool of statements relevant to the measurement of an attitude and then eliminating from the pool statements that are vague and/or nondiscriminating.[32] While a comprehensive discussion of this process is beyond our scope, let us look at an example to gain an intuitive understanding of it.

Suppose Safeway wants to develop a 20-item scale to measure customer attitudes toward different supermarkets. The first step is to develop a large number of items, say 100, similar to the six statements shown in Exhibit 11.4. There are no rules for generating the initial pool of items, except that they should reflect the entire range of factors likely to influence customer attitudes. Managerial judgment and exploratory research, such as informal discussions with supermarket employees and customer focus groups, can be helpful in generating a broad range of items. A procedure similar to the one outlined next can be used in reducing the initial 100-item pool to a final 20-item instrument.

A questionnaire containing the initial 100 items, each with five possible response categories ranging from "strongly agree" to "strongly disagree," is administered to a representative sample of customers. These customers are asked to rate Safeway (or any other supermarket) on each statement by checking one of the five response categories. The categories are then numbered 1 through 5, with higher numbers reflecting more favorable perceptions. Since there are 100 items, a respondent's total score (summed across all items) can range from 100 to 500. Further, since the initial item pool was designed to reflect various aspects relevant to customer attitudes, the total score can be viewed as a rough indicator of the respondent's overall attitude—the higher the score, the more favorable is the attitude. This total score plays a crucial role in condensing the initial pool of items into an appropriate concise scale.

To illustrate, consider the following total scores of two respondents, A and B, as well as their scores on two individual items, i and j:

Respondent	Score on Item i	Score on Item j	Total Score
A	3	4	428
B	3	1	256

[32] General procedures for generating an initial item pool and then narrowing it are discussed by Churchill, "A Paradigm for Developing Better Measures." For a specific illustration of how a Likert scale is developed, see William J. Lundstrom and Lawrence M. Lamont, "The Development of a Scale to Measure Consumer Discontent," *Journal of Marketing Research,* 8 (November 1976), pp. 373–381.

On the basis of the total scores, A has a more favorable attitude than B. By looking at their scores on items *i* and *j*, we see that item *i* is a poor discriminator and item *j* is a good discriminator between the two respondents. Item *j* is thus likely to be a better indicator of attitudes and hence more useful in a multiple-item scale. If we extend this insight across all statements and respondents, we see that items on which respondents' scores correlate strongly with the respondents' total scores are better candidates for inclusion in the final scale than other items. Therefore of the 100 initial items, the 20 items with the highest correlations between individual scores and total scores are chosen to form the final scale.

This scale development process can be quite laborious if it is to be done in an organized fashion. Nevertheless, such a systematic approach is essential for constructing a valid, reliable, and sensitive Likert scale.

The final scale can be used to measure customer attitude toward different supermarkets, as follows: A questionnaire containing the 20-item scale is administered to an appropriate sample of respondents, and their total scores are computed. Since there are 20 items, each with a five-point scale, the total scores will range from 20 to 100; the higher the respondents' scores, the more favorable are their attitudes. Also, the average total scores (across all respondents) for the various supermarkets can be compared to get a feeling for customers' relative attitudes toward them. For instance, if supermarkets XYZ and ABC have average total scores of 40 and 80, respectively, we can infer that customer attitude toward ABC is more favorable than that toward XYZ. However, we *cannot* infer that customer attitude toward ABC is *twice* as favorable as that toward XYZ, because the scores on each scale item, and hence the total scores, have only interval-scale properties, at best. The 20-item scale can also be used to monitor customer attitudes toward different supermarkets over time by administering it to representative samples of customers at different times and examining the changes in average attitude scores for each supermarket.

Semantic-differential scale

The format for the semantic-differential scale originated from work done some three decades ago by Osgood, Suci, and Tannenbaum to investigate the perceived meanings of words and concepts.[33] The initial semantic-differential-scaling procedure has since been modifed by marketing researchers to measure consumer attitudes.[34] The *semantic-differential scale* is similar to the Likert scale in that it consists of a series of items to be rated by respondents. However, there are some key differences, as the six semantic-differential scale items in Exhibit 11.5 demonstrate.

---

[33] Details about this work are given in Charles E. Osgood, George J. Suci, and Percy H. Tannenbaum, *The Measurement of Meaning* (Urbana, Ill.: University of Illinois Press, 1957).
[34] See, for example, William A. Mindak, "Fitting the Semantic Differential to the Marketing Problem," *Journal of Marketing*, 25 (April 1961), pp. 29–33.

Exhibit 11.5

Semantic-differential scale items

1. Friendly checkout clerks	___:___:___:___:___:___:___	Unfriendly checkout clerks
2. Slow-moving checkout lines	___:___:___:___:___:___:___	Fast-moving checkout lines
3. Low prices	___:___:___:___:___:___:___	High prices
4. Wide product assortment	___:___:___:___:___:___:___	Narrow product assortment
5. Inconvenient store hours	___:___:___:___:___:___:___	Convenient store hours
6. Confusing store layout	___:___:___:___:___:___:___	Clear store layout

Exhibit 11.5 highlights three basic features of a typical semantic-differential scale:

1. It consists of a series of bipolar adjectival words or phrases (rather than complete statements, as in the case of a Likert scale) that pertain to the attitude object.
2. Each pair of opposite adjectives is separated by a seven-category scale, with neither numerical labels nor verbal labels other than the anchor labels.
3. While some individual scales have favorable descriptors on the right-hand side, the other scales are reversed, with favorable descriptors appearing on the left-hand side. The rationale for the reversals is similar to the rationale for having a mixture of favorable and unfavorable statements in a Likert scale.

On each item making up a semantic-differential scale, respondents are asked to check one of the seven categories that best describes their views about the attitude object along the continuum implied by the bipolar adjectives. Once responses are obtained on all items, an overall attitude score for each respondent can be computed through a procedure similar to the one used with Likert scales. The seven categories can be numerically coded, say 1 through 7 (making sure to reverse code items that are reversed), and overall attitude scores can be obtained by summing the coded responses on the individual items. The interpretation of these scores is similar to the interpretation of scores generated through a Likert scale.

A more common application of the semantic-differential scale, however, is to develop a *pictorial profile* of the attitude object(s) based on the mean ratings on the individual items (median ratings if each seven-category scale is assumed

Exhibit 11.6

Pictorial profiles based on semantic-differential ratings

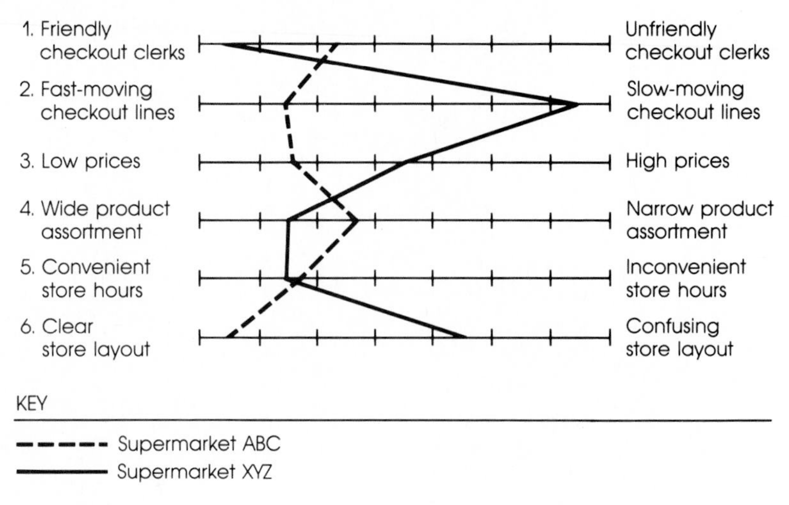

to have only ordinal properties; researchers typically assume the scale to have interval properties, however). Exhibit 11.6 presents hypothetical pictorial profiles for two supermarkets. To facilitate interpretation of the profiles, one usually places all the favorable descriptors on the same side of these diagrams.

According to Exhibit 11.6 customers apparently have a more favorable overall attitude toward supermarket ABC than toward supermarket XYZ. Notice that the overall profile for ABC is in general closer to the left end (i.e., more favorable end) of the scales. When we look at specific items, we see that ABC has a significant edge over XYZ with respect to speed of checkout lines and store layout; it is also perceived to be superior with respect to prices. Store XYZ is perceived to be better than ABC in terms of friendliness of checkout clerks, product assortment, and operating hours; however, ABC does not appear to be at a significant disadvantage along these dimensions.

The semantic-differential scale has considerable practical appeal because profiles like the ones in Exhibit 11.6 can pinpoint a particular firm's relative strengths and weaknesses as perceived by customers. The profiles can thus have useful, immediate managerial implications. Not surprisingly, the semantic differential is the most widely used attitude-scaling technique according to one recent survey.[35] Generating a useful and comprehensive set of adjectival pairs necessary for an effective semantic-differential scale is not always as easy as it may seem. The constraints and caveats mentioned in the context of developing effective Likert scales are relevant here as well.

---

[35] Greenberg, Goldstucker, and Bellenger, "What Techniques Are Used?"

Exhibit 11.7

Stapel scale items

	+5		+5		+5		+5		+5		+5
	+4		+4		+4		+4		+4		+4
	+3		+3		+3		+3		+3		+3
	+2		+2		+2		+2		+2		+2
Friendly checkout clerks	+1	Slow checkout lines	+1	Low prices	+1	Wide product assortment	+1	Inconvenient store hours	+1	Confusing store layout	+1
	−1		−1		−1		−1		−1		−1
	−2		−2		−2		−2		−2		−2
	−3		−3		−3		−3		−3		−3
	−4		−4		−4		−4		−4		−4
	−5		−5		−5		−5		−5		−5

Stapel scale

The *Stapel scale* is really a variation of the semantic-differential scale. The format of a typical Stapel scale is illustrated by the six items presented in Exhibit 11.7. Notice that the items in Exhibits 11.4, 11.5, and 11.7 correspond to the same set of supermarket traits. A comparison of these exhibits should reveal the key format differences between the Likert, semantic-differential, and Stapel scales.

The Stapel scale has four distinctive features:

1. Each item has only one word or phrase indicating the dimension it represents.
2. Each item has 10 response categories.
3. Each item is a forced-choice scale since it has an even number of categories.
4. The response categories have numerical labels but no verbal labels.

Typical instructions for responding to a Stapel scale, say one that pertains to Safeway, are as follows:

INSTRUCTIONS: In the following items, select a *plus* number for words that you think describe Safeway accurately. The more accurately you think the word describes Safeway, the larger the *plus* number you should choose. Select a *minus* number for words you think do not describe Safeway accurately. The less accurately you think a word describes Safeway, the larger the *minus* number you should choose. Therefore you can select any number from +5, for words you think are very accurate, to −5, for words you think are very inaccurate.[36]

[36] Adapted from Irving Crespi, "Use of Scaling Technique in Surveys," *Journal of Marketing,* 25 (July 1961), p. 71.

Data obtained through Stapel scales can be analyzed by using procedures similar to the ones we discussed under semantic-differential scales. Overall attitude scores can be computed for the respondents by summing their ratings on the individual items. Alternatively, pictorial profiles of the attitude objects can also be constructed from the mean (or median) respondent ratings on each item.

One apparent advantage of the Stapel scale is that one does not have to develop complete statements or come up with pairs of bipolar words or phrases—tasks that can get to be very tedious. Nevertheless, the Stapel scale is not as widely used as the other two types, perhaps because its format and instructions appear to be relatively more complex. However, this reason for the infrequent use of the Stapel scale is speculative. In fact, one controlled study found no significant differences between the Stapel and semantic-differential formats in terms of ease of administration and the quantified attitude estimates obtained.[37] According to another study, attitude measures generated by Likert, semantic-differential, and Stapel scales were all quite similar.[38] Therefore the final choice of a particular scale format should be based on practical considerations unique to a research setting.

A couple of final comments concerning the multiple-item scales discussed here are in order. First, the overall attitude scores generated through them are no more than interval-scaled. Therefore, while such scores can be used to compare the attitudes of different groups of individuals at a given time, or to track changes in the attitudes of the same group of respondents over time, computing and interpreting their ratios are inappropriate. Second, the three standard scale formats discussed do not exhaust all possibilities. Since each multiple-item scale is merely a collection of many single-item scales, one can create a large variety of multiple-item scale formats by varying the structure of the individual rating scales along one or more of the dimensions we discussed earlier in the "Self-Report Measures of Attitudes" section. Which format is best depends on the circumstances surrounding a research setting.

SUMMARY

The process of measurement in survey research involves quantifying responses by assigning appropriate numbers to them. However, numbers assigned to survey responses may not possess all the properties commonly attributed to the number system. How closely quantified responses resemble the number system depends on whether they are nominal-, ordinal-, interval-, or ratio-scaled. Nominal-scaled responses have virtually none of the properties of the number system;

[37] Del I. Hawkins, Gerald Albaum, and Roger Best, "Stapel Scale or Semantic Differential in Marketing Research?" *Journal of Marketing Research,* 11 (August 1974), pp. 318–322.
[38] Dennis Menezes and Norbert F. Elbert, "Alternative Semantic Scaling Formats for Measuring Store Image: An Evaluation," *Journal of Marketing Research,* 16 (February 1979), pp. 80–87.

ratio-scaled responses have all of them; and ordinal- and interval-scaled responses fall in between. Nominal- and ordinal-scaled responses are called nonmetric data because the concept of differences, or distances between numbers, is meaningless for such scales. Interval- and ratio-scaled responses, by virtue of the distance property they possess, are labeled metric data.

Virtually all variables encountered in marketing research surveys can be classified as attributes, behavior, beliefs, or attitudes. Of these four, beliefs and attitudes, whose measurement is the primary focus of this chapter, are relatively vague and defy precise definition or measurement. Debate still rages over whether they can be measured at the interval level or only at the ordinal level. Nevertheless, scales used to measure such variables are almost always assumed to have interval properties.

Attitudes have been defined in a number of different ways. But the various definitions seem to agree that attitudes relate to certain inner dispositions of people and that they are multifaceted. These general traits of attitudes have two important implications for their measurement. First, attitudes can only be inferred from indirect measurements. Second, to be effective, an attitude measurement procedure must attempt to tap the various facets capable of influencing overall attitudes.

Five broad, indirect methods for measuring attitudes are available: observing overt behavior, analyzing reactions to partially structured stimuli, evaluating performance on objective tasks, monitoring physiological responses, and using self-report measures. The last method is the most direct of the five approaches and is also the most widely used.

Self-report measures of attitudes typically involve the use of rating scales. A researcher can choose from a wide variety of rating scales, which differ on such dimensions as graphic versus itemized formats, comparative versus noncomparative assessments, forced versus nonforced response choices, balanced versus unbalanced response choices, labeled versus unlabeled response choices, number of scale positions, and measurement level of the data obtained. The choice of an appropriate format for a research project must take into account the nature of the variable to be measured, the ability of respondents to make mental judgments, and the types of analyses to be performed on the collected data.

To be useful, attitude scales must satisfy three crucial criteria: validity, reliability, and sensitivity. Validity refers to whether a scale truly and fully measures an attitude. It can be assessed in several different ways, including examination of a scale's content or face validity, construct validity (convergent and discriminant validity), and predictive validity. Reliability focuses on the consistency or stability of scores generated by a scale. Two commonly used criteria for reliability assessment are test-retest reliability and split-half reliability. Sensitivity of an attitude scale is the extent to which it is capable of discriminating between respondents with different attitudes. In general, multiple-item scales are better than single-item scales on all three criteria.

Three popular multiple-item attitude scales are the Likert, semantic-differential, and Stapel scales. Of the three, the semantic-differential scale is the most widely used, perhaps because of its practical appeal and the visually effective profile diagrams that can be constructed from the data generated. Despite the format differences across the three scales, there are apparently no significant differences in the attitudes inferred from the data generated through them. Therefore a researcher can choose the scale format that best meets the practical requirements of a situation.

QUESTIONS

1. Discuss the advantages and limitations of quantifying survey responses.
2. What are the four key levels of measurement? What mathematical operations are and are not permissible on data from each type of scale?
3. From a survey of users and nonusers of its products, one firm came up with the following inferences:
   a. On the average, users are only half as old as nonusers.
   b. The image that users have of our company is twice as positive as that of nonusers.

   Critically evaluate the meaningfulness and legitimacy of these inferences.
4. Briefly discuss, with concrete examples, whether attitudes are more difficult or less difficult to measure than behavior.
5. What is meant by saying that attitudes are multifaceted? Explain your answer with a specific example.
6. Other than self-report measures, what are the four general methods for inferring attitudes? For each method, state one limitation that you consider to be most serious.
7. "Of all rating scales, graphic rating scales provide the most precise and accurate measures of attitudes." Discuss this statement.
8. When should an itemized rating scale have unbalanced response choices? Why?
9. Why will using verbal labels for all intermediate categories on an itemized rating scale sometimes lead to a violation of the interval assumption for the data gathered?
10. Define *scale validity, reliability,* and *sensitivity.*
11. Briefly describe the various methods of validity assessment.
12. Can an attitude scale be sensitive if it is not reliable? Why or why not?
13. Explain why a multiple-item scale is a more sensitive measure of attitudes than a single-item scale.
14. Suppose a restaurant in your city wants to ascertain the image it has in the minds of its patrons. Construct a five-item scale to measure the perceived image of the restaurant, using each of the multiple-item formats we discussed. Make sure that the five items under each format correspond to the same five dimensions.
15. Which of the three multiple-item scales you constructed in Question 14 would you recommend to the restaurant? Why?

CASES FOR PART FOUR

CASE 4.1

People's National Bank

People's National Bank is located in a city with a population of about 90,000. Its main competitors for consumer accounts in the area are two other banks—First Security Bank and Midtown Bank & Trust—and two savings and loan associations—Prudent Savings Association and Security Savings & Loan. People's National Bank is about the same size (in terms of total assets) as the two competing banks but is somewhat bigger than the two savings and loan associations.

The primary services offered by People's National Bank include checking accounts, savings accounts, mortgage loans, personal or installment loans, trust services, safety deposit boxes, and 24-hour standard financial transactions through automatic-teller machines (ATMs). The other area banks and savings and loan associations also offer these same basic services.

Since the various competing financial institutions in the area offer fairly similar services, the president of People's National Bank, John Goodman, was interested in finding out the extent to which customers were loyal to a given financial institution and how they perceived the five major banks/savings and loan associations in the city. He therefore requested Patricia Stewart, vice president for consumer services, to conduct a mail survey of about 500 current customers of People's National Bank. If this survey revealed anything of significance, Ms. Stewart was to conduct a similar survey of noncustomers of People's National Bank to see if similar significant findings emerge.

In his request to Ms. Stewart, Mr. Goodman outlined several specific types of information he would like to see after the survey was conducted and the data analyzed. These items were as follows:

1. What proportion of our bank's current customers use the services of one or more of our main competitors?
2. For which service(s) do our current customers go to our competitors the most?
3. Which of our competitors has the largest proportion of our customers as its customers as well?
4. What is the average number of area financial institutions with which a typical customer of ours has dealings?
5. How do our customers perceive People's National Bank vis-à-vis our competitors along the following dimensions?
   a. Locational convenience,
   b. Convenience of hours of operation,

c. Friendliness of contact personnel,
d. Speed of transactions,
e. Accuracy of transactions,
f. Appearance of facilities,
g. Range of services offered,
h. Technological advancement.

6. How important is each of the above dimensions to our customers?
7. Do customer perceptions of financial institutions along the various dimensions (item 5) and evaluations of the relative importance of those dimensions (item 6) differ according to a customer's sex, age, education, income, and years of association with People's National Bank?

The mail survey questionnaire was to be sent to a random sample of 500 names and addresses selected from the current customer base of People's National Bank. A business reply envelope would also be sent for returning the questionnaires to the bank.

QUESTIONS

1. Design a suitable mail questionnaire (including a cover letter and all necessary instructions) that can meet the information needs of Mr. Goodman.
2. On the basis of Mr. Goodman's overall objective implied in the list, is the proposed mail survey the most appropriate first step? If not, what else would you propose?
3. What are the pros and cons of limiting the proposed survey to just People's National Bank's customers?

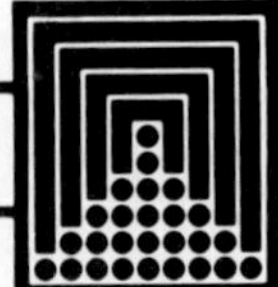

CASE 4.2

Bankers Life and Casualty Company

The marketing research department of Bankers Life and Casualty Company, headquartered in Northbrook, Illinois, conducted a mail survey of new buyers of the company's auto and homeowners/renters insurance. The questionnaire used in this survey was in the form of a booklet that was professionally prepared. The first page of this booklet (i.e., the outside of the front cover) contained the cover letter, which is reproduced here as Exhibit 1.

The questionnaire began on the inside front cover and was 10 pages long. These 10 pages are reproduced (in condensed form) as Exhibit 2. (*Note:* The first two pages of this questionnaire appeared as Exhibit 6.2 in Chapter 6).

QUESTIONS

1. What are the strengths and weaknesses of the cover letter shown in Exhibit 1?
2. Critically evaluate the mail questionnaire (Exhibit 2) on dimensions such as format, wording, ease of answering, and question sequencing.

Exhibit 1

Bankers cover letter

BANKERS MULTIPLE LINE/BANKERS LIFE AND CASUALTY

New Policyowner
Attitude Survey Questionnaire

Dear Policyowner:

We are delighted that you have decided to purchase your new policy from Bankers. As a new policyowner, we would like to get better acquainted with you and your insurance needs, so that we may serve you better in the future. To maintain your privacy, this questionnaire will be kept strictly confidential, and your responses will be used for statistical purposes only. When you have completed this questionnaire, please mail it back in the stamped pre-addressed envelope provided.

Thank you very much.

Sincerely,

Naava Grossman
Manager, Market Research

P.S. We have enclosed a pen for your convenience in filling out the questionnaire. Please keep the pen—it's a small way of thanking you.

Courtesy of Marketing Research Department, Bankers Life and Casualty Company, 1000 Sunset Ridge Road, Northbrook, IL 60062.

Exhibit 2

Bankers questionnaire

BANKERS MULTIPLE LINE/BANKERS LIFE AND CASUALTY NEW POLICYOWNER ATTITUDE SURVEY QUESTIONNAIRE

(1-4)
(5)

Throughout this questionnaire you will see questions asking about "Bankers". These questions are about *both* Bankers Life and Casualty *and* Bankers Multiple Line.

1. **How long have you been a Bankers policyowner?** (6)

   I am a new policyowner .... ☐ 1
   Less than one year .... ☐ 2
   One year or more, but less than five .... ☐ 3
   Five years or more .... ☐ 4

2. **The following question asks about the types of insurance coverage you now own.**

   A. In Column A please check the type(s) of policy (or policies) you just purchased from Bankers.

   B. In Column B please check each type of policy you already owned from Bankers.

   C. In Column C please check each type of group coverage you have (at work, or elsewhere).

   D. In Column D please check each type of policy you own with other companies. (Aside from group coverage).

	A. New Policy	B. Other Bankers Policies	C. Group Coverage	D. Other Policies	
	(7)	(8)	(9)	(10)	
Life	☐	☐	☐	☐	1
Health	☐	☐	☐	☐	2
Annuity	☐	☐	☐	☐	3
Auto	☐	☐	☐	☐	4
Homeowner/Renters	☐	☐	☐	☐	5
Disability Income	☐	☐	☐	☐	6
Other? ________	☐	☐	☐	☐	7

3. **Did your new Bankers policy replace a policy you had before?** (11)

   Yes ☐ 1 No ☐ 2

4. **From what company did you purchase your old policy?** ________ (12-13)

   I did not have this coverage before. ☐ 99

(*continued*)

5. **How long ago did you purchase your old policy?**

(14)

Within the last two years .... ☐ 1
Two to five years ago .... ☐ 2
Over five years ago .... ☐ 3
I did not have this coverage before .... ☐ 4

6. **Had you heard of Bankers before buying your new policy?**

(15)

Yes .... ☐ 1
No .... ☐ 2
Don't Recall .... ☐ 3

7. **Based on your knowledge of Bankers, by reputation or personal experience, how would you rate it in each of these areas:**

	Above Average 1	Average 2	Below Average 3	Don't Know 4	
Financially sound	☐	☐	☐	☐	(16)
A large, well known company	☐	☐	☐	☐	(17)
Offers good policies at reasonable cost ...	☐	☐	☐	☐	(18)
Has competent, well trained agents	☐	☐	☐	☐	(19)
Answers inquiries promptly and fully	☐	☐	☐	☐	(20)
Pays claims promptly and fairly	☐	☐	☐	☐	(21)
Serves the needs of senior citizens	☐	☐	☐	☐	(22)
Serves the needs of families	☐	☐	☐	☐	(23)
Other________________	☐	☐	☐	☐	(24)

8. **Before buying this policy, had you ever been contacted by a Bankers agent? Please check all that apply.**

(25)

Yes, within the last year .... ☐ 1
Yes, over a year ago .... ☐ 2
No, never contacted before .... ☐ 3
Can't recall .... ☐ 4

9. **Had you or a member of your family ever bought insurance from this agent before?**

(26)

Yes .... ☐ 1
No .... ☐ 2
Can't recall .... ☐ 3

10. **What led to the purchase of your new Bankers policy?**

(27)

A Bankers agent called on me .... ☐ 1
I contacted Bankers .... ☐ 2
I received a mailing from the company .... ☐ 3
Other .... ☐ 4

(continued)

11. How would you rate the Bankers agent in each of these areas?

	Excellent 1	Good 2	Fair 3	Poor 4	
A. Being courteous and businesslike	☐	☐	☐	☐	(28)
B. Having a thorough knowledge of insurance	☐	☐	☐	☐	(29)
C. Describing policies, costs, etc., clearly and openly..................	☐	☐	☐	☐	(30)
D. Helping you select the right coverage	☐	☐	☐	☐	(31)
E. Following through to get your policy issued to you smoothly and quickly ...	☐	☐	☐	☐	(32)

12. Based on your experience with the agent who sold you this policy, would you buy insurance from him or her again?

	(33)	
Yes	☐	1
No..............................	☐	2
Maybe	☐	3

13. Which of the following statements were true in your case when you decided to buy your Bankers policy?

	True in my case 1	Not true in my case (or does not apply) 2	
A. My Bankers policy gives me better coverage than my old policy..................	☐	☐	(34)
B. The Bankers agent did a better job than the agent of my old company............	☐	☐	(35)
C. A friend or relative recommended Bankers.	☐	☐	(36)
D. I have had good experience with Bankers.	☐	☐	(37)
E. My old company just raised the rates.	☐	☐	(38)
F. I now have all my insurance with Bankers.	☐	☐	(39)
G. I have had bad experience with my old company.	☐	☐	(40)
H. I saved money with Bankers.	☐	☐	(41)

I. Other important reasons why I decided to purchase from Bankers were ________ (42)

____

14. Besides Bankers and your previous company, did you get a quote from any other insurance company?

	(43)	
Yes	☐	1
No..............................	☐	2

(continued)

15. Below are examples of services that a person might receive after becoming a Bankers policyholder. Please indicate how interested you are in receiving that kind of service.

	Very Interested	Somewhat Interested	Not Interested	
	1	2	3	
A. Reviews to determine whether your coverages are adequate for your current needs.	☐	☐	☐	(45)
B. Reviews to make sure your policy information is up to date (addresses, drivers, home additions, etc.)	☐	☐	☐	(46)
C. Information about additional options or other insurance products offered by Bankers.	☐	☐	☐	(47)

16. Would you ever be interested in discussing any of the following with a Bankers agent? (Check all that apply)

(48)

Life Insurance . . . . ☐ 1
Health Insurance . . . . ☐ 2
Disability Income . . . . ☐ 3
Annuities . . . . ☐ 4
Auto Insurance . . . . ☐ 5
Homeowners/Renters . . . . ☐ 6
Other ______________________________ . . . . . . ☐ 7
No interest . . . . ☐ 8

17. How often would you like to have someone from Bankers get in touch with you to review your insurance?

(49)

At least once a year . . . . ☐ 1
Once every year or two . . . . ☐ 2
Only at my request . . . . ☐ 3

18. Should the contact be by: (Check all that apply)

(50)

Mail . . . . ☐ 1
Telephone . . . . ☐ 2
Personal visit . . . . ☐ 3
None of the above . . . . ☐ 4

19. For most questions about your Bankers insurance coverage, would you prefer to deal with:

(51)

The agent who sold you this policy . . . . ☐ 1
Any Bankers agent . . . . ☐ 2
The company directly . . . . ☐ 3
Other ______________________________ . . . . . . ☐ 4

(*continued*)

20. Approximately, how much do you spend per month on all types of insurance? (52)

Less than $10 .... ☐ 1
$10 - $49 .... ☐ 2
$50 - $99 .... ☐ 3
$100 - $200 .... ☐ 4
Over $200 .... ☐ 5

21. Please check the statement below that best describes how you feel about your insurance expenditures. (53)

I have about the right amount of insurance and it fits my budget .... ☐ 1
I have about the right amount of insurance, but it is a strain on my budget .... ☐ 2
I need more insurance, and I could fit more into my budget .... ☐ 3
I need more insurance, but I cannot afford any more .... ☐ 4

22. What state do you live in? ______________________ (54-55)

23. What is your age? (56)

Under 25 .... ☐ 1
25 - 34 .... ☐ 2
35 - 49 .... ☐ 3
50 - 64 .... ☐ 4
65 or over .... ☐ 5

24. Are you: (57)

A. Male .... ☐ 1
Female .... ☐ 2

(58)

B. Married .... ☐ 1
Single .... ☐ 2
Divorced or Separated .... ☐ 3
Widowed .... ☐ 4

25. Do you have any children living at home? (59)

Yes .... ☐ 1
No .... ☐ 2

26. Do you live in: (60)

A rural area .... ☐ 1
A small town (under 50,000 pop.) .... ☐ 2
A city (50,000 - 500,000 pop.) .... ☐ 3
A metropolitan area (over 500,000 pop.) .... ☐ 4

(*continued*)

27. What is your education?

	(61)	
Some high school or less	☐	1
High school graduate	☐	2
Some college	☐	3
College graduate or more	☐	4

28. Approximately, what is your family income?

	(62)	
Less than $10,000	☐	1
$10,000 - $19,999	☐	2
$20,000 - $29,999	☐	3
$30,000 - $39,999	☐	4
$40,000 or more	☐	5

29. How many adult individuals contribute to your family income?

	(63)	
One person	☐	1
Two persons	☐	2
Three or more	☐	3

30. What is your primary occupation?

	A. Self (64-65)	B. Spouse (66-67)	
Business owner	☐	☐	1
Professional, technical	☐	☐	2
Farm manager	☐	☐	3
Other executive or manager	☐	☐	4
Sales clerk, clerical worker	☐	☐	5
Sales representative	☐	☐	6
Craftsworker, foreman, machine operator	☐	☐	7
Laborer, service worker, farm worker	☐	☐	8
Student	☐	☐	9
Homemaker	☐	☐	10
Retired	☐	☐	11
Other______________	☐	☐	12

31. How many people are employed at the business where you work?

	(68)	
Less than 5	☐	1
5 - 10	☐	2
11 - 24	☐	3
25 - 50	☐	4
More than 50	☐	5

32. Do you own your own home or do you rent?

	(69)	
Own	☐	1
Rent	☐	2

(continued)

33. Which of the following changes have occurred in your life in the last year? Please check all that apply. (70-71)

- Changed residence .... ☐ 1
- Bought a home .... ☐ 2
- Bought a car .... ☐ 3
- Started a business .... ☐ 4
- Changed jobs .... ☐ 5
- Been promoted .... ☐ 6
- Retired .... ☐ 7
- Had a child .... ☐ 8
- Got married .... ☐ 9
- Other ________________ .... ☐ 10
- None .... ☐ 11

If you would like to make any additional comments, please write them in the space below, or enclose an extra sheet. (72)

Thank you very much for your time and help.

Courtesy of Marketing Research Department, Bankers Life and Casualty Company, 1000 Sunset Ridge Road, Northbrook, IL 60062.

CASE 4.3

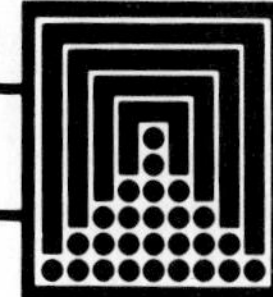

Hershey Chocolate Company (B)

Background information about this company and the alternative recipe study it conducted are described in the Hershey Chocolate Company (A) case. The purpose of this case is to examine the data collection instruments used in the recipe study. Two different questionnaires were used in this study: one to conduct the shopping mall intercept interview and the other to conduct the callback telephone survey. These two questionnaires are shown in Exhibits 1 and 2, respectively.

QUESTIONS

1. Identify the strengths and weaknesses of the two questionnaires.
2. What changes, if any, would you make in either of the questionnaires? Why?

Exhibit 1

Recipe study, mall placement

TIME STARTED: ______:______ ( ) AM ( ) PM

Hello, I'm ________________ from Interviewing Services. We're making a study with women today.

1a. First, are you the female head of your household?
1( ) Yes 2( ) No (TERMINATE AND TALLY)

1b. Are you between the ages of 18 and 49?
1( ) Yes 2( ) No (TERMINATE AND TALLY)

1c. How many children, if any, under 17 years of age do you have living at home?
\# OF CHILDREN: ________________________ -9
(IF NONE, TERMINATE AND TALLY)

1d. Do you or anyone else in your household work for an advertising agency, a marketing research company or a manufacturer, distributor or retailer of candy?
1( ) Yes (TERMINATE AND TALLY) 2( ) No

1e. Which, if any, of the following products have you used in the past few months? (READ LIST)

Pillsbury flour	1( ) Yes	2( ) No	-10
Land O'Lakes Butter	1( ) Yes	2( ) No	-11
Peanut Butter Chips	1( ) Yes	2( ) No	-12

IF YES TO PEANUT BUTTER CHIPS, RESPONDENT QUALIFIES FOR USER QUOTA.
ASK Q. 2 NEXT.

1f. IF NOT PEANUT BUTTER CHIPS USER, ASK:
Have you done any baking from scratch in the past few months?

13-

	Yes	1
(TERMINATE AND TALLY)	No	2
	N/A	9

1g. Does your family like baked peanut butter flavored desserts or snacks?

14-

	Yes	1
(TERMINATE AND TALLY)	No	2
	N/A	9

2. CHECK QUOTA:

15-

Peanut Butter Chips user	1
Scratch baker	2

3a. HAND RESPONDENT BOARD #231.
Please look at this picture and read the recipe written beside it. Take all the time you want to study the picture and recipe.

ALLOW RESPONDENT TIME.

How much does this appeal to you in terms of being appetizing? POINT TO DESSERT/SNACK IN THE PICTURE. Would you say it is:

(continued)

16-

Very appealing	5
Somewhat appealing,	4
Neither appealing nor unappealing,	3
Somewhat unappealing, or	2
Very unappealing?	1

3b. Why is it (NAME ANSWER TO #3a) to you? (PROBE)

____ 17-18 __ __

____ 19-20 __ __

____ 21-22 __ __

____ 23-24 __ __

____ 25-26 __ __

27-28 __ __

3c. If you were reading a magazine and saw this recipe, how likely do you think you would be to make it? Would you be:

29-

Very likely to make it,	5
Somewhat likely to make it,	4
Neither likely nor unlikely to make it,	3
Somewhat unlikely to make it, or	2
Very unlikely to make it?	1

TAKE BACK BOARD.

4a. HAND RESPONDENT BOARD #479.

Please look at this picture and read the recipe written beside it. Take all the time you want to study the picture and recipe.

ALLOW RESPONDENT TIME.

How much does this appeal to you in terms of being appetizing? POINT TO DESSERT/SNACK IN THE PICTURE. Would you say it is:

30-

Very appealing,	5
Somewhat appealing,	4
Neither appealing nor unappealing,	3
Somewhat unappealing, or	2
Very unappealing?	1

(continued)

4b. Why is it (NAME ANSWER TO #4a) to you? (PROBE)

______________________________ 31-32 _ _
______________________________ 33-34 _ _
______________________________ 35-36 _ _
______________________________ 37-38 _ _
______________________________ 39-40 _ _
41-42 _ _

4c. If you were reading a magazine and saw this recipe, how likely do you think you would be to make it? Would you be:

43-

Very likely to make it,	5
Somewhat likely to make it,	4
Neither likely nor unlikely to make it,	3
Somewhat unlikely to make it, or	2
Very unlikely to make it?	1

TAKE BACK BOARD.

5a. HAND RESPONDENT BOARD #658.
Please look at this picture and read the recipe written beside it. Take all the time you want to study the picture and recipe.
ALLOW RESPONDENT TIME.
How much does this appeal to you in terms of being appetizing? POINT TO DESSERT/SNACK IN THE PICTURE. Would you say it is:

44-

Very appealing,	5
Somewhat appealing,	4
Neither appealing nor unappealing,	3
Somewhat unappealing, or	2
Very unappealing?	1

5b. Why is it (NAME ANSWER TO #5a) to you? (PROBE)

______________________________ 45-46 _ _
______________________________ 47-48 _ _
______________________________ 49-50 _ _
______________________________ 51-52 _ _
______________________________ 53-54 _ _
55-56 _ _

(continued)

5c. If you were reading a magazine and saw this recipe, how likely do you think you would be to make it? Would you be:

57-

Very likely to make it,	5
Somewhat likely to make it,	4
Neither likely nor unlikely to make it,	3
Somewhat unlikely to make it, or	2
Very unlikely to make it?	1

TAKE BACK BOARD.

6a. SHOW RESPONDENT ALL 3 BOARDS.
Now that you have seen all three recipes, which one would you be <u>most</u> likely to use?

58-

#231 (Semi-Sweet Chocolate Chips, regular cookie)	1
#479 (Semi-Sweet Chips, bar cookie)	2
#658 (Syrup, brownie)	3

6b. Why would you be most likely to make that one? (PROBE)

_______________ 59-60 __ __
_______________ 61-62 __ __
_______________ 63-64 __ __
_______________ 65-66 __ __
_______________ 67-68 __ __
69-70 __ __

7a. I would like to give you a copy of this recipe, Peanut Butter Chips and (NAME PRODUCT CHOSEN IN Q. 6a) so that you can make this recipe at home. In addition for your cooperation, we will give you $5.00 and the two products.

We would like you to make the recipe in the next few days and we will call you to see how much you liked the recipe.

1( ) Will cooperate 2( ) Will not cooperate (TERMINATE AND TALLY)

7b. When would be the best day and time to call you within the next 3 or 4 days?

DAY: _______________ TIME: _______________
<u>MUST</u> BE WITHIN NEXT 4 DAYS.

7c. What is your telephone number? _______________
<u>MUST</u> BE GIVEN TO QUALIFY.

8a. And a few final questions for classification purposes. Including yourself, how many people are there in your household?

IN HOUSEHOLD: _______________ 71-72

(continued)

8b. Into which of the following age groups do you fall? (READ LIST)

73-

18 to 19	1
20 to 29	2
30 to 39	3
40 to 49	4

8c. And into which of the following groups does your total household income fall? HAND CARD TO RESPONDENT. Just read me the appropriate letter.

74-

"A" Under $10,000	1
"B" $10,000 to $14,999	2
"C" $15,000 to $19,999	3
"D" $20,000 to $24,999	4
"E" $25,000 to $29,999	5
"F" $30,000 or more	6

9a. GIVE RESPONDENT RECIPE, PRODUCTS AND $5.00.
Here is the recipe, two of the ingredients, and $5.00. We will call you on (NAME ANSWER TO Q. 7b) to get your reactions to the recipe.

9b. CHECK RECIPE AND PRODUCTS PLACED:

75-

#231 (Peanut Butter Chips and Semi-Sweet Chocolate Chips, regular cookie)	1
#479 (Peanut Butter Chips and Semi-Sweet Chips, bar cookie)	2
#658 (Peanut Butter Chips and Syrup, brownies)	3

TIME ENDED: ______:______ ( ) AM ( ) PM 76-77 __ __

RESPONDENT ______________________________

ADDRESS ______________________________

CITY ______________ STATE ______________ ZIP ______________

INTERVIEWER ______________________________ 78-79

DATE ______________ 80-1

Courtesy of Hershey Foods Corporation.

Exhibit 2

Recipe study callback

TIME START: _____:_____ ( ) AM ( ) PM

CHECK RECIPE:

	4-
#231 (Peanut Butter Chips and Semi-Sweet Chocolate Chips, regular cookie)	1
#479 (Peanut Butter Chips and Semi-Sweet Chips, bar cookie)	2
#658 (Peanut Butter Chips and syrup, brownies)	3

Hello, I'm ____________ from Interviewing Services. May I please speak with (NAME RESPONDENT)?.

1a. First, did you make the recipe using the ingredients we gave you at the Mall the other day?

		5-
(#2 NEXT)	Yes	1
	No	2

1b. IF NO:
Are you planning to make the recipe in the next few days?

		6-
	Yes	1
(TERMINATE AND TALLY)	No	2

1c. IF YES:
When can I call you to get your reactions to the recipe?
DAY: ______________________ TIME: ______________________

2a. How easy was the recipe for you to make—would you say it was:

		7-
(#3a NEXT)	Very easy to make,	5
	Somewhat easy to make,	4
	Neither easy nor difficult,	3
	Somewhat difficult to make, or	2
	Very difficult to make?	1

(continued)

2b. IF SOMEWHAT/VERY DIFFICULT:
What did you find difficult about making it? (PROBE)

_______________ 8- 9 __ __
_______________ 10-11 __ __
_______________ 12-13 __ __
_______________ 14-15 __ __
_______________ 16-17 __ __

3a. Did the finished product taste:

18-

	Better than you expected,	3
(#3c NEXT)	About the same as you expected, or	2
	Not as good as you expected?	1

3b. IF BETTER/NOT AS GOOD:
In what way was it (NAME ANSWER TO #3a)?

_______________ 19-20 __ __
_______________ 21-22 __ __
_______________ 23-24 __ __
_______________ 25-26 __ __
_______________ 27-28 __ __
29-30 __ __

3c. Did you serve this as:

A snack for yourself and family,	01	31-32 __ __
Dessert for yourself and family,	02	33-34 __ __
A snack for guests,	03	35-36 __ __
Dessert for guests,	04	
A special occasion, or (SPECIFY) ______		
Something else? (SPECIFY) ______		

(*continued*)

4a. How likely do you think you will be to make this recipe again. Would you say you will:

37-

(#4c NEXT)	Definitely make it again,	5
	Probably make it again,	4
GO TO RESPONDENT INFORMATION AT BOTTOM OF PAGE	May or may not make it again,	3
	Probably not make it again, or	2
	Definitely not make it again?	1

4b. IF PROBABLY/DEFINITELY NOT MAKE AGAIN:
Why do you think you won't make it again? (PROBE)

__________ 38-39 _ _

__________ 40-41 _ _

__________ 42-43 _ _

__________ 44-45 _ _

__________ 46-47 _ _

(GO TO RESPONDENT INFORMATION AT BOTTOM OF PAGE)

4c. IF DEFINITELY/PROBABLY MAKE AGAIN:
What was the one thing you liked most about this recipe?

__________ 48-49 _ _

__________ 50-51 _ _

__________ 52-53 _ _

__________ 54-55 _ _

__________ 56-57 _ _

58-59 _ _

TIME ENDED: ____:____ ( ) AM ( ) PM 60-61 _ _

RESPONDENT __________ PHONE __________

ADDRESS __________

CITY __________ STATE __________ ZIP __________

INTERVIEWER __________ 62-63

DATE __________ 64-79 (BLANK)

80-2

STAPLE TO BACK OF APPROPRIATE PLACEMENT INTERVIEW.

Courtesy of Hershey Foods Corporation.

PART FIVE

DESIGNING THE SAMPLE AND COLLECTING THE DATA

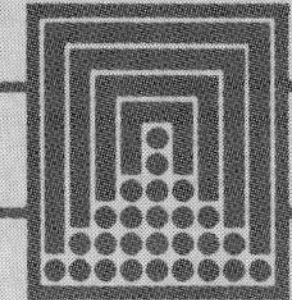

FROM THE MANAGER'S DESK

TOM BENEDICT, JR., is marketing research analyst with Blue Cross and Blue Shield of Iowa. Mr. Benedict is responsible for the direction and implementation of marketing research for Blue Cross and Blue Shield of Iowa. Prior to holding his present position, Tom served as a marketing research coordinator for the company. Tom's work experience also includes an internship with Northwest Community Hospital.

Tom Benedict received his B.A. from Iowa State University and is currently working toward his M.B.A. at Drake University. Tom is a member of the American Marketing Association and a contributing author to its publications.

QUESTION: What are your views on the relative importance and roles of probability- and nonprobability-sampling methods in practical marketing research projects?

RESPONSE: The dynamics of the change occurring in the health care industry within the past few years have clearly advanced the need for marketing research to the forefront. As major players in the industry, we recognize our responsibility to provide greater insight into how the public views its health. Typically, we solicit information through surveys in which probability- as well as nonprobability-sampling procedures are utilized.

Despite its importance, sampling remains shrouded in mystery. There is no question that sampling has a certain mystique. A few sources contributing to its mystique include complex models for determining sample size requirements, various probability- and nonprobability-sampling methods, and a preoccupation with techniques to increase survey response rates. In general, however, we have found that the basic, simple sampling procedures are well suited for most practical research projects.

Perhaps the most important determinant in choosing between using a probability- or a nonprobability-sampling procedure is the nature of the issue to be researched. Since research questions are often imprecise, time must be spent in formulating a researchable question. The more well-defined the question, the easier it will be to choose an appropriate method.

On the basis of our experience and judgment, nonprobability sampling should be reserved for use in exploratory-research efforts, such as focus group interviews or sampling a particular customer prototype. Recent studies have employed judgment-sampling procedures in situations where customers who chose to enroll in a health maintenance organization were asked to cite reasons for that decision. This particular method works well in small samples; however, it is less effective in larger samples.

Most of our research is designed to utilize probability-sampling procedures. The availability of a large customer base and an advanced system for generating customer file information provide the necessary sampling frame from which probability samples can be drawn. Since our research typically focuses on topics such as changes in benefits, public policy issues, and legislative issues, and since it has the potential to alter our relations with external constituencies, the research must be objective and must reflect the opinions of the marketplace. In our view, using less than a probability-sampling procedure is analogous to applying a nonparametric procedure when a more stringent examination is feasible and required. [*Note:* Nonparametric procedures are discussed in this book in Chapter 17.]

Regardless of which sampling method is employed, attention should be given to ensuring that the data collected are accurate. The effects of nonresponse bias, especially in mail surveys, can substantially jeopardize the usefulness of the results. For this reason we typically conduct telephone surveys when using a probability sample so as to minimize bias.

In short, the choice between probability- and nonprobability-sampling methods in practical research should be guided by the research purpose and the nature of the research situation. Each method has an important role to play and will be beneficial when used in the right context.

12

Introduction to Sampling

23P

WHAT IS SAMPLING?

Consider the following items:

ITEM: The ABC News–Harris Survey is a study that is done three times a week in order to constantly monitor the reactions of the American public to a wide variety of economic, political, social, and other issues. The importance and popularity of this survey is evident from its being widely cited in newspapers as well as on radio and TV. Each ABC News–Harris Survey is based on responses from 1600 adults spread over 200 locations across the country.[1]

ITEM: The A. C. Nielsen Company's Neilsen Retail Index offers valuable sales and brand share data on a regular basis to manufacturers of a wide variety of consumer products such as food, drugs, and cosmetics. These sales and brand share estimates are based on a representative sample of 1600 stores scattered across the country.[2]

One important feature common to most research studies emerges from these items: Insights and inferences that are crucial to decision makers can be based on data from a *sample* of units, which is quite small in size compared with

[1] "Survey Methodology," a brochure prepared by Louis Harris and Associates, 630 Fifth Avenue, New York, NY 10020.

[2] "Management with the Nielsen Retail Index," a brochure prepared by the A. C. Nielsen Company, Nielsen Plaza, Northbrook, IL 60062.

the size of the total group of units of interest to the decision makers. What is termed as *sampling* is the starting point of the inferential process involved in marketing research studies.

DEFINITION. ***Sampling*** **is the selection of a fraction of the total number of units of interest to decision makers, for the ultimate purpose of being able to draw general conclusions about the entire body of units.**

DEFINITION. **The entire body of units of interest to decision makers in a situation is known as the** ***population,*** **or** ***universe.***

Note that in marketing research studies the meaning of the term *population* is not restricted to people per se. Rather, it is used to denote any group of units—human or nonhuman—about which researchers or decision makers want to make some inferences. For instance, the implied population in the studies conducted to determine the Nielsen Retail Index is a collection of non-human units—all grocery, drug, and similar stores.

The basic reason sampling is an important component of most marketing research projects is that a study based on a sample of units has distinct advantages over a *census study*, which involves examining every unit in a population. Let us now examine those advantages.

SAMPLING VERSUS CENSUS STUDIES

One of the main advantages of a sampling study is its lower cost relative to a census study. A key factor that directly affects the data collection and data analysis costs in any research project is the number of units studied. Irrespective of whether the data collection method in a research project involves a personal-interview survey, a telephone survey, a mail survey, or an observation, the larger the number of units from which data are obtained, the greater are the data collection costs and the data analysis costs (because of the larger volume of data that have to be analyzed). In most real-life research projects the population sizes are prohibitively large, and the money allocated for research is too limited for conducting census studies.

A second advantage of a sampling study over a census study is in terms of the time needed for a research project. Given a set of limited resources for conducting research (e.g., money, fieldworkers to collect the data, facilities to code and analyze the data) the research will take longer to complete if it involves a census study rather than a sampling study. As we have seen in earlier chapters, data that are not obtained on a timely basis may not be relevant for decision making; worse still, the use of such data may result in erroneous decisions.

By now you are probably wondering: "Well, a census study is more expensive and time-consuming than a sampling study; but isn't it more *accurate* than a sampling study, since it obtains data from each and every unit within a population?" Surprisingly, the answer to that question is, "Not necessarily." By its definition, a census study involves looking at every unit in a population. However, the accuracy of data obtained from a study depends not only on the number of population units included in it but also on a host of other factors related to the process of collecting the data. For instance, in Chapter 6, when we discussed the relative merits of the different methods of administering questionnaires (namely, personal interviews, telephone interviews, and mail surveys), we got a glimpse of certain types of biases that might be present in some of those methods. Such biases are types of nonsampling errors that can occur even in census studies.

The *total error* associated with a research project may contain one or both of the following:

1. *Sampling error* that will occur in any project involving a sampling study, merely because only a sample of the population is studied (sampling error will be discussed in detail later in this chapter).
2. Other *nonsampling errors* that may occur during the process of data collection and analysis.

Nonsampling errors can arise from a multitude of factors, such as poor questionnaire construction, ill-trained fieldworkers, errors on the part of respondents, and errors in coding responses. We will discuss nonsampling errors in greater detail in Chapter 15. The best way for a researcher to minimize nonsampling errors is to have adequate control over the entire process of data gathering, coding, and analysis—for example, by using properly trained fieldworkers, by giving them proper instructions, and by closely supervising their work. A sampling study, by virtue of its limited scope when compared with a census study, is much more likely to offer a researcher such control.

Let us look at an example to illustrate this point. Suppose you want to do a census study of "all homes in the United States that have video recorders," using personal interviews to gather the data that you need. A population like this one will contain at least a few million units. Consequently, even if you have enough time and money to conduct a census study, you will probably have difficulty identifying enough *qualified* interviewers, let alone recruiting them, training them, and supervising them adequately. A researcher planning to conduct a census study under such circumstances will have to use marginally qualified personnel and settle for reduced control over the research. Huge nonsampling errors can result, which will more than offset the absence of any sampling error.

Therefore in most cases a well-conducted sampling study, in spite of some unavoidable sampling error, is likely to have a lower total error than a census study. This conclusion is supported by a somewhat surprising activity of the U.S. Census Bureau; the bureau actually conducts some controlled sampling studies *to verify the accuracy* of the data generated by its decennial population census studies.

In addition to the cost, time, and accuracy advantages that we have discussed so far, sampling studies have another indirect benefit over census studies in situations involving human populations. Because of the increasing use of research studies by a variety of institutions, people are becoming more likely to be requested to participate in surveys. Consequently, fresh respondents—that is, those who have not participated in any research surveys—are becoming harder to find than ever before. Indeed, a recent survey conducted by Walker Research, Inc., discovered that over half the United States adult population had participated in some research project or another, and that about a fourth of the United States adult population had taken part in some survey within the past year.[3]

Using fresh respondents in research projects is beneficial for two reasons:

1. A fresh respondent is more likely to agree to cooperate with a researcher and provide the needed data than one who is tired of participating in research surveys.
2. A respondent who has participated in several research surveys may, in effect, be a professional respondent. That is, such a respondent may unintentionally, or even deliberately, give biased responses, which in turn can add to nonsampling errors.

What does this discussion of fresh respondents have to do with our discussion of sampling versus census studies? Census studies increase the chances of multiple survey participation by respondents in many human populations that are probably already being oversampled. Hence in the interest of conserving the available pool of fresh respondents in the long run, a sampling study is preferable over a census study.

CONDITIONS FOR DOING CENSUS STUDIES IN MARKETING

Though census studies have several important limitations, we do not mean to say that they should never be conducted in marketing situations. Notice that the cost, time, and accuracy drawbacks of a census study will not be significant *if the population is small.* For example, populations such as "all neurosurgeons in the Chicago metropolitan area," "all savings and loan associations in Arkansas," and "all manufacturers who have a need for gold in its raw form" are unlikely to contain a large number of units. In research projects involving small populations, a census is certainly feasible from a cost, time, and accuracy standpoint. However, the feasibility of a census study in a situation does not necessarily imply that it must be conducted, as the next example shows.

[3] "1982 Industry Image Survey Results," *The Marketing Researcher* (Walker Research, Inc., 8000 Knue Road, Indianapolis, Ind. 46250), Spring 1983, p. 3.

EXAMPLE: Consider a hypothetical population consisting of 200 banks in a certain region. Let us say we want to determine the average number of tellers employed per bank in this population of banks. Now a census study of the banks will be feasible, given the relatively small size of the population. However, suppose we know that all the 200 banks are *identical* in terms of the number of tellers each uses, although we do not know what that number is. Given this knowledge about the nature of the population of banks, should we do a census study? We would be wasting our resources if we did. Since we know that all the banks are identical, all we need to do is study a sample of just *one* bank and find out the number of tellers it employs.

The point of this example is that whether or not a census study is *necessary* depends on the extent of variability among the population units with respect to the variable(s) about which data are needed in a research project.

In summary, two conditions must be met for a census study to be appropriate: (1) the feasibility condition and (2) the necessity condition. A census study will be *feasible* whenever a population is relatively small. A census study will be *necessary* only when the population units are extremely varied, that is, when each population unit is likely to be very different from all the other units. Consequently, the use of census studies in marketing is usually limited to industrial or institutional customer populations—that is, situations in which marketers may be interested in studying relatively small but highly varied populations. The next example illustrates the point.

EXAMPLE: The XYZ Company is a major producer of a special kind of chemical that is used by 100 manufacturers of plastic products. Each of these 100 manufacturers accounts for a significant portion of XYZ's sales; moreover, each of them uses the chemical for totally different applications. Currently, XYZ is considering adding a new ingredient to its chemical that is supposed to improve the chemical's performance characteristics. But it first wants to get the reactions of its customers to the addition of the new ingredient. The situation faced by XYZ is appropriate for conducting a census study of its customers: The population is relatively small, and, more importantly, it consists of a very diverse group of manufacturers whose individual reactions are likely to be quite important to XYZ.

PROBABILITY VERSUS NONPROBABILITY SAMPLING

The subject matter of the rest of this chapter and the next two chapters relates to various methods for picking a sample of units from a given population. So let us preview two basic sampling procedures that are available to researchers: (1) probability sampling and (2) nonprobability sampling.

A researcher using a probability-sampling procedure does not play a role in determining which *specific* population units are chosen to be part of a sample; that is, the researcher has no say in deciding whether or not each individual population unit is included in the sample. In probability sampling the researcher merely specifies some *objective scheme* for choosing units from a population. Once the scheme has been laid out, the selection of the sample units is independent of the personal preferences or biases of the researcher. Each population unit is assigned an objective probability of being selected on the basis of the specified sampling scheme (the probability of selection may or may not be the same for all population units, as we will see in the next chapter).

DEFINITION. ***Probability sampling*** **is an objective procedure in which the probability of selection is known in advance for each population unit.**

Nonprobability sampling is more judgmental than objective in the sense that the selection of individual population units is not done on a strictly chance basis; a researcher's subjective judgment does play a role in determining which specific population units get included in the sample. Hence determining an objective probability of selection for each population unit beforehand is impossible.

DEFINITION. ***Nonprobability sampling*** **is a subjective procedure in which the probability of selection for each population unit is unknown beforehand.**

The remainder of this chapter provides a detailed discussion of simple random sampling, which is a form of probability sampling. The various concepts discussed for simple random sampling are also relevant for the more advanced probability-sampling methods covered in Chapter 13. Nonprobability-sampling methods are discussed in Chapter 14.

DEFINITION OF SIMPLE RANDOM SAMPLING

Simple random sampling is the least sophisticated probability-sampling method for selecting a specified number of units from a population. A formal definition of simple random sampling is as follows:

DEFINITION. ***Simple random sampling*** **is a procedure in which every possible sample of a certain size within a population has a known and *equal* probability of being chosen as the study sample.**

EXAMPLE: Consider a hypothetical population containing just four stores: A, B, C, and D. Suppose we want to pick a sample of two stores from this population by using a simple-random-sampling procedure. Let us first enumerate every possible sample of size two. Six different samples, each containing two stores, are possible within our population; and since the population itself is quite small, we can easily identify and list those samples:

1. AB	**3.** AD	**5.** BD
2. AC	**4.** BC	**6.** CD

We can now write down the six sample combinations on six identical pieces of paper, fold the pieces of paper so that they are indistinguishable, drop them in a hat (or drum or whatever), mix them up thoroughly, pull one out randomly, and use the sample indicated. This procedure is a simple-random-sampling procedure because it assigns an equal probability of selection (namely, $\frac{1}{6}$) for every sample of size two.

Though the sampling procedure outlined in the example illustrates the definition of simple random sampling, it has serious drawbacks from a practical standpoint. For instance, consider a situation in which we want to pick a sample of two stores from a population of 40 (rather than 4) stores. The total number of possible samples of size two in this situation is 780. Imagine the amount of effort required to just enumerate all the 780 possible samples. In real-life situations, where population sizes and the desired sample sizes are usually large, a shortcut method that is much easier than this procedure is used, as discussed next.

CHOOSING A SIMPLE RANDOM SAMPLE IN PRACTICE

The practical approach for choosing a simple random sample is based on the following important fact: Picking a sample of size n by selecting n units at random from a population is *statistically equivalent* to first identifying all possible samples of size n in the population and then picking one of those samples randomly. In other words, one does not need to enumerate all possible samples when one wants to use simple random sampling. The easier procedure of randomly picking the desired number of units, one at a time, automatically guarantees an equal probability of selection for every possible sample of the desired size. Hence in our earlier example, instead of identifying the six possible samples, we can simply pick two of the four stores randomly—either by using a procedure similar to dropping the four store labels in a hat and drawing two of them randomly, or by using a random-number table, which is discussed below.

A random-number table consists of a group of digits that are arranged in random order; that is, any row, column, or diagonal in such a table contains digits that are sequenced in no systematic order. Table 12.1 is a table of random numbers. In this table the grouping of digits into 5-by-5 clusters is merely to facilitate reading and has no other significance.

Table 12.1

Table of random numbers

40743	39671	07812	42293	41539	40998	95829	11436	40890	16406
80833	23016	38342	03628	21313	46364	11934	82901	46587	41614
10743	34555	49339	36401	90000	77565	95132	93536	81876	59673
88103	46176	35968	10648	22427	22321	77904	76877	51829	55779
53976	43761	61725	49408	42200	98000	91259	42759	10504	14307
31230	41200	43973	62146	70245	39856	24029	38382	09225	49848
29249	48104	47431	26302	71090	63395	91312	25044	99955	66663
56588	28502	31317	37819	98119	50860	51639	55193	95055	06864
35438	73223	44149	70587	40561	50406	53423	82627	51266	42584
19793	30194	42198	59868	92882	74022	37797	93500	41877	17477
56865	63701	22341	37891	16351	88371	47968	97437	70400	93943
72201	03668	70611	47954	69660	26741	74733	00810	01152	52801
15890	96036	21583	04417	17438	76876	51807	27263	84521	55808
19983	27843	69758	61186	38368	39769	31722	68252	09347	04839
81126	95633	42617	16726	14259	08045	01691	16800	30293	23518
51823	40608	51380	58207	33716	53619	11038	31730	22239	08272
07454	92103	51564	21146	28807	00764	13854	73228	49968	94276
03375	95032	65271	71876	25947	84015	67464	28424	07995	48746
91374	36275	90717	56396	24855	99138	12491	52901	73174	48511
41086	67186	22605	15775	73647	64586	35994	54814	29835	64245
60431	24886	80034	96476	82831	20348	30157	73453	26122	09458
15899	81159	28224	17790	96251	30142	57206	30095	52935	43568
10052	05764	51779	47543	26866	02152	04707	54037	49744	59947
95657	52708	94879	12367	22228	06005	86391	78208	72906	31788
57337	25309	03169	95668	29124	14437	04837	91244	82967	67869
64988	98506	70398	68695	95970	76676	49086	09069	70654	39241
07387	98150	49313	08281	32958	15356	73356	71642	16187	92525
55762	30946	42835	27282	53450	01402	82937	48344	74237	85740
67720	48010	98907	44585	16464	28870	23885	18085	00278	93300
86803	62206	09160	81182	99671	17224	74272	31011	79866	45546
41693	81849	08818	65391	64726	42923	25449	98540	68914	56626
82145	50140	45227	37427	70649	26962	55693	11543	49701	84694
01600	81297	00713	88645	02774	44711	91565	63908	06488	00086
42718	96176	52680	93215	04964	03641	61251	40361	20291	12116
73397	35616	04020	70326	93138	26497	86161	13730	22414	84924
13100	63938	07302	89521	07910	03230	17163	13913	83881	42522
98505	42693	34714	41842	12051	05483	11279	45705	10644	17043
04274	62158	83986	36968	05792	14755	91042	78940	58215	92301
68619	63767	65875	39595	78214	45903	52216	29857	14521	79177
95445	76259	32639	45690	62614	40656	62956	93663	40034	49455
96721	33899	78824	46185	36809	45441	86203	37607	91375	73237
02879	89258	65507	31638	32510	76979	41048	41712	37650	16736
26176	86786	12324	17380	24938	97032	45054	98632	05148	78244
62199	72262	44802	58198	95923	36412	67574	33290	25200	51556
47013	04898	63931	28253	62793	81973	20581	18977	98348	93521
30448	34027	58753	78128	05239	72236	67343	01778	97089	63183
10561	14780	82473	64810	81448	37989	15817	81860	32942	57614
99651	20030	31874	43927	05097	94280	01378	48137	13308	43065
32483	25721	47734	00809	00371	37366	11124	70027	46199	44451
26341	11426	78027	49249	00137	92846	77094	38012	42631	93977

Reprinted from Page 349 of A MILLION RANDOM DIGITS WITH 100,000 NORMAL DEVIATES, by The Rand Corporation, New York: The Free Press, 1955. Copyright 1955, 1983 by The Rand Corporation. Used by permission.

EXAMPLE: Let us see how we can use this table to select two stores from our population of four stores. First, we number the stores 1 through 4, as follows:

1. A **2.** B **3.** C **4.** D

Then we go through these steps:

1. Randomly start with some digit in the table.
2. Read down (or up) the column (or row or diagonal) containing the digit.
3. Pick the stores corresponding to the digits that are read until the desired number of stores is selected.

For instance, suppose we start with the second row in the first column of the table and decide to read down the diagonal. The starting digit is 8. There is no number as large as 8 in our population list since there are only four stores in it. We simply move on to the next digit on the diagonal, which is 0; we ignore this digit also since it does not correspond to any store in our population. The next digit is 1, which corresponds to store A. We pick A and proceed in a similar fashion until we have a sample of size two. The random numbers selected for this particular sequence are 1 and 4. The sample derived from this sequence consists of stores A and D.

EXAMPLE: As another illustration of using the random-number table, consider a situation in which we want to pick a simple random sample of 10 counties from a population containing 60 counties. Here we number the counties 00 through 59 (the starting number 00 is chosen arbitrarily; the first population element can very well be designated as 01 or 10—or any other number, for that matter). We randomly start with any two-digit number in the table, say the first two digits in row 16 of the table, which are 51. If we now read down this two-digit column, our simple random sample of 10 counties contains those numbered 51, 07, 03, 41, 15, 10, 57, 55, 01, and 42. The sequence of random numbers that yields this sample is boxed in the table.

In this computer age a researcher can obtain electronic help in choosing a simple random sample. Many computers have pseudo-random-number generators that can readily provide a set of random numbers within any desired range. Unless the sample size is relatively small, computerized selection of a simple random sample is faster and easier than manual selection using a random-number table. Computer selection is particularly helpful in telephone surveys requiring a random sample of respondents. Nowadays, special computer programs are available to perform random-digit dialing, in which telephone numbers are randomly selected and dialed by a computer within an area covered by a prespecified three-digit telephone number prefix.

The preceding sample selection procedure assigns an equal probability of selection for *every unit* in the population. Indeed, a key property of simple random sampling is that every population unit is just as likely to end up in the chosen sample as any other unit. So why is simple random sampling not defined as "a procedure in which each population unit has a known and equal chance of being chosen for the sample"? This definition is somewhat simpler than the formal definition given earlier. However, the reason for not defining simple random sampling in this way is that the property of each population unit's having an equal probability of selection is not unique to simple random sampling. There are other probability-sampling methods (e.g., proportionate stratified random sampling, to be discussed in the next chapter) that also possess this property. Hence the apparently simpler definition does not unambiguously portray the key statistical process underlying simple random sampling—that is, the process of guaranteeing the same probability of selection for *every sample of a given size,* which is unique to simple random sampling.

SAMPLING ERROR AND SAMPLING DISTRIBUTION

The basic purpose of sampling is to generate sample data that can be used to infer something about the nature of the population. For instance, from data collected from a cross section of families living in a city, we can estimate the mean income of the population of families in the city, the proportion of families with microwave ovens, and the like. However, unless we conduct a census study (i.e., a study of *all* the families in the city), we cannot pinpoint the actual mean family income, the exact proportion of families with microwave ovens, and so on. The reason we cannot do so is the presence of sampling error, which is discussed in the next section.

Sampling error

The actual, or true, population mean value or population proportion for any variable (e.g., income, product ownership) is referred to as a *parameter.* An estimate of it from sample data is referred to as a *statistic.* Whenever a sampling procedure is used to estimate a population parameter, there may be some discrepancy between the sample statistic and the actual (but unknown) parameter value, no matter how objectively and carefully the sample is chosen. Such a discrepancy is commonly called sampling error.

DEFINITION. ***Sampling error*** **is the difference between a statistic value that is generated through a sampling procedure and the parameter value, which can only be determined through a census study.**

Knowledge of the *magnitude* of the sampling error is essential for ascertaining how precisely the population parameter can be estimated from a sample statistic value. But we cannot accurately determine the magnitude of the sampling error associated with a sampling process for two reasons: (1) We do not know the true population parameter value (if we already did, there would be no need for any sampling study), and (2) the sample statistic value itself may vary from sample to sample within the same population (more will be said on this variation in the next section). Hence we can only estimate the average amount of sampling error associated with a given sampling procedure. An important statistical concept that is critical for estimating sampling error is sampling distribution, which is discussed next.

Sampling distribution

Consider a population consisting of just 10 families. Suppose the annual expenditures of the 10 families for eating out are as shown in Table 12.2. Here the population mean expenditure for eating out (i.e., the population *parameter* value) is $275. Suppose we want to estimate the population parameter on the basis of data from a simple random sample of just 2 families.

There are 45 possible samples of size two in this population. For any sample the value of the sample mean expenditure for eating out (i.e., the sample *statistic* value) will depend on the families included in it. Table 12.3 contains a partial list of the various samples of size two, along with their sample mean expenditures for eating out. Notice that the sample mean values span a range—from $75 to $475—and that some mean values (such as $275) occur more frequently than others, since a greater number of samples yield those mean values. Thus, theo-

Table 12.2
Expenditures for eating out for a hypothetical population

FAMILY NUMBER	ANNUAL EXPENDITURE FOR EATING OUT ($)
1	50
2	100
3	150
4	200
5	250
6	300
7	350
8	400
9	450
10	500

Table 12.3
Partial list of possible samples and sample means

SAMPLES OF TWO FAMILIES	SAMPLE MEAN VALUES ($)
1, 2	75
1, 6; 2, 5; 3, 4	175
1, 10; 2, 9; 3, 8; 4, 7; 5, 6	275
5, 10; 6, 9; 7, 8	375
9, 10	475

retically, if we were to pick samples of size two over and over again from this population and compute the sample mean value each time, we would observe a range of mean values, with certain values showing up more often than others. This phenomenon underlies the sampling distribution concept.

DEFINITION. A *sampling distribution* is a representation of the sample statistic values—obtained from every conceivable sample of a certain size chosen from a population by using a specified sampling procedure—along with the relative frequency of occurrence of those statistic values.

Exhibit 12.1 represents the sampling distribution associated with a simple-random-sampling procedure for picking samples of 2 families from our popula-

Exhibit 12.1
Sampling distribution for simple random samples of two units

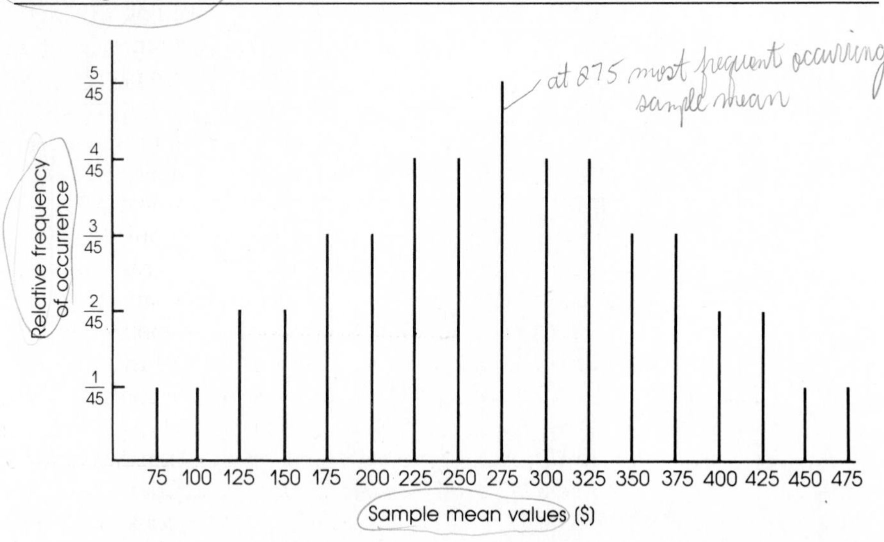

tion of 10 families. The horizontal axis in this exhibit portrays the possible range of mean values, and each vertical line indicates the relative frequency of occurrence of a corresponding sample mean value. For instance, if we pick many samples of size two and compute the sample mean for each, approximately $\frac{3}{45}$ (or about 6.7%) of those values will be \$175. That is, three independent samples yield a sample mean value of \$175 (see Table 12.3). And since each of these samples has the same selection probability (namely, $\frac{1}{45}$), the relative frequency (or probability) of occurrence for a sample mean value of \$175 is given by

$$\tfrac{1}{45} + \tfrac{1}{45} + \tfrac{1}{45} = \tfrac{3}{45}.$$

We emphasize that the sampling distribution concept is a theoretical concept in the sense that in real life we will only pick *one* random sample, rather than a large number of random samples that are needed to construct a sampling distribution. Nevertheless, an understanding of this concept is essential since it forms the basis for estimating a population parameter from a sample statistic value. The nature of the sampling distribution associated with a sampling procedure is the key to estimating the sampling error generated by the procedure.

The sampling distribution diagramed in Exhibit 12.1 has two noticeable features:

1. The most frequently occurring sample mean values cluster around the population parameter value of \$275.
2. Extreme sample mean values, although they are possible, are not very likely to occur..

These features are common to all sampling distributions. Repeated selection of random samples from the same population will yield sample statistic values such that the closer a value is to the population parameter value, the more often it will occur.

In our hypothetical illustration the population size of 10 families is relatively small and hence restricts the total number of possible sample mean values. For this reason the sampling distribution shown in Exhibit 12.1 is discrete and has a somewhat spiked appearance. If the population size is larger and more varied (as is normally the case in real life), a greater variety of sample compositions, and hence a greater variety of sample mean values, will be possible. Consequently, the sampling distribution will contain a much larger number of vertical lines and will have a denser appearance than the one shown in Exhibit 12.1.

When an infinite number of sample compositions are possible, the range of sample mean values can be considered to be *continuous* rather than *discrete*; that is, the sample mean can be considered as being able to take on any value rather than only certain specific values, like \$75, \$100, and \$125 in our example. The sampling distribution for a continuous variable is usually shown as a ***histogram*** rather than as a diagram like Exhibit 12.1 that indicates the probability of

Exhibit 12.2

Sampling distribution shown as a histogram

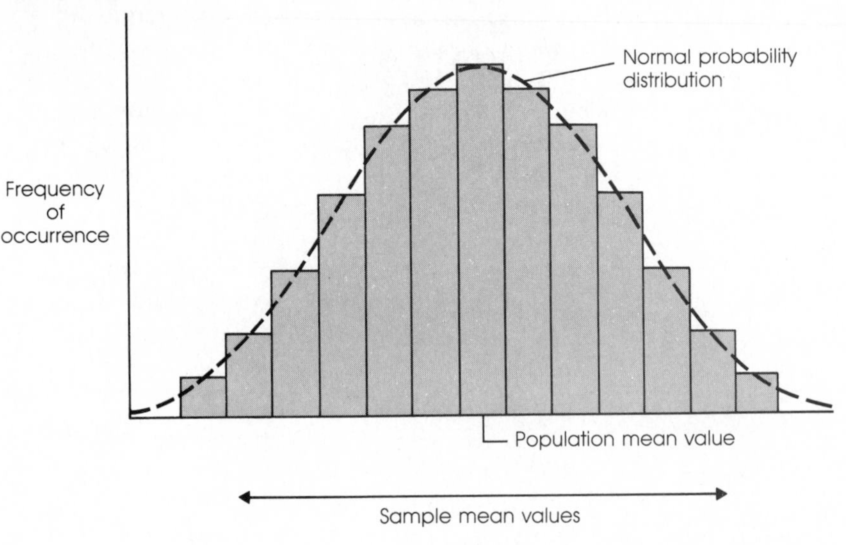

occurrence of *every possible* value of the variable. An example of a histogram representing the sampling distribution of the sample mean is shown in Exhibit 12.2.

In Exhibit 12.2 the height of each rectangle denotes the total frequency of occurrence of all sample mean values included within the range defined by the two vertical sides of the rectangle. Thus the histogram portrays the frequency of occurrence for different *ranges* of sample mean values rather than for *each possible* sample mean value. However, notice that the probability distribution diagram in Exhibit 12.1 and the histogram in Exhibit 12.2 have the same general shape. Indeed, the histogram can be approximated by a bell-shaped curve, as shown by the dotted line in Exhibit 12.2. Such a smooth curve is sometimes called the *theoretical* sampling distribution.

The sampling distribution curve has an important characteristic based on a theorem called the *central limit theorem:* For a sufficiently large sample size (in practice, a sample size of 30 or more), the sampling distribution curve for sample means associated with a sampling procedure will be centered on the population parameter value and will have all the properties of a *normal probability distribution.* (i.e., the so-called normal curve).[4]

[4] For a discussion of the properties of a normal probability distribution, see any introductory statistics textbook, such as D. R. Anderson, D. J. Sweeney, and T. A. Williams, *Introduction to Statistics—An Applications Approach* (St. Paul, Minn.: West, 1981).

Let us use the symbol μ to represent the true population mean value, the symbol $\bar{x}$ to represent a sample mean value, and the symbol $\sigma_{\bar{x}}$ to represent the *standard deviation of the different sample mean values* that will be obtained through repeated selection of samples from the same population. We can interpret $\sigma_{\bar{x}}$ as an average amount of sampling error associated with the sampling procedure. Traditionally, it is referred to as the *standard error of the mean.*

If the theoretical sampling distribution behaves like the normal probability distribution, a *confidence statement* like the following can be made: "If we repeatedly pick random samples of a given size from a population, we can predict that a certain percentage (say, q%) of the sample mean values will be within the range given by $\mu \pm z_q\sigma_{\bar{x}}$," where z_q is the standard normal-deviate value corresponding to q%. The z-values can be read from a normal probability table such as the one shown in Appendix B. Alternatively, the following statement can also be made: "If we pick *one* random sample of a given size from a population, we can predict with q% confidence (or certainty) that the mean value for that sample will be within the range given by $\mu \pm z_q\sigma_{\bar{x}}$." This latter statement forms the basis for estimating confidence intervals for population parameter values.

CONFIDENCE-INTERVAL ESTIMATION

The preceding section illustrated how certain confidence statements can be made about sample statistic values given that the population parameter value (μ) and the standard error ($\sigma_{\bar{x}}$) are known. However, in practice, neither μ nor $\sigma_{\bar{x}}$ is known. Moreover, our purpose is to predict, with a certain degree of confidence, the range of values within which the population parameter is likely to be, given data from just *one* random sample. We can accomplish this purpose by drawing upon the theoretical principles discussed in the preceding sections and by making some approximations.

Confidence intervals for population mean values

The z-value corresponding to a *two-tailed* q-value of 95% is 1.96 (see Appendix B). Notice the emphasis on *two-tailed*; this term underscores that a confidence interval is symmetric about the mean (or proportion), and therefore the z-value corresponds to the tail portion of a normal curve covering an area equivalent to $(100 - q) \div 2$. This two-tailed nature of confidence intervals is *implied* throughout the discussion hereafter.

Now, as we saw earlier, we can be 95% confident that any sample mean value ($\bar{x}$) will be within the range $\mu \pm 1.96\sigma_{\bar{x}}$. That is, we can be 95% confident about the accuracy of the following expression:

$$\mu - 1.96\sigma_{\bar{x}} \leq \bar{x} \leq \mu + 1.96\sigma_{\bar{x}}. \tag{12.1}$$

Expression (12.1) can be rewritten in the form of two separate components:

$$\mu - 1.96\sigma_{\bar{x}} \leq \bar{x}, \tag{12.1a}$$
$$\mu + 1.96\sigma_{\bar{x}} \geq \bar{x}. \tag{12.1b}$$

Let us now rewrite (12.1a) and (12.1b) as follows:

$$\mu \leq \bar{x} + 1.96\sigma_{\bar{x}}, \tag{12.2a}$$
$$\mu \geq \bar{x} - 1.96\sigma_{\bar{x}}. \tag{12.2b}$$

Expressions (12.2a) and (12.2b) can be combined into a single expression:

$$\bar{x} - 1.96\sigma_{\bar{x}} \leq \mu \leq \bar{x} + 1.96\sigma_{\bar{x}} \tag{12.2}$$

In comparing Eq. (12.2) with (12.1), notice that $\bar{x}$ and μ have switched places. Thus the preceding algebraic manipulations have resulted in the derivation of a *useful* confidence interval. Specifically, we have derived a lower and an upper bound within which we can be 95% confident that the population parameter (μ) will fall. This interval is really the type of *confidence interval* that we are looking for.

Unfortunately, Eq. (12.2) does have one catch from a practical standpoint—namely, we do not know the value of $\sigma_{\bar{x}}$. However, from statistical theory we can obtain an approximate estimate of the standard error of the sample mean (say $s_{\bar{x}}$) if we know the standard deviation (say s) of the data obtained from the units in our random sample. The expression for the *standard deviation* is as follows:[5]

$$s = \sqrt{\frac{\sum_{i=1}^{n}(x_i - \bar{x})^2}{n-1}},$$

where

n = number of units in the sample,

x_i = data obtained from each sample unit *i*,

$\bar{x}$ = sample mean value, given by $\sum_{i=1}^{n} \frac{x_i}{n}$.

[5] A few remarks about the expression for the standard deviation are in order. First, the $n - 1$ in the denominator (rather than n) ensures that the sample standard deviation is an *unbiased* estimate of the population standard deviation. Second, a "finite population correction factor" is applied to this expression when the sample size is relatively large compared with the population size. Third, more convenient computation formulas are available if one wants to calculate the sample standard deviation by hand. Further information on these issues can be found in most basic statistics textbooks; see, for instance, Anderson, Sweeney, and Williams, *Introduction to Statistics.*

There is a simple relationship between $s_{\bar{x}}$ and s, namely,

$$s_{\bar{x}} = \frac{s}{\sqrt{n}}.$$

Thus given $\bar{x}$ and $s_{\bar{x}}$ (both of which can be computed by using sample data), we can construct a 95% confidence interval for the population mean, as follows:

$$\bar{x} - 1.96s_{\bar{x}} \leq \mu \leq \bar{x} + 1.96s_{\bar{x}}.$$

That is, we can be 95% confident (or 95% certain) that the population parameter that we are looking for will be in the range given by $\bar{x} \pm 1.96s_{\bar{x}}$.

It was no accident that a value of 95% was picked for q in the preceding illustration of the procedure for constructing confidence intervals. Most practical applications of sampling customarily involve the use of a 95% confidence interval. However, the same procedure can be used to construct other kinds of confidence intervals; one simply chooses an appropriate z_q-value (from the normal probability table) corresponding to whatever confidence level may be desired. For instance, a 99% confidence interval for the population mean is given by $\bar{x} \pm 2.575s_{\bar{x}}$, since the z-value corresponding to a confidence level of 99% is 2.575 (Appendix B).

Let us look at a numerical problem to illustrate the construction of confidence intervals.

PROBLEM: A simple random sample of 100 men's clothing stores was chosen from the population of such stores in a city. The average annual sales of men's suits in this sample was 1278 units, and the standard deviation of sales was 399 units. Construct a 95% confidence interval for the average annual sales of men's suits in the *population* of stores.

In this problem $n = 100$, $\bar{x} = 1278$ units, and $s = 399$ units. Thus

$$s_{\bar{x}} = \frac{s}{\sqrt{n}} = \frac{399}{\sqrt{100}} = \frac{399}{10} = 39.9 \text{ units.}$$

The 95% confidence interval is

$$\begin{aligned} \bar{x} \pm 1.96s_{\bar{x}} &= 1278 \pm (1.96)(39.9) \\ &= 1278 \pm 78.204 \\ &= 1278 \pm 78, \text{ approximately.} \end{aligned}$$

From the sample data we can be 95% confident that the average annual sales of men's suits, across *all* men's clothing stores in the population, is between 1200 and 1356 units.

Confidence intervals for population proportions

The parameters of interest in some research projects may include population *proportions* (e.g., proportion of households in a city that own video recorders, proportion of firms in a region that employ more than 50 people). In such instances one must construct confidence intervals for population proportions from sample data. The procedure for determining such confidence intervals is quite similar to the one we discussed for population mean values. However, the symbolic notation used and the computation of the standard error are somewhat different. The following notation is customary for confidence intervals for population proportions:

π = true population proportion (i.e., the parameter value),
p = proportion obtained from a single sample (i.e., the statistic value),
s_p = estimate of the standard error of the sample proportion.

The 95% confidence interval for the population proportion is given by

$$p - 1.96s_p \leq \pi \leq p + 1.96s_p, \qquad (12.3)$$

where

$$p = \frac{\text{number of sample units having a certain feature}}{\text{total number of sample units (i.e., } n\text{)}}$$

and

$$s_p = \sqrt{\frac{p(1-p)}{n}}.$$

Notice that we only need to know the sample proportion and the sample size to be able to estimate the standard error s_p.

PROBLEM: A simple random sample of 100 grocery stores was chosen from *all* grocery stores in a city. Only 64 of the 100 stores carried potted plants; that is, the proportion of stores in the sample that carried potted plants was .64. Construct a 95% confidence interval for the *population* proportion of stores carrying potted plants.

In this problem $n = 100$ and $p = .64$. So

$$s_p = \sqrt{\frac{p(1-p)}{n}} = \sqrt{\frac{(.64)(.36)}{100}} = .048.$$

The 95% confidence interval is, then,

$$\begin{aligned} p \pm 1.96 s_p &= .64 \pm (1.96)(.048) \\ &= .64 \pm .09408 \\ &= .64 \pm .09\text{, approximately} \end{aligned}$$

This confidence interval can also be expressed in *percentage* terms: 64% ± 9%. In other words, we can be 95% confident that between 55% and 74% of all grocery stores in the city carry potted plants.

DETERMINING SAMPLE SIZE

A basic purpose of sampling is to estimate population parameter values as accurately as possible. We have already seen that we cannot know for sure what a population parameter value is unless we do a census study. The only way to "predict" a parameter value from sample data is to come up with an estimate in the form of a confidence interval, usually the 95% confidence interval. For a given confidence level the tighter, or more compact, the confidence interval, the more *precise,* and hence more useful, the interval estimate will be.

For instance, consider two sampling studies, say A and B, that are conducted to estimate the proportion of a target market that has tried a recently introduced product. Suppose the results of the two studies are as follows: From study A one can be 95% confident that the proportion of all target customers who have tried the product is between .48 and .52; from study B one can be 95% confident that the proportion of all target customers who have tried the product is between .35 and .65. Notice that the two confidence intervals imply that the sample proportion obtained through each study is the same, namely, .50.

If you are a product manager, which of these two studies will you consider to be more useful for decision-making purposes? Study A is apparently superior, because the interval estimate derived from study A is more precise. It implies that you can be reasonably certain that about half your target market has tried your new product, thereby providing you with a precise evaluation of the effectiveness of your marketing strategy for your product. The interval estimate obtained from study B contains little, if any, useful information. It merely indicates that you can be reasonably certain that the proportion of your target market that has tried your new product can be as low as .35 or as high as .65. This information is not really helpful in evaluating the effectiveness of the marketing strategy to launch the product.

In short, to be managerially useful, a confidence-interval estimate must be as compact as possible. That is, the term that is subtracted from and added to the sample statistic value (namely, the ± term) must be as small as possible. This point has key implications regarding certain factors that play a role in sample size determination, as discussed next.

Factors influencing sample size

Let us examine the composition of the ± term that is used in the construction of confidence intervals. This term is $z_q s_{\bar{x}}$ when we are dealing with population mean values, and it is $z_q s_p$ when we are dealing with population proportions. We know that $s_{\bar{x}}$ = (sample standard deviation) $\div \sqrt{n}$. The expression for s_p is $\sqrt{p(1-p)} \div \sqrt{n}$; however, $\sqrt{p(1-p)}$ is nothing but the sample standard deviation for a proportion. Hence, irrespective of whether we are interested in constructing confidence intervals for population means or population proportions, the general expression for the ± term is

$$z_q \times \frac{\text{sample standard deviation}}{\sqrt{n}},$$

where z_q is the standard normal deviate corresponding to the desired confidence level and n is the sample size.

This expression for the ± term is central in determining how compact or how wide a confidence interval will be. By simply examining this expression, we can gain some insights about factors that play a role in determining the sample size for a study.

First, the desired degree of compactness of the confidence interval—usually known as the desired *precision level*—plays a role in determining sample size. Other things remaining the same, the greater the desired precision level, the smaller the acceptable magnitude for the ± term is, and hence the larger the sample size should be.

Given a certain desired precision level, the larger the values of z_q, of the sample standard deviation, or of both, the larger the sample size should be. That is, if the numerator of the expression is large, the denominator must be correspondingly large in order to keep the magnitude of the expression small. Thus a second factor that must be considered in determining sample size is the z_q-value, or the desired *confidence level,* on which the value of z_q depends. Other things remaining the same, the more confidence we want to have in the interval estimate, the larger the z_q-value will be, and hence the larger the sample size should be. For instance, the z-values associated with the 95% and 99% confidence levels are 1.96 and 2.575, respectively. Thus if we desire a 99% confidence interval (rather than a 95% confidence interval) but want it to have the *same* width, or degree of precision, as a 95% confidence interval, we need to pick a larger sample than what we would need for constructing the 95% confidence interval.

The sample standard deviation is another key variable in the expression for the ± term. What does a large or a small standard deviation mean? Standard deviation is a summary measure of how much the data provided by individual sample units differ from the overall central tendency of the total sample (i.e., the sample mean or proportion). The standard deviation of a sample is a measure of how diverse or similar the individual units that make up the sample are; the larger the standard deviation, the greater is the diversity of the units included in the sample. Since a simple random sample is supposed to be an objective representation of the population, we can view the sample standard deviation as being an approximate measure of the extent of variability or similarity of units in the population itself. Hence a third factor that must be considered in determining sample size is the *degree of variability* across the population units. Other things remaining the same, the greater the degree of variability within the population, the larger the sample size should be.

Last, but not least, the *resources available* (e.g., time and money) for conducting a study must also be considered in determining sample size. The available resources are quite critical because, in practice, they place an upper limit on sample size. After all, if resources are unlimited, we can simply pick the largest possible sample, or even do a census study, and not even worry about determining sample size. Such an ideal situation rarely, if ever, exists in real life. Although decision makers may desire a certain level of confidence in research results and want the results to have a specified degree of precision, the fulfillment of their desires often is constrained by a lack of resources. In many real-life situations the budget available becomes the sole determinant of sample size.

Sample size determination methods

In the preceding section we discussed, in a qualitative fashion, the various factors that can influence sample size determination. This section focuses on using quantitative estimates of some of those factors to determine numerical values for sample sizes in different situations.

An important point we must discuss at the outset is that the estimation of numerical values for sample sizes requires a researcher to make certain assumptions and provide certain inputs that are crucial to the meaningfulness of the estimated sample sizes. A researcher, in collaboration with the relevant decision maker, must provide the following inputs in order to determine the sample size for a study:

1. The desired *precision level,* that is, the magnitude of the ± term that the researcher (or decision maker) is willing to tolerate. For example, a decision maker may want to estimate the mean age of a target market within four years, or the decision maker may want to estimate the percentage of a population that owns microwave ovens within a margin of error of ±5%.
2. The desired *confidence level,* that is, the degree of confidence that the decision maker wants to have in the interval estimate.
3. An *estimate* of the degree of variability in the population, expressed in the form of a *standard deviation.*

Given a desired precision level (say c), a desired confidence level (say q), and an estimate of the standard deviation (say s), we can write the following equation:

$$c = \frac{z_q s}{\sqrt{n}}. \tag{12.4}$$

We can square both sides of Eq. (12.4) and rewrite it as follows:

$$n = \frac{z_q^2 s^2}{c^2}. \tag{12.5}$$

Equation (12.5) can be used to determine sample size, irrespective of whether the objective is to estimate a population mean or a population proportion. The following problem demonstrates its application in a situation involving estimation of a population mean.

PROBLEM: A marketing manager of a frozen-foods firm wants to estimate the average annual amount that families in a certain city spend on frozen foods per year. He wants the estimate to be within ±$10. When such an interval estimate is constructed, he wants to be able to have 99% confidence in it. He estimates that the standard deviation of annual family expenditures on frozen foods is about $100. How many families must be chosen for this study?

In this problem c = $10, s = $100, and $z_q = 2.575$ (corresponding to a confidence level of 99%). Notice that c and s are expressed in the *same units,* namely dollars; c and s must be specified in the same units before solving any problem of this kind. We can solve for the value of n by using Eq. (12.5):

$$n = \frac{(2.575)^2(100)^2}{(10)^2} = 663 \text{ families, approximately.}$$

Although the preceding numerical solution to our problem is straightforward, there is a critical catch hidden in the problem; this catch relates to the estimate of the standard deviation of expenditures on frozen foods. How did the manager obtain this estimate? If it is merely an educated guess, how much trust can we place on its accuracy? What impact will this guessed value have on the sample size estimate? The impact can be great. For instance, even if the manager's estimate falls short of the true standard deviation by a mere $10 (i.e., if the true value of the standard deviation is $110 instead of the assumed value of $100), the actual sample size required will be approximately 802 families, and hence the estimated sample size of 663 will be off by 139 families.

The point is that the estimated sample size is very sensitive to even minor errors in the assumed value of the standard deviation. In many real-life situations, where estimates of standard deviations are often merely based on intuitions, using Eq. (12.5) to estimate sample sizes is meaningless. Thus sample size formulas do not have very wide application in practice.

Can a manager or a researcher do better than estimate the standard deviation through subjective judgment? Better estimates are available under certain circumstances:

1. If a study similar to the one being contemplated has been done in the past, the researcher may be able to use the standard deviation obtained from that study.
2. If enough time and money are available, a pilot study using, say, 30 or so units can be conducted simply to estimate the standard deviation of the variable.
3. If the minimum and maximum values of the variable in the population are known, *and* if the variable values for the population units can be assumed to be *normally distributed,* the standard deviation can be estimated as follows:

$$s = \frac{\text{maximum value} - \text{minimum value}}{6}.$$

This expression is derived as follows: Given a group of numbers that are normally distributed, almost all the numbers will be included in the interval formed by the group mean $\pm$ 3 standard deviations. In other words, the difference between the largest and smallest numbers in the group should be approximately equal to six standard deviations.

Though the three circumstances outlined here may yield better estimates of the standard deviation than those based on subjective judgment, a researcher would be wise to bear in mind that such estimates are still only approximations and cannot be expected to be totally error-free.

Let us now consider sample size determination in situations involving estimation of population proportions. As mentioned earlier, Eq. (12.5) can be used to determine sample size when the objective is to estimate a population proportion. However, estimating the standard deviation for this parameter is perhaps even more complex than estimating the standard deviation for a population mean. By definition, the standard deviation of a proportion is expressed in terms of the proportion itself; that is, $s = \sqrt{p(1-p)}$. Hence to estimate s, we need to estimate p, which is what the study, when completed, is supposed to find out.

Of course, if resources permit, one can conduct a pilot study to estimate p and then use that estimate to determine the sample size for the final study. However, a more meaningful approach to use in problems involving proportions is to determine an upper limit for the sample size that can guarantee an interval estimate that has the desired precision level *and* confidence level. How can we determine this upper limit? If we examine the general sample size formula given by Eq. (12.5), we see that for given values of c and z_q, n will take on its maximum value when s assumes its maximum value. For proportions the value of s is largest when $p = .5$, and that largest value is given by

$$s = \sqrt{.5(1 - .5)} = \sqrt{(.5)(.5)} = .5.$$

Hence the upper limit for sample size, $n_{\max}$, can be computed by using the following equation:

$$n_{\max} = \frac{.25z_q^2}{c^2}. \tag{12.6}$$

PROBLEM: A health agency wants to estimate the proportion of smokers among school students in the United States. The agency wants the estimate to be accurate within ±.02 and wants to have 95% confidence in the interval estimate. A pilot telephone survey of 50 high school students showed that 20 of them smoked. Estimate the required sample size for the final study from the given data. What should the sample size be if the desired precision and confidence levels are to be *guaranteed*?

In this problem $c = .02$ and $z_q = 1.96$. An estimate of s (from the pilot survey) is

$$\sqrt{\tfrac{20}{50}\left(1 - \tfrac{20}{50}\right)} = \sqrt{(.4)(.6)} = \sqrt{.24}.$$

So

$$n = \frac{z_q^2 s^2}{c^2} = \frac{(1.96)^2(\sqrt{.24})^2}{(.02)^2}$$

$$= 2305 \text{ students, approximately.}$$

The maximum sample size is

$$n_{\max} = \frac{.25z_q^2}{c^2} = 2401 \text{ students.}$$

By this time you probably have noticed that one important factor—the available resources—is conspicuously absent in the sample size formulas that we discussed. However, available resources often modify the estimated sample sizes. If resources are plentiful, the sample sizes that are estimated by using the formulas should be feasible. However, if resources are limited, one may not be able to pick as large a sample as dictated by a sample size formula. For instance, if the required sample size for a study is 1500 units, but resources are available for only 1000 units, the researcher has no choice other than to pick 1000 units. Under such circumstances the sample size is dictated by the available resources, and the researcher or decision maker will simply have to accept a lower precision level (i.e., a higher value for c) or a lower confidence level (i.e., a lower value for z_q) than desired.

PRACTICAL LIMITATIONS OF SIMPLE RANDOM SAMPLING

Although simple random sampling is the most basic probability-sampling method, it has certain drawbacks in terms of its practical usefulness. A key requirement for simple random sampling is that a complete list of population units be available. For many real-life populations—for example, the target market for perfumes, or all stores that sell paper towels and napkins—such lists may be difficult and expensive to put together. In some situations obtaining an accurate list of population units may even be impossible.

A second difficulty arises when the population and sample sizes are relatively large, which is usually the case in most practical situations. To pick a simple random sample of 100 units from a population of 500 units, by using a random-number table or some other suitable random procedure, may not be very difficult. However, the sample selection task will be laborious if we want to randomly pick a sample of, say, 1000 units from a population of 100,000 units—unless the population list is computerized, in which case the computer can generate a simple random sample relatively easily.

A third problem with simple random sampling is that, by definition, it guarantees an equal probability of selection for every possible sample of a certain size. Hence a simple random sample can turn out to be an extreme sample. For instance, if we pick a simple random sample of two units from the hypothetical population shown in Table 12.2, the sample may well be an extreme sample, such as families 1 and 2 or families 9 and 10, which will lead to a sample statistic estimate that is very far away from the population parameter. Of course, if we repeatedly sample from the same population, on the average we should get a good estimate of the population parameter. However, in practice we only pick *one* sample and hope that it is not an extreme sample. Unfortunately, if we use simple random sampling, our hope may not be fulfilled.

Because of these difficulties, and because there are other probability-sampling methods that can overcome at least some of these difficulties, simple random sampling is not very widely used in practical settings. However, our lengthy discussion of simple random sampling in this chapter does serve a useful purpose; namely, it lays the statistical groundwork that is basic to *all* probability-sampling techniques and is a foundation for more sophisticated probability-sampling techniques.

SUMMARY

Most marketing research projects use sampling, which is the first step in the process of making inferences about a total group of units known as a population. A population of interest to a researcher can be a collection of human or nonhuman units. A census study is one in which every population unit is examined.

When a research population is relatively large, a sampling study is likely to be less expensive, faster, and more accurate than a census study. Furthermore, given the rapidly increasing number of research surveys of human populations, sampling studies can help minimize the depletion of the pool of fresh respondents. Fresh respondents are vital for the successful completion of surveys and for the accuracy of survey results.

Census studies have a place in marketing research projects when they may be both feasible *and* necessary. The feasibility and necessity conditions for conducting a census study will be satisfied by a population that is relatively small and contains units that are distinctly different from one another.

There are two basic procedures for selecting a sample from a given population. One is probability sampling, in which the selection of individual population units is independent of a researcher's judgment or biases. The other procedure is nonprobability sampling, in which a researcher's subjective judgment does play a role in the selection of individual population units.

Simple random sampling is the most basic form of probability sampling. It involves assigning an equal probability of selection to every possible sample of a given size in a population. However, the actual selection of a simple random sample can be done by randomly picking the desired number of units from the population. This procedure is statistically equivalent to first identifying all possible samples of the desired size and then picking one of those samples at random.

Every sampling procedure has a sampling distribution associated with it. The sampling distribution shows how a sample statistic varies across random samples of a given size chosen from the same population. The nature of the distribution associated with a sampling procedure determines the extent of its sampling error. The sampling error can be quantified as the standard deviation of the sample statistic value obtained through repeated sampling; this quantified estimate is known as the standard error.

According to the central limit theorem, when the sample size is sufficiently large, the sampling distribution associated with a sampling procedure displays the properties of a normal probability distribution. This theorem allows us to construct confidence intervals for a population parameter value (mean or proportion) from a sample statistic value.

The sample size for a study must be based on the desired precision level, the desired confidence level, the degree of variability in the population to be studied, and the available resources. Formulas can be used to determine the required sample size for a study. However, the sample size provided by such a formula is very sensitive to the standard deviation estimate used in it. Since estimating accurately the standard deviation prior to conducting a study is difficult, caution must be exercised in using sample size formulas. Moreover, the sample size formulas we discussed do not directly take into account the resources available for a study. In real life the available resources often place an upper limit on sample size, and hence one may not always be able to pick as large a sample as dictated by a sample size formula.

Simple random sampling does have some practical limitations. However, the principles and statistical theory underlying it form the foundation for the advanced sampling techniques to be discussed in the next chapter.

QUESTIONS

1. "When you want to pick a simple random sample of 50 units from a population of 1000 units, you do *not* need to enumerate all possible samples of 50 units." Discuss this statement.
2. What is wrong with defining *simple random sampling* as "a procedure in which each population unit has a known and equal chance of being included in the sample"? Give a more correct definition of simple random sampling.
3. Briefly discuss the distinction between *parameter* and *statistic,* using a suitable example, and define *sampling error.*
4. Define *sampling distribution.* What properties does a sampling distribution curve associated with a random-sampling procedure have? Be specific.
5. a. A simple random sample of 400 undergraduate students in Exmont University had an average grade point ratio of 2.2, with a standard deviation of 2. The sample was chosen randomly by a computer from a university record containing the names and grade point ratios of all undergraduate students in Exmont University. The sample mean and the standard deviation were also calculated and reported by the computer. Construct a 95% confidence interval for the average grade point ratio of Exmont's undergraduate population.
   b. If you were asked to start from scratch and estimate the average grade point ratio *parameter,* would you use the same procedure as in part a? Or would you use a different procedure? Explain your answer. (*Hint:* Consider the pros and cons of a census study versus a sampling study.)
6. a. A marketer wants to be 95% confident that the per capita family income in a certain area is *at least* \$10,000 before deciding to locate a retail outlet in the area. A simple random sample of 81 families chosen from the area had a mean income of \$12,000, with a standard deviation of \$9000. Should the marketer locate a retail store in the area?
   b. Will your answer be different if the marketer raises the minimum per capita income requirement from \$10,000 to \$10,500? Why or why not?
7. a. Firm XYZ introduced a new product in a test market area. Six months after the product had been introduced, a random telephone survey of 100 households in the area indicated that 20 of them had tried the product. Construct a 95%

confidence interval for the percentage of all households in the test area that had tried the new product.

b. Suppose XYZ's goal is "to ensure that at least 75% of the households in the test area try our new product within 12 months after introduction." What recommendation(s) would you make to XYZ from the results in part a?

8. Mr. J. R. Soper, a presidential candidate, does not want to campaign in any state in which he is not almost certain (i.e., 99% confident) that at least 30% of all registered voters are already in favor of him. A random telephone survey of 900 registered voters in state A showed that 360 of them favored Mr. Soper. Should Mr. Soper campaign in state A?

9. State the four factors that should be considered in determining the sample size for any study, and indicate in what way each factor influences sample size.

10. A charitable organization is considering whether it should launch a fund-raising telethon. However, before making a "go or no-go" decision, the organization wants to conduct a national telephone survey of households to estimate the average contribution that a household will make in response to the fund-raising telethon. The organization wants to be 95% confident in the interval estimate derived from the survey, and it desires the estimate to be within ±$10. The standard deviation of charitable contributions in response to similar telethons in the past is about $150. How many households should the organization interview in its telephone survey?

11. The XYZ Company wants to conduct a study to estimate, within ±5%, the percentage of households in Texas that have microwave ovens. Moreover, XYZ wants to have 99% confidence in the interval estimate. A pilot study of 100 households in typical Texas communities found that 30 of them had microwave ovens. What sample size should XYZ use for its study?

12. A study conducted in 1970 showed that family expenditures on travel and entertainment ranged from a low of $100 to a high of $2500 per year. Although the *range* of current family expenditures on travel and entertainment is likely to be the same as in 1970, the *mean* expenditure is likely to have changed substantially. Suppose you want to estimate the current mean expenditure within ±$20, and you desire a confidence level of 95% for your estimate. How many families would you interview regarding their travel and entertainment expenditures?

13. What would your answer to Question 11 be if XYZ wanted to *guarantee* an interval estimate within ±5% at a 99% confidence level?

14. Briefly discuss the practical constraints that limit the usefulness of formulas for determining sample size.

15. Describe the practical limitations of simple random sampling.

13

Advanced Probability-Sampling Methods

PROPORTIONATE STRATIFIED RANDOM SAMPLING

This chapter builds on the previous one by discussing several advanced probability-sampling techniques with the aid of statistical concepts and principles developed earlier. The chapter also presents a comparison of the various probability-sampling methods and discusses their advantages and disadvantages.

In simple random sampling, for a given sample size, *any* combination of population units is just as likely to become the actual sample as any other combination of the same size. Hence the actual study sample may turn out to be an extreme sample that does not adequately represent the population. The example discussed next illustrates this possibility.

EXAMPLE: Suppose the administrators of some university, say Kirkwood University, want to determine the attitudes of their students toward various aspects of the university. Kirkwood University's student body, which is the population of interest here, contains 10,000 students—consisting of 3000 freshmen, 3000 sophomores, 2000 juniors, and 2000 seniors—and we want to select a sample of 500 students for conducting the attitude survey. If we use simple random sampling to pick 500 students, there is no guarantee that the chosen sample will adequately represent the four classification segments of the student body. In fact, simple random sampling may yield a sample in which all 500 students are from the *same* student classification group. In this case the sample will be an extreme one. An extreme sample is not desirable since we cannot use it to generalize the survey results to the entire student body.

An approach to avoid selecting extreme samples is to use a stratified random sampling procedure. *Stratified random sampling* is a probability sampling method in which the chosen sample contains units from various key segments, or strata, of a population. One form of this method is proportionate stratified random sampling, discussed next.

Proportionate stratified random sampling ensures proportionate representation from every population segment, thereby preventing the selection of extreme samples. The following steps are involved in proportionate stratified random sampling:

1. The population of interest is divided into *homogeneous* strata on the basis of some appropriate population characteristic.
2. The total study sample is allocated across the population strata in such a way that the number of units allocated to each stratum is *proportionate* to the size of the stratum.
3. The allocated number of units is selected from each stratum by using a simple-random-sampling procedure.

In step 1 the research population is segmented into strata (or groups). The basis for stratifying the population is some appropriate characteristic. What kind of population characteristic will qualify as being appropriate? First, it must be one that is likely to be associated with the data to be collected through the research study. It must be *relevant* to the study, in the sense that one can expect the responses from the sample units to be *similar within each stratum* but *different across various strata.* The rationale for this requirement will become clear a little later. Second, data about the characteristic must be readily available for each population unit *before* one conducts the study—that is, the characteristic must be *operational*—so as to facilitate the grouping of population units into the various strata.

The Kirkwood University example can be used to illustrate the properties of a characteristic that is appropriate for stratifying a population. Suppose we want to use proportionate stratified random sampling for selecting a sample of Kirkwood University students. Recall that the main objective of the university administrators is to ascertain students' attitudes toward the university. One characteristic that is likely to be associated with a student's attitudes is his or her classification—that is, whether the student is a freshman, sophomore, junior, or senior—since it reflects the nature and the scope of the student's experience at the university. For instance, the attitudes of seniors may be different from those of freshmen by virtue of the seniors' longer exposure to the university's environment. Hence classification is a relevant characteristic for the study of students' attitudes. Is it also operational? Yes, it is; the classification of each student can be identified from university records, and the student population can be easily divided into the four strata, *before* one conducts the study. Thus student classification satisfies both requirements of an appropriate characteristic.

Table 13.1
Proportionate allocation of total sample of Kirkwood University students

POPULATION STRATA	NUMBER OF POPULATION UNITS	NUMBER OF SAMPLE UNITS ALLOCATED
Freshmen	3,000	150
Sophomores	3,000	150
Juniors	2,000	100
Seniors	2,000	100
Total	10,000	500

The second step in proportionate stratified random sampling involves allocating the total sample across the population strata. This allocation is done on a proportionate basis, using the following expression:

$$\begin{array}{l}\text{number of}\\ \text{units allocated}\\ \text{to a stratum}\end{array} = \frac{\begin{array}{c}\text{number of population}\\ \text{units in the stratum}\end{array}}{\begin{array}{c}\text{total number of units}\\ \text{in the population}\end{array}} \times \text{total sample size.}$$

Table 13.1 illustrates the proportionate allocation of the total sample of 500 students in the Kirkwood University example.

After the total sample is allocated, each population stratum is treated as a subpopulation, and a simple random sample of the specified number of units is chosen from each subpopulation to make up the total study sample.

In proportionate stratified random sampling the key to avoiding extreme samples is the assignment of *similar* population units to the *same* stratum and *dissimilar* population units to *different* strata. Since units that are similar will all be within the same stratum, the total sample cannot be an extreme one consisting of like units. Moreover, the selection of units from every stratum ensures adequate representation in the total sample from different segments of the population. Hence the important point is that the relevant population strata be formed in such a way that they are homogeneous within themselves but different from one another.

Sampling distribution and sampling error

What impact will the procedure used in proportionate stratified random sampling have on the sampling distribution associated with it? Recall that a *sampling distribution* represents the relative frequency of occurrence of the values of a sample statistic when samples of a certain size are repeatedly chosen from the same population. If we select samples over and over again from a population by using proportionate stratified random sampling, we can expect the variation in the sample statistic value across the different samples to be less than it would be if we used a sampling procedure that allows for the possibility of extreme samples. Ensuring adequate representation of the population in any one sample is equivalent to ensuring that numerous samples chosen from the same population are as similar to one another as possible. Hence we can expect the sampling distribution of proportionate stratified random sampling to be more compact than one associated with a procedure allowing extreme samples. Therefore the *sampling error,* or *standard error,* of a proportionate-stratified-random-sampling procedure will also be relatively small, since it is simply an estimate of the extent to which the sample statistic value will vary from sample to sample.

Comparison with simple random sampling

As we have seen, for a given sample size proportionate stratified random sampling will result in a tighter sampling distribution and a lower sampling error than will simple random sampling. To illustrate this point further, let us once again consider the hypothetical population of 10 families presented in Chapter 12. In Chapter 12 we discussed the selection of a simple random sample of 2 families from this population in order to determine the mean family expenditure for eating out. Suppose we want to use proportionate stratified random sampling to select a sample of 2 families from the same population. One characteristic that will be relevant as a basis for stratifying the population is family income, since we can expect it to be associated with family expenditure for eating out. However, in real life, family income data for each population unit may not be readily available *before* one conducts a study. But for the sake of illustration, let us assume that we know whether each family in our hypothetical

Table 13.2
Stratification of a hypothetical population

POPULATION STRATA	FAMILY NUMBER	ANNUAL EXPENDITURE FOR EATING OUT ($)
Below-average income	1	50
	2	100
	3	150
	4	200
	5	250
Above-average income	6	300
	7	350
	8	400
	9	450
	10	500

Table 13.3

Mean values for all possible proportionate stratified random samples

POSSIBLE SAMPLES OF TWO FAMILIES	SAMPLE MEAN VALUES ($)
1, 6	175
1, 7; 2, 6	200
1, 8; 2, 7; 3, 6	225
1, 9; 2, 8; 3, 7; 4, 6	250
1, 10; 2, 9; 3, 8; 4, 7; 5, 6	275
2, 10; 3, 9; 4, 8; 5, 7	300
3, 10; 4, 9; 5, 8	325
4, 10; 5, 9	350
5, 10	375

population is above average or below average with respect to income. Specifically, suppose families 1 through 5 have below-average incomes and families 6 through 10 have above-average incomes. Table 13.2, which is a modified version of Table 12.2, shows the stratification of the population on the basis of family income.

For proportionate stratified random sampling the total sample of two units is allocated equally between the two strata, since they contain the same number of population units. The study sample will then consist of one unit chosen randomly from each stratum. Notice that this procedure will exclude certain sample combinations. For example, sample combinations (1, 2), (2, 4), (6, 7), and (9, 10) will not be selected through proportionate stratified random sampling. Notice also that every sample combination that is possible will have representation from each income stratum.

Table 13.3 shows the mean expenditures for eating out for the various samples of two families that can be chosen through proportionate stratified random sampling. Compare the distribution of sample mean values shown in Table 13.3 with the distribution of mean values of simple random samples of two families chosen from the same population (Table 12.2 and Exhibit 12.1 in Chapter 12). What major differences do you see between the two?

The distribution of mean values obtained through proportionate stratified random sampling differs in two distinct ways from that obtained through simple random sampling:

1. Extreme sample means do not occur for proportionate stratified random sampling. The range of possible mean values is $175 to $375 in proportionate stratified random sampling; the range is $75 to $475 in simple random sampling.

2. Sample mean values that are close to the true population mean value (i.e., the population parameter) are more likely to occur with proportionate stratified random sampling than with simple random sampling. For example, the probability of a sample mean value being exactly equal to the population mean value of \$275 is $\frac{5}{25}$, or $\frac{1}{5}$, when proportionate stratified random sampling is used. The probability is a mere $\frac{5}{45}$, or $\frac{1}{9}$, when simple random sampling is used.

Exhibits 13.1(a) and 13.1(b) graphically demonstrate the differences between the two sampling distributions for our hypothetical population.

Exhibit 13.2 shows the general nature of the *theoretical* sampling distributions for simple random samples and proportionate stratified random samples of equal sizes chosen from the same population. Although both sampling distributions are centered on the population mean value, and both possess the properties of a normal probability distribution, the one associated with proportionate stratified random sampling is narrower and steeper than the one associated with simple random sampling. This result reiterates our earlier inference that for a given sample size a proportionate stratified random sample will result in a smaller sampling error (or standard error) than a simple random sample. Thus any confidence-interval estimate for the population parameter will be more

Exhibit 13.1
Sampling distributions

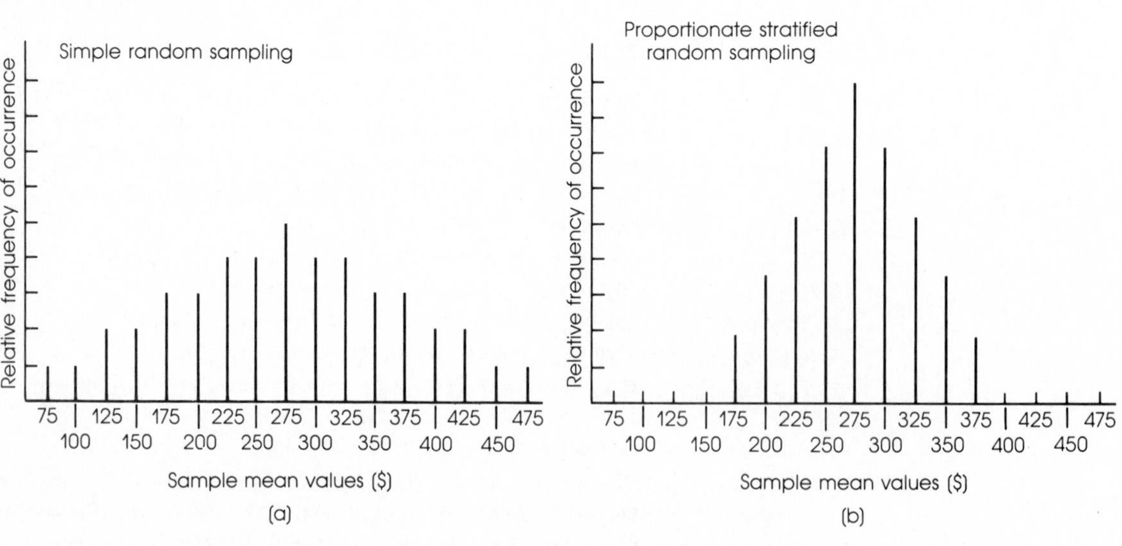

Exhibit 13.2

Theoretical sampling distribution curves

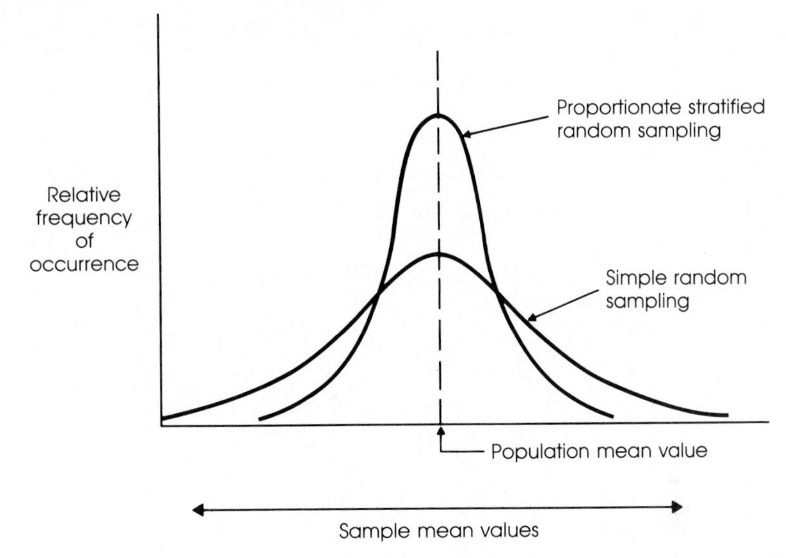

precise if it is based on data obtained through a proportionate stratified random sample rather than a simple random sample.

Relative statistical efficiency

The *statistical efficiency* of a sampling procedure is a measure of how good it is in terms of the sampling error associated with it. Specifically, one sampling procedure is statistically more efficient than another procedure if for a given sample size it results in a smaller sampling error. A sampling procedure that is statistically more efficient than another will also result in a more precise confidence-interval estimate, since the amount of sampling error and the level of precision are inversely related to each other (as we saw in Chapter 12). Alternatively, we can consider a sampling procedure that is statistically more efficient than another as one that requires a *smaller sample* (than the other procedure) in order to provide the *same level of precision* for a confidence-interval estimate.

Clearly, from our discussion in the previous section, proportionate stratified random sampling is statistically more efficient than simple random sampling. In general, the greater the ability of a sampling procedure to prevent the selection of extreme or skewed samples from a population—or, alternatively, the greater the ability of a sampling procedure to yield samples that are each representative of the population and are thus as similar to one another as possible—the higher will be its statistical efficiency.

Confidence-interval estimation

In this section we will focus on the estimation of 95% confidence intervals for population parameter values—means or proportions—although a similar procedure can also be used for constructing other confidence intervals, such as a 99% confidence interval. The confidence-interval estimation method associated with proportionate stratified random sampling is not totally different from the one we discussed in conjunction with simple random sampling; however, it requires some additional computations. Specifically, it involves the following steps:

1. Determine the sample statistic value (mean or proportion) and the corresponding standard error for each population stratum. Recall that any population stratum can be viewed as a subpopulation from which a simple random sample is chosen. Data obtained from each such simple random sample are used to compute a mean (or proportion) and the associated standard error.
2. Combine the sample statistic estimates for the various strata to obtain an overall statistic value.
3. Combine the standard-error estimates for the various strata to obtain an overall standard-error value.
4. Use the following expression to construct the 95% confidence interval for the population parameter:

$$\begin{aligned}95\% \text{ confidence interval} &= \text{overall statistic value}\\ &\quad \pm 1.96(\text{overall standard error})\end{aligned}$$

Confidence intervals for population means. Let $\bar{x}_k$ be the sample mean and s_k be the corresponding standard deviation for any population *stratum k*. The overall sample mean, say $\bar{x}_{\text{st}}$, is estimated by combining the sample means for the various strata:

$$\bar{x}_{\text{st}} = \sum_{k=1}^{L} w_k \bar{x}_k = w_1\bar{x}_1 + w_2\bar{x}_2 + \cdots + w_L\bar{x}_L,$$

where

$$L = \text{total number of strata into which the population is divided,}$$

$$w_k = \frac{\text{number of population units in stratum } k}{\text{total number of units in the population}}.$$

To estimate the overall standard error, say $s_{\bar{x}_{st}}$, we must estimate the standard errors for the individual population strata, which is accomplished as follows:

$$s_{\bar{x}_k} = \frac{s_k}{\sqrt{n_k}} \quad \text{for} \quad k = 1, 2, \ldots, L,$$

where

$s_{\bar{x}_k}$ = standard error for stratum k,
n_k = number of units selected for the sample from stratum k.

We can now estimate the overall standard error by using the following expression:

$$s_{\bar{x}_{st}} = \sqrt{\sum_{k=1}^{L} w_k^2 s_{\bar{x}_k}^2} = \sqrt{w_1^2 s_{\bar{x}_1}^2 + w_2^2 s_{\bar{x}_2}^2 + \cdots + w_L s_{\bar{x}_L}^2}.$$

The 95% confidence interval for the population mean is given by

$$\bar{x}_{st} \pm 1.96 s_{\bar{x}_{st}}.$$

Let us look at a numerical example in order to illustrate the procedure.

PROBLEM: A professional organization consisted of a population of 3000 marketing executives, of whom 2100 had bachelor's degrees and the rest had master's degrees. A random sample of 100 executives was chosen from this population by using a proportionate-stratified-random-sampling procedure. From a survey of this sample the following results were obtained: The mean annual income of the bachelor's degree stratum was \$25,000, with a standard deviation of \$1500; the mean annual income of the master's degree stratum was \$36,000, with a standard deviation of \$2000. Determine the 95% confidence interval for the mean annual income of the members of the entire organization.

The population of interest in this problem is divided into two strata; let stratum 1 be the bachelor's degree stratum and stratum 2 be the master's degree stratum. Notice that $L = 2$ in this case. The total sample of 100 executives is allocated *proportionately* between the two strata. Therefore

$$n_1 = \frac{2100}{3000} \times 100 = 70,$$

$$n_2 = \frac{900}{3000} \times 100 = 30.$$

From the data given in the problem, we can see that $\bar{x}_1 = \$25{,}000$; $s_1 = \$1500$; $\bar{x}_2 = \$36{,}000$; and $s_2 = \$2000$. The weights for the two strata are

$$w_1 = \frac{2100}{3000} = .7,$$
$$w_2 = \frac{900}{3000} = .3.$$

The overall mean is

$$\begin{aligned}\bar{x}_{\text{st}} &= w_1\bar{x}_1 + w_2\bar{x}_2\\ &= (.7)(25{,}000) + (.3)(36{,}000)\\ &= 17{,}500 + 10{,}800 = \$28{,}300.\end{aligned}$$

The standard errors associated with the two strata are

$$s_{\bar{x}_1} = \frac{s_1}{\sqrt{n_1}} = \frac{1500}{\sqrt{70}},$$
$$s_{\bar{x}_2} = \frac{s_2}{\sqrt{n_2}} = \frac{2000}{\sqrt{30}}.$$

The overall standard error is

$$\begin{aligned}s_{\bar{x}_{\text{st}}} &= \sqrt{w_1^2 s_{\bar{x}_1}^2 + w_2^2 s_{\bar{x}_2}^2}\\ &= \sqrt{(.7)^2\frac{(1500)^2}{70} + (.3)^2\frac{(2000)^2}{30}}\\ &= \sqrt{27{,}750} = \$167, \text{ approximately.}\end{aligned}$$

The 95% confidence interval is

$$\$28{,}300 \pm 1.96(\$167) = \$28{,}300 \pm \$327, \text{ approximately.}$$

From the sample data we can be 95% confident that the mean annual income of the organization's members is between \$27,973 and \$28,627.

Confidence intervals for population proportions. The procedure for computing confidence intervals for proportions is the same as the one for means, except for some changes in the notation used. We will use the following notation when the variable of interest is a proportion:

$$\begin{aligned}p_k &= \text{sample proportion estimated from stratum } k,\\ s_k &= \text{standard deviation associated with stratum } k\\ &= \sqrt{p_k(1 - p_k)},\end{aligned}$$

$$s_{p_k} = \text{standard error associated with stratum } k$$
$$= \frac{s_k}{\sqrt{n_k}} = \sqrt{\frac{p_k(1-p_k)}{n_k}},$$
$$p_{st} = \text{overall proportion}$$
$$= w_1p_1 + w_2p_2 + \cdots + w_Lp_L,$$

where L is the total number of strata and the w's are weights as defined in the previous section. Also,

$$s_{p_{st}} = \text{overall standard error}$$
$$\sqrt{\ = w_1^2s_{p_1}^2 + w_2^2s_{p_2}^2 + \cdots + w_L^2s_{p_L}^2}.$$

The 95% confidence interval is

$$p_{st} \pm 1.96s_{p_{st}}.$$

PROBLEM: A population of interest to a marketer consists of 100,000 retail outlets. This population contains 20,000 large outlets (stratum 1), 30,000 medium outlets (stratum 2), and 50,000 small outlets (stratum 3). A proportionate stratified random sample of 1000 outlets was chosen from this population and studied. The researcher found that 60 large outlets, 150 medium outlets, and 300 small outlets in the sample were closed for business on Sundays. Determine the 95% confidence interval for the population proportion of outlets closed on Sundays.

In this problem there are three distinct strata ($L = 3$). Furthermore, the total sample of 1000 is allocated as follows:

$$n_1 = \frac{20{,}000}{100{,}000} \times 1000 = 200,$$
$$n_2 = \frac{30{,}000}{100{,}000} \times 1000 = 300,$$
$$n_3 = \frac{50{,}000}{100{,}000} \times 1000 = 500.$$

Hence $p_1 = 60/200 = .3$; $p_2 = 150/300 = .5$; and, $p_3 = 300/500 = .6$. Also,

$$w_1 = \frac{20{,}000}{100{,}000} = .2, \qquad w_2 = \frac{30{,}000}{100{,}000} = .3, \qquad w_3 = \frac{50{,}000}{100{,}000} = .5;$$
$$p_{st} = w_1p_1 + w_2p_2 + w_3p_3$$
$$= (.2)(.3) + (.3)(.5) + (.5)(.6)$$
$$= .06 + .15 + .3 = .51;$$
$$s_{p_1} = \sqrt{\frac{p_1(1-p_1)}{n_1}} = \sqrt{\frac{(.3)(.7)}{200}} = \sqrt{\frac{.21}{200}},$$

$$s_{p_2} = \sqrt{\frac{p_2(1 - p_2)}{n_2}} = \sqrt{\frac{(.5)(.5)}{300}} = \sqrt{\frac{.25}{300}},$$

$$s_{p_3} = \sqrt{\frac{p_3(1 - p_3)}{n_3}} = \sqrt{\frac{(.6)(.4)}{500}} = \sqrt{\frac{.24}{500}},$$

$$s_{p_{st}} = \sqrt{w_1^2 s_{p_1}^2 + w_2^2 s_{p_2}^2 + w_3^2 s_{p_3}^2}$$

$$= \sqrt{(.04)\left(\frac{.21}{200}\right) + (.09)\left(\frac{.25}{300}\right) + (.25)\left(\frac{.24}{500}\right)}$$

$$= \sqrt{.00237} = .0154, \text{ approximately.}$$

The 95% confidence interval is

$$.51 \pm 1.96(.0154) = .51 \pm .0302.$$

One can be 95% confident that the proportion of outlets closed on Sundays is between .48 and .54. Alternatively, one can be 95% confident that between 48% and 54% of the 100,000 retail outlets remain closed on Sunday.

DISPROPORTIONATE STRATIFIED RANDOM SAMPLING

In proportionate stratified random sampling the basis for allocating the total sample across the population strata is the size of each stratum. The larger the number of units in a stratum, the bigger is the sample chosen from it. However, this procedure is not necessarily the *best* way to allocate the total sample. To understand why, recall our discussion in Chapter 12 about the various factors that influence the determination of sample size. One of those factors was the *degree of variability within a population.* We saw that the greater the degree of variability, the larger the sample size should be so as to ensure the desired levels of confidence and precision. We can extend this principle to individual population strata, which are after all subpopulations. If one stratum contains more diverse units, and hence exhibits a greater degree of variability than another stratum of the same size, a larger number of units must be chosen from the former than from the latter. Thus the degree of variability within a population stratum, rather than its size, is a more appropriate basis for allocating the total sample.

Disproportionate stratified random sampling consists of the same basic steps as proportionate stratified random sampling, but with one major difference in the second step: The total sample is allocated on the basis of relative variabilities, rather than sizes, of the population strata. A potential constraint in this procedure is that one may not know in advance whether the degree of diversity of the population units (with respect to the variables to be studied) differs from one stratum to another, and, if so, by how much. Consequently, in real-life situations proportionate, rather than disproportionate, stratified random sampling is more commonly used. When variances within strata are not known, though, a more sensible procedure may be to draw samples of equal rather than proportionate size from each stratum. However, proportionate samples do have a certain intuitive appeal to clients or research users, thereby leading to the relatively wider use of proportionate stratified sampling in real-life studies. Furthermore, standard canned computer programs for analyzing data from stratified samples typically assume proportionate allocation of the total sample. Nevertheless, note that proportionate stratified random sampling implicitly assumes that the larger the size of a stratum, the greater is the degree of diversity among the units within it—an assumption that may not be necessarily true. The following example illustrates this point.

EXAMPLE: Suppose we want to ascertain the political views of a population of registered voters in a certain community by conducting a survey of 100 voters. Let us say that 50% of this population consists of Democrats, 40% consists of Republicans, and the remaining 10% consists of independents. If we were to use proportionate stratified random sampling, our sample would contain 50 Democrats, 40 Republicans, and 10 independents. However, a sample of 10 units would probably not adequately reflect the diversity of views that independents might be holding. Indeed, the diversity of political views across voters is likely to be much greater in the stratum of independents than in either the stratum of Democrats or the stratum of Republicans. Thus a better way to utilize the total sample of 100 voters is to reallocate some sample units to the stratum of independents from the other two strata. For instance, a sample consisting of 30 Democrats, 30 Republicans, and 40 independents may be more appropriate than a strictly proportionate sample.

For a given sample size disproportionate stratified random sampling will provide a better representation of the total population than proportionate stratified random sampling. This representation is accomplished by sampling *more than proportionately* (relative to their sizes) those strata that are more diverse than others. Hence disproportionate stratified random sampling will be *statistically more efficient* than proportionate stratified random sampling. If the degrees of variability across the strata are different *and known,* disproportionate, rather than proportionate, stratified random sampling must be used. Although quantitative procedures for allocating the total sample on the basis of the degree of stratum variability are available, they are beyond the scope of this textbook.

The A. C. Nielsen Company uses a form of disproportionate stratified ran-

Exhibit 13.3

Disproportionate stratified random sampling used by A. C. Nielsen Company

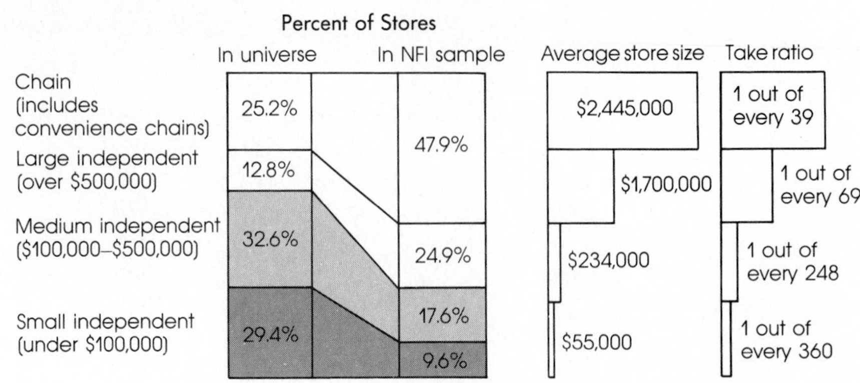

Source: "Management with the Nielsen Retail Index System," a brochure published by the A. C. Nielsen Company, Nielsen Plaza, Northbrook, Ill., p. 11. Courtesy of the A. C. Nielsen Company.

dom sampling in selecting stores that provide the data for the Nielsen Retail Index System. Exhibit 13.3 illustrates the disproportionate-sampling plan that Nielsen uses. Notice that the chain and the large-independent strata are sampled more than proportionately relative to their sizes, while the medium-independent and the small-independent strata are sampled less than proportionately relative to their sizes. Notice also that the "take ratio," which is the selection probability of a store in each stratum, varies from stratum to stratum.

If proportionate sampling were used, the percentage distribution of stores across the strata in the Nielsen sample would be *identical* to the percentage distribution in the universe; moreover, the take ratio would be the same in all the four strata. The rationale for Nielsen's use of disproportionate sampling is that the chain and the large-independent strata account for the purchases of a much larger number of households and exhibit a greater variety in terms of the nature and the volume of those purchases, when compared with the other two strata. Hence the disproportionate allocation of stores is likely to provide a more accurate representation of purchases of the entire population than a proportionate allocation.

SIMPLE CLUSTER SAMPLING

Simple cluster sampling (sometimes known merely as cluster sampling) involves the following steps:

1. The population is divided into subpopulations, or clusters of units.
2. A simple random sample of a few clusters is selected.
3. *All* the units in the selected clusters are studied; that is, a census of each selected cluster is conducted.

Although step 1 of simple cluster sampling resembles the first step of stratified random sampling (proportionate or disproportionate), the two sampling procedures are quite different. While the total sample in stratified random sampling consists of a sample of units from each subpopulation (stratum), the total sample in simple cluster sampling consists of *all the units within a sample of subpopulations* (clusters). Since simple cluster sampling does not involve selecting units from every cluster, its ability to provide a sample that adequately represents a population depends on the extent to which the clusters themselves are each representative of the population. Ideally, each cluster must be a miniature population; each must adequately reflect the degree of heterogeneity (or variability) in the population and, hence, be as similar to the other clusters as possible. Thus the nature of the subpopulations formed in simple cluster sampling is quite the opposite of the nature of the subpopulations formed in stratified random sampling. While the clusters in the simple cluster sampling must be internally *heterogeneous* and *similar* to one another, the strata in stratified random sampling must be internally *homogeneous* and *different* from one another.

A major advantage of simple cluster sampling is the ease of sample selection relative to other probability-sampling methods. For example, suppose we have a population of 20,000 units from which we wish to select a sample of 500 units. Choosing a sample of that size through simple random sampling or stratified random sampling will require a cumbersome procedure like selecting 500 suitable numbers from a random-number table. But if the population is divided into, say, 80 clusters of 250 units each, we can select the sample relatively easily by using simple cluster sampling; we only need to pick randomly two clusters and study all the units in those chosen clusters. However, the ease of sample selection in simple cluster sampling must be weighed against the potential difficulty in forming clusters that are miniature populations. In most real-life situations a researcher will be hard-pressed to form clusters that are each heterogeneous enough to reflect the true nature of the population. The amount of work needed to form such clusters may more than offset the ease of sample selection.

Can we draw any conclusions about the relative statistical efficiency of simple cluster sampling from this discussion? Recall that the statistical efficiency of a sampling procedure depends on its ability to draw a *representative* sample from a population. Hence simple cluster sampling is likely to have relatively low statistical efficiency, unless the individual clusters are representative of the population. Unfortunately, forming clusters by grouping similar units (as in the case of stratified random sampling) is often much easier than devising clusters that are each sufficiently varied to mirror the population. Nevertheless, because of the ease of sample selection in simple cluster sampling, the temptation to use it may be quite high even when the clusters are not representative of the population. However, anyone wanting to use it must be prepared to pay a price in terms of reduced statistical efficiency and the consequent imprecise estimates. In fact, if the clusters are very different in composition from one another and consist of similar units within each, the statistical efficiency of simple cluster sampling may even be lower than that of simple random sampling.

To preserve the ease-of-use benefit associated with simple cluster sampling and, at the same time, make it statistically efficient, researchers must limit its practical application to research populations that can be easily divided into representative clusters. Though such populations are rare, they may be found in a few research projects, as illustrated in the following example.

EXAMPLE: Consider a situation in which the population consists of all the names listed in a certain city's telephone book. Let us say that there are 20,000 names in the telephone book, listed alphabetically in 200 pages, 100 names on each page. Suppose we want to choose a sample of 400 names for the research study. In this situation we can treat the 200 pages as representative clusters of the population, randomly choose any four pages, and combine all the names in those four pages to form the sample. This cluster-sampling procedure is obviously easier than other procedures such as simple random sampling. But will it also be as statistically efficient as simple random sampling? Yes, it will be if we assume that the alphabetical listing of names is as good as a random listing of names for the purpose of the research.

Although the assumption of this example may be reasonable, it may not hold up under *all* circumstances, as illustrated next.

EXAMPLE: Let us say that the purpose of a research project is to study several ethnic- and culture-related aspects of people in a certain area. Moreover, suppose some large ethnic groups of people live in this area. Consequently, the last names of many individuals belonging to certain ethnic groups may all begin with the same letter. A case in point is North Orange County, California. The telephone book for this area has more Nguyen (Vietnamese) surnames than Smith surnames. Thus if the research is to be conducted in North Orange County, names listed in the telephone book cannot be considered to be a random listing. Simple cluster sampling may be inappropriate here since any sample derived through it may underrepresent or overrepresent some critical segments of the population. For instance, what if the Nguyen page in the North Orange County telephone book happens to be one of the randomly chosen clusters? The result will be a nonrepresentative sample and reduced statistical efficiency.

SYSTEMATIC SAMPLING

Systematic sampling, as the name implies, is an organized procedure for selecting a sample from a list that contains all the population units. Specifically, it involves these steps:

1. A *sampling interval k* is determined as follows:

$$k = \frac{\text{number of units in the population}}{\text{number of units desired in the sample}}.$$

2. *One unit* between the first and *k*th units in the population list is randomly chosen.
3. The randomly chosen unit and *every kth unit* thereafter are designated as part of the sample.

To illustrate the procedure, consider a population list of 1000 units (numbered 1 through 1000) from which we wish to select a sample of 50 units. The sampling interval k is $1000/50 = 20$. To select the first unit for our sample, we randomly pick one number between 1 and 20, say 17. So our sample will consist of the population units numbered 17, 37, 57, . . . , 997. Notice that only the starting unit for the sample (unit 17) is randomly selected; the rest are "systematically" selected from the population list. Hence the starting unit completely determines the rest of the sample. For instance, if our initial random number happened to be 12, the units numbered 32, 52, . . . , 992 would automatically become part of the sample. Thus systematic sampling is equivalent to randomly picking *one cluster* of units (e.g., a cluster consisting of units 17, 37, 57, . . . , 997, or units 12, 32, 52, . . . , 992) from the population and considering *all* the units in that cluster as part of the sample. Conceptually, then, systematic sampling is a form of simple cluster sampling, although one need not actually divide the population into clusters if one wants to pick a systematic sample.

The most obvious attraction of systematic sampling is its simplicity relative to the other methods that we have seen: Given a population list, only one random number is required in order to select a sample from it. A less obvious benefit of systematic sampling is that in most practical applications its statistical efficiency is no lower than that of simple random sampling and can be as high as that of proportionate stratified random sampling. This benefit of systematic sampling, coupled with its simplicity, makes it very appealing from a researcher's standpoint.

The statistical efficiency of systematic sampling will vary depending on the *order* in which the population units are arranged in the list from which the sample is chosen. If the units are arranged in some random order (e.g., a population of industrial firms listed alphabetically), a systematic-sampling procedure will yield a sample that is equivalent to a simple random sample; hence its statistical efficiency will be as good as that of simple random sampling. Its statistical efficiency will be as good as that of proportionate stratified random sampling if the population units are ordered according to some relevant characteristic—one that is likely to be associated with the variables to be studied. For instance, let us say that the purpose of a research project is to estimate the average marketing expenditures of industrial firms, and that the population list of firms is ordered according to firm size, from the largest firm to the smallest, or vice versa. In this situation a systematic-sampling procedure will automatically result in proportionate representation from various size categories of industrial firms. Consequently, its statistical efficiency will be as good as that of proportionate stratified random sampling.

Systematic sampling does have one potential problem that although it arises infrequently in real life, can be quite serious when it does arise. The statistical efficiency of systematic sampling will be drastically reduced if the population list contains a certain periodicity (e.g., if every tenth unit in the list is similar) and if the periodicity happens to be equal to the sampling interval k, a multiple of the sampling interval (e.g., $2k$ or $3k$), or an integral fraction of the sampling interval (e.g., $k/2$ or $k/3$). The following example illustrates this problem.

EXAMPLE: The ABC Company, an appliance manufacturer, has a 24-hour, toll-free hot line that consumers can call if they have questions or complaints about its appliances. During the past year ABC has maintained detailed records, on an hour-by-hour basis, of the number and nature of toll-free calls it received.

Suppose ABC wants to estimate the average number of product complaint calls received per hour during the past year from each state in the United States. Moreover, suppose going through all the thousands of call records that ABC has in its files is too expensive. Hence the researcher wishes to select a *sample* of one-hour records from the chronologically arranged population of all such records.

An easy way to select a sample from the chronological listing of records is to use systematic sampling. However, there is a built-in periodicity in such a population listing: Every 24th unit will correspond to the same hour in the day. Consequently, if the sampling interval happens to be related to this built-in periodicity—sampling intervals of 12, 24, or 48, for example—a systematic sample of one-hour records will not be representative of all one-hour records; it will consist merely of records corresponding to exactly the same hour, or the same few hours, of each day. Such a sampling procedure will be statistically inefficient and lead to imprecise estimates, since we can expect the number and the origin of complaint calls to vary from hour to hour within a day.

The potential problem of periodicity in a population is not insurmountable. An alert researcher who suspects some hidden periodicity can avoid the problem through two different means. First, the researcher can use a sampling interval that is independent of the suspected periodicity—for instance, a sampling interval such as 10, 25, or 50 in the situation faced by ABC. Second, the researcher can scramble the population list so as to break up any periodicity and thus convert it to a random listing. However, the second approach will be cumbersome and hence may neutralize the simplicity of systematic sampling. Moreover, if maintaining a chronological or ordered list of population units is essential for other purposes, the researcher may not be able to scramble it just for the sake of using systematic sampling.

AREA SAMPLING

Area sampling is another type of cluster sampling in which clusters are formed on the basis of the *geographic location* of the population units. A form of area sampling that is analogous to simple cluster sampling is *one-stage area sampling*. It involves the following steps:

1. Segment a total geographic area of interest (e.g., a city or a state) into subareas (e.g., city blocks, census tracts, or counties).
2. Select a few of the subareas randomly.
3. Study *all* the units (e.g., households, retail outlets, or financial institutions) in the selected subareas.

As in the case of simple cluster sampling, a key advantage of one-stage area sampling is its simplicity. It is, perhaps, even a little easier to use than simple cluster sampling since the clusters (subareas) are usually *predefined* by their geographic orientation. A researcher therefore needs to exert little effort in segmenting the population. Unfortunately, a very serious drawback of one-stage area sampling is that the final sample is not likely to be representative of the population of units. The units within any geographic subarea (e.g., households within the same city block) will be quite similar to one another on a number of characteristics. As a result, in terms of statistical efficiency, conducting a census of a few randomly chosen subareas will be a relatively poor sampling procedure.

A form of area sampling that is statistically more efficient than one-stage area sampling is *two-stage area sampling,* which differs from the former in the following way: Instead of the researcher's picking *all* the units from the randomly chosen subareas, only a *sample* of units is randomly picked from each of them. As its name implies, this procedure involves two distinct stages of random sampling: Stage 1 is a random selection of a sample of subareas; and stage 2 is a random selection of a sample of units from each chosen subarea. For a given sample size two-stage area sampling allows the researcher to examine a wider, more representative geographic area than one-stage area sampling; hence it will be statistically more efficient. However, on the negative side, two-stage area sampling will generally require more time and money than one-stage area sampling, owing to the wider geographic area to be covered.

Let us look at an example to illustrate the area-sampling concepts that we have discussed so far.

EXAMPLE: Suppose a television station in a certain city wants to conduct a survey related to the TV-viewing behavior of households in the city. Assume that the city consists of 5000 city blocks, each of which contains 20 households. Suppose a sample of 200 households is to be chosen for the study through area sampling. Table 13.4 shows seven different combinations of city blocks (stage 1 units) and households from city blocks (stage 2 units) for obtaining a total sample of 200 households.

Plan A is a one-stage area-sampling plan; plans B through G are two-stage area-sampling plans. Notice that for a sample of 200 households plan A will be least representative of all households in the city, while plan G will be most representative. In terms of relative statistical efficiency, plan A will be the worst, plan G will be the best, and the others will be in between.

How do the seven plans compare in terms of the effort and the resources needed to implement them? We can expect the ranking of the plans here to be the reverse: plan A best, plan G worst, and the others in between. Clearly, a choice between one-stage and two-stage area-sampling plans, or a choice from among alternative two-stage area-sampling plans, has to be based on the degree of statistical efficiency or precision desired as well as the resources available for the research.

In some research projects *multistage area sampling*, which is merely an extension of two-stage area sampling, can be used. For instance, suppose we

Table 13.4

Alternative sampling plans for a study of TV-viewing behavior

SAMPLING PLAN	NUMBER OF STAGE 1 UNITS TO BE SELECTED	NUMBER OF STAGE 2 UNITS TO BE SELECTED FROM EACH CHOSEN STAGE 1 UNIT
A	10	20
B	20	10
C	25	8
D	40	5
E	50	4
F	100	2
G	200	1

want to choose a sample for a nationwide study of households in the United States. We can use multistage area sampling by randomly selecting (1) a sample of counties from a population of all counties in the United States; (2) a sample of towns and cities from each selected county; (3) a sample of census tracts from each selected town or city; and (4) a sample of households from each selected census tract. In general, for a given number of units to be selected from a specified geographic area, the greater the number of sampling stages, the greater will be the statistical efficiency and the resources required.

The methods we have discussed so far in this section illustrate the basic concepts underlying area sampling. However, they are based on some simplifying assumptions and do not exactly mirror area sampling as it is used in practice. For instance, in our treatment of two-stage area sampling we implicitly (and conveniently) assumed that each stage 1 unit had the *same* number of stage 2 units. Is this assumption valid? In many real-life situations it will not be. When the number of stage 2 units in each stage 1 unit is not the same, the stage 1 units have to be realigned or their selection probabilities have to be adjusted according to their relative sizes.

To illustrate these modifications briefly, let us again consider the example dealing with TV-viewing behavior.

EXAMPLE: Suppose the 5000 city blocks making up the total area of interest in this study are not all of the same size. Specifically, suppose 2000 city blocks have 20 households each, another 2000 city blocks have 40 households each, and the remaining 1000 city blocks have 60 households each. One way of choosing an area sample of 200 households under these circumstances is to first realign the city blocks so as to create a new set of stage 1 units of equal size. For instance, city blocks with 40 households can each be split into two subareas with 20 households in each subarea; similarly, city blocks with 60 households can each be split into three subareas. This procedure results in a new set of 9000 stage 1 units (2000 + 2000 × 2 + 1000 × 3) with 20 households in each. The desired sample of 200 households can now be chosen by using a two-stage area-sampling plan similar to the ones in Table 13.4.

In situations where geographic realignment of stage 1 units is not feasible, an alternative approach called *probability-proportional-to-size area sampling* can be used. In this procedure the original stage 1 units are not altered; rather, their probabilities of selection are adjusted to be proportional to the number of stage 2 units in them. In our illustration city blocks with 40 households will be twice as likely (and those with 60 households will be three times as likely) to be chosen in the first stage of sampling as city blocks with 20 households. The number of households selected in the second stage from each chosen city block will still be the same. To illustrate, suppose we want to choose 200 households by using plan E in Table 13.4 (i.e., selection of 50 city blocks followed by selection of 4 households from each). We can use probability-proportional-to-size area sampling by following these steps:

1. Number the city blocks 1 through 5000.
2. For each city block with 20 households, drop *one* piece of paper with its number written on it into a hat; drop *two* such pieces of paper into the hat for each city block with 40 households; drop *three* such pieces of paper into the hat for each city block with 60 households.
3. Draw 50 pieces of paper randomly from the hat.
4. Randomly select 4 households from each city block whose number is drawn.

The resulting sample of 200 households will provide a more accurate geographic representation of the city than a sample derived through a procedure that did not adjust the selection probabilities for the city blocks according to the number of households in them.

As the preceding modified two-stage area-sampling illustrations demonstrate, there are several complex variations of the procedures described in this section that are frequently necessary in practical applications of area sampling.

COMPARISON OF THE VARIOUS METHODS

Statistical efficiency

Can we rank-order the various probability-sampling methods in terms of their relative statistical efficiency? To come up with a clear-cut ranking of all those methods will be somewhat difficult. The specific purpose of a research project vis-à-vis the nature of the research population involved in it (e.g., the degree of variability within the population with respect to the research questions to be addressed) can make one sampling technique statistically more efficient than another *in that research project* but not necessarily in other projects. However, we can make some generalizations about the relative statistical efficiency of different sampling methods, bearing in mind that there may be exceptions to those generalizations in a few unique situations.

In general, for a given population stratified random sampling will be statistically more efficient than simple random sampling. Disproportionate stratified random sampling will be statistically more efficient than proportionate stratified random sampling. Simple cluster sampling will be worse than simple random sampling, unless the individual clusters can be viewed as random samples from the research population. The statistical efficiency of systematic sampling will be at least equal to that of simple random sampling and can be as high as that of proportionate stratified random sampling. However, it will be lower than that of simple random sampling if the sampling interval is related to any periodicity embedded in the population list. One-stage area sampling will be statistically less efficient than simple random sampling. When an area-sampling plan has two or more stages, all we can say is that its statistical efficiency will be directly related to its ability to produce a sample that adequately represents diverse geographic segments within the total area of interest. While the statistical efficiency of such a plan will be higher than that of one-stage area sampling, it may or may not be higher than that of other probability-sampling techniques.

Practical considerations

Not all probability-sampling methods may be equally practical in any research project. Certain factors affect the feasibility of and the effort involved in implementing them. First, unless a complete list of all population units is available, simple and stratified random sampling as well as systematic sampling cannot be used. In this regard simple cluster sampling and area sampling are somewhat more feasible because a complete list of units will be required only for the subpopulations that get selected. Second, the feasibility of some sampling plans depends on the amount of prior knowledge about a population that a researcher has. For instance, both proportionate and disproportionate stratified random sampling require data on some relevant population characteristic in order for the researcher to stratify the population; additionally, disproportionate stratified random sampling requires knowledge about the degree of variability within each stratum. Two-stage area sampling, if done properly, requires knowledge about the number of stage 2 units in each stage 1 unit. Third, although every probability-sampling method involves random selection at some point, the effort needed to identify the units for a sample varies widely across the methods. For example, in simple and stratified random sampling *each* unit must be randomly picked; in contrast, only the *first* unit needs to be randomly picked in systematic sampling.

In summary, no sampling technique can be labeled the best in terms of relative statistical efficiency *and* feasibility. The choice of the most appropriate sampling technique for a research project must be based on a careful evaluation of the nature of the population involved, the degree of precision desired for the estimates, and the amount of resources available for the research.

SUMMARY

This chapter discussed several probability-sampling techniques other than simple random sampling, namely, stratified random sampling (proportionate and disproportionate), simple cluster sampling, systematic sampling, and area sampling (one-stage, two-stage, and multistage). A sizable segment of this chapter was devoted to proportionate stratified random sampling; the material there focused on extending the sampling principles and theory that we covered under simple random sampling in Chapter 12. Specifically, we discussed the nature of the sampling distribution and the estimation of confidence intervals associated with proportionate stratified random sampling vis-à-vis those associated with simple random sampling. For a given sample size proportionate stratified random sampling will have a tighter sampling distribution and will result in a more precise confidence-interval estimate than simple random sampling; that is, it will have greater statistical efficiency.

We did not explicitly examine confidence-interval estimation procedures for sampling techniques other than proportionate stratified random sampling; nor did we look at procedures for determining the required sample sizes for any of the advanced probability-sampling techniques. Although estimation formulas, which are somewhat more complex than the ones we have presented in Chapter 12 and in this chapter, are available for these purposes, a discussion of such formulas is beyond the scope of this textbook.

With respect to the relative statistical efficiency of the various sampling techniques, although some general statements can be made, an unambiguous rank ordering of all the techniques is not possible. Also, the extent to which a sampling technique is practical in a research setting will depend on factors such as the availability of a complete list of population units, the amount of prior knowledge about a population that a researcher has, and the effort needed versus the resources available to identify the sample units. Hence the choice of an appropriate technique depends to a considerable extent on the specific characteristics of and constraints in a research setting.

QUESTIONS

1. Summarize the steps involved in proportionate stratified random sampling.
2. Briefly discuss, with a suitable example, the two properties that a population characteristic must possess if it is to be appropriate for use in stratified random sampling.
3. In what ways does the sampling distribution associated with proportionate stratified random sampling differ from that associated with simple random sampling? Why?
4. Develop a logical argument to indicate why a confidence-interval estimate based on proportionate stratified random sampling will be more precise than one based on simple random sampling.
5. Define *statistical efficiency,* and indicate when one sampling procedure can be considered to be statistically more efficient than another.
6. A population of 10,000 families consists of two strata: a low-income stratum with 6400 families and a high-income stratum with 3600 families. A proportionate stratified random sample of 100 families was surveyed from this population. For the low-income stratum the mean annual expenditure for eating out was \$300, and the standard deviation was \$100. For the high-income stratum the mean was \$500, and the standard deviation was \$100. Determine the 95% confidence interval for the population mean expenditure.

7. The population of 50,000 employed adults in a city fell into the following strata: (1) 10,000 who had college degrees, (2) 15,000 who had high school diplomas but no college degrees, and (3) 25,000 who had not completed high school. A proportionate stratified random sample of 1000 individuals from this population showed the following: Those in stratum 1 had a mean income of $20,000, with a standard deviation of $1500. Those in stratum 2 had a mean income of $10,000, with a standard deviation of $1200. Those in stratum 3 had a mean income of $8000, with a standard deviation of $1000. What is the 95% confidence interval for the mean income of all employed adults in the city?
8. The relevant population for a study consisted of two strata: males and females. Exactly half of the population was male. A sample of 800 people was chosen from this population by using proportionate stratified random sampling. A survey of this sample indicated that 40% of the males and 20% of the females had college degrees. Estimate the 95% confidence interval for the percentage of individuals with college degrees in the population.
9. A food marketer wanted to determine the percentage of grocery stores in a certain area stocking more than three brands of catsup. There are 500 large, 1500 medium-sized, and 3000 small grocery stores in the area. A proportionate stratified random sample of 100 stores was examined. Six of the large stores, 9 of the medium-sized stores, and 15 of the small stores in the sample stocked more than three brands of catsup. Construct the 95% confidence interval for the percentage of all grocery stores stocking more than three brands of catsup.
10. What is the basic difference between proportionate and disproportionate stratified random sampling? Why does this difference make the latter procedure statistically more efficient than the former?
11. How would you describe the difference between an ideal stratum in stratified random sampling and an ideal cluster in simple cluster sampling? Explain your answer.
12. Briefly discuss the relative merits and drawbacks of simple cluster sampling.
13. List the steps involved in systematic sampling. Why is systematic sampling really a form of simple cluster sampling?
14. "The statistical efficiency of systematic sampling will never be lower than that of simple random sampling." Discuss this statement.
15. Describe the problem of periodicity in systematic sampling, and indicate ways it can be avoided.
16. Briefly discuss the pros and cons of one-stage area sampling and of two-stage area sampling.
17. What are the practical considerations that may favor one probability-sampling method over another in a research setting? Give an example to illustrate each consideration.

14

Nonprobability-Sampling Methods

Nonprobability sampling is a subjective procedure in which the probability of selection for the population units cannot be determined. It cannot be determined because in nonprobability sampling the selection of sample units from a population is not done on a strictly chance basis, as it is in probability sampling. An important feature of nonprobability sampling is that it offers researchers greater freedom and flexibility in selecting the individual population units than does probability sampling. Before examining this feature, let us first discuss the basic types of nonprobability-sampling methods.

CONVENIENCE SAMPLING

DEFINITION. ***Convenience sampling* is a procedure in which a researcher's convenience forms the basis for selecting a sample of units.**

All of us have been and continue to be exposed to numerous applications of convenience sampling during our daily routines. For instance, you have probably come across several situations similar to the ones in the following examples.

EXAMPLE: The administrators of your college have just announced a sharp increase in tuition fees for the next year, citing rapidly increasing administrative costs as the main reason for the increase. This announcement is covered in the evening news program of your local TV station. The TV reporter covering this news item says, "While some of the students feel that the ten percent fee hike is justified, most of them consider it to be unfair." Then as apparent support for this conclusion, the reporter is shown standing in a certain part of campus and talking to several students, one at a time, about their reactions to the proposed tuition fee increase.

EXAMPLE: One of your marketing professors is interested in studying the impact of the size of print advertisements on the degree of awareness they are likely to create for the brands advertised. This professor has developed a set of hypothetical advertisements of different sizes for a variety of products, along with a questionnaire to measure the extent of brand awareness among consumers exposed to the advertisements. To pretest the research instrument, the professor asks the members of your class to examine the advertisements and then respond to the questionnaire.

EXAMPLE: As you enter a shopping mall, you see a group of individuals passing out questionnaires to every adult entering the mall. The questionnaire is from your local government. It concerns the attitudes of local residents toward atmospheric pollution and their reactions to the possibility of increased taxes that may be needed to enforce strict pollution controls. You are asked to take just a few minutes to fill out the questionnaire and drop it in the box that is conspicuously placed in the shopping mall entrance. You notice that while a few shoppers fill out the questionnaire and drop it in the box, many others are just walking off with unfilled questionnaires.

The use of responses from a *sample* of individuals is evident in each of these examples. However, in contrast to the methods of probability sampling, notice that in each case the "researcher"—namely, the TV news reporter in the first example, the marketing professor in the second example, and the local government in the third example—was apparently willing to make some inferences on the basis of inputs from whatever sample was *conveniently available*. The researcher made no effort to locate and use inputs from a representative sample of units.

Invariably, there will be some major difference between the population as implied by a convenience sample and the ideal population.

DEFINITION. **An *implied population* is the collection of units to which any generalization from the actual sample is restricted.**

DEFINITION. **The *ideal population* is the collection of units that is most pertinent for the research; it is the population to which generalizations from the research should be desired.**

The implied and ideal populations in the three examples differ as follows:

Example	Population Implied by the Convenience Sample	Ideal Population of Interest
1. Students' reactions to proposed fee hike	Students who happened to be in the vicinity where the TV news reporter was conducting interviews on campus	All students who will have to pay higher tuition fees during the next year
2. Pretesting research instrument	College students with at least some awareness of marketing tools, who may or may not be potential buyers of the types of products included in the test advertisements	All individuals who are likely to be potential buyers of the types of products included in the test advertisements
3. Public opinion survey about pollution	Adults who went to the shopping mall and were willing to fill out the questionnaires passed out	All adults who live within the jurisdiction of the local government

The population implied by a convenience sample can differ from the ideal population in two important ways. First, the implied population may *exclude* certain *relevant units* that are of interest to the researcher. Second, the implied population may *include* certain *irrelevant units* that are not likely to be of interest to the researcher. Illustrations of the types of relevant units excluded

Example	Relevant Units Excluded	Irrelevant Units Included
1. Students' reactions to proposed fee hike	Students unwilling to be interviewed on camera Students not present on campus when the TV reporter was there	Students who will not be affected by the tuition fee increase, such as students who will graduate by next year and students who will be on tuition waiver scholarships when the fee increase takes effect
2. Pretesting research instrument	Nonstudent consumers with no formal education about marketing tools	Students who are not potential buyers of the advertised products
3. Public opinion survey about pollution	Local residents who did not go to the mall when the survey was being conducted Local residents who did go to the mall but did not have time to fill out the questionnaire	Visitors who are not residents of the local area but who happened to go to the mall when the survey was being conducted

Exhibit 14.1

Discrepancy between implied and ideal populations in convenience sampling

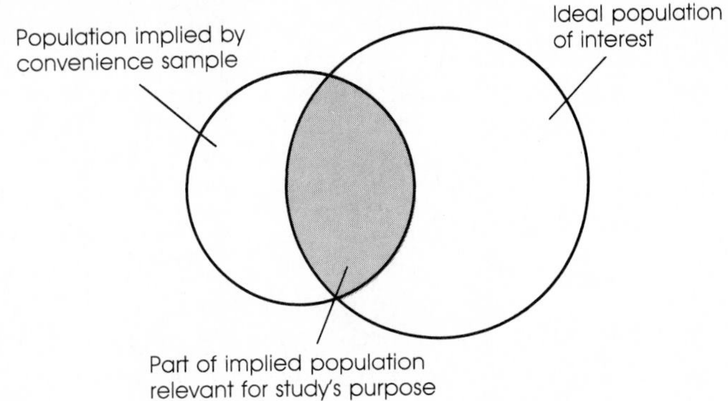

from, and of irrelevant units included in, the implied population in each of our three examples are given in the following list.

How good is a convenience sample in terms of serving the ultimate purpose of sampling, which is to be able to make some generalizations about a population (i.e., the ideal population)? The answer to this question depends on the extent of discrepancy between the ideal population and the population implied by a convenience sample. Exhibit 14.1 graphically illustrates the discrepancy between the two types of populations. The larger the shaded area in Exhibit 14.1, the more representative the convenience sample will be of the ideal population. Unfortunately, a researcher using convenience sampling has little control over how large the shaded area will be, because the researcher takes whatever respondents he or she can conveniently get. Consequently, there is no way of controlling the nature of the sample in terms of the types of respondents included in it. Indeed, in convenience sampling a researcher cannot even identify the nature of the implied population *until after such a sample has been selected and studied.*

JUDGMENT SAMPLING

Judgment sampling is similar to convenience sampling, except that it is more refined. In convenience sampling a researcher does not exert any effort to obtain a representative sample. Such effort is expended in judgment sampling.

DEFINITION. ***Judgment sampling* is a procedure in which a researcher exerts some effort in selecting a sample that he or she feels is most appropriate for a study.**

The definition implies that a researcher, on the basis of his or her subjective judgment, will deliberately select certain kinds of units and avoid others. For this reason judgment sampling is also known as *purposive sampling*.

Let us take another look at the TV news story example. If the TV news reporter were to seek out some officers from various student organizations and obtain their reactions to the proposed fee hike, instead of merely interviewing a conveniently available sample of students, he or she would be using a judgment-sampling procedure. Whether a judgment sample is better (i.e., more representative of the ideal population) than a convenience sample will depend on how sound the judgment of the researcher is in selecting the sample units. To the extent that officers of student organizations may be well informed about the feelings of the general student body, a judgment sample of student officers may be more representative than a convenience sample of students. In practical situations the researcher will, or *should,* be knowledgeable about the nature of the relevant or ideal population for a study. Hence, although a judgment sample will require greater researcher effort, it will generally be more appropriate than a convenience sample.

Judgment sampling involves the deliberate choice of each sample unit. Assuming that the researcher is knowledgeable about the ideal population for a study and uses sound judgment in selecting the sample units, *irrelevant* units are unlikely to be included in a judgment sample. However, there is no guarantee that a judgment sample will adequately represent all *relevant* segments of the ideal population, as illustrated in the following example.

EXAMPLE: Consider the judgment sample of student officers in our TV news story. Since student officers supposedly represent various student groups, the reporter may reasonably assume that they will be relevant sample units, especially if they are asked to express their perceptions of what the students in general feel about the proposed fee hike. However, can the perceptions of a sample of student officers capture the feelings of *all* segments of the student body? Most likely, they will not. For instance, the perceptions of a student officer sample may not adequately reflect the views of independent students who do not belong to any student organization.

The point of this discussion is that the population implied by a judgment sample, while not likely to contain any irrelevant segment, usually will be only a *subset* of the ideal population. Exhibit 14.2 demonstrates this feature graphically.

THE USE OF CONVENIENCE AND JUDGMENT SAMPLES

Even though convenience and judgment samples are unlikely to provide perfect representations of the ideal population for a study, they can be used under

Exhibit 14.2

Discrepancy between implied and ideal populations in judgment sampling

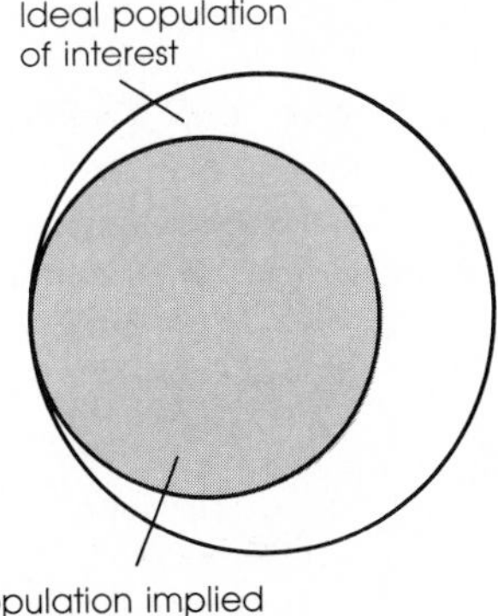

certain conditions. Such samples may be appropriate when the basic purpose of a research study is to generate some initial insights rather than to make any generalizations. Exploratory-research projects, which we discussed in Chapter 4, often involve the use of convenience sampling or, if time and other resources permit, judgment sampling. The next example gives an illustration.

EXAMPLE: While developing Underalls—the panty hose with built-in underpants—the Hanes Company initially tested it among its women employees and obtained their reactions to it. This preliminary research suggested product benefits and promotional appeals that were further tested through additional research. The sample of women employees was clearly a convenience sample since it was most conveniently available to the Hanes management. Nevertheless, it was an appropriate sample since the purpose of the research was merely to obtain some initial reactions to the product.[1]

Judgment sampling will also be appropriate when the sample size for a research project is relatively small, as is usually the case in exploratory research. For instance, judgment sampling is often used in selecting respondents for focus group interviews.

EXAMPLE: One of the services offered by Burke Marketing Research, Inc., a leading commercial marketing research firm, is focus group interviewing. Burke conducts most of its focus group interviews in Cincinnati, where it is

[1] "Underalls' Success Due to 'Flanking Strategy,' Product Idea, Positioning," *Marketing News,* November 14, 1980, p. 11.

headquartered, and each group interview typically involves 8 to 10 people. The respondents for the group interviews are obtained from local organizations such as churches, schools, and clubs.

Burke has used over 500 different organizations in the Cincinnati area to obtain respondents for its focus groups. In the judgment of Burke's researchers:

> This large number of organizations allows a degree of pre-selection of respondents. Any sample can be made *reasonably representative* [emphasis added]. Organizations tend to fall within specific age, sex, socio-economic and regional limits and a proper selection of the groups can achieve a satisfactory balance of these factors. . . . Burke gets a great deal of cooperation from the many organizations.[2]

Thus depending on the nature of the subject matter to be covered in a focus group interview, Burke selects some appropriate local organizations and requests them to provide individuals with certain desired characteristics. In short, Burke uses judgment samples for its focus group interviews.

The following important, but perhaps counterintuitive, point is implicit in this example: When a research study involves the use of a small number of sample units, a carefully chosen judgment sample may be better able to provide a proper mix of units for the study than even a probability sample.

You may find this statement hard to believe. However, consider for a moment that you are the marketing manager of a firm that wants to test-market a new product in six different metropolitan areas in the United States. You have to select the six areas from a population of all standard metropolitan statistical areas (SMSAs) in the United States. Would you select the six SMSAs on the basis of your subjective judgment, or would you prefer to select them on the basis of some probability-sampling method, say simple random sampling?

If you use simple random sampling, there is no guarantee that the particular sample of six SMSAs chosen will be representative of the total United States market. For instance, the six SMSAs chosen by using simple random sampling may all turn out to be in California, New York, or some other limited geographic region (recall our discussion of the limitations of simple random sampling). But if you use your judgment to select the six SMSAs, you can at least attempt to balance your sample in terms of market size, geographic location, and other market characteristics that you consider relevant. Clearly, a judgment sample of six SMSAs, although not a scientifically chosen sample, may be more appropriate for test-marketing purposes than a simple random sample (or any other type of probability sample, for that matter).

[2] "Group Interviewing," a brochure published by Burke Marketing Research, Inc., 2600 Victory Parkway, Cincinnati, OH 45206. Pp 5–6.

QUOTA SAMPLING

Quota sampling is the most refined form of nonprobability sampling and is often used in practice, especially in studies involving personal interviewing. Hence we will discuss it in some detail. Quota sampling resembles stratified random sampling (Chapter 13) and possesses certain features of judgment and convenience sampling as well. Quota sampling involves the following steps:

1. The population is divided into segments (typically referred to as *cells*) on the basis of certain *control* characteristics.
2. A *quota* of units to be selected from each population cell is determined from the judgment of the researchers and/or decision makers.
3. The interviewers for the study are instructed to fill the quotas assigned to the cells but are given some freedom in selecting the sample units.

A newspaper subscriber survey that the author was involved in made use of quota sampling. This survey was conducted at the request of the management of a newspaper in a medium-sized city in the Midwest. Management wanted information about subscribers' reactions to the newspaper and the relative popularity of various sections of it. The relevant population for this study was considered to be all adult newspaper subscribers who lived within city limits. Personal interviews were to be conducted with 300 newspaper subscribers; the sample size of 300 was based on time and cost considerations. A list of addresses of all households that subscribed to the newspaper was available from internal records.

The newspaper's management felt that reader reaction could vary depending on the sex of the reader and the section of the city in which the reader lived. Management believed that geographic location was a good surrogate indicator of the socioeconomic and educational characteristics of the city's residents. Hence sex and geographic location constituted the two control characteristics used in this study. The city was divided into five geographic segments, each of which was further divided into two cells on the basis of sex. As a result, ten population cells were formed. Table 14.1 shows the ten cells along with the quotas established for each of them.

Five interviewers were employed for conducting the survey, one for each geographic segment. The interviewers were given the addresses of the subscribing households located in the respective segments assigned to them. They were each asked to select 60 households and interview an adult male reader in 30 of them and an adult female reader in the remaining 30. As a safeguard against the interviewers choosing all the households from just a small section of the areas assigned to them, they were further instructed not to choose more than 4 households from any one street. Notice that even with the constraints imposed on the interviewers, they still had some freedom in selecting the households; for instance, they could, at their discretion, choose four conveniently located households (e.g., neighboring households) on any one street.

Table 14.1
Quota-sampling plan for the newspaper subscriber survey

GEOGRAPHIC SEGMENT	SEX	
	Male	Female
I	30	30
II	30	30
III	30	30
IV	30	30
V	30	30

Total sample size = 300

This example illustrates the general steps involved in quota sampling. Let us now examine some similarities and differences between quota sampling and other sampling methods, especially stratified random sampling. In the previous chapter we saw that the stratified-random-sampling procedure starts with dividing the population of interest into *homogeneous strata* on the basis of some appropriate population characteristic. This step resembles the first step in quota sampling: The cells and the control characteristics in quota sampling are similar to the homogeneous strata and appropriate characteristic in stratified random sampling, respectively. However, there are some major differences between quota sampling and stratified random sampling. Though each control characteristic in quota sampling must be relevant to the proposed study—that is, it must be one that is likely to be associated with the responses to the study questions—data about the characteristic need not be available for the population units *before* one conducts the study. Recall that in stratified random sampling, data on the characteristic that serves as the basis for stratification must be available beforehand in order to facilitate the grouping of population units into the various strata and to facilitate the probabilistic selection of the designated number of units from each stratum.

In quota sampling the sample units are selected on a *subjective* rather than on a *probabilistic* basis; the only requirement of the procedure is that a designated number of units (i.e., a quota of units) possess the characteristics of each cell, irrespective of how the units are actually chosen. In quota sampling the data on control characteristics are obtained through screening questions or merely through observation (e.g., when sex is a control characteristic) *after* each potential respondent is contacted. The data are then used to determine the eligibility of each respondent for the study. The following example illustrates these features of quota sampling.

EXAMPLE: Consider a study of consumer attitudes toward social welfare programs. Suppose the respondents for this study are to be selected through a

Table 14.2
Quota-sampling plan for a survey of attitudes toward social welfare programs

	HIGHEST EDUCATION LEVEL			
AGE	Less Than High School	High School Diploma	Some College	College Degree
18–30	100	100	100	100
31–45	100	100	100	100
46–60	100	100	100	100
Over 60	100	100	100	100

Total sample size = 1600

quota-sampling plan in which the age and the education level of consumers are the control characteristics. The details of this quota-sampling plan are shown in Table 14.2. The first two questions in the questionnaire used in this study will be screening questions that ask for the respondent's age and education level. Each interviewer will subjectively select a respondent and ask him or her the screening questions. From the responses to the screening questions the interviewer can decide whether or not the respondent is eligible for the study. Specifically, interviews with respondents who are under 18 years of age and respondents who belong to cells whose quotas have already been filled will be terminated at this stage.

Advantages and disadvantages

Quota sampling does not require prior knowledge about the cell to which each population unit belongs; as a result, it has two distinct advantages over stratified random sampling. First, it is easier to execute than a stratified-random-sampling procedure in which every population unit must be placed in the appropriate stratum before the actual sample selection can begin. Second, the lower a priori data requirements of quota sampling often allow a researcher to use two or more control characteristics in defining the population cells. The resultant benefit is that a researcher can control a quota sample's representativeness on several relevant population characteristics. In contrast, stratified random sampling typically, although not always, involves the use of just one characteristic as the basis for stratifying the population.

Quota sampling is superior to both convenience and judgment sampling in terms of sample representativeness. If the control characteristics used in designing a quota-sampling plan are relevant as far as the research questions are concerned, the *ideal* population of interest and the population *implied* by a quota sample will be very similar. Indeed, we can expect the ideal and the implied populations to overlap completely, at least with respect to the control characteristics.

The relative simplicity of quota sampling, when compared with probability-sampling techniques such as stratified random sampling, and its ability to provide representative samples that are much better than mere convenience or judgment samples have made it a popular technique in real-life research studies.

However, quota sampling does have some potential limitations that we must be aware of. First, it lacks the statistical precision and generalizability that probability-sampling procedures possess. We will have more to say about this later in the chapter when we discuss the features of probability and nonprobability sampling in general.

Second, increasing the number of control characteristics in order to improve a sample's representativeness can sharply lower quota sampling's flexibility and make it prohibitively expensive to locate the respondents needed to fill the various cell quotas. For instance, suppose we want to add a third control characteristic to the quota-sampling plan outlined in Table 14.2. Specifically, let us say that in addition to age and education level, we want to include a respondent's income as a control characteristic with the following four levels: less than \$15,000; \$15,000 to less than \$30,000; \$30,000 to less than \$50,000; and \$50,000 or over. What will happen to the number of population cells in Table 14.2 if income is added as the third control characteristic? It will increase from 16 to 64. Each of the existing 16 cells will have to be further divided into 4 cells corresponding to the four levels of income. For the total sample size of 1600 respondents, the effort and the resources needed to implement a 64-cell quota-sampling plan will be substantially higher than those needed for the 16-cell quota-sampling plan. A much larger number of respondent contacts made by interviewers implementing a 64-cell quota-sampling plan may be wasted since each respondent will have to qualify for the sample on the basis of three rather than two characteristics. For instance, locating 100 respondents who are over 60 years of age and have college degrees will be relatively easier than locating 25 such respondents from each of the four income groups.

Third, even if several control characteristics are used in designing a quota sample, the sample that is actually obtained may still be biased. Quota sampling, by permitting some freedom in the selection of the actual sample units, offers interviewers an incentive to select the most convenient sample, as long as they do not violate the quota constraints. Consequently, they may make little or no effort to contact respondents who are hard to reach or difficult to talk to, such as those who live in very rich or very poor neighborhoods. Thus a quota sample may suffer from some serious biases with respect to relevant population characteristics that are not explicitly used in forming the population cells. The real-life example described next shows that this problem can occur even in carefully designed quota samples.

EXAMPLE: The National Purchase Diary Panel is maintained by NPD Research, Inc., a leading commercial marketing research firm that specializes in continuously monitoring consumer purchases of food, household products, and personal-care products. The NPD collects product purchase data from a sample of consumers who are requested to keep track of their households' purchases. The members of this diary panel are recruited by using an elaborate quota-sampling plan. Specifically, NPD has designed a 288-cell population matrix on the basis of the following five control characteristics: (1) family size, (2) age of housewife, (3) income, (4) in or out of SMSA, and (5) census division. The NPD uses the utmost care in selecting the panel members and maintaining the representativeness of its panel over time. However, by NPD's own admission:

> All panels suffer some nonrepresentivity through non-inclusion of illiterates and semi-literates, foreign speaking families, etc. . . . And, the representation of blacks is only about half of what it should be . . despite costly efforts by NPD in recent years to increase the black population on the panel.[3]

The point is that although the population implied by a quota sample should be quite similar to the ideal population on the control characteristics, one must be cautious in generalizing the findings of a quota-sampling study. To illustrate, suppose sex, age, and education are used as control characteristics in selecting a quota sample of respondents for a study on people's attitudes toward birth control. Let us say the interviewers in this study correctly filled their quotas with interviews conducted in their own neighborhoods. But as luck would have it, all the interviewers happened to live in Catholic neighborhoods. In this case the study's findings, although based on a sample that satisfied all the specified controls, obviously cannot be generalized with a high degree of assurance.

Determining cell quotas

The total sample size for a study using a quota-sampling plan is usually based on how varied the population is, the depth to which various subsegments of the population are to be studied, and, most importantly, the resources available for the study. For a given total sample size, though, there is no standard procedure for dividing it into quotas for the population cells. In fact, the determination of individual-cell quotas is an area in which a researcher's judgment plays a key role. For instance, in the newspaper subscriber survey discussed earlier, the total sample of 300 respondents was allocated *equally* among the 10 population cells. In contrast, NPD uses a sophisticated scheme in setting quotas for the 288 cells represented by its diary panel. Specifically, NPD establishes quotas in such

[3] "Sharpening Marketing Decisions with Diary Panels," a brochure published (in 1975) by NPD Research, Inc., 900 West Shore Road, Port Washington, N.Y., p. 20.

Table 14.3
Comparison of NPD sample with United States population

FAMILY SIZE	PERCENTAGE OF HOUSEHOLDS	
	NPD Sample	U.S. Census
2	37.9%	39.0%
3–4	41.4%	40.6%
5+	20.7%	20.4%
Total	100.0%	100.0%

a way that on each control characteristic the distribution of panel households is approximately *proportionate* to the distribution of all households in the United States (as determined by the latest available United States census data). For example, on the dimension of family size the NPD sample and the total United States population have the percentage distribution shown in Table 14.3.

Thus researchers using quota sampling are free to establish individual-cell quotas on the basis of their best judgment about the composition of each cell and its relative importance in the overall study. As a rule of thumb, however, a quota of at least 30 units per cell is established in most real-life studies.

PROBABILITY- VERSUS NONPROBABILITY-SAMPLING METHODS

Precision

The most significant advantage of probability sampling over nonprobability sampling relates to the ability to estimate how confident one can be about a study's results. Indeed, to estimate confidence intervals for population parameters from sample data is permissible only if the sample is a probability sample. Confidence-interval estimation may not be appropriate when data are gathered from a nonprobability sample. Recall that the *central limit theorem* and the theory of *normal probability distributions* form the basis for confidence-interval estimation. The application of these statistical principles is legitimate only when the sampling procedure is such that, theoretically, repeated samples chosen from the same population will yield sample statistic values that follow a *predictable* distribution, namely, a normal probability distribution. Only probability sampling, through its objectivity, can *guarantee* a process that will generate a predictable distribution pattern for the sample statistic.

To gain further insight into this advantage of probability sampling, consider that nonprobability sampling requires neither precise definition of the ideal population nor the identification of all units within it before sample selection takes place. Consequently, the only population that a nonprobability sample represents is the one it implies *after* the sample selection has taken place. Furthermore, owing to the subjectivity involved in selecting the sample units, the implied population itself could vary depending on the actual procedures and persons employed in selecting the sample. For instance, suppose a male researcher picks a judgment sample of respondents for a study of the public's opinions about sexual freedom. The population represented, or implied, by this judgment sample will most likely be different from a population implied by a judgment sample chosen by a female researcher. Furthermore, it is hard to predict in what ways and to what extent the populations implied by the two judgment sample will most likely be different from a population implied by a Hence making any projections, in the form of confidence-interval estimates for the population parameters, from data obtained from a nonprobability sample is inappropriate and dangerous. When a nonprobability sample is used in a study, the safest approach for a researcher to take is to draw some preliminary insights after carefully examining the nature of the population implied by the particular sample chosen and the nature of the ideal population.

Time and cost

In general, probability-sampling methods will be more time-consuming and expensive than nonprobability-sampling methods, for two reasons:

1. Probability sampling requires an accurate specification of the population and an enumeration of the units within it.
2. The selection of sample units using a probability-sampling procedure must precisely follow an objective scheme that is prespecified.

Let us now examine these two reasons in greater detail. We must point out at the outset, though, that to define and enumerate accurately some populations may be easy. For example, a population consisting of "all dentists in Chicago" can be easily identified and listed by using the yellow pages of a telephone book or a current directory of dentists in the area. Unfortunately, in practice, research involving such simple populations are the exception rather than the rule. Populations such as "all smokers in California," "all households with children under six years of age," and "all business firms that have their own computers," which cannot be easily identified accurately, are typical of populations encountered in many research projects. Hence a researcher who wants to use probability rather than nonprobability sampling must be prepared to spend greater time and effort prior to sample selection.

Even if an accurate research population list is readily available, some time and effort will normally be needed to make contact with the *particular* units specified by the probability-sampling procedure used. For instance, suppose simple random sampling is to be used to select 100 households from a city for a personal-interview survey. The households selected through simple random sampling may be located in widely dispersed sections of the city. Consequently, contacting a simple random sample of 100 households may require greater time and expense than contacting, say, a judgment sample of 100 households. Moreover, for some households identified through simple random sampling, the interviewer may have to make several callbacks before being able to contact suitable respondents. In contrast, if some nonprobability sampling is used, there will be virtually no need for callbacks, since the interviewer does not have any objectively determined set of households to be contacted.

Determining which sampling method to use

In general, the choice between probability and nonprobability sampling involves a trade-off between the capability to generalize the sample results to the population with a *known* degree of accuracy and the lower time/cost requirements. A researcher whose primary concern is to be able to make quantitative inferences about population parameters (as is usually the case in conclusive-research projects) must use some form of probability sampling. However, time and financial constraints may force the researcher to deviate from a *rigid* probability-sampling procedure; if so, extreme caution must be used in projecting the sample results to the population. When a research project is primarily exploratory, some form of nonprobability sampling will be adequate.

Identifying the most appropriate sampling plan for a given project may not always be as clear-cut as these guidelines appear to indicate. Though nonprobability-sampling methods usually have a time and cost advantage over probability-sampling methods, the advantage may not exist in every research situation. Some sophisticated quota-sampling plans, for instance, may be just as time-consuming and expensive as probability-sampling plans. The quota-sampling scheme used by NPD in recruiting members for its diary panel is a case in point. Furthermore, in many situations a hybrid-sampling plan—one that incorporates aspects of both probability- and nonprobability-sampling methods—may be most appropriate, as illustrated by the following example.

EXAMPLE: Consider a study for which a representative sample of households from a metropolitan area is needed. In this study a hybrid-sampling plan, consisting of two-stage area sampling followed by quota sampling, can be used to select the desired sample of respondents. Specifically, area sampling, which only requires a list of geographic segments rather than a list of all households in the metro area, can be used initially to select a sample of census tracts and a certain number of city blocks from each selected census tract. The interviewers for the study can then be given a quota of households

Exhibit 14.3

Sample selection for the Gallup Omnibus

The Gallup Organization, Inc., maintains a national probability sample of 300 interviewing areas that is used for all Omnibus surveys. Each survey week, 1,500 individuals are personally interviewed. An independent sample of individuals is selected for each interviewing wave.

The sampling procedure is designed to produce an approximation of the U.S. civilian adult population living in private households, excluding those persons living in institutions such as prisons or hospitals or those living on military bases. Survey data can be applied to this population for the purpose of projecting percentages to numbers of people.

The design of the sample is that of a replicated, probability sample down to the block level in the case of urban areas, and to segments of townships in the case of rural areas. Approximately three hundred sampling points, that is, clusters of blocks or rural segments, are used in each survey. Interpenetrating samples can be provided for any given study when appropriate.

The sample design included stratification by these four size-of-community strata on the basis of Census data: Central cities of population 1,000,000 and over; 250,000 to 999,999; 50,000 to 249,999; all other populations. Each of these strata was further stratified into seven geographic regions. Within each city size–regional stratum, the population was arrayed in geographic order and zoned into equal-sized groups of sampling units. From this array of data, pairs of localities were randomly selected in each zone, with probability of selection proportional to size producing two replicated samples of localities.

Within localities so selected for which the requisite population data are reported, sub-divisions were drawn with probability of selection proportional to size of population. In all other localities, small definable geographic areas were selected with equal probability.

Separately for each survey, within each sub-division so selected for which block statistics are available, a sample of blocks is drawn with probability of selection proportional to the number of dwelling units. In all other sub-divisions or areas, blocks or segments are drawn with equal probability.

In each cluster of blocks and each segment so selected, a randomly selected starting point is designated on the interviewer's map of the area. Starting at this point, interviewers are required to follow a given direction in the selection of households until their assignment is completed.

Only one interview per household is conducted. Interviewing hours are restricted to times when adult men and women are most likely to be at home. Provision is made for a "times-at-home" weighting to allow for persons not at home when the interviewer calls.

Source: "The Gallup Omnibus," a brochure published (in 1975) by the Gallup Organization, Inc., 53 Bank Street, Princeton, NJ 08540. Used by permission.

to be interviewed from each chosen city block. If desired, further quotas within each city block can be established with respect to other control characteristics, such as sex of the respondent and size of the household.

The point here is that depending on the objectives of the research and the resources available for conducting it, a researcher can pretty much improvise a suitable sampling plan. Such hybrid-sampling plans are used frequently in practice.

However, pure probability-sampling techniques, despite their time and cost requirements, are also used in real-life projects, although perhaps less frequently. Sophisticated probability-sampling techniques are used especially by large commercial marketing research firms that maintain national samples or panels that can be readily accessed for conducting periodic research surveys. The Gallup Organization, for example, offers a business service called the Gallup Omnibus. The service is a national survey conducted every two to four weeks, using personal in-home interviews. Questions that are custom-designed to fit the requirements of individual clients can be included in the national survey in any desired month of the year. The survey's results are projectable to the United States adult civilian population 18 years and older.[4] The sample for the Gallup Omnibus is chosen through an elaborate probability-sampling plan, as described in Exhibit 14.3.

SUMMARY

Convenience sampling and judgment sampling are two very basic forms of nonprobability sampling. Both methods are rather crude. While convenience sampling is done purely on the basis of a researcher's convenience, judgment sampling involves at least some researcher effort to select a representative sample. In both methods the population implied by the actual sample chosen may differ greatly and systematically from the ideal population. However, this discrepancy is likely to be somewhat less if judgment sampling is used, in the sense that a population implied by a judgment sample is not likely to contain any irrelevant units. Convenience and judgment sampling may be appropriate methods when the sole purpose of a research project is to generate some initial insights. Also, judgment sampling is an ideal technique when the sample size for a study is extremely small.

Quota sampling is a refined form of nonprobability sampling that has some features of stratified random sampling, although it also involves the use of judgment in selecting the sample units. The population implied by a quota sample should be quite similar to the ideal population, at least with respect to

[4] "The Gallup Omnibus," a brochure published (in 1975) by the Gallup Organization, Inc., 53 Bank Street, Princeton, N. J.

the control characteristics. Nevertheless, a quota sample may still suffer from serious biases owing to nonrepresentativeness on dimensions that are not explicitly included as controls. The relative flexibility of quota sampling and its ability to provide reasonably representative samples have made it a popular technique. However, quota-sampling plans that involve too many control characteristics, and hence numerous population cells, may lose their advantage over probability-sampling plans with respect to ease of execution. There is no standard or universally used scheme for dividing the total sample for a quota-sampling study into individual quotas for the population cells; this area is left to the discretion of the researcher.

The major advantage of probability sampling over nonprobability sampling relates to the level of confidence one can have in a study's results. Specifically, quantitative generalizations about the population on the basis of sample data, in the form of confidence-interval estimates, are permitted *only if* probability sampling is used. Hence studies using nonprobability sampling can only lead to qualitative statements, in the form of hunches or hypotheses, about the population. However, nonprobability-sampling methods are, in general, less time-consuming and less expensive than probability-sampling methods.

The choice between probability and nonprobability sampling for a study hinges on the study's objectives as well as the resources available for conducting the study. Furthermore, hybrid-sampling plans can be devised to fit the unique circumstances surrounding a particular research project. Hybrid plans are frequently used in practice, although pure probability-sampling plans are also used in real-life studies, especially by large commercial marketing research firms.

QUESTIONS

1. Define *convenience sampling, implied population,* and *ideal population.* In what ways can the population implied by a convenience sample differ from an ideal population? Are such differences likely to be serious?
2. Briefly discuss the differences between convenience sampling and judgment sampling.
3. Describe, with suitable examples, the circumstances in which convenience sampling and judgment sampling are appropriate.
4. List the steps involved in quota sampling. Summarize the basic procedural differences between quota sampling and stratified random sampling.
5. Discuss the pros and cons of quota sampling relative to stratified random sampling.
6. "In quota sampling the determination of individual-cell quotas is subjective." Discuss this statement.
7. Briefly discuss the advantages and limitations of nonprobability sampling relative to probability sampling.
8. Is a researcher's choice of sampling plans restricted to one of the standard probability- or nonprobability-sampling plans? Discuss your answer, giving a suitable example.

9. For each of the following situations, suggest a specific sampling plan—probability, nonprobability, or hybrid sampling—and justify your selection. Also briefly describe how the sample should be selected in each situation.
   a. A political candidate for the U.S. Senate is in a very tight race with her opponent. Election day is 10 weeks away, and this candidate wants to get a weekly reading of how much registered voters prefer her to her opponent.
   b. A large independent discount department store carries 20,000 different products. The manager of the store wants to know whether store customers are experiencing any difficulty in locating the products they are looking for.
   c. The president of an electronic-products firm wants to know what the field of computer chip technology will look like five years from now.
   d. The school district in a metropolitan area has 30 elementary schools spread across the area. The superintendent of the school district wants to ascertain the opinions of parents in the area about the quality of elementary school education their children are receiving.

15

Data Collection: Fieldwork and Potential Errors

The usefulness of a research project will depend to a large extent on the overall quality of the data generated. One key factor influencing data quality is sampling error. In Chapter 12 we defined *sampling error* as the difference between a statistic value that is generated through a sampling procedure and the population parameter value that can only be determined through a census study. In other words, a certain amount of sampling error is bound to be present in studies that involve collecting data from only a part of the population. As we saw in Chapters 12 and 13, from data from a sample (assuming it is a probability sample), one can only obtain an *interval estimate* of a population parameter, rather than an exact *point estimate,* because of the presence of sampling error. The higher the sampling error, the less precise (or wider) the interval estimate will be.

While confidence-interval estimates explicitly take into account sampling error, they do not reflect a number of other errors that can occur *irrespective* of the sampling procedure and sample size employed. These errors are called *nonsampling errors* and can arise even in census studies. We will discuss several types of nonsampling errors a little later. Strategies we discussed in earlier chapters for reducing sampling error, such as using a statistically efficient probability-sampling technique, will have little or no effect in reducing nonsampling errors. The following section examines the distinction between sampling and nonsampling errors in greater detail.

SAMPLING VERSUS NONSAMPLING ERRORS

Sampling error

EXAMPLE: In March 1983, Yankelovich, Skelly and White, Inc., conducted a survey for *Time* magazine. According to *Time*:

> The survey polled 1,008 registered voters from March 1 to 3. The sampling error is plus or minus 3%. . . . [According to this survey] 36% of those questioned believed that cheating on income taxes is becoming more common. More unsettling, 43% found it "acceptable" to barter goods and services without reporting it on the tax forms, and 26% found it acceptable not to report cash payments as income.[1]

The error of ±3% in this example is the maximum *sampling error* associated with any percentage estimate obtained from a sample of 1008 at a 95% confidence level. Let us see how the ±3% is derived. Recall from our discussion in Chapter 12 that the standard deviation, and hence standard error (which is a measure of sampling error), will be highest when $p = .5$, or 50%. Thus the maximum sampling error in the *Time* magazine example can be derived by estimating the standard error when $p = .5$ and computing the ± term associated with a 95% confidence interval:

$$\text{maximum standard error} = \sqrt{\frac{(.5)(1 - .5)}{1008}} = \sqrt{\frac{.25}{1008}} = .0157, \text{ or } 1.57\%.$$

At the customary confidence level of 95%, a standard error of 1.57% implies a sampling error of $\pm(1.96)(1.57) = \pm 3.08\%$, or approximately ±3%. For percentage estimates that are greater or lower than 50%, the error will be lower than 3%. Therefore 3% represents the upper bound on sampling error associated with *any* percentage estimate from that sample.

We must bear in mind that sampling error merely captures the extent of *chance,* or *random, fluctuations* in estimates. These fluctuations can occur from sample to sample when repeated samples (of the same size) are chosen by using the same procedure. Sampling error is only a function of the fact that a sample (rather than the entire population) is chosen for a study. It says little about the truthfulness of the collected data. The lower the variation across estimates obtained from different samples, the lower the sampling error will be.

What is the magnitude of the sampling error in a study that involves conducting a census rather than choosing a sample? It is zero, because in a census study the "sample" is the population itself. Hence repeated measures of the entire population should yield identical estimates.

[1] "Cheating by the Millions," *Time,* March 28, 1983, p. 27.

In studies involving sampling the amount of sampling error can be reduced by using a sampling procedure that has high statistical efficiency and/or by increasing the sample size. Table 15.1 illustrates the magnitudes of sampling errors associated with various percentage estimates based on simple random samples of different sizes. Notice in Table 15.1 that for any given sample size the sampling error is highest for an estimate of 50%. Also notice that the sampling error associated with any percentage estimate decreases as sample size increases.

Nonsampling errors

One general way of distinguishing between sampling and nonsampling errors is to say that while sampling error relates to *random variations,* which can be estimated in the form of standard error, nonsampling error typically results in some *systematic bias* that invariably is difficult, if not impossible, to estimate. Strictly speaking, some nonsampling errors may be variable errors and may cancel each other; however, such errors are assumed to be random and are thus not distinguishable from sampling error. For the sake of simplicity we will include only those errors that lead to systematic biases (i.e., definite upward or downward biases) under the label "nonsampling errors."[2] The following discussion illustrates the distinction between sampling and nonsampling errors.

Consider an executive club consisting of 10,000 members. You are interested in estimating the average contribution made by club members to charitable organizations on the basis of a survey of 100 members. Suppose the true average contribution (i.e., population parameter value) is $500. A probability sample of 100 club members will yield an average contribution estimate that will most likely be either lower or higher than $500. Moreover, if numerous probability samples of 100 members are chosen repeatedly, they will provide a range of average contribution estimates. However, as we saw in Chapters 12 and 13, the center of that range (or the *mean* of all the average contribution estimates) will coincide with the parameter value of $500. The mean will coincide with the parameter value because sampling error, which is the source of fluctuations across different sample estimates, is *random*; that is, high and low average contribution estimates will even out exactly and result in a grand mean value of $500, the true average contribution. In statistical terminology the sample average is said to be an *unbiased estimate* of the population average.

Thus far we have implicitly assumed that each club member will *truthfully* report his or her contribution amount. Suppose this assumption is incorrect. Specifically, let us say that every club member overstates his or her contribution

---

[2] For further discussion on this subject, see Leslie Kish, *Survey Sampling* (New York: Wiley, 1965), especially Chap. 13, "Biases and Nonsampling Errors," pp. 509–573. For a study showing that nonsampling error can be a significant component of total error, see Henry Assael and John Keon, "Nonsampling vs. Sampling Errors in Survey Research," *Journal of Marketing,* 46 (Spring 1982), pp. 114–123.

Table 15.1

Sampling errors for estimates of percentages at the 95% level of confidence

SAMPLE SIZE	1% OR 99%	2% OR 98%	3% OR 97%	4% OR 96%	5% OR 95%	6% OR 94%	8% OR 92%	10% OR 90%	12% OR 88%	15% OR 85%	20% OR 80%	25% OR 75%	30% OR 70%	35% OR 65%	40% OR 60%	45% OR 55%	50%
25	4.0	5.6	6.8	7.8	8.7	9.5	10.8	12.0	13.0	14.3	16.0	17.3	18.3	19.1	19.6	19.8	20.0
50	2.8	4.0	4.9	5.6	6.2	6.8	7.7	8.5	9.2	10.1	11.4	12.3	13.0	13.5	13.9	14.1	14.2
75	2.3	3.2	3.9	4.5	5.0	5.5	6.2	6.9	7.5	8.2	9.2	10.0	10.5	11.0	11.3	11.4	11.5
100	2.0	2.8	3.4	3.9	4.4	4.8	5.4	6.0	6.5	7.1	8.0	8.7	9.2	9.5	9.8	9.9	10.0
150	1.6	2.3	2.8	3.2	3.6	3.9	4.4	4.9	5.3	5.9	6.6	7.1	7.5	7.8	8.0	8.1	8.2
200	1.4	2.0	2.4	2.8	3.1	3.4	3.8	4.3	4.6	5.1	5.7	6.1	6.5	6.8	7.0	7.0	7.1
250	1.2	1.8	2.2	2.5	2.7	3.0	3.4	3.8	4.1	4.5	5.0	5.5	5.8	6.0	6.2	6.2	6.3
300	1.1	1.6	2.0	2.3	2.5	2.8	3.1	3.5	3.8	4.1	4.6	5.0	5.3	5.5	5.7	5.8	5.8
400	0.99	1.4	1.7	2.0	2.2	2.4	2.7	3.0	3.3	3.6	4.0	4.3	4.6	4.8	4.9	5.0	5.0
500	0.89	1.3	1.5	1.8	2.0	2.1	2.4	2.7	2.9	3.2	3.6	3.9	4.1	4.3	4.4	4.5	4.5
600	0.81	1.1	1.4	1.6	1.8	2.0	2.2	2.5	2.7	2.9	3.3	3.6	3.8	3.9	4.0	4.1	4.1
800	0.69	0.98	1.2	1.4	1.5	1.7	1.9	2.1	2.3	2.5	2.8	3.0	3.2	3.3	3.4	3.5	3.5
1000	0.63	0.90	1.1	1.3	1.4	1.5	1.7	1.9	2.1	2.3	2.6	2.8	2.9	3.1	3.1	3.2	3.2
1200	0.57	0.81	0.99	1.1	1.3	1.4	1.6	1.7	1.9	2.1	2.3	2.5	2.7	2.8	2.8	2.9	2.9
1500	0.51	0.73	0.89	1.0	1.1	1.2	1.4	1.6	1.7	1.9	2.1	2.3	2.4	2.5	2.5	2.6	2.6
2000	0.44	0.61	0.75	0.86	0.96	1.0	1.2	1.3	1.4	1.6	1.8	1.9	2.0	2.1	2.2	2.2	2.2
2500	0.40	0.56	0.68	0.78	0.87	0.95	1.1	1.2	1.3	1.4	1.6	1.7	1.8	1.9	2.0	2.0	2.0
3000	0.36	0.51	0.62	0.71	0.79	0.87	0.99	1.1	1.2	1.3	1.5	1.6	1.7	1.7	1.8	1.8	1.8
4000	0.31	0.44	0.54	0.62	0.69	0.75	0.86	0.95	1.0	1.1	1.3	1.4	1.4	1.5	1.5	1.6	1.6
5000	0.28	0.40	0.49	0.56	0.62	0.68	0.77	0.85	0.92	1.0	1.1	1.2	1.3	1.4	1.4	1.4	1.4

Example — If a sample of 500 respondents resulted in a percentage of 75%, we can be sure 95 times out of 100 that the true percentage is between 78.9% and 71.1% (75.0% ± 3.9%).

Source: Adapted from a table presented in "AIM: A Monthly Omnibus Research Service," a descriptive brochure prepared by R. H. Bruskin Associates, Market Research, 303 George Street, New Brunswick, N.J. 08903, p. 35. Used by permission.

by $50. Under this revised assumption numerous probability samples of 100 members will still yield a range of average contribution estimates. But the mean of such estimates will *not* be $500. It will, instead, be $550; each sample average estimate will be inflated by $50. Thus the inaccurate reporting by club members will introduce a *systematic error* in the sample estimate.

A systematic error will lead to a *nonzero* net bias (either an upward or downward bias) in the sample estimate. Notice that even if the various club members overstate their contributions by *differing* amounts, there will still be an upward systematic bias in the sample estimate. Thus as long as questions exist about the accuracy of the responses provided by the club members, any estimate of their average contribution will be biased owing to nonsampling error.

Nonsampling error cannot be reduced by increasing the sample size. Indeed, when nonsampling error is present, even a census of the population will result in a biased estimate. For instance, if every club member overstates his or her contribution by $50, the average estimated contribution based on a census will be $550, in contrast to the true value of $500. In other words, nonsampling errors can never be overcome by increasing the sample size.

Inaccurate reporting by respondents is not the only source of nonsampling errors. They can occur because of a variety of factors, as discussed in the next section.

TYPES OF NONSAMPLING ERRORS

Sampling frame error

A *sampling frame* is a specific list of population units from which the sample for a study is chosen. For instance, suppose Sears wants to survey a sample of its credit card customers. It can readily generate a complete list of individuals who have Sears' credit cards. This list will constitute a sampling frame from which a desired number of individuals can be chosen. In this example the sampling frame is identical to the ideal population, namely, all Sears' credit card customers. In many other studies, however, generating an exact sampling frame may be quite difficult. Consequently, such studies may suffer from sampling frame error.

DEFINITION. ***Sampling frame error* is a bias that occurs when the population as implied by the sampling frame differs in a systematic fashion from the ideal population.**

Consider a situation in which a marketer wants to conduct a telephone survey of residents of a city. An obvious sampling frame from which to choose a sample for the survey is the city's phone book. However, if we examine the appropriateness of the phone book as a sampling frame, two potential problems become evident: (1) The phone book does not contain residents with unlisted numbers, and (2) it does not contain those who do not have telephones. Given this discrepancy between the ideal population and the proposed sampling frame, a key question that arises is whether the discrepancy is serious. In other words, are the residents included in the phone book likely to differ in a systematic fashion from those not included? Yes, they are. Indeed, a research project conducted by Pacific Northwest Bell Telephone Company to examine the nature of this discrepancy gave the following conclusions:

> The results of [this project highlight] the problems inherent in using telephone directories as sampling frames. . . . In using telephone directories for sampling, systematic biases are introduced. . . . If households with unlisted numbers are systematically excluded, the resulting sample will be somewhat older, more rural, more white, more educated, more retired and more white-collar than the universe of households with telephone service.[3]

Clearly, surveys based on a sample of telephone numbers selected from a phone book will invariably contain sampling frame error. This error is a form of nonsampling error because even a census of residents with listed telephones will not yield completely accurate data. The survey results will be systematically and significantly different from those that *would* have been obtained had the sampling frame contained the entire population.

A point that needs emphasizing here, however, is that sampling frame error is not necessarily a serious problem whenever the sampling frame and the ideal population are not *identical.* In certain situations even an incomplete sampling frame may adequately represent all relevant segments of the ideal population. Consequently there may be no appreciable sampling frame error. The following example illustrates this point.

EXAMPLE: The management of a retail discount store wants to survey a sample of the store's customers who use credit cards to pay for their purchases made in the store. The store has a list of names and telephone numbers of its customers who paid with credit cards during the past month. Will this list be a valid sampling frame, although it obviously does not contain *all* customers of the store who had paid for their purchases using credit cards? It most likely will be a valid sampling frame since there is no a priori reason to believe that the *composition* of customers using credit cards will vary significantly from month to month.

Unfortunately, situations in which an incomplete or partial sampling frame is an adequate representation of the ideal population are quite rare in real life.

---

[3] Patricia E. Moberg, "Biases in Unlisted Phone Numbers," *Journal of Advertising Research,* 22 (August/September 1982), pp. 54–55.

Exhibit 15.1 illustrates key aspects of the nature of sampling frame error in the case of an ideal population that has four distinct segments.

Exhibit 15.1(a) shows a sampling frame that overrepresents two segments of the ideal population and underrepresents the other two. The sampling frame depicted in Exhibit 15.1(b), in addition to having a bias similar to the one in Exhibit 15.1(a), also contains units that are not included in the ideal population and hence are irrelevant. Exhibit 15.1(c) shows an incomplete sampling frame; but since it accurately represents the four population segments, it does not have sampling frame error. In Exhibit 15.1(d) the sampling frame and ideal population are identical. Of these four situations the sampling frames in Exhibits

Exhibit 15.1

Key aspects of sampling frame error

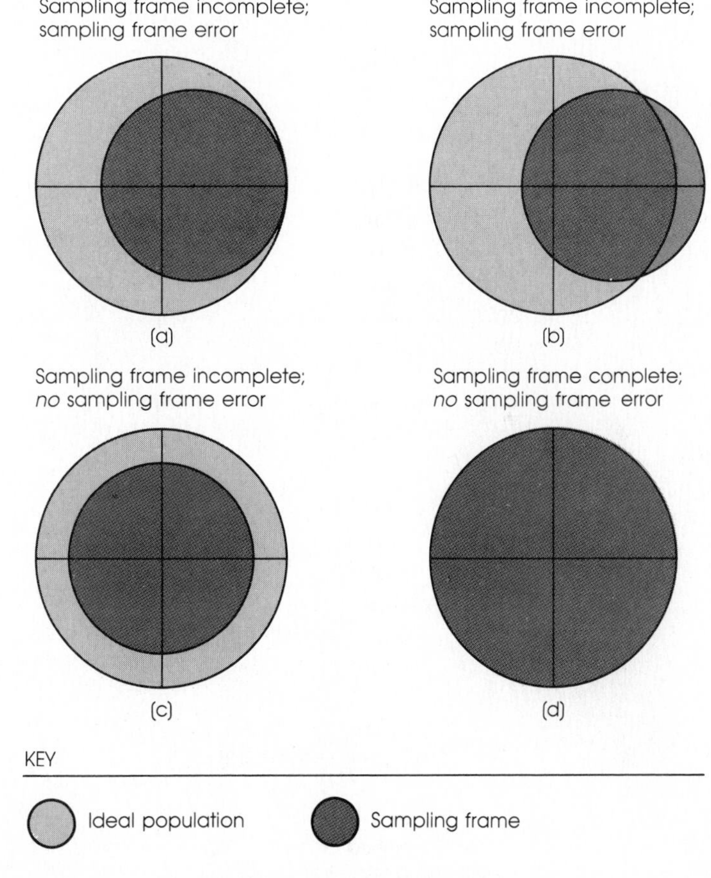

15.1(a) and 15.1(b) occur much more frequently than those in Exhibits 15.1(c) and 15.1(d) in practical marketing research projects.

In Chapter 14 we saw that it is difficult to draw valid inferences about the ideal population from a nonprobability sample. This problem arises because of the discrepancy that frequently exists between the ideal population and the population implied by the nonprobability sample. Our discussion thus far clearly indicates that even studies using probability samples will suffer from a similar drawback if there is any sampling frame error, that is, if the sampling frame is like the ones shown in Exhibits 15.1(a) and 15.1(b).

Nonresponse error

Nonresponse error, as the term implies, relates to studies in which responses are not obtained from all the units in the *planned sample.* The planned sample is the set of units initially chosen from a sampling frame. For reasons we will discuss later, the *final sample* obtained in a study can be significantly different from the planned sample. When it is, the study's findings will suffer from nonresponse error.

DEFINITION. ***Nonresponse error*** **is a bias that occurs when the final sample differs in a systematic way from the planned sample.**

Consider a research study whose objective is to obtain information about various aspects of the television-viewing behavior of the public. Suppose questionnaires are mailed in this study to a random sample of 500 individuals chosen from a representative sampling frame. As we saw in Chapter 6, mail surveys are often plagued by poor response rates. In the current study, let us say responses are obtained from 200 respondents, for a 40% response rate. Does this rate, by itself, imply a significant nonresponse error? It does not necessarily, because the existence of nonresponse error depends more on the *nature* of the discrepancy between the planned and final samples than on the response rate. For instance, if the final sample of 200 respondents does not differ in any systematic way from the planned sample of 500—that is, if the final sample is *representative* of the planned sample—there would be no noticeable nonresponse error.

Alternatively, suppose only those with plenty of time on their hands took the trouble to respond to the mail survey. In other words, let us say the final sample was dominated by respondents who had more leisure time than the typical individual in the planned sample. Would the results of the study now be valid for the general public? They most likely would not be, since we can expect people's television-viewing behavior to be strongly associated with the amount of leisure time they have. Consequently, if the final sample differed systematically from the planned sample with respect to leisure time, nonresponse error would make the study's inferences erroneous.

Two important points emerge from our discussion of nonresponse error thus far:

1. Nonresponse error can occur even if there is no sampling frame error. Even choosing a probability sample from a representative sampling frame cannot guarantee there will be no nonresponse error.
2. The presence of nonresponse error depends on the composition of the final sample vis-à-vis the planned sample. A response rate of less than 100% does not necessarily imply there is nonresponse error.

Exhibit 15.2 illustrates these points by using a sampling frame that adequately represents relevant segments of an ideal population and a planned sample that is representative of the sampling frame.

The occurrence of nonresponse error is not limited to studies involving mail surveys. Personal-interview surveys and telephone surveys are also susceptible to nonresponse error, despite the fact that response rates in such surveys are usually higher than in mail surveys. As we have already seen, nonresponse error is a function of the nature (rather than the *number*) of the units responding to a survey. Two potential sources of nonresponse error in personal and telephone surveys are as follows:

1. Not-at-home problem. Invariably, a few respondents specified by the planned sample will not be available when the interviewer attempts to make contact with them. Nonresponse error will occur if not-at-home respondents are significantly different on relevant dimensions from the respondents in the planned sample.
2. Respondent refusal problem. Even if all the respondents in the planned sample are available when the interviewer makes contact, the possibility always exists that some respondents will refuse to participate in the survey. Indeed, real-life situations in which there are *no* respondent refusals are quite rare. Refusal rates of at least 10% occur in most studies. Again, nonresponse error will be present when the respondents who refuse to participate differ systematically from the planned sample of respondents.

Data error

The validity of research findings depends not only on the extent of sampling frame and nonresponse errors but also on the extent of errors that can occur during the course of data collection, analysis, or interpretation. We will use the term *data error* to denote any such error. Sometimes, the term *measurement error* is used to denote all errors that occur during, or because of, the data-gathering process. Errors due to not-at-homes, for instance, would be included

Exhibit 15.2

Key aspects of nonresponse error

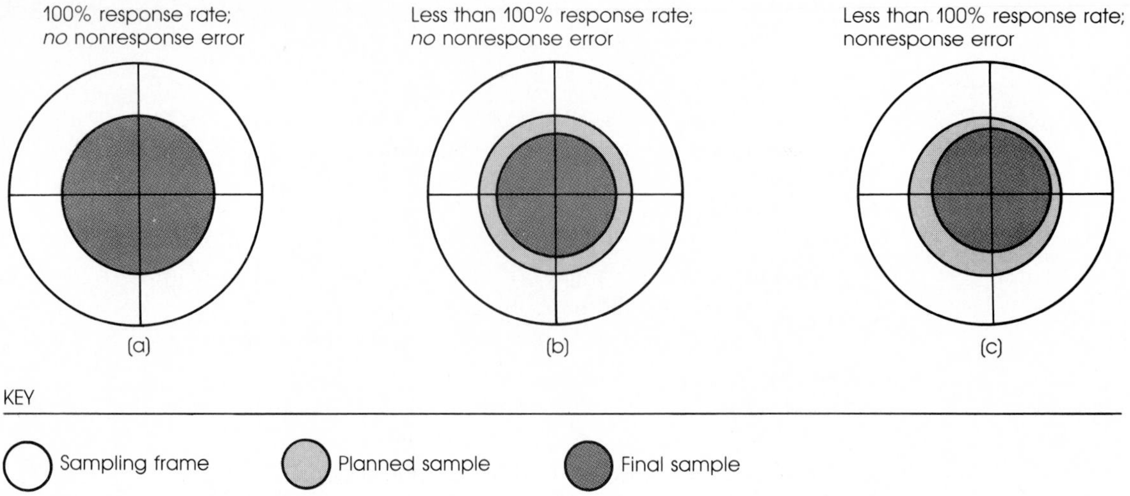

under measurement error. We will use the term *data error* so as to distinguish clearly the errors that are directly related to the collected data from the errors that occur because of sampling frame or nonresponse problems.

DEFINITION. ***Data error*** **is any systematic bias that occurs during data collection, analysis, or interpretation and hence reduces the accuracy of inferences made about the ideal population.**

The factors contributing to data error are so numerous that discussion of an exhaustive list is beyond the scope of this book. Hence we will focus on a few that are illustrative of the various types of data errors.

One major source of data error is the respondent. In our earlier discussion of nonsampling error we saw that a systematic bias resulted when respondents inflated the magnitude of their charitable contributions. Such deliberate distortion of responses is a form of data error. Sensitive questions that invite socially acceptable answers—for example, questions about the extent to which respondents obey the law—are particularly prone to this form of data error.

Respondents may sometimes be forced to give distorted answers unintentionally. Questions that are difficult for a respondent to answer are prime candidates for distorted or erroneous responses. The following question was found in an Annual Constituent Questionnaire sent out by a U.S. congressman not too long ago:

> Do you believe people you know and associate with who receive benefits under a federal program would accept reductions in those benefits if reductions were necessary to balance the budget and make a tax cut possible and if the burden of such reductions was shared by all recipients of benefits under all federal programs?
>
> __________ Yes   __________ No   __________ Undecided

It is doubtful whether an average person could comprehend such a question, let alone provide a meaningful response to it. Hence the extent to which the respondents' answers to this question reflect their true feelings is open to debate.

Another potential cause of data error is the person who conducts a telephone or personal interview. For instance, even in our informal conversations with others, we often modify the scope and content of what we say according to the nature and the mood of the person who is conversing with us. We can expect such modification to occur to an even greater extent in an interview setting where a respondent is engaging in a formal conversation with an interviewer who is most likely a stranger. In fact, studies have shown that the nature of physical and social characteristics of the interviewer and those of the respondent can have a significant impact on responses.[4] Even such things as an interviewer's appearance and tone of voice can affect the responses. Thus the characteristics of the interviewer can inadvertently lead to data error in the form of distorted responses. Unfortunately, as is usually the case with many forms of data error, detecting the existence, let alone the magnitude, of such distortion is difficult.

A more direct way in which interviewers may lead to data error is through *cheating*. Serious data error will result when less-than-scrupulous interviewers even partially fill out questionnaires by themselves. However, thanks to a variety of control procedures that we will discuss later, the threat of cheating by interviewers can be reduced to a large extent.

Data errors can also occur because of sloppiness in recording, analyzing, and interpreting the data collected. For instance, mistakes may be made by interviewers in recording responses, especially those to open-ended questions. Or mistakes may be made by coders in transferring the data from questionnaires to computers. Inappropriate interpretation can also lead to data error in the

[4] See, for example, Robert L. Kahn and Charles L. Cannell, *The Dynamics of Interviewing* (New York: Wiley, 1957), pp. 193–196; see also U. S. Bureau of the Census, "Evaluation and Research Program of the U.S. Censuses of Population and Housing, 1960," in *Effects of Interviewers and Crew Leaders*, Series ER60, no. 7 (Washington, D.C.: U.S. Government Printing Office, 1968).

form of invalid inferences. Often such errors are quite subtle, as the next example points out.

EXAMPLE: The XYZ Company, the producer of brand A pain reliever, surveyed a probability sample of doctors regarding their opinions about pain relievers. One of the questions used in the survey was the following:

Would you recommend the use of brand A to your patients who suffer from aches and pains?

_________Yes   _________No

Analysis of responses to this question showed that 75% of the doctors surveyed said yes; the rest said no. From this analysis XYZ Company made the following inference: "Three out of four doctors surveyed recommend brand A for their patients who suffer from aches and pains."

Is the inference made by XYZ Company valid? At first glance it appears to be. However, some doubt arises about its meaning, and hence accuracy, when one critically examines the *wording* of the question used in the survey. For instance, consider the following alternative wording for the same question:

Which brand of pain reliever would you recommend the most to your patients who suffer from aches and pains?

_________Brand A

_________Brand B

_________Brand C

.

.

.

_________Other_________________(Please specify.)

The alternative wording obviously offers greater latitude of response for the doctors than the wording used in the survey, which forced the doctors to say yes or no to brand A. Consequently, one can argue that the only valid inference that can be drawn from the survey's findings is something like this: "Three out of four doctors surveyed *do not object* to the use of brand A by their patients who suffer from aches and pain." Alternatively, unless 75% of the doctors checked brand A in response to the revised question, one could not legitimately make the inference that YXZ Company made. The point here is that the danger of some form of data error exists even long after the data is collected and coded.

In summary, the *total error* in any research project is a combination of sampling and nonsampling errors. Of these errors only sampling error can be influenced by the choice of sample size and the sample selection procedure to be used. Nonsampling errors consist of sampling frame error, nonresponse error, and data error. The next section discusses ways of controlling the various forms of nonsampling errors.

CONTROLLING NONSAMPLING ERRORS

Sampling frame error

The only way to guarantee the absence of sampling frame error is to have a *complete* sampling frame when you begin a study. However, developing a complete sampling frame may often be tedious or impossible. Consider the situation presented in the following example.

EXAMPLE: Home Sales Company, a real estate brokerage firm, wants to conduct a personal-interview survey of a sample of people who have bought their homes within the past year. Home Sales, as well as all other realtors in its area of operation, subscribe to a service known as the Multiple-Listing Service, which has a list of all buyers who purchased homes listed through local realtors during the past year. Home Sales has ready access to this list.

Will this list adequately represent all those who bought homes within the past year? It will be a complete sampling frame only if the population of interest is defined as the buyers of homes *listed through realtors.* In other words, missing from this list are all those who bought their homes directly from the owners. Admittedly, direct buyers are usually only a small fraction of all home buyers. However, their characteristics and decision-making behavior are likely to be significantly different from those who bought their homes through realtors. Hence excluding them can lead to serious sampling frame error if the ideal population consists of *all* home buyers.

The only way to overcome this error is to develop a complete sampling frame, perhaps by going through the records of the tax offices in the area. This process will be more cumbersome than using the readily available sampling frame, but it is necessary if sampling frame error is to be avoided.

Sampling frame error can also be reduced in some situations by modifying an available sampling frame that is incomplete. For instance, we saw earlier that a phone book is invariably an incomplete sampling frame when the ideal population is the general public. One way of overcoming this problem, at least partially, is to use a technique called *plus-one dialing.* In plus-one dialing a fixed integer (usually 1) is added to each telephone number chosen from the phone book, and the revised telephone number is dialed. In theory, plus-one dialing amounts to using a sample of numbers chosen from a *modified* sampling frame, which is constructed by increasing each telephone number in the original sampling frame by a fixed number. The rationale behind plus-one dialing is that the modified sampling frame will constitute an adequate cross section of listed and unlisted numbers, thus leading to a reduction in sampling frame error.

Another technique used to reduce sampling frame error in telephone surveys is *random-digit dialing.* This technique involves randomly dialing the last four digits of telephone numbers within each telephone exchange included in the area of interest. For instance, a random sample of telephone numbers can be obtained from any exchange (say 555) by randomly generating the X's in 555–XXXX and avoiding any duplication of numbers already chosen. With the advent of high-speed computers and computerized telephone dialing, random-digit dialing is easy and quick to use if one has the appropriate equipment. Sievers Research Company, for example, uses random-digit dialing in its Omniview service, which is a regular monthly survey of a national probability sample of adults.[5]

Neither plus-one dialing nor random-digit dialing can completely eliminate sampling frame error when the ideal population is *all* households—those with and those without telephones. That is, any telephone survey, irrespective of the technique used to select the numbers, can only represent households that have telephone service.

Nonresponse errors

Mail surveys. Nonresponse errors in mail surveys can be reduced by increasing the response rate in such a way as to make the final sample reasonably representative of the planned sample. A number of approaches have been found useful in increasing response rates. For example, several studies have shown the following techniques effective in this regard: the inclusion of cash or other incentives with the questionnaire; the mailing of follow-up questionnaires or reminders; and the use of first-rate postage (e.g., first-class mail, special delivery) to mail the questionnaire.[6]

Of course, employing any of these techniques adds to the cost of conducting a mail survey. Moreover, the available research evidence is not clear about the impact of these response rate improvement techniques on the *composition* of respondents in the final sample. A potential danger is that some of these techniques may increase the size, but not necessarily the representativeness, of the final sample, as indicated in the next example.

---

[5] "Check on America with OMNIVIEW," a brochure prepared by Sievers Research Company, 2111 Huntington Drive, San Marino, Calif. 91108.

[6] Leslie Kanuk and Conrad Berenson, "Mail Surveys and Response Rates: A Literature Review," *Journal of Marketing Research,* 12 (November 1975), pp. 440–53; Arnold S. Linsky, "Stimulating Responses to Mailed Questionnaires: A Review," *Public Opinion Quarterly,* Spring 1975, pp. 82–101; Don A. Dillman, *Mail and Telephone Surveys* (New York: Wiley, 1978).

EXAMPLE: The National Purchase Diary Panel of NPD Research Inc., contains families who are requested to keep a diary of their purchases and mail the diaries to NPD at regular intervals. The NPD uses *gifts* (rather than cash or cashlike items such as coupons or trading stamps) to encourage panel families to make entries in their diaries and mail them in regularly. The following rationale provided by NPD for using gifts as incentives illustrates the "potential danger" alluded to earlier:

> Compensating families via gifts is superior to using trading stamps, although stamps are less expensive and this method is used by one competitive panel. Our research shows stamp savers are atypical of the population (greater price sensitivity) and their choice of stores is obviously influenced by the availability of stamps.[7]

Thus nonresponse error may be a problem in mail surveys even if the response rate is adequate. Hence if at all possible, one should compare the composition of the planned sample with that of the final sample—or, alternatively, the composition of respondents with that of nonrespondents—on characteristics that are relevant to the study. If the comparison reveals substantial differences between the two groups, the researcher should exercise caution in interpreting the results of the study, owing to the possible presence of nonresponse error.

The author was involved in a research project aimed at generating information about new-product-planning activities of manufacturing firms in the United States. A random sample of 500 manufacturing firms was chosen, and a questionnaire (along with a cover letter) was mailed to the president of each firm. The sample of 500 firms was the planned sample. A second questionnaire (follow-up) was mailed to those firms that had not responded within five weeks. A total of 107 firms returned properly filled-out questionnaires; this sample was the final sample. Nonresponse error was a concern in this study, especially since the effective response rate was only a little over 21%. Fortunately, data were available for both the planned and the final sample on certain key characteristics that were likely to be associated with new-product-planning activities. One such characteristic was the type of industry to which each firm belonged. Table 15.2 offers a comparison of the firms in the planned and final samples on this characteristic.[8]

Although there are differences in the composition of the two samples (as indicated by the percentage figures in Table 15.2), they do not appear to be major. Moreover, these differences were not statistically significant on the basis of a chi-square test (we will discuss chi-square tests in Chapter 17). Since the

[7] "Sharpening Marketing Decisions with Diary Panels," a brochure prepared (in 1975) by NPD Research, Inc., 900 West Shore Road, Port Washington, NY 11050, p. 22.

[8] For additional details about this study, see Leigh Lawton and A. Parasuraman, "The Impact of the Marketing Concept on New Product Planning," *Journal of Marketing,* 44 (Winter 1980), pp. 19–25.

Table 15.2

Comparison of the planned and final samples in the new-product-planning study

	COMPOSITION OF PLANNED SAMPLE		COMPOSITION OF FINAL SAMPLE	
INDUSTRY TYPE	Number of Firms	Percentage of Firms	Number of Firms	Percentage of Firms
Food and tobacco	46	9	11	10
Textile	43	9	12	11
Lumber and furniture	33	7	5	5
Paper and printing	43	9	8	8
Chemical and petroleum	38	8	7	7
Rubber, leather, and glass	40	8	9	8
Metal	94	19	15	14
Machinery	106	21	27	25
Transportation, measuring instruments, and miscellaneous	57	11	13	12
Total	500		107	

Note: All percentages have been rounded off; hence they may not add to exactly 100%.

planned and final samples were similar in composition, we concluded that nonresponse error was negligible.

Telephone and personal-interview surveys. As we discussed earlier, two primary sources of nonresponse error in telephone and personal-interview surveys are the not-at-home and respondent refusal problems. When interviewers encounter a not-at-home situation, they are often tempted to substitute the chosen home with a neighboring dwelling where a respondent is available (or with the next number if a telephone survey is being conducted). This procedure may seem sound. However, it is only sound in terms of ensuring an adequate sample size. It may actually increase rather than decrease the nonresponse error. Consider the following example.

EXAMPLE: Jane is an interviewer who is conducting personal interviews of women in order to ascertain their attitudes toward day-care centers for children. She has a list of households (as designated in the planned sample) that she is supposed to contact. It is 10 A.M. and Jane has already made contact with and interviewed three nonworking women in the first three houses specified on her list. Jane is now at the fourth address on her list, but there is nobody home. However, she notices a similar house just across the street, and a couple of children are playing in the front yard of that house. The presence of children indicates somebody is home. Jane is wondering whether she should substitute the house across the street for the fourth house on her list. What do you think she should do?

If Jane does make the substitution, she will probably find another nonworking housewife, whereas the person who is not at home in the designated house is likely to be a working woman. If Jane makes a number of such substitutions (from the appearance of houses), the final sample will be biased because it will be dominated by nonworking housewives; the final sample, although similar in size to the planned sample, will be sharply different in terms of composition. The result will be serious nonresponse error. We can expect a woman's attitude toward day-care centers, which is the key variable in the study, to differ depending on whether or not she is a working woman.

The use of *callbacks* and *differential scheduling of interview times* to make contact with hard-to-reach respondents are more effective in reducing nonresponse error than the substitution of available respondents for the not-at-homes. For example, Belden Associates, a commercial marketing research firm, uses both these strategies to reduce nonresponse error in personal-interview surveys that are a part of a Continuing Market Study (CMS) service offered to newspaper publishers. According to Belden Associates:

> In samples employing call-backs, interviewers must make a maximum of three calls (one original and two call-backs) to complete the interview with a selected respondent. . . . To reflect possible variations in consumer behavior by day of the week, interviewing is spread out Tuesday through Saturday (thus representing Monday-through-Friday "yesterday" newspaper exposure). To improve the chances of finding all types of people at home, interviewing is conducted approximately between 5:00 and 9:30 P.M. on weekdays and noon to 4:30 P.M. on Saturdays.[9]

Callbacks and differential scheduling (or spreading out) of interview times will add to the cost of a study. Moreover, they do not guarantee the completion of the total number of interviews specified in the planned sample. Nevertheless, nonresponse error in a study employing these techniques will be lower than in studies not employing them or in studies using substitution of respondents for not-at-homes, as illustrated by the diagrams in Exhibit 15.3. The amount of nonresponse error in Exhibit 15.3(a) is lower than it is in Figure 15.3(b) or 15.3(c). Also notice that the nonresponse error in Exhibit 15.3(b) is higher than in Exhibit 15.3(c), despite the final sample size in 15.3(b) being as large as the planned sample size.

The respondent refusal problem is difficult to avoid, especially in telephone

[9] "The Belden Continuing Market Study: The Indianapolis '74 Newspaper Audience," a brochure prepared (in 1975) by Belden Associates, 2900 Turtle Creek Plaza, Dallas, TX 75219, p. D in the "Technical Notes" section.

Exhibit 15.3

Effects of strategies used to handle not-at-homes

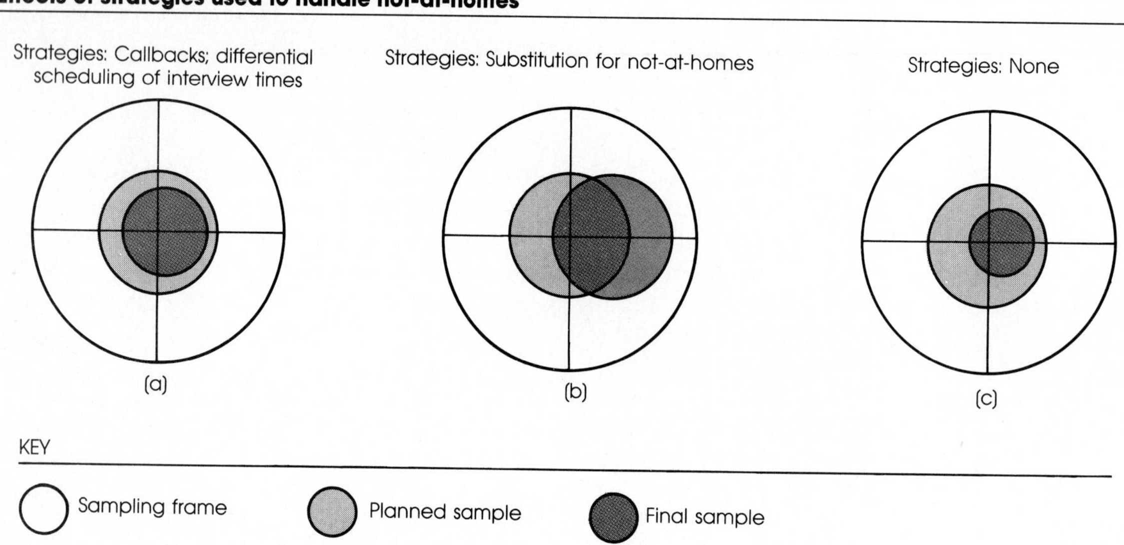

surveys. At least in personal-interview surveys, once the interviewer comes face to face with a respondent, it may be psychologically hard for the respondent to say no. In telephone surveys, though, the respondent can easily decline to participate by just hanging up. There are two reasons for respondent refusals: (1) The time when the interviewer makes contact is inconvenient for the respondent, and (2) the respondent is reluctant to participate for reasons other than convenience.

Refusals stemming from inconvenient interview timing can be handled to some extent in a fashion similar to the handling of not-at-homes—through callbacks and judicious scheduling of the initial contacts at times likely to be convenient to respondents. Refusals occurring because of respondent resistance are tougher to handle. However, offering incentives (monetary or nonmonetary) and using well-qualified interviewers who are trained to overcome respondent objections may be helpful.[10]

Refusals due to respondents' resistance to the survey itself have a special bearing on the plus-one and random-digit dialing strategies for overcoming sampling frame errors in telephone surveys. While telephone surveys using

[10] For example, one technique that has been used with some success to overcome respondent objections is the foot-in-the-door technique; see Jonathan L. Freedman and Scott C. Frazer, "Compliance Without Pressure: The Foot-in-the-Door Technique," *Journal of Personality and Social Psychology,* October 1966, pp. 195–202.

these strategies may be able to minimize sampling frame error, research evidence (and perhaps even intuition) indicates that these surveys may still encounter serious nonresponse error owing to refusals. For instance, one of the conclusions of the research project conducted by Pacific Northwest Bell that we mentioned earlier was as follows:

> Even if respondents with nonpub[lished] numbers are contacted, they are more likely to refuse to be interviewed, and less likely to answer all the questions than are respondents with listed telephone numbers. Evidently, their desire for privacy extends to surveys. These response rate data provide clues to the characteristics of nonrespondents. Nonrespondents to surveys probably differ from respondents in systematic ways.[11]

Nonresponse error can be minimized, but it cannot be completely avoided in most surveys. Sound research practice requires careful consideration of this potential limitation in drawing inferences and making recommendations. Moreover, a good research report must explicitly disclose the implications of nonresponse error (or any other error, for that matter). Disclosure will enable the report's audience to exercise caution in interpreting the research findings. Exhibit 15.4 provides an example of an explicit disclosure made by Walker Research, Inc., in a report describing its Industry Image Survey. This survey is conducted once every two years, using a national probability sample of adults, to determine the public's opinions about the marketing research industry.

Incorporating effects of nonresponse errors into sample results. Our discussion thus far focused on procedures for minimizing nonresponse errors and for ascertaining whether such errors could be a problem in studies just completed. In some situations the researcher may be able to estimate the effects of nonresponse errors on at least certain key variables and then adjust the sample results accordingly.[12]

For instance, suppose only n sample units from a planned sample of N units respond to a survey dealing with recreation. Let the mean value for a key variable (e.g., expenditures per year on record albums) be $\overline{X}_1$ for respondents and $\overline{X}_2$ for nonrespondents—and, of course, at this stage $\overline{X}_2$ is unknown. The correct mean value for the planned sample (say $\overline{X}$) is

$$\overline{X} = \frac{n\overline{X}_1 + (N - n)\overline{X}_2}{N}.$$

Sometimes, a rough estimate of $\overline{X}_2$ may be available through secondary sources. For instance, when some information about the demographic profile of

---

[11] Moberg, "Biases in Unlisted Phone Numbers," pp. 54–55.

[12] For references related to statistical treatment of the effects of nonresponse errors, see *Statistical Adjustment for Nonresponse in Sample Surveys: A Selected Bibliography with Annotations* (Monticello, Ill.: Vance Bibliographies, 1979).

Exhibit 15.4

Acknowledging sampling frame and nonresponse errors

Limitations of Findings

The findings of the 1982 Industry Image Survey are limited by the normal biases associated with contact and refusal rates inherent in all research studies. Because this project was conducted by telephone, it is not necessarily representative of non-telephone owning households. Further, some potential for nonresponse bias may be involved since some consumers refused to participate in this study, as shown in the following table.

Representative Sample
Refusal Summary

	1982	1980	1978
Total refused	432	346	477
Percent refused	46%	41%	49%
At introduction	30%	16%	22%
During interview	16%	25%	27%
Completed interview	499	500	500
Percent complete	54%	59%	51%

These limitations should be kept in mind when reading the findings of this survey.

Source: "1982 Industry Image Survey Results," *The Marketing Researcher* (published by Walker Research, Inc.), Spring 1983, p. 7. Used by permission.

nonrespondents is available, past studies or music industry sources can be consulted to obtain an approximate estimate of a variable such as expenditures on record albums made by the nonrespondent group. If $\overline{X}_2$ differs greatly from $\overline{X}_1$, the formula can be used to adjust $\overline{X}_1$ so as to obtain a more accurate estimate of the sample mean $\overline{X}$.

Alternatively, an attempt can be made to estimate $\overline{X}_2$ through an intensive follow-up of a small random sample of nonrespondents. For instance, a sample of nonrespondents to a mail survey can be contacted by telephone or in person and requested to answer a relatively small set of key questions on the original survey. Data thus gathered can be used to estimate $\overline{X}_2$. Again, if $\overline{X}_2$ differs greatly from $\overline{X}_1$, the formula can be used to adjust the results obtained from the initial group of respondents. The ability to make such an adjustment depends on factors such as whether nonrespondents can be identified, whether adequate resources are available for intensive follow-up efforts, and whether nonrespondents cooperate when recontacted. In any case, the preceding discussion highlights an important point: When a researcher does not make any adjustment of $\overline{X}_1$, a critical assumption being made is that $\overline{X}_1$ is not significantly different from $\overline{X}_2$. The accuracy of the sample results and the inferences stemming from them will be questionable when this assumption is not valid.

Data error

Data errors due to respondents' providing distorted answers (either intentionally or unintentionally) are difficult to control directly. However, an examination of why respondents distort their answers may reveal strategies for minimizing such errors. The motivation for deliberately distorting responses is likely to be high when the respondent perceives a question to be sensitive or a question invites a socially desirable answer; the respondent is irritated by the questionnaire or the questioning process as a whole and wants to frustrate the researcher; and/or a question is difficult for the respondent to answer. How can one avoid, or at least minimize, the incidence of these conditions?

Questions about sensitive issues obviously cannot be avoided if the purpose of a research project requires that such issues be examined. However, the *degree* of sensitivity of the questions as perceived by the respondents can be minimized by carefully adhering to the guidelines for good questionnaire construction, which we discussed in Chapter 10. For instance, of the following two alternative wordings of an income question, a respondent will perceive alternative A to be somewhat more sensitive than alternative B.

A. What is your annual gross income (before taxes)?

$______________

B. Indicate your annual gross income (before taxes) by checking the appropriate category:

__________ Less than $10,000

__________ $10,000 to less than $15,000

__________ $15,000 to less than $20,000

__________ $20,000 to less than $25,000

__________ $25,000 to less than $30,000

__________ $30,000 to less than $35,000

__________ $35,000 to less than $40,000

__________ $40,000 or more

Question B will only yield categorical data (i.e., nonmetric data) on income; question A should ideally yield more refined income data (i.e., metric data). However, since question A is somewhat more threatening than question B from the respondent's point of view, the answers to it may be seriously distorted. Nevertheless, the apparent refined nature of the data may give the researcher a false sense of accuracy and prompt the computation of statistics such as the mean income. However, if the data are distorted, the computed statistics will be biased, resulting in erroneous inferences. Another potential drawback of question A is that more respondents are likely to refuse to answer it than to answer question B.

A variety of other strategies, several of which were described under questionnaire design (Chapter 10), are available to minimize deliberate as well as unintentional response distortions. These strategies include the following techniques:

1. Train interviewers to establish rapport with respondents.
2. Choose interview times that are convenient for respondents.
3. Avoid the use of leading questions (i.e., questions that invite a certain type of response irrespective of how a respondent actually feels).
4. Do not ask sensitive questions early in the interview.
5. Make the questionnaire interesting and easy for respondents.
6. Pretest the questionnaire.

Taking precautions to minimize data errors caused by respondents is especially important, since such errors are much harder to detect than sampling frame or nonresponse errors. As we established earlier, for sampling frame and nonresponse errors one can indirectly ascertain their extent after a study has been completed—for example, by comparing the sampling frame with the ideal population and/or by comparing the planned sample with the final sample—and modify one's inferences accordingly. No such after-the-fact adjustment of inferences is possible when there are data errors caused by respondents because of the difficulty in uncovering the presence and the magnitude of such errors.

A potential source of error in telephone and personal-interview surveys, as well as in observation studies, is the interviewer. (Although we will be using the term *interviewer* hereafter, some of the interviewer errors we will discuss may also be relevant for studies using the observation method to gather data.) The keys to minimizing data errors stemming directly from interviewers are *selection, training,* and *supervision.* Substantial data errors may result if enough time and energy are not devoted to these activities. Thus serious efforts must be made *to prevent* (rather than *to cure,* after the fact) interviewer errors. Similar to the errors made by respondents, data errors caused by interviewers are hard to detect and measure. One possible exception is *interviewer cheating,* which can be detected in some situations, as we will see shortly. However, even if interviewer cheating is detected, the researcher usually only has the option of discarding (rather than correcting) the data generated by the interviewer. While this option may be better than inadvertently using the erroneous data, it is also an expensive option owing to data wastage.

Recognizing the seriousness of interviewer biases, many reputable marketing research firms take elaborate steps for controlling such biases. For example, according to Walker Research, Inc.:

> We believe comprehensive training is a key factor in data collection quality and have developed training programs that are among the best in the industry. Walker training programs include a unique three-level interviewer training, specialized study training, CRT [Cathode Ray Tube] interviewing training, supervisor training and travelling supervisor training.
>
> Interviewer candidates throughout our network are evaluated for verbatim reading and listening skills. Only those candidates who meet Walker's rigid standards are hired and trained to probe, clarify, and record responses the WALKER WAY.[13]

As another example, Louis Harris and Associates offers its clients a regular service called Harris Perspective Service, which is designed

> to provide corporations with timely and relevant information necessary to evaluate the social and political climate they operate within, and to help make sound business decisions regarding corporate policy, planning, marketing, and communications.[14]

This service is based on data obtained through personal interviews of a random sample of the American public. Before using the collected data, the firm takes specific steps to detect and handle interviewer cheating:

> Interviews are validated for each Perspective study. Interviewers send the name, address, and phone number (if available) of respondents to a validation service selected by the Harris firm. In New York, the Harris firm makes up a list of five study questions which are given to the validation service. Approximately 20% of each interviewer's respondents, randomly chosen, are contacted by the validation service (generally by telephone, but by mail if necessary) and asked the study questions. If there is any doubt about the authenticity of an interviewer's work, all of his or her interviews are carefully checked.[15]

In addition to proper selection, training, and supervision, the following techniques can also be helpful in reducing sloppiness on the part of interviewers and the incidence of interviewer cheating:

- Keep the interviewers' task as simple as possible and make sure they clearly understand it. For instance, a complex questionnaire or a complicated sample selection procedure can be very frustrating to interviewers and may motivate them to cheat. As Boyd, Westfall, and Stasch correctly observed:

[13] "The Walker Way . . . To Quality Research," a brochure prepared by Walker Research, Inc., 800 Knue Road, Indianapolis, IN 46250.
[14] "Opinion Research for Business: Harris Perspective Service 1979," a brochure prepared by Louis Harris and Associates, 630 Fifth Avenue, New York, NY 10020 p. 28.
[15] Ibid.

"Many investigators are coming to the conclusion that cheating is as much a problem of morale as morals."[16]

- Provide interviewers with adequate compensation. Contacting strangers, convincing them to participate, and eliciting responses from them is not easy, especially in a face-to-face situation and especially when a study deals with sensitive subject matter. The mental and physical strains on interviewers are likely to be quite high. Consequently, if they think their compensation is inadequate, the chances of their cutting corners during the fieldwork are likely to increase.

Some obvious data errors, such as inconsistent responses to different questions, can be detected through the use of appropriate editing and coding procedures (more will be said on this subject in the next chapter). For instance, in response to a question about store patronage, if a respondent claimed to have never been to store ABC, but later in the questionnaire acknowledged buying brand X, which is only available in store ABC, there is obviously data error in the form of response distortion. Such errors have to be eliminated before data analysis can begin. The best way to avoid errors in analyzing the data and interpreting the findings is to understand the nature of the data (e.g., whether they are ordinal or interval) and the quality of the data (e.g., whether they suffer from any nonresponse error) *before* one begins the data analysis. Researcher objectivity is crucial in minimizing errors in the data analysis and interpretation stages of a research project.

SUMMARY

The total error in a research project consists of sampling and nonsampling errors. Table 15.3 recapitulates the different types of errors and summarizes strategies for controlling them.

Sampling error is random and is quantifiable if a probability-sampling method is used. Moreover, sampling error can be reduced by increasing the sample size and/or by using a rigorous sampling procedure with high statistical efficiency.

Nonsampling errors introduce systematic biases that are usually quite hard to detect, let alone measure. Three major forms of nonsampling errors are sampling frame error, nonresponse error, and data error. These errors stem from a variety of sources. The popular saying that prevention is better than a cure is particularly pertinent to handling many forms of nonsampling error that are difficult to uncover and correct after they have occurred.

A final point worth emphasizing is that the numerous errors that can occur

[16] Harper W. Boyd, Ralph Westfall, and Stanley F. Stasch, *Marketing Research Text and Cases* (Homewood, Ill.: Irwin, 1981), p. 378.

Table 15.3

Summary of potential errors in research projects

TYPE OF ERROR	WAYS OF MINIMIZING ERROR
SAMPLING ERROR	
(Occurs when a sample, rather than the entire population, is studied)	• Increasing the sample size • Using a statistically efficient sampling plan; i.e., making the sample as representative of the population as possible
NONSAMPLING ERROR	
Sampling frame error (Occurs when the sampling frame is not representative of the ideal population)	• Starting with a complete sampling frame • Modifying the sampling frame to make it representative of the ideal population (e.g., using plus-one dialing in telephone surveys)
Nonresponse error (Occurs when the final sample is not representative of the planned sample)	• Mail surveys: Increasing response rates through the use of incentives, follow-up mailings, etc. (*Caution:* Increase in response rate per se may not reduce nonresponse error) • Telephone and personal-interview surveys: Making callbacks and spreading out the time blocks during which interviews are conducted
Data error (Occurs because of distortions in the data collected as well as mistakes in data coding, analysis, or interpretation)	• Ensuring that the questionnaire is good—i.e., is simple, unbiased, etc. • Proper selection, training, and supervision of interviewers • Keeping the interviewers' task simple and making it clear to them • Giving adequate compensation to the interviewers • Using sound editing and coding procedures • Taking into account the nature and quality of the data in analyzing and interpreting them

in a research project have implications not only for researchers but also for research users (managers or decision makers in general). Very often decision makers are content with knowing that a study employed random sampling and surveyed a large sample of units. However, as we have seen, these criteria are not capable of capturing the total error that can occur in a research project. Hence a decision maker should carefully examine a number of issues, such as the following questions, before drawing any conclusions from the research findings.

- What sampling frame was used?
- What are the characteristics of the respondents?
- What follow-up methods were used to reach nonrespondents?
- How do the respondents compare with nonrespondents on characteristics relevant to the research study?
- What were the extent and the nature of the training and supervision received by the interviewers?

A good research report should already have the answers to questions like these. If a report fails to address methodological issues adequately, a decision maker must ask the researcher(s) for additional information. Such information will be very helpful in determining how much faith one can have in the research findings. Similarly, even when evaluating a research proposal, decision makers will benefit from asking probing questions about whether and to what extent controls have been built into the proposed research design in order to handle potential errors.

QUESTIONS

1. "The higher the statistical efficiency of a sampling procedure, the higher will be the quality of the data collected from a sample chosen by using that procedure." Discuss this statement.
2. Define *sampling* and *nonsampling error.* What effect will these errors have on the estimate of a population parameter value from sample estimate values?
3. Define and briefly discuss *sampling frame error.* Give an example of your own to illustrate it.
4. Define *nonresponse error.* Will nonresponse error occur whenever certain sample units fail to respond to a survey? Why or why not?
5. State and briefly describe the two main sources of nonresponse error in personal and telephone surveys.
6. Define *data error,* and illustrate it with two different examples.
7. Briefly discuss the ways in which sampling frame error can be reduced. Illustrate your answer with examples.
8. Name two ways in which the response rates to mail surveys can be increased. Does the resulting higher response rate mean lower nonresponse error? Why or why not?
9. In what ways can the not-at-home problem be handled? Which of these ways would you recommend? Why?
10. "Nonresponse error can be reduced but not eliminated in most surveys." Discuss this statement.
11. Discuss the role that good questionnaire design can play in reducing nonsampling errors.
12. Develop an argument in support of the following statement: "Of the three major forms of nonsampling error, data error is the most serious."

13. Briefly describe the various interviewer-related strategies that can be used to reduce nonsampling errors.

14. Can the research user play any role in ensuring that the information generated from a research project is of high quality? Explain your answer.

15. In Chapter 2 we discussed certain limitations of the studies conducted by Twedt and Krum regarding the incidence of marketing research departments. What specific types of nonsampling errors do those limitations correspond to? Why?

16. Are there any ethical issues implicit in the example involving XYZ Company (producer of brand A pain reliever) presented in this chapter? If so, what are they? (*Hint:* Review the section on marketing research ethics in Chapter 2.)

CASES FOR PART FIVE

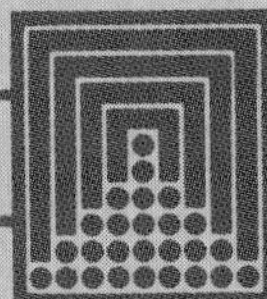

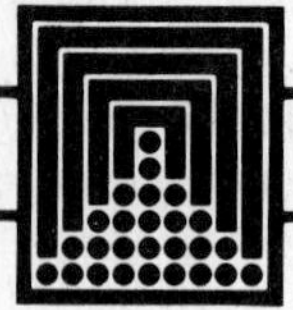

CASE 5.1

Dexter's Department Stores

Dexter's Department Stores is a chain of 150 upscale department stores operating in ten different states in the United States. The company's president and CEO, Don Dexter, has been concerned for quite some time about a growing phenomenon in the field of retailing in general and in Dexter's case in particular—namely, that fewer male business graduates are attracted to careers in retailing than female business graduates. While over half of all business graduates are males, apparently less than 20% of them are considering retailing as an attractive career option.

THE COMPANY'S RECRUITING EFFORTS

Every year, Dexter's Department Stores recruits graduates from several major universities in each of the ten states in which it has operations as well as from a few well-known universities outside these states. In all, Dexter's recruiters visit 40 college campuses regularly—at least once each year. They also recruit at a few other campuses but not on a regular basis. During the past year they filled 50 job openings at Dexter's Department Stores with business graduates. All 50 graduates were from the 40 campuses the recruiters visited regularly. Of these 50 graduates only 8 were males.

RESEARCH PROBLEM

Mr. Dexter has been quite pleased with the quality of the female graduates his company hired. In fact, several of the females hired within the past three or four years have rapidly risen to high-level managerial positions as a result of their excellent performance. Nevertheless, Mr. Dexter was puzzled and intrigued by the less-than-enthusiastic response from male business school graduates to his company's supposedly aggressive recruiting efforts on college campuses. He wanted to know why a highly successful company like Dexter's Department Stores was having difficulty in attracting male business graduates.

Specifically, he wanted to gain insight into the relative perceptions of male and female business school seniors about a career in retailing in general and one with Dexter's Department Stores in particular. He also wanted to get a feeling for how male and female business school seniors rated retailing careers vis-à-vis careers in such fields as selling and advertising.

Mr. Dexter therefore asked his director of personnel to look into the broad issue of female versus male college seniors' views about retailing careers. The director of personnel, in turn, requested a commercial marketing research firm to draw up a research proposal for examining the issues that Mr. Dexter was interested in. Several weeks later, the research firm submitted a proposal that detailed a formal, structured telephone survey of 1000 business school seniors across the country. The procedure for selecting the 1000 respondents suggested by the research firm is described in the next section.

SAMPLING PLAN

The section of the proposal that dealt with sampling read as follows:

> We will first obtain a list of all universities/colleges in the United States that have a four-year degree program in business administration. We expect that there will be about a thousand such universities. We will pick a systematic sample of 20 universities from this list. If there are 1000 universities in the list, for example, we will pick every 50th university on the list, after randomly picking the first one.
>
> We will then get the student telephone directories from the 20 chosen universities. From each telephone directory five pages will be chosen at random, and from each chosen page 10 business school seniors' names and telephone numbers will be chosen at random for conducting the survey. Appropriate adjustments will be made in this last stage to ensure that 5 of the 10 seniors selected from each page are males.
>
> In summary, 50 business school seniors—25 males and 25 females—will be randomly chosen from each of 20 college campuses, which, in turn, will have been chosen from a list of all campuses with four-year business programs. The resulting total sample of 1000 seniors will give us an adequate, unbiased cross section of students for the telephone survey.

QUESTIONS

1. How would you describe the proposed sampling plan in terms of the various sampling techniques we have presented? Explain your answer.
2. Critically evaluate the proposed sampling plan. What are its advantages and disadvantages? Is the plan appropriate for or consistent with the types of information Mr. Dexter desires?
3. What alternative sampling plan would you propose? Why?
4. Comment on the appropriateness of conducting a structured telephone survey of 1000 seniors. If you think it is appropriate, explain why. If you think it is inappropriate, what alternative approach would you suggest, and why?

CASE 5.2

Northwest Bank of Woodcreek (A)

Northwest Bank of Woodcreek (NBW) is the largest of three banks in Woodcreek, a city with a population of 120,000. The NBW recently asked a local marketing research firm to conduct a competitive study of area financial institutions. Specifically, the top management of NBW wanted information on the financial-patronage habits of local residents and their perceptions of financial institutions in Woodcreek. To satisfy top management's overall information needs, the research firm specified the following more detailed objectives:

1. To investigate the market shares of the financial institutions in Woodcreek for several types of financial services.
2. To explain why Woodcreek residents chose to deal with the financial institutions they are presently associated with.
3. To determine the extent of bank switching and the reasons for switching.
4. To uncover the perceived advantages and disadvantages of the three primary institutions in Woodcreek, banks, savings and loan associations, and credit unions.
5. To determine the extent of awareness and use of, and interest in electronic-banking services.
6. To examine the extent of recognition for the slogans and the symbols of the banks and the savings and loan associations in Woodcreek.
7. To determine the perceived images of the major Woodcreek banks.
8. To examine the demographic profiles of customers of the various financial institutions.
9. To describe the patronage patterns in Woodcreek, census tract by census tract.
10. To determine if and how the customers of rival institutions can be attracted to Northwest Bank of Woodcreek.

SAMPLING PLAN

The research firm proposed a personal-interview survey of 400 residents chosen from various census tracts in Woodcreek (the city has a total of 25 census tracts). The following paragraphs excerpted from the final report submitted by the research firm describe the sampling plan used.

> So that the results of this study might provide an accurate representation of the true viewpoints of Woodcreek residents, care had to be taken in the questionnaire design, in the sample selection, and in the execution of the study. The population of interest was defined as the residents of the city of Woodcreek. However, since not all residents are equally valuable as banking customers, the study deliberately underrepresented the census tracts that were low-income areas. The population of each census tract was determined from United States census data, and a stratified random sample was drawn from the Woodcreek City Directory.
>
> Our sample was drawn so as to have a composition similar to that of the population of Woodcreek, with the exception of the planned underrepresentation of certain low-income census tracts. Census tracts 1 and 23 were eliminated because of their low-income level and very small population. In the remaining low-income tracts (2, 3, 6, 7, 9, and 18) half as many respondents were drawn as would have been had these tracts been fully represented in the sample [a map of Woodcreek showing the various census tracts was included in the report].
>
> Professional interviewers were used to conduct the personal interviews.

ACTUAL SAMPLE

The following description of the sample that provided the data for the study appeared in the research firm's final report.

> A total of 393 usable questionnaires were obtained from the 400 residents surveyed. Overall, the demographic characteristics of the sample surveyed seemed to have met our expectations. Consequently, we feel confident that the sample is representative enough to draw meaningful conclusions from the information obtained. As can be seen from an examination of the demographic characteristics contained in Table 1, all demographic groups are adequately represented. The 65-and-over age-group is slightly overrepresented, and the under-25 age-group is somewhat underrepresented. Feedback from our interviewers indicated that this result occurred because of the differences in the availability and willingness of these age-groups to participate in the survey. However, this slight deviation is not serious enough to significantly affect the conclusions drawn from the study.

QUESTIONS

1. What label would you place on the sampling plan used by the research firm? Critically evaluate the sampling plan in light of the objectives of the study and the composition of the actual sample obtained.
2. If you were to do this study over again, what specific sampling procedure(s) would you use? Justify your answer.

Table 1

Demographic characteristics of the sample surveyed

CHARACTERISTICS	CATEGORIES	PERCENTAGE OF RESPONDENTS IN EACH CATEGORY
Sex	Male	36.6
	Female	63.4
Age of household head	Under 25	7.9
	25–34	21.1
	35–44	19.6
	45–54	16.3
	55–64	16.3
	65 and over	17.6
	Refused to answer	1.2
Marital status	Married	79.9
	Single (includes separated or divorced, and widowed)	20.1
Education level of highest-educated spouse	Less than high school	6.9
	Attended high school	8.7
	High school graduate	44.0
	High school + some college	20.1
	College degree or beyond	19.6
	Refused to answer	0.7
Household annual income	Less than $5,000	16.0
	$5001–$10,000	15.8
	$10,001–$15,000	21.1
	$15,001–$20,000	19.1
	$20,001–$25,000	7.4
	$25,001–$30,000	5.1
	Over $30,000	3.3
	Refused to answer	12.2
Length of stay in Woodcreek	Less than 6 months	3.1
	6 months–less than 1 year	1.0
	1 year–less than 2 years	2.3
	2 years and over	93.6

Note: All numbers in this table represent percentages based on a total sample of 393 respondents.

CASE 5.3

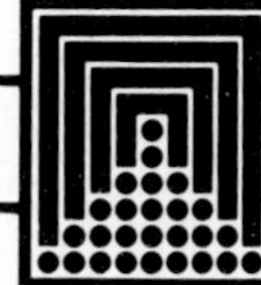

Phoenix Newspapers, Inc.

Phoenix Newspapers, Inc., publisher of two major Phoenix area newspapers—the *Arizona Republic* and the *Phoenix Gazette*—has a long tradition of community involvement and service. As a service to local organizations and the business community, the company publishes an annual brochure called "Inside Phoenix." This brochure is based on a comprehensive study of Phoenix area residents and contains a wealth of information particularly useful as a resource tool for planning and marketing. The annual Phoenix Market Study on which "Inside Phoenix" is based is conducted by the Marketing Research Department of Phoenix Newspapers, Inc. The year 1982 marked the 28th publication of "Inside Phoenix." A description of the methodology used in the 1982 Phoenix Market Study is excerpted here from "Inside Phoenix 1982."

PHOENIX MARKET STUDY METHODOLOGY

The 1982 Phoenix Market Study is a comprehensive media/market study of the Phoenix SMSA (Standard Metropolitan Statistical Area). A broad range of data including demographic characteristics, newspaper, radio and television audiences, and product and shopping data were collected from a common group of respondents. The wealth of available data provides the opportunity for a wide range of analyses, including media penetration singularly and in schedules, market segmentation, product and audience profiles, cross-shopping patterns, and numerous other cross-tabulations of the data.

In order to obtain this data, three different questionnaires were used. An initial telephone interview was used to collect audience data on radio, television, daily and weekly newspapers and magazines. In addition, travel data and grocery shopping information along with demographic characteristics were obtained.

Case material was provided courtesy of Phoenix Newspapers, Inc., P.O. Box 1950, Phoenix, AZ 85001.

Each respondent was mailed a self-completion questionnaire which contained questions about leisure time and vacation activity, stores and shopping centers, automotive equipment, alcoholic beverage and other market products areas.

Finally, each respondent was telephoned a second time. This second telephone interview was, first of all, a validation of the initial telephone interview. In addition, the daily and Sunday newspaper questions were asked again, thus producing a larger data base for audience estimates, and also the necessary input for estimating multiple reach and frequency.

SAMPLE DESIGN AND EXECUTION

The survey represented all adults 18 years of age and older residing in telephone households in Maricopa County. Persons living in nonhousehold types of accommodations, such as student dormitories, military bases, and institutions of various types, were excluded.

The interviewing was carried out between September 9 and October 17, 1981. All interviewing was done from Tuesday through Saturday, primarily in the late afternoon and evening to accommodate working men and women.

Random-digit dialing was used to represent telephone households. A random selection of four-digit numbers was selected from each exchange, proportionate to the household listings in that exchange. These were used as "seed" numbers, to which random numbers were added. This produced a random sample of both listed and unlisted numbers. Within each telephone household one adult was randomly designated as the respondent. No substitution was permitted. Callback procedures at different times of the day and different days of the week were used to obtain interviews with designated respondents. The completed sample representing 61.3% of the sample frame includes 2313 respondents, of whom 1152 are men and 1161 are women.

A self-executing questionnaire concerning shopping and purchasing behavior was mailed to each eligible respondent. A dollar bill was used as an incentive and a reminder mailing was used as a prompt. 1518 questionnaires were obtained using these methods, or 65.6%.

Each respondent was telephoned a second time at least eight days after the initial interview. The second interview was a validation technique and also provided additional newspaper audience data completed with 1869 respondents, or a completion rate of 80.8%.

SAMPLING DEVIATIONS

It should be remembered that, as with all surveys, the findings are subject to the ever-present laws of chance. As such, there will be a few findings that will depart from the true levels by an uncomfortably wide margin. Fortunately, by these same laws of chance, the number of these departures will be relatively small. Users of the data should bear in mind that the findings are subject to sampling tolerance, and these tolerances should be taken into consideration when critical evaluations are made.[1]

[1] Reprinted with permission from *Inside Phoenix 1982* published by Phoenix Newspapers, Inc.

QUESTIONS

1. Critically evaluate the sampling procedures used in conducting the 1982 Phoenix Market Study.
2. Quantify the sampling tolerance (i.e., sampling error) associated with percentage estimates derived from data provided by (a) all respondents; (b) male respondents; (c) female respondents.
3. Are there likely to be any errors other than sampling error in the 1982 Phoenix Market Study? If so, what are they, and how serious are they likely to be?

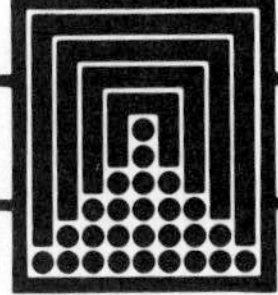

CASE 5.4

McCaw Cablevision

The community of Bryan–College Station, located in central Texas, was served for a number of years by two competing cable television companies, Community Cablevision and Midwest Video Corporation. But in early 1984 both companies were bought by McCaw Communications, Inc., a company based in Bellevue, Washington. McCaw Communications decided to merge the two companies into a single unit called McCaw Cablevision.

One of several potential problems associated with merging the two independent companies was that the companies had been offering their respective subscribers somewhat different sets of channels as part of their basic channel packages. McCaw Cablevision therefore had to decide which channels should be included in, and which should be excluded from, a new basic package to be offered to all subscribers. To aid in designing its basic package, McCaw Cablevision decided to seek input from the community in the following way.

In late May 1984 McCaw Cablevision bought a full-page ad in the Bryan–College Station *Eagle*, the community's daily newspaper. This ad briefly described the merger and sought the public's preferences concerning a number of different channels that could be included in the basic package. Specifically, part of the ad read as follows:

> McCaw is merging the two previous cable company line-ups into a single line-up. And, after counting in the channels we're required to carry by federal and local rules, we have room left for six others. So we want your favorites.

Exhibit 1

McCaw Cablevision coupon

Dear McCaw Cablevision,
Here are the six channels I'd most like to see on the new McCAW BASIC CABLE line-up.

1) ____________________
2) ____________________
3) ____________________
4) ____________________
5) ____________________
6) ____________________

The following channels are must carry channels (and will automatically appear with the above six picks):
KBTX (Channel 3/CBS) Bryan/College Station
KCEN (Channel 6/NBC/ABC) Waco
KAMU (Channel 15/PBS) Bryan/College Station
Government Access
Education Access

____
Name

____
Address

____
City

Plug in your six choices from the list provided. Mail to McCaw Cablevision, 426 Tarrow Drive, Suite 105, College Station, Texas 77840 by June 15, 1984.

Clip and mail immediately.

Source: Courtesy of McCaw Communications Companies, Inc., Bellevue, Wash.

We can't guarantee each of your choices will make our final list. But we'll take the six most popular picks, then plug them into our new McCAW BASIC CABLE line-up. And soon you'll be watching your favorite channels on your new McCAW BASIC CABLE.[1]

The text of the ad was accompanied by a list of 19 different cable channels. Readers were requested to select 6 of these channels they would most like to see on the new McCAW Basic Cable lineup and to list those preferences on a coupon that accompanied the ad. A copy of the coupon is shown in Exhibit 1.

QUESTIONS

1. What sampling frame and sampling method are implied in the procedure used by McCaw Cablevision to seek the community's cable channel preferences?
2. What is your evaluation of the procedure used and the usefulness of the data generated through it? Justify your answer. If you feel the procedure was not sound, what do you think should have been done differently?

[1] Bryan–College Station *Eagle*, May 27, 1984, p. 3A.

PART SIX

DATA ANALYSIS

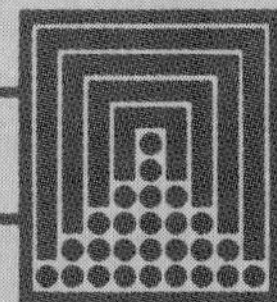

FROM THE MANAGER'S DESK

GEOFFREY STEVENS is administrator of special projects for San Diego Gas and Electric Company. Mr. Stevens graduated from the University of Michigan (B.A.) and the Annenberg School of Communications, University of Pennsylvania (M.A.). He has conducted marketing research for the education, publishing, cable television, and utility industries.

QUESTION: What is the most sophisticated or complex data analysis technique that you have come across, and what is your assessment of this technique? What is the simplest data analysis technique you have come across, and what is your assessment of it?

RESPONSE: In my experience perhaps the most sophisticated application I have seen has been the use of regression and factor analysis to model consumer behavior. The result was less than favorable.

In this specific case a group of consultants prepared elaborate clusters of attitudinal variables, combining several years of data from a tracking study. They talked at great length about the significant correlations they were receiving. A closer examination of the data, however, revealed that all of these factors combined explained less than 4% of the total variance in the data. In summation, while their findings were intellectually interesting, they were nearly useless from a decision-making perspective.

What was disconcerting in this study was not their effort but that their formal presentation did not even mention what percentage of variance was explained. They did not educate their audience about what their findings really meant, and that is not honest.

In short, don't confuse your audience. If you use a sophisticated technique, make sure you explain what it does and how to interpret it. The burden is on you to explain what your results mean, not on your audience to interpret your techniques. With sophisticated techniques you take a gamble. You gain increased precision in understanding your data, but you take on the added responsibility of explaining to others what you are doing and why.

The simplest data analysis technique I have seen is the basic market research technique involving a standard cross-tabulation printout. By scanning the cross-tabulations, one can quickly examine commonsense hypotheses. Although not elegant, it is efficient and easy to understand.

Whether straightforward or sophisticated techniques are used, the rules are the same. Have a clear idea of what you are researching; develop testable hypotheses in a suitable research design; analyze your data thoroughly, going from simple techniques to the more complex; and finally and most importantly, communicate your findings to your users in terms they can understand and use for decision-making purposes.

16

Quality Control and Initial Analysis of Data

As demonstrated in the previous chapter, a variety of errors can occur during fieldwork. Such errors, if not detected and corrected, will lower data quality and cast serious doubt on conclusions stemming from analysis of the data. While certain fieldwork errors can be prevented through precautionary measures such as proper questionnaire design and adequate interviewer training, unanticipated errors can and frequently do occur. Failure to quickly discover and remedy those errors will result in meaningless or misleading data.

For example, a descriptive-research project the author was associated with involved a personal-interview survey of a quota sample of 500 adult respondents. The purpose of the project was to obtain data on life-style variables like leisure time activities, reading habits, and television-viewing behavior. Several seemingly professional interviewers were recruited to gather the data. Sex was one of the quota controls, and the interviewers were instructed to divide their interviews evenly between males and females. The questionnaire, though lengthy, was fairly structured and straightforward. Moreover, no difficulties or complaints were voiced by the interviewers during data collection. As a result, the researchers in charge grew complacent and did very little checking of the completed questionnaires immediately after receiving them from the field. The only periodic checking they did was a cursory examination of interviewers' quota sheets to verify whether adequate progress was being made toward filling the various cell quotas. The questionnaires were not scrutinized until well after all of them had been returned.

A careful examination of the questionnaire data revealed that 25 questionnaires had *both* male and female categories checked under the item "respondent's sex." Yet the interviewers had been assigned quotas of 50% male and 50% female respondents, and these quotas had apparently been adhered to. Additional investigation traced all 25 questionnaires to the same interviewer, who, unfortunately, had moved out of the area by that time. Therefore the only clue to these strange responses was the following additional notation the interviewer had made on one of the questionnaires:

___X___ Male Husband; answered most of the questions

___X___ Female Wife; answered certain leisure activity questions

Evidently, this interviewer did not restrict the interview to just one person in households where both husband and wife were willing to participate in the survey. Conducting part of the interview with a male and part of it with a female was a serious error; all 25 interviews had to be discarded. However, this mistake might have been an honest mistake since the formal quota-sampling instructions asked the interviewers to *contact* (apparently interpreted by this particular interviewer as "make initial contact with") 50% males and 50% females. The point is, irrespective of whether the mistake was an honest one, it could, and *should,* have been caught and corrected much earlier than it was. Discovering fieldwork errors and attempting to correct them early in the project is discussed in the next section.

EDITING

The term *editing,* as used in marketing research, refers to the process of examining completed questionnaires and taking whatever corrective action is needed to ensure that the data are of high quality. It is a sort of quality control check that is performed when the data are still in raw form. As we saw in Chapter 15, some fieldwork errors can be prevented through sound questionnaire design and good control over interviewers. Despite researchers' best efforts, however, rarely is data collection flawless.

Editing is essential for detecting and correcting data collection problems before it is too late. To illustrate, the problem that occurred in the life-style research study could have been minimized and perhaps completely solved by a preliminary edit, also known as a field edit.

DEFINITION. **A *preliminary,* or *field, edit* is a quick examination of completed questionnaires in the field, usually on the same day they are filled out.**

In the life-style research study even a cursory examination of completed questionnaires immediately after the researcher received them from the interviewers would have pinpointed the interviewer who was checking both male and female on some questionnaires. The errant interviewer could then have been reinstructed about the quota-sampling requirements and asked to repeat the defective interviews, using correct procedures. Even if repeating the interviews was not feasible, the mistake could have been prevented from occurring in subsequent interviews. Therefore the number of wasted interviews would have been much lower than 25.

A field edit has two objectives: to ensure that proper procedures are being followed in selecting respondents, interviewing them, and recording their responses; and to remedy fieldwork deficiences before they turn into major problems. Obviously, *speed* is crucial for an effective field edit: It must be done while the study is still in progress—preferably at the end of each interviewing day, and especially at the end of the first day of interviewing. Indeed, in central-location, CRT-controlled telephone interviewing—such as that conducted by Market Facts' National Telephone Center discussed in Chapter 6 (see Exhibit 6.4)—some field editing can and should be done by a supervisor as the interviews are taking place.

Illustrations of typical problems a field edit is capable of revealing include *inappropriate respondents* (as in the life-style research study discussed earlier), *incomplete interviews* (e.g., one or several questions left unanswered for no apparent reason), and *illegible* or *unclear responses* (especially in the case of open-ended questions). Upon uncovering problems of this nature, the field editor, who is usually the person in charge of supervising the fieldwork, must seek an explanation from the interviewer *immediately,* when the interview is still fresh in the interviewer's mind.

A second stage of editing, known as the final edit, or office edit, is conducted after all the field-edited questionnaires are received in a central location. In CRT-controlled telephone interviewing there are typically no physical questionnaires, and the collected data are directly stored in computer memory. Final editing of such data can be done with the aid of a computer (this topic is discussed later).

DEFINITION. A *final,* or *office, edit* involves verifying response consistency and accuracy, making necessary corrections, and deciding whether some or all parts of a questionnaire should be discarded.

An office edit is more thorough than a field edit, and the task of an office editor is somewhat more complex than that of a field editor. The following cases are illustrative of the types of problems an office editor may have to deal with.

- Case 1. A respondent who said he was 18 years old but indicated that he had a Ph.D. when asked for his highest level of education.
- Case 2. On a questionnaire containing 30 Likert scale items, a respondent "strongly agreed" with *all* of them.
- Case 3. In response to the question "What is the most expensive purchase you have made within the past one month?" three respondents gave the

following answers: respondent 1, "a new car"; respondent 2, "a vacation in Hawaii"; respondent 3, "water, gas, and electricity for my household use."

In case 1 the responses to the age and education questions appear to be inconsistent. For an 18-year-old to hold a Ph.D. degree is highly unlikely (although not impossible). Therefore the office editor has to examine a number of alternative explanations for this unusual pair of responses. Was the respondent lying about his age, his education, or both? Did the interviewer make a recording error? Or was the respondent truly brilliant, in which case the answers would be accurate? Perhaps the only way to find out which of these explanations is correct is to look for clues in the respondent's answers to other questions. For instance, if the respondent had indicated that his job title was "director of R&D" and that he had 10 years of work experience, his age as recorded would seem to be in error. Under these circumstances the editor should designate the age of this respondent as a "missing value" (more on missing values later).

Case 2 involves a set of responses that are too consistent. As we saw in Chapter 11, Likert scales invariably contain a mixture of positive and negative items. Therefore a respondent who agreed with all such items was obviously being frivolous and providing invalid answers. In this case the office editor may have no alternative other than throwing the entire questionnaire out.[1]

The situation in case 3 depicts a different type of editing problem—namely, consistency or comparability of responses *across* questionnaires to the same question. While the answers given by all three respondents are legitimate, they appear to be based on different frames of reference. The major issue facing the office editor is deciding how these diverse responses should be coded (coding will be discussed in detail in the next section). For instance, should each such response be treated as a separate category, or should only tangible-product purchases (e.g., respondent 1's answer) be treated as separate categories, with all other purchases lumped under a miscellaneous category? The specific information objectives of the study play a critical role in coding responses. In fact, before commencing the editing process, the researcher should establish a detailed set of guidelines, preferably in writing, for interpreting and categorizing open-ended responses.

The specific editing problems covered in the preceding discussion are certainly not exhaustive. Exhibit 16.1 contains a more comprehensive list of problems that an editor should look for and deal with when they do occur. Notice that several of the problems listed in Exhibit 16.1 can be handled at the field-editing stage.

---

[1] Reversing the wording of some items is but one way of attempting to uncover less-than-truthful respondents. Other approaches include deliberately planting certain questions (sometimes referred to as "sleeper" questions) intended to reveal whether a respondent is too consistent or not consistent enough. For a discussion of one such approach, see Robert S. DuBoff, "Produce More Accurate Projections with 'Consistency Filtering' Technique," *Marketing News,* January 6,1984, Section 1, pp. 16–17.

Exhibit 16.1

A list of problems that editing can help uncover

1. Improper field procedures.
   (a) Wrong questionnaire form used.
   (b) Interview inadvertently not taken.
2. Incomplete interviews.
   (a) Questions not asked.
   (b) Directions not followed (proper segments of the questionnaire were not administered).
3. Improperly conducted interviews.
   (a) The wrong respondent interviewed (e.g., son instead of father).
   (b) Questions misinterpreted by interviewer or respondent.
   (c) Evidence of bias or influencing of answers.
   (d) Failure to probe for adequate answers or the use of poor probes.
   (e) Interviewer apparently does not understand what type of responses constitute an answer to the actual question asked; or does not understand what the objective of the question is, and thus accepts an improper frame of reference for the respondent's answer.
   (f) Interviewer's illegible writing and/or style.
   (g) Interviewer recorded information which identified a respondent whose anonymity should have been protected.
   (h) Other evidence of need for training or instructions to be given to interviewer (e.g., failure to write down probes, wrong abbreviations, failure to follow directions).
4. Technical problems with the questionnaire or interview.
   (a) Space was not provided for needed information.
   (b) The presence of unanticipated or unusually frequent extreme responses to questions, indicating a possible need for rewording of certain questions.
   (c) Inappropriate or unworkable interviewer instructions not detected in the pretest.
   (d) The order in which questions were asked introduces confusion, resentment, or bias into the respondent's answers.
5. Respondent rapport problems.
   (a) Frequent refusal to answer certain questions.
   (b) Reports of abnormal termination of the interview (or presence of hostility) due to sensitive questions.
   (c) Evidence that respondent and interviewer are playing the "game" of "What answer do you want me to give?"
   (d) Evidence that the presence of other people in the interview situation is causing problems.
6. Consistency problems that can be isolated and reconciled.
   (a) Contradictory answers (e.g., reports no savings in one section of the interview but reports interest from bank accounts in another section).
   (b) Misclassification (e.g., mortgage debt improperly reported as installment debt).
   (c) Impossible answers (e.g., reports paying $600 for a new Edsel in 1970—the car should have been recorded as a "used" car; or weekly income reported on the income-per-month line).
   (d) Unreasonable (and probably erroneous) responses (e.g., reports borrowing $2000 for two years to buy a car but reported monthly payments multiplied by 24 months are less than $2000; or house value is reported as being $90,000 while income is $2000 per year and the respondent claims less than a high school education).

Source: John A. Sonquist, William C. Dunkelberg, *SURVEY AND OPINION RESEARCH: Procedures for Processing and Analysis*, © 1977, pp. 43–44. Reprinted by permission of Prentice-Hall, Inc., Englewood Cliffs, N.J.

A few final points about editing should be discussed. First, a number of potential editing problems can be avoided through careful planning *before* fieldwork begins. Preventing ambiguous, inappropriate, or incorrect responses is better than attempting to cure data errors after they occur. Editing is not a panacea for all data quality problems, and it is a serious mistake to view it as such.

Second, when the collected data are already in computer memory—as in the case of CRT-assisted interviews—editing can be done thoroughly and efficiently. Editing tasks that are difficult or impossible to accomplish manually, especially in large-scale surveys, can be done easily through computer editing. For instance, a computer can be programmed to check for such things as whether response values are within prespecified ranges, whether responses to key questions are consistent with those to related questions, or whether a respondent's pattern of answers deviates substantially from the average pattern of answers. Problem responses and respondents can thus be brought to the office editor's attention quickly. A computer can be used even for editing tasks that cannot be accomplished automatically by a computer, such as in deciding what to do with widely disparate open-ended responses like the ones depicted in case 3 earlier. An office editor scanning the responses on a CRT screen will be more efficient than one wading through a bulky set of questionnaires. In fact, an office editor who uses a computer will have at his or her fingertips answers to queries like the following: How many open-ended responses to question XX contain such and such word(s)? How many respondents gave more than a 10-word answer to question YY? What is the most frequently mentioned response to the "other" category in question ZZ? The capability and productivity of the office editor can thus be increased immensely.

Third, the role editing can play in improving data quality is much more restricted in mail surveys than in personal-interview or telephone surveys. As we saw in Chapter 6, a mail survey researcher has little control over data collection once the questionnaires are mailed out. Therefore, the only editing possible in mail surveys is a limited office edit.

In most survey research projects the process of editing, especially the office edit, goes hand in hand with the process of coding, to which we now turn.

CODING

The term *coding* broadly refers to the set of all tasks associated with transforming edited questionnaire responses into a form that is ready for analysis. Our emphasis here will be on questionnaires used in conclusive-research projects which invariably involve large sample sizes and computer data analyses. As we saw in Chapter 4, exploratory-research projects are characterized by fairly informal data collection and analysis procedures. Hence a formal coding process is typically not necessary in such projects.

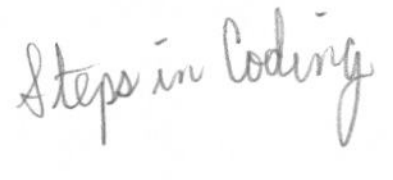

We can view coding as the following sequence of steps:

1. Transforming responses to each question into a set of meaningful categories.
2. Assigning numerical codes to the categories.
3. Creating transformed variables, if needed.
4. Transferring the data to coding sheets (this step is needed only in situations where data are not directly entered into computer memory).
5. Creating a data set suitable for computer analysis.

In discussing these steps, we will use as an illustration a research study (hereafter referred to as the "survey of United States firms") conducted by the author. The primary purpose of this study was to ascertain the emphasis placed by United States firms on marketing research. A six-page questionnaire was mailed to the marketing departments of a random sample of 1000 firms in the United States. Completed questionnaires were returned by 261 firms. The first two pages of the six-page questionnaire are reproduced in Exhibit 16.2 and will be used to illustrate the various coding steps.

Transforming responses into meaningful categories

How difficult and time-consuming this step is depends on the degree to which the questionnaire is structured. As we have already seen in earlier chapters, a structured question is precategorized—that is, it has a set of fixed-response categories. Responses to a nonstructured or open-ended question have to be grouped into a meaningful and manageable set of categories, a task that can be laborious if the respondents' answers vary widely.[2]

Consider for a moment the partial questionnaire presented in Exhibit 16.2. The questions listed are completely structured, with two exceptions: Question 4 in part I has an open-ended "other" category; question 3 in part II is open-ended. However, neither of these questions posed any major coding difficulty.

The "other" category in question 4 in part I was checked by only one firm. Had numerous firms checked this category, and had the self-descriptions provided by such firms fallen into distinct groups, splitting the "other" category into several separate categories would have been necessary. A large number of respondents checking the "other" category, however, would have strongly suggested that the question was bad—that is, the specific response categories provided were not exhaustive enough (as they should be if a question is good) to

[2] An especially good discussion of the difficulties in coding answers to open-ended questions is given in Claire Selltiz, Marie Jahoda, Morton Deutsch, and Stuart W. Cook, *Research Methods in Social Relations* (New York: Henry Holt, 1959), Chap. 11.

Exhibit 16.2

Two pages of the questionnaire used in the survey of United States firms

Part I: Please answer the following general questions about your firm and industry.

1. What is the total number of full-time employees in your firm?

   __________ Fewer than 100

   __________ 100–499

   __________ 500–999

   __________ 1000–1499

   __________ 1500 or more

2. What is your firm's annual sales revenue?

   __________ Less than $5 million

   __________ $5 million to less than $10 million

   __________ $10 million to less than $25 million

   __________ $25 million to less than $100 million

   __________ $100 million or more.

3. How many different product and/or service categories does your firm currently market?

   __________ Fewer than 10

   __________ 10–24

   __________ 25–49

   __________ 50–99

   __________ 100 or more

4. Of the following categories, check *one* category that *best* describes the type of industry to which your firm belongs.

   __________ Consumer goods manufacturers

   __________ Industrial goods manufacturers

   __________ Consumer and industrial goods manufacturers

__________ Retailers

__________ Wholesalers/industrial distributors

__________ Financial institutions

__________ Firms offering services (other than financial)

__________ Other ______________________________
(please specify)

5. How would you rate the overall degree of competition among firms within your industry? Please circle the number that best describes your opinion:

Very intense	Intense	Moderate	Weak	Very weak
5	4	3	2	1

6. Would you say that the relative market position or competitive strength of your firm (when compared with other firms in your industry) is above average, average, or below average? Please check one of the following:

__________ Above average __________ Average
__________ Below average

Part II: Questions in this part relate to marketing research activities of your firm.

1. Does your firm have at least one full-time employee whose *primary* duties/responsibilities relate to marketing research?

__________ Yes __________ No

2. Does your firm have a separate marketing research department?

__________ Yes __________ No

3. Approximately what percentage of your total marketing expenditures were used for marketing research expenditures (including the purchase of commercial marketing research services, if any) during the last year?

__________ %

If you indicated 0%, skip to Question 5; otherwise, please continue with Question 4.

cover the bulk of the respondents. In other words, a well-designed question with an "other" category is unlikely to pose any major coding problem.

Question 3 in part II, though open-ended, sought a numerical response. Numerical responses are already coded in quantified form and hence can be directly transferred to coding sheets, without collapsing them into a set of categories. In fact, collapsing numerical responses into a parsimonious set of categories will generally lead to a loss of information and hence is not usually advisable. In this particular case, converting the responses given in percentages (which are ratio data) into a set of response categories—for example, 0% to less than 10%, 10% to less than 20%, and so on—would have lowered the measurement level of the data to ordinal.

In establishing response categories for open-ended questions, one must ensure that the categories are *mutually exclusive* (i.e., nonoverlapping) and *collectively exhaustive* (i.e., every response given fits into one of the categories). Response categories for structured questions should already possess these characteristics (recall the discussion in Chapter 10 on constructing multiple-category questions).

A special problem in coding responses to open-ended as well as structured questions relates to the treatment of "don't know" responses. A "don't know" might be a legitimate response; that is, the respondent could not honestly answer the question. Or it might be an interviewing failure; that is, the respondent had an answer but for some reason did not divulge it.[3] An editor/coder must ascertain which of these two interpretations of "don't know" is correct. Unfortunately, this task is not easy, except in certain cases. For instance, a "don't know" answer to the question "Do you have any credit cards?" is most likely an interviewing failure. But a "don't know" answer to the question "Do you favor or oppose spending public funds to support certified abortion clinics?" may or may not be an interviewing failure.

There are no rules for the *best* way to treat "don't know" responses. One approach used by some researchers is to distribute the "don't know"s among the other response categories, in proportion to the number of responses already in each of those categories. Another approach is to infer an actual response for each "don't know"—that is, to make an educated guess about what the answer might have been had the respondent not said "don't know"—on the basis of the answers to other questions. For example, a respondent's likely income bracket might be subjectively estimated from his or her age, education level, and occupation. However, both these approaches are fraught with questionable assumptions and hence are of dubious validity. A safer and more defensible approach is to simply classify the "don't know"s as a separate response category. And if legitimate "don't know"s can be distinguished from those that are interviewing

[3] Hans Zeisel, *Say It with Figures* (New York: Harper & Row, 1968), Chap. 4, contains a good discussion of these two types of "don't know"s and ways of handling them.

failures, one should report the latter separately as missing values, a topic discussed next.

A *missing-value category,* as the name implies, is used to code questions for which answers should have been obtained but were not for some reason. A missing value can stem from a respondent's refusal to answer a question, an interviewer's failure to ask a question or record an answer, or a "don't know" that does not seem legitimate. Sound questionnaire design, tight control over fieldwork, and a thorough field edit can help reduce, but not necessarily eliminate, the occurrence of missing values. Questions plagued by a large number of missing values, however, are invariably indicative of a poorly designed questionnaire and/or shoddy fieldwork. In such a case caution must be exercised during subsequent analysis and interpretation of the data gathered.[4]

Assigning numerical codes

The next stage in the coding process is to assign appropriate numerical codes to responses that are not already in quantified form. The purpose of numerical coding is to facilitate computer manipulation and analysis of the responses. In Exhibit 16.2 the response categories in questions 1, 2, 3, 4, and 6 in part I and questions 1 and 2 in part II need to be assigned numerical codes.

The issue of assigning numbers to responses was covered at length in Chapter 11 and will not be discussed here. Nevertheless, we reemphasize that the scale or measurement level reflected by the numerical codes depends on the way a question is asked and the nature of the variable it is attempting to measure. Table 16.1 summarizes the measurement levels achieved by responses to the various questions in Exhibit 16.2. The researcher must keep these measurement levels in mind while analyzing and interpreting the quantified responses.

Creating transformed variables

Each question in Exhibit 16.2 represents a distinct variable. Question 1 in part I, for instance, represents a firm's size as measured by the number of full-time employees. Question 2 in part I also represents a firm's size, but as measured by annual sales revenue. Variables like these are directly defined by the questionnaire data and hence can be labeled *raw variables.* A researcher may sometimes

[4] Several ways of handling missing values (similar to those mentioned in this chapter for handling "don't know"s) are available. For a good discussion of these approaches, see John A. Sonquist and William C. Dunkenberg, *Survey and Opinion Research: Procedures for Processing and Analysis* (Englewood Cliffs, N.J.: Prentice-Hall, 1977). This book is an excellent general source for editing and coding procedures.

Table 16.1

Measurement levels of the responses to the questions used in the survey of United States firms

QUESTION NUMBER	CONSTRUCT MEASURED BY QUESTION	MEASUREMENT LEVEL OF RESPONSE
Part I, question 1	Number of employees	Ordinal
Part I, question 2	Annual sales revenue	Ordinal
Part I, question 3	Number of product/service categories	Ordinal
Part I, question 4	Industry type	Nominal
Part I, question 5	Industry competition intensity	Ordinal; perhaps can be assumed to be interval
Part I, question 6	Firm's competitive position	Ordinal; perhaps can be assumed to be interval
Part II, question 1	Full-time employee in charge of marketing research	Nominal
Part II, question 2	Separate marketing research department	Nominal
Part II, question 3	Percent allocation to marketing research	Ratio

want to create *transformed variables,* which are essentially new variables constructed from data on raw variables.

To illustrate, suppose we want to compare the results of the survey of United States firms across the following two subsamples: firms with at least 500 full-time employees *and* an annual sales revenue of at least $25 million, and all other firms. To sort the survey results according to these subsamples, we must create a new dichotomous variable, say X, with values 1 or 2, such that $X = 1$ for each firm whose coded response to question 1 is 3, 4, or 5 *and* whose coded response to question 2 is 4 or 5 (assuming that response categories to both questions are coded 1 through 5); and $X = 2$ for all other firms. The variable X is a transformation of the raw variables implied by questions 1 and 2.

An important point concerning transformed variables is that they do not always have to be created at this stage of the coding process. In fact, more often than not, variable transformations are accomplished by a computer after data on raw variables have been coded and stored in computer memory. Virtually all standard computer programs are capable of creating transformed variables, as needed, just prior to data analysis. However, in certain situations it may be expedient and efficient to generate values for transformed variables as and when the raw variables are being coded (such a situation is illustrated in the next section).

Transferring data to coding sheets

The numerically coded responses pertaining to raw and transformed variables are transferred to a common set of coding sheets in order to facilitate the process of data entry into a computer. However, coding sheets are not used when the data are entered directly into computer memory, as in the case of CRT-controlled interviewing. Computers typically read data from so-called *data records,* each of which can accommodate a number of numerical digits. Up until the late seventies these records were primarily in the form of punched cards. At the present time, however, data are invariably stored on computer disks or tapes, which are more efficient data storage units and are easier to handle than a bulky deck of punched cards. Irrespective of whether the data input into the computer is through cards, optical-scan sheets, disks, or tapes, the data are arranged as a series of fixed-length records. Coding sheets are helpful in organizing the data in this fashion before getting them on to an appropriate computer input medium.

Exhibit 16.3 shows one of several coding sheets used to record the data generated in the survey of United States firms. Each row of numbers on this coding sheet represents all the answers given by one respondent. In this study each data record consisted of 80 columns (or spaces). Only 58 columns of an 80-column record were needed to summarize the answers of each respondent (notice that columns 59 through 80 are blank in Exhibit 16.3). However, when longer questionnaires are used, several records (i.e., several rows on the coding sheet) may be needed to code the answers of each respondent.

A detailed set of instructions, preferably in writing, is essential if one is to avoid errors in transferring data from questionnaires to coding sheets. Table 16.2 lists the coding instructions pertaining to the partial questionnaire shown in Exhibit 16.2.

Although Exhibit 16.3 and Table 16.2 are self-explanatory, several key features deserve some discussion. First, the entries under the "Variable Name" column in Table 16.2 were the symbols used in the survey of United States firms to identify the respective variables during computer analysis. Since variable names are no more than identification labels, they can be chosen to fit a researcher's preferences, as long as they do not violate any restrictions imposed by the specific computer programs to be used.

Second, variables V1, V2, V3, and V4 are transformed variables, derived from the raw data. For each respondent the coder had to assign a value for each of these variables before transferring the data to coding sheets. For instance, to determine a respondent's value for V2, the coder would glance through part I of the respondent's questionnaire and count the number of questions left unanswered. While this procedure appears cumbersome, it really was not, since the questionnaire was quite short, with a relatively small number of questions in each part. Of course, values for V2 could have also been generated later, at the

Exhibit 16.3

Illustrative coding sheet used in the survey of United States firms

1	2	3	4	5	6	7	8	9	10	11	12	13	14	15	16	17	18	19	20	21	22	23	24	25	26	27	28	29	30	31	32	33	34	35	36	37	38	39	40	41	42	43	44	45	46	47	48	49	50	51	52	53	54	55	56	57	58	59	60	61	62	63	64	65	66	67	68	69	70	71	72	73	74	75	76	77	78	79	80
0	2	6		0	8	0	0	1	2	0	3	1	1	2	4	3	3	1	1													1	0	1	0													4		7		1	2	4	8	5	8																						
0	2	7		0	9	0	0	0	1	0	1	3	4	4	5	5	2	1	1													1	0	1	0	3	3	5	7	5	7	7	7	7	7	3	6	4	6	5		2	2	2	6	2	6																						
0	2	8		1	0	0	0	0	0	0	0	1	2	4	5	5	2	1	1	0	0	0										1	1	1	1	4	6	5	7	5	7	7	7	4	7	2	6	3	6	6	2	1	1	2	4	2	4																						
0	2	9		1	0	0	0	0	0	0	0	1	2	5	5	4	3	1	1	0	0	0										1	1	1	1	2	2	2	2	2	3	6	4	5	5	3	7	6	4	6	6	1	2	0	3	3	1																						
0	3	0		0	9	0	0	0	0	0	0	1	1	3	4	4	2	1	1	0	0	0										1	1	1	1	3	5	6	6	5	6	7	5	5	4	2	5	6																																
0	3	1		1	0	0	0	0	0	0	0	5	5	3	1	5	2	2	2	0	0	7	0	5	0	0	2	5	0	2	5	1	0	2	2	3	4	5	5	4	6	6	4	5	4	2	5	3	3	4	6	2	4	2	0	3	0																						
0	3	2		1	1	0	0	0	0	0	0	1	1	2	5	4	3	1	1	0	0	0										1	1	1	1	6	5	6	6	7	7	7	7	6	6	2	6	6	5	4	6	4	2	0	9	0	9																						
0	3	3		1	0	0	0	0	0	0	0	2	4	1	5	4	2	1	1	0	0	0										1	1	1	1	5	2	7	7	7	6	6	7	7	7	2	6	4	5	2	4	1	2	0	4	1	4																						
0	3	4		0	9	0	0	0	3	0	0	3	4	1	2	3	3	2	1	0	0	1	0	9	0	0	0	5	0	0	5	1	1	1	1	5				5	6	6	6	3	2	2	7	7	5	5	6	4	4	2	9	4	0																						
0	3	5		1	1	0	0	0	0	0	0	1	1	5	3	4	2	1	1	0	0	0										1	1	1	1	5	7	7	7	7	7	7	7	7	6	2	5	4	6	6	7	5	1	1	2	6	2																						
0	3	6		1	1	0	0	0	0	0	0	1	2	1	1	4	3	1	1	0	0	0										1	0	2	0	6	3	5	6	6	6	6	7	5	3	3	3	6	4	4	4	1	2	0	5	1	1																						
0	3	7		1	0	0	0	0	0	0	0	2	4	1	2	4	3	2	1	0	2	5	0	2	5	0	5	5	0	2	0	1	1	2	1	2	3	4	7	5	7	7	7	7	4	2	5	6	6	6	6	4	4	1	7	2	9																						
0	3	8		0	9	0	0	0	0	0	0	1	2	1	8	4	3	1	1	0	0	0										1	0	1	0	4	5	6	7	7	7	7	6	7	7	3	6	5	5	5	7	1	1	0	1	0	1																						
0	3	9		1	0	0	1	1	3	0	2	1	1		4	5	3	1	1													1	1	1	1												7	2	5	2			1	4	0	4	5																						
0	4	0		1	0	0	0	0	0	0	0	2	5	2	5	4	2	1	1	0	0	5	0	8	0	0	1	0	0	1	0	1	1	2	2	1	1	4	7	4	7	7	7	6	1	3	7	5	6	6	4	1	2	1	8	3	3																						
0	4	1		1	4	0	0	0	0	0	0	2	4	1	4	5	3	1	1	0	0	0										1	1	1	1	3	3	5	5	5	5	5	5	5	3	2	7	3	6	5	7	5	1	0	8	3	0																						
0	4	2		0	9	0	0	0	0	0	0	2	2	2	2	4	2	2	1	0	1	5	0	7	5	0	1	5	0	1	0	1	1	2	2	3	3	5	6	3	6	6	7	6	4	3	6	4	7	6	7	3	1	1	5	3	5																						
0	4	3		1	0	0	0	0	0	0	0	2	2	1	1	2	2	1	1	0	0	0										1	1	1	1	3	2	3	6	6	3	6	7	7	4	1	7	6	3	3	7	1	1	3	2	3	2																						
0	4	4		1	1	0	0	0	0	0	0	2	4	5	5	4	3	2	1	0	0	5	0	3	5	0	6	0	0	0	5	1	1	2	1	4	1	7	5	5	6	7	7	5	6	3	3	4	4	1	6	1	2	2	7	3	0																						
0	4	5		1	0	0	0	0	0	0	0	2	4	4	1	5	3	2	1	0	0	0										1	1	1	1	7	2	7	7	7	7	7	7	7	7	2	7	4	7	6	7	3	2	0	6	1	6																						
0	4	6		1	1	0	0	0	1	0	0	1	2	3	4	4	3	1	1	0	0	0										1	0	1	0		5	6	6	6	6	5	6	7	7	2	6	7	6	6	6	2	3	2	3	3	3																						
0	4	7		0	9	0	0	1	0	0	0	1	1	1	7	3	3	1	1	0		2	0	2	0	0	4	0	0	4	0	1	1	1	1											2	6	4	6	6	7	1	1	2	5	3	1																						
0	4	8		1	0	0	0	0	0	0	0	1	1	1	5	5	2	1	1	0	0	0										1	1	1	1	4	1	4	7	4	7	7	7	7	4	2	7	4	6	6	2	1	1	2	0	3	5																						
0	4	9		1	0	0	0	0	0	0	0	1	3	5	5	5	2	1	1	0	0	0										1	1	1	1	4	4	5	4	5	7	7	6	4	6	2	7	6	7	6	7	3	8	1	9	2	5																						
0	5	0		1	0	0	0	0	0	0	0	1	1	2	4	4	3	2	1	0	0	0										2	2	1	0	3	3	5	5	5	6	6	7	4	4	3	7	4	6	6	7	3	9	0	2	0	4																						

Note: The numbers in the first row of the coding sheet merely indicate column numbers.

Table 16.2
Coding instructions for the questionnaire used in the survey of United States firms

COLUMN NUMBERS ON CODING SHEET	DESCRIPTION OF ITEM TO BE CODED	QUESTION NUMBER	VARIABLE NAME	RANGE OF PERMISSIBLE NUMERICAL CODES*
01–03	ID number for responding firm	—	—	001–261
04		—	—	—
05–06	Speed of response—number of days between questionnaire mail-out date and postmark date on returned questionnaire	—	V1	01–60
07–08	Item omission in part I (i.e., number of questions left unanswered that should have been answered)	— transformed variables	V2	00–06
09–10	Item omission in part II	—	V3	00–22
11–12	Item omission in part III	—	V4	00–09
13	Number of employees	Part I, question 1	V5	1–5 (5 = 1500 or more)
14	Annual sales revenue	Part I, question 2	V6	1–5 (5 = $100MM or more)
15	Number of product/service categories	Part I, question 3	V7	1–5 (5 = 100 or more)
16	Industry type	Part I, question 4	V8	1–8 (8 = other)
17	Industry competition intensity	Part I, question 5	V9	1–5 (5 = very intense)
18	Firm's competitive position	Part I, question 6	V10	1–3 (3 = above average)
19	Existence of full-time employee in charge of marketing research	Part II, question 1	V11	1–2 (2 = yes)
20	Existence of separate marketing research department	Part II, question 2	V12	1–2 (2 = yes)
21–23	Percent allocation to marketing research	Part II, question 3	V13	000–100 (*Note:* Round fractional percentages exceeding 10% to nearest whole number—e.g., 16.8% should be coded as .17. Round fractional percentages below 10% to one or two decimal places—e.g., 1.25% should be coded as 1.3, .175 should be coded as .18)

*When any variable has a missing value, leave the corresponding coding sheet columns blank.

analysis stage, by programming the computer to check each question and add the number of missing values. However, in this study the researcher felt that accomplishing the variable transformation by hand would be just as easy as programming the computer to do it.

Third, to see the interrelationships among the survey questionnaire (Exhibit 16.2), the coding instructions (Table 16.2), and the coding sheet (Exhibit 16.3), consider firm 50, and try to infer its responses from the numerical codes in the coding sheet. You should see that firm 50 responded to the survey in 10 days (columns 5–6); answered all questions in all three parts (columns 7–12); had fewer than 100 full-time employees (column 13); had annual sales revenue of less than $5 million (column 14); marketed between 10 and 24 product/service categories (column 15); was a retailer (column 16); operated in an industry characterized by intense competition (column 17); was competitively above average (column 18); had at least one full-time employee with marketing research responsibilities (column 19); had no separate marketing research department (column 20); and allocated little or none of its previous year's marketing expenditures specifically for marketing research (columns 21–23).

Fourth, notice that each survey question listed in Table 16.2 has just one corresponding raw variable; that is, responses to each question translate into data on only a single variable. The reason is that each question in the survey of United States firms had one, and *only one,* possible response. The one-question/one-variable feature is not universal, however. A question allowing ***multiple*** responses will need as many variables as there are possible responses. The following question is a case in point:

> Which of the following countries have you visited during the past 12 months?
>
> ________Canada
>
> ________England
>
> ________France
>
> ________Germany
>
> ________Japan
>
> ________Mexico

As few as zero or as many as six categories can be checked in response to this question. Simply assigning a series of numerical codes to the six response categories (say 1 through 6) and treating them as pertaining to a single variable will be inadequate for coding purposes. It will be inadequate because this question is, in effect, asking respondents *six* separate questions: "Did you visit Canada during the past 12 months?" "Did you visit England during the past 12 months?" And so on. Therefore six variables, each relating to a specific country and having two possible values—for example, 1 = "no" and 2 = "yes"—will be needed. Furthermore, six columns must be set aside in the coding sheets (and/or computer data records) to record responses to this question. Clearly, the process of coding questions with multiple responses is somewhat complex and hence requires special attention.

Finally, as has been mentioned before, in not all studies are coding sheets necessary in transferring data from questionnaires to appropriate computer records. Sometimes, all the necessary coding instructions—for example, the specific record column(s) in which each response is to be coded—are printed on the questionnaires. In such instances the questionnaire data can be directly transferred through a computer terminal to cards, disks, or tapes. Moreover, in computerized interviews using CRT terminals, which are becoming increasingly popular, responses are coded and stored in computer memory as the interviews are taking place, eliminating the need for printed questionnaires as well as coding sheets.

Creating a data set

A *data set,* also known as a *data file,* is a logical outcome of the preceding stage in the coding process. It is merely an organized collection of the data records created earlier. Each sample unit for which data are available within a data set is typically called a *case,* or *observation.* When the sample size is n (i.e., the number of observations = n) and the total number of variables embedded in the questionnaire is m, the resulting data set can be conceptually viewed as an $n \times m$ matrix of numbers, as illustrated by Table 16.3.

When coded data records are transferred to a computer, they are stored in computer memory in a format similar to the format in Table 16.3. Each x_{ij} in the table is a number and represents the coded response for the ith sample unit on

Table 16.3
Structure of a data set

	VARIABLES						
OBSERVATIONS	1	2	$\cdots$	j	$\cdots$	m
1	x_{11}	x_{12}	$\cdots$	x_{1j}	$\cdots$	x_{1m}
2	x_{21}	x_{22}	$\cdots$	x_{2j}	$\cdots$	x_{2m}
$\vdots$	$\vdots$	$\vdots$	$\vdots$	$\vdots$	$\vdots$	$\vdots$
i	x_{i1}	x_{i2}	$\cdots$	x_{ij}	$\cdots$	x_{im}
$\vdots$	$\vdots$	$\vdots$	$\vdots$	$\vdots$	$\vdots$	$\vdots$
n	x_{n1}	x_{n2}	$\cdots$	x_{nj}	$\cdots$	x_{nm}

the *j*th variable. Data analysis can begin once a data set is available in computer memory. Any desired computer-generated variable transformations are obtained at this time by using the data already in the data set. Such transformations will increase the size of the data set. For example, if two transformed variables are created by using the data set in Table 16.3, two more columns of numbers will be added to it. Thus an expanded data set in the form of an $n \times (m + 2)$ matrix will result.

One final comment before we move on to the next section: While the chapter material so far has described editing and coding in some detail, it does not constitute a comprehensive treatment of those topics. The details of tasks like designing coding forms, hiring qualified editors/coders, and verifying their work are beyond the scope of this text. Good discussions of these topics can be found elsewhere, however.[5]

PRELIMINARY DATA ANALYSIS

Before analyzing a data set by using sophisticated techniques, a researcher should get a feeling for what the data are like. The purpose of preliminary data analysis is to reveal features of the basic composition of the data that have been collected. Preliminary analysis may also provide useful insights pertaining to the research objectives and suggest meaningful approaches for further analysis of the data.

Preliminary data analysis involves examining the *central tendency* and the *dispersion* of the data on each variable in the data set. The measurement level of a variable—that is, whether the variable is nominal, ordinal, interval, or ratio—has a bearing on which measures of central tendency and dispersion will be appropriate for it. Table 16.4 summarizes the commonly used measures for different types of variables.

Note that Table 16.4 lists the same measures of central tendency and dispersion for interval and ratio data. Almost no statistical techniques have been developed specifically for ratio data; therefore they are invariably analyzed by using techniques developed for interval data. Ratio data, of course, have all the properties of interval data, as discussed in Chapter 11. Furthermore, the measures listed in Table 16.4 for nominal and ordinal data can be computed for interval and ratio data as well. Similarly, nominal data measures are also permissible for ordinal data.

A simple way of uncovering the central tendency and/or dispersion of data for virtually any variable is to construct a one-way table for it. This topic is discussed next.

---

[5] See, for example, Charles S. Mayer, "Quality Control," in *Handbook of Marketing Research,* ed. Robert Ferber (New York: McGraw-Hill, 1974), pp. 2–160 to 2–177; in the same handbook, see also Philip S. Sidel, "Coding," pp. 2–178 to 2–199.

Two-way tabulation

The objectives of most research studies include an examination of relationships among key variables. For instance, one crucial issue in the survey of United States firms was whether a firm's size was associated with how much money it allocated to marketing research. Two-way tabulation is a useful preliminary step in understanding the nature of the association between a pair of variables. For two-way tabulation to be meaningful, however, the data on each variable must be coded into a fixed set of categories, and the number of categories should not be large. Therefore two-way tables are particularly appropriate for categorical (i.e., nominal- or ordinal-scaled) variables. Of course, two-way tables are also appropriate for interval- or ratio-scaled variables that have been transformed into ordinal-scaled variables with a limited number of categories.

Constructing a *two-way table* involves breaking down the number of responses in each category of one variable into the categories of the second variable. This process is the simplest form of *cross-tabulation,* which refers to simultaneous tabulation of data on two or more variables. Standard computer programs capable of cross-tabulating data on any combination of variables in a data set are available for virtually all computers.

Table 16.7 summarizes the results of cross-tabulating two transformed variables in the survey of United States firms: a three-category "size" variable (less than 100 employees, 100 to 499 employees, and 500 or more employees); and a

Table 16.7
Association between firm size and allocation to marketing research

	ALLOCATION TO MARKETING RESEARCH		
NUMBER OF FULL-TIME EMPLOYEES	Nothing	Some Funds	ALL FIRMS
Less than 100	92 (77%) (64%)	27 (23%) (29%)	119 (100%)
100 to 499	41 (57%) (29%)	31 (43%) (33%)	72 (100%)
500 and over	10 (22%) (7%)	36 (78%) (38%)	46 (100%)
All Firms	143 (100%)	94 (100%)	237* (total sample)

Note: Numbers without parentheses are the actual number of firms in each cell. The percentage figures in parentheses listed below and beside each of these numbers are based on the corresponding column and row totals.

*This value is less than 261 because of the 24 missing values for the "marketing research allocation" variable.

two-category "marketing research allocation," variable (firms allocating nothing to marketing research, and those allocating some funds to marketing research). Several key features of Table 16.7 deserve to be highlighted.

First, notice that the two-way table is based on a total sample of only 237 firms. This total occurs because 24 of the 261 responding firms did not answer the question dealing with allocation to marketing research, although all of them indicated the number of employees they had. An important general caveat underlies this feature—namely, the total sample size available for cross-tabulating two variables is constrained by the variable with the larger number of missing values (this maximum, effective sample size may be further reduced by missing values on the other variable). Therefore, even if just one of the two variables has a large number of missing values, the resulting two-way table may be misleading. Under such circumstances one should exercise caution in interpreting the table, especially if respondents with missing values on the variable in question are likely to differ markedly from other respondents.

Second, as shown in Table 16.7, we customarily report the responses falling within each cell as raw frequencies as well as percentages. Percentages are easy to compare and hence are helpful in gaining insight into the relationship between the variables being cross-tabulated. A simple glance at the cell percentages in Table 16.7 suggests the presence of an association between the size of a firm, as measured by number of employees, and whether it allocated any money to marketing research. Considering the percentages based on the row totals indicates that larger firms seem more likely to have allocated some funds to marketing research than smaller firms. While 78% of the firms in the "500 and over" size category had allocated some funds to marketing research, only 43% of the firms in the "100 to 499" category and 23% of the firms in the "less than 100" category had done so. Similarly, considering the percentages based on the column totals, firms allocating some funds to marketing research appear to be larger than firms allocating no funds to marketing research. One assumption implicit in these inferences, however, is that the 24 firms with missing values were not substantially different from the 237 firms on which the two-way table is based. That is, had it been possible to construct a two-way table for the full sample of 261 firms, the pattern of percentages in that table would have been similar to those in Table 16.7.

Third, the cell frequencies in Table 16.7 are expressed as percentages of row totals as well as column totals. (Almost all computer-generated two-way tables also express the cell frequencies as percentages of the total sample size, although these percentages may not be as helpful in uncovering possible associations between variables.) While both sets of percentages appear to be consistent (i.e., they both lead to the same conclusion concerning the association between a firm's size and its allocation for marketing research), they are not necessarily equally meaningful. An important question here is, In which direction (row or column) is it most meaningful to compute percentages for the cell frequencies? A general, intuitively appealing guideline is *to compute percent-*

ages in the direction of the presumed causal variable.[9] In other words, when we can logically view one of the two variables being cross-tabulated as a *possible cause* of the other, we should base the percentages on the response totals in corresponding categories of the causal variable. Note the emphasis on "possible cause." As pointed out earlier in this book (especially in Chapter 4), cross-tabulation of data gathered through descriptive research can only suggest, but not prove, cause and effect between variables.

Let us examine Table 16.7 in light of this guideline. To view a firm's size as influencing its allocation to marketing research, rather than the other way around, seems more logical. Therefore, it is more meaningful to interpret the table by using the row percentages (those reported to the right of the raw cell frequencies) than the column percentages. Moreover, Table 16.7 will look less cluttered, but still convey the same substantive information, if the column percentage figures are omitted.

The general guideline for computing percentages in two-way tables has a couple of potential problems. First, which of the two variables is the likely causal variable may not always be clear. For instance, in the survey of United States firms, consider the cross-tabulation of data on firms' competitive positions (variable V10 in Table 16.2) and their allocations to marketing research. Whether a firm is competitively weak, average, or strong may have a bearing on how much it spends on marketing research (e.g., weaker firms may feel they do not have as much to spend and hence may allocate little or nothing to marketing research). In contrast, a firm's expenditures on marketing research may influence its relative competitive strength (e.g., firms may be competitively weak *because* of their failure to spend enough on marketing research). Thus the general guideline will not be helpful when there is no clear basis for presuming a particular direction of causality between the variables. In such cases a researcher should compute and report percentages in both directions.

Second, a more subtle, and perhaps more serious, limitation of the general guideline is that it may be inappropriate when the sample is not representative of the population with respect to the presumed causal variable, as in the case of certain types of quota sampling. To illustrate, consider a study aimed at generating descriptive profiles of households with and without personal computers. Because of the relative novelty of personal computers, a random representative sample of households may not contain a sufficient number of households with personal computers. Therefore, assume that a quota sample of 1000 households—500 with and 500 without personal computers—is chosen, and data are collected on their demographic characteristics. Also, suppose the cross-tabulation of data on household income and personal-computer ownership is as shown in Table 16.8.

[9] For a comprehensive discussion of this issue, see Hans Zeisel, *Say It with Figures* (New York: Harper & Row, 1968), Chap. 3; see also Loether and McTavish, *Descriptive Statistics for Sociologists,* pp. 177–182.

Table 16.8

Association between household income and ownership of personal computers

	OWNERSHIP OF PERSONAL COMPUTERS		
HOUSEHOLD INCOME	Households With	Households Without	ALL HOUSEHOLDS
High income ($25,000 or more)	400 (67%) (80%)	200 (33%) (40%)	600 (100%)
Low income (Less than $25,000)	100 (25%) (20%)	300 (75%) (60%)	400 (100%)
All households	500 (100%)	500 (100%)	1000 (total sample)

The presumed causal variable in this case is household income. Therefore, if we follow the general guideline—compute percentages in the direction of the causal variable—we will examine the percentages based on the row totals and make the following inference: "High-income households are much more likely to own personal computers than low-income households. Specifically, a high-income household is about 2.7 times (67% vs. 25%) as likely to own a personal computer as a low-income household." Strictly speaking, however, such an inference (especially the latter part of it) may be misleading since the sample is not necessarily representative of the population of households with respect to income. No attempt was made during sample selection to control for household income. Therefore the income distribution within the sample is purely a consequence of the particular mix of households with and without personal computers chosen for the study. While inferences stemming from the percentages based on row totals are true for this sample, they cannot be generalized confidently to the population of households.

Percentages based on the column totals in Table 16.8, in contrast, are meaningful because the sampling procedure deliberately controlled the representation of households with respect to ownership of personal computers. Hence inferences such as the following make more sense and are more generalizable than those made earlier: "Eight out of ten households with personal computers are likely to be high-income households, whereas only four out of ten households without personal computers are likely to be high-income households. In other words, a household with a personal computer is twice as likely to be a high-income household as one without a personal computer."

The preceding discussion suggests the following exception to the general guideline: When the sample is nonrepresentative with respect to the logical causal variable, but is controlled with respect to the other variable, percentages must be based on response category totals for the latter variable.

In conclusion, the most meaningful way to compute percentages in two-way tables can be summarized as follows: Compute percentages in the direction of the presumed causal variable *if* the sample is representative on that variable. If it is *not,* compute percentages in the direction of the variable on which the sample is explicitly controlled. When the likely direction of causality is ambiguous, compute and report percentages in both directions.[10]

Precautions in interpreting two-way tables

Two-way tabulation, though helpful in uncovering relationships, has a few pitfalls that can easily lead a careless researcher to unwarranted conclusions. A frequent temptation when a two-way table shows evidence of a relationship, especially when one of the two variables is presumed to influence the other, is to view it as conclusive evidence of a *causal* relationship. This temptation must be resisted, however, since to infer causation from association is risky unless such evidence stems from a controlled experimental study. Two-way tables can, at best, only *suggest* the possibility of a causal relationship.

Another caveat in interpreting two-way tables is to watch out for small cell sizes and to be wary of percentages that are unaccompanied by the raw totals on which they are based. Consider the following two-way table based on a survey of 200 hospital patients:

	Smokers	Nonsmokers
Patients with lung cancer	40%	20%
Patients without lung cancer	60%	80%
	100%	100%

This table appears to confirm what is commonly believed to be true: Smokers are more likely than nonsmokers to contract lung cancer. Specifically, the table shows that smokers are twice as likely (40% vs. 20%) to contract lung cancer. But assume for a moment that you have no prior knowledge of a possible link between smoking and contracting lung cancer. In other words, suppose this table is the first piece of evidence you are seeing about smoking and lung cancer. Would you now infer that smokers are twice as likely as nonsmokers to contract lung cancer? You should not, not before ascertaining how many in the sample of 200 were smokers. For instance, even if there were only 5 smokers in the sample, 2 of whom had lung cancer, the percentages in the first column would be correct. But you could not put much trust in those figures. So before you jump to conclusions about results from two-way tables (especially when the evidence is consistent with your preconceived notions), ensure that the individual cell sizes, in addition to the overall sample size, are sufficiently large.

[10] Zeisel, *Say It with Figures,* and Loether and McTavish, *Descriptive Statistics for Sociologists,* contain several examples of the correct way to calculate percentages in two-way tables under different circumstances. Also, Huff, *How to Lie with Statistics,* highlights several pitfalls related to percentages in general.

Finally, and perhaps most importantly, two-way tables, by definition, are constructed by using data on just two variables at a time. While this feature makes the tables easy to interpret, it also increases the risk of drawing erroneous inferences, because the relationship between two variables may often depend on *other* variables. For example, the nature and the extent of association between students' intelligence levels and their test grades in a course may depend on factors like course content, effort exerted by students, and test format. Mak-

Table 16.9

Associations between number of cars owned, household income, and household size

(a) Number of Cars Owned Versus Household Income

HOUSEHOLD INCOME	NUMBER OF CARS OWNED		ALL HOUSEHOLDS
	2 or Less	More than 2	
$25,000 or more	300 (60%)	200 (40%)	500 (100%)
Less than $25,000	200 (40%)	300 (60%)	500 (100%)

(b) Number of Cars Owned Versus Household Income and Household Size

HOUSEHOLD INCOME	HOUSEHOLD SIZE	NUMBER OF CARS OWNED		ALL HOUSEHOLDS
		2 or Less	More than 2	
$25,000 or more	4 or less	260 (87%)	40 (13%)	300 (100%)
	More than 4	40 (20%)	160 (80%)	200 (100%)
Less than $25,000	4 or less	150 (60%)	100 (40%)	250 (100%)
	More than 4	50 (20%)	200 (80%)	250 (100%)

(c) Number of Cars Owned Versus Household Size

HOUSEHOLD SIZE	NUMBER OF CARS OWNED		ALL HOUSEHOLDS
	2 or Less	More than 2	
4 or less	410 (75%)	140 (25%)	550 (100%)
More than 4	90 (20%)	360 (80%)	450 (100%)

ing inferences about the association between intelligence levels and test grades without taking into account such outside factors is risky.

In situations where a pair of variables being cross-tabulated may be influenced by other variables, the evidence presented by the two-way table may just tell part of the story. This point is an important one, but it is frequently overlooked. We will therefore discuss it in detail, using as illustration the cross-tabulations (based on hypothetical data from a survey of 1000 households) shown in Table 16.9.

Let us examine Table 16.9(a). The evidence in this two-way table seems to suggest a negative association between a household's income and the number of cars it owns: Low-income households are more likely to own more than two cars than are high-income households. But this counterintuitive finding may be due to other outside factors, such as household size, which, indeed, can have a bearing on the number of cars owned.

Table 16.9(b) is a three-way table that provides simultaneous examination of the relationships of household income and household size to the number of cars owned. It is an expanded version of Table 16.9(a) in which each cell of Table 16.9(a) is split into two cells according to household size. In Table 16.9(b), examine the two rows pertaining to households with more than 4 individuals. The percentages in these two rows are identical and suggest that *irrespective of income level,* 4 out of 5 large households are likely to own more than 2 cars. In other words, there seems to be *no association* between household income and number of cars owned for large households. Now examine the two rows pertaining to households with 4 or less individuals. The percentages in these two rows still suggest a negative association between household income and number of cars owned: While 40% of the households in the low-income category own more than 2 cars, only 13% of the households in the high-income category do so. This somewhat puzzling finding may be due to yet another variable, such as the *types* of cars owned. For example, while small households with high incomes are less likely to own more than 2 cars, the cars they do own may be more expensive than those owned by low-income households.

In short, although the three-way table, Table 16.9(b), has not completely explained the unexpected finding in the preceding two-way table, Table 16.9(a), it certainly sheds further light on the relationships being examined. Specifically, it provides the following additional insights:

1. The relationship between household income and number of cars owned is moderated by household size. While there is still a negative relationship for small households, there is no relationship for large households.
2. Within each household income group, large households are more likely to own more than 2 cars than small households.

The second insight further suggests that household size, when compared with household income, may be more closely and directly associated with number of cars owned. This suggestion is supported by the two-way tabulation of data on household size and number of cars owned in Table 16.9(c).

The cross-tabulations in Table 16.9 convey an important general message: *A two-way table may not always tell the whole story about the nature of the relationship between a pair of variables.* Sometimes, an apparent relationship evidenced by a two-way table may be spurious and may be explainable by incorporating other relevant variables into the tabulation. Similarly, an apparent *absence* of association between two cross-tabulated variables does not necessarily mean they are unrelated. Critical variables excluded from the table may be masking a relationship that really does exist, as illustrated by the following discussion.

Suppose a sample of 400 grocery stores is surveyed, and data are gathered for a certain brand of detergent on three variables: unit sales, promotional expenditure, and price. On the basis of these data the stores are classified as being above or below the median on each of the three variables. In other words, each store is labeled as "above the median" or "below the median" with respect to the detergent's sales, with respect to the promotional expenditure for it, and with respect to its price. The cross-tabulations of these categorical data are shown in Table 16.10.

Let us examine Table 16.10(a), the two-way tabulation of sales and promotional expenditure. This table shows no association between promotional expenditure and sales, a rather unusual finding. Since price can also influence sales, the particular set of prices used by the sample of stores may be masking the association between promotional expenditure and sales. Table 16.10(b), which is a three-way table incorporating price, confirms such a masking effect. From the numbers in the first and third rows of this table (both rows relating to stores having above-median prices), we see that stores with above-median promotional expenditures are more likely (33% vs. 25%) to enjoy above-median sales than other stores. A similar conclusion is suggested by the second and fourth rows (both relating to stores with below-median prices): Stores with higher promotional expenditures are more likely (75% vs. 67%) to enjoy higher sales. In short, when price is held constant, there is a direct association between promotional expenditure and sales. Thus incorporation of price as a third variable into the original two-way table has helped reveal an important relationship that would otherwise have gone unnoticed.

The illustrations in Tables 16.9 and 16.10 imply that the larger the number of variables included in the cross-tabulated data, the smaller is the risk of making erroneous inferences. That is, three-way tables are better than two-way tables, four-way tables (having four variables cross-tabulated simultaneously) are better than three-way tables, and so on. Unfortunately, while this implication is theoretically sound, it is not always easy to implement. Even a modest increase in the number of variables included in a cross-tabulation will sharply increase the number of cells in the table. This increase will, in turn, reduce the number of

Table 16.10

Associations between sales, promotional expenditure, and price

(a) Sales Versus Promotional Expenditure

PROMOTIONAL EXPENDITURE	SALES		ALL FIRMS
	Above the Median	Below the Median	
Above the median	100 (50%)	100 (50%)	200 (100%)
Below the median	100 (50%)	100 (50%)	200 (100%)

(b) Sales Versus Promotional Expenditure and Price

PROMOTIONAL EXPENDITURE	PRICE	SALES		ALL FIRMS
		Above the Median	Below the Median	
Above the Median	Above the Median	40 (33%)	80 (67%)	120 (100%)
	Below the Median	60 (75%)	20 (25%)	80 (100%)
Below the Median	Above the Median	20 (25%)	60 (75%)	80 (100%)
	Below the Median	80 (67%)	40 (33%)	120 (100%)

sample units per cell, since the total sample size is fixed. As pointed out earlier, drawing inferences from tables with small cell sizes can be dangerous.

Furthermore, even assuming that the total sample size is large enough to warrant going beyond two-way tabulation, identifying the *most appropriate* third variable to add to the table may not always be easy. When several variables seem to be equally worthy of inclusion as the third variable, a researcher may be tempted to construct all possible three-way tables to see which variable is most useful. This approach is generally not recommended, however, since it will usually be laborious and may amount to no more than an aimless fishing expedition.

That cross-tabulations may quickly become unwieldy and meaningless underlines the need to plan ahead and map out a systematic analysis strategy well in advance. Sound exploratory research, including a thorough review of past studies related to the topic being researched, is extremely useful in developing hypotheses about the nature of the variables of interest and the relationships among them. Such hypotheses, at least in the form of informal hunches, are essential in deciding which two-way tables to construct and which of those to expand by incorporating other relevant variables. Moreover, recognizing that an apparent relationship may be spurious—or that an apparent lack of relationship may be suspect—is not possible without the benefit of prior hypotheses. In short, a researcher with no hypotheses but hoping to gain insights through cross-tabulations is like a compassless ship hoping to go from point A to point B. If the ship ever gets to point B, it will only be after a great deal of inefficiency in the form of numerous miscues and wasted resources.

SUMMARY

Editing is a quality control check on the raw data; it involves inspection and any necessary correction of completed data collection forms. A preliminary stage of editing, known as the field edit, is conducted when the data are being collected. Its purpose is to verify that interviewers are following proper procedures and to correct any fieldwork problems before it is too late. A more comprehensive edit, known as the final, or office, edit, is conducted after all the completed questionnaires are returned to a central office. Major responsibilities of an office editor include checking for response consistencies within and across questionnaires, deciding on appropriate ways to handle "don't know" responses and missing values, and classifying open-ended responses.

The process of coding immediately follows, or often overlaps with, the office edit. It includes classifying open-ended responses into mutually exclusive and collectively exhaustive categories, and assigning numerical values to response categories that are not already in quantified form. Coding sheets are helpful in transferring the response data to a computer input medium, such as punched cards, disks, or tapes. Once the data are stored in an appropriate computer medium, a data set, or data file, can be created in computer memory just prior to data analysis. A data set is a matrix of numbers in which each row contains the coded answers given by a single respondent (typically referred to as a case or observation).

A good practice is to conduct a preliminary analysis to get an initial idea about the nature of the data. Preliminary analysis involves obtaining and examining the central tendency and the dispersion of the data for all variables (including transformed variables) of interest. The choice of the most appropriate measure of central tendency and dispersion to use depends on whether the variables are nominal, ordinal, interval, or ratio.

A rather simple way to ascertain what the data look like is a one-way tabulation, that is, the frequency distribution of responses for each variable. In addition to revealing the general nature of the data, one-way tables are helpful in detecting certain types of coding errors; comparing the distribution of data on a variable with other relevant distributions, such as the overall population distribution and the distributions of similar variables; and suggesting meaningful variable transformations.

Two-way tabulation involves breaking down the number of responses in each category of one variable into the categories of a second variable. The purpose of a two-way tabulation is to explore the extent and the nature of possible associations between pairs of variables. The numbers in a two-way table are usually reported as raw frequencies and percentages. A general guideline for computing percentages in a two-way table is to compute them in the direction of the presumed causal variable. However, if the presumed causal variable is not clear-cut, one should compute the percentages in both directions. Also, if the sample is not representative of the population with respect to the presumed causal variable, computing percentages in the opposite direction is more meaningful.

While two-way tables can provide valuable insights about relationships between variables, they can easily mislead an unwary researcher. Thus the following precautions are worth bearing in mind: First, two-way tables can suggest, but cannot convincingly show, cause and effect between variables. Second, two-way tables with very small cell sizes, or those that present the evidence solely in percentages, may be suspect. Third, evidence in a two-way table of a particular type of relationship, or lack thereof, between two variables is not necessarily conclusive.

Relevant variables excluded from a two-way table may lead to a spurious relationship or may mask a true relationship. When external variables are suspected of playing a role in a relationship, a researcher should construct and examine appropriate three-way, or even larger, tables. Unfortunately, inadequate sample sizes and lack of information about which external variables to include often pose practical constraints in constructing multiway tables. Moreover, numerous cross-tabulations may overwhelm a researcher. Therefore the researcher should have at least a tentative analysis plan beforehand specifying which cross-tabulations will be constructed and how detailed each will be. Formulating a clear-cut analysis plan requires adequate exploratory research capable of leading to hypotheses concerning the variables of interest.

QUESTIONS

1. Briefly discuss the similarities and differences between a *field edit* and an *office edit*.
2. "Editing plays no role in acting as a quality control check on mail survey data." Discuss this statement.
3. What are the two types of "don't know" responses? Give an example of each.
4. What advantages does computer-assisted editing have over completely manual editing?
5. Why do questions permitting multiple responses require special attention during coding?

6. What are *variable transformations,* and what purposes can they serve?
7. Transform variable V13 in the survey of United States firms into an appropriate three-category new variable (excluding the missing-value category) that reflects varying ranges of allocations to marketing research. Explain your rationale. Also, construct a one-way table for the new variable.
8. Refer to Exhibits 16.2 and 16.3 and Table 16.2. Derive a descriptive profile of firm 45 on variables V1 through V13.
9. Define these terms: *case, record, data set.*
10. What are three potential uses of one-way tabulation?
11. What is a *skewed distribution?* Suppose two ordinal variables, each with eight categories, have extremely skewed distributions. What type of variable transformation would you create for the two variables so as to make their cross-tabulation meaningful? Briefly explain your answer.
12. What is the general principle for computing percentages in two-way tables? What are the two exceptions to this principle?
13. What are the three major precautions that should be taken in interpreting two-way tables?
14. From the information in Table 16.10, construct a two-way tabulation of the detergent's price and its unit sales. Is there a relationship between these two variables? If so, what is its nature? If not, why not?
15. What are the practical constraints involved in constructing and interpreting multiway tables? Summarize the general implication of these constraints in a sentence or two.

17

Hypothesis Testing and Its Role in Data Analysis

DESCRIPTIVE VERSUS INFERENTIAL ANALYSIS

The data analysis procedures discussed in Chapter 16—namely, computing measures of central tendency and dispersion, as well as constructing one-way, two-way, and multiway tables—help the researcher summarize the general nature of the study variables and the interrelationships among them. Such preliminary-analysis procedures are descriptive and can provide valuable insights, as demonstrated by the examples in the previous chapter. In fact, certain research studies may require no more than descriptive analysis of the data. In many studies, however, one must go beyond descriptive analysis in order to verify specific statements, or *hypotheses,* about the population(s) of interest. Data analysis aimed at testing specific hypotheses is usually called *inferential analysis.* This chapter describes the general procedure involved in hypothesis testing, discusses the role of hypothesis testing in data analysis, and outlines several hypothesis tests frequently encountered in marketing.

OVERVIEW OF HYPOTHESIS TESTING

A useful starting point for discussing hypothesis testing is to consider the following situations, which illustrate critical questions typically faced by decision makers.

SITUATION A: Karen, product manager for a line of apparel, is wondering whether to introduce the product line into a new market area. A recent survey of a random sample of 400 households in that market showed a mean income per household of $13,000. On the basis of past experience and of comprehensive studies in current market areas, Karen strongly feels that the product line will be adequately profitable only in markets where the mean household income (across *all* households) is greater than $12,000. Should Karen introduce the product line into the new market?

SITUATION B: Tom, advertising manager for a frozen-foods company, is in the process of deciding between two TV commercials, X and Y, for a new frozen food to be introduced shortly. Commercial X runs for 20 seconds, and commercial Y runs for 30 seconds. Therefore for a given number of exposures, commercial Y will be more expensive than commercial X. Tom feels that commercial Y will also be more effective in creating awareness for the new product, but he is not sure.

The two commercials were recently shown during identical TV programs in two comparable test cities (only one of the two was shown in each city). After the commercials were shown, a random sample of 200 adults was interviewed by telephone in each city. In the city in which commercial X was shown, 40 of the 200 respondents were aware of the new frozen food; that is, the awareness rate for commercial X was 20%. In the other city the awareness rate for commercial Y was 25%. Can Tom conclude that commercial Y will be more effective in the total market for the new frozen food?

What features do situations A and B have in common? Clearly, in order to reach a final decision, both Karen and Tom have to make a general inference from sample data. However, making generalizations from sample data is a feature implicit in virtually all conclusive-research projects and hence is not unique to situations A and B. As we have seen in the chapters on sampling (Chapters 12, 13, and 14), the purpose of any sampling study is to learn *something* about the population.

A more distinctive feature of situations A and B, one that is more directly relevant to hypothesis testing, is that each situation implies a criterion on which the final decision depends. In situation A the criterion is the mean income across all households in the new market area under consideration. Specifically, if the mean population household income is greater than $12,000, Karen should introduce the product line into the new market. In situation B the criterion is the relative degrees of awareness likely to be created by the two commercials in the population of all adult consumers. Specifically, Tom should conclude that commercial Y is more effective than commercial X only if the anticipated population awareness rate for Y is greater than that for X.

Stated differently, Karen's decision making in situation A is equivalent to either accepting or rejecting the following hypothesis: "The population mean household income in the new market area is greater than $12,000." Similarly, Tom's decision making in situation B is equivalent to either accepting or rejecting the following hypothesis: "The potential awareness rate that commercial Y can generate among the population of consumers is greater than that which commercial X can generate." A situation calling for formal hypothesis testing will usually stipulate a specific criterion for choosing between alternative inferences or courses of action. However, as we will see later, certain types of hypothesis tests may not have a criterion as clear-cut as the criteria in situations A and B. Furthermore, in many real-life situations final decisions may depend on several factors rather than on a single, clear-cut criterion; situations A and B have been simplified intentionally to highlight the salient features of hypothesis testing.

Null and alternative hypotheses

The first step, after one recognizes that a particular decision situation requires formal hypothesis testing, is to state a null hypothesis and an alternative hypothesis. We will use the symbols H_o and H_a to denote the null and alternative hypotheses, respectively. Before discussing the specific meanings of H_o and H_a, we make one general comment about stating hypotheses: Hypotheses always pertain to *population* parameters or characteristics rather than *sample* characteristics. It is the population, *not* the sample, that we want to make an inference about from limited data. Although this point may seem obvious, in the author's experience, students often get confused about it when formally stating and interpreting hypotheses.

The null and alternative hypotheses complement each other; they are mutually exclusive and collectively exhaustive. In other words, the two hypotheses are stated in such a way that H_a will not be accepted if the sample evidence strongly supports H_o. Similarly, H_a will be accepted if the sample evidence is strong enough to reject H_o. In situation A, with μ denoting the population mean household income, the two hypotheses are as follows:

$$H_o: \mu \leq \$12{,}000;$$
$$H_a: \mu > \$12{,}000.$$

In situation B, with the symbols π_X and π_Y denoting the potential awareness rates capable of being generated by commercials X and Y, respectively, the two hypotheses are as follows:

$$H_o: \pi_Y \leq \pi_X;$$
$$H_a: \pi_Y > \pi_X.$$

The two hypotheses in situation B can also be (and usually are) stated as follows:

$$H_o: \pi_Y - \pi_X \leq 0;$$
$$H_a: \pi_Y - \pi_X > 0.$$

For situations A and B you are probably wondering how one decides which hypothesis is the null and which is the alternative. This issue is somewhat tricky and depends to a large extent on the nature of the decision to be made. However, the following three guidelines, at least one of which should be relevant in most situations, will be helpful in properly stating H_o and H_a:

1. Of the two hypotheses, the null should be stated more conservatively; that is, failure to reject H_o from the sample evidence should preserve the status quo. Situation A illustrates the use of this guideline. The product line will not be introduced into the new market area (i.e., status quo will be maintained) if H_o is not rejected.
2. If the decision maker expects that a particular hypothesis will be supported by the sample evidence, then that hypothesis should be viewed as H_a. (Verify that this guideline is the underlying rationale for the statement of H_o and H_a in situation B.)
3. If one of the two hypotheses implies strict equality (e.g., μ = \$12,000 or $\pi_Y = \pi_X$), then that hypothesis should be treated as H_o, irrespective of what the preceding two guidelines might suggest.

For instance, in situation B, suppose Tom has no prior reason for believing that one commercial will be more effective than the other. Also, suppose he expects the two commercials to be equally effective. In this case the proper way to state the hypotheses is as follows:

$$H_o: \pi_Y = \pi_X \quad \text{or} \quad \pi_Y - \pi_X = 0;$$
$$H_a: \pi_Y \neq \pi_X \quad \text{or} \quad \pi_Y - \pi_X \neq 0.$$

Type I and Type II errors

Inferences stemming from hypothesis testing are subject to error since the testing procedure relies on sampling data. One cannot be entirely certain whether a hypothesis is true or false unless a study involving a census is undertaken.

Consider situation A, for instance. Whether or not H_o (i.e., $\mu \leq$ \$12,000) is true cannot be ascertained for sure unless the income of every household in the new market area is obtained, a task that is bound to be impractical, if not impossible. Therefore, Karen's decision about whether H_o is true or false has to be based solely on the sample evidence. The sample mean income ($\bar{x}$) of \$13,000 suggests that H_o may be false. Unfortunately, however, even when the population mean value is as low as \$12,000 (i.e., μ = \$12,000, in which case H_o will still be true), one can obtain a sample mean value as high as \$13,000. As we discussed in Chapter 12, mean values of samples selected repeatedly from a given population will fall on *either* side of the population mean and form a

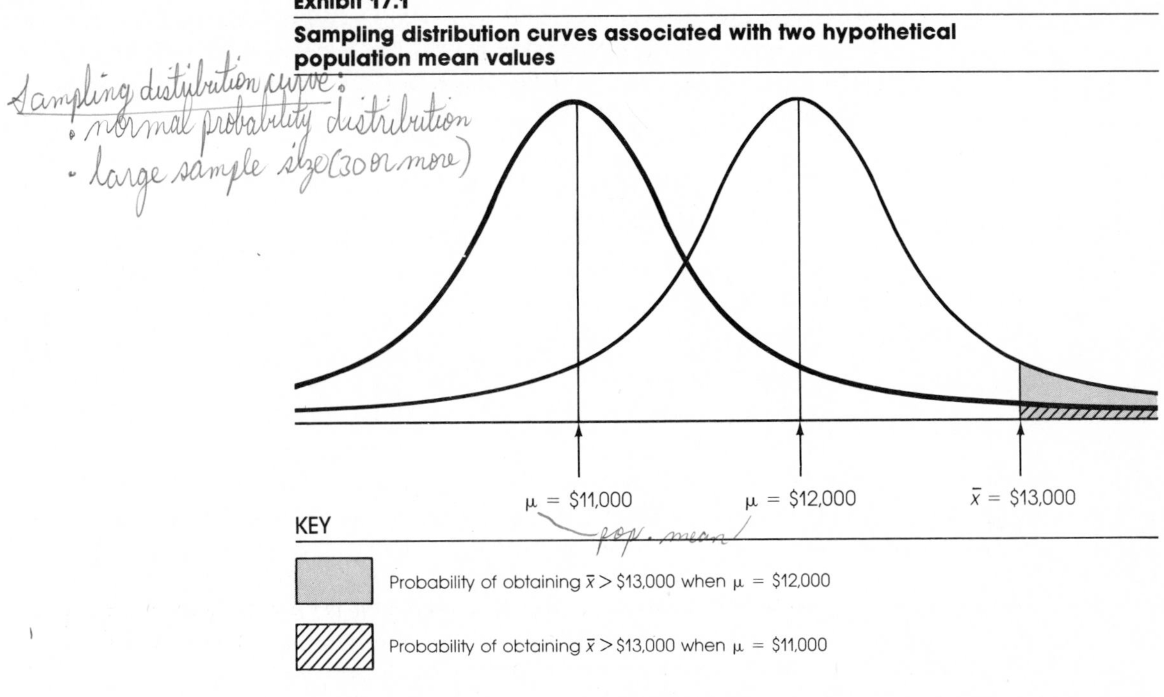

Exhibit 17.1

Sampling distribution curves associated with two hypothetical population mean values

distribution (called the sampling distribution) around it. Hence one cannot rule out the possibility of obtaining a sample mean of \$13,000 when H_0 is true.

Examine Exhibit 17.1, which shows the sampling distribution curves associated with two hypothetical population mean values—μ = \$11,000 and μ = \$12,000—both of which are consistent with the null hypothesis. As this exhibit demonstrates, there is some chance of obtaining a sample mean value of \$13,000 *or more* under each of the two circumstances. Thus Karen will be making a mistake if she rejects H_0 and the population mean happens to be \$12,000 or less. Such a mistake is called a Type I error.

DEFINITION. **A *Type* I *error* is committed if the null hypothesis is rejected when it is true.**

What if Karen decides not to reject H_0 from the sample evidence that $\bar{x}$ = \$13,000? Can her inference then be considered to be error-free? Her inference will still not be error-free because a population with a mean value greater than \$12,000 (i.e., $\mu >$ \$12,000, in which case H_0 will be false) is obviously capable of yielding a sample with a mean value of \$13,000. In fact, a sample mean value of \$13,000 (or more) has a higher probability of occurring when H_0 is false than when it is true. You can verify this statement by superimposing on the curves of Exhibit 17.1 another sampling distribution curve centered on, say, $\mu = \$12{,}500$. Therefore Karen will again be making a mistake if she does not reject H_0 and the population mean happens to be more than \$12,000. Such a mistake is called a Type II error.

DEFINITION. **A *Type II error* is committed if the null hypothesis is *not* rejected when it is false.**

Type I error and significance level

From the preceding discussion we see that Karen *may* commit an error no matter what final inference she makes. A Type I error may occur if she rejects H_0, and a Type II error may occur if she does not reject H_0. Karen's dilemma is not as hopeless as it seems, however. Because although Type I and Type II errors cannot be entirely avoided, the probability of occurrence of one of them can be constrained to be within an acceptable level. Virtually all hypothesis-testing procedures place a limit on the probability of committing a Type I error. This limit is specified by the researcher or decision maker and, as we will see a little later, forms the basis for deciding when to reject H_0 and when not to do so. The term *significance level* refers to the upper-bound probability of a Type I error.

DEFINITION. **The *significance level* associated with a hypothesis-testing procedure is the maximum probability of rejecting H_0 when using that procedure and H_0 is actually true.**

The symbol α (Greek letter alpha) is typically used to denote the significance level. The complement of the significance level (i.e., $1 - \alpha$) is called the *confidence level.*

Let us now examine the role played by the significance level in deciding when to reject H_0. In situation A, suppose Karen does not want to allow more than a 5% chance of rejecting H_0 when $\mu \leq \$12{,}000$ (i.e., $\alpha = .05$). In other words, she does not want to reject H_0 unless the sample evidence is overwhelmingly against it. The significance level is the key in deciding what type of evidence can be considered as being "overwhelmingly against" H_0.

Intuitively, sample mean ($\bar{x}$) values greater than \$12,000—that is, $\bar{x}$-values on the right-hand side of the sampling distribution centered on $\mu = \$12{,}000$—suggest that H_0 may be false. And, more importantly, the farther away to the right $\bar{x}$ is, the stronger is the evidence against H_0. Therefore beyond some critical $\bar{x}$-value, say $\bar{x}_c$, Karen should be able to conclude that the evidence is overwhelmingly against H_0. Specifically, she should choose $\bar{x}_c$ such that any sample whose mean exceeds $\bar{x}_c$ has less than a 5% chance of having come from a population

Exhibit 17.2
Identifying the critical sample mean value

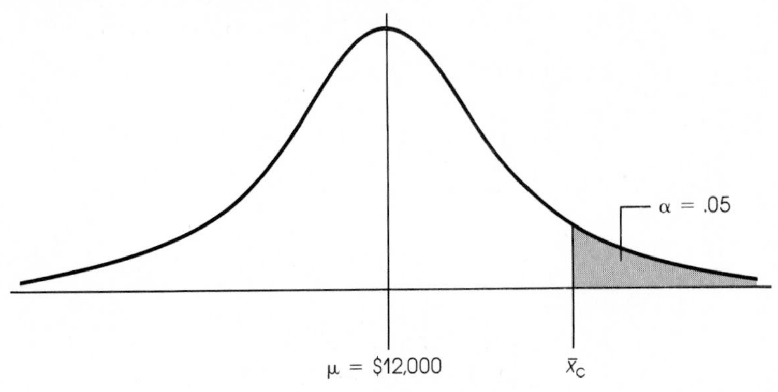

whose mean is $12,000 or less. This criterion is shown graphically in Exhibit 17.2.

How does one select an appropriate significance level (or confidence level) for a hypothesis test? For instance, in situation A, how or why did Karen choose a significance level of .05? The choice of a particular significance level is subjective and depends on the nature of the problem as well as on the degree of risk the decision maker is willing to take. The following example illustrates this point.

EXAMPLE: Consider two firms, ABC and XYZ, each considering introducing a new product that radically differs from its current product line. Company ABC has a well-established customer base and enjoys a distinct reputation for its existing product line. In contrast, XYZ has neither a loyal clientele nor a distinct image for its present products. Which of these two firms should be more cautious in making a decision to introduce the new product?

Intuitively, we feel that ABC should be more cautious, since it apparently has more to lose than XYZ by making a hasty go-ahead decision. Stated differently, ABC perhaps should not set a higher significance level (or lower confidence level) than XYZ, if both firms are to make a go–no-go decision on the basis of a suitable hypothesis test using sample data pertaining to potential customer acceptance of the new product. Of course, the willingness of management of the two firms to assume risk also plays a role: Generally, the more risk-averse management is, the lower the significance level should be.

In summary, the choice of a suitable significance level for a hypothesis test is, or should be, situation-specific. There is no standard significance level that is equally appropriate under all circumstances. In other words, although many hypothesis tests use seemingly standard significance levels of .01, .05, or .10, there is nothing sacred about these numbers. It is not a capital crime to use a significance level of, say, .20 or .30, if the circumstances warrant it.

Decision rule for rejecting the null hypothesis

At this point, reviewing certain key sampling distribution concepts discussed in Chapter 12 is helpful. Recall that the sampling distribution curve will have properties of the normal probability distribution when the sample size is sufficiently large (in practice, a sample size of 30 or more). Furthermore, when the sampling distribution is centered on μ and has a standard deviation of $\sigma_{\bar{x}}$ (traditionally referred to as the standard error), any sample mean value ($\bar{x}$) can be expressed as an equivalent standard normal deviate z, given by

$$z = \frac{\bar{x} - \mu}{\sigma_{\bar{x}}}.$$

When $\sigma_{\bar{x}}$ is unknown, which is usually the case, it is approximately estimated by $s_{\bar{x}}$, the standard error of the sample mean, given by $s_{\bar{x}} = s/\sqrt{n}$, where s is the sample standard deviation and n is the sample size. Therefore the expression for z can be modified as follows:

$$z = \frac{\bar{x} - \mu}{s_{\bar{x}}}.$$

The sampling distribution associated with z is a *standard* normal curve (i.e., one with a mean of zero and a standard deviation of one). The areas, or probabilities, under the standard normal curve corresponding to various values of z are tabulated in Appendix B at the end of the book.

Let us return now to situation A. Suppose the standard deviation of household income for the sample of 400 households is \$8000. The standard error of the mean ($s_{\bar{x}}$) is given by

$$s_{\bar{x}} = \frac{s}{\sqrt{n}} = \frac{\$8000}{\sqrt{400}} = \frac{\$8000}{20} = \$400.$$

The critical mean household income $\bar{x}_c$ can now be computed through the following two steps:

1. Determine the critical value of z, say z_c, such that the area to its right under the standard normal curve is α, which is .05 in this case. From Appendix B, $z_c = 1.645$.
2. Substitute the value of z_c into the general expression for z and solve for $\bar{x}_c$ under the assumption that H_o is "just" true.

A note about the term *just true* is needed here. When H_o is stated as an inequality (as it is in situation A), it can be true for a *range* of population parameter values. It is "just" true, or "barely" true, when the population parameter is exactly equal to the hypothesized value. Furthermore, the probability of committing a Type I error is greatest when H_o is just true. You can verify this statement by superimposing on the curve of Exhibit 17.2 several sampling distribution curves centered on values of μ less than \$12,000. Therefore calculating the value of $\bar{x}_c$ when H_o is just true guarantees that the probability of committing a Type I error will be no more than the specified significance level (α).

In situation A, H_o is just true when μ = \$12,000. The expression for z_c is

$$z_c = \frac{\bar{x}_c - \mu}{s_{\bar{x}}}.$$

Rearranging the terms in the above expression gives

$$\begin{aligned}\bar{x}_c &= \mu + z_c s_{\bar{x}} = \$12{,}000 + 1.645 \times \$400 \\ &= \$12{,}000 + \$658 = \$12{,}658.\end{aligned}$$

Karen's decision rule can be stated as follows: "If the sample mean household income is greater than \$12,658, reject the null hypothesis and introduce the product line into the new market area." The same decision rule can also be stated in terms of z-values, as follows: "If the z-value corresponding to the sample mean household income is greater than 1.645, reject the null hypothesis and introduce the product line into the new market area." In general, the latter format is used to specify the decision rule for rejecting H_o, because it is cast in terms of a standard test statistic.

DEFINITION. The *test statistic* is a standard variable whose value is computed from sample data and compared with a critical value (obtained from an appropriate probability table) to decide whether or not to reject the null hypothesis.

Every hypothesis test has a corresponding test statistic, which depends on the sampling distribution involved. Since the sampling distribution in situation A has the properties of the normal probability distribution, the appropriate test statistic is the z-variable. The value of the test statistic is simply the z-value corresponding to $\bar{x}$ = \$13,000:

$$\begin{aligned}z &= \frac{\bar{x} - \mu}{s_{\bar{x}}} = \frac{\$13{,}000 - \$12{,}000}{\$400} \\ &= \frac{\$1000}{\$400} = 2.5.\end{aligned}$$

Clearly, Karen should reject H_o from the sample evidence since $\bar{x} > \bar{x}_c$ and $z > z_c$. In other words, she should introduce the product line into the new market area. If she does so, the probability of her committing a Type I error will be less than .05, as shown in Exhibit 17.3.

The intuitive notion underlying this hypothesis test is embedded in the following question: "What are the chances that a sample mean income as high as \$13,000 (or a test statistic value as high as 2.5) will have occurred when the true population mean income is \$12,000 or less?" The answer to this question in situation A is, "Less than 5%, the subjectively selected significance level." Therefore from the sample evidence the hypothesis that the population mean income is \$12,000 or less is not tenable and should be rejected.

The probability of obtaining an $\bar{x}$-value as high as \$13,000 or more when μ is only \$12,000 is given by the area under the distribution curve to the right of $z = 2.5$. From Appendix B this probability is only .0062. This value is sometimes called the *actual* significance level of the test, to distinguish it from α, which is the preset, maximum significance level. The actual significance level of .0062 in this case means that the odds are less than 62 out of 10,000 that the sample mean income of \$13,000 would have occurred entirely due to chance (i.e., when the population mean income is \$12,000 or less).

Type II error and power

The hypothesis-testing procedure discussed thus far has focused exclusively on limiting the probability of a Type I error. This emphasis does not mean that Type II errors are unimportant. The risk of committing a Type II error (i.e., failing to reject H_o when it is false) is very real and is present in all hypothesis tests. Indeed, as will be shown in this section, lowering the probability of a Type I error will increase the probability of a Type II error.[1] Researchers invariably constrain the probability of a Type I error to be within a small, prespecified significance level and let the probability of a Type II error fall where it may. This point is noteworthy because it highlights a bias inherent in the traditional hypothesis-testing procedure—namely, it reflects the posture of giving the null hypothesis the benefit of the doubt and rejecting it only when the sample evidence is strongly against it.

To illustrate the impact of a prespecified significance level (α) on the probability of Type II error, let us once again consider Karen's decision rule based on $\alpha = .05$: "Reject H_o if the sample mean exceeds \$12,658." Assume for a moment that H_o is actually false. Specifically, suppose the true population mean (μ) is \$12,500, with a standard error the same as before. Also, suppose a fresh random sample of 400 households is to be selected. Can this sample, when selected,

[1] Several interesting analogies highlighting the trade-off between Type 1 and Type II errors are discussed in Robert Hooke, *How to Tell the Liars from the Statisticians* (New York: Dekker, 1983), pp. 67–70.

Exhibit 17.3
Critical value for rejecting the null hypothesis

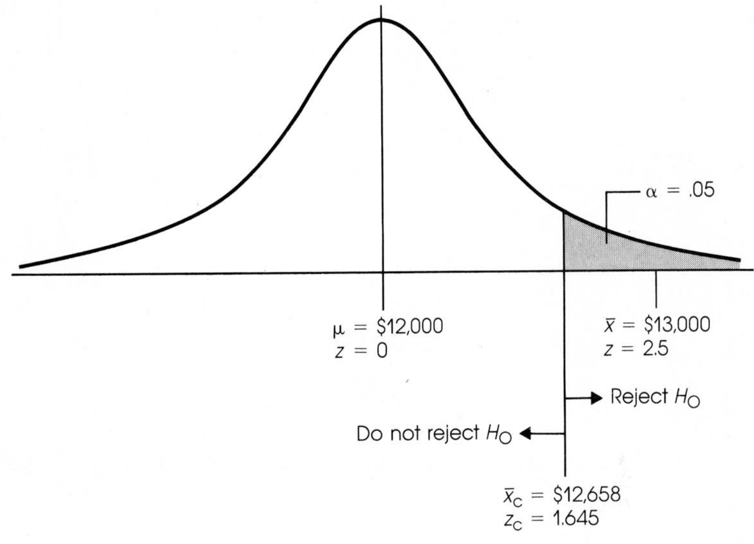

yield a mean value less than or equal to $12,658? Yes, it can, as shown by Exhibit 17.4(a).

The shaded area under the sampling distribution curve centered on μ = $12,500 in Exhibit 17.4(a) is the probability of obtaining a sample mean less than or equal to $12,658. Since according to Karen's decision rule, H_o will *not* be rejected when $\bar{x} < \$12,658$, the shaded area is also the probability of a Type II error. The symbol β (Greek letter beta) is typically used to denote the probability of a Type II error. The quantity $(1 - \beta)$, which is the probability of avoiding a Type II error, is called the power of the test, or simply power.

DEFINITION. The *power* of a hypothesis test is the probability of rejecting H_o (based on the decision rule for the test) when H_o is false.

Although the actual values of β and power can be calculated in this case, we will not attempt to do so since the calculation procedure is quite cumbersome.[2] Rather, we will graphically examine the impact of changes in α and in the true population mean on β and power.

What will happen to the value of β in Exhibit 17.4(a) if α is lowered from .05

[2] Most basic statistics texts discuss the procedure for calculating power. See, for example, Morris Hamburg, *Statistical Analysis for Decision Making* (New York: Harcourt Brace Jovanovich, 1977), pp. 271–275.

Exhibit 17.4

Impact of α and μ on β and the power of the test

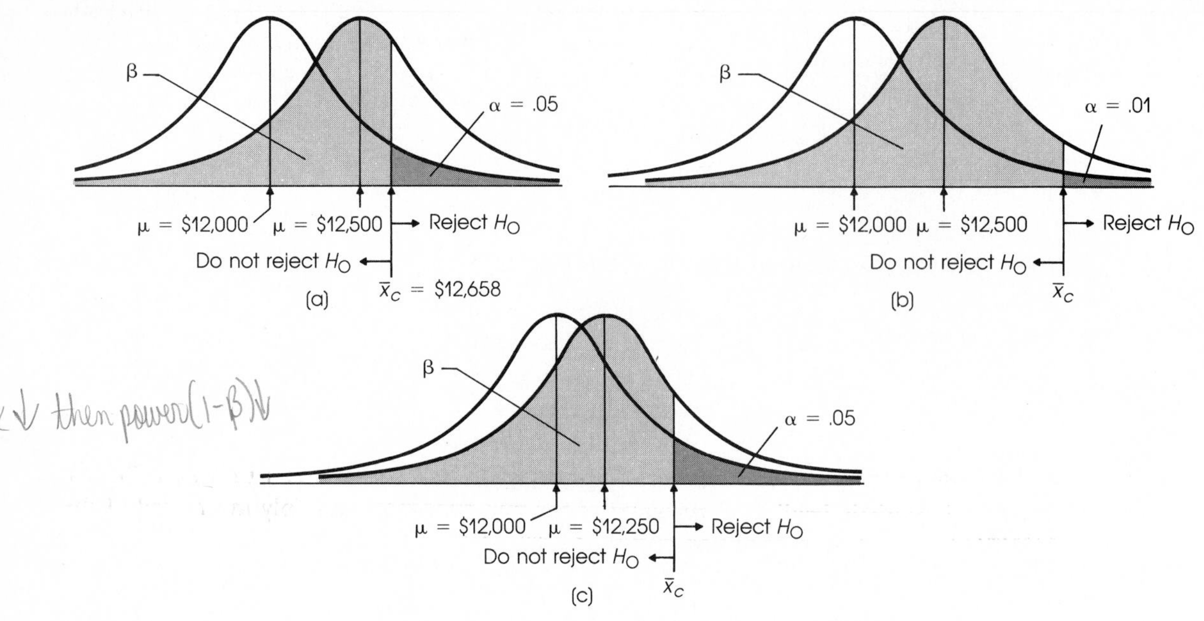

to, say, .01? The impact of this change is shown in Exhibit 17.4(b). Comparing Exhibits 17.4(a) and 17.4(b), we see that β increases and power decreases when α decreases. In other words, the probabilities of Type I and Type II errors are *inversely* related. (However, the sum of the α and β probabilities does *not* equal 1, as is often mistakenly believed.) This inverse relationship also makes intuitive sense: The smaller the value of α, the stronger is the evidence needed to reject H_o and, therefore, the greater are the chances of failing to reject H_o when it should be. The preceding point highlights the danger inherent in the blind choice of a small value for the significance level (e.g., .05): It implicitly assumes that the *opportunity cost* of making a no-go decision is negligible—or at least is not as severe as the cost of incorrectly making a go decision. Such an assumption may be questionable in many real-life settings.

Will β and power change if we assume that the true population mean is $12,250 instead of $12,500, as assumed earlier? A comparison of Exhibits 17.4(a) and 17.4(c) answers this question: With the changed assumption about the population mean, β increases and power decreases. This finding implies the following important generalization: When H_o is false, the values of β and power depend on how false H_o really is. The closer it is to being true (i.e., the closer the actual population mean is to the originally hypothesized mean), the higher β

will be and the lower power will be. Therefore β and power depend not only on the prespecified significance level (i.e., α) but also on the actual (but unknown) value of the population parameter. This complexity of the concept of power is a key reason why hypothesis-testing procedures merely focus on limiting the probability of a Type I error, without explicitly incorporating the probability of a Type II error. In fact, in certain hypothesis tests (e.g., the chi-square tests to be discussed later), computing the value of power is impossible.

Table 17.1 provides a summary of the key concepts and terms related to errors involved in hypothesis testing.

One-tailed versus two-tailed tests

The procedure we used to set up a decision rule for Karen in situation A involved what is known as a *one-tailed hypothesis test.* The term *one-tailed* signifies that all $\bar{x}$- or z-values that would cause Karen to reject H_0 are on just one tail of the sampling distribution (i.e., $\bar{x} > \$12{,}658$, or $z > 1.645$).

DEFINITION. **A** ***one-tailed hypothesis test*** **is one in which values of the test statistic leading to rejection of the null hypothesis fall only in one tail of the sampling distribution curve.**

Whenever the null hypothesis involves an inequality (i.e., $\leq$ or $\geq$), it is said to be a *directional hypothesis.* The corresponding hypothesis test will be one-tailed.

If the null hypothesis involves a strict equality (i.e., =), it is *nondirectional.* For instance, consider the following pair of hypotheses:

$$H_0: \mu = \$12{,}000;$$
$$H_a: \mu \neq \$12{,}000.$$

Table 17.1
Summary of errors involved in hypothesis testing

INFERENCE BASED ON SAMPLE DATA	REAL STATE OF AFFAIRS	
	H_0 Is True	H_0 Is False
H_0 Is True	Correct decision Confidence level = $1 - \alpha$	Type II error P (Type II error) = β*
H_0 Is False	Type I error Significance level = α†	Correct decision Power = $1 - \beta$

* For a given value of α, β and power will depend on how false H_0 really is.
† Term α represents the maximum probability of committing a Type I error.

Intuitively, both very high and very low values of $\bar{x}$ should lead to rejection of H_o. Therefore the decision rule for rejecting H_o will have *two* critical $\bar{x}_c$ values—one below $12,000 (say $\bar{x}_{c1}$) and the other above $12,000 (say $\bar{x}_{c2}$). The decision rule will be, "Reject H_o if $\bar{x} < \bar{x}_{c1}$ *or* if $\bar{x} > \bar{x}_{c2}$." As shown in Exhibit 17.5, $\bar{x}$-values in either tail of the curve imply that H_o should be rejected.

DEFINITION. A *two-tailed hypothesis* test is one in which values of the test statistic leading to rejection of the null hypothesis fall in both tails of the sampling distribution curve.

A two-tailed hypothesis test has one special implication: The significance level specified for the test must be allocated equally to each tail of the sampling distribution curve. In other words, when the significance level is α, the two critical test statistic values must be established in such a way that the tail portion of the sampling distribution curve beyond each critical value corresponds to a probability of $\alpha/2$. This allocation is illustrated in Exhibit 17.5. We will look at a more detailed example involving a two-tailed hypothesis test later.

In practice, whether a hypothesis test should be one-tailed or two-tailed depends on the nature of the problem. A one-tailed test is appropriate when the decision maker's interest centers primarily on one side of the issue. For example, is the proportion of customers preferring our brand over competitors' brands greater than .3? Is customer response to our coupon campaign greater in city A than in city B? Is our current advertisement less effective than the proposed new advertisement? A two-tailed test is appropriate when the decision maker has no a priori reason to focus on one side of the issue. For example, is the average useful life for our appliance as perceived by consumers different

Exhibit 17.5

Critical sample mean values for a two-tailed test

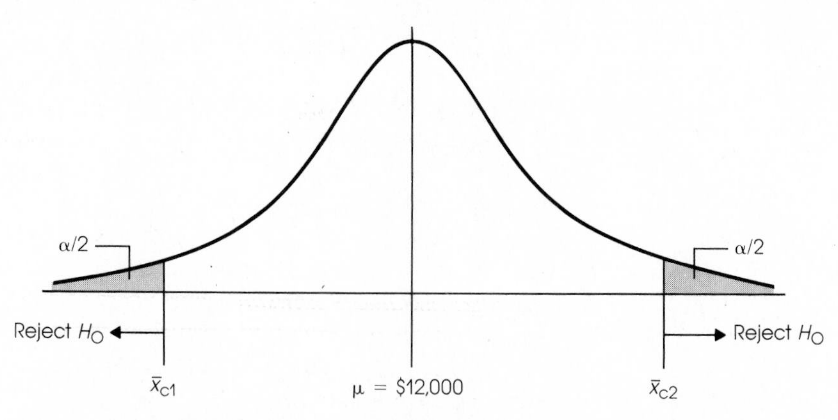

from the objectively determined average life of 10 years? Is test market C different from test market D in terms of average household incomes? Is the satisfaction level of salespeople over 30 years of age different from that of salespeople 30 years of age or younger?

Up to this point we have discussed several key terms and concepts pertaining to hypothesis testing. In particular, the calculations we have performed for situation A illustrate how a hypothesis test is conducted. The procedures followed in those calculations are representative of hypothesis testing in general. In summary, the sequence of tasks involved in a typical hypothesis test are as follows:

- Step 1. Set up H_o and H_a.
- Step 2. Identify the nature of the sampling distribution curve and specify the appropriate test statistic. *Note:* In situation A the sampling distribution was the normal curve and the test statistic was the z-variable. But as we will see later, depending on the specific problem, the appropriate sampling distribution and test statistic will vary.
- Step 3. Determine whether the hypothesis test is one-tailed or two-tailed.
- Step 4. Taking into account the specified significance level, determine the critical value (*two* critical values for a two-tailed test) for the test statistic from the appropriate statistical table.
- Step 5. State the decision rule for rejecting H_o.
- Step 6. Compute the value for the test statistic from the sample data.
- Step 7. Using the decision rule specified in step 5, either reject H_o or reject H_a.

We will use this sequence of steps as the basic framework in describing the various hypothesis tests to be covered subsequently.

ROLE OF HYPOTHESIS TESTING IN DATA ANALYSIS

The scenarios in situations A and B presented earlier were such that the key issue facing the decision maker in each situation could be readily stated as a formal hypothesis. However, in not all situations will the need to test specific hypotheses be that apparent. Nevertheless, virtually all data analysis techniques to be discussed in the next two chapters involve hypothesis testing, at least indirectly. In other words, hypothesis testing may be viewed as an integral (although not always formally stated) part of most analysis procedures that go beyond merely describing the nature of the data. Therefore we will review at this point certain key determinants of the appropriate analysis technique (and hence the appropriate hypothesis test) to use in a given situation.

Three factors are crucial in choosing an appropriate analysis procedure:

(1) number of variables to be analyzed; (2) number of groups (samples) from which data on the variables have been collected; and (3) the nature of the data collected on each variable. Analysis procedures are broadly classified as being univariate or multivariate, depending on the first factor, that is, the number of variables involved. As the terms imply, *univariate analysis* is appropriate when just one variable is the focus of the analysis, and *multivariate analysis* is appropriate when two or more variables are to be analyzed simultaneously. The label *bivariate* (rather than multivariate) *analysis* is often used when the analysis involves just two variables.

Within each of the two broad categories (i.e., univariate and multivariate), the relevant research questions—and hence the specific analysis techniques and hypothesis tests to be used—will be influenced by whether the data are from a single sample or more than one sample. Table 17.2 presents four scenarios involving different combinations of number of variables and number of samples. An illustrative research question calling for some form of hypothesis testing is also included under each scenario.

In scenarios A and B the illustrative research questions imply a need to investigate *differences.* That is, is there a difference between the mean income of videocassette owners and the general population mean income of $15,000? Is there a difference between the purchase rates of households receiving cents-off coupons and those not receiving the coupons? In general, hypothesis tests encountered in analyzing data on a single variable will involve the examination of differences of some sort. The specific hypothesis tests to be covered in the remainder of this chapter will all be of the univariate type.

When two or more variables are analyzed simultaneously, investigating *associations* between the variables is usually of primary interest. This research purpose is indicated by the illustrative research questions in scenarios C and D (both calling for multivariate techniques). Several multivariate (especially bivariate) techniques for analyzing associations between variables, as well as a few corresponding hypothesis tests, will be covered in the next two chapters.

In addition to number of variables and number of samples involved, a third factor affecting the choice of analysis techniques is the nature of the data collected. Particularly relevant in this regard is the measurement level of the data, that is, whether they are nominal, ordinal, interval, or ratio. As was discussed in Chapters 11 and 16, nominal and ordinal data (i.e., nonmetric data) are not as powerful or versatile as interval and ratio data (i.e., metric data). Therefore, only relatively crude statistical analyses can be performed with nonmetric data when compared with metric data.

The types of analyses and hypothesis tests appropriate for nonmetric data are typically labeled as *nonparametric procedures.* Statistical procedures that are nonparametric require only minimal assumptions about the nature of the data, especially with respect to their measurement level and the shape of their distribution.

Table 17.2

Examples of situations calling for univariate and multivariate analysis

NUMBER OF SAMPLES	NUMBER OF VARIABLES: One (Univariate)	Two or More (Multivariate)
One	Scenario A. A sample of households with videocassette recorders is chosen and each household's income is measured Illustrative research question: Is the mean income of households with videocassette recorders different from the mean general population household income of, say, $15,000?	Scenario C. A university surveyed a sample of its undergraduate students and collected data on demographic characteristics, academic performance, study habits, and extracurricular activities Illustrative research question: Are students' grade point ratios associated with age, number of hours per day spent studying, and number of parties attended per week?
Two or more	Scenario B. A food marketer monitored the number of packages of cake mix purchased over a period of time by two different samples of households, those that received a 50-cents-off coupon for the product and those that did not receive the coupon Illustrative research question: Is the mean purchase volume of households receiving the coupon different from that of households not receiving the coupon?	Scenario D. A bank gathered data on age, education, income, and occupation for three different groups of loan customers: (1) Those who always made their monthly payments on time; (2) those who defaulted on their payments once during the past 12 months; and (3) those who defaulted more than once during the past twelve months Illustrative research question: Is there any association between a customer's loan repayment behavior and his or her demographic characteristics? Alternatively, given data on a customer's age, education, income, and occupation, how well can one predict which of the three types of loan repayment behavior the customer is likely to exhibit?

Analysis techniques suitable for metric data are said to be *parametric procedures*. The use of most parametric methods requires data with at least interval-scale properties and having a distribution that resembles the normal probability distribution.[3]

[3] Further discussion of the assumptions that must be met for use of parametric and nonparametric methods, as well as the pros and cons of the two methods, is beyond the scope of this text. However, several excellent books are available for those interested in such a discussion. See, for example, Sidney Siegel, *Nonparametric Statistics for the Behavioral Sciences* (New York: McGraw-Hill, 1956); Jean Dickinson Gibbons, *Nonparametric Methods for Quantitative Analysis* (New York: Holt, Rinehart and Winston, 1976).

In short, as a general rule, nonparametric procedures are appropriate for nominal and ordinal data, and parametric procedures are appropriate only for interval and ratio data. We will discuss several procedures of each type in this and the next two chapters.[4]

SPECIFIC HYPOTHESIS TESTS

This section deals with certain univariate hypothesis tests that are used quite frequently. One point is noteworthy before we look at those tests: We customarily describe a hypothesis test in terms of the test statistic it involves. Consider, for instance, the hypothesis test conducted under situation A (i.e., the situation where Karen had to decide whether or not to introduce the product line into the new market area). Recall that the test statistic for that hypothesis test was the z-variable (standard normal deviate), or the z-statistic, as it is usually called. The name for the hypothesis test itself in this case is the z-test. The specific hypothesis tests we will discuss in this section are summarized in Table 17.3.[5]

Chi-square goodness-of-fit test

The general purpose of the *chi-square goodness-of-fit test* is to see whether the distribution of data on a nominal-scaled variable is consistent with what one would expect if the sample had come from a prespecified population. The research question the test is capable of answering can be stated as follows: "Is the population implied by the distribution of sample data likely to be the same as some prespecified population?" (Recall that in Chapter 14 we defined an *implied population* as the collection of units to which any generalization from the actual sample would be restricted.) A question like this one may arise under a variety of circumstances, as the next two examples illustrate.

EXAMPLE A: A social worker surveyed a random sample of respondents and measured their attitudes toward a variety of community welfare programs. Since people's ethnic backgrounds are likely to be associated with their attitudes toward welfare programs, the social worker wishes to verify

[4] Selecting an appropriate analysis technique in a situation can be more complex than what our discussion here may suggest. However, a comprehensive presentation of all the intricacies involved in choosing a proper analysis procedure is too involved for a basic textbook like this one. An excellent discussion—one that gives a step-by-step flow diagram for selecting a technique after taking into account a variety of considerations—is given in Frank M. Andrews, Laura Klem, Terrence N. Davidson, Patrick M. O'Malley, and Willard L. Rodgers, *A Guide for Selecting Statistical Techniques for Analyzing Social Science Data* (Ann Arbor, Mich.: Institute for Social Research, 1981).

[5] The hypothesis tests listed in Table 17.3 are not meant to be exhaustive. Discussions of a greater variety of tests are given in many standard statistics books, such as Hamburg, *Statistical Analysis,* and Andrews, Klem, Davidson, O'Malley, and Rodgers, *Guide for Selecting Statistical Techniques.*

Table 17.3

Frequently used univariate hypothesis tests

TYPE OF DATA	ILLUSTRATIVE NULL HYPOTHESES	APPROPRIATE TEST STATISTIC	NAME OF TEST
Nominal	H_o: The observed frequency distribution is statistically equivalent to some expected frequency distribution	Chi-square	Chi-square goodness-of-fit test (nonparametric)
Ordinal	Same as for nominal data	Kolmogorov-Smirnov D	Kolmogorov-Smirnov test (nonparametric)
Interval or ratio	H_o: $\mu \leq \mu_o$ (where μ_o is some given value)	t	t-test* (parametric)
	H_o: $\pi \geq \pi_o$ (where π_o is some given value)	z	z-test (parametric)
	H_o: $\mu_1 - \mu_2 = 0$ (where μ_1 and μ_2 refer to two different populations)	t	t-test* (parametric)
	H_o: $\pi_1 - \pi_2 \leq 0$ (where π_1 and π_2 refer to two different populations)	z	z-test (parametric)

* Although the t-test is the technically correct test for hypotheses involving population means, the z-test can be used when the sample sizes are sufficiently large (in practice, $n \geq 30$).

whether the sample's (and hence the implied population's) ethnic mix is consistent with that of the actual population residing in the community.

EXAMPLE B: A restaurant added four different fruit pies to its menu and monitored the unit sales of each over a period of time. Data on unit sales, broken out by type of pie, are now available. The restaurant's manager wants to know whether or not the sales data imply an equal customer preference for each type of pie. The underlying research question is whether the distribution of customer preferences implied by the sales data is consistent with one that might be expected from a population whose preferences are evenly divided across the four types of pies.

The chi-square goodness-of-fit test is appropriate in both examples. In each example the test involves comparing the actual sample distribution (or *observed distribution,* as it is usually called) with an *expected* sample distribution in order to see whether the two differ significantly. The expected sample distribution describes the manner in which the sample data would have been distributed if the sample had come from a prespecified population.

To illustrate, suppose these additional details about example B are available: The restaurant sold 600 fruit pies during one month. The observed distribution of sales was as follows:

Apple pies	180
Cherry pies	120
Peach pies	160
Blueberry pies	140
Total	600

The expected distribution in this case is derived by reallocating the total sales of 600 pies under the assumption of equal customer preference for all four varieties. The expected distribution of sales is as follows:

Apple pies	150
Cherry pies	150
Peach pies	150
Blueberry pies	150
Total	600

Let us now perform a chi-square goodness-of-fit test in the context of this example, assuming a significance level of .05 and following the seven-step procedure outlined earlier.

Step 1: State H_o and H_a. The null hypothesis can be stated in two different, but conceptually equivalent, forms:

> H_o: The observed and expected distributions of pie sales are statistically equivalent.

Or

> H_o: Customer preference for the four types of pies are identical.

The alternative hypothesis is

> H_a: The observed and expected distributions of pie sales are not statistically equivalent.

Or

> H_a: Customer preferences for the four types of pies are not identical; that is, preferences for at least two of the pies are significantly different.

Step 2: Identify the test statistic. Since the sample data are in nominal form, only a nonparametric test is appropriate for deciding whether to reject H_o or H_a. Specifically, the test statistic is the chi-square (χ^2) statistic, whose sampling distribution resembles the chi-square probability distribution. (Discussing the nature of the chi-square distribution and why it is the appropriate sampling distribution in this case is beyond the scope of this textbook.)

Step 3: Determine whether the test is one-tailed or two-tailed. Hypothesis tests involving the chi-square statistic (at least the ones we will be dealing with) are *all* one-tailed. We will simply treat the preceding statement as a given, since the rationale for it is beyond our scope. Thus the test in our example will be one-tailed.

Step 4: Determine the critical test statistic value. Two pieces of data are needed to determine the critical chi-square value (χ_c^2): The significance level (α, which is specified to be .05 in this case) and the so-called degrees of freedom (d.f.). The appropriate degrees of freedom in a univariate chi-square test are given by $k - 1$, where k is the number of nominal categories in the sample data distribution. Since there are four categories of pies in our example,

$$\text{d.f.} = 4 - 1 = 3.$$

Refer to the standard chi-square table in Appendix C. The critical chi-square value (χ_c^2) when $\alpha = .05$ and d.f. $= 3$ is 7.81.

Step 5: State the decision rule. The decision rule for chi-square tests is generally of the following form: "Reject H_o if χ^2 (computed from sample data) is greater than χ_c^2." In our example, if the computed value of χ^2 exceeds 7.81, the restaurant manager should conclude that customer preferences for at least two of the pies are different.

Step 6: Determine the test statistic value. The computed value of the test statistic in chi-square goodness-of-fit tests is derived by using the following expression:

$$\chi^2 = \sum_{i=1}^{k} \frac{(O_i - E_i)^2}{E_i},$$

where O_i and E_i are the observed and expected *frequency counts,* respectively. Examining this expression carefully shows that the lower the discrepancies between the observed and the expected frequency counts, the lower the computed value of χ^2 will be. When the observed and the expected frequency distributions are identical, $\chi^2 = 0$. Therefore the smaller the computed value of χ^2, the weaker the evidence against H_o will be. Notice that this result is consistent with the general decision rule, that is, to reject H_o only when χ^2 is large enough to exceed χ_c^2.

The emphasis here on *frequency counts* is noteworthy. Chi-square values should always be computed by using the raw number of units (as opposed to percentages or proportions of units) falling in each category. In our example we compute

$$\chi^2 = \frac{(180 - 150)^2}{150} + \frac{(120 - 150)^2}{150} + \frac{(160 - 150)^2}{150} + \frac{(140 - 150)^2}{150}$$
$$= 6.0 + 6.0 + .67 + .67 = 13.34.$$

Step 7: Reject H_o or H_a. Since $\chi^2(=13.34) > \chi^2_c(=7.81)$, the restaurant manager should reject H_o and conclude that customer preferences for the four types of pies are *not* identical. In fact, the computed χ^2 value (13.34) is so high that the probability of making a Type I error (i.e., the *actual* significance level) is less than .005 (verify this result by using Appendix C). Stated differently, if consumer preferences were indeed identical for the four types of pies, a chi-square value of 13.34 would have occurred less than five times in a thousand.

One final point about chi-square goodness-of-fit tests is in order. These tests are not meaningful when the *expected* frequency counts are too small. A rule of thumb is to ensure that each category has an expected frequency count of at least five units. Therefore, if the prespecified population is likely to be very sparse in certain categories and dense in others, the total sample size must be large enough to ensure an adequate expected sample frequency count in each category.

The rationale for the minimum expected frequency count requirement can be summarized as follows: Since the expected frequency count (E_i) appears in the denominator of the expression for χ^2, several categories with low expected frequency counts will artificially inflate the computed value of χ^2. This inflated value, in turn, may lead to the rejection of H_o without guaranteeing that the probability of a Type I error will be within α.

Kolmogorov-Smirnov test

The *Kolmogorov-Smirnov test* is appropriate for examining the fit between observed and expected frequency distributions of data when the variable is ordinal-scaled. Consider the following situation:

EXAMPLE: Suppose a random sample of 200 households drawn from a certain population has the following income distribution:

Less than \$10,000	60
\$10,000 to less than \$20,000	50
\$20,000 to less than \$30,000	40
\$30,000 to less than \$40,000	30
\$40,000 or more	20
Total	200

Also, suppose census data indicate that the percentages of population households in the five income categories (going from lowest to highest) are as follows: 35%, 30%, 15%, 10%, and 10%. On the basis of this data, is the sample representative of the population with respect to household income?

To answer the question posed in this example, we can, of course, perform a chi-square goodness-of-fit test by generating an expected frequency distribution of the sample of 200 households, using the census proportions, and comparing it with the observed frequency distribution. However, the chi-square goodness-of-fit test will not take into account that the variable categories are ordinal rather than nominal. In other words, the more refined quality of the available data will essentially be wasted if such a test is used.

Here is where the Kolmogorov-Smirnov test comes in. The Kolmogorov-Smirnov test is conceptually very similar to the chi-square goodness-of-fit test. In both tests the hypothesis statements are identical, and the decision rules for rejecting H_0 are of the same form. However, there are some key differences in the computational procedures. Specifically, in a Kolmogorov-Smirnov test the observed and expected distributions are expressed as *proportions* (rather than frequency counts) and are converted to *cumulative* distributions before comparisons are made. These two steps are summarized in Table 17.4 for our example.

The appropriate test statistic in this case is the Kilmogorov-Smirnov D-statistic, whose value is given by

$$D = \max |OCP_i - ECP_i|,$$

where D is the *maximum absolute discrepancy* (across all categories) between the observed cumulative proportion and the corresponding expected cumula-

Table 17.4
Derivation of observed and expected cumulative proportion distributions of household incomes

INCOME CATEGORY (i)	OBSERVED FREQUENCY (O_i)	OBSERVED PROPORTION (OP_i)	EXPECTED PROPORTION* (EP_i)	OBSERVED CUMULATIVE PROPORTION (OCP_i)	EXPECTED CUMULATIVE PROPORTION (ECP_i)
1	60	0.30	0.35	0.30	0.35
2	50	0.25	0.30	0.55	0.65
3	40	0.20	0.15	0.75	0.80
4	30	0.15	0.10	0.90	0.90
5	20	0.10	0.10	1.00	1.00
	200	1.00	1.00		

* Based on census data.

tive proportion. (From now on the specific steps in the hypothesis-testing procedure will not be explicitly stated; however, you should be able to recognize them.)

For a significance level of .05, the critical value of the test statistic (D_c) can be approximated by the following expression, provided the sample size (n) is 36 or more:

$$D = \frac{1.36}{\sqrt{n}}.$$

When n is less than 36 and/or when α is different from .05, one can refer to standard tables that are available for determining the critical values of D for any given α and n.[6]

The decision rule in a Kilmogorov-Smirnov test is, "Reject H_o if $D > D_c$." In our example the maximum absolute discrepancy between the observed and expected cumulative proportions occurs for the second income category (see Table 17.4):

$$D = |.55 - .65| = .10.$$

Assuming $\alpha = .05$,

$$D_c = \frac{1.36}{\sqrt{200}} = \frac{1.36}{14.14} = .096.$$

Since $D > D_c$, H_o should be rejected: The sample chosen *cannot* be considered to be adequately representative of the population with respect to household income.

Unlike the chi-square goodness-of-fit test, the Kolmogorov-Smirnov test does not have any minimum expected frequency requirement for each category. Moreover, the computational procedure is somewhat less cumbersome. These additional advantages of the Kolmogorov-Smirnov test further favor its use when the variable categories are ordinal.[7]

Test for a single mean

We have already examined in detail one instance where the focus was on hypotheses about a single mean. Specifically, in situation A described earlier, we

[6] For further details, see, for example, Siegel, *Nonparametric Statistics.*

[7] For a more complete and theoretically rigorous discussion of the relative merits of the Kolmogorov-Smirnov test, see, for example, Gibbons, *Nonparametric Methods,* pp. 75–77. This reference also describes several other applications of the Kolmogorov-Smirnov test.

tested the following hypotheses:

$$H_o: \mu \leq \$12{,}000;$$
$$H_a: \mu > \$12{,}000.$$

Therefore we do not need to repeat the entire procedure here. Some clarification is needed, however, concerning the proper test statistic and critical value to use when conducting tests involving single means. Recall that in situation A the test statistic we used was the z-statistic (standard normal deviate). Our use of the z-statistic was actually an approximation, because the theoretically correct sampling distribution for sample means is the *t-distribution,* and the appropriate test statistic is the *t-statistic.* Fortunately, when the sample size is 30 or more the t-distribution closely resembles the standard normal curve. Hence our use of the z-statistic in situation A was justified.

If the sample size in situation A was, say, only 25 instead of 400, the z-statistic would no longer be appropriate. The correct test statistic is the t-statistic, defined as

$$t = \frac{\bar{x} - \mu}{s_{\bar{x}}}.$$

Also, the critical test statistic value (t_c) must be obtained from a t-table (Appendix D at the end of this book). The value of t_c depends not only on α but also on the number of degrees of freedom. The t-statistic associated with a single sample mean has $n - 1$ degrees of freedom, where n is the sample size.

To illustrate the use of the t-statistic, let us rework some of the steps in the problem for situation A, assuming $n = 25, \bar{x} = \$13{,}000$ (same as before) and $s = \$8000$ (same as before). From the t-table in Appendix D, $t_c = 1.71$ for $\alpha = .05$ and d.f. $= 24$. Hence the decision rule is, "Reject H_o if $t > 1.71$." Let us now compute the value of t from the sample data:

$$t = \frac{13{,}000 - 12{,}000}{8000/\sqrt{25}} = \frac{1000}{1600} = .625.$$

Since the computed value of t is less than 1.71, H_o *cannot* be rejected. In other words, Karen should not introduce the product line into the new market area.

Notice that this conclusion contradicts the one we arrived at earlier after performing a z-test in the same situation (except for the larger sample size). However, bear in mind that by failing to reject H_0 based on the t-test we may be committing a Type II error. Indeed, in general, when everything else remains the same, the smaller the sample size, the less likely it is that H_o will be rejected, the higher will be the β-probability, and the lower will be the power. Since traditional hypothesis-testing procedures only limit the probability of committing a Type I error, one has to be cautious in interpreting a finding that H_o cannot be rejected on the basis of a small-sample-size hypothesis test.

Test for a single proportion

Consider the following scenario:

EXAMPLE: Ms. Jones is marketing vice president for Peripherals, Inc., a firm that sells a variety of personal-computer accessories under the brand name Comp-Ease. She is wondering whether she should yield to a request from Mr. Berry, the advertising manager, for a substantial increase in the firm's advertising budget. Mr. Berry had just surveyed a random sample of 100 personal-computer owners and found that only 20 of them had heard of the Comp-Ease name. In making his plea for an increased advertising budget, Mr. Berry had described the sample awareness rate of .2 as being "shamefully low." Ms. Jones, however, feels that the .2 awareness rate is not all that bad, especially since the Comp-Ease line had been introduced only recently. In any case, she is reluctant to increase the advertising budget unless Mr. Berry can show "beyond a reasonable doubt" (i.e., with less than a 5% chance of error) that the true awareness rate for the Comp-Ease name across all personal-computer owners is less than .3. Should Ms. Jones increase the advertising budget on the basis of Mr. Berry's survey results?

The key decision in this scenario boils down to testing the following hypotheses about the population proportion (π is the symbol for population proportion) of personal-computer owners who are aware of the Comp-Ease name:

$$H_o: \pi \geq .3;$$
$$H_a: \pi < .3.$$

The theoretically correct sampling distribution for sample proportions is the binomial distribution. However, for a sufficiently large sample size the binomial distribution resembles the normal distribution, and the z-statistic can be used as the test statistic. How large a sample size is "sufficiently large"? A rule of thumb is that n must be large enough to make each of the following quantities equal at least 10: $n\pi$ and $n(1 - \pi)$, where the value of π is its value when H_o is just true. In our scenario, $n = 100$ and $\pi = .3$. Hence $n\pi$ and $n(1 - \pi)$ are both greater than 10, and the z-statistic, as defined below, can be used as the test statistic:

$$z = \frac{p - \pi}{\sqrt{\pi(1 - \pi)/n}},$$

where p is the sample proportion. Notice that the denominator of this expression is really the standard error of the sample proportion. However, in contrast to the standard error in the test for the mean, where we had to approximate $\sigma_{\bar{x}}$ by $s_{\bar{x}}$ (which, of course, can only be determined after the sample standard deviation is computed), the standard error of the proportion is known exactly once π and n are specified.

Since only small values of p relative to π (or relatively large *negative* values of z) will lead to the rejection of the H_o stated earlier, this hypothesis test is one-tailed, as shown in Exhibit 17.6. The critical test statistic value (z_c) is negative because the shaded tail corresponding to rejection of H_o is on the left-hand side of the sampling distribution centered on $\pi = .3$, or $z = 0$ (the z-value at the center of a normal probability distribution is always zero; z-values on the left-hand side of the distribution are all negative, while those on the right-hand side are all positive). From Appendix B, $z_c = -1.645$ for $\alpha = .05$. The appropriate decision rule here is, "Reject H_o if $z < -1.645$." Using $p = .2$, $\pi = .3$, and $n = 100$, we can compute the value of z:

$$z = \frac{.2 - .3}{\sqrt{(.3)(.7)/100}} = \frac{-.1}{.046} = -2.174$$

Since $-2.174 < -1.645$, we reject H_0; The sample awareness rate of .2 is too low to support the hypothesis that the population awareness rate is .3 or more. In

Exhibit 17.6

Hypothesis test related to proportion of personal-computer owners

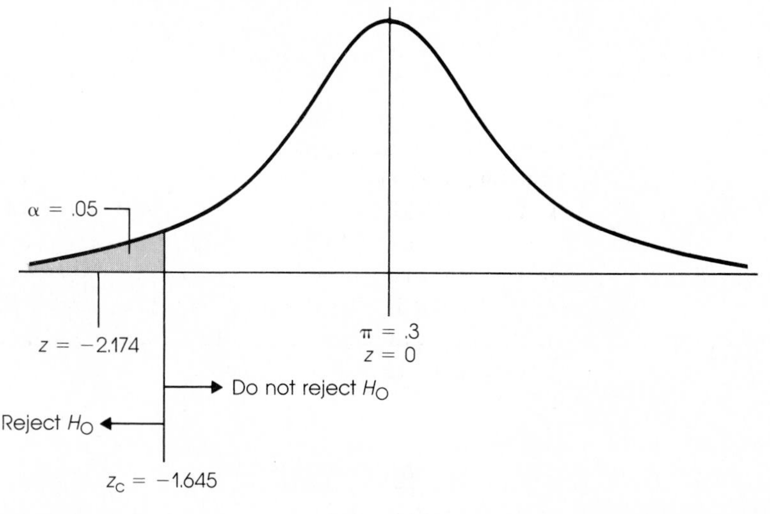

other words, Mr. Berry apparently has a legitimate request, and Ms. Jones should increase the advertising budget.

Test of two means

Consider the situation described in the following example.

EXAMPLE: A health service agency has designed a public service campaign to promote physical fitness and the importance of regular exercise. Since the campaign is a major one, the agency wants to make sure of its potential effectiveness before running it on a national scale. To conduct a controlled test of the campaign's effectiveness, the agency has identified two similar cities: City 1 will serve as the test city, and city 2 will serve as a control city. A preliminary random survey of 300 adults in city 1 and 200 adults in city 2 was conducted to measure the average time per day spent on some form of exercise by a typical adult in each city. The survey showed that this average was 30 minutes per day (with a standard deviation of 22 minutes) in city 1 and 35 minutes per day (with a standard deviation of 25 minutes) in city 2. From these results, can the agency conclude confidently that the two cities are well matched for the controlled test? The agency does not want to allow more than a 5% chance of inferring that the cities are *not* matched when they truly are matched.

This situation is typical of those that require testing hypotheses involving two means. Let us denote the population means in city 1 and city 2 as μ_1 and μ_2, respectively. The survey results in the two cities can be summarized as follows, using our customary notation:

City 1:	$n_1 = 300$	$\bar{x}_1 = 30$	$s_1 = 22$
City 2:	$n_2 = 200$	$\bar{x}_2 = 35$	$s_2 = 25$

The hypotheses are

$$H_o: \mu_1 = \mu_2 \quad \text{or} \quad \mu_1 - \mu_2 = 0;$$
$$H_a: \mu_1 \neq \mu_2 \quad \text{or} \quad \mu_1 - \mu_2 \neq 0.$$

In a two-means hypothesis test, when the sample sizes are sufficiently large (i.e., $n_1 > 30$ and $n_2 > 30$), the sampling distribution for the difference between sample means resembles the normal probability distribution, and the test statistic is the *z*-statistic, given by

$$z = \frac{(\bar{x}_1 - \bar{x}_2) - (\mu_1 - \mu_2)}{\sqrt{s_1^2/n_1 + s_2^2/n_2}}.$$

Both n_1 and n_2 are greater than 30 in our example. The z-statistic can therefore be used as the test statistic.

Since the null hypothesis is in the form of a strict equality, the hypothesis test is two-tailed, and hence we have to identify two critical values of z, one for each tail of the sampling distribution. The probability corresponding to each tail is .025, since $\alpha = .05$. From Appendix B the z-value associated with a tail probability of .025 is 1.96. The decision rule is, "Reject H_o if $z < -1.96$ or if $z > 1.96$."

Let us now compute the value of z from the survey results and under the customary assumption that the null hypothesis is true (i.e., $\mu_1 - \mu_2 = 0$):

$$z = \frac{(30 - 35) - (0)}{\sqrt{(22)^2/300 + (25)^2/200}} = \frac{-5}{\sqrt{1.61 + 3.13}}$$
$$= \frac{-5}{\sqrt{4.74}} = \frac{-5}{2.18} = -2.29.$$

Since $z < -1.96$, we should reject H_o. Therefore the health service agency cannot confidently assume that the current levels of exercising activity of residents in the two cities are identical. A pictorial summary of this hypothesis test is shown in Exhibit 17.7.

In addition to the assumption of a large sample size, the use of the z-statistic in a hypothesis test involving two means requires the assumption of *indepen-*

Exhibit 17.7

Hypothesis test related to mean exercising in two cities

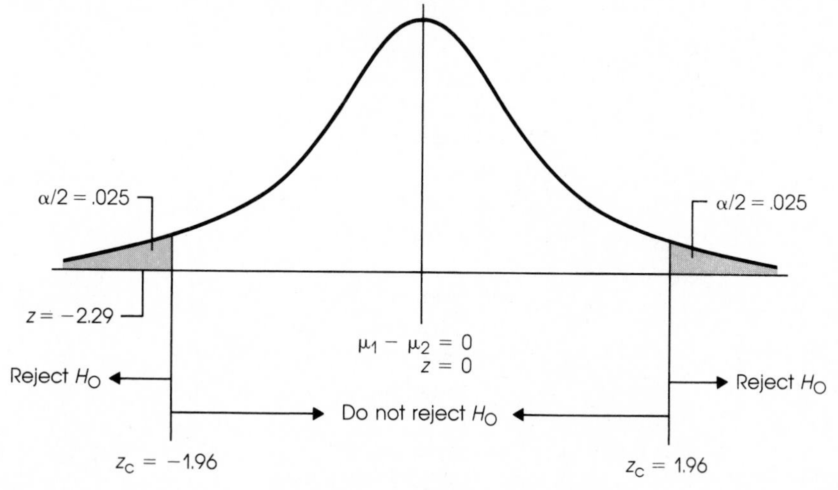

dent samples; that is, the samples must be chosen independently of each other. Thus, for example, the z-test is not appropriate for checking whether there is a statistically significant difference between two mean values obtained at different times from the *same* sample. Under such circumstances a different hypothesis-testing procedure, which we will discuss a little later, should be used.

Furthermore, just as in the case of a single-mean hypothesis test, when one or both sample sizes are small (i.e., $n_1 < 30$ or $n_2 < 30$), a t-test rather than a z-test should be conducted. Using the t-statistic in a two-means hypothesis test requires two additional assumptions, however:

1. The two populations from which the samples are selected are each normally distributed with respect to the variable.
2. The two populations have equal variances.

These assumptions are usually taken for granted. Ideally, however, they should be verified to ensure that conducting a t-test is legitimate. Procedures for verifying the assumptions from sample data are available but will not be discussed here.[8]

When the two above assumptions, along with the assumption of independent samples, are satisfied, the appropriate test statistic is

$$t = \frac{(\bar{x}_1 - \bar{x}_2) - (\mu_1 - \mu_2)}{s^*(\sqrt{1/n_1 + 1/n_2})},$$

with d.f. $= n_1 + n_2 - 2$. In this expression s^* is the *pooled standard deviation,* given by

$$s^* = \sqrt{\frac{(n_1 - 1)s_1^2 + (n_2 - 1)s_2^2}{n_1 + n_2 - 2}}$$

The procedure for conducting the t-test is quite similar to the one for conducting the z-test. To illustrate the use of the t-statistic, let us assume that the sample sizes for city 1 and city 2 in the health service agency survey were only 20 and 10, respectively, but that means and standard deviations were the same as before. Thus:

$$n_1 = 20 \quad \bar{x}_1 = 30 \quad s_1 = 22$$
$$n_2 = 10 \quad \bar{x}_2 = 35 \quad s_2 = 25$$

The degrees of freedom for the t-statistic are

$$\text{d.f.} = n_1 + n_2 - 2 = 20 + 10 - 2 = 28.$$

[8] These procedures can be found in most basic statistics textbooks, such as Neil Weiss and Matthew Hassett, *Introductory Statistics* (Reading, Mass.: Addison-Wesley, 1982).

From Appendix D the critical value of t with 28 degrees of freedom for a tail probability of .025 is 2.05. Therefore the decision rule is, "Reject H_o if $t < -2.05$ *or* if $t > 2.05$." The pooled standard deviation is

$$s^* = \sqrt{\frac{(20-1)(22)^2 + (10-1)(25)^2}{20+10-2}}$$

$$= \sqrt{\frac{9196 + 5625}{28}} = \sqrt{\frac{14821}{28}}$$

$$= \sqrt{529}\text{ (approximately)} = 23.$$

So the test statistic is

$$t = \frac{(30-35)-(0)}{23(\sqrt{\frac{1}{20}+\frac{1}{10}})} = \frac{-5}{23(\sqrt{.05+.1})}$$

$$= \frac{-5}{23(.39)} = \frac{-5}{8.97} = -.56.$$

Since t is neither less than -2.05 nor greater than 2.05, we cannot reject H_o. In other words, the sample evidence is not strong enough to conclude that the two cities differ in terms of levels of exercising activity of their residents. As was pointed out under t-tests for single means, however, this inference must be viewed with a good deal of caution because the small sample sizes greatly increase the possibility of a Type II error.

Test of two means when samples are dependent

The testing procedures in the preceding section can be used only when the two samples are chosen independently of each other. However, marketers often need to check for significant differences between two mean values when the samples are not independent. For instance, "On the basis of a survey of husband-wife households, is there a significant difference between the mean attitude score of husbands and that of wives toward our product?" Marketers also may want to check differences between two mean values when the two sets of data are from the same sample. For example, "On the basis of consumer panel data, is the mean frequency of use for our product among panel households significantly higher after the coupon campaign than before?" In either case a modified hypothesis-testing procedure is necessary, as discussed next. The following example illustrates a practical situation in which the modified procedure is needed.

EXAMPLE: A retail chain ran a special promotion in a representative sample of 10 of its stores, hoping to boost sales substantially. Weekly sales per store

Table 17.5
Sales per store before and after a promotional campaign

	SALES PER STORE ($\times$ \$1000)		
STORE NUMBER (i)	Before Promotion (X_{bi})	After Promotion (X_{ai})	CHANGE IN SALES ($\times$ \$1000) ($X_{di} = X_{ai} - X_{bi}$)
1	250	260	10
2	235	240	5
3	150	151	1
4	145	140	−5
5	120	124	4
6	98	100	2
7	75	70	−5
8	85	95	10
9	180	200	20
10	212	220	8
Total			50

before and after the introduction of the special promotion are shown in Table 17.5. The key question now is whether the sample evidence in Table 17.5 is strong enough to support management's a priori hunch that the special promotion would lead to a significant increase in sales.

For this example the "before" and "after" sales data (X_{bi} and X_{ai}, respectively) are clearly not independent since they are from the same sample of stores. The hypothesis-testing procedure in situations like these calls for first computing *difference* scores for pairs of related sample data; in our example these differences are the X_{di} values in the last column of Table 17.5. This step essentially collapses what appear to be two-sample data into a set of single-sample difference scores. The rest of the procedure is similar to the hypothesis-testing procedure for a single mean.

Let μ_d represent the population *mean change* in sales per store. Since management had a prior expectation that the special promotion would be effective, that expectation should be consistent with the alternative hypothesis (recall the guidelines specified at the beginning of this chapter for properly specifying the null and alternative hypotheses). Therefore:

$$H_o: \mu_d \leq 0;$$
$$H_a: \mu_d > 0.$$

The sample estimate of μ_d is $\bar{x}_d$, given by

$$\bar{x}_d = \frac{\sum_{i=1}^{n} X_{di}}{n},$$

where n is the sample size. In our example, the summation in the numerator is the total of the difference scores in the last column in Table 17.5 (i.e., 50) and $n = 10$. Therefore $\bar{x}_d = 5$.

The sampling distribution for $\bar{x}_d$ is the t-distribution, and the test statistic is

$$t = \frac{\bar{x}_d - \mu_d}{s/\sqrt{n}},$$

with $(n - 1)$ degrees of freedom, and where s is the standard deviation of the difference scores and is given by

$$s = \sqrt{\frac{\sum_{i=1}^{n} (X_{di} - \bar{x}_d)^2}{n - 1}}.$$

Given the way H_o and H_a are stated, only relatively high values of $\bar{x}_d$ (or t) will lead to the rejection of H_o. Hence the hypothesis test is one-tailed, as shown in Exhibit 17.8, in which a significance level of .05 has been assumed. From

Exhibit 17.8

Hypothesis test related to change in weekly sales per store

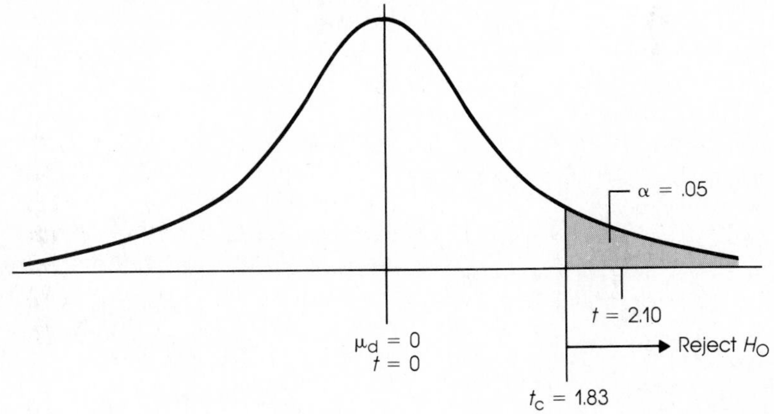

Appendix D the critical value of t with $n - 1 = 9$ degrees of freedom, for a one-tail probability of .05, is 1.83. The decision rule then is, "Reject H_o if $t > 1.83$."

The standard deviation of the difference scores (s) in our example turns out to be 7.53. We can now compute the value of the test statistic:

$$t = \frac{\bar{x}_d - \mu_d}{s/\sqrt{n}} = \frac{5 - 0}{7.53/\sqrt{10}}$$

$$= \frac{5}{2.38} = 2.10.$$

Since $t > 1.83$, we reject H_o and conclude that the mean change in sales per store was significantly greater than zero. In other words, the special promotion was indeed effective.

Tests of two proportions

We will use the data in situation B (described earlier in the chapter) to illustrate hypothesis tests involving two proportions. In situation B, recall that Tom, the advertising manager for a frozen-foods company, is wondering whether commercial Y will be more effective than commercial X. The commercials were run in two comparable test cities. Subsequent surveys in the two cities showed that the sample awareness rates for commercials Y and X were 25% and 20%, respectively.

Using the subscript 1 for symbols pertaining to commercial Y and the subscript 2 for symbols pertaining to commercial X, we can summarize situation B as follows:

Sample sizes:	$n_1 = 200$	$n_2 = 200$
Sample proportions:	$p_1 = .25$	$p_2 = .20$

The hypotheses are

$$H_o: \pi_1 \leq \pi_2 \quad \text{or} \quad \pi_1 - \pi_2 \leq 0;$$
$$H_a: \pi_1 > \pi_2 \quad \text{or} \quad \pi_1 - \pi_2 > 0.$$

When the two samples are sufficiently large in a test involving two proportions, the sampling distribution of the difference between sample proportions can be assumed to be the normal probability distribution, and the z-test is appropriate. A rule of thumb for ensuring that the sample sizes are adequate is to verify that each of the following quantities is at least 10: n_1p_1, $n_1(1 - p_1)$, n_2p_2, and $n_2(1 - p_2)$. The data in situation B satisfy these requirements. Hence the z-test is appropriate. The test statistic is given by

$$z = \frac{(p_1 - p_2) - (\pi_1 - \pi_2)}{\sigma_{p_1 - p_2}},$$

where $\sigma_{p_1-p_2}$ is the population standard error for the difference between proportions. Since $\sigma_{p_1-p_2}$ is invariably unknown, it is estimated by the sample standard error ($s_{p_1-p_2}$), as follows:

$$s_{p_1-p_2} = \sqrt{PQ\left(\frac{1}{n_1} + \frac{1}{n_2}\right)},$$

where P is the weighted proportion across both samples and Q is its complement:

$$P = \frac{n_1p_1 + n_2p_2}{n_1 + n_2}$$

$$Q = 1 - P$$

The null hypothesis in situation B will be rejected only for certain positive values of the quantity $p_1 - p_2$. Therefore the hypothesis test is one-tailed. Assuming the customary significance level of .05, the critical value of z (from Appendix B) is 1.645. The decision rule is, "Reject H_o if $z > 1.645$."

To compute the value of z from the sample data, we first have to compute P and Q, then $s_{p_1-p_2}$ and z:

$$P = \frac{200(.25) + 200(.2)}{200 + 200} = \frac{50 + 40}{400} = \frac{90}{400} = .225$$

$$Q = 1 - .225 = .775$$

Exhibit 17.9

Hypothesis test related to awareness generated by two commercials

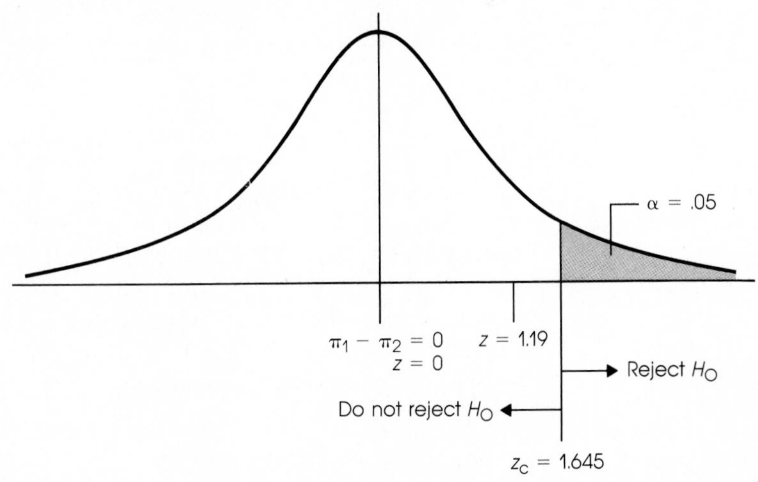

$$s_{p_1-p_2} = \sqrt{(.225)(.775)(\tfrac{1}{200} + \tfrac{1}{200})}$$
$$= \sqrt{(.225)(.775)(\tfrac{1}{100})} = \sqrt{.00174} = 0.42$$
$$z = \frac{(.25 - .20) - (0)}{.042} = \frac{.05}{.042} = 1.19$$

Since $z < 1.645$, we *cannot* reject H_o. Therefore the sample evidence is not strong enough to suggest that commercial Y will be more effective than commercial X. The results of our hypothesis test in situation B are pictured in Exhibit 17.9.

SUMMARY

An analysis procedure that goes beyond merely describing what the sample data look like is called inferential analysis, and it invariably involves some form of hypothesis testing. Situations calling for hypothesis testing will have a prespecified criterion on which a final decision, or inference, hinges. This criterion plays a key role in the formal statement of the null and alternative hypotheses.

Two kinds of errors are possible in testing hypotheses about population characteristics based on sample data: A Type I error, which refers to rejecting the null hypothesis when it is actually true, and a Type II error, which refers to failing to reject the null hypothesis when it is false. Traditional hypothesis-testing procedures place an upper bound on the probability of a Type I error—called the significance level α—but do not explicitly control Type II error. When α is lowered, however, the probability of a Type II error (called β) will increase and power (which is $1 - \beta$) will decrease. The value of β depends not only on α but also on how false the null hypothesis really is.

The general procedure for testing hypotheses consists of the following steps:

1. Set up H_o and H_a (in accordance with the guidelines stated in the chapter).
2. Identify the nature of the sampling distribution of the variable and specify the appropriate test statistic.
3. Determine whether the hypothesis test is one-tailed or two-tailed (in general, a test will be one-tailed when H_o does not involve a strict equality).
4. Specify the critical value(s) for the test statistic, depending on the preset significance level.
5. State the decision rule for rejecting H_o.
6. Compute the value of the test statistic from sample data.
7. Compare the test statistic value with the critical value(s) and decide whether or not to reject H_o.

Hypothesis testing is an integral, although sometimes an implicit, part of virtually all statistical analyses that go beyond mere data description. Therefore factors that affect the choice of an appropriate analysis technique are also germane to selecting suitable hypothesis tests. Three such factors are crucial: number of variables, number of groups or samples, and measurement level of the data. Analyses and hypothesis tests pertaining to just one variable are univariate; those pertaining to two or more variables are multivariate (they are sometimes described as bivariate when just two variables are involved). Typically, examining differences of some sort is the focus of univariate analyses and hypothesis tests. In contrast, multivariate analyses and hypothesis tests usually involve associations between variables. Nonparametric tests are used when the data are nonmetric (nominal or ordinal), and parametric tests are used when the data are metric (interval or ratio).

In this chapter we discussed several univariate hypothesis tests; the first two were nonparametric and the rest were parametric. The specific tests covered were as follows:

1. The chi-square goodness-of-fit test for comparing the observed and expected frequency distributions of a nominal-scaled variable.
2. The Kolmogorov-Smirnov test for comparing the observed and expected frequency distributions of an ordinal-scaled variable.
3. The z-test for a single mean when the sample size is large.
4. The t-test for a single mean when the sample size is small.
5. The z-test for a single proportion (valid only when the sample size is large).
6. The z-test for two means when both samples are large.
7. The t-test for two means when either sample is small.
8. The t-test for two means when the samples are dependent.
9. The z-test for two proportions (valid only when both samples are large).

The risk of committing a Type II error is especially high in the t-tests involving small sample sizes.

QUESTIONS

1. Can data gathered through a descriptive-research project be useful in conducting inferential analysis? Why or why not? (Refer to Chapter 4 and refresh your memory about what is meant by descriptive research.)
2. What are Type I and Type II errors? Explain the relationship between these two types of errors.
3. What will happen to the probability of committing a Type II error when the significance level is increased from, say, .05 to .1? Illustrate your answer by setting up a

hypothetical pair of null and alternative hypotheses and by constructing an appropriate set of sampling distribution diagrams.

4. Suppose H_o in a particular setting is that the proportion of households in an area using brand A toothpaste is at least .4. The significance level for testing H_o is .05. Will the power of this hypothesis test be higher if the true population proportion is .35 than if it is .25? Illustrate your answer with a suitable diagram.
5. What will be the power of the test in the situation depicted in the Question 4 if the true population proportion is .45? Why?
6. "Hypothesis-testing procedures, given their statistical rigor, are free of decision maker subjectivity." Discuss this statement.
7. Set up H_o and H_a for the two illustrative scenarios presented in Table 17.2 under the column labeled "Univariate."
8. A firm wanted to test four alternative types of packaging—A, B, C, and D—for one of its products. Specifically, it wanted to determine whether there was any significant difference in consumer preference across the four types of packaging. It conducted a consumer preference test in which a sample of 200 consumers participated. Each participant was shown the four types and asked to pick the one that he or she preferred the most. The results of this test were as follows: Of the 200 consumers, 40 preferred A, 55 preferred B, 60 preferred C, and 45 preferred D. From these results, can one conclude with 95% confidence that there is some significant difference in preferences across the four types of packaging?
9. The representative sample selected for a mail survey of businesses had the following distribution of types of firms: 20% industrial-goods manufacturers, 30% consumer goods manufacturers, 25% retailing firms, and 25% service firms. A total of 1000 questionnaires were mailed, but responses were obtained only from 280 firms, consisting of 65 industrial-goods manufacturers, 75 consumer goods manufacturers, 55 retailing firms, and 85 service firms. Assuming that the type of firm is likely to have a major bearing on the questionnaire responses, can one be 95% confident that there was no significant *nonresponse error?* (For a definition of nonresponse error, see Chapter 15.)
10. From census information the households in a certain city have the following distribution with respect to the number of people in them:

Category	Number of People	Percentage of Households
A	1	10%
B	2	30%
C	3	30%
D	4	20%
E	More than 4	10%

A sample of 500 households chosen from the city was distributed across the five categories as follows: A = 30, B = 100, C = 160, D = 120, E = 90. Can this sample be considered statistically equivalent to the population with respect to household size (at a significance level of .05)?

11. The Miller Cereal Company has been running an advertising campaign for one of its brands for quite some time. It wants to continue running the campaign only if at least 20% of the target audience is now aware of the brand; otherwise, it wants to discontinue the campaign. A just-completed survey of a random sample of 400

customers in the target audience showed that 75 of them were aware of the advertised brand. Should the Miller Cereal Company discontinue the advertising campaign on the basis of this evidence? Assume that if the company does decide to discontinue the campaign, it wants to be 95% confident that it is making the correct decision.

12. Questions 6a and 6b in Chapter 12 are problems dealing with estimating confidence intervals. Rework those problems by using the hypothesis-testing framework discussed in this chapter. Are the conclusions stemming from the hypothesis-testing procedure the same as those stemming from the confidence intervals estimated earlier? Why or why not?

13. The XYZ Company wants to advertise its product in a magazine only if the average age of the magazine's readership is greater than 30. A random sample of 100 readers of the magazine had an average age of 32, with a standard deviation of 10. Suppose the firm does not want more than a 5% chance of making the mistake of advertising in the magazine when the magazine is really inappropriate. Set up, and test, a suitable pair of hypotheses, and indicate whether the firm should advertise in the magazine.

14. The ABC Company is currently selling brand Z through 2000 retail outlets across the United States. To strengthen Z's market position, ABC's objective is to make it one of the three highest selling brands in each of the 2000 outlets. One of ABC's options for achieving this goal is to cut the retail selling price of Z. However, it wants to cut the retail price only if analysis of last year's sales indicates that Z is the number 4 brand or worse in more than 50% of the stores. The company plans to check the brand's position by obtaining information on its sales from a random sample of 400 stores. In its decision making from this sample information, ABC does not want more than a 5% chance of cutting price when Z indeed holds one of the top three positions in at least 50% of the 2000 stores. Suppose 212 of the 400 stores surveyed indicated that Z's sales performance was number 4 or worse. Should the price be cut on the basis of this sample information?

15. A sample of 400 female consumers of a product had a mean age of 30 with a standard deviation of 4, and a sample of 500 male consumers had a mean age of 28 with a standard deviation of 5. Can the mean ages of the female and male populations of consumers be considered significantly different at a significance level of .05?

16. A new product was promoted to two similar target markets, using two *different* advertising media: Medium 1 was used for market 1, and medium 2 was used for market 2. After the promotional campaign was over, a random sample of 200 people was surveyed from market 1, and a random sample of 300 people was surveyed from market 2. Of the market 1 sample 150 were aware of the new product, while of the market 2 sample 210 were aware of the new product. Using this evidence, test the null hypothesis that medium 2 is at least as effective as, if not better than, medium 1 in terms of generating awareness among consumers (at the .05 significance level).

18

Techniques for Examining Associations: Chi-square, Correlation, and Regression

The previous chapter covered several univariate techniques and hypothesis tests for investigating the statistical significance of two categories of *differences:* differences between the frequency distribution/mean/proportion pertaining to a variable measured from a single sample and the corresponding expected or preset values; and differences between the frequency distributions/means/proportions pertaining to a variable measured from two samples. The focus of this chapter is on the investigation of *associations* between two or more variables. Specifically, it discusses several multivariate techniques for analyzing data obtained from a single sample. Certain other multivariate techniques, including some for analyzing data from two or more samples, are covered in the next chapter. The first technique we will look at is an extension of the two-way tabulation procedure discussed in Chapter 16.

CHI-SQUARE CONTINGENCY TEST

The *chi-square contingency test* is a widely used technique for determining whether there is a statistically significant relationship between two categorical (nominal or ordinal) variables. (While the chi-square test only requires nominal data, it can also be used to analyze associations between two ordinal-scaled variables or one nominal- and one ordinal-scaled variable.) Recall that a mere visual inspection of a two-way tabulation of data can suggest whether or not the variables are associated with each other. The chi-square contingency test is a means of formally checking the relationship between such variables. It is a hypothesis test much like the chi-square goodness-of-fit test discussed in the previous chapter. To illustrate the chi-square contingency test, let us consider the following scenario.

EXAMPLE: The marketing manager of a cosmetics company is reviewing the results of a survey of adult women. The survey involved a random sample of 500 respondents and was conducted in a metropolitan area representative of the company's target market area. He is intrigued by one table, which is a cross-tabulation of data on the working status of respondents and the dollar amount per month they spend on cosmetics. Table 18.1 presents this cross-tabulation. Can the marketing manager infer that there is an association between working status and expenditure on cosmetics?

The percentage breakdowns in Table 18.1 do suggest an association between the two variables. And the association does appear to be somewhat intriguing, with those working part-time spending more on cosmetics than either of the other two categories of respondents. However, is this result trustworthy, or could the association have occurred in this sample purely by chance? A chi-square contingency test of the following hypotheses can answer this question:

H_o: There is no association between working status and expenditure on cosmetics (i.e., the two variables are independent of each other).

H_a: There is some association between working status and expenditure on cosmetics (i.e., the two variables are not independent of each other).

Conducting the test

Just as in the chi-square goodness-of-fit test, computing the test statistic in the chi-square contingency test involves comparing the actual, or observed, cell frequencies in the cross-tabulation (also called the *contingency table* in this context) with a corresponding set of expected cell frequencies. The expected

Table 18.1

Two-way tabulation of working status and expenditures on cosmetics

	WORKING STATUS			
EXPENDITURES ON COSMETICS	Working Full-Time	Working Part-Time	Not Working	TOTAL
Less than $10	30 (21.4%)	20 (12.5%)	60 (30%)	110
$10 to $25	55 (39.3%)	60 (37.5%)	65 (32.5%)	180
Over $25	55 (39.3%)	80 (50%)	75 (37.5%)	210
Total	140 (100%)	160 (100%)	200 (100%)	500

cell frequencies are generated under the assumption that the null hypothesis is true. In other words, they are generated by asking the following question: "How would the total sample have partitioned itself into the various cells if the two variables were truly unrelated in the population?" The expected cell frequency (E_{ij}) for any cell defined by the ith row and jth column in the contingency table is given by

$$E_{ij} = \frac{n_i n_j}{n},$$

where n_i and n_j are the marginal frequencies—that is, the total number of sample units in category i of the row variable and category j of the column variable, respectively.

The rationale for this expression is based on probability theory and is quite intuitive. The probability that any given respondent within the sample will be in category i of the row variable is n_i/n. Similarly, the probability that this same respondent will be in category j of the column variable is n_j/n. Therefore, if the row and column variables are independent, the joint probability of the respondent being in both row category i and column category j is given by $(n_i/n)(n_j/n)$. For the total sample of n respondents the expected value (number of respondents) one should find in cell ij if H_o is true is given by $(n)(n_i/n)(n_j/n)$, which simplifies to $n_i n_j/n$.

Using this expression, we can compute an E_{ij}-value for each cell. Table 18.2 contains the expected cell frequencies corresponding to the various cells in Table 18.1. The row (as well as column) totals in Table 18.2 are identical for both the observed and expected frequencies. This feature is always true and is helpful in verifying whether the expected cell frequencies have been computed correctly. A discrepancy between the observed and the expected frequency totals in

Table 18.2

Observed and expected cell frequencies for the working status/cosmetics expenditures table

EXPENDITURES ON COSMETICS	WORKING STATUS			TOTAL
	Working Full-Time	Working Part-Time	Not Working	
Less than $10	30 (30.8)	20 (35.2)	60 (44)	110
$10 to $25	55 (50.4)	60 (57.6)	65 (72)	180
Over $25	55 (58.8)	80 (67.2)	75 (84)	210
Total	140	160	200	500

Note: In each cell ij the number without parentheses is the observed cell frequency (O_{ij}) and the number in parentheses is the expected cell frequency (E_{ij}).

any row or column is indicative of some error in computing the expected cell frequencies.

The value of the *chi-square test statistic* in a contingency test is obtained by using the following formula:

$$\chi^2 = \sum_{i=1}^{r} \sum_{j=1}^{c} \frac{(O_{ij} - E_{ij})^2}{E_{ij}},$$

where r and c are the number of rows and columns, respectively, in the contingency table. Notice that this formula closely resembles the one we used for the chi-square goodness-of-fit test. The only difference between the two is that the expression here has a double summation sign and uses double subscripts because it relates to two categorical variables. Also, the number of degrees of freedom associated with this chi-square statistic are given by the product $(r - 1)(c - 1)$. In our example

$$\text{d.f.} = (3 - 1)(3 - 1) = 4.$$

Assuming a significance level of .05, the critical chi-square (χ^2_c) value from Appendix C for 4 degrees of freedom is 9.49. Furthermore, a chi-square contingency test of independence between two variables is always a one-tailed test. Therefore the decision rule is, "Reject H_o if $\chi^2 > 9.49$."

The computed value of the test statistic is

$$\begin{aligned}\chi^2 &= \frac{(30 - 30.8)^2}{30.8} + \frac{(20 - 35.2)^2}{35.2} + \frac{(60 - 44)^2}{44} \\ &\quad + \frac{(55 - 50.4)^2}{50.4} + \frac{(60 - 57.6)^2}{57.6} + \frac{(65 - 72)^2}{72} \\ &\quad + \frac{(55 - 58.8)^2}{58.8} + \frac{(80 - 67.2)^2}{67.2} + \frac{(75 - 84)^2}{84} \\ &= .021 + 6.564 + 5.818 + .420 + .100 + .681 \\ &\quad + .246 + 2.438 + .964 \\ &= 17.252.\end{aligned}$$

Since the computed chi-square value is greater than the critical value of 9.49, we can reject the null hypothesis. In other words, the apparent relationship between working status and expenditure on cosmetics revealed by the sample data is unlikely to have occurred because of chance.

That the chi-square contingency test only requires categorical data for ascertaining whether two variables are associated is a great advantage and has contributed to its wide use. However, it does have one potential limitation. For the test to be meaningful, there is a requirement for a minimum expected cell frequency (i.e., minimum E_{ij}). A commonly suggested rule of thumb is that no cell should have an expected frequency of less than one and no more than a fifth of the cells should have expected frequencies of less than five. The rationale here is similar to the rationale we discussed in the previous chapter for the chi-square goodness-of-fit test. Too many low expected frequencies will artificially inflate the computed chi-square value and may lead to the rejection of H_0 when such a conclusion is not warranted.

In practical terms, the minimum–expected frequency requirement implies that the test may not be meaningful when the observed *marginal* frequencies of one or both variables (i.e., the $n_{i\cdot}$- or $n_{\cdot j}$-values) are very small for certain categories. In some cases, however, one may be able to combine adjacent variable categories in such a way that the collapsed category has a large enough marginal frequency.

For example, suppose we want to conduct a chi-square contingency test to see whether there is an association between annual family income and the number of television sets owned by families; the data are gathered from a random sample of 250 families. Also, suppose family income is measured as a five-category variable and number of TVs owned is measured as a four-category variable; their observed marginal-frequency distributions are as shown in Table 18.3(a).

The last category of each variable has relatively few units, as shown in Table 18.3(a). The effect of these low observed frequencies on the expected cell frequencies is shown in Table 18.3(b). The last row–last column cell in this table has an expected frequency of only .2. Also, more than 20% of the cells in the table have expected frequencies of less than 5. The chi-square contingency test is therefore inappropriate for examining the association between the two variables in their present form.

Notice, however, that the categories of both variables are ordinal. Hence we can meaningfully combine the last two categories of each to form a single category with an adequate marginal frequency. The revised variable categories have large enough marginal totals to yield expected cell frequencies that satisfy the rule of thumb, as indicated in Table 18.3(c).

The ordinal nature of the variables in this example facilitated combining adjacent categories as desired. However, when a variable's categories do not follow a logical ordering—for example, those of race or ethnic background—combining categories may not always make sense. Furthermore, combining categories will result in a loss of degrees of freedom, which, in turn, will weaken the test. Another limitation of the chi-square contingency test is that it is inappropriate for examining the association between two measurements of the same variable taken at two different times (e.g., the brand preferences of a consumer panel before and after a major promotional campaign for one of the brands).[1]

[1] One nonparametric test that can be used to measure the significance of a change between a before and an after measure of the same variable is the McNemar test; for details, see Sidney Siegel, *Nonparametric Statistics for the Behavioral Sciences* (New York: McGraw-Hill, 1956), pp. 63–67.

Table 18.3
Association between family income and number of TVs owned

(a) Observed Marginal-Frequency Distributions

FAMILY INCOME	FREQUENCY	NUMBER OF TVs OWNED	FREQUENCY
1. Less than $10,000	100	1. One	80
2. $10,000 to less than $25,000	50	2. Two	90
3. $25,000 to less than $40,000	50	3. Three	70
4. $40,000 to less than $55,000	45	4. Four or more	10
5. $55,000 or more	5		
Total	250	Total	250

(b) Expected Cell Frequencies in a Two-Way Tabulation

FAMILY INCOME CATEGORIES	NUMBER OF TVs OWNED CATEGORIES				TOTAL
	1	2	3	4	
1	32	36	28	4	100
2	16	18	14	2	50
3	16	18	14	2	50
4	14.4	16.2	12.6	1.8	45
5	1.6	1.8	1.4	0.2	5
Total	80	90	70	10	

(c) Expected Cell Frequencies with Collapsed Variable Categories

FAMILY INCOME CATEGORIES	NUMBER OF TVs OWNED CATEGORIES			TOTAL
	1	2	3	
1	32	36	32	100
2	16	18	16	50
3	16	18	16	50
4	16	18	16	50
Total	80	90	80	

Finally, the chi-square contingency test will only indicate whether or not there is a statistically significant relationship between two variables, without providing a meaningful quantitative measure of the strength of the relationship. This limitation can be overcome to some extent by computing certain additional statistics, as described in the next section.

Measuring the degree of association in contingency tables

When the null hypothesis of independence between variables is rejected in a chi-square contingency test, some feeling for the degree of association between the two variables can be obtained by computing a *contingency coefficient* (C) as follows:

$$C = \sqrt{\frac{\chi^2}{n + \chi^2}},$$

where χ^2 is the computed chi-square value and n is the total sample size. In the example pertaining to Table 18.2,

$$C = \sqrt{\frac{17.252}{500 + 17.252}} = .183.$$

The lowest possible value of C is zero, which will occur when $\chi^2 = 0$ (i.e., when there is absolutely no relationship between the two variables). Unfortunately, the upper limit on C is not fixed; it depends on the number of rows and columns in the contingency table and is not necessarily unity. Interpreting the computed value of C is therefore not easy.[2]

When the number of rows and the number of columns in a contingency table are equal, however, the maximum value of C is given by $\sqrt{(r - 1)/r}$, where r is the number of rows (or columns). Since the contingency table in our example has three rows and three columns, the maximum possible value of C is $\sqrt{\frac{2}{3}}$, or .816. This value suggests that the association between working status and expenditure on cosmetics is quite weak; the C-value is only .183 when its range is from 0 (no relationship) to .816 (perfect relationship).

Given the difficulty in interpreting the contingency coefficient, especially when the number of rows and columns in the table are different, a somewhat more useful measure, called *Cramer's V-statistic,* has been proposed. The expression for this statistic is

$$V = \sqrt{\frac{\chi^2}{n(f - 1)}},$$

[2] For further discussion of the difficulty in interpreting the contingency coefficient, see Siegel, *Nonparametric Statistics,* pp. 200–201.

where χ^2 and n are defined as before and f is the smaller of the number of rows and columns in the contingency table, that is, $f = \min(r, c)$. The quantity $n(f - 1)$ is the maximum value that the computed χ^2 can possibly attain for any $r \times c$ contingency table. Therefore $V = 0$ when there is no relationship and $V = 1$ when there is a perfect relationship. Hence, at least from an intuitive standpoint, V is a better measure of degree of association than the contingency coefficient C.[3] In our example

$$V = \sqrt{\frac{17.252}{500(3 - 1)}} = .131.$$

This value of V is consistent with our earlier inference that the degree of association between the two variables is quite weak.

A word of caution about the contingency coefficient and Cramer's V-statistic is in order. Although they seem like precise measures of association between variables, there is a certain amount of arbitrariness built into them. That is, the number of categories created for each variable and how those categories are defined can greatly influence the configuration of the contingency table—and hence the values of these statistics—for the *same* set of raw data.

To illustrate, consider Table 18.4(a). Categorical data on two variables, age and brand of soft drink most preferred, obtained from a sample of 90 respondents are cross-tabulated in Table 18.4(a). This table implies a perfect association between the two variables. Therefore the contingency coefficient C will attain its maximum value of .816 (since the table has three rows and three columns), and Cramer's V-statistic will also attain its maximum value of 1. Let us assume for a moment that 15 of the 30 respondents in the 20–35 age category are 35 years old, and that 15 of the 30 respondents in the 36–50 age category are 50 years old. Also, suppose the following slightly modified age categories are used in constructing the contingency table:

20–34 (instead of 20–35)
35–49 (instead of 36–50)
50 and over (instead of over 50)

With the redefined age categories, the cross-tabulation of the same data will look like the contingency table shown in Table 18.4(b). This table clearly does not suggest as perfect a relationship between the two variables as does Table 18.4(a). Therefore, the contingency coefficient and Cramer's V-statistic corresponding to Table 18.4(b) will be lower than their maximum possible values (you can verify this result).

In short, numbers representing the degree of association on the basis of a contingency table can be very sensitive to how the table is constructed. They are

[3] For additional details, see, for example, Jean Dickinson Gibbons, *Nonparametric Methods for Quantitative Analysis* (New York: Holt, Rinehart and Winston, 1976), pp. 330–339.

Table 18.4

Association between age and brand of soft drink most preferred

(a) Original Contingency Table

AGE	MOST PREFERRED BRAND			TOTAL
	A	B	C	
20–35	30	0	0	30
36–50	0	30	0	30
Over 50	0	0	30	30
Total	30	30	30	

(b) Contingency Table with Revised Age Categories

AGE	MOST PREFERRED BRAND			TOTAL
	A	B	C	
20–34	15	0	0	15
35–49	15	15	0	30
50 and over	0	15	30	45
Total	30	30	30	

hence not as precise as measures of association for metric-scaled variables (called correlation coefficients, which we will discuss a little later). After all, as we saw earlier, analysis of nonmetric data cannot yield as rich and refined results as analysis of metric data.

SPEARMAN CORRELATION COEFFICIENT

The chi-square contingency test and the corresponding *C*- and *V*-statistics can be used for examining the association between variables whose categories are ordinal. However, a more powerful measure of association between two ordinal variables, called the *Spearman correlation coefficient* (r_s), can be computed when the data are refined enough to rank the sample units 1 through *n* on each variable. Consider the following example.

EXAMPLE: Over the past several years an industrial marketing firm has been hiring all its salespeople from among the graduates of 10 business schools in the vicinity of its headquarters. To ascertain whether there is any association between the relative prestige of the 10 schools and the performance of the graduates hired from each, the firm's sales managers developed a sub-

Table 18.5

Association between school prestige and performance of graduates

BUSINESS SCHOOL (i)	RANKING OF SCHOOL'S PRESTIGE (SP_i)	RANKING OF PERFORMANCE OF SCHOOL'S GRADUATES (GP_i)	DIFFERENCE BETWEEN RANKS ($d_i = SP_i - GP_i$)	SQUARED DIFFERENCE (d_i^2)
1	10	8	2	4
2	7	3	4	16
3	9	7	2	4
4	1	2	−1	1
5	6	9	−3	9
6	2	4	−2	4
7	3	5	−2	4
8	8	10	−2	4
9	5	6	−1	1
10	4	1	3	9

$$\sum_{i=1}^{10} d_i^2 = 56$$

jective ranking of the perceived prestige levels of the 10 schools and the performance levels of the groups of graduates recruited from these schools. These rankings are shown in the second and third columns of Table 18.5. What is the degree of association between the prestige levels of the schools and the sales performance levels of their graduates hired by this company?

A Spearman correlation coefficient is appropriate for answering the question posed in this situation. It is a widely used measure of association between two sets of ranks. The formula for computing it is

$$r_s = 1 - \frac{6\sum_{i=1}^{n} d_i^2}{n(n^2 - 1)},$$

where d_i is the difference between the ith sample unit's ranks on the two variables and n is the total sample size. Notice that $r_s = 1$ when the sum of the d_i^2 values is zero, that is, when the two sets of ranks are identical.[4] The range of

[4] For a discussion of the derivation and interpretation of the formula for r_s, see Siegel, *Nonparametric Statistics,* pp. 202–213. This text also discusses the treatment of tied ranks.

possible values for r_s is +1 (perfect direct association) to −1 (perfect inverse association), with a value of 0 signifying no association.

As shown in the last column of Table 18.5, the value of $\Sigma\, d_i^2$ in our example is 56. Therefore

$$r_s = 1 - \frac{(6)(56)}{10(100 - 1)} = 1 - .339 = .661.$$

The r_s-value of .661 suggests at least a moderate association between the two sets of ranks. Is this association statistically significant? Answering this question involves assuming that the 10 schools are a random sample from a population of business schools and testing these hypotheses:

$$H_o: \rho_s = 0;$$
$$H_a: \rho_s \neq 0;$$

where ρ_s is the population correlation coefficient between the two sets of ranks. When $n \geq 10$, the following *test statistic* will have a *t-distribution* with $n - 2$ degrees of freedom:

$$t = r_s \sqrt{\frac{n - 2}{1 - r_s^2}}.$$

This hypothesis test is a two-tailed test. Assuming a significance level of .05, the critical values of t for 8 degrees of freedom (d.f. $= n - 2 = 10 - 2 = 8$) are +2.31 and −2.31. Hence the decision rule is, "Reject H_o if $t > 2.31$ *or* if $t < -2.31$." In the present example

$$t = .661 \sqrt{\frac{10 - 2}{1 - (.661)^2}} = .661 \sqrt{\frac{8}{1 - .437}}$$
$$= (.661)(3.770) = 2.49.$$

Since $t > 2.31$, we reject H_o and conclude that there is a true association between the prestige of business schools and the job performance of its graduates. In other words, the sample correlation of .661 is unlikely to have occurred because of chance.

Note that the basis for determining r_s is the computation of differences between pairs of ranks, an operation that is apparently inconsistent with the notion that it is inappropriate to place any meaning on the magnitude of the difference between numbers forming only an ordinal scale. Indeed, in computing r_s one is implicitly assuming that the differences between ranks on the two variables can be meaningfully compared. If such an assumption is unreasonable, the Spearman correlation coefficient may be misleading.

PEARSON CORRELATION COEFFICIENT

The *Pearson correlation coefficient* (also known as the *Pearson product-moment correlation*) is appropriate for measuring the degree of association between variables that are interval- or ratio-scaled. It is a more refined measure than the ones we have discussed so far. The Pearson correlation coefficient is insightful in its own right and also plays a key role in advanced multivariate analysis procedures.

To illustrate the computation and interpretation of the Pearson correlation coefficient, let us consider some data gathered by a firm selling Bright detergent in numerous market areas nationwide. Table 18.6 contains data from a sample of 20 market areas for the following variables: the revenues generated by sales of Bright during a one-month period, the advertising expenditures for Bright dur-

Table 18.6
Data gathered by marketer of Bright detergent

MARKET AREA	DOLLAR SALES OF BRIGHT (THOUSANDS)	ADVERTISING EXPENDITURES FOR BRIGHT ($)	NUMBER OF COMPETING DETERGENTS
1	5	500	15
2	10	1300	8
3	6	500	14
4	20	1500	5
5	15	1000	9
6	9	900	10
7	11	500	12
8	18	1300	4
9	22	1700	6
10	7	600	13
11	24	1900	2
12	14	1200	8
13	16	1500	6
14	17	1400	7
15	23	1800	1
16	8	700	11
17	12	1000	10
18	13	1200	7
19	21	1600	7
20	19	1600	3

ing that period, and the number of competing detergent brands being sold in each market area.

Notice that the data in Table 18.6 are metric data; indeed, all three variables are ratio-scaled. Therefore as a first step in understanding the association between any two of the variables, we can plot the corresponding data on a two-dimensional graph. Such a plot is called a *scatter diagram,* and it can indicate how closely and in what fashion the variables are associated. Exhibit 18.1 shows a scatter diagram of the sales and advertising data; Exhibit 18.2 shows a plot of sales versus number of competing brands.

The scatter diagram in Exhibit 18.1 clearly shows a direct relationship between dollar sales and advertising expenditures: In general, the higher the advertising expenditures, the higher the sales are. Also, the swarm of points in the diagram seems to follow a *linear trend.* We will have more to say about this linear trend later when we discuss regression analysis. However, we note here that the existence of a linear scatter is a prerequisite for the meaningfulness of the Pearson correlation coefficient, because it is only designed to capture the extent of linear association between variables.

Exhibit 18.1

Scatter diagram of sales and advertising data

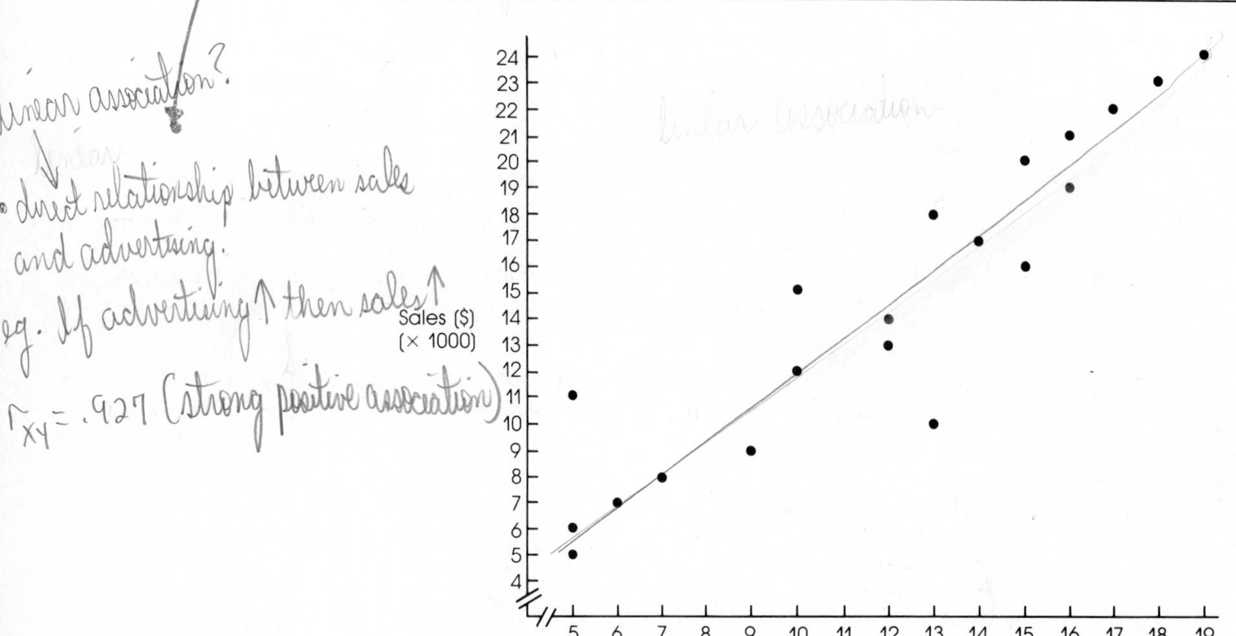

Exhibit 18.2

Scatter diagram of sales and number of competing brands data

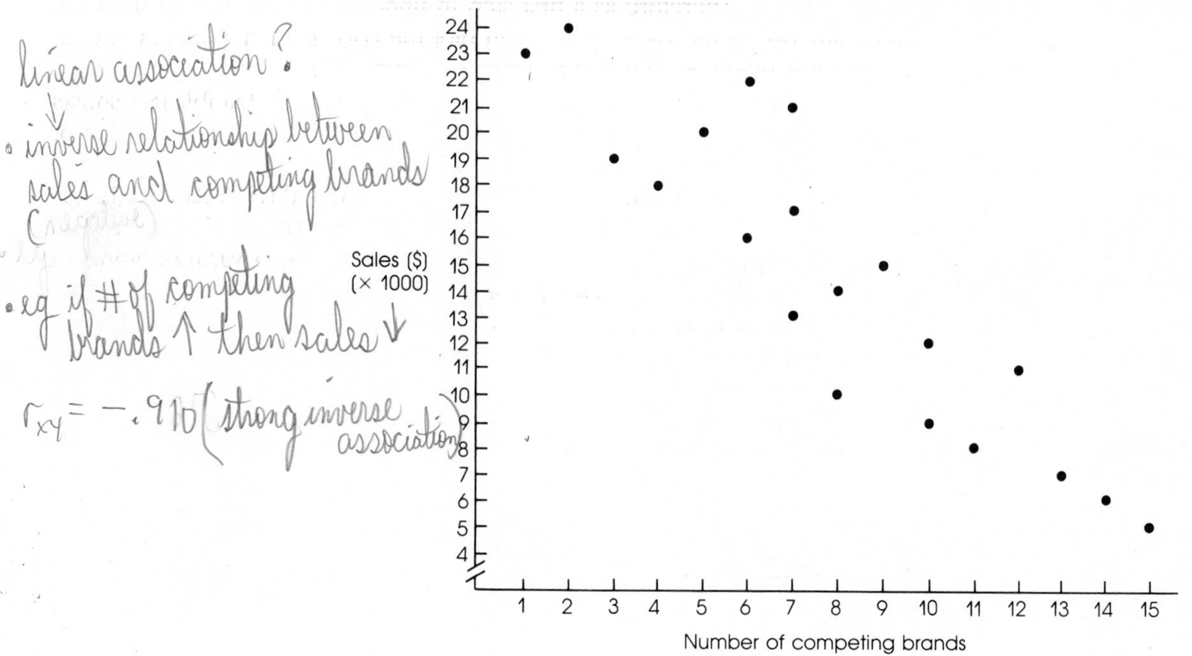

Two other key assumptions that must be met, especially for making statistical inferences based on the Pearson correlation coefficient, are the following:

1. The two variables have a bivariate normal distribution. That is, the population is such that all units with a given value of one variable have values on the second variable that are normally distributed.
2. The variance of the normal distribution of one variable at any given value of the other variable remains the same across various values of the latter variable.

These assumptions are hard to verify by using sample data and are often taken for granted.[5]

The scatter diagram in Exhibit 18.2 also displays an underlying linear association between sales and number of competing brands. Notice, however, that this

[5] Further discussion of these assumptions can be found in many statistics textbooks; see, for example, David R. Anderson, Dennis J. Sweeney, and Thomas A. Williams, *Introduction to Statistics: An Applications Approach* (St. Paul, Minn.: West, 1981), pp. 343–345.

trend is an inverse one; that is, in general, the greater the number of competing brands, the lower the sales of Bright are. Exhibit 18.2 thus suggests a fairly strong, but negative, association between sales and number of competing brands.

The direction and the degree of association between two variables shown graphically by a scatter diagram, such as the ones in Exhibits 18.1 and 18.2, can be quantified in a single number, which is the Pearson correlation coefficient. When the two variables are labeled X and Y, the Pearson correlation coefficient (r_{XY}) between them is given by

$$r_{XY} = \frac{\sum_{i=1}^{n} (X_i - \bar{X})(Y_i - \bar{Y})}{(n - 1)s_X s_Y},$$

where n is the sample size (total number of data points), X_i and Y_i are values for any sample unit i, $\bar{X}$ and $\bar{Y}$ are means, and s_X and s_Y are standard deviations. The derivation of this formula and a discussion of the rationale underlying its interpretation are provided in the appendix to this chapter.

Correlation coefficients are easily calculated by using readily available computer packages once a data set (such as the one in Table 18.6) has been created. But if one wants to calculate correlation coefficients by hand, a shortcut formula that is easier to use than the expression given here is available in basic statistics textbooks.[6]

Pearson correlation coefficients, like Spearman coefficients, can range from +1 to −1. The sign of a correlation coefficient indicates the direction of association, while its magnitude indicates the strength of association. In our example the correlation between sales and advertising turns out to be .927. This value reaffirms the strong positive association suggested by the scatter diagram in Exhibit 18.1. Consistent with our interpretation of the scatter diagram in Exhibit 18.2, the correlation between sales and number of competing brands is −.910 (a strong inverse association).

The sample correlation coefficient r can itself serve as the test statistic in conducting a two-tailed test of the following hypotheses:

$$H_o: \rho = 0;$$
$$H_a: \rho \neq 0;$$

where ρ is the population correlation coefficient. The degrees of freedom associated with r are $n - 1$, and its critical values are tabled in Appendix E. In our example, for $\alpha = .05$ and 19 degrees of freedom (d.f. $= n - 1 = 19$), the critical values are $r_c = +.433$ and $r_c = -.433$. The decision rule is, "Reject H_o if $r > .433$ *or* if $r < -.433$." Applying this decision rule to the .927 correlation between

[6] See, for example, Anderson, Sweeney, and Williams, *Introduction to Statistics,* p. 357.

sales and advertising and to the −.910 correlation between sales and number of competing brands, we should reject H_0 in both cases.

While Pearson correlation coefficients are extremely helpful in uncovering bivariate associations, there are two important caveats concerning their use. First, a low sample correlation (or a failure to reject H_0) does not necessarily mean there is *no* association; it only implies an absence of *linear* association. Exhibit 18.3 illustrates this point. The scatter diagram in this figure clearly shows a strong U-shaped relationship between X and Y. Yet the Pearson correlation coefficient in this case will be close to zero, since there is no discernible linear trend when the data points are considered together. The moral: Even if the Pearson correlation coefficient is very small or not statistically significant, one should explore the possible presence of a *nonlinear* association, especially when intuitive or theoretical considerations suggest that the variables may be related. Perhaps the simplest way of exploring a nonlinear association is to plot and visually examine a scatter diagram.

Second, as has been pointed out earlier in the book, existence of a correlation by itself is not sufficient to infer causation between variables. For instance, the correlation of .927 between sales and advertising does not necessarily imply that increased advertising expenditures will lead to increased sales, although it is tempting to draw such a conclusion. The only thing this correlation says is that

Exhibit 18.3

Scatter diagram showing a nonlinear association between variables

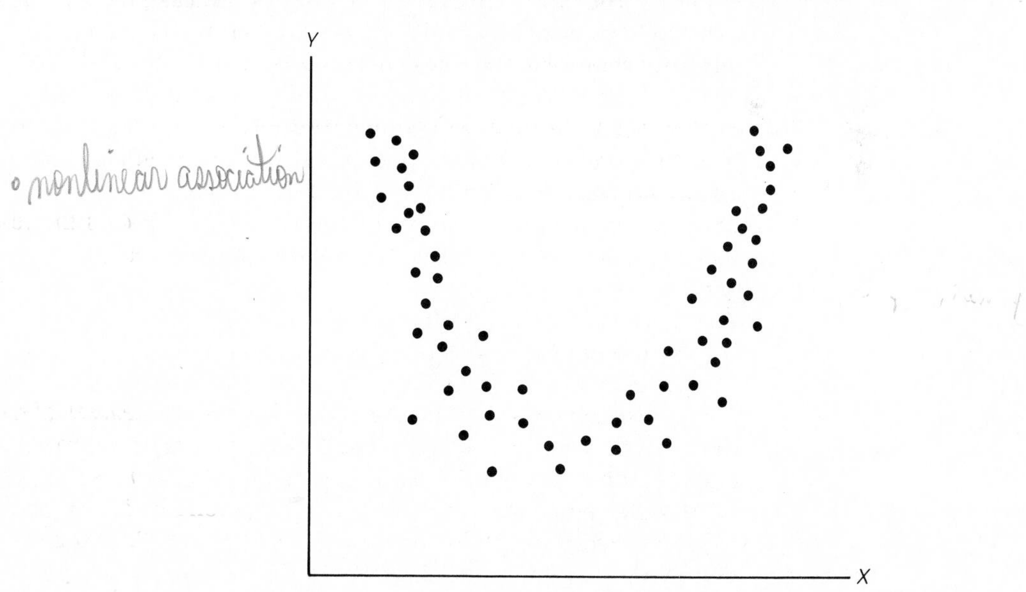

the data on the two variables follow a very similar pattern in the 20 markets studied. But this pattern may be a result of a causal linkage going from sales to advertising, rather than the other way around. For example, anticipation of a certain level of sales in each market may have dictated a correspondingly low or high advertising expenditure level. Thus unless all other relevant factors are controlled or accounted for, to infer a certain direction of causality between variables simply on the basis of a correlation coefficient is dangerous.

SIMPLE REGRESSION ANALYSIS

Simple *regression analysis* is somewhat similar to the procedure involved in computing the Pearson correlation coefficient between two variables. A technique called *multiple regression* analysis is not unlike simple regression analysis, but it involves examining associations among more than two variables. We will cover multiple regression analysis in the next section after laying the foundation for the general regression technique in this section.

Correlation and regression analyses have a lot in common. Nevertheless, there are a few subtle differences between the two in terms of purpose and assumptions.

First, while correlation analysis focuses on summarizing the degree and the direction of association between variables as a single number, the purpose of regression analysis is to generate a mathematical function or equation linking those variables. The resulting equation is called a *regression equation.*

Second, when we are examining the association between two variables, the notion of a presumed causal variable is much more germane to regression analysis than to correlation analysis. (Recall that we introduced the concept of a presumed causal variable in Chapter 16 while discussing two-way tabulations.) Specifically, in simple regression analysis we must designate one of the two variables as the *independent variable,* which is also known as an explanatory or predictor variable. The variable so designated is often presumed to be a cause of the other, and it is conventionally plotted along the *X*-axis in a scatter diagram. The second variable—the one presumed to be influenced by the independent variable—is appropriately called the *dependent* (or sometimes criterion) *variable,* and it is traditionally plotted along the *Y*-axis.

Third, while the assumptions about statistical properties of the input data necessary for correlation analysis are, in general, also required for regression analysis, there is one major difference: In regression analysis only the dependent variable is random; the independent variable is implicitly treated as a fixed variable. Stated differently, in generating the input data for regression analysis, one is supposed to set the independent variable (being presumed as a causal factor) at a variety of specific or fixed levels, at each of which one observes the nature of the distribution of values for the dependent variable. Furthermore, the dispersion (or variance) of dependent-variable values at each level for the independent variable should be approximately the same. That is, if one were to measure the width of a scatter diagram (i.e., swarm of points) in the vertical direction at various locations along the *X*-axis, such widths should be roughly equal. Although these requirements are not always strictly met in practice, they are important to the theory underlying the derivation and interpretation of a mathematical relationship between the dependent and the independent variables.[7]

DERIVING A REGRESSION EQUATION

A scatter diagram is useful for developing a conceptual understanding of the process involved in constructing a regression equation. We will once again use the data on sales and advertising and the corresponding scatter diagram in Exhibit 18.1 for this purpose. Between sales and advertising, suppose management has reason to presume that the latter is the likely causal variable; that is, advertising expenditures for Bright detergent in the 20 market areas were not influenced by past or anticipated sales of Bright. Advertising is hence the independent variable and is plotted along the *X*-axis in Exhibit 18.1. Sales, the implied dependent variable, is plotted along the *Y*-axis. The resulting scatter diagram's linear trend can be summarized by constructing an appropriate upward-sloping straight line through it. Any straight line constructed on a two-dimensional graph can be mathematically represented by the following type of equation linking the *X*- and *Y*-variables:

$$Y = a + bX,$$

where a and b are constants. An equation of this form is what regression analysis of data is intended to generate.

How does one construct an appropriate straight line through the scatter diagram? One obvious approach is to visually scan the scatter diagram and subjectively construct a line that appears to fit it well. The problem with this approach, however, is that it is unlikely to produce one unique line; several different lines may all seem to fit the scatter diagram equally well, as Exhibit 18.4 demonstrates. Clearly, then, a more objective procedure is needed to identify *the* best-fitting line. One such widely used procedure, called the *least-squares approach,* is discussed in the appendix to this chapter.

Statistical packages available on most computers are capable of performing least-squares regression analysis. They can provide the values of a and b as well as a variety of statistics for evaluating the regression equation. Exhibit 18.5 shows

[7] Further discussion of the rationale for this requirement and the extent to which one can deviate from it without reducing the meaningfulness of the resulting regression equation is beyond the scope of this textbook; consult an advanced multivariate statistics book, such as J. Johnston, *Econometric Methods* (New York: McGraw-Hill, 1984).

Exhibit 18.4
Several subjectively constructed regression lines

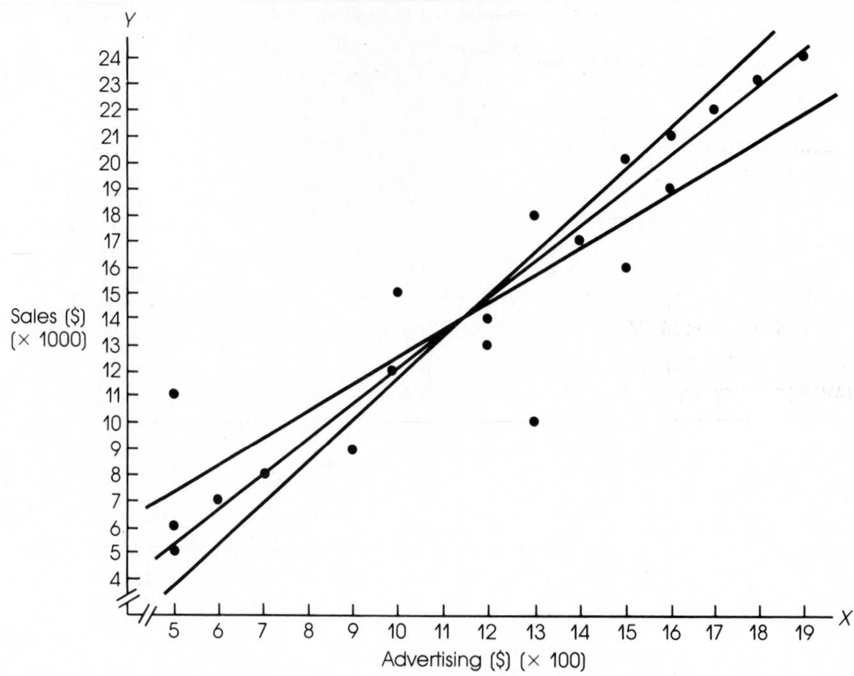

the computer output (produced by an SPSS program) for the regression analysis of the sales and advertising data.

We have not yet discussed all the regression analysis concepts necessary for fully understanding this output. Hence we will be making reference to this exhibit as and when we cover each concept. Here, let us simply get the values of a and b from the exhibit. These values are shown under the column labeled B in the lower half of the output. Specifically, the number corresponding to ADVTG (the name given to the advertising variable in this program) in this column is the value of b. The number immediately below that number is the value of a. Rounding these values to three decimal places, we have

$$a = .163,$$
$$b = 1.210.$$

The regression equation is

$$\hat{Y}_i = .163 + 1.210X_i,$$

Exhibit 18.5

SPSS computer output for simple regression analysis of sales and advertising data

MULTIPLE REGRESSION

DEPENDENT VARIABLE. . SALES VARIABLE LIST 1
VARIABLE(S) ENTERED ON STEP NUMBER 1. . ADVTG REGRESSION LIST 1

		ANALYSIS OF VARIANCE	DF	SUM OF SQUARES	MEAN SQUARE	F
MULTIPLE R	0.92716					
R SQUARE	0.85962	REGRESSION	1.	571.64576	571.64576	110.22127
ADJUSTED R SQUARE	0.85182	RESIDUAL	18.	93.35424	5.18635	
STANDARD ERROR	2.27736					

VARIABLES IN THE EQUATION

VARIABLE	B	BETA	STD ERROR B	F
ADVTG	1.209832	0.92716	0.11524	110.221
(CONSTANT)	0.1634874			

VARIABLES NOT IN THE EQUATION

VARIABLE	BETA IN	PARTIAL	TOLERANCE	F

MAXIMUM STEP REACHED

STATISTICS WHICH CANNOT BE COMPUTED ARE PRINTED AS ALL NINES.

where $\hat{Y}_i$ is the value of sales (in thousands of dollars) *predicted* by the regression equation for an advertising expenditure level of X_i (in hundreds of dollars).

When $X_i = 0$, $\hat{Y}_i = .163$, which is the constant a. The a in a regression equation is known as the *Y-intercept* and represents the predicted value of the dependent variable corresponding to a value of zero for the independent variable.

The constant b, representing the coefficient of X_i, is known as the *slope* of the regression equation. The slope has a very important interpretation: *It represents the change in the predicted value of the dependent variable per one-unit change in the independent variable,* assuming that all other variables likely to influence the dependent variable remain the same. In our example, since sales are measured in thousands of dollars and advertising expenditures are measured in hundreds of dollars, the value of 1.210 for b implies the following: If advertising expenditures are increased (or decreased) by \$100 (which constitutes one unit of advertising), sales can be predicted to increase (or decrease) by \$1210 (which constitutes 1.210 units of sales), assuming no other relevant factor changes.

EVALUATING THE REGRESSION EQUATION

We have seen that the least-squares procedure will yield the best possible straight line and corresponding regression equation for a given data set. However, when the data set leads to a scatter diagram that is widely dispersed, as opposed to falling within a relatively narrow linear band that follows an upward- or downward-sloping trend, the usefulness of the resulting regression equation is questionable. Stated differently, the least-squares procedure will always yield a regression equation; but how trustworthy the equation is depends on how compact the scatter diagram is and how closely it resembles a linear trend.

To illustrate, consider the two scatter diagrams shown in Exhibit 18.6. Suppose a least-squares analysis of either diagram results in the same regression equation (i.e., same *a*- and *b*-values). But, intuitively, the regression equation stemming from the scatter diagram of Exhibit 18.6(a) will be more trustworthy and valuable than one stemming from the diagram of Exhibit 18.6(b). Clearly, then, we need objective criteria for evaluating the *goodness* of the regression equation. One such criterion is called the *coefficient of determination,* denoted by R^2. The coefficient of determination is a global measure of how much better predictions of the dependent variable made with the aid of the regression equation are than those made without.

For a given value of X, what is the best prediction of Y *without* using the regression equation? The best prediction should be $\overline{Y}$, the mean value of the dependent variable. While $\overline{Y}$ will greatly underpredict some actual values and greatly overpredict others, on the average (over a number of such predictions), the overpredictions and underpredictions will cancel out.

For any given value of X_i the deviation between the actual and the mean values of Y—that is, $(Y_i - \overline{Y})$—is called the *total deviation in Y.* The sum of the total squared deviations—that is, $(Y_i - \overline{Y})^2$ added across all data points in the scatter diagram—is a measure of the variation in Y about its mean value. This sum is conventionally called the *total sum of squares,* denoted by SS_T. Part of SS_T can be accounted for, or explained, when an appropriate regression equation is

Exhibit 18.6

Two identical regression lines based on different scatter diagrams

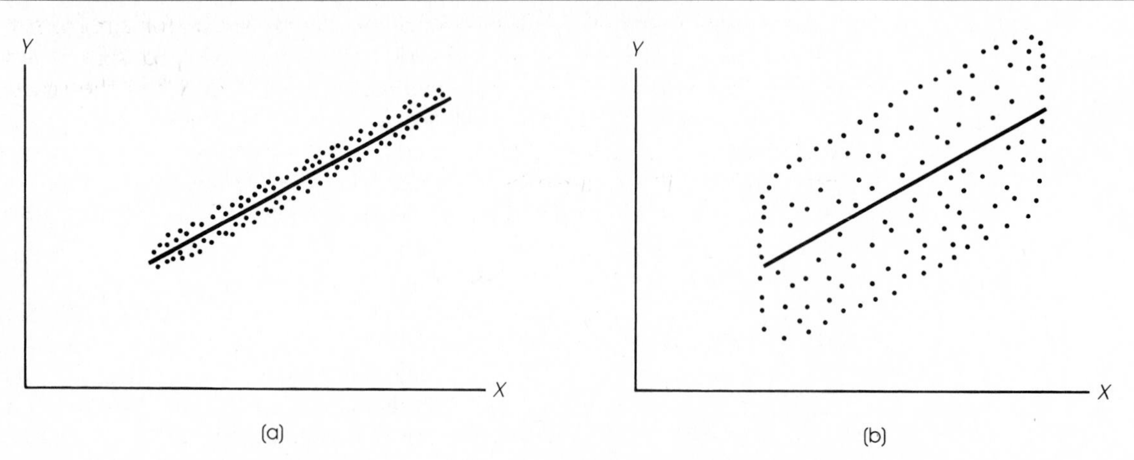

available. The variance thus explained is called the *regression sum of squares,* SS_R. The variance left unexplained by the regression equation is called the *residual,* or *error, sum of squares,* SS_E. It can be shown that $SS_T = SS_R + SS_E$. The procedure for doing so is called partitioning the total sum of squares, which is illustrated briefly in the chapter appendix.

The least-squares procedure fits a straight line through the scatter diagram such that SS_E has the smallest possible value. Since SS_T is fixed by the input data on Y, the SS_R corresponding to the best-fit line will have the highest possible value. Intuitively, the higher the value of SS_R for a given value of SS_T, the better the regression equation should be. Therefore a good way to see whether a regression equation is trustworthy is to examine the ratio between SS_R and SS_T, which is exactly what the coefficient of determination R^2 accomplishes:

$$R^2 = \frac{\text{variance explained by the regression equation}}{\text{total variance}} = \frac{SS_R}{SS_T}.$$

The right-hand half of the computer output in Exhibit 18.5 contains the values of SS_R and SS_E under the heading SUM OF SQUARES. Rounding the values to three decimal places, we obtain

$$SS_R = 571.646$$
$$SS_E = 93.354$$
$$SS_T = SS_R + SS_E = 665$$
$$R^2 = \frac{SS_R}{SS_T} = \frac{571.646}{665} = .860$$

Thus from the regression equation in our example, advertising expenditures can be said to explain about 86% of the total variance in sales.

The range of possible values for R^2 is from 0 to 1. The R^2 for a regression equation corresponding to a scatter diagram that displays no apparent upward- (or downward-) sloping linear trend will be close to zero. When the scatter diagram forms a perfectly horizontal swarm of points, the regression line will coincide with a horizontal line constructed at $Y = \bar{Y}$. Predictions based on such a regression line will, of course, be no better than those given by $\bar{Y}$, and hence R^2 will be zero. What will R^2 be when all the data points in a scatter diagram fall exactly on a downward- or upward-sloping straight line? In such a case SS_E will be zero, SS_R will be the same as SS_T, and R^2 will be 1.

The value of R^2 we computed as the ratio SS_R/SS_T is also shown in Exhibit 18.5, next to the label R SQUARE. The ADJUSTED R SQUARE value immediately below it is a corrected value that takes into account the number of data points available for constructing the regression line vis-à-vis the number of independent variables. The adjusted R^2 will invariably be lower than the original R^2. Discussion of why and how this correction is made is beyond the scope of this textbook.[8] Hereafter, for interpretive purposes we will examine only the unadjusted R^2-values.

The item labeled MULTIPLE R in the computer output is simply the square root of R^2. It is generally known as the *multiple correlation coefficient* and represents the overall degree of association between the dependent and independent variables. Since there are only two variables in our example, the multiple correlation coefficient of .927 is equivalent to the Pearson correlation coefficient between sales and advertising. In any bivariate regression analysis the square of the Pearson correlation coefficient between the dependent and independent variables will be the same as the value of the coefficient of determination.

Testing the significance of R^2

The R^2-value is an important measure of how trustworthy a regression equation is: The higher the R^2-value, the more trustworthy the equation is. Nevertheless, the regression equation and its R^2-value are based only on sample data. Thus depending on the nature of the data, one may sometimes obtain a high R^2-value when there is really no association between the dependent and independent variables in the *population*. For instance, suppose data on sales and advertising expenditures are obtained from a sample of just two markets chosen at random from a population of all such markets. A scatter diagram of these data will consist of just two points. We can fit a straight line through these points no matter where they are on the two-dimensional graph. Thus R^2 will be 1 since the fit will be perfect. But we cannot trust this regression line to be an accurate representation of any underlying association between sales and advertising. Thus a high R^2-value by itself is necessary *but not sufficient* to conclude that a regression equation is trustworthy.

A suitable test is needed to verify whether a nonzero R^2-value stemming from a sample regression line is truly reflective of an underlying linear association in the population. Whether a sample R^2-value is significantly greater than zero can be checked by computing the following *F-statistic:*

$$F = \frac{SS_R/k}{SS_E/n - k - 1},$$

where k is the number of independent variables included in the equation and n is the sample size (i.e., the number of data points).

To determine the critical value of F, we need to specify two types of degrees

[8] For details, see any advanced book on regression analysis, such as Ronald J. Wonnacott and Thomas H. Wonnacott, *Econometrics* (New York: Wiley, 1970), p. 311.

of freedom associated with the F statistic: the numerator degrees of freedom, given by k, and the denominator degrees of freedom, given by $n - k - 1$. Critical values of F are tabled in Appendix F for the customary significance level (α) of .05. In our example $k = 1$ and $n - k - 1 = 18$. For these numerator and denominator degrees of freedom, the critical value of F from Appendix F is 4.41. The decision rule implied in this F-test is to *reject* the null hypothesis that R^2 is not significantly greater than zero if the computed F-statistic value is *greater* than its critical value.

The computed F-statistic value in our example is given by

$$F = \frac{571.646/1}{93.354/18} = \frac{571.646}{5.186} = 110.229.$$

Since this F is greater than the critical F, we can infer that the R^2-value of .860 is statistically significant—it is unlikely to have occurred because of some idiosyncrasy in the sample data.

Now that we have covered the mechanics of conducting an F-test, let us formally define a couple of other important concepts implicit in the test, concepts that will be helpful in understanding certain other techniques to be covered later. One such concept is the *mean square,* which is simply a sum-of-squares value divided by its corresponding degrees of freedom. Both the numerator of the F-statistic (SS_R/k) and its denominator ($SS_E/n - k - 1$) are thus mean squares. Specifically, SS_R/k is the *regression mean square* and can be interpreted as the average sum of the squared variations explained per independent variable. Term $SS_E/n - k - 1$ is the *error mean square* (or *residual mean square*) and can be roughly interpreted as the average sum of the squared variations (per data point) left unexplained by the regression equation. With these interpretations you can see why a high regression mean square and a low error mean square, and the resulting high F-value, will tend to support an inference that the R^2-value is statistically significant. The mean square values and the corresponding F-value are provided by the computer output (see Exhibit 18.5). These values differ slightly from those we calculated earlier because of rounding.

The square root of the error mean square is called the *standard error of the regression.* Conceptually, it is a sort of standard deviation of the portion of the variation in the dependent variable left unexplained by the independent variable (or variables in a multiple regression equation). The conventional notation used for the standard error associated with a simple regression equation is $s_{Y/X}$. It is given by

$$s_{Y/X} = \sqrt{\frac{SS_E}{n - k - 1}}.$$

The value of the standard error ($s_{Y/X}$) is shown in the computer output (Exhibit 18.5) as 2.277, which is the square root of the error mean square value of 5.186. The concept of standard error is crucial in constructing confidence intervals around the predictions made by a regression equation. It is also relevant for evaluating whether the slope is significantly different from zero, as discussed next.

Testing the significance of the slope

An important element of evaluating the usefulness of a regression equation is checking whether the coefficient associated with an independent variable is significantly different from zero. A regression equation based on sample data (namely, $\hat{Y}_i = a + bX_i$) is a crude reflection of an underlying population regression equation, $\hat{Y}_i = \alpha + \beta X_i$, which can be constructed if data from all the population units are available. In other words, the slope b is merely a sample estimate of the population parameter β. Testing the statistical significance of the slope involves testing the following hypotheses:

$$H_o: \beta = 0,$$
$$H_a: \beta \neq 0.$$

The appropriate test statistic here is a t-statistic defined as

$$t = \frac{b - \beta}{s_b},$$

where s_b is the standard error associated with b and is given by

$$s_b = \sqrt{\frac{s_{Y/X}^2}{(n - 1)s_X^2}},$$

where s_X is the standard deviation of the independent variable whose slope is being evaluated. The degrees of freedom for the t-statistic are $n - k - 1$ (d.f. = 18 in our example), and the hypothesis test is two-tailed. The critical values of t from Appendix D for a significance level of .05 are +2.10 and −2.10. Therefore we should reject H_o if $t > 2.10$ or if $t < -2.10$.

Before computing t, we need to determine s_b. The standard deviation of advertising (s_X) turns out to be 4.534. Hence

$$s_b = \sqrt{\frac{(2.277)^2}{(20 - 1)(4.534)^2}} = .115$$

This value is shown under STD ERROR B in the computer output in Exhibit 18.5. Thus t is

$$t = \frac{b - \beta}{s_b} = \frac{1.210 - 0}{.115} = 10.522$$

Since $t > 2.10$, we can reject H_o and conclude that the slope of 1.210 is significantly different from zero.

In simple regression analysis the t-test for checking the significance of b is equivalent to the F-test for checking the significance of R^2. Indeed, the t-statistic value is simply the square root of the F-statistic value associated with R^2 (you can verify this statement in our example). The equivalence of the two tests can also be seen by picturing the nature of the true regression line when β is zero: The line will be perfectly horizontal, implying thereby that R^2 should be zero. Similarly, when the true R^2 is zero, β should also be zero. In multiple regression analysis, however, there is one overall F-test but several t-tests, one for each b-value. Therefore the notion of equivalence between the F-test for R^2 and the t-tests is not very meaningful (this topic is discussed more fully later).

One final comment concerning the computer output in Exhibit 18.5: The number under the heading BETA is *not* the value of the true regression line's slope, β. Rather, it is simply the *standardized regression coefficient,* that is, the b-value when the data on all the variables are standardized (reduced to a mean of zero and a standard deviation of one) before performing the least-squares regression analysis. Standardized regression coefficients are useful in multiple regression analysis because their magnitudes can be compared across independent variables so as to gain insight into the relative influence of each on the dependent variable.

PRACTICAL APPLICATIONS OF REGRESSION EQUATIONS

Thus far we have covered quite a few details about constructing, interpreting, and evaluating regression equations. Let us now pause to look at some practical applications of simple regression equations before we discuss multiple regression equations.

Let us assume that a regression equation is trustworthy—that is, has a high enough and statistically significant R^2-value. (There is no rule telling us what R^2-value can be considered to be high enough; for practical purposes, however, R^2-values of around .7 or higher are usually adequate.) The regression equation can be helpful in two ways.

First, the regression coefficient, or slope, can indicate how sensitive the dependent variable is to changes in the independent variable. To illustrate, suppose the firm marketing Bright detergent currently spends $2000 on advertising the detergent in a particular market. It is considering a 20% reduction in its advertising budget and wants to know by how much sales revenue might decline in this market as a result. The information the firm desires can be obtained from the slope b of the regression equation we derived:

$$b = 1.210,$$

which, taking into account the units of measurement of X and Y, means that sales revenue will decline by $1210 for every $100 reduction in advertising expenditures. Also

$$\begin{aligned}\text{proposed reduction in advertising expenditures} &= 2000 \times .2\\ &= \$400.\end{aligned}$$

Therefore

$$\text{anticipated decline in sales revenue} = \frac{1210 \times 400}{100} = \$4840.$$

Second, the regression equation is a forecasting tool for predicting the value of the dependent variable for a given value of the independent variable. For example, suppose the firm marketing Bright wants to forecast sales revenue from a market in which it intends to spend $750 on advertising the detergent. The needed forecast can be obtained by simply substituting the value of 7.50 for X_i (recall that advertising expenditures are expressed in hundreds of dollars in the regression equation) into the regression equation and solving for $\hat{Y}_i$:

$$\begin{aligned}\hat{Y}_i &= .163 + 1.210X_i = .163 + 1.210(7.5)\\ &= .163 + 9.075 = 9.238.\end{aligned}$$

Since sales revenue is expressed in thousands of dollars in the regression equation, the forecast in dollars is given by

$$9.238 \times 1000 = \$9238.$$

Most practical applications of regression analysis revolve around some form of forecasting. Not all applications are for forecasting sales, however. The examples in Table 18.7 demonstrate a wide variety of circumstances in which regression analysis can provide valuable insights. This table briefly describes three scenarios in which the decision makers may benefit by conducting appropriate simple regression analyses. The table also suggests a pair of relevant dependent and independent variables for each scenario.

Table 18.7
Illustrative scenarios calling for regression analysis

SCENARIO	POSSIBLE DEPENDENT VARIABLE	POSSIBLE INDEPENDENT VARIABLE
Curtis is a construction industry lobbyist in an area of the country that is economically depressed. His current charge is to convince local government officials to vote in favor of several tax concessions for the construction industry. He is wondering whether he can generate any concrete evidence to show that increased construction activity (presumably spurred by the proposed tax concessions) would greatly benefit the state.	Number of people unemployed or the unemployment rate; data on this variable may be gathered from a sample of areas from around the country.	Number of construction permits issued or number of ongoing construction projects; data on this variable should be gathered from the same sample areas.
Carol, chief librarian in a major university, is eager to increase the number of students borrowing books from the library as well as the number of books borrowed per student. However, she feels that she needs some persuasive evidence to show how increased borrowing of books might benefit them.	Cumulative grade point ratio; data on this variable should be gathered for a sample of students who have borrowed books in the past.	Number of books borrowed; assuming that the library has records of the books borrowed by students, data on this variable can be obtained from those records for the same sample of students.
Jack, an officer in an association in charge of putting together and promoting industrial trade shows, is wondering about the nature and the extent of the impact that the number of exhibitors in a trade show has on trade show attendance.	Number of people visiting a trade show; from the association's past records data on this variable can be obtained for a representative sample of trade shows.	Number of exhibitors in a trade show; here, again, the necessary data can be obtained from past records.

PRECAUTIONS IN USING REGRESSION ANALYSIS

The wide popularity of regression analysis and the ready access to computer programs capable of performing it offer a strong temptation to researchers to rush into using the technique without ascertaining whether it is appropriate and without giving much thought to its pitfalls. However, potential users of regression analysis must be aware of several key limitations that, if ignored, can result in erroneous inferences. This section will discuss the limitations in the context of simple regression analysis; the same limitations are also applicable to multiple regression analysis (to be discussed in the next section).

First, just as in the case of correlation analysis, regression analysis is only capable of capturing *linear* associations between dependent and independent variables. The regression technique we have covered is not appropriate when the scatter diagram does not display a meaningful linear trend.[9] Whenever possible, one should first plot the data on the relevant variables and examine the nature of the scatter diagram.

Second, a regression equation with a significant R^2-value does not necessarily imply a *cause-and-effect* association between the independent and dependent variables. This point is particularly noteworthy; the convention of labeling one variable "dependent" and the other "independent" may persuade careless researchers into thinking that the former is definitely caused by the latter when the regression results are statistically significant. But the fact of the matter is that a particular direction of causality between two variables must stem from prior knowledge and theoretical considerations, rather than from mathematical manipulation of data on the variables. Thus specification of which is the dependent variable and which is the independent variable is done by the *researcher,* not by the regression technique. Therefore the results of a regression analysis cannot be expected to reveal the direction of causality.

To illustrate, consider the second scenario in Table 18.7. Suppose Carol, the librarian, conducts a regression analysis of data on cumulative grade point ratio (dependent variable) and number of books borrowed (independent variable) and obtains a statistically significant R^2-value of .9. Does this result mean high grade point ratios are a result of increased borrowings from the library? The inference does not necessarily follow. Although Carol may be tempted to make such an inference, the following inference is also a plausible explanation for the regression results: Students borrowing a large number of books may have done so *because* they were studious and had high grade point ratios to begin with. In other words, Carol can switch the dependent and the independent variables in the regression equation and still obtain an equally high R^2-value.

Third, a regression equation may not yield a trustworthy prediction of the

[9] Modifications of the basic technique are available for dealing with situations involving nonlinearity, but they are beyond the scope of this textbook. For details, see Wonnacott and Wonnacott, *Econometrics,* Chap. 4.

dependent variable when the value of the independent variable at which the prediction is desired is outside the range of values used in constructing the equation. For example, the range of advertising expenditures used in deriving the regression equation for Bright detergent's sales was $500 to $1900. We take a risk in using this regression equation to predict sales revenue corresponding to an advertising expenditure level of, say, $50 or $2500. We do not know whether the scatter diagram would follow the same linear trend if it were extended at either end by plotting new data points. In fact, even within the original range of independent-variable values, prediction errors will increase as we move away from the sample mean ($\bar{X}$) value in either direction.

The regression equation's prediction for a given value of the independent variable is merely a *point estimate.* We can construct a *prediction interval* (similar to the 95% confidence intervals discussed in Chapter 12) around each such estimate. A 95% prediction interval, for instance, is the range of values within which we can be 95% confident that the actual value of the dependent variable (corresponding to the given value of the independent variable) will fall. We will not discuss the formulas needed to construct prediction intervals.[10] But the resulting intervals at various levels of the independent variable form a sort of hourglass shape, as shown in Exhibit 18.7.

Fourth, a regression equation based on relatively few data points cannot be trusted. As we saw earlier, a simple regression equation based on just two data points will have an R^2-value of 1, no matter where those points are. Sample size and, hence, the number of data points available are especially critical in multiple regression analysis. Including too many independent variables when the sample size is small will lead to an artificially high R^2-value. A rule of thumb is to have at least ten sample units for every independent variable included in the equation.

Fifth, the ranges of data on the dependent and the independent variables can affect the meaningfulness of a regression equation. The ranges for both variables must be sufficiently wide if the regression equation is to be useful. Deriving a meaningful regression line when data on either variable span only a narrow range will be difficult. The need for a sufficient degree of dispersion in the data is succinctly stated by Loether and McTavish:

> Clearly, if there is no variation in the dependent variable, there is nothing to explain. Thus there are relatively few studies of the number of heads humans are born with. Given some variation, we can ask why, and introduce independent variables to help explain. There is also no progress to be made in explanation unless independent variables have some variation. If there were no variation in independent variables, then only one prediction would always be made for the dependent variable, which would hardly help account for differences in scores on the dependent variable.[11]

---

[10] For these formulas and the rationale underlying them, see, for instance, Anderson, Sweeney, and Williams, *Introduction to Statistics,* pp. 352–355.

[11] Herman J. Loether and Donald G. McTavish, *Descriptive Statistics for Sociologists: An Introduction* (Boston: Allyn and Bacon, 1974), p. 360.

Exhibit 18.7

Prediction intervals corresponding to a regression line

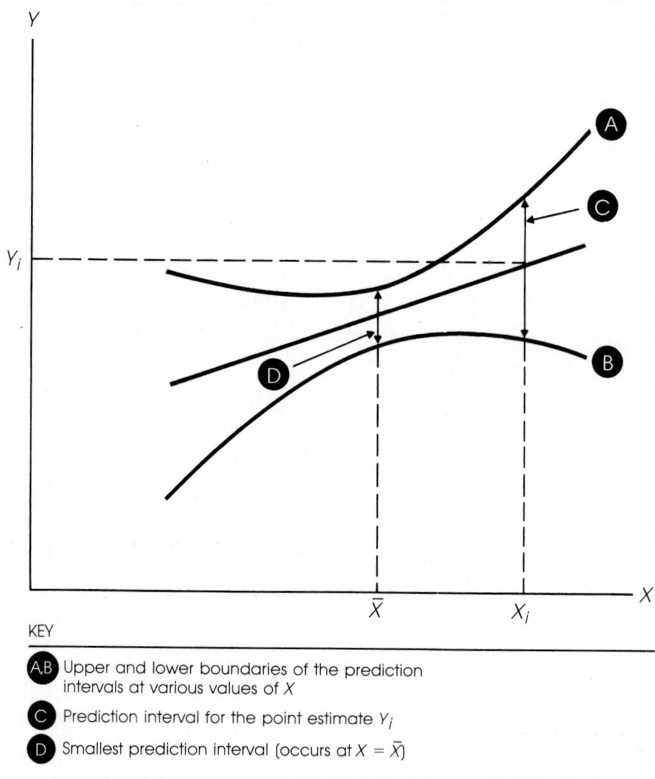

MULTIPLE REGRESSION ANALYSIS

Multiple regression analysis is useful when more than one independent variable is likely to be associated with a dependent variable and ascertaining the contribution of all such independent variables in accounting for variation in the dependent variable is necessary. A multiple regression equation with k independent variables can be written as follows:

$$\hat{Y}_i = a + b_1X_{1i} + b_2X_{2i} + \cdots + b_kX_{ki},$$

where $\hat{Y}_i$ is the predicted value of the dependent variable for some unit i; X_{1i}, X_{2i}, . . . , X_{ki} are values on the independent variables for unit i; $b_1, b_2, \ldots, b_k$ are the regression coefficients (slopes) for the corresponding independent variables; and a is the Y-intercept representing the prediction for Y when all independent variables are set to zero. The slopes b_1 through b_k have the same interpretation as in simple regression analysis. For instance, b_k represents the change in Y per unit change in X_k, assuming the values of all other variables remain the same.

The Y-intercept and slopes are determined by using a least-squares procedure similar to the one we discussed for simple regression analysis. Their values can be readily obtained by using standard computer packages once a data set (like the one in Table 18.6) has been created.

Advertising expenditures for Bright detergent was the only independent variable in the regression equation discussed in the preceding section. But as we saw when we discussed correlation analysis, number of competing brands was also strongly associated with Bright's sales. Therefore examining a regression equation with both advertising and number of competing brands as independent variables may be interesting. The SPSS computer output for the multiple regression analysis of the data set in Table 18.6 is shown in Exhibit 18.8.

Advertising expenditures and number of competing brands are denoted as ADVTG and NCOMP, respectively, in the computer output. Except for the addition of one row corresponding to NCOMP, the format of this computer output is the same as the format of the simple regression analysis output (Exhibit 18.5). Using Y to represent sales (in thousands of dollars), X_1 to represent ADVTG (in hundreds of dollars), and X_2 to represent NCOMP (in actual number of competing detergent brands), we can write the regression equation as

$$\hat{Y} = 8.854 + .808X_1 - .498X_2$$

Exhibit 18.8

SPSS computer output for a multiple regression analysis of the data in Table 18.6

MULTIPLE REGRESSION

DEPENDENT VARIABLE. . SALES — VARIABLE LIST 1

VARIABLE(S) ENTERED ON STEP NUMBER 1. . NCOMP ADVTG — REGRESSION LIST 3

		ANALYSIS OF VARIANCE	DF	SUM OF SQUARES	MEAN SQUARE	F
MULTIPLE R	0.93421					
R SQUARE	0.87274	REGRESSION	2.	580.37308	290.18654	58.29317
ADJUSTED R SQUARE	0.85777	RESIDUAL	17.	84.62692	4.97805	
STANDARD ERROR	2.23116					

VARIABLES IN THE EQUATION

VARIABLE	B	BETA	STD ERROR B	F
NCOMP	−0.4975703	−0.32847	0.37579	1.753
ADVTG	0.8081323	0.61931	0.32371	6.232
(CONSTANT)	8.854438			

VARIABLES NOT IN THE EQUATION

VARIABLE	BETA IN	PARTIAL	TOLERANCE	F

ALL VARIABLES ARE IN THE EQUATION

STATISTICS WHICH CANNOT BE COMPUTED ARE PRINTED AS ALL NINES.

In this equation the subscript i is omitted from the variables for simplicity. Also, the values of a (8.854), b_1 (.808), and b_2 (−.498) are obtained directly from the computer output. The negative sign of b_2 stems from the inverse relationship between sales of Bright and number of competing brands (see Exhibit 18.2).

The R^2-value for this multiple regression equation is .873. Thus advertising expenditures and number of competing brands *together* account for a little over 87% of the total variation in sales of Bright. The F-statistic value for this R^2 is 58.293, with degrees of freedom $k = 2$ for the numerator and $n - k - 1 = 17$ for the denominator. The critical F-value for a significance level of .05 is 3.59 (from Appendix F). Since the calculated F-value is greater than the critical value, we can infer that the R^2-value is statistically significant and that the regression equation is trustworthy.

A statistically significant R^2-value in multiple regression analysis does not necessarily mean that all regression coefficients (the b's) are significantly different from zero. Each b-value must be checked separately for statistical significance, using a t-test similar to the one for checking the significance of a simple regression coefficient. Since there are two independent variables in our multiple regression equation, we must test two sets of hypotheses:

1. $H_o: \beta_1 = 0$ and $H_a: \beta_1 \neq 0$.
2. $H_o: \beta_2 = 0$ and $H_a: \beta_2 \neq 0$.

The squared value of the t-statistic for each regression coefficient is shown as an F-value in the computer output in Exhibit 18.8 (recall that the t-statistic is the square root of the corresponding F-statistic). The degrees of freedom for the t-statistic are $n - k - 1 = 17$. Assuming a significance level of .05, the critical values for t for a two-tailed hypothesis test are 2.11 and −2.11 (from Appendix D). The actual t-values for b_1 and b_2 can be derived from their corresponding F-values shown in Exhibit 18.8. For b_1

$$t = \sqrt{6.232} = 2.496$$

For b_2

$$t = -\sqrt{1.753} = -1.324$$

(the negative sign is included because b_2 is negative).

Comparing these t-values with the critical t-values, b_1 is significantly different from zero, but b_2 is not. In other words, according to our multiple regression results, while advertising apparently has a significant association with sales, the number of competing brands does not. This finding is somewhat puzzling because, as we saw earlier, the Pearson correlation coefficient between sales and number of competing brands is quite high (−.909) and statistically significant. The explanation for this apparent anomaly lies in the fact that the two indepen-

Exhibit 18.9

SPSS computer output for a pairwise correlation analysis of the data in Table 18.6

	SALES	ADVTG	NCOMP
SALES	1.00000	0.92716	−0.90889
ADVTG	0.92716	1.00000	−0.93721
NCOMP	−0.90889	−0.93721	1.00000

dent variables are strongly associated with each other. This association can be seen by scanning the last two columns in the data set shown in Table 18.6. Furthermore, the Pearson correlation coefficient between the two variables turns out to be −.937. When independent variables in a multiple regression equation are highly correlated among themselves, the problem of *multicollinearity* is said to exist. Interpretation of individual regression coefficients is very difficult and can be misleading when multicollinearity is present, as we will see in the next section.

MULTICOLLINEARITY'S IMPLICATIONS

Multicollinearity is a frequently encountered problem. Evidence of its presence must be checked for before one interprets a multiple regression equation. Most computer packages will provide a matrix of correlations among all variables as part of the regression analysis output. Exhibit 18.9 contains the matrix of correlations printed by the SPSS program used to derive the multiple regression equation for the sales of Bright.

The high correlation between ADVTG and NCOMP in Exhibit 18.9 implies that interpreting their regression coefficients is risky. Every user of the multiple regression technique must examine such a correlation matrix and exercise caution in interpreting the coefficient (slope) of any independent variable that is strongly associated with one or more other independent variables.

A comprehensive discussion of the rationale underlying the difficulty in interpreting regression coefficients when there is multicollinearity is beyond our scope.[12] However, we can intuitively see why there is difficulty if we reexamine the general interpretation of a regression coefficient: It is the change in the dependent variable per unit change in the independent variable, *assuming all other variables remain the same*. The emphasized words here refer to a condition that cannot be met when there is multicollinearity. That is, a high correlation between two independent variables implies that a change in one will be accompanied simultaneously by a corresponding change in the other. Hence one will have difficulty sorting out the *individual* contributions of the indepen-

[12] An excellent treatment of this issue is given in R. B. Darlington, "Multiple Regression in Psychological Research and Practice," *Psychological Bulletin,* 69 (1968), pp. 161–182.

dent variables in accounting for variations in the dependent variable.[13] So interpreting the magnitudes of the regression coefficients as accurate measures of the dependent variable's sensitivity to changes in corresponding independent variables will not be meaningful.

The simple and multiple regression analyses of the data related to Bright detergent yielded two different values for the regression coefficient of advertising expenditures. It was 1.210 in the simple regression analysis (Exhibit 18.5) and .808 in the multiple regression analysis (Exhibit 18.8), despite the fact that the same set of data on sales and advertising was used in both cases. The lower *b*-value in the multiple regression analysis is due to advertising's high correlation with number of competing brands. Neither the regression coefficient of .808 for ADVTG nor the regression coefficient of −.497 for NCOMP have a clear-cut interpretation because of the extensive overlap between the two variables. Had the correlation between them been weak, advertising's regression coefficient in the multiple regression analysis would have been close to its original value of 1.210.

The presence of multicollinearity does not necessarily mean that the regression equation is useless. As long as the R^2-value is high and statistically significant, the equation can still be used for predicting Y if one is given values for all the independent variables. One caveat, however, is that the relative values of the independent variables for which the prediction is desired must be consistent with the general pattern of values in the data set used to derive the multiple regression equation.

For instance, consider the multiple regression equation derived for the sales of Bright. The input data on advertising and number of competing brands (Table 18.6) are never *both* high or low. For this reason the two variables have a strong negative correlation. If we want to predict Bright's sales for a pair of new values of the independent variables, one of them must be high and the other low for the prediction to be meaningful. Thus, for example, the equation's prediction of sales when advertising is $650 and number of competing brands is 2 is unlikely to be trustworthy—both values are low vis-à-vis the range of values in the data set.

Multicollinearity is not the only potential limitation of multiple regression analysis. The precautions we discussed under simple regression analysis apply to multiple regression analysis as well, and they must be heeded to avoid making misleading inferences.

A few final remarks about regression analysis: Despite the rather extensive treatment of the technique in this chapter, we have only covered the fundamentals necessary to give you a basic understanding of it, including its capabilities

[13] A technique called *partial correlation analysis* is available for examining the association between a dependent and an independent variable after statistically factoring out the effect of other independent variables. For details, see Fred N. Kerlinger and Elazar J. Pedhazur, *Multiple Regression in Behavioral Research* (New York: Holt, Rinehart and Winston, 1973), Chap. 5.

and limitations. There is much more to regression analysis than what a textbook of this nature can possibly cover. Not covered here are topics such as transforming data on variables to make them satisfy the assumptions of regression analysis. (One topic—that of including categorical independent variables in a regression analysis by transforming them into dummy variables—will be covered in the next chapter when we discuss analysis of variance.) While such topics are not relevant for all regression applications, students wishing to gain a comprehensive understanding of regression analysis will benefit from additional reading.[14]

SUMMARY

This chapter dealt with procedures for ascertaining and interpreting associations between variables. A frequently used technique for examining associations when data on the variables are nonmetric (nominal or ordinal) is the chi-square contingency test. It involves comparing the observed cell frequencies in a two-way table (called a contingency table) with corresponding expected cell frequencies computed under the null hypothesis of no association between the variables. Certain minimum cell frequency requirements must be met for the chi-square contingency test to be meaningful. Also, this test by itself only indicates whether or not two variables are significantly related. When this test leads to the rejection of the null hypothesis of independence, some idea about the degree of association between the variables can be obtained by computing the contingency coefficient C or Cramer's V-statistic. However, these measures of association are somewhat arbitrary. Their values are sensitive to how the variable categories are defined and how many rows and columns the contingency table has.

The Spearman correlation coefficient r_s is a better measure of association when the data on variables are ordinal and are in the form of ranks of the sample units on each variable. This coefficient will range from $+1$ to -1, with a value of zero signifying no correlation. Its statistical significance can be verified by conducting a t-test.

The Pearson correlation coefficient is a widely used measure of association between metric (interval or ratio) variables. It is a number ranging from $+1$ to -1 and summarizes the degree of compactness as well as the direction of a scatter diagram, which is a plot of the data on the variables. Whether this correlation coefficient is significantly different from zero can be determined easily, given its value, the sample size, and a desired significance level. A limitation of the Pearson correlation coefficient is that it can only capture the degree of linear association between variables. Furthermore, evidence of a strong cor-

[14] Several books on regression analysis are available, such as Kerlinger and Pedhazur, *Multiple Regression,* and Johnston, *Econometric Methods.*

relation by itself does not constitute evidence of causality in any particular direction.

Simple regression analysis is similar to correlation analysis except that it generates a mathematical relationship (called the regression equation) between one variable designated as the dependent variable (Y) and another designated as the independent variable (X). An independent variable is typically assumed to influence the dependent variable in some fashion. The regression equation, $\hat{Y}_i = a + bX_i$, is derived by fitting a straight line through the scatter diagram so as to minimize the error sum of squares (SS_E). This procedure is called the least-squares technique and is available from several computer packages. The constant a is called the Y-intercept, and the regression coefficient b is called the slope. The slope has an important interpretation: It is the change in the predicted value of Y per unit change in X, when all other variables likely to influence X remain the same.

Several indicators are available to check the usefulness of a regression equation. One that is commonly examined is the coefficient of determination R^2. The value of R^2 can range from 0 to 1 and is a measure of the proportion of the total variance in Y that is accounted for by predictions made by the regression equation. The higher the R^2-value, the better the regression equation is. The statistical significance of R^2 can be checked by using an F-test. The square root of R^2 is called the multiple correlation coefficient. In bivariate regression analysis the multiple correlation coefficient is the same as the Pearson correlation coefficient. A related measure of goodness of a regression equation is the standard error of the estimate, $s_{Y/X}$, which is a sort of average variation in Y left unexplained by the regression equation. The smaller the value of $s_{Y/X}$, the better the regression equation is.

Another way to evaluate a regression equation is to see whether the slope is significantly different from zero. A t-test is employed for this purpose. The F-test for the significance of R^2 and the t-test for the significance of b are equivalent in simple regression analysis.

Two practical applications of simple regression analysis are to ascertain changes in the dependent variable when the independent variable changes by a specified amount, and to predict the value of the dependent variable for a given value of the independent variable. In interpreting and using the regression equation, however, researchers must keep several potential pitfalls in mind. Regression analysis by itself cannot establish causality between variables. Regression equations based on nonlinear scatter diagrams, on a limited number of data points, or on data spanning relatively narrow ranges are unlikely to be meaningful. Also, making predictions of the dependent variable for values of the independent variable that fall outside the range of data used in deriving the regression equation is risky.

Multiple regression analysis is a logical extension of simple regression analysis and involves two or more independent variables. The analytical procedures and the interpretation of the results are quite similar in both cases. The limitations of simple regression analysis apply to multiple regression analysis as well. A key difference between the two techniques is that statistical significance of the R^2-value of a multiple regression equation (based on an F-test) does not automatically mean that all the regression coefficients (b-values) are significantly different from zero. Each regression coefficient must be individually evaluated by using a t-test. Furthermore, a potentially serious problem in multiple regression analysis is multicollinearity—that is, the presence of strong correlations among independent variables. When multicollinearity exists, caution must be exercised in interpreting the values of individual regression coefficients.

QUESTIONS

1. From a survey of 1000 families the following two-way table was constructed:

	Owned Product X	
Income Level	Yes	No
Hi	200	150
Med	150	100
Lo	150	250
	500	500

Is there a statistically significant relationship between income level and ownership of product X, at the 95% confidence level?

2. A random sample of 500 consumers in a certain county consisted of 300 males and 200 females. Of the males in the sample 200 were smokers, and of the females 50 were smokers. On the basis of this evidence, is there a statistically significant relationship (at the 95% confidence level) between the sex of consumers in this county and whether or not they smoke?

3. What are the potential limitations of the chi-square contingency test?

4. Compute and interpret the contingency coefficient and Cramer's V-statistic for the problems in Questions 1 and 2. Is the contingency coefficient more meaningful than Cramer's V-statistic (or vice versa) in either case? Why or why not?

5. What major caveat should one bear in mind in computing and interpreting numbers apparently representing the *degree* of association between categorical variables that have been cross-tabulated to produce a contingency table?

6. Ace Chemicals, Inc. (ACI), selected 15 of its customer firms at random and rank-ordered them from highest (rank 1) to lowest (rank 15) on the basis of their volumes of purchases from ACI. It then rank-ordered these same 15 firms according to how formalized the firms' purchasing operations were (rank for most formalized = 1 and rank for least formalized = 15). For the firms ranked 1 through 15 in terms of purchase volumes, the following ranks reflect the degree of formalized purchasing operations, respectively: 3, 5, 2, 1, 4, 8, 10, 7, 6, 11, 9, 13, 15, 14, 12. In other words, the firm with the largest purchase volume ranked third with respect to formalized purchasing operations, the firm with the second largest purchase volume ranked fifth with respect to formalized purchasing operations, and so on. Compute the Spearman correlation coefficient between customer purchase volume from ACI and formalization of customers' purchasing operations. (If you have access to a computer, use it to derive the Spearman correlation coefficient with the aid of a canned computer program.) How do you interpret this correlation coefficient?

7. Is the correlation coefficient you computed in Question 6 statistically significant? Why or why not?
8. The sales manager of a firm administered a standard, multi-item job satisfaction scale to a sample of the firm's sales force. The manager then correlated the satisfaction scores with the ages of the salespeople in the sample. The Pearson correlation coefficient between satisfaction and age turned out to be .08. On the basis of this evidence the sales manager came to the following conclusions: "A salesperson's age has hardly anything to do with his or her satisfaction. Furthermore, as salespeople get older, they continue to have the same average levels of job satisfaction." Would you agree or disagree with the sales manager's conclusions? Explain your answer.
9. Compute the Pearson correlation coefficient for the data in Question 6 (using a canned computer program, if possible). How does this coefficient compare with the Spearman correlation coefficient computed earlier? From this comparison, what inference can you make about marketing researchers' often assuming ordinal data to have interval properties?
10. What are the key differences between simple regression and correlation analyses?
11. Clearly summarize, in a sentence or two, what the least-squares approach to regression analysis does.
12. Exhibit 18.10 shows the SPSS output for the simple regression analysis of the data on sales (SALES, expressed in thousands of dollars) and number of competing detergents (NCOMP) given in Table 18.6. Notice that the format of Exhibit 18.10 is identical to that of Exhibit 18.5. Use the output of Exhibit 18.10 to answer the following questions.
    a. Identify the Y-intercept and slope values, and interpret those values.
    b. Write the regression equation linking predicted sales of Bright and the number of competing detergent brands.

Exhibit 18.10

SPSS computer output for a simple regression analysis of sales and number of competing brands

MULTIPLE REGRESSION

DEPENDENT VARIABLE. . SALES
VARIABLE(S) ENTERED ON STEP NUMBER 1. . NCOMP

VARIABLE LIST 1
REGRESSION LIST 2

MULTIPLE R	0.90889	ANALYSIS OF VARIANCE	DF	SUM OF SQUARES	MEAN SQUARE	F
R SQUARE	0.82809	REGRESSION	1.	549.34783	549.34783	85.50000
ADJUSTED R SQUARE	0.81643	RESIDUAL	18.	115.65217	6.42512	
STANDARD ERROR	2.53478					

VARIABLES IN THE EQUATION

VARIABLE	B	BETA	STD ERROR B	F
NCOMP	−1.376812	−0.90889	0.14890	85.500
(CONSTANT)	25.37681			

VARIABLES NOT IN THE EQUATION

VARIABLE	BETA IN	PARTIAL	TOLERANCE	F

MAXIMUM STEP REACHED

STATISTICS WHICH CANNOT BE COMPUTED ARE PRINTED AS ALL NINES.

c. What is the R^2-value associated with the regression equation? Is it statistically significant? Why or why not?
d. Verify that $R^2 = SS_R/SS_T$, and give a verbal interpretation of the R^2-value.
e. Circle the number representing the Pearson correlation coefficient between the two variables.
f. Verify that the square root of the error mean square is the standard error of the regression.
g. Is the slope of the regression equation statistically significant? Why or why not?
h. Use the implied regression equation to predict sales for Bright in a market where it will have 18 competing detergent brands. Is this prediction meaningful? Explain your answer.
i. Bright currently has five competing detergent brands in a certain market area. The firm expects three additional competing brands to enter the market in the near future. What impact will the new detergent brands have on Bright's monthly dollar sales in this market area? What precautions should you take in interpreting the estimated impact?

13. What is multicollinearity? What implications does the presence of multicollinearity have for the interpretation and use of a regression equation?

14. You are given the following results for a regression analysis of a dependent variable (Y) and two independent variables (X_1 and X_2) from a sample of 30 observations:

Means	$\bar{Y} = 3000$	$\bar{X}_1 = 100$	$\bar{X}_2 = 150$
Standard deviations	$S_Y = 25$	$S_{X_1} = 30$	$S_{X_2} = 20$
Correlation coefficients	$r_{YX_1} = .75$	$r_{YX_2} = .95$	$r_{X_1X_2} = .8$
Estimated regression equation	$\hat{Y} = 1000 + 5X_1 + 10X_2$		
$R^2 = .91$	F-value associated with $R^2 = 5.67$		

a. Is the R^2-value statistically significant? Why or why not?
b. Can you meaningfully determine the change in Y when X_1 is increased by one unit? If you can, what is the change in Y? If you cannot, why not?
c. What proportion of the variance of Y is *not* explained by the regression equation? What does this result say about how good the regression equation is?

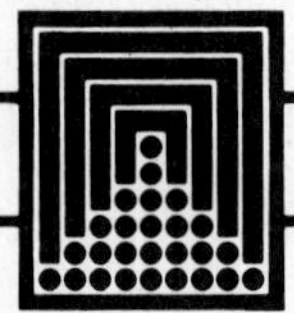

APPENDIX TO CHAPTER 18

Some Technical Details about Correlation and Regression Analysis

DERIVATION AND INTERPRETATION OF PEARSON CORRELATION COEFFICIENT

The purpose of this section is to develop the expression for the Pearson correlation coefficient and, at the same time, to provide the rationale underlying its interpretation. To accomplish this purpose, we will start with the scatter diagram in Exhibit 18.1 (included in the body of the chapter), which shows a plot of advertising expenditures against sales revenue.

Exhibit A.18.1 shows the same scatter diagram as in Exhibit 18.1, but it is partitioned into four quadrants by constructing two new axes, one perpendicular to the original X-axis at the mean value of advertising expenditures ($\bar{X}$) and the other perpendicular to the original Y-axis at the mean value of sales ($\bar{Y}$). For each data point in Exhibit A.18.1, the uppercase coordinates (X, Y) refer to the raw data, and the lowercase coordinates (x, y) refer to deviations of the raw data from their respective mean values. The coordinates (x, y) are central to determining the Pearson correlation coefficient.

Consider the four illustrative data points *a, b, c,* and *d* in quadrants I, II, III, and IV, respectively. What can we say about the product xy for each of these data points? For data point a both x_a and y_a are positive. Therefore $x_a y_a$ is also positive. Indeed, the xy-product is positive for all data points in quadrant I. Now examine data point c in quadrant III. Since both x_c and y_c are negative, their product $(x_c y_c)$ is positive. Thus the product of the deviations x and y is positive for all data points in quadrants I and III—the points that, in general, are most consistent with a linear, upward-sloping trend, signifying a positive association between the variables.

Data points in quadrants II and IV are off-diagonal relative to the linear, upward-sloping trend. Intuitively, if too many data points fall in quadrants II and

Exhibit A.18.1

Plot of deviations of sales and advertising data from their respective means

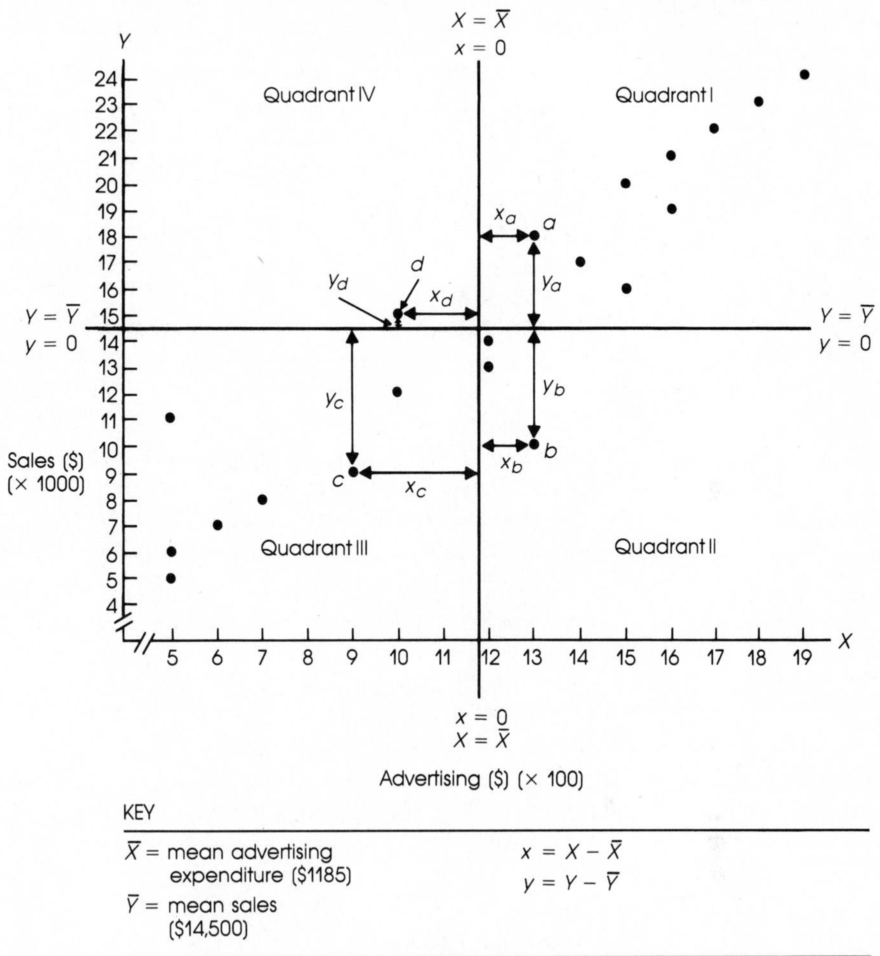

IV, the evidence of a direct positive association between the variables will be weakened. Not accidentally, the product xy is negative for all data points in these two quadrants. For instance, for data point b, x_b is positive but y_b is negative, and for data point d, x_d is negative but y_d is positive. Thus the product of the deviations will be negative in both cases.

Keeping in mind the foregoing discussion about the nature of the data points in the four quadrants, examine the following quantity, which is called the *covariance* of X and Y and denoted as Cov(X, Y):

$$\text{Cov}(X, Y) = \frac{\sum_{i=1}^{n} x_i y_i}{n - 1},$$

where n is the sample size (total number of data points). The Cov(X, Y) is an average measure of the degree to which X and Y move together. Clearly, the larger the number of data points in quadrants I and III, the higher the value of Cov(X, Y) will be. In contrast, the larger the number of data points in quadrants II and IV, the smaller the value of Cov(X, Y) will be. Alternatively, a large positive value for Cov(X, Y) will signify a strong direct association between X and Y, and a large negative value for Cov(X, Y) will signify a strong inverse association between X and Y.

Although Cov(X, Y) is a quantitative measure of the degree of association between variables, one problem in interpreting it is that it can be arbitrarily increased by merely changing the units of measurement for the variables. For example, by using cents instead of dollars for both sales and advertising in the expression for Cov(X, Y), the value of the covariance between the two can be increased by a factor of 10,000. Hence for a clear interpretation of covariance, its value must be made independent of the units in which the variables are measured. This independence can be accomplished by standardizing the variables. The resulting standardized covariance is the Pearson correlation coefficient, given by the following expression:

$$r_{XY} = \frac{\sum_{i=1}^{n} x_i y_i}{(n - 1) s_X s_Y},$$

where s_X and s_Y are the standard deviations of the two variables. The value of r_{XY} can range from $+1$ to -1.

LEAST-SQUARES REGRESSION ANALYSIS

This section briefly reviews how the least-squares approach derives the best-fitting regression line for a given scatter diagram. The rationale underlying the least-squares approach stems from the implied primary purpose of a regression equation, namely, to predict values of the dependent variable (Y) for given values of the independent variable (X), *with errors as small as possible.*

Consider the upward-sloping line in Exhibit A.18.2, which contains the same scatter diagram as in Exhibit 18.1 presented in the chapter. For any given value of X, say X_i, we can predict a Y-value, say $\hat{Y}_i$, using the line in Exhibit A.18.2. However, $\hat{Y}_i$ will not necessarily coincide with the actual value Y_i corresponding

Exhibit A.18.2
Prediction errors and explained variation associated with a regression line

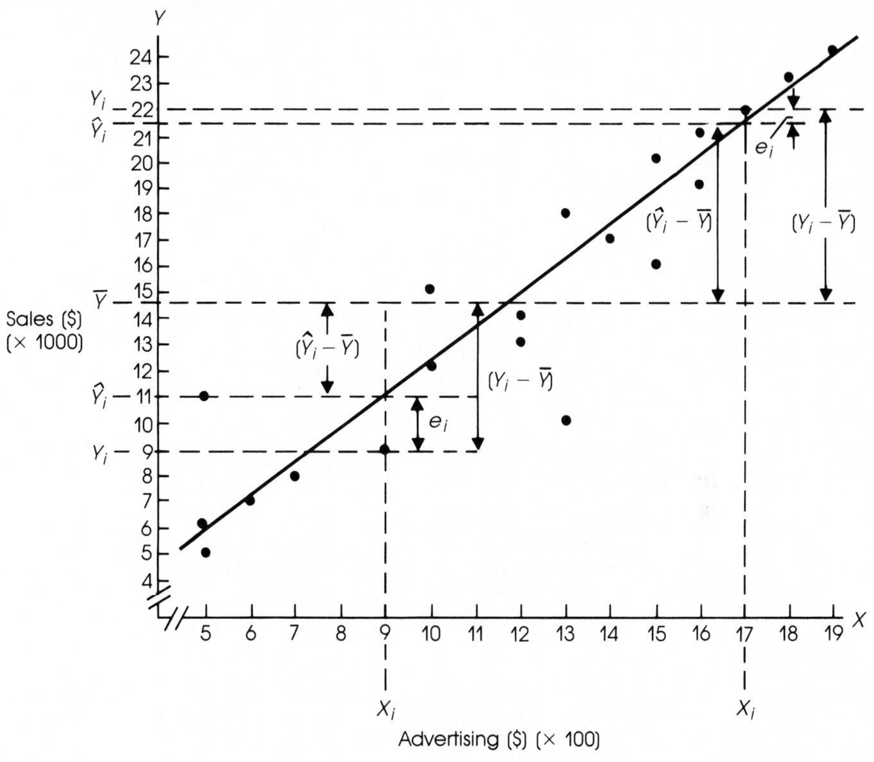

to X_i. Thus using this line to predict a Y-value for a given X_i-value will lead to a *prediction error* (e_i), defined as

$$e_i = Y_i - \hat{Y}_i.$$

Illustrative prediction errors pertaining to two data points are shown in Exhibit A.18.2. The quantities $(\hat{Y}_i - \overline{Y})$ and $(Y_i - \overline{Y})$ in this exhibit are discussed in the next section of the appendix. Notice that prediction errors corresponding to data points above the line will be positive, and those corresponding to data points below the line will be negative. Furthermore, different straight lines, such as the ones in Exhibit 18.4 presented in the chapter, will result in different sets of prediction errors.

What the least-squares approach does is pick the line that *minimizes the sum of the squared* prediction errors across all data points. In other words, the values of the constants a and b in the equation representing this line (i.e., $Y = a + bX$) are chosen so as to make the quantity Σe_i^2 as small as possible. The mathematics involved in deriving the optimum values of a and b is too complex to include here. But the resulting formulas for computing the constants are

$$b = \frac{\sum_{i=1}^{n} X_i Y_i - \left(\sum_{i=1}^{n} X_i\right)\left(\sum_{i=1}^{n} Y_i\right) \Big/ n}{\sum_{i=1}^{n} X_i^2 - \left(\sum_{i=1}^{n} X_i\right)^2 \Big/ n},$$

$$a = \frac{1}{n}\left(\sum_{i=1}^{n} Y_i - b \sum_{i=1}^{n} X_i\right).$$

Once the values of a and b are known, they can be substituted into the regression equation, $\hat{Y}_i = a + bX_i$, where $\hat{Y}_i$ is the predicted dependent-variable value for a given value of X_i for the independent variable.

PARTITIONING THE TOTAL SUM OF SQUARES

Take another look at Exhibit A.18.2. How do the predictions made with the aid of the regression line (i.e., the $\hat{Y}_i$'s) compare with the best prediction that could be made in the absence of the regression line (i.e., $\bar{Y}$)? Clearly, predictions based on the regression line are generally much closer to the actual Y-values. Although the regression line's predictions are not perfect, they are able to account for a substantial part of the total deviation in Y. As demonstrated by Exhibit A.18.2, the following relationship holds for any given value X_i of the independent variable:

$$\begin{aligned}(Y_i - \bar{Y}) &= (\hat{Y}_i - \bar{Y}) + (Y_i - \hat{Y}_i) \\ &= (\hat{Y}_i - \bar{Y}) + e_i.\end{aligned}$$

This relationship, written in words, is

total deviation = deviation explained by regression line
+ deviation unexplained by regression line.

Using this relationship as a starting point, we can show that

$$\sum_{i=1}^{n} (Y_i - \bar{Y})^2 = \sum_{i=1}^{n} (\hat{Y}_i - \bar{Y})^2 + \sum_{i=1}^{n} e_i^2$$

Each term in this expression represents the summation of a particular type of squared deviation and is hence called a *sum of squares:*

$\sum_{i=1}^{n} (Y_i - \bar{Y})^2$	*Total* sum of squares; a measure of the total *variance* in the dependent variable; denoted as SS_T
$\sum_{i=1}^{n} (\hat{Y}_i - \bar{Y})^2$	*Regression* sum of squares; represents the portion of the variance explained by the regression equation; denoted as SS_R
$\sum_{i=1}^{n} e_i^2$	*Error* (or sometimes residual) sum of squares; represents the portion of the variance unexplained by the regression equation; denoted as SS_E

The procedure involved in deriving the relationship $SS_T = SS_R + SS_E$ is called *partitioning the total sum of squares.* It is fundamental to regression analysis and to a technique called analysis of variance, to be covered in the next chapter.

19

Overview of Other Multivariate Techniques

The preceding chapter discussed a variety of techniques for examining associations, including regression analysis, which is a very widely used multivariate procedure. However, there are many other multivariate techniques, some of which are relatively new and becoming increasingly popular. The purpose of this chapter is to introduce you to several of them and to provide an intuitive understanding of each.

The specific techniques to be described are analysis of variance (ANOVA), automatic interaction detector (AID), discriminant analysis, factor analysis, cluster analysis, multidimensional scaling, and conjoint analysis. Since these techniques are rather complex, to cover them comprehensively is beyond the scope of this textbook. There are more to the techniques—in terms of sophisticated extensions and analytical nuances—than will be discussed here. You should bear this caveat in mind while reading the chapter.

ANALYSIS OF VARIANCE

Analysis of variance (ANOVA) is closely related to regression analysis in that its purpose is also to examine the relationship between dependent and independent variables. There is, however, one basic difference between the two techniques: While both dependent and independent variables are metric (i.e., interval or ratio) in regression analysis, only the dependent variable is metric in analysis of variance; the independent variable is categorical (i.e., nominal or ordinal). ANOVA is therefore especially appropriate in situations where the independent variable is set at certain specific levels (called *treatments* in an ANOVA context) and metric measurements of the dependent variable are obtained at each of those levels. Not surprisingly, ANOVA procedures are often employed to analyze data from marketing experiments in which different groups of units (e.g., stores) are exposed to various levels of an experimental treatment (e.g., amount of in-store promotion for a brand) and are measured on some criterion variable (e.g., sales of the brand). Let us look at a specific example to understand what ANOVA does.

EXAMPLE: A grocery store chain wanted to evaluate the price sensitivity of sales of its store brand of vegetable oil. Twenty-four of the chain's stores in a certain region were chosen at random to participate in an experimental study involving the following three treatments:

1. Store brand sold at the regular price.
2. Store brand sold at 50¢ off the regular price.
3. Store brand sold at 75¢ off the regular price.

Eight of the 24 stores were randomly assigned to the first treatment, another 8 were randomly assigned to the second treatment, and the rest were assigned to the third treatment. Sales of the store brand of vegetable oil were monitored for a week in each store. The data thus gathered are summarized in Table 19.1.

Price is the independent variable (nonmetric, with three categories) in Table 19.1. Unit sales, which is ratio-scaled, is the dependent variable. The basic question now is whether the cents-off treatments had any significant impact on

Table 19.1

Unit sales data under different pricing treatments

TREATMENT	REGULAR PRICE ($j = 1$)	50¢ OFF ($j = 2$)	75¢ OFF ($j = 3$)
Unit sales in each store			
(Y_{ij})	37	46	46
	38	43	49
	40	43	48
	40	45	48
	38	45	47
	38	43	48
	40	44	49
	39	44	49
Number of stores (n_j)	8	8	8
Mean sales ($\bar{Y}_{.j}$)	38.75	44.13	48.00

sales. One way of checking this question is to look for evidence of significant differences in mean sales between *pairs* of treatment groups, using the t-test procedure discussed in Chapter 17. A problem with this approach is that a separate t-test is required for each possible pair of treatments. We would have to conduct three t-tests in our example, a potentially cumbersome procedure. The task would be even more laborious when there are more treatment levels. ANOVA is a better approach to use when multiple sample means are to be compared to see whether at least one of them is significantly different from one or more of the others. It provides a one-shot, global test for detecting significant differences between treatment group means.

When there are k treatment groups or samples, ANOVA can aid in testing the following hypotheses:

H_0: $\mu_1 = \mu_2 = \cdots = \mu_k$.

H_a: At least one μ is different from one or more of the others.

Here the μ's are means of the dependent variable in the populations represented by the corresponding treatment groups. The test statistic in this case is an F-statistic based on the concept of partitioning the total sum of squares, introduced while discussing regression analysis in Chapter 18. The following general notation is helpful in developing an understanding of what the F-statistic in ANOVA represents:

Y_{ij} = dependent variable value for sample unit i in treatment group j;
$\bar{Y}_{.j}$ = mean value for treatment group j;
$\bar{Y}_{..}$ = grand mean value (across all units in all treatment groups);
n_j = number of sample units in treatment group.

The total deviation of any sample unit's value from the grand mean is $(Y_{ij} - \bar{Y}_{..})$. This total deviation can be written as

$$(Y_{ij} - \bar{Y}_{..}) = (Y_{ij} - \bar{Y}_{.j}) + (\bar{Y}_{.j} - \bar{Y}_{..}).$$

With the above expression as a starting point, it can be shown that

$$(Y_{ij} - \bar{Y}_{..})^2 = (Y_{ij} - \bar{Y}_{.j})^2 + (\bar{Y}_{.j} - \bar{Y}_{..})^2. \quad (19.1)$$

Summing Eq. (19.1) across all units in any treatment group j yields

$$\sum_{i=1}^{n_j} (Y_{ij} - \bar{Y}_{..})^2 = \sum_{i=1}^{n_j} (Y_{ij} - \bar{Y}_{.j})^2 + n_j(\bar{Y}_{.j} - \bar{Y}_{..})^2. \quad (19.2)$$

Now summing Eq. (19.2) across all treatments yields

$$\sum_{j=1}^{k}\sum_{i=1}^{n_j}(Y_{ij}-\bar{Y}_{..})^2=\sum_{j=1}^{k}\sum_{i=1}^{n_j}(Y_{ij}-\bar{Y}_{.j})^2+\sum_{j=1}^{k}n_j(\bar{Y}_{.j}-\bar{Y}_{..})^2. \tag{19.3}$$

The left-hand term in Eq. (19.3) is the *total sum of squares* (SS_T) representing the variation across all units and all treatments. The first term on the right-hand side is called the *within sum of squares* (SS_W). It is a measure of variation in dependent-variable values within the treatment groups. The second term on the right-hand side is called *between sum of squares,* or sum of squares attributable to the treatments (SS_{TR}). Term SS_{TR} is a weighted measure of variation in values between treatment groups.

It follows that $SS_T = SS_{TR} + SS_W$. Notice the similarity between this expression and the expression $SS_T = SS_R + SS_E$ that we derived in the regression analysis discussion. The treatment sum of squares (SS_{TR}) is analogous to the explained variation (SS_R) under regression analysis, and the within sum of squares (SS_W) is analogous to the residual (or unexplained) variation (SS_E). Intuitively, if the experimental treatments (independent variable) had little impact on the Y-values (dependent variable), we would expect SS_{TR} to be small. For a given value of SS_T, a small SS_{TR} would imply a large SS_W. Just as in regression analysis, a comparison of SS_{TR} and SS_W, taking into account their appropriate degrees of freedom, is the basis for the F-statistic in ANOVA. When there are k treatments, the degrees of freedom associated with SS_{TR} and SS_W are $(k - 1)$ and $(n - k)$, respectively, where n is the total number of units across all treatments. Therefore

$$F=\frac{SS_{TR}/k-1}{SS_W/n-\mathrm{k}}.$$

The numerator and denominator of F are mean squares corresponding to the variation owing to the treatments and chance variation owing to sampling, respectively. To see whether the experimental treatments had a significant impact on the dependent measure, the computed value of F is checked against an appropriate critical value from the F table. Hypothesis H_o is rejected if the computed value exceeds the critical value.

Returning to the data in Table 19.1, let us conduct an ANOVA to see whether at least one of the treatment means (shown in the last row of the table) is significantly different from one or more others. Although we can compute the necessary F-value by hand, using the formulas just derived, it is more convenient to use one of the readily available computer packages for this purpose. Given the raw dependent-variable values for each treatment (i.e., the Y_{ij}-values), a computer program can perform ANOVA efficiently and provide a rich variety of output information. The computer output resulting from analyzing the raw data in Table 19.1 by using the SPSS ANOVA program is shown in Exhibit 19.1.

The names SALES and TREAT were used for the dependent and independent variables in the computer program (they are shown in the output just below the heading). A tabular array such as the one in Exhibit 19.1, showing various sums of squares, degrees of freedom, mean squares, F-values, and their corresponding significance levels, is usually called an ANOVA table. Its format is similar to the formats we saw in the regression analysis computer outputs (Exhibits 18.5 and 18.8).

The number 137.447 shown under F in the row labeled TREAT in Exhibit 19.1 is the computed F-value we are looking for. It is the ratio of the mean square value of 172.625 associated with TREAT (that is, $SS_{TR}/k - 1$) and the mean square value of 1.256 associated with RESIDUAL (that is, $SS_W/n - k$). The critical F-value with 2 numerator degrees of freedom and 21 denominator degrees of freedom at the traditional significance level of .05 is only 3.47 (from Appendix F). We should therefore reject H_0 and conclude that at least one of the treatment means is significantly different from one or more others. Indeed, in this case we need not even have determined the critical value of F to arrive at the above conclusion, since the ANOVA output shows the actual significance level of the F-test—the value 0.000 under the column SIGNIF OF F. This value means there is a less than a .001 probability of obtaining an F-value as high as 137.447 by chance when TREAT has no impact on SALES. In other words, there is less than one chance in thousand of committing a Type I error by rejecting H_0 on the basis of the available evidence.

Some additional explanation of the output in Exhibit 19.1 is in order. Perhaps you are wondering why there are three identical rows of numbers (the first three rows) in the computer output. While there was just one independent variable in our illustration, we can examine the impact of two or more indepen-

Exhibit 19.1

SPSS computer output for ANOVA analysis of the data in Table 19.1

ANALYSIS OF VARIANCE

SALES BY TREAT

SOURCE OF VARIATION	SUM OF SQUARES	DF	MEAN SQUARE	F	SIGNIF OF F
MAIN EFFECTS	345.250	2	172.625	137.447	0.000
TREAT	345.250	2	172.625	137.447	0.000
EXPLAINED	345.250	2	172.625	137.447	0.000
RESIDUAL	26.375	21	1.256		
TOTAL	371.625	23	16.158		

24 CASES WERE PROCESSED.
0 CASES (0.0 Pct) WERE MISSING.

dent variables by using ANOVA. The row labeled MAIN EFFECTS refers to results aggregated over *all* independent variables considered in a given situation. Since TREAT was the only independent variable in this case, numbers in the first and second rows of the computer output are the same. (Had there been more than one independent variable, there would have been additional rows of numbers under the row corresponding to TREAT, one row for each additional variable.) The row labeled EXPLAINED refers to the total of individual, or main, effects of independent variables as well as any effects due to *interactions* between them (interaction effects are described later). Again, since our example involves only one independent variable, there is no interaction effect. Hence the numbers in the TREAT and EXPLAINED rows are identical. The RESIDUAL row corresponds to variance in the dependent variable not accounted for by the independent variables and their interactions. So the sum of squares and degrees of freedom in the EXPLAINED and RESIDUAL rows must add to the corresponding numbers in the TOTAL row (verify this result in Exhibit 19.1).

Now that we know TREAT had a significant impact on SALES, which specific treatment group means are significantly different? Visual inspection of the three treatment group means suggests that each may differ significantly from the other two. An extension of the ANOVA technique—called constructing and evaluating *contrasts*—is available to verify the statistical significance of differences between any pair of treatment means. We will not cover the details of this extension.[1] Most computer programs for performing ANOVA offer an option for evaluating specific treatment differences.

The similarity between the expressions for the total sum of squares (SS_T) under ANOVA and regression analysis was pointed out earlier. The appendix to this chapter discusses further the correspondence between the two techniques with the help of dummy-variable regression, which is used when one or more independent variables are categorical.

ADVANCED ANOVA PROCEDURES

The ANOVA procedure illustrated in the preceding section is a rather basic one called a *one-way, completely randomized ANOVA.* The "one-way" descriptor refers to the fact that only one independent variable—price, with three treatment levels—was involved. The procedure was "completely randomized" in that the 24 sample stores were allocated to the three treatment levels in a purely random fashion. This ANOVA procedure is the one typically used for analyzing data stemming from a completely randomized experimental design (discussed in Chapter 9). Sophisticated extensions of this basic ANOVA procedure are

[1] A good discussion of contrasts is given in William C. Guenther, *Analysis of Variance* (Englewood Cliffs, N.J.: Prentice-Hall, 1964).

available for analyzing data from the more advanced experimental designs described in Chapter 9. In this section we will briefly describe several such extensions.[2]

Randomized-block ANOVA

One limitation of the completely randomized experimental design used in the grocery store chain example is that no explicit effort was made to control for the potential effects of extraneous factors (e.g., store size) on unit sales of the vegetable oil. Although random allocation of the sample stores to the three treatments should even out such effects, there is no guarantee that it would be successful in doing so. For instance, stores allocated to the 50¢-off and 75¢-off treatments can, by chance, be larger than those allocated to the regular-price treatment. If so, the observed differences in mean sales across the three groups of stores cannot be unambiguously attributed to the pricing treatments. One way of guarding against such a possibility is to use a randomized-block experimental design.

As we saw in Chapter 9, in a randomized-block design the stores will not be allocated to three treatments on a completely random basis. Rather, they will first be arranged according to size. The three largest stores will then be assigned randomly to the three treatments. Thus one store from the matched threesome of stores is guaranteed to be in each treatment group. Successive threesomes of stores from the arranged list will be assigned to the three treatments in a similar fashion. The result will be eight blocks of stores (each block representing a different store size category), with stores within each block randomly assigned to the three treatments. Blocking in experimentation is analogous to stratification in sampling. Just as stratified random sampling is statistically more efficient than simple random sampling, the randomized-block design is better than the completely randomized design in terms of detecting differences between treatment groups.

The format of the raw data set generated through a randomized-block design will be similar to that of Table 19.1, but with one key difference: Each row of data will now correspond to a set of three stores of roughly equal size. Store size in this case is called a *blocking factor*. Randomized-block ANOVA achieves its advantage over completely randomized ANOVA by the way it partitions the total variation in the dependent variable (that is, SS_T). Rather than splitting SS_T simply into between (or treatment) and within (or unexplained) sums of squares, it further splits the within sum of squares into a sum of squares due to the blocking factor (SS_b) and a residual or error sum of squares (SS_e). Therefore in a randomized-block ANOVA,

$$SS_T = SS_{TR} + SS_b + SS_e.$$

[2] An excellent reference source for learning more about the various ANOVA procedures is Guenther, *Analysis of Variance*.

The only unexplained variance is hence the error variance (SS_e), which in any given situation will invariably be lower than the unexplained variance if a completely randomized design is to be used (that is, SS_W). Also, the *F*-statistic (ratio of treatment mean square to error mean square) for checking the significance of the treatment effects will be higher when a randomized-block ANOVA is used. So the likelihood of rejecting the null hypothesis of no effect due to the treatment variations, when it is false, will be higher. Thus randomized-block ANOVA is *more powerful* in terms of being able to detect differential impacts due to the treatment levels.

The computer output for a randomized-block ANOVA will look similar to the output in Exhibit 19.1, except that it will list separate sums of squares, degrees of freedom, and mean squares for the treatment variable, blocking factor, and residual. It will also list separate *F*-values for the treatment variable and blocking factor so that the statistical significance of the impact of each on the dependent variable can be ascertained.

Latin-square ANOVA

Latin-square ANOVA is a procedure that permits simultaneous control of the effects of *two* extraneous factors, and it is useful for analyzing data coming from a Latin-square experimental design (described in Chapter 9). To review this design, consider the grocery store chain example. Suppose unit sales of vegetable oil can be affected by not only store size but also store location. The Latin-square design will be appropriate in this situation to evaluate the true effects of the pricing treatments. One major requirement for using the Latin-square design is that the number of levels of each blocking factor and the number of main treatment groups must be identical. Hence in our example we must have exactly three categories of store size (e.g., large, medium, and small) and three categories of store location (e.g., urban, suburban, and rural).

From the three levels of each blocking factor a 3×3 matrix of 9 cells, representing all possible combinations of blocking-factor levels, is created. Next, starting with one cell at random, we assign pricing treatments to stores in the various cells such that each treatment appears once, and only once, in each row and column of the matrix. Unit sales are then measured in each cell and analyzed to ascertain the impact of the pricing treatments.

In a Latin-square ANOVA the part of SS_T not attributable to the treatments are split *three* ways: a sum of squares due to the row blocking factor (SS_r), a sum of squares due to the column blocking factor (SS_c), and a residual, or error, sum of squares (SS_e). Therefore

$$SS_T = SS_{TR} + SS_r + SS_c + SS_e.$$

Since in a Latin-square ANOVA the effects of two blocking factors are filtered out of the unexplained variance, the residual (or error) sum of squares (SS_e) is likely to be further reduced and the power to detect differential treatment effects increased, in comparison with the randomized-block procedure. The computer output for a Latin-square ANOVA will be similar to that for a randomized-block ANOVA. It will enable one to perform separate statistical-significance testing of the impact of the row blocking factor, the column blocking factor, and the main-treatment variable.

Factorial ANOVA

The factorial ANOVA is used to analyze data from a factorial-design experiment—that is, one intended to investigate the impact of *more than one* categorical independent variable on a metric-scaled dependent variable. A factorial design is thus a multiway design. We will review and illustrate this design by using our grocery chain example. Suppose we want to investigate the impact of an in-store, point-of-purchase display on unit sales of vegetable oil in addition to the pricing factor already described. Also, suppose the presence and the absence of the point-of-purchase display are the two treatment levels for this new factor. When we consider the two factors simultaneously, six *combinations* of treatment levels are possible: presence or absence of the point-of-purchase display with each of the three pricing treatments (regular price, 50¢ off, and 75¢ off). Sample stores can now be allocated to the six treatment levels, and unit sales can be monitored and analyzed to provide insight into the impact of the two factors.

When several factors, each with several levels, are involved in a factorial design, the number of possible combination levels and hence treatment groups can become numerous. In this case the cost of studying a subsample of units under each combination level may be prohibitive. Fortunately, procedures (which we will not discuss here) are available for systematically selecting and studying just a few of the levels and still being able to gain insight into the impact of all the factors.[3]

In our example we can, of course, use two separate one-way designs—one to study the impact of price and the other to study the impact of the point-of-purchase display. However, a major limitation of this approach is that it will not indicate possible interaction effects of the two factors on unit sales. An *interaction effect* is said to be present when the impact of a treatment level of one factor varies across treatment levels of another factor. For instance, suppose the 50¢-off pricing treatment is more effective than the regular-price treatment in the absence of the point-of-purchase display, but the two treatments are equally effective when the point-of-purchase display is present. In this case the two factors are said to interact with each other in influencing the dependent variable.

In factorial ANOVA the between sum of squares across all treatment combinations (six such combinations in our example), denoted as SS_{TR}, is split into

[3] See, for example, Charles W. Holland and David W. Cravens, "Fractional Factorial Experimental Designs in Marketing Research," *Journal of Marketing Research,* 10 (August 1973), pp. 270–276.

sums of squares attributable to each treatment variable separately and to interactions between treatment variables. If we label the treatment variables in a two-way ANOVA as P and Q, we can represent the partitioning of the total sum of squares as follows:

$$\begin{aligned} SS_T &= SS_{TR} + SS_e \\ &= SS_P + SS_Q + SS_{PQ} + SS_e, \end{aligned}$$

where SS_P and SS_Q correspond to the main effects of the two treatments, SS_{PQ} corresponds to the interaction effect between them, and SS_e is the error sum of squares.

The computer output for a factorial ANOVA will indicate the value of each SS-component in the expression for SS_T along with its associated degrees of freedom and mean square value. It will also provide separate F-values for ascertaining the significance of each main effect and the interaction effect.

A factorial experimental design is more efficient than several one-way designs in that it costs about the same and yet provides richer information. This design is also quite versatile in terms of allocating units to treatments and incorporating blocking factors. Units can be allocated by using a completely randomized procedure (as in the very first design we looked at), a randomized-block procedure, or a Latin-square procedure; partitioning of the total sum of squares and the resulting ANOVA will vary accordingly.

Analysis of covariance (ANCOVA)

Analysis of covariance is simply a variation of the ANOVA procedures and is intended to remove the effects of extraneous variables on the dependent variable. ANCOVA is especially suitable for situations where one cannot explicitly control an extraneous variable, as is possible in, say, a randomized-block design. One key requirement of ANCOVA is that metric data must be available for sample units on each extraneous variable to be included in the analysis.

To illustrate what is involved in ANCOVA, let us once again look at the one-way, completely randomized experimental design for investigating the effect of price on unit sales. As we saw earlier, one extraneous variable that could influence unit sales in addition to price is store size. Suppose metric data are available on store size (e.g., square feet of area), but for some reason we cannot use a randomized-block design to block out the effect of this extraneous factor. With metric data on unit sales and store size for all the sample stores, we can treat the former as a dependent variable and the latter as an independent variable and perform a regression analysis. Using the resulting regression equation, we can predict unit sales for each sample store and also compute a *residual,* representing the difference between the actual and predicted unit sales. We can thus generate a set of residual values for stores in each treatment group.

What do the residual values represent? They are simply the portion of unit sales not accounted for by store size. Stated differently, the residuals are data on the dependent variable that are no longer contaminated by the effects of store size. Therefore by analyzing these residuals (rather than the raw unit sales) through ANOVA, we should get a clearer picture of the pricing-treatment effects.

The modified ANOVA procedure illustrates the essence of ANCOVA. Stated simply, ANCOVA is ANOVA performed on dependent-variable residuals generated by regressing data on the extraneous variables against the raw data on the dependent variable. The extraneous factors included in an ANCOVA procedure are appropriately called *covariates*.

AUTOMATIC INTERACTION DETECTOR

The *automatic interaction detector* (AID) is a technique useful in identifying a set of key categorical independent variables that are most closely associated with a metric-scaled dependent variable. It is especially suitable for identifying market or customer segments and their distinguishing characteristics. To understand what AID does, as well as its capabilities and limitations, consider the following situation.

EXAMPLE: The Consumer Credit Company (CCC), a firm with over a million credit card holders, has gathered data on the following five variables for a random sample of 1000 of its customers:

1. Charge volume, defined as the total dollar amount charged to a card holder's account during the past year.
2. Highest education level, defined as less than high school diploma, high school diploma, bachelor's degree, or graduate degree.
3. Annual income, defined as less than \$25,000, \$25,000 to \$50,000, or more than \$50,000.
4. Number of years since card was issued, defined as less than 2 years, 2 to 5 years, or over 5 years.
5. Sex, defined as male or female.

The company wants to know the relative importance of variables 2 through 5 in accounting for variation in charge volume across its credit card customers. It also wants to construct distinguishing descriptive profiles, using variables 2 through 5, for segments that differ markedly with respect to charge volumes.

The AID technique is ideal for providing the desired information from the data gathered by CCC. Notice that charge volume, the dependent variable implicit in this situation, is metric-scaled (ratio-scaled, to be exact), while the four independent variables, 2 through 5, are categorical. This data format is similar to the format for ANOVA. Indeed, as we will see shortly, ANOVA is an integral part of the overall AID procedure.

The following steps are involved in conducting an AID analysis. First, all meaningful binary splits of the total sample are identified on each independent variable considered separately. A *binary split* is a split that results in two mutually exclusive and collectively exhaustive subsamples. For independent variables with just two categories (e.g., sex), only one binary split is possible. For those with more than two categories (e.g., annual income), several binary splits are possible. For instance, for the specific categories used by CCC to collect data on annual income, two meaningful binary splits based on that variable are possible: less than $25,000/$25,000 or more, and $50,000 or less/more than $50,000. At the end of the first step AID would thus have identified a number of ways of dividing the total sample into two subsamples.

Second, with each binary split as a pair of treatment groups, AID uses an ANOVA procedure to calculate a between sum of squares representing the amount of variation in the dependent variable accounted for by the binary split. One between sum of squares is calculated for each binary split identified in the previous step.

Third, the binary split with the highest between sum of squares—that is, the one offering two subsamples that are maximally differentiated on the dependent variable—is designated as the initial split of the total sample. Of all the independent variables included in the analysis, the one associated with the initial split is most critical in accounting for variation in the dependent variable.

Fourth, the two subsamples obtained in the initial split are further divided into two groups each, using a procedure similar to the first three steps. This process is repeated until subsample sizes or between sums of squares become too small for further splitting to be meaningful.

An AID analysis is laborious, involving a large number of calculations. It is therefore virtually always conducted with the aid of a computer. The primary output of this analysis is an AID tree, such as the one shown in Exhibit 19.2 for the CCC example.

The income level of card holders—specifically, the "more than $50,000/$50,000 or less" split—is most fruitful in accounting for variation in charge volume. However, the next most critical independent variable is not clear-cut. It is education level in the upper part of the AID tree and number of years since card was issued in the lower part. This sort of ambiguity is a limitation of the AID technique.[4]

Also, notice that while the upper part of the AID tree does not branch out beyond the second iteration, the lower part involves one more round of splits based on sex for one subsample and education level for the other. That is, any part of an AID tree can stop growing when the subsample sizes or between sums

[4] For a discussion of other limitations, see Peter Doyle and Ian Fenwick, "The Pitfalls of AID Analysis," *Journal of Marketing Research,* 12 (November 1975), pp. 408–413.

Exhibit 19.2

AID tree for the CCC example

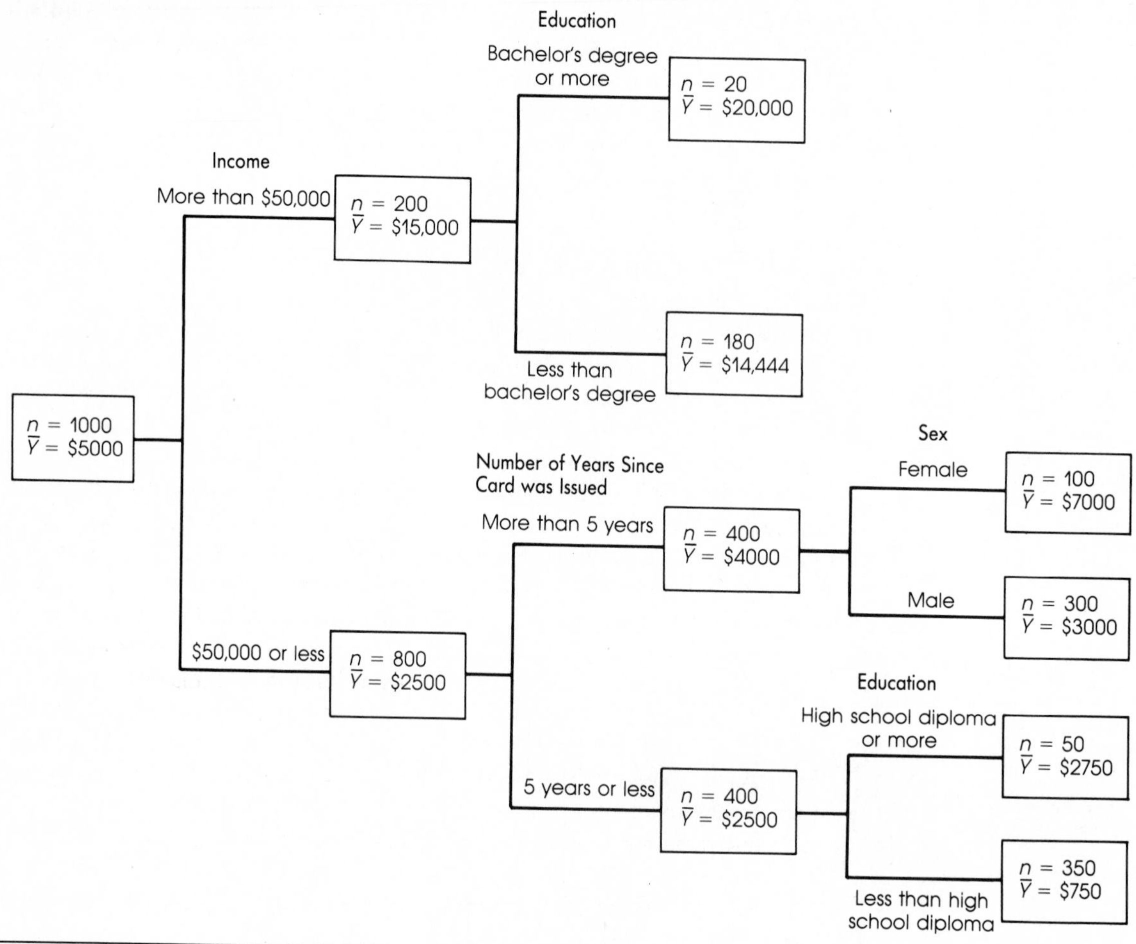

of squares become too small. In fact, a key requirement for a useful AID analysis is a large initial sample size (much larger than for other multivariate techniques) so that subsamples will have sufficient numbers of units to facilitate further splitting. Thus depending on the nature of the particular sample and the manner in which it starts splitting, the number of critical independent variables and their positions in the branching sequence can vary. This susceptibility of the AID technique to sampling idiosyncrasies is a potential drawback.[5]

[5] This point is well discussed in Doyle and Fenwick, "Pitfalls of AID Analysis."

Despite its limitations, the AID technique can provide at least preliminary insights. In the CCC example, for instance, the customer segment with the highest charge volume consists of individuals earning over $50,000 a year and holding at least bachelor's degrees. At the other extreme, the segment with the lowest charge volume is characterized by customers with annual incomes of $50,000 or less who have held their cards for five years or less and whose education level is less than a high school diploma. Such insights will be helpful to CCC when it formulates its future marketing strategies. Because of its usefulness, the AID technique has been applied in a variety of situations.[6]

DISCRIMINANT ANALYSIS

Discriminant analysis, like the AID technique, deals with identifying the distinguishing features of subgroups of units that are maximally separated on some dependent variable. However, the two techniques differ in a couple of critical ways.

First, while in AID analysis the number and the nature of subgroups are determined by the technique itself (as the various sample-splitting iterations occur), in discriminant analysis the subgroups are *prespecified* (e.g., heavy, moderate, and light users of a product; homeowners and renters; viewers and nonviewers of a television program). Thus the dependent variable in discriminant analysis is categorical, and there are as many prespecified subgroups as there are categories. Also, the independent variables are typically metric-scaled, in contrast to the categorical independent variables in AID analysis.

Second, while the basic purpose of AID analysis is to describe the subgroups in terms of the independent variables, the purpose of discriminant analysis also includes classification of new units into one of the subgroups, given the new units' values on the independent variables.

To illustrate discriminant analysis, consider the following example.

EXAMPLE: A computer manufacturer wants to see whether household income (X_1) and the number of years of formal education of the household head (X_2) are useful in clearly distinguishing households owning personal computers from those not owning personal computers. If X_1 and X_2 seem to be crucial determinants of personal-computer ownership, the firm also wishes to be able to determine whether a prospective customer household is likely to buy a personal computer, given the household's values on X_1 and X_2. The firm has gathered data on X_1 and X_2 for two random samples of households,

[6] For a recent application involving identification of key determinants of the export marketing behavior of firms, see S. Tamer Cavusgil and John R. Nevin, "Internal Determinants of Export Marketing Behavior: An Empirical Investigation," *Journal of Marketing Research,* 18 (February 1981), pp. 114–119.

Exhibit 19.3

Scatter plot of income and education data for personal-computer owners and nonowners

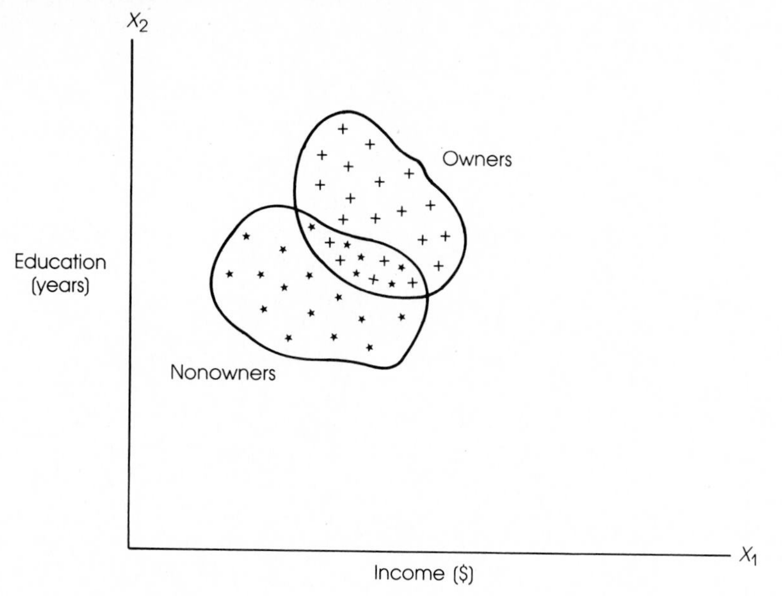

an owner sample and a nonowner sample. These data are plotted on the two-dimensional graph shown in Exhibit 19.3.

Two enclosed areas are shown in Exhibit 19.3, one containing primarily households with personal computers and the other containing primarily households without personal computers. Although the two areas overlap, the extent of overlap does not seem to be substantial. Intuitively, this exhibit implies that income and education are good discriminators between households with and those without personal computers. Minimal overlap between groups, as in Exhibit 19.3, is a critical requirement if discriminant analysis is to be fruitful.

The task of discriminant analysis now is to utilize the two groups of data points to quantify the relative importance of X_1 and X_2 in discriminating between the two sets of households, and to develop a criterion for classifying prospective households as potential owner or nonowner households. The key to accomplishing this twofold task is to develop an appropriate *discriminant function,* which is simply a linear combination of X_1 and X_2, specified as

$$v_1X_1 + v_2X_2,$$

where v_1 and v_2 are constants called *discriminant weights,* or *coefficients.* Given the values of v_1 and v_2 (we will see shortly how these are determined), we can compute a number summarizing the linear combination for each sample household. This number is called a household's *discriminant score,* which we will denote as its Y-score. For any household h,

$$Y_h = v_1X_{1h} + v_2X_{2h}.$$

Let us now turn to the determination of v_1 and v_2. Theoretically, an infinite number of combinations of v_1- and v_2-values are possible. Furthermore, depending on these values, the Y-scores for the sample households will vary. What discriminant analysis does is to select v_1 and v_2 in such a way that the variation in the Y-scores *between* the two groups of households is made as large as possible relative to variation in the Y-scores *within* them. In other words, v_1 and v_2 are chosen so as to maximize the ratio of between to within sums of squares corresponding to Y-scores. The mathematical details of this maximization are beyond our scope. Suffice it to say that the discriminant function is the linear combination of the independent variables that offers the best separation (least overlap) of Y-scores between the prespecified groups.

A graphical interpretation of a discriminant function of the form $v_1X_1 + v_2X_2$ is as follows: It is a family of parallel straight lines in a two-dimensional graph with X_1 and X_2 as axes. Each straight line in the family corresponds to a specific Y-score. Therefore the Y-scores of data points on the same straight line will be identical, but Y-scores of data points on different straight lines will vary. In fact, we can measure the Y-scores along a line perpendicular to the family of lines representing the discriminant function. This perpendicular line is called the *discriminant axis* and represents the dimension along which maximum separation between the two groups occurs. Stated differently, projections on the discriminant axis of the data points corresponding to the two groups will be clustered together within each group and spread apart between groups. The graphical interpretation of the discriminant function and discriminant scores is illustrated in Exhibit 19.4.

Using the discriminant function

The weights v_1 and v_2 can be interpreted as signifying the relative importance of X_1 and X_2 in being able to discriminate between the two groups, provided both independent variables are measured in the same units. When the measurement units are different (as in our example), one must obtain standardized weights, say v_1^* and v_2^*, as follows:

$$v_1^* = v_1s_1, \qquad v_2^* = v_2s_2,$$

Exhibit 19.4

Discriminant function and discriminant scores

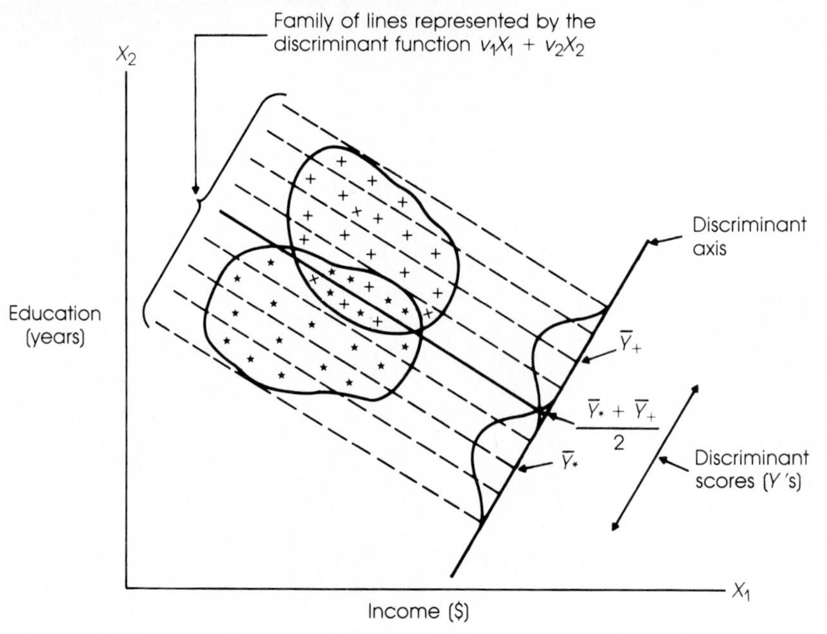

where s_1 and s_2 are *pooled standard deviations* for X_1 and X_2, respectively. The pooled standard deviation s_k for any variable X_k can be computed by using the formula mentioned in Chapter 17 in the discussion of hypothesis testing related to two population means. Using the subscripts 1 and 2 to refer to the two samples, we have

$$s_k = \sqrt{\frac{(n_1 - 1)s_{k1}^2 + (n_2 - 1)s_{k2}^2}{n_1 + n_2 - 2}}.$$

Use of this formula requires the assumption of equal X_k variances in the populations implied by the two samples.

The correspondence between the discriminant weights and the relative importance of the two independent variables in the discriminant function is demonstrated graphically by the two extreme situations depicted in Exhibit 19.5.

Classification of a new household with the discriminant function is quite straightforward. Given X_1- and X_2-values for a new unit, a Y-score is computed for it by using the discriminant function:

$$Y_{\text{new}} = v_1X_{1,\text{new}} + v_2X_{2,\text{new}}.$$

Exhibit 19.5

Relative importance of independent variables in a discriminant function

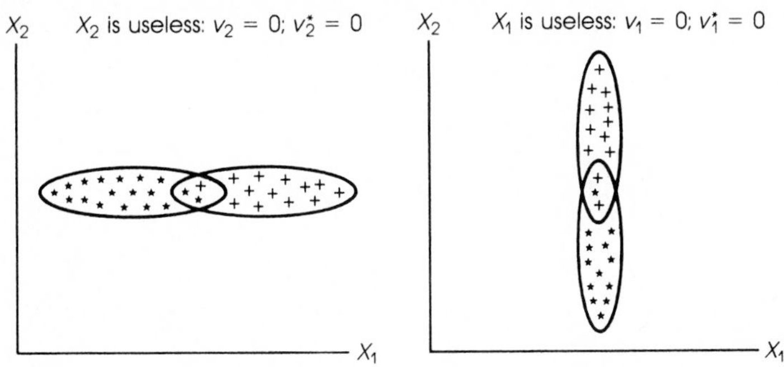

Then Y_{new} is compared with the mean discriminant scores, $\bar{Y}_*$ and $\bar{Y}_+$, for the two groups, which are computed as follows:

$$\bar{Y}_* = v_1\bar{X}_{1*} + v_2\bar{X}_{2*},$$
$$\bar{Y}_+ = v_1\bar{Y}_{1+} + v_2\bar{X}_{2+}.$$

The new household is assigned to the owner group if Y_{new} is closer to $\bar{Y}_+$ than to $\bar{Y}_*$; if not, it is assigned to the nonowner group. Another way of stating this assignment criterion is as follows: Compare Y_{new} with a *critical discriminant score,* Y_{cri}, defined as

$$Y_{cri} = \frac{\bar{Y}_* + \bar{Y}_+}{2}.$$

If $Y_{new} > Y_{cri}$, assign the household to the owner group; if not, assign it to the nonowner group. This allocation rule implicitly assumes that the cost of misallocation is the same for both groups. That is, erroneously classifying a potential owner as a nonowner will cost the same as classifying a potential nonowner as a owner. When the costs of misallocation are different, a more sophisticated classification criterion (not discussed here) is needed.[7] The solid line in the family of lines in Exhibit 19.4 is the critical discriminant line.

To illustrate the use of a discriminant function, suppose the data collected by the computer manufacturer on households with and without personal com-

[7] For details about this classification criterion and other aspects of discriminant analysis, see Donald F. Morrison, "Discriminant Analysis," in *Handbook of Marketing Research,* ed. Robert Ferber (New York: McGraw-Hill, 1974), pp. 2.442–2.457.

puters and the results of analyzing such data are as follows (the subscript + refers to personal-computer-owner households and the subscript * refers to nonowner households):

Sample sizes	$n_+ = 20$	$n_* = 20$
Sample means	$\overline{X}_{1+} = \$30{,}000$	$\overline{X}_{1*} = \$20{,}000$
	$\overline{X}_{2+} = 18$ years	$\overline{X}_{2*} = 16$ years
Standard deviations	$s_{1+} = \$6000$	$s_{1*} = \$5000$
	$s_{2+} = 4$ years	$s_{2*} = 6$ years
Discriminant weights	$v_1 = .009;\ v_2 = 3.25$	
Discriminant function	$.009X_1 + 3.25X_2$	

[Programs are available in several computer packages (e.g., SPSS) for deriving a discriminant function given the prespecified groupings of the sample units and data on the independent variables for each of those units.]

The firm, in addition to wanting to know the relative importance of income (X_1) and education (X_2) in discriminating between personal-computer-owner and nonowner households, wishes to classify a prospective household with $X_1 =$ \$28,000 and $X_2 = 15$ years into one of the two groups.

Since X_1 and X_2 are measured in different units, the discriminant weights v_1 and v_2 must be standardized through multiplication by the corresponding pooled standard deviations s_1 and s_2:

$$s_1 = \sqrt{\frac{(n_+ - 1)s_{1+}^2 + (n_* - 1)s_{1*}^2}{n_+ + n_* - 2}}$$

$$= \sqrt{\frac{(19)(6000)^2 + 19(5000)^2}{38}} = \$5522.68,$$

$$s_2 = \sqrt{\frac{(n_+ - 1)s_{2+}^2 + (n_* - 1)s_{2*}^2}{n_+ + n_* - 2}}$$

$$= \sqrt{\frac{(19)(4)^2 + 19(6)^2}{38}} = 5.10 \text{ years},$$

$$v_1^* = s_1v_1 = (5522.68)(.009) = 49.70,$$

$$v_2^* = s_2v_2 = (5.10)(3.25) = 16.52.$$

Comparing v_1^* with v_2^*, we can say that household income is about three times as important as education of the household head in distinguishing between personal-computer-owner and nonowner households.

To classify the prospective household, we need to determine its Y-score and compare it with Y_{cri}:

$$\begin{aligned}
Y_{\text{new}} &= v_1 X_{1,\text{new}} + v_2 X_{2,\text{new}} \\
&= (.009)(28{,}000) + (3.25)(15) \\
&= 252 + 48.75 = 300.75, \\
\bar{Y}_+ &= (.009)(30{,}000) + (3.25)(18) \\
&= 270 + 58.5 = 328.5, \\
\bar{Y}_* &= (.009)(20{,}000) + (3.25)(16) \\
&= 180 + 52 = 232, \\
Y_{\text{cri}} &= \frac{\bar{Y}_+ + \bar{Y}_*}{2} = \frac{328.5 + 232}{2} = 280.25.
\end{aligned}$$

Since $Y_{\text{new}} > Y_{\text{cri}}$, we should classify the prospective household as a potential owner of a personal computer.

Evaluating a discriminant function

The preceding discussion of discriminant analysis has not considered the issue of how trustworthy the resulting discriminant function is. However, tests are available for checking the statistical significance of a discriminant function as well as its discriminant weights. These tests are similar to the ones we discussed for regression analysis.[8] Since both regression analysis and discriminant analysis involve forming linear combinations of independent variables, the potential limitations of regression analysis and the precautions to be taken in interpreting its results are applicable to discriminant analysis as well.

For a discriminant function that is statistically significant, an intuitive approach for evaluating its practical usefulness is to construct and examine what is usually called a confusion matrix. A *confusion matrix* indicates the degree of correspondence, or lack thereof, between the actual groupings of the sample units and the predicted groupings obtained by classifying the same units through the discriminant function. The confusion matrix corresponding to our illustration (Exhibit 19.4) is shown in Table 19.2.

Numbers on the diagonal going down from left to right in the confusion matrix refer to sample units correctly classified. A summary indicator of a discriminant function's predictive ability is the following ratio, called the ***hit rate***:

$$\frac{\text{total number of correctly classified units}}{\text{total sample size}}.$$

The hit rate for the confusion matrix in Table 19.2 is

$$\frac{17 + 16}{20 + 20} = \frac{33}{40} = .825.$$

[8] For further details, see Morrison, "Discriminant Analysis."

Table 19.2

Confusion matrix corresponding to Exhibit 19.4

ACTUAL GROUPINGS	PREDICTED GROUPINGS	
	Households With Personal Computers	Households Without Personal Computers
Households with Personal Computers	17	3
Households without Personal Computers	4	16

Thus our illustrative discriminant function is able to correctly classify 82.5% of all sample households.

Note that the hit rate calculated here is based on the same set of sample units used to construct the discriminant function. Hence it is likely to be somewhat biased in favor of the function. A more stringent way to measure a discriminant function's predictive ability is to construct the function by using part (say one-half or two-thirds) of the sample and to compute the hit rate on the basis of predictions for the units in the remainder of the sample. Being able to use this approach, of course, depends on how large the sample size is.

How good is the hit rate (prediction accuracy) of 82.5%? The answer depends on how accurately one can classify the units by chance (i.e., without using the discriminant function). The extent to which correct classifications can be made purely by chance is a function of the relative sizes of the two actual groups. In our example both groups are of the same size (i.e., 20), implying that the a priori probability of any sample unit being a personal-computer owner is .5. Also, our objective is to classify the units into owners and nonowners. So suppose we toss a fair coin for each unit and classify the unit as a personal-computer owner if we observe heads (nonowner, if we observe tails). We will be correct 50% of the time, and therefore our prediction accuracy by chance will be 50%. Therefore the hit rate of 82.5% for our discriminant function appears to be quite good.

What if the two groups are not of the same size? For instance, suppose the nonowner group is three times as large as the owner group (i.e., $n_+ = 10$ and $n_* = 30$)? Now the a priori probability of a sample unit being a personal-computer owner is .25. Therefore if we want to classify each unit as either an owner or a nonowner without the aid of a discriminant function, we can use the following procedure: For each unit, draw a random number between 1 and 100. If the number is between 1 and 25, classify the unit as an owner; if not, classify the unit as a nonowner. The chance prediction accuracy in this case can be shown to be

$$P^2 + (1 - P)^2,$$

where P is the proportion of units in one group and $(1 - P)$ is the proportion of units in the other. When $P = .25$, the chance prediction accuracy is $(.25)^2 +$

$(.75)^2 = .625$, or 62.5%. A hit rate of 82.5% compared with a chance prediction accuracy of 62.5% is still not bad, although it is worse than it is when the two groups are of equal size—that is, $P = .5$ (verify that the chance prediction accuracy is 50% when $P = .5$).

In general, the more dissimilar the sizes of the two original groups, the lower is the ability of a discriminant function to outperform a chance classification scheme that relies merely on the relative group sizes. Such a chance classification scheme implies the use of what is usually called the proportional chance criterion. There is another chance classification scheme that uses the so-called maximum chance criterion, in which *all* the units are classified into the larger of the two a priori groups. Thus when a sample of 40 units has 10 owners and 30 nonowners, classifying all 40 units as nonowners will result in a maximum prediction accuracy of 75%. The maximum chance criterion is unrealistic, however, since putting all units into just one group defeats the very purpose of identifying distinct group memberships.

Final remarks

Our treatment of discriminant analysis centered on situations where the total sample is divided into two groups on the basis of some prespecified criterion. However, discriminant analysis is not limited to just two-group situations. It is capable of generating discriminant functions for classifying units into more than two prespecified groups. While the rationale underlying multiple-group discriminant analysis is similar to that underlying the two-group case, further details of the technique are too complex to be included in this textbook.

Discriminant functions are not restricted to just two independent variables either. The sole reason for including only two independent variables in our discussion was to keep it simple and to facilitate graphical interpretation of what the technique does. Discriminant functions can and often do contain more than two independent variables. The general form for a discriminant function with k variables is

$$v_1X_1 + v_2X_2 + \cdots + v_kX_k.$$

Discriminant analysis has been used in a wide variety of settings, although it is not as popular as regression analysis or analysis of variance.[9] The potential for applying discriminant analysis is great, however, given marketers' ever-present need for defining customer segments, identifying critical characteristics capable of distinguishing among them, and classifying prospective customers into appro-

[9] See Barnett A. Greenberg, Jac L. Goldstucker, and Danny N. Bellenger, "What Techniques Are Used by Marketing Researchers in Business? *Journal of Marketing,* 41 (April 1977), pp. 62–68; A. Parasuraman, "A Study of Techniques Used and Clients Served by Marketing Research Firms," *European Research,* 10 (October 1982), pp. 177–185.

priate segments.[10] Rumor has it that even the Internal Revenue Service has developed a sophisticated discriminant function to help classify tax returns into those worthy of an IRS audit and those that are not.

FACTOR ANALYSIS

The multivariate techniques discussed so far fall under the general label of *dependence techniques* because they involve analyzing data sets in which one variable is designated as the dependent variable and the rest are treated as independent variables. The techniques to be covered in the remainder of this chapter are *interdependence techniques;* that is, the dependent- and independent-variable designations are not necessary for their use. Interdependence techniques treat all variables in a data set equally and search for underlying patterns within the data set. The first interdependence technique we will discuss is factor analysis, which is perhaps the most frequently used among all such techniques.

Factor analysis is essentially a data and variable reduction technique. For metric-scaled data on a large number of variables, factor analysis generates a smaller number of variables, called *factors,* which captures as much information as possible from the original data set. The factors are formed by taking advantage of interrelationships among the original variables. Factor analysis typically begins by examining a matrix of pairwise correlations among the original variables and explores ways of combining them into factors such that each factor primarily represents a cluster of maximally correlated variables. The mechanics of analyzing correlations to derive the factors will not be covered here.[11] Rather, our primary focus will be on providing an intuitive understanding of what factor analysis does and how its results can be interpreted and used.

Intuitive Explanation

To examine the procedure of factor analysis, let us first consider this hypothetical situation:

EXAMPLE: Star Brands, Inc. (SBI), a manufacturer of a variety of home appliances and electronic products, recently conducted a survey of customers owning Star products. The purpose of the survey was to find out how

---

[10] One marketing research firm specializes in using discriminant analysis to advise clients on what characteristics distinguish likers of their brands from dislikers, and how to reposition the brands so as to convert dislikers into likers. See Lorin Zissman and John Morton, "Brand Maximization Analysis Clarifies Product Repositioning Opportunities," *Marketing News,* January 22, 1982, Section 1, pp. 4–5.

[11] The following texts provide good discussions of the technical details concerning factor analysis: Jum C. Nunnally, *Psychometric Theory* (New York: McGraw-Hill, 1978); Harry H. Harman, *Modern Factor Analysis* (Chicago: University of Chicago Press, 1967).

customers felt about SBI in general and about specific Star products in particular. The survey involved numerous evaluative statements that respondents answered by using a seven-point scale on which the higher the number, the more favorable was the evaluation.

A variety of rating scales were discussed in Chapter 11. Recall that data obtained through rating scales are typically assumed to have interval-scale properties. Factor analysis requires data that are at least interval-scaled.

Although factor analysis typically involves analyzing data on a large number of statements (variables) simultaneously, let us just consider the following two statements from the SBI survey in order to illustrate graphically the rationale underlying the technique:

1. I have been satisfied with the Star products I have purchased.
2. When I have to purchase a home appliance in the future, it will likely be a Star product.

Customer ratings on each statement can be considered as data on a single variable. Let S_1 and S_2 denote the variables implicit in the two statements. A plot of the survey data on S_1 and S_2 is shown in Exhibit 19.6.

Exhibit 19.6

When factor analysis will be beneficial

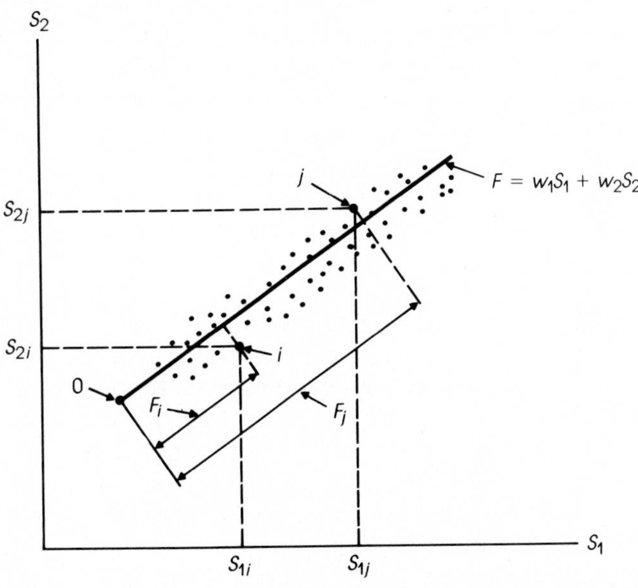

Clearly S_1 and S_2 are highly correlated. In other words, ratings on the two statements are largely redundant since they apparently represent very similar customer sentiments. Therefore we should be able to combine them into ratings along just one dimension without any significant loss of information embedded in the raw data set. This combination is exactly what factor analysis of the data on S_1 and S_2 will accomplish. The straight line labeled F in Exhibit 19.6 is a factor and represents the dimension along which measurements can be made for all sample units from an arbitrary origin such as point 0 shown on the line. These measurements are called *factor scores.* Two such factor scores, F_i and F_j, are shown in the exhibit for respondents i and j.

What does a comparison of the factor scores for respondents i and j with their ratings on S_1 and S_2 reveal? Clearly, the higher a respondent's rating on S_1 *or* S_2, the higher the respondent's factor score is in an almost proportionate fashion. Exhibit 19.6 further suggests that the close correspondence between the two original sets of ratings and the factor scores can be generalized to the entire sample. In factor analysis terminology S_1 and S_2 are said to have high factor loadings on F.

DEFINITION. A *factor loading* is the Pearson correlation coefficient between an original variable and a factor.

In short, having data on just F for the sample respondents is virtually as good as having separate ratings on S_1 and S_2. What Exhibit 19.6 demonstrates graphically for just two variables is the foundation underlying factor analysis and can be generalized to more than two variables: Given data on a large number of variables, *at least some of which are highly correlated with one another,* factor analysis can provide a more parsimonious set of factors with little loss of information. The emphasis on correlations among the original variables in the preceding sentence is noteworthy: Factor analysis will not do much good if the original variables are poorly correlated.

This limitation of factor analysis is demonstrated in Exhibit 19.7, in which S_1 and S_2 are poorly correlated. Poor association between factor scores and S_1 and S_2 ratings is illustrated by the fact that all data points along line *ab* (with S_1 ratings ranging from S_{1a} to S_{1b} and S_2 ratings ranging from S_{2a} to S_{2b}) will have the same factor score F_{ab}.

The factor scores along dimension F in Exhibit 19.7 do not correlate strongly with the data on either S_1 or S_2. The factor F thus does a poor job of capturing the essence of the original data set. We can make F parallel to the S_1 axis, as shown by line FS_1, so that the factor scores will perfectly correspond with the S_1 ratings. Unfortunately, factor scores along FS_1 will reflect nothing about the ratings on S_2. We would have to construct another perpendicular factor, such as FS_2, to capture the S_2 ratings. But by doing so, we would defeat the purpose of factor analysis, namely, data and variable reduction. Obviously, using the original two variables themselves is sensible if two factors are needed to

Exhibit 19.7

When factor analysis will not be beneficial

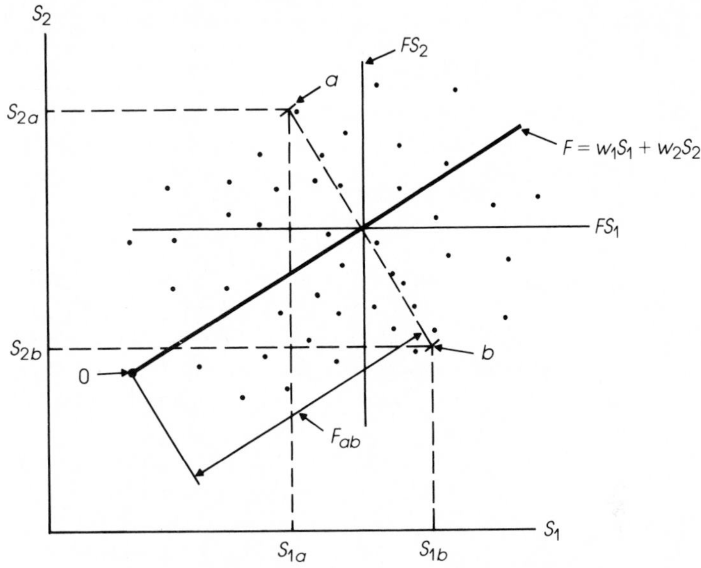

fully capture the gist of the raw data. Thus factor analysis is not always guaranteed to accomplish its intended purpose.

Returning to Exhibit 19.6, what interpretation can we place on factor F? Mathematically, it is a linear combination that accounts for almost all the variation in S_1 and S_2:

$$F = w_1S_1 + w_2S_2,$$

where w_1 and w_2 are weights determined by the factor analysis procedure. But does it have any *substantive* meaning? In other words, since F is a new, combined variable, what *name* can we give it? The issue of naming factors is highly subjective and hence somewhat controversial. Invariably, users of factor analysis simply choose a label on the basis of any common thread running through the original variables that have high loadings on it. So naming a factor can be very difficult when variables with high loadings on it have little in common, which is not an unusual occurrence in factor analysis applications and thus is a potential limitation of the technique. In our illustration S_1 represents satisfaction with Star products and S_2 represents likelihood of future purchases of Star products. Hence we can perhaps consider F as *trust* in Star products. Someone else looking at Exhibit 19.6 may come up with a label other than trust, however.

Factor analysis output and its interpretation

As you would expect, canned computer programs are available to perform factor analysis. These programs typically conduct the analysis after standardizing the variables (i.e., converting each to a mean of zero and variance of one). The primary output of such programs is a *factor-loading matrix.* To illustrate this matrix, let us assume that a factor analysis is conducted on ratings given by owners of Star videocassette recorders (VCRs) on six statements included in the SBI survey. These statements (designated as variables X_1 through X_6) and their factor-loading matrix are shown in Table 19.3.

Table 19.3 implies that two factors (F_1 and F_2) have been constructed by analyzing data on variables X_1 through X_6. In general, as many factors as there are variables can be derived from an original data set. Computer programs allow factor analysis users to specify the number of factors to be extracted. Of course, the smaller the number of factors that can adequately reflect the information in the original data set the better.

One important feature of factor analysis that is crucial in interpreting its results is that the factors themselves are *independent.* In other words, the technique constructs factors in such a way that the correlation between any pair of

Table 19.3
Factor-loading matrix based on data from study of Star customers

FACTOR LOADINGS	FACTORS		ACHIEVED COMMUNALITIES
	F_1	F_2	
X_1: I did not mind paying the high price for my Star VCR	0.89	0.15	.815
X_2: I am pleased with the variety of things that a Star VCR can do	0.16	0.86	.766
X_3: I hardly ever worry about anything going wrong with my Star VCR	0.18	0.94	.916
X_4: My friends are very impressed with the Star VCR	0.96	0.06	.926
X_5: The Star VCR has the latest technology built into it	0.09	0.88	.782
X_6: No other brand of VCR even comes close to matching the Star VCR	0.92	0.17	.875
Eigenvalues: Standardized variance explained by each factor	2.626	2.454	
Proportion of the total variance explained by each factor	0.438	0.409	

extracted factors will be zero. Thus there is no overlap or redundancy of information among the factors.

The numbers in Table 19.3 under the column heading "Factors," through the sixth row, are factor loadings. Thus, for instance, the correlation coefficient between X_1 and F_1 is .89; that between X_1 and F_2 is .15. Recall from Chapter 18 that the squared correlation coefficient between two variables is the proportion of variance in one accounted for by the other. Therefore $(.89)^2$ is the variance in X_1 accounted for by F_1, and $(.15)^2$ is the variance in X_1 accounted for by F_2. Since there is no duplication of information between F_1 and F_2, the variance in X_1 extracted by both factors considered together is $(.89)^2 + (.15)^2 = .815$. This value is called the achieved communality for X_1. The achieved communalities for all six variables are listed in the last column of Table 19.3.

DEFINITION. The *achieved communality* for any original variable represents the proportion of variance in it accounted for by all the extracted factors.

Achieved communalities for the original variables are given by summing the squared factor loadings corresponding to each variable. They shed light on the extent to which a reduced set of factors is able to reflect the data on each original variable. The two factors in our example account for over 75% of the variance in each of the six variables, suggesting thereby that the factor analysis has been quite effective.

Numbers in the row labeled "Eigenvalues" in Table 19.3 summarize the amount of information captured by each factor.

DEFINITION. The *eigenvalue* of any factor is the total standardized variance accounted for by the factor.

Eigenvalues of the extracted factors are given by summing the squared factor loadings corresponding to each factor. The total standardized variance in the original data set is simply the number of variables, since each variable has a variance of one. The total standardized variance in our example is 6. Therefore, the proportion of variance extracted by F_1 is its eigenvalue divided by 6, or $2.626/6 = .438$. Similarly, the proportion of the total variance extracted by F_2 is .409. These proportions are shown in the last row of Table 19.3. The proportion of the total original variance extracted by the two factors together is .847 (or 84.7%). This result is another indication that the factor analysis has been quite effective.

Let us now turn to interpretation of F_1 and F_2. The first factor is strongly correlated with X_1, X_4, and X_6 and weakly correlated with X_2, X_3, and X_5. The second factor is strongly correlated with X_2, X_3, and X_5 and weakly correlated with X_1, X_4, and X_6. These results are somewhat fortunate; factor loadings will not always be so clean as to suggest that key variables making up one factor have little in common with another factor.[12] What do X_1, X_4, and X_6 have in common? Not minding the product's high price (X_1), impressing friends with the product (X_4), and viewing the product as being vastly superior to competing products (X_6) suggest that the common dimension underlying them can be called a *prestige* factor. Similarly, satisfaction with the products' capabilities (X_2), lack of worry about the product failing (X_3), and believing that the product is technologically advanced (X_5) imply that F_2 can perhaps be labeled as a *performance* factor. However, as we pointed out earlier, these labels are subjective and may be challenged by others as being inappropriate.

Not all factor loadings have to be positive, as in Table 19.3. After all, they are correlation coefficients and can range from -1 to $+1$. The features the original variables are measuring and the nature of the interrelationships among them will have an impact on the signs of the factor loadings. For instance, if a statement such as "Star VCRs are technologically behind the times" had been included in the SBI survey, its loading on factor F_2 in Table 19.3 would most likely have been negative. Intuitively, a negative factor loading means that the variable is representing something that is contrary to what the overall factor dimension represents.

Potential applications

Factor analysis has several different applications. First, it can be used in developing parsimonious, yet comprehensive, multiple-item scales for measuring various marketing constructs. This application is perhaps the most frequent one, judging from published research reports and articles. In Chapter 11 we saw that the process of developing a multiple-item scale (e.g., a Likert scale for measuring attitudes) typically starts with generating a large set of statements related to a topic. Factor analysis can be helpful in reducing the set of statements to a concise instrument and, at the same time, ensuring that the retained statements adequately reflect critical aspects of the construct being measured. The following example illustrates this application.

EXAMPLE: A public utility company wants to develop a 15-item scale to measure the attitudes of its customers toward nuclear power. The company has already generated an initial pool of 100 items concerning nuclear power. Further, it has data on these items in the form of ratings obtained through a pilot survey of customers.

---

[12] When the initial factor-loading matrix is difficult to interpret, one can sometimes make the pattern of loadings clearer through a process called *factor rotation*. Details of factor rotation are complex and can be found in advanced texts, such as Nunnally, *Psychometric Theory*, and Harmon, *Modern Factor Analysis*.

One approach to constructing the final 15-item scale is to use factor analysis in the following fashion: As was stated in Chapter 11, attitudes are generally believed to have three distinct dimensions, cognitive, affective, and behavioral.[13] One can therefore conduct a factor analysis of the initial pool of 100 items and extract three factors from it. An examination of the resulting factor-loading matrix and the key items making up each factor can indicate whether the three attitude dimensions are adequately covered by the initial set of items. If they are, the five items with the highest loadings on each factor can be chosen for the final 15-item scale.[14]

A second application of factor analysis is to bring into bold relief the nature of distinct dimensions underlying an existing data set and hence offer managerial insights that may not emerge otherwise—insights that can be helpful in developing market segmentation and marketing-mix strategies. For instance, the factor-loading matrix pertaining to the SBI survey data (Table 19.3) implies that prestige and performance may be two critical criteria underlying customer evaluations of Star VCRs. This finding, in turn, suggests that SBI may benefit by building its promotional strategy for Star VCRs around the themes of prestige and performance.

Third, the ability of factor analysis to convert a large volume of data into a set of factor scores on a limited number of *uncorrelated* factors makes the technique ideal for use in conjunction with other analysis procedures such as multiple regression and discriminant analysis. Suppose 20 closely related independent variables are to be included in a multiple regression equation. Two potential problems here are multicollinearity and the lack of a sufficient number of observations. An effective way of circumventing both problems is to perform a factor analysis of the 20 independent variables. Since the variables are closely related, just a few factors, say 4, should capture most of the information in the independent-variable data set. The 4 uncorrelated factors can be treated as independent variables, and their factor scores can be used as raw data for the multiple regression analysis.[15]

---

[13] See, for example, Carl E. Black and Kenneth J. Roering, *Essentials of Consumer Behavior* (Hinsdale, Ill.: Dryden Press, 1976), pp. 220–222.

[14] A number of applications of factor analysis in scale development have been reported in the marketing literature; see, for example, Robert W. Ruekert and Gilbert A. Churchill, Jr., "Reliability and Validity of Alternative Measures of Channel Member Satisfaction," *Journal of Marketing Research,* 21 (May 1984, pp. 226–233).

[15] Despite the versatility and mathematical sophistication of factor analysis, subjective decisions made by users of the technique play a critical role in how meaningful its applications are. For a discussion of these decisions and their impact on the final outcomes, see William D. Wells and Jagdish N. Sheth, "Factor Analysis," in *Handbook of Marketing Research,* ed. Robert Ferber (New York: McGraw-Hill, 1974), pp. 2.248–2.471; see also David A. Aaker, "Factor Analysis: An Exposition," in *Multivariate Analysis in Marketing,* ed. David A. Aaker (Palo Alto, Calif.: Scientific Press, 1981), pp. 163–171.

CLUSTER ANALYSIS

As the name of this technique implies, the basic purpose of *cluster analysis* is to segment objects (e.g., customers, market areas, and products) into groups so that objects within each group are similar to one another on a variety of characteristics. Cluster analysis is potentially valuable in market segmentation studies in which the objective is to identify distinct customer groups. Indeed, the AID analysis for identifying customer segments that we discussed earlier can be viewed as a clustering procedure. However, AID analysis is a dependence technique since each binary split in the AID tree is based on a prespecified criterion variable (e.g., charge volume in Exhibit 19.2). In this respect AID analysis is somewhat different from traditional cluster analysis, which strives to identify *natural groupings* of objects on the basis of their values on a number of variables without designating any of them as a dependent variable. The following example illustrates this point.

EXAMPLE: A firm offering recreational services wants to enter a new region of the country. It recently surveyed a large sample of households in this region and gathered data on over a hundred characteristics including demographics, expenditures on recreation, leisure time activities, and interests of household members. The firm wants to identify one or several household segments that are likely to be most responsive to its advertising and to its services.

One way for the firm to identify such segments is to conduct a cluster analysis of the data it has gathered. The results of this analysis will reveal clusters of households where each cluster contains households that have similar data on the measured characteristics and where each cluster differs markedly from other clusters. Examining the composition of individual clusters will aid the firm in deciding which clusters to target and how best to reach them through its advertising.[16]

How does cluster analysis work? Several clustering procedures are available, each based on a somewhat different set of complex computer routines.[17] But the basic principle underlying them is the same and involves measuring the

---

[16] Several marketing research firms specialize in performing cluster analysis to identify useful customer segments for their clients. For a discussion of several such firms and the services they offer, see Doris Walsh, "Cluster Demographics Can Target Consumers but Zip-Code Groupings May Not Be Accurate," *Marketing News,* May 13, 1983, Section 1, pp. 24–25.

[17] For additional details, see Ronald A. Frank and Paul E. Green, "Numerical Taxonomy in Marketing Analysis: A Review Article," *Journal of Marketing Research,* 5 (February 1968), pp. 83–98. Also, a variation of the factor analysis procedure we discussed can be used for clustering *objects* (instead of variables). This analysis is called Q-factor analysis, to distinguish it from traditional factor analysis, which is called R-factor analysis.

Exhibit 19.8

Clusters formed by using data on two characteristics

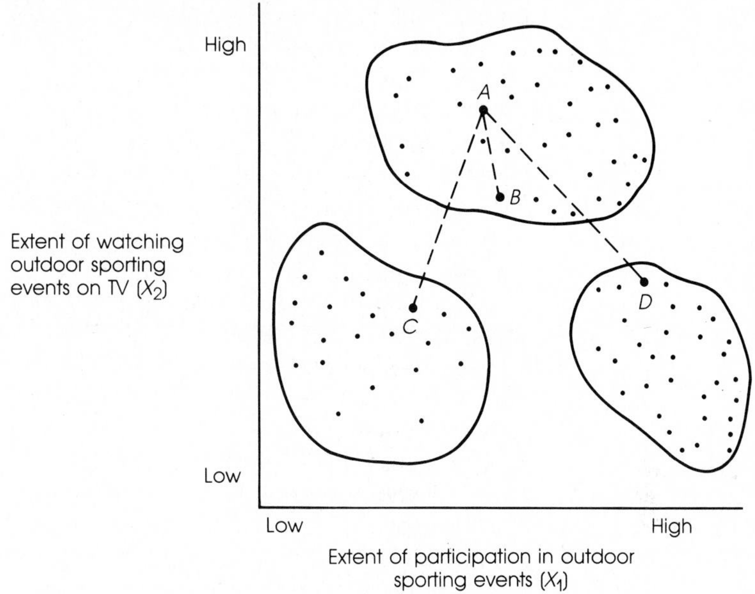

similarity between objects on the basis of their values on the various characteristics. Similarity between objects is often ascertained through some *distance measure,* which can best be illustrated in the context of a situation involving just two clustering characteristics. Suppose data are available for a sample of individuals on the two variables described below:

- The extent to which they participate in outdoor sporting events (X_1).
- The extent to which they watch outdoor sporting events on TV (X_2).

Data on X_1 and X_2 are plotted on a two-dimensional graph in Exhibit 19.8.

Each point in Exhibit 19.8 represents one individual. The physical distance between any pair of points is *inversely* related to how similar the corresponding individuals are when their X_1- and X_2-values are considered together. Thus individual *A* is more like *B* than either *C* or *D*. From a comparison of all such interpoint distances, Exhibit 19.8 reveals three distinct clusters.

Constructing clusters from a scatter plot—that is, determining how many distinct clusters there are and to which cluster each data point should be assigned—is an iterative, trial-and-error process. Complex computer algorithms are available for this purpose and must be used if the clustering is to be done in an efficient, systematic fashion. The mechanics underlying the computer algorithms are quite involved and vary across algorithms. However, the basic idea behind all of them is to start with some arbitrary cluster boundaries and modify them progressively until a stage is reached where the average interpoint distances within clusters are as small as possible relative to average distances between clusters. This logic of minimizing interpoint distances within clusters and maximizing them across clusters also applies to situations where a large number of variables form the basis for clustering. However, to display clusters graphically in more than two dimensions is difficult.

The use of cluster analysis is not limited to segmenting customers. It can also be used to segment objects such as geographic market areas or brands within a product category. One application of cluster analysis, for instance, involved segmenting 88 standard metropolitan areas in the United States into homogeneous clusters on the basis of several economic and demographic characteristics of the areas. The results, which revealed 18 distinct clusters, can be valuable to marketers who want to select similar markets for conducting controlled research studies.[18] A variety of other marketing applications of cluster analysis are summarized in a review article on this topic.[19]

MULTIDIMENSIONAL SCALING

Multidimensional scaling is most often used in marketing to identify key dimensions underlying customer evaluations of products or brands. The technique is intended to infer the underlying dimensions from a series of similarity and/or preference judgments provided by customers about objects (products, brands, etc.) within a given set. In this respect multidimensional scaling does somewhat the reverse of what cluster analysis does: While cluster analysis groups objects according to similarities inferred from data on prespecified dimensions, multidimensional scaling infers underlying evaluative dimensions from similarities and/or preferences indicated by customers. Data on perceived similarities or preferences can be in the form of ranks (i.e., nonmetric) or in the form of more refined ratings (i.e., metric). Multidimensional-scaling approaches are available for analyzing nonmetric as well as metric input data; one may also analyze data on similarities and preferences separately or on both simultaneously. Going into the details of these analysis variations is beyond our scope.[20] To get an intuitive

[18] Paul E. Green, Ronald E. Frank, and Patrick J. Robinson, "Cluster Analysis in Test Market Selection," *Management Science,* April 1967, B–387 to B–400.

[19] Girish Punj and David W. Stewart, "Cluster Analysis in Marketing Research: Review and Suggestions for Application," *Journal of Marketing Research,* 20 (May 1983), pp. 134–148.

[20] For further information and technical details concerning multidimensional scaling, see Paul E. Green and Frank J. Carmone, *Multidimensional Scaling* (Boston: Allyn and Bacon, 1970); Paul E. Green, "Marketing Applications of MDS: Assessment and Outlook," *Journal of Marketing,* 39 (January 1975), pp. 24–31.

Table 19.4
Similarity rankings of six department stores

	K-MART	PENNEYS	SEARS	WALMART	WARDS	WOOLWORTH
K-MART		12	11	1	7	3
PENNEYS			5	15	4	10
SEARS				13	6	14
WALMART					9	2
WARDS						8

Note: Numbers are ranks indicating perceived similarities between pairs of stores; the smaller the number, the more similar the pair of stores is.

idea of what multidimensional scaling does, we will use a simple example involving analysis of similarities provided in the form of ranks.

EXAMPLE: A customer is given a set of six department stores and asked to express how similar each store is to the others. Specifically, the customer is asked to compare *pairs* of stores and rank the pairs from most similar to least similar. Since there are six stores, 15 distinct pairs of stores are possible. The ranks given by the customer are shown in Table 19.4.

Multidimensional scaling, like cluster analysis, is an iterative, trial-and-error process that can be carried out by using one of several available computer programs.[21] If the data in Table 19.4 are subjected to multidimensional scaling, the technique will attempt to generate a geometric configuration of the stores such that distances between pairs of stores are as consistent as possible with the customer's similarity ranks—that is, the pair of stores ranked 15th are farthest apart, the pair of stores ranked 14th are next farthest apart, and so on.

An important feature of this approach is that it attempts to represent objects in a geometric space with the *least* possible number of dimensions necessary to make the resulting configuration consistent with the similarity ranks. For instance, suppose three objects, A, B, and C, are such that a respondent perceives A and B to be most similar (rank = 1), B and C to be least similar (rank = 3), and A and C to be somewhere in between (rank = 2). These similarity rankings can be easily transformed into a corresponding geometric configuration in just *one* dimension, as follows:

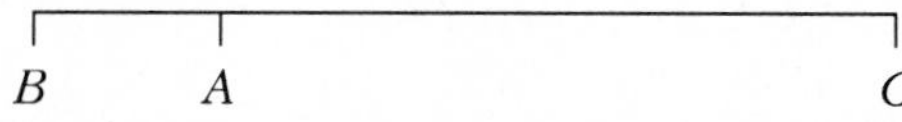

[21] For a description of these programs, see Paul E. Green and Vithala R. Rao, *Applied Multidimensional Scaling: A Comparison of Approaches and Algorithms* (New York: Holt, Rinehart and Winston, 1972).

Exhibit 19.9

Multidimensional map of department stores based on similarity rankings

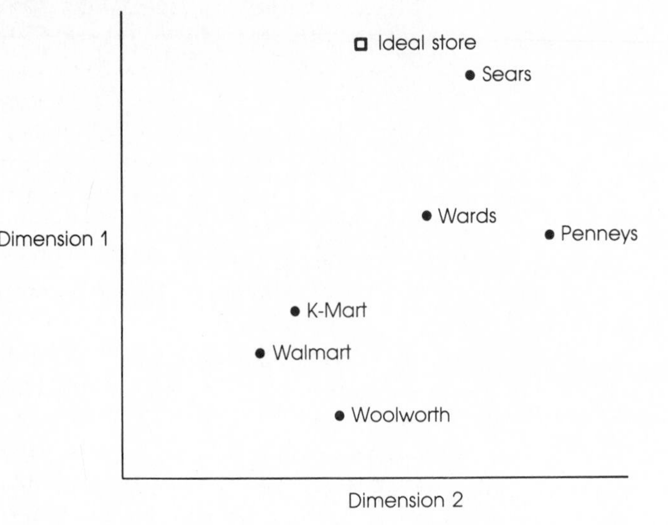

However, as the number of objects increases, a higher-dimensional space may be necessary to represent the objects so that interobject distances are consistent with perceived similarity rankings.

Conceptually, this technique starts by arraying objects on a straight line (one dimension). If the object cannot be positioned on this line in accordance with perceived similarities between them, it adds another perpendicular line and moves the objects around in two-dimensional space to see whether a configuration that is reasonably consistent with the similarity rankings can be obtained.[22] If it cannot be obtained, the technique adds a third dimension, reconfigures the objects in three-dimensional space, and so on. Exhibit 19.9 shows a two-dimensional configuration of the six stores in which the interstore distances are consistent with the input rankings shown in Table 19.4.

Ignoring for the moment the point marked Ideal store, what insight does Exhibit 19.9 offer? To answer this question, we must know what the two dimensions represent. Labeling the dimensions is quite subjective, however, and is hence a potential problem area. It basically involves inspecting the relative position of the objects along each dimension and inferring what the dimension

[22] What is reasonably consistent is based on a measure called the *stress index,* whose value is provided by most multidimensional-scaling programs after each iteration. For details about the stress index, see J. B. Kruskal, "Multidimensional Scaling by Optimizing Goodness of Fit to a Nonmetric Hypothesis," *Psychometrika,* March 1964, pp. 1–27.

is most likely to represent on the basis of one's prior knowledge about the objects themselves.

When the six stores in our example are arrayed along the horizontal dimension (dimension 1), Walmart is closest to the origin and Penneys is farthest from the origin. From what we know about the stores, we can perhaps label dimension 1 as price, with prices increasing from left to right along the dimension. Likewise, dimension 2 can be interpreted as representing number of product lines or product variety, with variety increasing from bottom to top. (Remember, however, that someone else looking at the same map may come up with a different set of labels for the two dimensions. Also, in some cases interpreting certain dimensions meaningfully may be impossible.)

Thus from Exhibit 19.9, which summarizes the results of applying multidimensional scaling to the customer's similarity rankings, we can infer that this particular customer implicitly used price and product variety as key criteria in comparing the six stores. These criteria may therefore be critical in influencing the customer's choice of department stores.

Now let us look at the position marked Ideal store in Exhibit 19.9. As its name suggests, this label signifies a hypothetical store most able to meet the customer's specific needs. The position of the ideal store can be derived by including it in the set of stores initially compared by the customer—in other words, by asking the customer to make pairwise comparisons among *seven* (six actual and one ideal) stores. From the position of the ideal store in Exhibit 19.9, Sears would appear to be most attractive and Woolworth least attractive to the customer. Insights like these will suggest changes in strategy and the dimensions along which such changes must be made in order to move a particular store closer to a customer's ideal store.

The store configuration shown in Exhibit 19.9 is derived from just one customer's perceived similarities among the stores and hence does not necessarily reflect the perceptions of other customers. For the same set of stores another customer's similarity rankings may produce an entirely different multidimensional map. Herein lies another practical limitation of multidimensional scaling (in addition to the problem of naming the dimensions): One may not be able to derive global inferences from the results of multidimensional scaling when the maps corresponding to different customers vary greatly, especially with respect to the number of dimensions in each. One way of tackling this problem is to identify *segments* of customers with fairly similar multidimensional maps by using an appropriate cluster analysis technique in conjunction with multidimensional scaling.[23] When properly conducted, multidimensional scaling can be helpful in areas such as product or brand positioning, market segmentation, and analysis of competing firms' positions within an industry.

---

[23] See, for example, Yoram Wind and Patrick J. Robinson, "Product Positioning: An Application of Multidimensional Scaling," in *Attitude Research in Transition,* ed. Russell I. Haley (Chicago: American Marketing Association, 1972), pp. 155–175.

CONJOINT ANALYSIS

Conjoint analysis (also called conjoint measurement) is a fairly recent variation of multidimensional scaling and is also much more practical. As suggested by the discussion in the preceding section, interpreting the results of multidimensional scaling is quite subjective and may not necessarily result in meaningful insights. Conjoint analysis differs from multidimensional scaling in certain key respects. First, respondents are asked to compare hypothetical rather than actual products, brands, and so on. Second, the hypothetical stimuli are descriptive profiles formed by systematically combining varying levels of certain key attributes. Thus while evaluative dimensions in multidimensional scaling are derived from the input data, the evaluative dimensions in conjoint analysis are the prespecified attributes themselves. The problem of naming the dimensions therefore does not exist in conjoint analysis. Third, the mathematical procedure underlying both techniques involves generating a geometric configuration of objects in multidimensional space on the basis of similarity or preference rankings.[24] But conjoint analysis goes a step further by deriving a set of *utility values* corresponding to various levels of each attribute. As we will see shortly, these utility values can be used to ascertain the relative importance of the attributes as well as the potential attractiveness to customers of different descriptive profiles or bundles of attributes.

We will now discuss briefly how conjoint analysis works.[25] The first step in performing conjoint analysis is to construct several descriptive profiles (i.e., hypothetical stimuli) by combining different levels of selected attributes. Suppose we want to assess the role played by the following attributes in customer evaluations of personal computers: price, memory (data storage capacity), and versatility (number of different tasks the computer can perform). Also, suppose we are particularly interested in evaluating three levels of price ($1000, $1500, and $2000), two levels of memory (64K and 128K), and four levels of versatility (4, 8, 12, and 16 different tasks can be performed). With these levels for the three attributes a total of 24 different descriptive profiles of personal computers are possible (3 levels of price × 2 levels of memory × 4 levels of versatility).

One approach to obtaining customer-preference-ranking data suitable for conjoint analysis is called the *two-factors-at-a-time,* or *trade-off, approach.* In this approach customers are asked to rank their preferences for various combinations of attribute levels, considering just a pair of attributes at a time. Consid-

---

[24] Like input data in multidimensional scaling, the input data in conjoint analysis can have one of several different formats. The most frequently used type of data is a set of preference rankings in conjoint analysis and similarity rankings in multidimensional scaling. For additional details, see Paul E. Green and V. Srinivasan, "Conjoint Analysis in Consumer Research: Issues and Outlook," *Journal of Consumer Research,* September 1978, pp. 103–123.

[25] An excellent article that discusses conjoint analysis in very readable terms is Paul E. Green and Yoram Wind, "New Way to Measure Consumers' Judgements," *Harvard Business Review,* July/August 1975, pp. 107–117.

Exhibit 19.10

Utility values for three personal-computer attributes

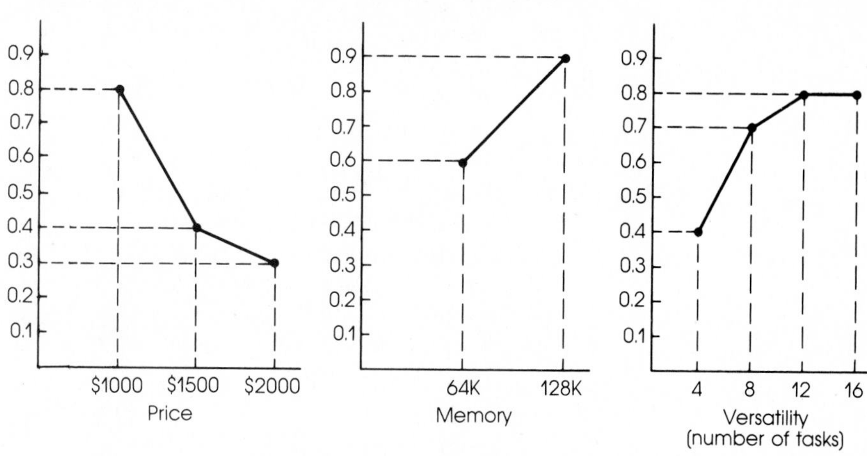

ering price and memory in our example, customers are asked to rank the six possible combinations of levels according to their preferences (most preferred = 1 and least preferred = 6). Similar sets of preference ranks can be obtained for the price-versatility and memory-versatility attribute pairs. Another way of obtaining customer-preference-ranking data is to use a *full-profile approach*. In this approach customers are asked to rank-order their preferences for the 24 different profiles representing all possible combinations of the three attributes.

The two-factors-at-a-time approach is easier for customers to comprehend and respond to, especially when numerous attributes are included in the analysis. This approach is somewhat unrealistic, however, because it involves presenting only partial stimuli to respondents. Hence there is some question about how meaningful the preference ranks will be. The full-profile approach is more realistic but may overwhelm respondents when the number of attributes is large.[26]

The output of conjoint analysis is a set of utility values corresponding to each attribute. The higher the utility value for a certain level of an attribute, the greater is a customer's preference for descriptive profiles containing that level. For instance, assume that the utility values plotted in Exhibit 19.10 are generated by a conjoint analysis of preference rankings given by one customer. This exhibit offers several interesting insights. As we would expect, the utility of price decreases for the higher price levels, while the utilities of memory and versatil-

[26] Further discussion of the two approaches is given in Green and Srinivasan, "Conjoint Analysis in Consumer Research."

ity go up with increases in their attribute levels. The relative importance of the three attributes can be ascertained by computing and comparing their respective *ranges* of utility values:

$$\begin{aligned}\text{range for price} &= 0.8 - 0.3 = 0.5,\\ \text{range for memory} &= 0.9 - 0.6 = 0.3,\\ \text{range for versatility} &= 0.8 - 0.4 = 0.4.\end{aligned}$$

Intuitively, a wide range of utility values should signify that customer preferences are quite sensitive to changes in the levels of the attribute. Hence in our illustration price is most critical, versatility is next most critical, and memory is least critical in influencing customer preferences for personal computers.

The utility values in Exhibit 19.10 can also be used to compare the potential attractiveness of different personal-computer configurations. For instance, is a personal computer with a 64K memory, capable of performing 8 different tasks, and costing $1500 likely to be more attractive to the customer than one with a 128K memory, capable of performing 12 different tasks, and costing $2000? This question can be answered by computing the total utility of the two hypothetical product configurations, as follows:[27]

total utility for the 64K, 8-task, $1500 personal computer

$$= 0.6 + 0.7 + 0.4$$
$$= 1.7,$$

total utility for the 128K, 12-task, $2000 personal computer

$$= 0.9 + 0.8 + 0.3$$
$$= 2.0.$$

Thus the latter combination of attributes is likely to be more attractive to the customer than the former.

Like the results in multidimensional scaling, the results in conjoint analysis are individual-specific. That is, a set of utility values are generated for *each* respondent. Utility values must therefore be pooled across respondents if generalizable inferences are to be made. Although pooling of utility values can be troublesome, several meaningful approaches have been developed for this purpose.[28] Some of these approaches can yield pooled utilities and also aid in estimating market shares for products with different combinations of attribute levels. For example, AT&T used conjoint analysis in conjunction with a com-

---

[27] This computation assumes that a simple, linear, additive conjoint model underlies the customer preference rankings. However, other conjoint models that may produce somewhat different results are also available. For a comparison of such models, see Ishmael Akaah and Pradeep K. Korgaonkar, "An Empirical Comparison of the Predictive Validity of Self-Explicated, Huber-Hybrid, Traditional Conjoint, and Hybrid Conjoint Models," *Journal of Marketing Research,* 20 (May 1983), pp. 187–197.

[28] See, for example, William L. Moore, "Levels of Aggregation in Conjoint Analysis: An Empirical Comparison," *Journal of Marketing Research,* 17 (November 1980), pp. 516–523.

puter simulator to identify the most attractive combination of attributes for a new data terminal and to predict its market share. Actual sales of this product after it was introduced showed that the market share prediction was very accurate.[29] A recent survey found that conjoint analysis has had several hundred commercial applications within the past few years.[30] The practical appeal of conjoint analysis results and the ready access to high-speed computers are likely to further increase the use of the technique in the future. Even some of the data collection problems associated with conjoint analysis—such as the difficulty in systematically formulating descriptive profiles when the number of attributes are numerous and in presenting the profiles without overwhelming the respondents—are being overcome by using computers to construct the stimuli, present them to respondents, record their preferences, and transfer the data immediately to a central computer's memory.[31]

SUMMARY

This chapter discussed a variety of multivariate techniques, broadly classified into dependence and interdependence techniques. The primary focus of the chapter was on providing a conceptual understanding of the techniques along with their potential applications and limitations. Table 19.5 briefly describes the nature and purpose of the various multivariate techniques we have looked at. This table should be helpful to you in choosing the most appropriate technique in situations calling for multivariate data analysis.

The seeming statistical sophistication of multivariate techniques, coupled with the ready access to computer programs incorporating the techniques, may tempt researchers to rush into using them without adequately considering their appropriateness in a given situation. Yielding to the temptation may lead to meaningless results, however.[32] One must also bear in mind that applications of multivariate techniques, despite their apparent quantitative rigor, may not be totally free of researcher subjectivity. For instance, it is up to the researcher to decide which independent variables to include in any application involving the use of dependence techniques. Yet the choice of a particular set of independent variables can greatly influence quantitative results and the inferences they imply.

[29] "Attitude Research, Conjoint Analysis Guided Ma Bell's Entry into Data-Terminal Market," *Marketing News,* May 13, 1983, Section 1, p. 13.

[30] Philippe Cattin and Dick R. Wittink, "Commercial Use of Conjoint Analysis: A Survey," *Journal of Marketing,* 46 (Summer 1982), pp. 44–53.

[31] An illustration involving computerized data collection is discussed in Linda D. Straube and Bridgid J. Michand, "Combine Microcomputer Interviewing with Conjoint Analysis to Study Pricing Strategies," *Marketing News,* May 13, 1983, Section 2, p. 10.

[32] For a discussion of caveats to bear in mind while using multivariate techniques, see Jagdish N. Sheth, "Seven Commandments for Users of Multivariate Methods," in *Multivariate Methods,* ed. Jagdish N. Sheth (Chicago: American Marketing Association, 1977), pp. 333–335.

Table 19.5

Summary of multivariate techniques

TYPE OF TECHNIQUE	USUAL FORM OF THE INPUT DATA	PRIMARY PURPOSE OF THE TECHNIQUE
DEPENDENCE TECHNIQUES		
Regression analysis	Dependent variable, metric Independent variable(s), metric	To ascertain the relative importance of independent variable(s) in explaining variation in the dependent variable; also to predict dependent-variable values for given values of the independent variable(s)
Analysis of Variance (ANOVA)	Dependent variable, metric Independent variable(s), nonmetric	To see whether different levels (treatments) of independent variable(s) have significantly different impacts on the dependent variable
Automatic interaction detector (AID)	Dependent variable, metric Independent variable(s), nonmetric	To identify distinct segments (defined in terms of independent-variable categories) that differ markedly with respect to dependent-variable values
Discriminant analysis	Dependent variable, nonmetric Independent variable(s), metric	To identify independent variables that are critical in distinguishing between subsamples defined by the dependent-variable categories; also to aid in classifying new units into one of the subsample categories
INTERDEPENDENCE TECHNIQUES		
Factor analysis	Metric	To reduce data on a large number of variables into a relatively small set of factors; also to identify key constructs underlying the original set of measured variables
Cluster analysis	Metric	To identify natural clusters of objects on the basis of similarities of the objects on a variety of characteristics
Multidimensional scaling	Nonmetric (similarity ranks based on comparisons of actual objects)	To identify key dimensions underlying respondent evaluations of products, brands, stores, etc.; also to determine the relative positions of the objects in multidimensional space
Conjoint analysis	Nonmetric (preference ranks based on comparisons of hypothetical stimuli formed by systematically varying selected attribute levels)	To derive utility values that respondents implicitly assign to various levels of key attributes used in evaluating objects; the utility values themselves aid in ascertaining the relative importance of the attributes and the potential attractiveness of descriptive profiles defined by different combinations of attributes

QUESTIONS

1. A marketer of a refrigerated fruit drink has developed three new package designs for the product that will enable the fruit drink to be stored at room temperature. The marketer wants to know if any or all of these package designs may result in significantly higher sales than the current package design that requires refrigerated storage. Suggest a suitable research approach to the marketer for realistically evaluating the alternative package designs. What technique(s) should be used to analyze the research data so as to fulfill the marketer's information needs? Explain the rationale for your answer.
2. Explain in simple words the distinction between a randomized-block ANOVA design and an ANCOVA design.
3. What is the primary marketing application of the AID technique? What are this technique's limitations?
4. Table 17.2 in Chapter 17 describes two scenarios requiring the use of multivariate analysis techniques. Suggest an appropriate multivariate technique for each scenario, and defend your choice.
5. A random sample of 600 respondents consisted of 300 users (group 1) and 300 nonusers (group 2) of a certain product. The means and standard deviations of the age (variable A) and income (variable B) of the respondents in the two groups are as follows:

Group 1	$\bar{A}_2 = 30$	$\bar{B}_1 = \$15{,}000$	$S_{1A} = 3$	$S_{2B} = \$100$
Group 2	$\bar{A}_2 = 40$	$\bar{B}_2 = \$20{,}000$	$S_{2A} = 4$	$S_{2B} = \$90$

A discriminant analysis of the age and income data for the two groups produced the following discriminant function:

$$Y = v_A A + v_B B \quad \text{where} \quad v_A = .10, \quad v_B = .01.$$

a. From the discriminant analysis, would you classify a person aged 25 with an income of \$18,000 as a user or a nonuser? Why?

b. Is one of the two independent variables more important than the other in discriminating between users and nonusers? If so, what exactly is the relative importance of one variable with respect to the other? If not, why not?

6. Describe in your own words what *factor analysis* is, and indicate the potential benefits it can offer.
7. Consider the following factor-loading matrix:

	F_1	F_2	F_3
X_1	.90	.02	.05
X_2	.80	.02	.10
X_3	.05	.90	.02
X_4	.03	.03	.95
X_5	.75	.05	.10
X_6	.10	.80	.05
X_7	.60	.06	.08
X_8	.05	.85	.03

a. What proportion of the total variance in the original set of variables is explained by the three factors taken together?

b. What are the achieved communalities for X_4 and X_7? How would you interpret these values?

c. Are the three factors easy to interpret? Why or why not?

8. Exhibit 18.9 in Chapter 18 contains the correlation matrix for three variables: sales revenue (SALES), advertising expenditures (ADVTG), and number of competing brands (NCOMP). Suppose the data on these three variables are subjected to factor analysis. Will one factor be able to account for a substantial portion of the variance in the original data set? Explain your answer. (If you have access to a computer, subject the raw data in Table 18.6 to factor analysis and see whether the results agree with your answer).

9. Refer to Question 8. Assuming that one factor is able to capture the essence of SALES, ADVTG, and NCOMP, what label will you place on that factor?

10. State how the following techniques differ from one another: (a) cluster analysis; (b) discriminant analysis; (c) the AID technique.

11. Why is conjoint analysis, a relatively recent technique, more popular in marketing practice than the traditional multidimensional scaling?

12. "Multivariate techniques, though mathematically sophisticated, are not free of researcher and/or decision maker subjectivity." Defend this statement by pointing out some subjective aspect of each technique we discussed.

13. A bank conducted a survey of customers and obtained preference rankings for various hypothetical bank profiles constructed by using the following characteristics and levels within each characteristic:

Operating hours:
A. 8 A.M. to 3 P.M. weekdays
B. 9 A.M. to 5 P.M. weekdays
C. 9 A.M. to 5 P.M. weekdays plus 9 A.M. to noon Saturdays

Automatic-teller machines (to facilitate routine transactions 24 hours every day):
A. Yes B. No

Monthly service charge:
A. None C. $15
B. $5 D. $20

Conjoint analysis of the data yielded the following utility values for various levels of each of the three characteristics:

- Operating hours: A = 0.3; B = 0.3; C = 0.8.
- Automatic-teller machines: A =0.6; B = 0.3.
- Monthly service charge: A = 1.0; B = 0.8; C = 0.4; D = 0.1.

a. Which of the three bank characteristics is most crucial in influencing customer preference? Why?

b. Will the bank benefit more by operating 8 A.M. to 3 P.M. weekdays, providing no automatic-teller machines, and assessing no monthly service charge, or by operating 9 A.M. to 5 P.M. weekdays plus 9 A.M. to noon Saturdays, providing automatic-teller machines, and assessing a monthly service charge of $15? What if the service charge is changed to $20 in the latter alternative?

APPENDIX TO CHAPTER 19

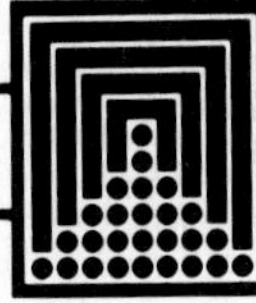

ANOVA and Dummy-Variable Regression

The purpose of this appendix is to demonstrate the conceptual correspondence between ANOVA and regression analysis and also to discuss *dummy variables,* which are necessary when data on one or more independent variables in a regression equation are categorical rather than continuous. Examples of categorical independent variables frequently encountered in marketing research studies include sex, ethnic background, marital status, and occupation.

Both ANOVA and regression analysis are meant to shed light on the influence of independent variables on some dependent variable. We have already seen certain computational similarities between the two techniques (e.g., the analogous total as well as partitioned sums of squares). We can gain a more thorough understanding of the equivalence between the two techniques by performing a regression analysis of our illustrative data in Table 19.1 presented in the chapter, using dummy independent variables. Before doing so, however, we need to know more about the concept of a dummy variable.

A dummy variable is defined as one that can only have a value of either 0 or 1. While independent variables in regression analysis are typically required to be at least interval-scaled, an exception to this general requirement is a 0–1 dummy variable. For reasons that we will not get into here, it is legitimate to include categorical independent variables in a regression equation as long as data on them can be coded as 0s and 1s. Suppose, for example, we want to include sex as an independent variable in a multiple regression equation for predicting the extent of use of a certain product. Since sex has only two categories, it naturally fits the description of a dummy variable. So we can include, in the regression equation, an independent variable, say S, coded as

$S = 0$ if respondent is male,
$S = 1$ if respondent is female.

What if a categorical independent variable has more than two categories, such as TREAT in our ANOVA example? We can still include it in a regression equation by creating a suitable *set* of dummy variables. Specifically, any variable with k categories can be recoded into a 0–1 format by forming $k - 1$ dummy variables. To illustrate, the three-category TREAT variable can be represented by two dummy variables, say DUMV1 and DUMV2, as follows:

TREAT	DUMV1	DUMV2
1. Regular price	0	0
2. 50¢ off	1	0
3. 75¢ off	0	1

Any sample store selling the product at regular price is equivalent to a store whose values on DUMV1 and DUMV2 are zero. Stores with the 50¢-off pricing treatment are uniquely identified by the combination DUMV1 = 1 and DUMV2 = 0. Similarly, stores with DUMV1 = 0 and DUMV2 = 1 are those with the 75¢-off pricing treatment. What we have done here is simply convert TREAT (coded as 1, 2, or 3) into two independent dummy variables in such a way that the three possible combinations of 0–1 values on them are uniquely associated with the three pricing treatment categories. A data set can now be created from the raw data in Table 19.1 in order to derive a multiple regression equation of the following form:

$$\hat{Y}_i = a + b_1X_{1i} + b_2X_{2i},$$

where $\hat{Y}_i$ is the predicted sales for any store i in the sample of 24 stores, X_{1i} is the DUMV1 value for store i, and X_{2i} is the DUMV2 value for store i. The data set suitable for regression analysis is shown in Table A.19.1.

The computer output stemming from regression analysis of the data set in Table A.19.1 (using SPSS) is shown in Exhibit A.19.1.

The right-hand side of Exhibit A.19.1 contains basically the same information as the ANOVA table shown in Exhibit 19.1 presented in the chapter. In fact, the numbers are identical except for a few minor discrepancies due to rounding. The F-value for testing the significance of R^2 in the regression analysis output is the same as the F-value for testing the significance of the treatment effects in the ANOVA table. The two procedures are thus statistically equivalent and lead to the same conclusion: There is a significant association between price and unit sales of the store brand of vegetable oil.

The interpretation of the regression coefficient (b-value) of a dummy variable is somewhat different from the traditional interpretation of slope—namely, that it is the change in the dependent variable per unit change in the independent variable, assuming all other variables remain the same. Since a dummy variable merely indicates the presence (1) or absence (0) of some attribute, the notion of a continuous unit change in the attribute is meaningless. Moreover,

Table A.19.1
Modified data set with dummy independent variables

STORE (i)	DEPENDENT VARIABLE, SALES (Y_i)	INDEPENDENT VARIABLES DUMV1 (X_{1i})	DUMV2 (X_{2i})
1	37	0	0
2	38	0	0
3	40	0	0
4	40	0	0
5	38	0	0
6	38	0	0
7	40	0	0
8	39	0	0
9	46	1	0
10	43	1	0
11	43	1	0
12	45	1	0
13	45	1	0
14	43	1	0
15	44	1	0
16	44	1	0
17	46	0	1
18	49	0	1
19	48	0	1
20	48	0	1
21	47	0	1
22	48	0	1
23	49	0	1
24	49	0	1

when several dummy variables are used to represent one independent variable (as in our example), the particular *combination* of 0s and 1s corresponding to each independent-variable category must be considered in interpreting the dummy-variable regression coefficients. In the grocery store chain illustration a 0–0 combination (i.e., DUMV1 = 0 and DUMV2 = 0) represents the regular-price treatment. This combination can be called the *base level* of the independent variable. In general, the base level is one for which *all* dummy variables representing the independent variable have a value of 0. It is the benchmark against which the effects of other levels are measured by examining the regres-

Exhibit A19.1

SPSS computer output for analysis of the data in Table 19.1, using dummy-variable regression

MULTIPLE REGRESSION

DEPENDENT VARIABLE. . SALES
VARIABLE(S) ENTERED ON STEP NUMBER 1. . DUMV1
DUMV2

VARIABLE LIST 1
REGRESSION LIST 1

		ANALYSIS OF VARIANCE	DF	SUM OF SQUARES	MEAN SQUARE	F
MULTIPLE R	0.96386	REGRESSION	2.	345.25000	172.62500	137.44550
R SQUARE	0.92903	RESIDUAL	21.	26.37500	1.25595	
ADJUSTED R SQUARE	0.92227					
STANDARD ERROR	1.12069					

VARIABLES IN THE EQUATION

VARIABLE	B	BETA	STD ERROR B	F
DUMV1	5.375000	0.64391	0.56035	92.012
DUMV2	9.250000	1.10812	0.56035	272.502
(CONSTANT)	38.75000			

VARIABLES NOT IN THE EQUATION

VARIABLE	BETA IN	PARTIAL	TOLERANCE	F

ALL VARIABLES ARE IN THE EQUATION

STATISTICS WHICH CANNOT BE COMPUTED ARE PRINTED AS ALL NINES.

sion coefficients. Specifically, the regression coefficient of any dummy variable has the following interpretation:

> Other things remaining the same, it represents the difference between the average dependent-variable value for units with a 1 on the dummy variable and the average dependent-variable value for the base level units.

To illustrate, the 1–0 combination of dummy-variable values (i.e., DUMV1 = 1 and DUMV2 = 0) represents stores receiving the 50¢-off pricing treatment. The regression coefficient for DUMV1 is 5.375 (see Exhibit A.19.1). This value represents the difference between the average unit sales of stores selling the vegetable oil at 50¢ off and the average unit sales of those selling it at regular price (base level):

average sales of stores selling at 50¢ off = 44.13

(see Table 19.1 presented in the chapter).

average sales of stores selling at regular price = 38.75

(see Table 19.1 presented in the chapter).

difference in average sales = 44.13 − 38.75 = 5.38,

which is the same as the *b*-value for DUMV1. The *b*-value of 9.25 for DUMV2 has a similar interpretation: Stores with a 1 on DUMV2 (i.e., those receiving the 75¢-off pricing treatment) on the average sell 9.25 units more than stores at the base level.

The statistical significance of the dummy-variable regression coefficients can be tested with the aid of the *F*-values reported in Exhibit A.19.1 and the testing procedure outlined in Chapter 18. It turns out that both coefficients are significant beyond the customary .05 significance level. Thus both the 50¢-off and the 75¢-off pricing treatments are significantly more effective in increasing unit sales than the regular-price treatment. In general, testing the statistical significance of dummy-variable regression coefficients is analogous to evaluating whether certain pairs of treatment effects are significantly different in ANOVA.[1]

The *a*-value (*Y*-intercept) in Exhibit A.19.1 is 38.75. That this value is the same as the average sales of base-level stores is not mere coincidence. In regression equations involving dummy as well as regular independent variables, the average dependent-variable value for base-level units (corresponding to a related set of dummy variables) will be part of the *Y*-intercept value. Since the regression equation in our example only has a pair of related dummy variables and no regular independent variables, the *Y*-intercept is identical to the average sales of base-level stores.

The foregoing discussion seems to suggest that categorical independent variables are not a constraint in conducting regression analysis since they can be readily converted into appropriate sets of dummy variables. A potential problem, however, is that too many dummy variables will sharply increase the number of observations and hence the sample size needed for the resulting multiple regression equation to be meaningful. Recall from Chapter 18 the rule of thumb calling for a minimum of 10 observations for every independent variable included in a regression equation. This rule of thumb applies to dummy variables as well.

Suppose, for instance, that three categorical independent variables, each with four levels, are to be included in a multiple regression equation after being converted to dummy variables. The number of dummy variables needed to represent the three variables in the regression equation is $(4 - 1) \times 3 = 9$. Unless the number of observations available is large enough to accommodate this many dummy variables, the regression equation will not be very useful. Furthermore, even when the sample size is sufficient, interpretation of the dummy-variable regression coefficients becomes more and more difficult as the number of categorical independent variables included in the regression increases. Thus dummy variables are not a panacea, and they must be used spar-

[1] For a more formal discussion of the equivalence of these significance tests, see Fred N. Kerlinger and Elazur J. Pedhazur, *Multiple Regression in Behavioral Research* (New York: Holt, Rinehart and Winston, 1973), pp. 119–121.

ingly. Whenever feasible, collecting refined data on independent variables to begin with is better than collecting categorical data and conducting regression analysis with dummy independent variables.

QUESTIONS

1. What is the basic difference between ANOVA and regression analysis? In what ways can the two techniques be considered similar?
2. In analyzing data from a certain consumer survey using regression analysis, the researcher feels that race is a critical independent variable. Data on race was gathered by using the following categories: white, black, Hispanic, American Indian, Asian, and other. Can the researcher include race as an independent variable in the regression analysis? If so, explain how. If not, why not?

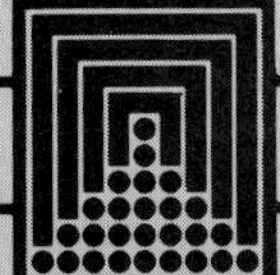

CASES FOR PART SIX

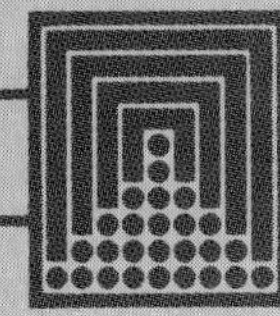

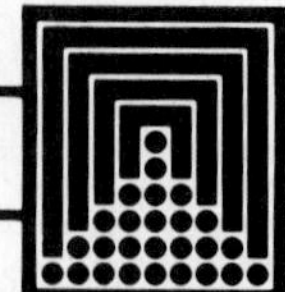

CASE 6.1

Northwest Bank of Woodcreek (B)

The case titled "Northwest Bank of Woodcreek (A)" listed several specific objectives of the competitive study conducted for NBW by a local marketing research firm. One of those objectives was, "To examine the extent of recognition received by the slogans and symbols of the banks and savings and loan associations in Woodcreek." Two banks and three savings and loan associations in Woodcreek compete with NBW. They are Public Bank & Trust (PB&T), Woodcreek Savings Bank (WSB), People's Mutual Savings & Loan (PMS&L), First Federal Savings & Loan (FFS&L), and Home Savings & Loan (HS&L).

All three banks and three savings and loans in Woodcreek have their own distinct symbols that they use in their advertisements: PB&T uses the picture of an owl; WSB uses three triangles apparently forming the letter *W;* NBW uses a line drawing depicting a series of faces; PMS&L uses three pillars; FFS&L uses an eagle; and HS&L uses a fireplace. The three banks and one of the three savings and loans also have distinct promotional slogans: PB&T was "The wide awake bank"; WSB uses "The bank designed with you in mind"; NBW uses "Everybody's bank"; HS&L uses "There's no place like home."

SYMBOL AND SLOGAN RECOGNITION

During the personal interviews of area residents, the interviewers obtained recognition measures for the symbols and slogans used by the various institutions. For the purpose of measuring symbol recognition, each respondent was given a six-page booklet in which each page contained one of the six symbols. After looking at each symbol, the respondent was asked to state the name of the financial institution to which the symbol belonged. To measure slogan recognition, the interviewer simply read one slogan at a time and asked the respondents to name the institution that used the slogan.

RESULTS

The results of the symbol and slogan recognition tests are summarized in Tables 1 and 2, respectively. In both tables two additional financial institutions—Mercer Bank & Trust (MB&T) and Principal Savings and Loan (PS&L)—are included. These financial institu-

Table 1

Recognition of symbols of institutions

SYMBOL	INSTITUTION USING SYMBOL	TYPE OF RESPONDENTS	PERCENT SAYING "DON'T KNOW"	PERCENT OF RESPONDENTS ATTRIBUTING SYMBOL TO								
				PB&T	WSB	NBW	PMS&L	FFS&L	PS&L	HS&L	MB&T	Other Institutions
Owl	PB&T	Customers	61.2	36.7	1.0	1.0	0.0	0.0	0.0	0.0	0.0	0.0
		Noncustomers	74.2	20.0	2.4	2.4	0.0	0.7	0.0	0.3	0.0	0.0
		All respondents	71.0	24.2	2.0	2.0	0.0	0.5	0.0	0.3	0.0	0.0
Three triangles	WSB	Customers	55.3	0.0	41.1	1.4	0.0	0.7	1.4	0.0	0.0	0.0
		Noncustomers	72.6	0.0	24.2	2.0	0.4	0.0	0.0	0.4	0.0	0.4
		All respondents	66.4	0.0	30.3	1.8	0.3	0.3	0.5	0.3	0.0	0.3
Faces	NBW	Customers	70.8	2.5	1.2	24.8	0.0	0.6	0.0	0.0	0.0	0.0
		Noncustomers	80.6	1.3	1.7	14.7	0.4	0.4	0.4	0.4	0.0	0.0
		All respondents	76.6	1.8	1.5	18.8	0.3	0.5	0.3	0.3	0.0	0.0
Three pillars	PMS&L	All respondents	83.3	0.3	2.3	1.5	9.2	0.8	2.0	0.3	0.8	0.0
Eagle	FFS&L	All respondents	83.7	0.8	1.0	2.8	0.0	11.5	0.0	0.0	0.0	0.3
Fireplace	HS&L	All respondents	16.5	0.3	0.3	0.8	0.0	0.8	0.0	81.4	0.0	0.0

Note: The percentages in rows labeled "All respondents" are based on a sample size of 393.

Table 2

Recognition of slogans of institutions

SLOGAN	INSTITUTION USING SLOGAN	TYPE OF RESPONDENTS	PERCENT SAYING "DON'T KNOW"	PERCENT OF RESPONDENTS ATTRIBUTING SLOGAN TO								
				PB&T	WSB	NBW	PMS&L	FFS&L	PS&L	HS&L	MB&T	Other Institutions
"The wide awake bank"	PB&T	Customers	74.5	22.4	1.0	2.0	0.0	0.0	0.0	0.0	0.0	0.0
		Noncustomers	81.4	10.2	2.7	2.4	0.3	0.3	0.7	0.3	1.7	0.0
		All respondents	79.6	13.2	2.3	2.3	0.3	0.3	0.5	0.3	1.3	0.0
"The bank designed with you in mind"	WSB	Customers	51.1	3.5	30.5	10.6	0.7	1.4	0.0	0.7	0.7	0.7
		Noncustomers	52.8	3.6	21.4	17.1	0.0	0.0	0.8	3.8	0.0	1.2
		All respondents	52.2	3.6	24.7	14.8	0.3	0.5	0.5	2.3	0.3	1.0
"Everybody's bank"	NBW	Customers	29.2	11.8	3.7	54.0	0.0	0.0	0.0	0.6	0.0	0.6
		Noncustomers	46.6	15.5	10.8	26.3	0.0	0.0	0.0	0.0	0.4	0.4
		All respondents	39.4	14.0	7.9	37.9	0.0	0.0	0.0	0.3	0.3	0.5
"There's no place like home"	HS&L	All respondents	10.9	0.3	0.5	0.3	0.3	0.5	0.5	86.8	0.0	0.0

Note: The percentages in rows labeled "All respondents" are based on a sample size of 393.

tions are located in an adjoining community (outside Woodcreek city limits) to which some respondents incorrectly attributed several of the symbols/slogans used by the institutions in Woodcreek.

For the three Woodcreek banks the overall recognition measures are also broken out for customers and noncustomers of each bank. As an aid in interpreting the numbers in the tables, a couple of illustrations are provided here. In Table 2, for instance, in the row starting with the slogan "There's no place like home," the number in the fourth column is 10.9. This number indicates that 10.9% of all respondents could not attribute this slogan to any institution. The number in the seventh column of the same row indicates that 0.3% of all respondents incorrectly attributed this slogan to NBW. The number in the eleventh column shows that 86.8% of all respondents correctly attributed the slogan to HS&L. For each of the three Woodcreek banks the percentage columns have three numbers for each slogan. For instance, the row starting with "Everybody's bank" has the numbers 54.0, 26.3, and 37.9 in the seventh column. These numbers indicate that 54.0% of the customers of NBW, 26.3% of the noncustomers of NBW, and 37.9% of all respondents (customers and noncustomers combined) correctly attributed this slogan to NBW.

QUESTIONS

1. How do you interpret the effectiveness of the symbols and slogans of the Woodcreek area financial institutions on the basis of the results reported in Tables 1 and 2? What recommendation(s) would you make to the NBW management?
2. What analysis procedures do you think were used in arriving at Tables 1 and 2? What other procedures or tests, if any, would you recommend for a better interpretation of the findings?
3. Critically evaluate the clarity and meaningfulness of the two tables.

CASE 6.2

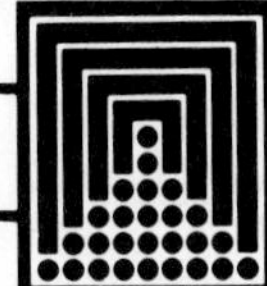

ITT's Image Advertising Campaign

The International Telephone and Telegraph Corporation (ITT), headquartered in New York, faced a serious image problem in the early seventies. A majority of the public was unaware of the firm and its variety of business activities. Furthermore, many of those who were aware of ITT had a rather blurred image of the firm, primarily because of confusion between the ITT and AT&T (American Telephone and Telegraph) names.

In 1974, ITT began a multiyear, multimillion-dollar advertising campaign aimed at building a distinct and favorable image for itself in the eyes of the public. The campaign involved a series of television and print ads that employed very creative approaches to convey memorable messages and slogans, such as "The best ideas are the ideas that help people." ITT's campaign won praise from advertising critics and received numerous awards and honors over the years, such as the CLIO and EFFIE awards. As of 1982, ITT was spending over $10 million on its corporate image-building campaign.

To assess the potential impact of the advertising campaign on the public, ITT retained the services of Yankelovich, Skelly and White, Inc., a marketing research firm well known for its expertise in conducting public opinion polls. Yankelovich, Skelly and White conducted a benchmark survey in 1974 to assess the public's views just before the start of the advertising campaign. The survey involved telephone interviews of a national sample of 1500 respondents. Similar surveys, using fresh random samples of respondents, were conducted at least once a year thereafter in order to monitor changes, if any, in the public's perceptions about ITT. A summary of the findings stemming from the surveys conducted during the period 1974 to 1978 is shown in Table 1.

For each attribute listed on the left-hand side of the table, the percentage figures correspond to respondents who felt that ITT possessed the attribute. For instance, while only 68% of the respondents in the January 1974 survey felt that ITT was one of the largest companies, 85% of the respondents in the November 1978 survey felt so.

The information in this case was provided by courtesy of International Telephone and Telegraph Corporation, 320 Park Avenue, New York, NY 10022.

Table 1

ITT Corporate strengths

ATTRIBUTE	PERCENT RESPONSE* November 1978	October 1977	October 1976	December 1975	December 1974	January 1974†	PERCENTAGE POINT DIFFERENCE October 1977	December 1975
One of largest companies	85	86	90	86	85	68	−1	−1
Very profitable	77	76	80	73	76	61	+1	+4
Makes quality products	76	77	82	74	75	54	−1	+2
Leader in technology	76	75	81	73	72	49	+1	+3
Develops many new products	73	74	75	68	67	46	−1	+5
Good stock to buy or own	70	70	72	62	53	52	=	+8
Leads in research and development to improve products	68	69	71	66	65	46	−1	+2
Reliable	66	70	73	63	64	48	−4	+3
Gives good value	56	58	62	56	56	43	−2	=
Cares about its customers	51	58	59	55	56	40	−7	−4
Pays good wages	47	51	50	47	44	34	−4	=
Cares about general public	46	51	50	42	43	31	−5	+4
Fair to employees of all races	44	48	48	45	42	34	−4	−1
Good labor relations	43	42	46	40	43	29	+1	+3
Interesting place to work	43	42	45	40	40	26	+1	+3
Gives women equal opportunity	42	44	45	43	40	29	−2	−1
Cares about community near plant	40	40	44	40	40	26	=	=
Good balance in profits/public interest	40	35	37	33	31	29	+5	+7
Honest, forthright advertising	39	42	44	37	39	27	−3	+2
Makes products safe without regulations	38	39	42	38	40	29	−1	=
Protects jobs of U.S. workers	37	36	41	39	38	27	+1	−2
Working to curb pollution	30	32	31	26	29	21	−2	+4
Solves social problems	22	23	24	21	23	19	−1	+1
Reduces prices when possible	19	19	18	18	18	12	=	+1
Tells all about itself, good and bad	17	13	16	15	16	11	+4	+2

* Multiple responses.
† Adjusted to account for variation in the method of asking the question.

QUESTIONS

1. What specific inferences can you draw about the advertising campaign's effectiveness on the basis of the results summarized in Table 1? Justify your answer.
2. What additional types of data and analyses might be helpful for evaluating the campaign's effectiveness?

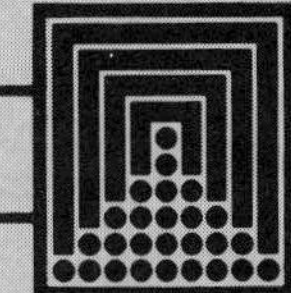

PART SEVEN

COMMUNICATING WITH RESEARCH USERS

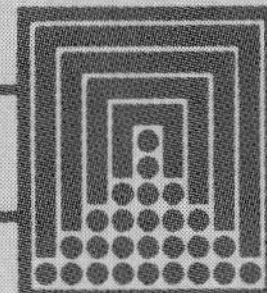

FROM THE MANAGER'S DESK

MARY B. STUPNIK is research manager for Harold Cabot & Company, Inc. Ms. Stupnik is responsible for the execution and analysis of research projects in support of Cabot Advertising's clients, which include companies as diverse as New England Telephone, Prime Computer, Fidelity Investments, and Anderson-Little Clothing Stores. Prior to joining Cabot in 1983, she was involved in retail market research for the Bank of New England Corporation as well as bank structure and competition analysis for the Federal Reserve Bank of Cleveland.

Ms. Stupnik received her A.B. in political science from John Carroll University (Cleveland, Ohio) and her master's degrees in economics and public administration from the Ohio State University.

QUESTION: What aspects of written research reports and/or oral presentations of research findings have bothered you most often? What aspects have impressed you most often?

RESPONSE: The importance of effectively communicating the results of marketing research cannot be stressed too strongly. The time, energy, and money devoted to even a small project is a lost investment if the eventual user of the research is unable to understand the results or to draw useful conclusions from them. While the usefulness of research results certainly depends on more factors than simply the way they are presented, ineffective written or oral presentations can substantially undermine the success of a project.

The centerpiece of every well-executed research report or presentation is a clear understanding of the audience with whom one is seeking to communicate and the willingness to communicate in terms that will satisfy that audience's needs. Each research report or presentation developed with this centerpiece in mind is impressive to me because it shows that the analytical skills of the researcher did not stop with the "numbers" but went beyond the data to reflect an awareness of the role of marketing research in the business decision-making process. As much as the process of doing research can in and of itself be a great source of satisfaction to the researcher, failure to separate oneself from that process and to place oneself in the shoes of the research user leads to many of the problems that often arise with respect to research presentations and reports.

One of the key problems with many research reports and presentations is the researcher's persistent use of technical language or research buzzwords that are often meant to reassure the user that, indeed, the researcher is competent in his or her field but, instead, serve as a barrier to effective communication. A result presented in commonly understood terminology is no less impressive or valid than one presented in jargonistic or technical terms. Furthermore, an easily understood result is more likely to be acted upon or raise more questions for the researcher to investigate.

Another problem that sometimes arises in research presentations is the researcher's failure to organize research issues or results in order of their importance to the audience. Just because a questionnaire was designed so that certain questions were asked before others does not mean that the issues studied in the research follow the order of the questionnaire in importance. The researcher's failure to organize issues in the order of their importance may simply lead to annoyance, but it also could lead to more serious consequences, such as misinterpretation of results or failure to recognize the most crucial conclusions.

Where do research conclusions end and recommendations begin? This question is important and should also be borne in mind by the researcher who is presenting results. The perspective of the researcher concerning what the results mean for particular business decisions is valuable and should be reported. However, these perspectives should be treated as recommendations and not reported as though they were the outcomes of the research itself. Failure to make this distinction can lead the users of the research to discount the validity of the results on the grounds that they are biased or politically motivated. Separating conclusions and recommendations makes the researcher more credible and a more valuable member of the business decision team.

From my experiences as a member of the research community, I feel that the abilities to understand the audience, communicate clearly, organize issues, and provide both conclusions and recommendations to the user are the hallmarks of successfully communicated research results. It goes without saying that the basics of professionalism, including everything from checking a report for typographical errors to honesty about the limits of the research design and results, must also be present.

20

Presentation of Research Results

Communicating the results of a research project to decision makers is the last step of the research process. Nevertheless, the position of this topic in the sequence of research steps is no indication of its importance. Indeed, whether and to what extent research findings have an impact on decision making critically depends on how well they are communicated. As we have seen in earlier chapters, a research project is worthless if decision makers do not act on its findings, no matter how accurately and thoroughly it is conducted.

Effective presentation is the critical difference between a written report's gathering dust—or an oral presentation's falling on deaf ears—and the research findings' being truly beneficial. Unfortunately, communication is perhaps the weakest link between researchers and research users—a point emphasized at the beginning of the book. The topics of this chapter should therefore be studied carefully, especially by budding researchers who may be captivated by the methodological aspects of marketing research and thus may neglect the aspect of communicating their findings effectively. When a sample of marketing managers were asked to give their best advice to college students interested in marketing research careers, many of them gave answers like the following:

> Develop a good ability to communicate well—both orally and in writing.
>
> Work very hard on written and verbal communication skills, especially on how to say a great deal in as few a number of words as possible.[1]

[1] A. Parasuraman and Deborah G. Wright, "A Study of Marketing Research Jobs for College Graduates: Implications for Educators," in *1983 AMA Educators' Proceedings,* eds. Patrick E. Murphy, Gene R. Laczniak, Paul F. Anderson, Russell W. Belk, O. C. Ferrell, Robert F. Lusch, Terence A. Shimp, and Charles B. Weinberg (Chicago: American Marketing Association, 1983), p. 184.

IMPORTANCE OF UNDERSTANDING THE AUDIENCE

Researchers invariably present a project's description and findings in the form of a written report. Frequently, they also supplement the written report with an oral presentation to highlight key findings and answer any questions decision makers may have. Regardless of whether a research is summarized in written or oral form, however, its potential impact depends on how well it is tailored to fit the background and needs of its audience. A report or presentation that is prepared without considering its intended audience is bound to be ineffective. While this point appears to be obvious, in real life it is not always heeded. As we saw in Chapter 1, researchers sometimes attempt to impress rather than *communicate with* decision makers. Misunderstanding between research providers and users is the inevitable result.

Gaining a good understanding of audience characteristics and needs is therefore the foremost step in writing a research report or preparing an oral presentation. Thus a researcher should explore questions like these: Individuals from which organizational levels are likely to read the report or attend the oral presentation? How busy are these individuals likely to be? How familiar are they with the project? What aspects of the project are they most likely to be interested in? Do they have the background and training to easily understand technical complexities and terminology related to the project?

Researchers may not always be able to find accurate answers to questions like the ones just posed. Nevertheless, being sensitive to these questions is a prerequisite for ensuring a good report or presentation. Moreover, when the audience consists of multiple groups with widely disparate backgrounds and interests, a researcher should prepare several separate reports or presentations, if feasible, in order to maximize the overall impact of a research project. The importance of being user-oriented at this final and *most critical* stage of a research project will become more evident in our subsequent discussion.[2]

The primary focus of this chapter will be on written reports. However, most of the points covered are germane to oral presentations as well. Certain guidelines critical for making good oral presentations will be stressed at the end of the chapter.

PREPARING EFFECTIVE WRITTEN REPORTS

Writing skills cannot be acquired overnight; they have to be cultivated through constant practice over a period of time. Similarly, the details for preparing good

[2] The importance of understanding the audience and how to do so effectively are discussed succinctly by Dianna Booher, *Would You Put That in Writing?* (New York: Facts On File, 1983), pp. 15–19.

written reports cannot be covered in a single chapter; numerous comprehensive books and manuals on report writing are available for that purpose. Therefore, our purpose here is merely to offer a checklist of key features that an effective research report should contain and to illustrate the importance of those features. Details on the variety of ways in which such features can be incorporated into a report are available in several of the references cited in this chapter.

The desirable features of a research report can be summarized in one mnemonic word, SIMPLE: *s*hort, *i*nteresting, *m*ethodical, *p*recise, *l*ucid, and *e*rror-free. These six features do overlap to some degree. However, each is important enough to be discussed separately.

Make it short

Decision makers usually have no more than a few hours to read a report summarizing a study that may have taken weeks or months to complete. Hence the report must be as succinct as possible. It should cover in detail only those aspects that are of interest to research users and have a direct bearing on their decision making. This task is more easily said than done, however. Having labored for long on a project, researchers may be tempted to explain everything they did, perhaps to obtain the audience's appreciation for their efforts. This temptation is likely to be strong among those unaccustomed to writing research reports. In his excellent book on report writing, William J. Gallagher states:

> In their exuberance, many inexperienced writers find it difficult to screen out irrelevancy. Anxious to display their new-found knowledge and laboring under the delusion that their education is unique, recent graduates of advanced programs in science and business administration are often guilty of including unnecessarily elaborate discussions of theory and technique even though the theory may be well-known and the method conventional. Other writers are often victims of a kind of narcissism. For example, they write at great length about the difficulty they encountered in obtaining the data, the implication being that only their ingenuity and persistence could have avoided abysmal failure. Others write *ad nauseam* about the sample selected even though it is immediately apparent that the sample is representative and valid. Still others include a wealth of information about apparatus and methods to protect themselves against the carping criticism of other members of their profession, even though these people are not included among the intended readers of the report.[3]

This quotation does not necessarily mean that technical or methodological details must be omitted from research reports. All it implies is that report writers must set aside their personal or psychological needs and focus on potential readers' needs instead. A report should, of course, include technical details if its

[3] William J. Gallagher, *Report Writing for Management* (Reading, Mass.: Addison-Wesley, 1969), pp. 87–88.

readers are likely to be interested in them. As mentioned earlier, a thorough understanding of the audience is essential for producing a concise, effective report.

How concise should a report be in order to be labeled "short"? There is no standard length for a report. The ideal length depends on the needs of the audience and hence will vary from one situation to another. The intent of the discussion in this section is not to suggest a standard page limit for research reports. Rather, it is to emphasize that a report must not contain material irrelevant to its intended audience—a piece of advice that is ignored more often than it is followed by report writers. In his article on writing good reports, Stewart Henderson Britt, a respected marketing scholar, observes:

> Errors of *too long* a report far exceed the number of instances of *too short* a report. You do not have to report every detail, and neither should you always give every finding equal relevance. You do not even have to have a table or a graph accompanying every statement of results, unless this adds to the information needed by your readers.[4]

Make it interesting

The editorial philosophy of *Decision Sciences,* a technical journal, offers the following advice to would-be contributors of articles:

> Authors should especially bear in mind the fact that the journal is not intended as a cure for insomnia, so the occasional injection of a little wit and/or thought-provoking asides will not be discouraged.[5]

This advice is relevant to all report writers, particularly to those prone to inundating their reports with confusing statistics, tables, and formulas. While a report does not have to be humorous or entertaining, it must be interesting enough to grab and maintain the attention of its readers. As we saw in Chapter 5, the current information explosion is making many managers drown in data. There is just too much competition for the time that managers can devote to research reports. Therefore an uninteresting report may not even be fully read, let alone have an impact on decision making.

How does one prepare an interesting report? A researcher can prepare an interesting report by understanding the audience and by writing in a style appealing to them;[6] by focusing the report's content on issues that are relevant

---

[4] Stewart Henderson Britt, "The Writing of Readable Research Reports," *Journal of Marketing Research,* 8 (May 1971), p. 266.

[5] "Editorial Philosophy," *Decision Sciences,* 16 (Spring 1985), p. vi.

[6] In addition to Gallagher's book, *Report Writing for Management,* a number of other books on writing style are available, such as Paul R. Timm, *Managerial Communication: A Finger on the Pulse* (Englewood Cliffs, N.J.: Prentice-Hall, 1980); Jessamon Dawe and William Jackson Lord, Jr., *Functional Business Communication* (Englewood Cliffs, N.J.: Prentice-Hall, 1968); William C. Himstreet and Wayne Murlin Baty, *Business Communications* (Belmont, Calif.: Wadsworth, 1973); Dianna Booher, *How to Write Your Way to Success in Business* (New York: Harper & Row, 1984).

to the audience and important for it to know, a point we stressed in the previous section; and by using suitable illustrations and visual aids, a topic we will discuss later.

Make it methodical

A written report must be well organized to avoid readers' confusion and facilitate their quick comprehension. The various sections within the report must be logically sequenced to ensure smooth transitions. The number of sections and the best way to arrange them depend to some degree on the nature of the project and of the audience. However, the following general outline should be helpful for structuring reports in most situations.[7]

1. Preliminary sections;
   A. Transmittal letter;
   B. Title page;
   C. Table of contents;
   D. Executive summary;

2. Body of the report;
   A. Purpose;
   B. Method;
   C. Findings;
   D. Conclusions (and recommendations if requested);

3. Addenda;
   A. List of references;
   B. Appendix.

Not all sections listed in this outline are necessary in every report. The following description of the outline discusses the role of the various sections.

Transmittal letter. As its name implies, the transmittal letter introduces the report to its audience. It typically follows the style of business letters and includes a brief description of the report's highlights. The contents of the executive summary section, which we will discuss shortly, can be incorporated into the transmittal letter if the entire report is brief. The transmittal letter is optional when the researcher personally delivers the report to its readers.

Title page. The title page contains the title of the study, the name/affiliation of the report's author, the date of the study, and the name/affiliation of the person

[7] This outline is adapted from Himstreet and Baty, *Business Communications,* p. 335; many ideas in the descriptions of individual components of the outline are also adapted from this source. This outline is not the only available outline; examples of some different outlines can be found in Timm, *Management Communication,* Dawe and Lord, *Functional Business Communication,* and Booher, *How to Write.*

requesting the study. An attractively laid out title page is important for making a good first impression on the reader.

Table of contents. When a report contains many sections, a table of contents helps the reader quickly locate any desired section. The contents page customarily does not include the title of the study; it is labeled "Table of Contents" or simply "Contents." When the body of the report contains numerous tables, figures, or other illustrations, a desirable feature is a separate page titled "List of Tables," "List of Figures," or the like, after the contents page.

Executive summary. The executive summary is a synopsis of the entire report and typically should be no more than a few pages long. Although an executive summary may not be necessary in every report, it should be included in lengthy and/or technically complex reports. It should describe succinctly the primary purpose of the study, the general methodology used, the significant findings, and the key conclusions/recommendations. It is often the only section of a report that busy executives, who may well be the people with final authority to act on the study's findings, will have time to read thoroughly. A carelessly written executive summary is bound to create a poor image of the study and hurt the chances of its findings having any impact. Writing an executive summary is therefore an important task. Viewing this task as one that can be accomplished in a hurry after completing the main report is incorrect. Ideally, the executive summary should be drafted first by carefully distilling from the study the main messages to be conveyed to readers. A tightly written executive summary, in addition to being desirable from the reader's standpoint, can aid the writer in drafting the full report: It can serve as a skeleton for structuring and fleshing out the body of the report.

Body of the report. The body offers readers a comprehensive picture of the study by discussing all phases of it. The outline presented earlier lists four sections under this segment. These sections can be divided into suitable subsections if they become lengthy or complex. Since the body of the report is essentially a report within a report, it should be written in accordance with the guidelines implied by the mnemonic SIMPLE.

Addenda. Addenda are relevant attachments referred to, but not included in, the body of a report. A typical addendum is a list of references. This list is necessary when numerous citations—data sources, past studies, articles, books, and so on—are made in the main report. When only a few citations are involved, they can simply be referenced in footnotes on the pages where they appear, thereby eliminating the need for a separate list of references. Another addendum to research reports is an appendix (or set of appendixes). Questionnaires, raw data tables, formulas, complex calculations, and similar items are usually placed at the end of a report as a set of appendixes. In general, any study-related material whose placement in the body of a report may be distracting rather than enlightening must be relegated to the appendix section.

Make it precise

A precise report is a *clear* report, one that is composed of unambiguous statements. It is also a *comprehensive* report, one that contains all the information necessary for readers to get a complete and true picture of the study. The first feature (i.e., clarity) is a function of writing style and report format, which we will discuss further in the following sections.

The second feature (i.e., comprehensiveness) involves providing enough details about the study—for example, nature of the sample, data collection procedures, analysis techniques—to help readers decide how valid and generalizable the study's findings are. Withholding such details can easily mislead readers. In terms of ensuring objectivity as well as being ethical, researchers have an obligation to inform research users about potential limitations of a study.

As we have seen throughout this book, to expect practical research projects to be *perfect* is unrealistic. Experienced research users are well aware of this shortcoming. Consequently, they are bound to view with skepticism reports that sound too good to be true. Contrary to what some researchers may believe, a report that acknowledges a study's limitations is likely to create a better impression about the study than a report that fails to do so.

Report writers must be careful, though, not to overdo the reporting of limitations by listing every little problem the study may have encountered. Doing so will not only lengthen the report unduly but also give the study a poor image. Furthermore, merely acknowledging all the limitations of a study does not make the study a good one. A study that is badly flawed because of researcher carelessness cannot be salvaged simply by detailing all its limitations.

In short, a report summarizing a *reasonably well conducted study*—one whose limitations were beyond the researcher's control—will be more credible when it mentions the key limitations than when it does not.

Make it lucid (clarity)

The lucidity of a report is critical to its effectiveness for several reasons. First, the clearer a report, the less time readers need to understand what it says and the more time they can spend *digesting* its contents. As was mentioned earlier, most managers can devote only a limited amount of time to research reports. Hence the more time they can devote to digesting, rather than simply understanding, a report's contents, the greater the potential impact of the report will be. Second, a report that lacks clarity runs the risk of confusing its readers and leading them to conclusions unwarranted by the study and unintended by the report writer.

Third, an unclear report can annoy its readers and create a poor image about the quality of the entire research project.

How does one prepare a clear report? In a general sense, clarity is simply a function of the other desirable report features we have already discussed or will discuss presently. A report that is short, interesting, methodical, precise, and error-free is bound to be clearer than one that does not possess these characteristics. There are, however, a few other, more specific guidelines for enhancing report clarity.

One prerequisite for developing a clear report is to thoroughly understand the audience and to write in a style compatible with its background. A frequent complaint of managers is that research reports are too technical. The source of this complaint is invariably the report writer's failure to pay adequate attention to the audience. Technically complex material may be clear to the report writer and may even be viewed as a means for impressing the reader. However, more often than not, such material will neither enlighten nor impress the reader. On the contrary, it is most likely to result in dismissal of the report as being too theoretical to be of practical value.

Devoting a little extra time and effort to translating technical statements into plain language can greatly improve report clarity, as the following illustrations demonstrate:

- Technical statement. Owing to severe multicollinearity between the independent variables (personal selling expenditures and advertising expenditures), it is difficult to interpret their regression coefficients (estimated beta values) and hence their impact on the dependent variable (sales).
- Plain-language translation. Since personal selling and advertising expenditures for our product have moved together closely in the past, to say which of these two types of expenditures may be responsible for changes in our product's sales is difficult.
- Technical statement. According to our analysis of the survey data, the difference between mean sales per store in regions A and B is statistically significant beyond an alpha level of .05, based on a two-tailed *t*-test.
- Plain-language translation. According to our analysis of the survey data, the odds are less than 5 in 100 that the observed difference between mean sales per store in regions A and B could have occurred merely by chance.

The preceding examples are not meant to suggest that a report should be written in a style that talks down to its readers. To use technical terminology (especially when it will help reduce a report's length) is appropriate *if* the audience consists of those who are familiar with such terminology. Indeed, explanations of technical aspects in lay terms may run the risk of insulting a sophisticated audience. The bottom line is that the nature of the audience determines how technical a report can get without losing clarity.

A rather straightforward way to improve the clarity of a report, regardless of the technical complexity level of the project it pertains to, is to use simple words and sentence structures.[8] However, the skill of writing in a simple yet effective style can be developed and strengthened only through practice. There are no shortcuts or formulas (although several have been suggested in books on effective written communications) that can guarantee simple and effective reports.[9] As Gallagher points out:

> Many respected writing authorities have inadvertently contributed to the myth of the magic formula by developing statistical norms and mathematical yardsticks based on word, sentence, and paragraph length to determine ease of reading and, by implication, effectiveness of writing. Although these formulas are intended only as broad guidelines, not as stimulants to creative effort, many writers have misinterpreted the intent. As a result, they have divorced content from form, ignored relationships between ideas, and blandly assumed that writing is a mechanical skill that can be acquired merely by keeping words and sentences short. Therefore, they often become concerned more with words than with thoughts.[10]

Last, but not least, the use of appropriate tables, charts, or figures can add to the clarity of a report by conveying the contents of written material much more effectively and parsimoniously. For instance, consider the following excerpt from an article published in a leading marketing journal (in this excerpt ES1 and ES2 refer to samples selected in two different studies):

> A comparison of the demographic profiles between ES1 and ES2 revealed no major differences. . . . In ES1, the typical respondent was white (85.5%), married (72.7%), male (66.8%), and employed in a white collar job (36.4%). Fifty-five percent of the respondents reported incomes of less than $20,000, 48.2% had completed high school or less, and 44% were under 45 years of age. In ES2, 59.7% were male, 70.2% were married, 28.9% held white collar jobs, and 81.8% were white. Approximately 43% of the sample were under 45, 53.2% reported having a high school education or less, and almost 50% stated that they had family incomes of less than $20,000 a year.[11]

---

[8] The references cited in footnote 7 offer numerous suggestions for writing reports in a style that is simple and readable.

[9] One formula that is frequently used to assess the clarity of written material is called the Fog Index, developed by Robert Gunning. Details on this formula are given in Robert Gunning, *The Technique of Clear Writing* (New York: McGraw-Hill, 1952).

[10] Gallagher, *Report Writing for Management,* p. 13.

[11] Richard M. Durand, Hugh J. Guffey, Jr., and John M. Planchon, "An Examination of the Random Versus Nonrandom Nature of Item Omissions," *Journal of Marketing Research,* 20 (August 1983), p. 307.

The information conveyed by this excerpt would have been much clearer had it been presented in tabular form, as follows:

Respondent Characteristic	Percentage of Respondents	
	ES1 Sample	ES2 Sample
White	85.5	81.8
Married	72.7	70.2
Male	66.8	59.7
White-collar employee	36.4	28.9
Income less than $20,000	55.0	50.0
High school education or less	48.2	53.2
Under 45 years of age	44.0	43.0

We will further discuss the use of tables and charts in the section on graphical illustrations.

Make it error-free

To make a good impression on readers, a report must be free of arithmetical, grammatical, and typographical errors, however minor they may be. While this point seems obvious, report writers frequently neglect to edit and proofread their work carefully. Checking a completed report thoroughly should take no more than a small fraction of the time taken to put the report together. Yet perhaps because of a premature feeling of relief that the task is done, writers often look over their final drafts hastily or not at all.

The price of carelessness can be quite high, however. Incorrectly typed numbers, percentages that do not add up right, misspelled words, and other minor errors are usually *major* annoyances to readers. These errors will distract readers and divert their attention from digesting a report's contents. Moreover, a report with several such errors will make readers skeptical about the quality of the project itself. Checking a report more than once, preferably with the help of someone good at editing and proofreading, is a wise and worthwhile investment of the report writer's time.

In summary, the key to maximizing a report's potential effectiveness is to make it SIMPLE: short, interesting, methodical, precise, lucid, and error-free. The next section describes a variety of ways of presenting data graphically so as to highlight the key insights embedded in them.

GRAPHICAL ILLUSTRATIONS

Research reports typically contain a variety of data whose main messages must be communicated to the audience clearly and quickly. As the example concerning the ES1 and ES2 samples showed, presenting data in tabular form is usually

Table 20.1
Market shares of six toothpaste brands

	MARKET SHARES (%)					
YEAR	Brand X	Brand A	Brand B	Brand C	Brand D	Brand E
1975	30	29	25	5	5	6
1976	22	35	22	7	6	8
1977	25	25	30	10	5	5
1978	25	29	28	8	6	4
1979	28	30	25	6	6	5
1980	25	28	28	6	7	6
1981	22	30	29	6	6	7
1982	22	27	32	7	7	5
1983	20	29	33	5	7	6
1984	18	28	34	7	8	5

more effective than describing them in the body of a report. A report's clarity can be further improved by recasting the data in tables into graphical illustrations (charts, graphs, etc.), especially when the tables are complex or confusing. Visually appealing graphical illustrations can also add to a report's communication effectiveness by giving its audience refreshing breaks from the monotony of words and numbers.

One's imagination is the only limit on the number of ways tabular data can be transformed into appropriate graphical illustrations. Nevertheless, there are really only a handful of basic charts and graphs, variations of which are frequently used. To describe these basic formats, let us consider the hypothetical data in Table 20.1 pertaining to market shares of six brands of toothpaste in a certain region.

Suppose Table 20.1 is presented to the manager in charge of marketing brand X. Close examination of the table should offer the manager several key insights. For example, the two dominant competitors of brand X are brands A and B, and brand X's market position has been weakening over the years. These insights, and others not immediately apparent from the table, can be communicated more efficiently and effectively through graphical illustrations such as the ones discussed next.

Pie charts

A *pie chart* is a circle divided into several slices whose areas are proportionate to the quantities to be represented on the chart. The relative sizes of the slices are shown as percentages. A pie chart is excellent for showing the decomposition of a total quantity into its components—for example, the contributions made by a firm's product lines to its sales or profits; the income distribution of households using a certain product; the allocation of a total budget to various expense categories; the market shares of firms within an industry or brands within a product category. Exhibit 20.1 illustrates two pie charts showing the market shares of the six toothpaste brands in 1975 and 1984.

The two charts in Exhibit 20.1 clearly show the loss of brand X's market share, apparently to brand B, between 1975 and 1984. Table 20.1 also offers the same insight, but it does not do so as vividly as Exhibit 20.1. While a single pie chart, by itself, can be quite revealing, a comparison of pie charts over time (e.g., as in Exhibit 20.1) or a comparison of related pie charts at the same point in time (e.g., pie charts showing the relative contributions of a firm's product lines to its sales and profits) can be even more insightful.

Using different shadings or colors for the various slices of a pie chart can improve its effectiveness. Also, limiting the number of slices to about six or seven is preferable. Too many slices will clutter the chart and diminish its visual impact. When a total quantity is made up of numerous components, one should lump minor components (i.e., those making relatively small individual contributions to the total) into an "Other" category so as to avoid overcrowding the chart.

Constructing a pie chart may not be helpful when the total is made up of numerous components, each contributing about equally to the total. For instance, when a firm's marketing budget is allocated to 20 different categories,

Exhibit 20.1

Pie charts of market shares in 1975 and 1984

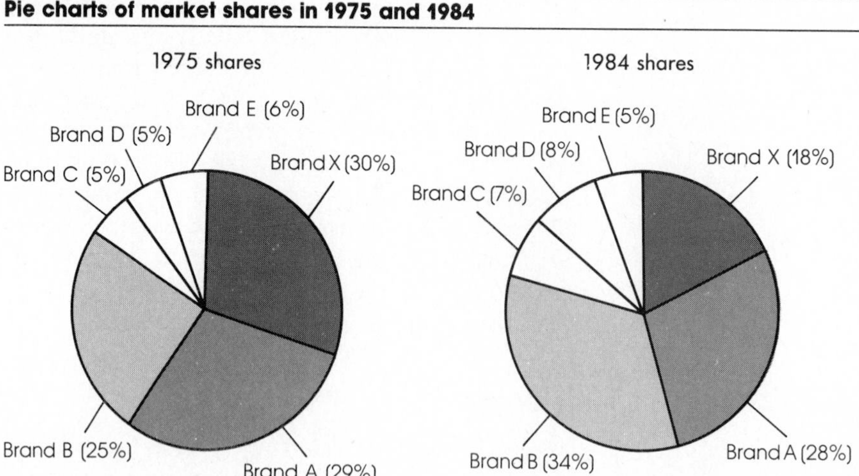

each accounting for about 4% to 6% of the budget, a pie chart is likely to be no better than a table showing the allocations.

In short, pie charts will be most effective when the number of components is relatively small and the relative sizes of those components are dissimilar. Constructing pie charts under other circumstances may merely add to the length of a report without improving its effectiveness.

Line charts

A *line chart* is a two-dimensional graph and is typically used to show movements in one or more items over time. The horizontal axis is customarily the time axis, and the vertical axis represents values of the items. Exhibit 20.2 is a line chart showing changes in market shares of the toothpaste brands during the period 1975 to 1984.

Exhibit 20.2 summarizes the data in Table 20.1 in a very revealing fashion. A glance at Exhibit 20.2 offers key insights (e.g., brand X's share has been steadily slipping, in almost symmetric contrast to brand B's increasing share) that only a very careful scrutiny of Table 20.1 will reveal.

For a line chart to be most effective, the trends corresponding to different items must be shown by lines of different color or of different form, as in Exhibit 20.2. And just as in the case of pie charts, one should not include more than a

Exhibit 20.2

Line chart of market shares from 1975 to 1984

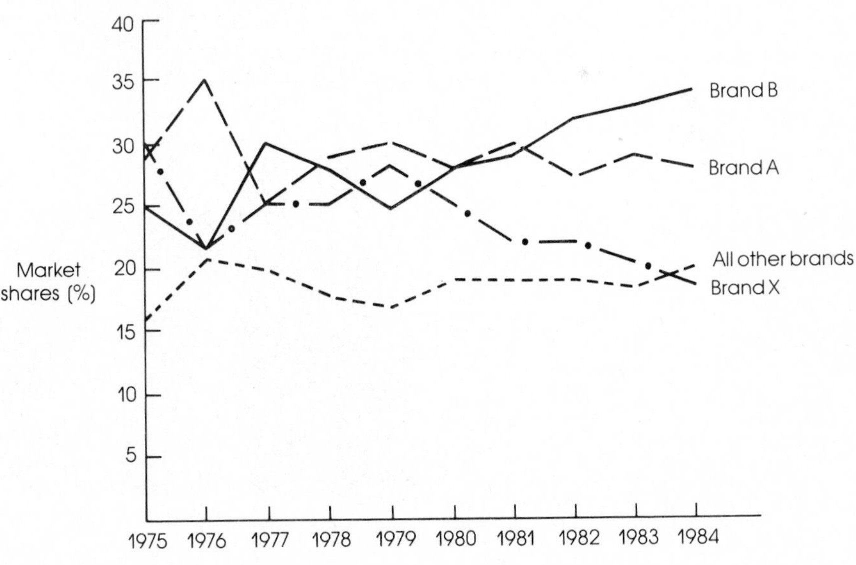

few items on a line chart. Too many lines on one chart will give it a crowded appearance and can cause confusion.

Stratum charts

A *stratum chart* is also a two-dimensional graph with time along the horizontal axis and values of the items to be plotted along the vertical axis. The area of the graph is divided into several horizontal layers, or strata, one corresponding to each item. At any given time the width of each stratum represents the relative magnitude of the corresponding item at that time. Exhibit 20.3 is a stratum chart summarizing the data in Table 20.1.

The lowest stratum in Exhibit 20.3 corresponds to brand X. The line defining the upper boundary of this stratum represents the same market share values as the brand X line in Exhibit 20.2. The second lowest stratum in Exhibit 20.3 corresponds to brand A. The line defining the upper boundary of this stratum represents the *sum* of the market shares of brands X and A. Similarly, the upper

Exhibit 20.3

Stratum chart of market shares from 1975 to 1984

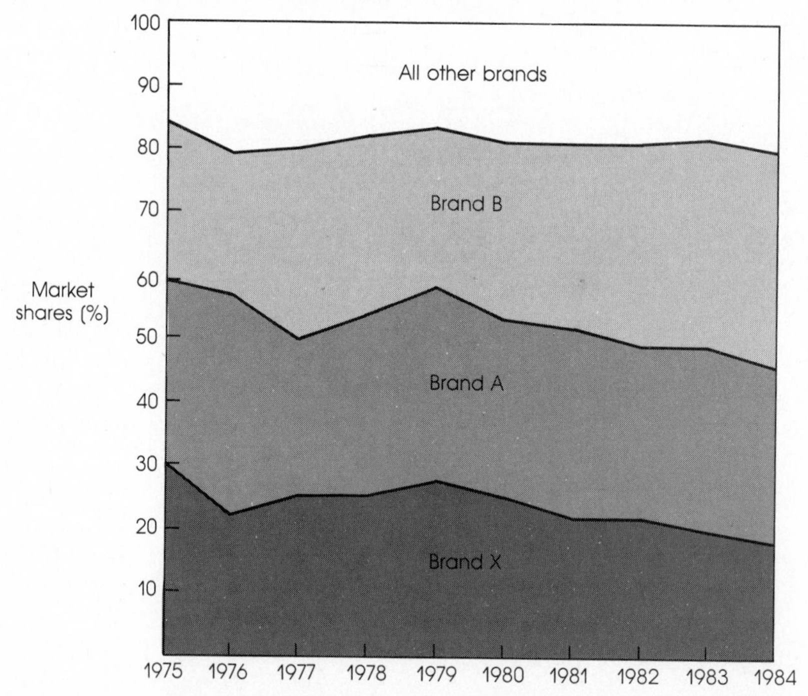

boundary of the third lowest stratum represents the combined share of brands X, A, and B.

Thus a stratum chart is a *cumulative line chart.* Also, its information content is similar to that of a series of pie charts constructed over a period of time. That is, it tracks the changes in relative magnitudes of the items over time. Just as with pie and line charts, having a fairly small number of items (strata) and making the strata distinct by using different colors or shadings are critical for a stratum chart's effectiveness.

Bar charts

A *bar chart,* as its name implies, consists of a series of bars (of equal thickness) whose heights (or lengths, if the bars are drawn horizontally) represent values of the items. Exhibit 20.4 contains two bar charts showing the market shares of the toothpaste brands in 1975 and 1984.

The information conveyed by Exhibit 20.4 is the same as that conveyed by Exhibit 20.1. How, then, does one decide whether to use a pie chart or a bar chart? There is no cut-and-dried answer to this question. A pie chart is preferable, however, when the values to be pictured are *relative* magnitudes (e.g.,

Exhibit 20.4

Bar charts of market shares in 1975 and 1984

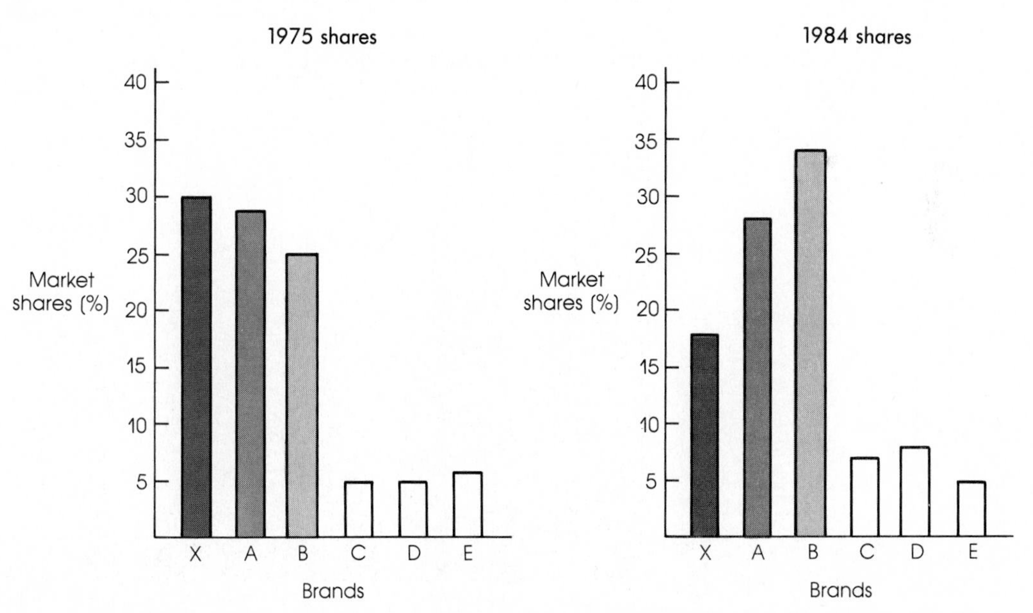

market shares, budget shares, and other types of percentages), since the concept of slicing up a pie seems intuitively appropriate for representing relative shares. Bar charts are appropriate for depicting *actual* or *absolute* magnitudes (e.g., sales of different product lines, expenditures on different marketing activities). The heights (or lengths) of the bars can be made to correspond to the absolute magnitudes of items; yet the areas occupied by the bars will provide a visual picture of relative magnitudes of the items.

Bar charts can also be used for showing changes over time by, for example, plotting time along the horizontal axis, constructing one vertical bar at each point in time, and dividing each bar into segments so that their heights correspond to the values of the items at that point in time. The visual impact of such a time series bar chart is similar to that of a stratum chart. Exhibit 20.5 shows a bar chart that conveys the same information as the stratum chart in Exhibit 20.3.

Pictograms

A *pictogram* is a special type of bar chart. It uses pictures of the items instead of the customary rectangular bars. The heights of the pictures correspond to the values of the items. A pictogram of the 1984 shares of the six toothpaste brands is shown in Exhibit 20.6.

The apparent advantage of a pictogram is that it is more appealing and interesting than a traditional bar chart. However, pictograms run the risk of

Exhibit 20.5

Bar chart of market shares from 1975 to 1984

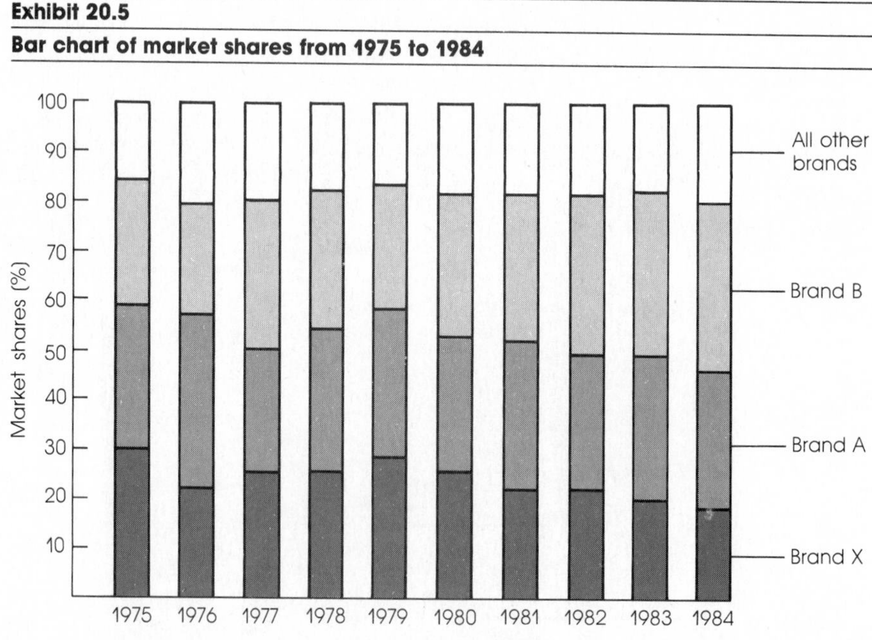

Exhibit 20.6

Pictogram of market shares in 1984

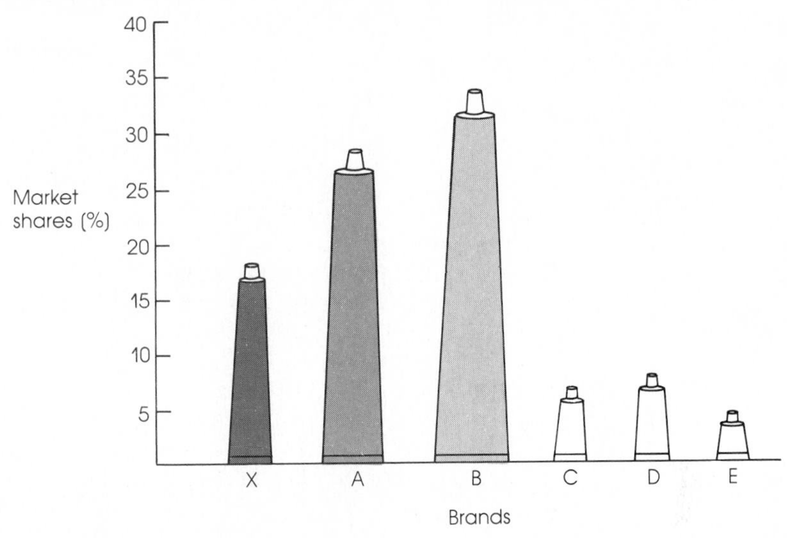

misleading the audience through visual exaggeration. For instance, consider the two tubes of toothpaste representing brands A and C in Exhibit 20.6. Consistent with the fact that brand A's share is four times as much as brand C's share in 1984 (28% versus 7%), the brand A tube is four times as tall as the brand C tube. But the *area* occupied by the brand A tube is over six times as large as the area occupied by the brand C tube. The point is that a pictogram may mislead those who draw inferences from the pictures' overall sizes rather than just their heights.[12]

Therefore a report using pictograms should ensure that the pictures do not mislead. Exhibit 20.6, for example, can be modified by representing the bars as stacks of *equal-sized* toothpaste tubes and varying the number of tubes in each stack to reflect different quantities. In this way the widths of the pictorial bars will be the same and only their heights will vary. Such a modified pictogram is shown in Exhibit 20.7.

Concluding comments

Graphical illustrations can make a report interesting and add to its clarity. The number of illustrations to use and the appropriate formats for them should be

[12] An interesting discussion of the pitfalls of pictograms, with several good examples, is given in Darrell Huff, *How to Lie with Statistics* (New York: Norton, 1954), Chap. 6, pp. 66–73.

Exhibit 20.7

Modified pictogram of market shares in 1984

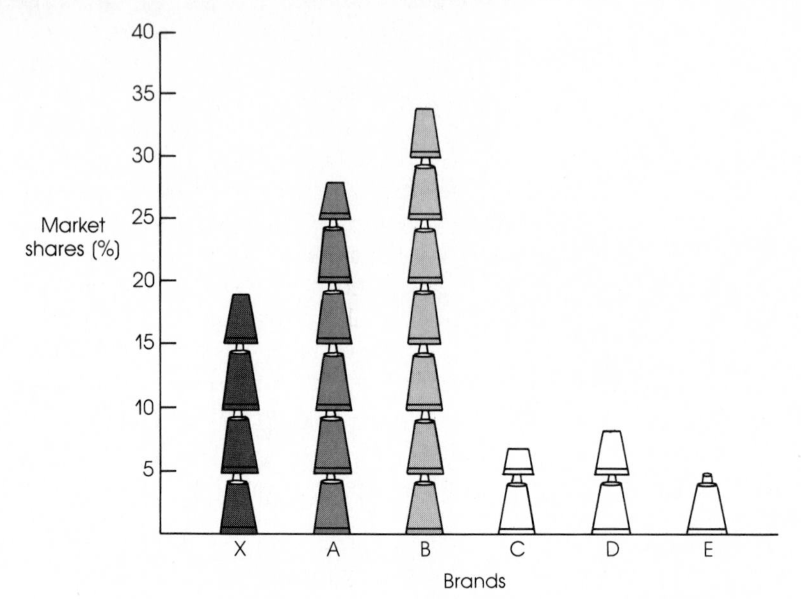

carefully determined so as to avoid confusing, meaningless, or misleading illustrations.[13] When the same results can be charted in a number of graphical formats, the researcher should draft, in rough form, several alternative charts and pick the most effective and least confusing one for the final report. The increasing access to personal computers and the availability of computer graphics software packages should be helpful here. Computer graphics programs can analyze data stored in memory and present the results in a variety of graphical formats. The user can peruse visual displays of the resulting pictures and obtain hard copies of the most effective ones. Machines are also available to create color photographs and transparencies or slides of computer-generated charts and graphs. Computer experts predict that in the near future "some graphics software will feature artificial intelligence that will be able to select automatically the most effective graph for a particular set of data."[14]

[13] For a discussion of situations where certain graphical illustrations are more appropriate than others, as well as the pros and cons of each, see Mary E. Spear, *Practical Charting Techniques* (New York: McGraw-Hill, 1969).

[14] "Management Warms Up To Computer Graphics," *Business Week,* August 13, 1984, p. 101.

ORAL PRESENTATIONS

Oral presentations, like written reports, must also be SIMPLE: short, interesting, methodical, precise, lucid, and error-free. However, making an effective oral presentation is in some ways more difficult than writing a good report because of the direct interaction with the audience. Any sign of faltering during an oral presentation will make an unfavorable impression on the audience and may lower the self-confidence of the presenter. An effective oral presentation requires meticulous preparation of what will be said and how it will be said. It also requires planning for contingencies like a breakdown of visual equipment or a series of tough questions from the audience. Even a thirty-minute presentation may therefore need many hours (or days) of preparation. Carefully planning and rehearsing an oral presentation is critical to its effectiveness.

Details for putting together and delivering a good oral report are beyond the scope of this textbook.[15] However, the following three general tasks, covered while discussing written reports, are especially important for the success of oral presentations:

1. Researching the audience—knowing who will be in the audience, understanding their backgrounds and information needs, and anticipating the questions they may ask.
2. Choosing the main points of the study to be covered during the presentation, while being careful not to select too many main points.
3. Making good use of visual aids—flip charts, transparencies, slides, and so on—to improve presentation clarity and maintain audience interest.

Concerning the third point, given the proliferation of technology and equipment for creating visual aids, such aids are expected by audiences and used by presenters in virtually all oral presentations. Indiscriminate use of visual aids is not likely to be of much help, however. They must be chosen and sequenced with care, with each one containing a simple, relevant message. Exhibit 20.8 provides a number of suggestions for the proper use of slides. Many of the suggestions are also relevant for ensuring the effectiveness of other forms of visual aids.

SUMMARY

Communicating the results of a research project to decision makers is the last step of the research process. It is by no means the least important step, however.

[15] A succinct discussion is given in Timm, *Managerial Communication,* Chap. 7.

Exhibit 20.8

Guidelines for effective use of slides

Word slides

- Keep them brief: Use key words only
- Use bullets and color to highlight key points
- Break up the information to make a series of slides (a progressive or "build" series). Use color to show the new line added to each slide.

Tabular slides

- Useful to show lists
- Keep items brief as possible; arrange them to fill the slide area so the type can be as large as possible.

Box charts

- Use for organization charts, flow charts
- Simplify to keep them legible
- Break up complex charts into a series. (Show flow chart divided by time periods; show organization chart with the overall chart and departmental "close up.")

Bar charts

- Use them for data arranged in segments (by month, year, etc.)
- Choice of vertical or horizontal bars (both within horizontal slide format)
- Add drop shadow for dimensional bars
- Show complex facts clearly by using multiple or segmented bars
- Divide extensive data into a progressive disclosure series.

Indeed, it may be the *most* important step in that the practical worth of a project is closely linked to how effectively its findings are communicated. The foremost step in communicating the results of a research project is to gain a good understanding of the audience and its information needs. Lack of awareness of the audience and its concerns is a frequent reason that many sound research projects do not have as much impact as they should.

The most common vehicle for communicating research findings is the written report. To be effective, a written report must be SIMPLE: short, interesting, methodical, precise, lucid, and error-free. These six features are interrelated, although each connotes certain distinct requirements:

Pie charts

- Use them to emphasize the relationship of the parts to the whole
- Select single pie or double pie
- Consider options such as drop shadow for dimensional effect, pulled-out slices, etc.
- Arrange the slices to make your point most effectively
- Divide the slice into a series if that improves effectiveness.

Line graphs and area graphs

- Use these to display trends or continuous data
- Decide whether line graph or area graph shows your point better
- Select baseline and scale for maximum effectiveness
- Use callouts to identify key points in graph
- Divide extensive data into a series of graphs.

Other graphics

- Computer technology can be used to produce many additional kinds of graphics and illustrations
- Since these can be stored in computer memory and recalled for reuse, they can be very economical
- Logos and illustrations can be used in subdued colors in the background, as "watermarks"—an effective way to add visual interest and continuity to a presentation
- Any previously created slides can be recalled from memory and combined to make new slides.

Source: From Leslie Blumberg, "For Graphic Presentations, Managers Focus on Slides," *Data Management,* May 1983, p. 23. Copyright and reprint permission granted by Data Processing Management Association. All rights reserved.

- Short. A report should discuss only those aspects of a study that are relevant and important from the reader's standpoint. Other aspects, such as methodological details that may fascinate researchers but frustrate readers, must be omitted or only briefly stated.

- Interesting. The style, format, and contents of a report must be able to win and maintain the attention of readers.

- Methodical. The sections of a report and their contents must be chosen with the readers in mind and arranged in a logical sequence. While there is no standard research report format, the outline suggested in the chapter should be helpful.

- Precise. A report must be clear and comprehensive. Clarity is a function of writing style and format. Comprehensiveness implies that the report must contain enough detail to provide an accurate, complete picture of the study; the report should acknowledge key limitations and how they may affect interpretation of the results.
- Lucid. The report must be written in language that is not likely to be foreign to its readers. It should use simple words and sentences, as well as appropriate tables and charts, so as to communicate its contents clearly and quickly.
- Error-free. Even seemingly minor arithmetical, grammatical, or typographical errors in a report may annoy its readers a great deal. Sufficient time and effort must be devoted to catching and correcting such errors before finalizing the report.

A variety of graphical illustrations—such as pie charts, line charts, stratum charts, bar charts, and pictograms—can be employed to enhance the clarity and effectiveness of a report. However, the number and types of graphical illustrations to use must be determined with care. Haphazard use of illustrations may merely add to a report's bulk; worse still, it may confuse or mislead readers.

In addition to submitting written reports, researchers often make oral presentations of their findings. Many of the guidelines for preparing good written reports apply to making effective oral presentations as well. Understanding the audience, distilling from the study the main messages to be conveyed, and making good use of appropriate visual aids are particularly germane for oral presentations. For a successful oral presentation adequate time and effort must be spent on planning and rehearsing it.

QUESTIONS

1. What are the major reasons that the last step—communicating research results—in the research process may well be the most important step?
2. Two desirable features of a written report are that it be short and precise. Is there likely to be any conflict between these two features? If so, how would you reconcile such a conflict? If not, why not?
3. "To have an impact on readers, a research report must be humorous and entertaining." Discuss this statement.
4. Why is the executive summary such a critical component of a research report?
5. Recast the following statements in less technical language:
   a. On the basis of our survey, the 95% confidence interval for the proportion of households with VCRs is $.4 \pm .05$.

b. The regression of sales (dependent variable) on advertising expenditures (independent variable) produced an R^2-value of .9, which was statistically significant ($F = 55.8, p < .01$).

6. Go through a business publication like *Business Week* or *Fortune* and pick out any three graphical illustrations. State what type of chart or graph each is, and critically evaluate it—that is, identify its positive and negative features.

7. Using the data in Table 20.1, compute the rate of change in market shares for brands X, A, and B from year to year (i.e., 1975 to 1976, 1976 to 1977, etc.). Diagram these changes by using a line chart and a bar chart. Which of these two charts is more effective in your opinion? Why?

8. Can a pie chart or a stratum chart be used to depict the market share changes computed in Question 7? Why or why not?

9. Ms. Smith, a researcher in XYZ Company, is delighted because management just informed her that she need only make a brief oral presentation of a study she recently completed; management does not want her to write a written report. "Thank goodness I don't have to go through the torture of writing up my findings!" she thinks. What advice would you give to Ms. Smith?

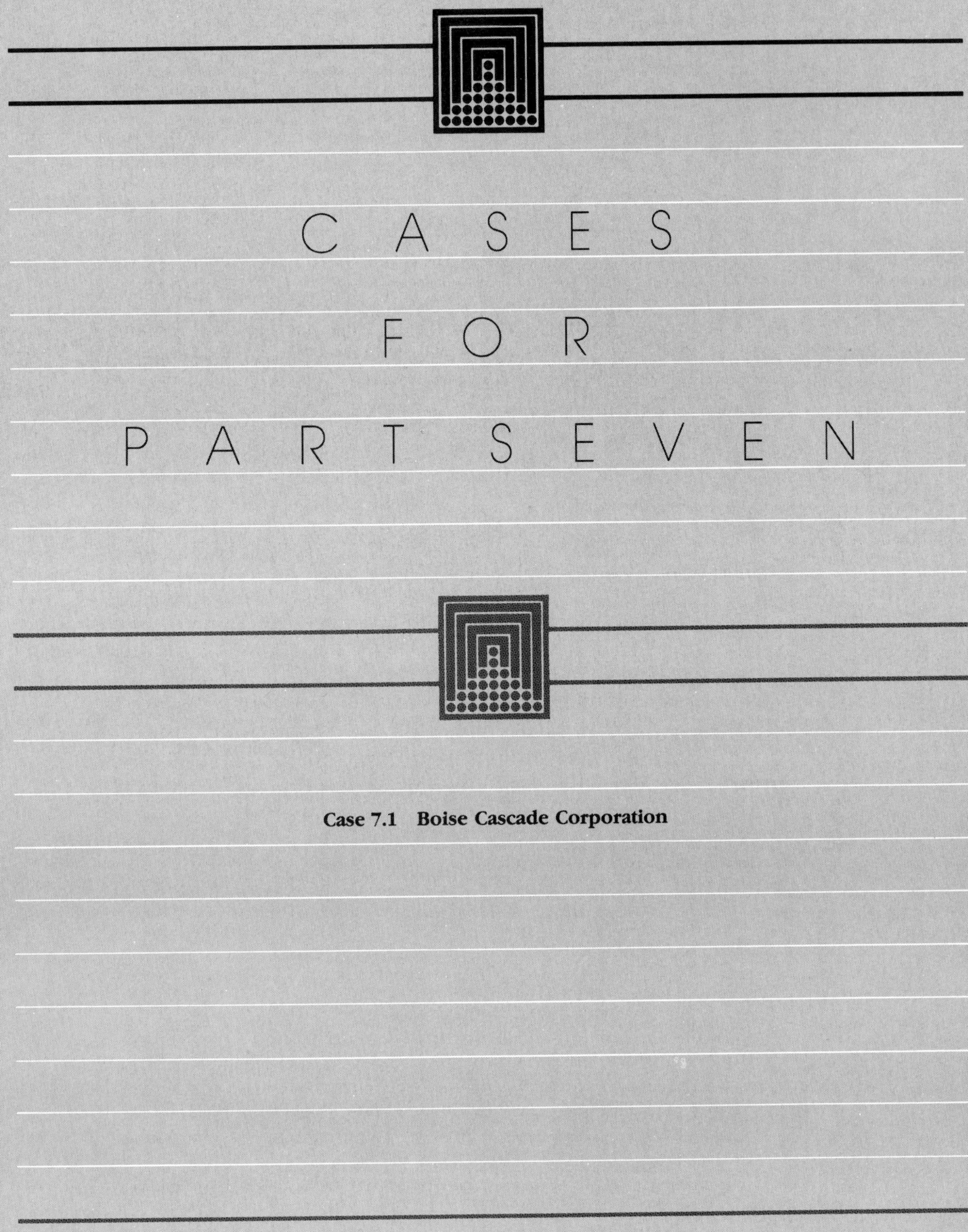

CASES FOR PART SEVEN

CASE 7.1

Boise Cascade Corporation

Gary Bush, marketing manager for the Paper Group of Boise Cascade Corporation, headquartered in Portland, Oregon, recently received a written report from a marketing research firm in the Chicago area. He had requested the firm to conduct a study to determine the paper-purchasing practices of the low-volume office copy machine market. The Paper Group had long been interested in formulating effective marketing strategies for penetrating this market. Mr. Bush hoped that the report submitted by the marketing research firm would provide some useful insights about this market.

The report was 28 typed pages long. An abbreviated version of the report is presented here. The title page of the report was the research firm's letterhead with the following information on it:

A PILOT STUDY OF PAPER PURCHASING PATTERNS

FOR SMALL VOLUME COPY MACHINES IN THE CHICAGO AREA

for BOISE CASCADE CORPORATION, PAPER GROUP, PORTLAND, OREGON

MARCH 1978

The subsequent parts of the report are given in the following sections (several of these parts are reproduced in their entirety; others are presented in abbreviated form).

SUMMARY

The average small volume copy machine user in this limited sample had 1.3 machines on the premises and almost half of them made less than 5,000 copies per month. However, because of several companies in the 30,000 to 50,000 per month range, the average usage was about 12,000 copies per month.

The median user orders three or four cases at a time every two or three months. Few users have more than one source of supply and over half the users prefer to buy their

Information in this case was provided courtesy of Boise Cascade Corporation, Paper Group, 1600 S.W. 4th Avenue, Portland, OR 97207.

paper from the copy machine manufacturer or dealer. More buy from paper wholesalers than from retail dealers/stationers.

The small user tends to be willing to pay more for the convenience and avoidance of risk by buying from the machine manufacturer, especially since the potential savings from "shopping around" are small. On the other hand the large (over 10,000 per month) user tended to buy from paper trade sources since the potential savings justify experimentation and risk. Thus, on a volume basis about two-thirds of the paper actually comes from paper distributors and dealers. Prices paid range from under \$20 to \$35 with the median price about \$30 per case.

Little brand choice is being exercised. Most buyers take the machine manufacturers private label or whatever brand the paper distributor recommends. The original decision as to the paper to buy is made by the owner or general manager of these small businesses, but reordering is done by secretaries or office managers who generally do not have the authority to change sources or paper brands. Service is not a factor since few respondents were dissatisfied with delivery times. However, avoidance of trouble was found to be a much greater consideration than price. A significant number of users (especially those with Xerox machines) have tried other brands and switched back because of problems.

Paper whiteness was found to be a factor, but not a crucial one to some users. Most users are not concerned with the convenience of buying paper from sources that sell other office supplies and prefer to deal with specialists.

Paper distributors are not actively seeking the small copy machine user. Most discourage orders for less than \$100.

Since there seem to be two different systems at work for the under and over 10,000 per month users, a two pronged marketing approach may be required to exploit this market.

TABLE OF CONTENTS

INTRODUCTION

Background and purpose

This study was designed to develop a preliminary insight into the low-volume office copy machine market and to assist Boise Cascade's Paper Group in the planning and development of marketing strategies and programs that would enable the profitable participation in that market.

Methodology

Information was gathered in a series of 50 personal interviews with the owners or office managers of 50 companies which had small volume plain paper copy machines on the premises using less than 50,000 copies per month (preferably in the 5–10,000 range). To keep travel costs low, all of the interviews were conducted in the greater Chicago metropolitan area.

As specified, we interviewed 5 companies each in the following 10 general small business areas:

Law	Real estate
Insurance	Consulting
Banks	Advertising
Brokers (stock)	Employment
Engineering	Medical

The companies were primarily service oriented businesses and did not include organizations involved in manufacturing or retail trade.

Respondents were screened and located by selection from Yellow Page listings or "cold" calls in office buildings where they might be found. Companies encountered using machines in the right size range, but utilizing coated paper, were not counted as interviews.

In addition, in order to gain some insight about the channels of distribution in the area, we also had conversations with Boise Cascade's regional sales manager and the following distributors in the Chicago area:

Boise Cascade Distributors	Other Distributors
Ace Paper Company	Bradner Smith & Company
Graham Paper Company	Hobart McIntosh Paper Company
Murnane Paper Company	Moser Schmidt Paper

The following is a list of the copy machine users interviewed.

[This list, containing 50 company names classified by type of business and labeled "Copy Paper Users Interviewed" is omitted here.]

Number of employees

The average number of employees was 43. This was pulled up somewhat by some larger institutions such as banks, hospitals, and stock brokers.

Segment	Range	Average
Law	9 to 15	12
Insurance	10 to 90	27
Banks	23 to 125	54
Stock brokers	11 to 230	105
Engineers	10 to 45	27
Real estate	12 to 200	75
Consulting	7 to 45	18
Advertising	10 to 32	21
Employment	8 to 90	35
Medical	5 to 150	58
Overall average		43

FINDINGS

Note: Please keep in mind that the following findings represent a first phase pilot study covering only a limited sample of service industry companies in the greater Chicago area running less than 50,000 copies per month each. Therefore, the findings must not be construed as being representative of the national copy market.

[The "Findings" section was on a separate page.]

Number of machines and copiers

The average respondent had 1.3 plain paper copy machines on the premises and 44% of them made less than 5,000 copies per month.

Number of Machines on Premises	Number of Companies	Percent
1	40	80
2	6	12
3	3	6
4	1	2
Total: 65 machines	50	100

Copies per Month	Number of Companies	Percent
0 to 5,000	22	44
5,001 to 10,000	12	24
10,001 to 15,000	4	8
15,001 to 20,000	3	6
20,001 to 30,000	5	10
30,001 to 40,000	2	4
40,001 to 50,000	2	4
	50	100

[The above format—i.e., a finding followed by one or more tables apparently to support the finding—was used in the original report in presenting all subsequent findings. Only the findings, not the tables, are shown in the remainder of the sections to conserve space.]

Types of copy machines

Almost two-thirds of the machines are Xerox. The 3100 and 4000 are the most popular models. Savin makes a good showing.

[Table omitted.]

Usage by market segment

Real estate, stock brokers and employment firms in the limited sample were found to be the largest copy paper users.

[Table omitted.]

- Total of about 600,000 copies per month used by these 50 firms on 65 machines.
- Average of 12,000 copies per firm.
- Average of 9,200 copies per machine.

Exhibit 1

Tentative model of the distribution of copy paper to low volume users in the Chicago area (widths of channels are proportional to paper volume)

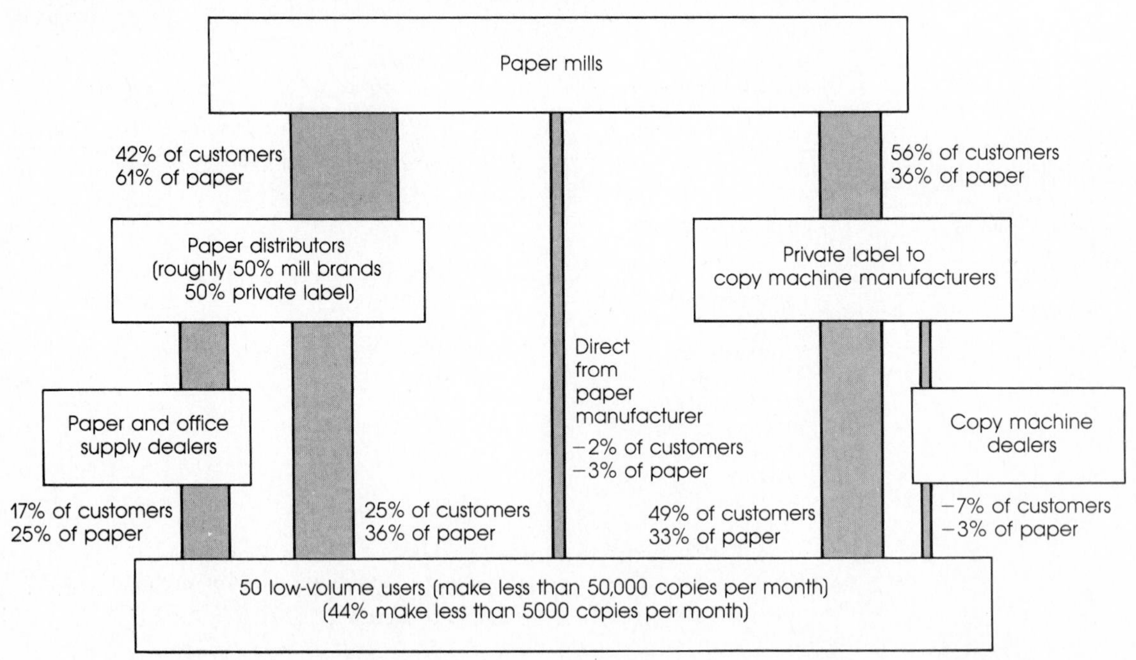

Order size and frequency for paper

About half of the respondents order less than four cases at a time every two or three months.

[Two tables omitted.]

Source of paper purchases (by number of users)

Few have more than one source of supply for copy paper. Over half of the customers are locked into buying paper from the machine supplier or dealer. The paper wholesaler is the next most important channel.

[Table omitted.]

Source of paper purchases (by volume of paper)

The large number of smaller users tend to buy from the machine manufacturer. But the fewer but larger customers who tend to buy from paper distributors account for two-thirds of the paper volume.

[Two tables omitted.]

[Following these tables was a one-page chart illustrating the distribution of copy paper. This chart is shown as Exhibit 1.]

Brand of paper used

Private labels predominate, especially those of machine manufacturers. Big paper producers' brand names account for less than 20% of the brands encountered.

[Table omitted.]

Brand specification

Almost half the users buy the machine makers' brand automatically. Most of the rest take whatever brand their paper supplier sends. There is very little brand choice being exercised.

[Table omitted.]

Price per case

At the higher volume levels, users are paying $20 to $25 per case. Smaller volume users pay $26 to as high as $34.50 per case. The median price is about $30.

[Table omitted.]

- Prices paid to Xerox ranged from $17 (under a national account) to $31.95. The average was $25.50.
- A few respondents reported paying over $50 per case, but backed down when pressed for verification. A paper distributor verified that some sales may be taking place at that price.

Purchasing and ordering decisions

The original purchasing decision is usually made at a managerial level at the time of machine selection. Re-ordering decisions are now made automatically at a lower level.

[Two tables omitted.]

The general scenario which emerges is: executive level attention to the selection of paper at the time of purchase of the machine. After that, routine ordering is delegated to a lower level. This arrangement is not usually altered unless there is a technical problem with the paper, poor service or a re-examination of costs (mostly at higher volume users) due to a purchasing agent's intervention or a cost cutting opportunity presented by a competing paper salesman. In our opinion, well under half the people who place the orders have the authority to choose the supplier.

How paper supplier was selected

Avoidance of risk/trouble, habit and friendship are far more important than price. There seems to be some justification for buying the machine maker's brand.

[Table omitted.]

- Service (delivery) not specifically mentioned as the prime reason, since most suppliers seemed to be providing reasonable service or respondents have switched in the past from suppliers with poor service.
- With few exceptions, low-volume Xerox customers consider their price and service reasonable. Quantities they buy are too small to justify shopping around.
- Larger volume users and larger firms are more likely to shop for price because of greater savings incentives and presence of a purchasing agent who is a more sophisticated buyer.
- There were so many instances where Xerox users have had poor experience with other brands of paper that it might be assumed that there is at least some basis to their belief that other brands don't work as well.

Comments on paper purchasing/problems

Most of the problems relate to how well the paper runs in the machines. Paper whiteness is a factor, but not a crucial one to some users.

Relevant comments:

> We never have a jamming problem with Xerox. Some other brands may work, but you're never sure till it's too late. Xerox delivers fast and the price isn't really out of line if you order in quantity.
>
> We had some paper sticking problems with Boise Cascade.

[Ten other such verbatim comments were included in the original report; they are omitted here.]

Purchase of other office supplies

There is no strong interest in buying copy paper from general office supply sources. However, most prefer to buy toner from the same source, particularly when it is the machine manufacturer.

[Table omitted.]

- Stationery is generally bought from a printer.
- Many who switched their paper source from the machine manufacturer continue to buy toner from them, because they consider the toner more critical than the paper for proper performance.
- About two-thirds of the respondents do not feel it is important to be able to buy other office supplies from the paper suppliers, and see no advantage in it.

  Better to deal with a specialist.

  Prefer several sources.

  Rather shop around.

  Prefer to match the machine.

- Those partial to "one-stop" shopping mentioned volume discounts rather than convenience as the principal reason.

Miscellaneous findings

The market is very competitive. Many of the firms, especially the larger ones, commented that they are continually beset by phone and personal calls from paper salesmen. Several also complained about unscrupulous "boiler room" shops with fraudulent deals. Only some of the very smallest users said they rarely saw a salesman.

Lid cartons are not a factor. Only one of the 50 companies claimed that the special Xerox lid carton was a factor (but not a ruling one). They are used in the office for storage. Surplus ones are taken home by office personnel for home storage.

Payments are by invoice. Only one respondent prepaid the order and one bought a prepaid discount coupon book. All others get invoices by mail. None pay C.O.D.

All orders are received by delivery service. None of the respondents pick up orders at a store or warehouse. All mentioned "delivery service" but did not seem clear as to whether it was the supplier's own truck or a common carrier. One mentioned United Parcel Service.

Few of the respondents read office magazines. Four mentioned reading "Office," two mentioned "Administrative Management," and one "Modern Office Procedures." Several answered "Business Week," "Time," and "Forbes."

Paper distributors

The paper distributors think the small volume trade is probably a growing area, but find it too costly to pursue.

[Several specific comments made by, and data pertaining to, each of the six distributors interviewed were included in this section; these comments took up about two pages of the original report.]

CONCLUSIONS AND RECOMMENDATIONS

This pilot study was conducted among a small sample of low-volume copy paper users in a very limited geographic area. Therefore its findings cannot be considered as providing a definitive or quantitative picture of paper purchasing patterns in the nation. However, we do feel that the study has served well to define the basic qualitative considerations of how the market "works" and to identify the issues that future research needs to focus on.

The principal conclusion is that the target group of 5,000 to 10,000 sheet per month users will be a "tough sell." They tend to stay with the copy machine maker's recommendations and are more interested in avoiding jams than in price. Also, it seems that they do not imagine the machine maker's private label to be better. . . . There were quite a few who ventured to try another brand and encountered enough trouble to switch back.

These small users purchases of 3 or 4 cases every 2 or 3 months is below the paper wholesalers' minimum order levels and wholesalers actively discourage their salesmen from seeking such business. This may be due to the fact that the Chicago market has a large number of large users, being served by some very large paper wholesalers. Therefore, this finding may not hold true in areas of lesser industrial concentration.

The second important conclusion is that the purchasing and ordering decisions are in separate hands. Among these users the business owner usually makes the original purchase decision, but the routine re-ordering is usually done by an office person. Salesmen who call are not likely to see the owner. They are more likely to see the office person who does not usually have the authority to change brands without clearing with the owner. Therefore, it begins to appear that any marketing approach may need two prongs:

1. Appeal to the office person to "do your boss a favor" and bring to his attention a cost cutting opportunity (via mailers, ads in office magazine, free samples for trial, etc.).

2. Appeal to the owner/manager to initiate exploration of saving up to $10 per case, not for some risky unknown brand, but for a well-known quality-image brand such as Boise Cascade (via ads in general business publications).

It can also be envisioned that the distribution strategy might also involve two approaches:

1. Sell the under 10,000 per month user that the wholesalers avoid via your Office Products Division, perhaps by a free 2 or 3 ream sample program to prove that it works as well as the machine maker's brand.
2. Develop a special marketing program to encourage the distributors to go after the 10 to 50,000 per month user, who (as it was shown) tend to be more ready to buy from a distributor on a price basis.

It was found that the larger users who were buying from paper wholesaler/distributors had unusually long relationships with them. . . . Many have bought from them for 10 or 15 years. Therefore, the duration of the relationship may justify some investment spending to develop this new business.

FUTURE RESEARCH

If the second phase of this research is to be pursued (200 telephone interviews on a national basis), we suggest that the sample not be limited to the 10 service industry segments used in this survey, since it eliminates small manufacturing and large retail establishments which may have purchasing agents and thus may do more sophisticated buying and pricing comparisons. If a list of small copy machine users can be purchased from a list source, a more representative national sample can be selected from it on an *n*th name basis.

It might also be important to do a survey of paper distributors and copy machine dealers around the country in order to find out how they view the market and what it would take to get them to support a Boise Cascade program to reach this market.

QUESTIONS

1. Critically evaluate the report submitted by the marketing research firm to Boise Cascade Corporation. What are the report's strengths and weaknesses?
2. In what ways does the report differ from the guidelines/format suggested in this chapter? If you were in charge of writing this report, would you have done anything differently? Why or why not?

APPENDICES

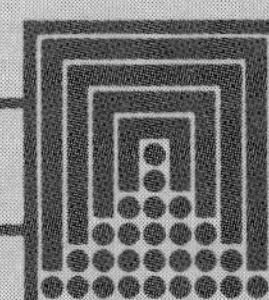

APPENDIX A

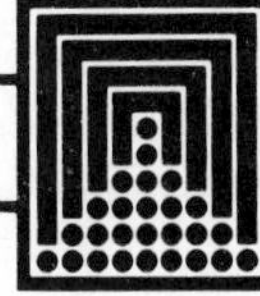

NPD Data Set and Analysis Exercises[1]

INTRODUCTION

This appendix provides and discusses a data set for illustrating a number of analysis concepts and techniques covered in this book, particularly in Chapters 16, 17, 18, and 19. The data set contains real-life data culled from purchase diaries filled out over a period of one year by a representative sample of 100 families. These families are from a consumer panel maintained by the NPD Research, Inc., of New York. A description of NPD's consumer panel and a sample page of NPD's purchase diary are contained in the appendix to Chapter 5.

The data set consists of 200 data records, two per family. The data on each family include certain demographic data and purchase data pertaining to four product categories: toilet tissue, frosting, cereal, and mayonnaise. The next section presents a more detailed description of the data set.

VARIABLES INCLUDED IN THE DATA SET

Demographic data

Data are available for the 100 families on the following 10 demographic characteristics (labeled as variables D1 through D10 for future reference):

1. Education of female head (D1),
2. Employment status of female head (D2),
3. Pet ownership (D3),
4. Type of residence (D4),
5. Residence ownership (D5),

[1] The author thanks NPD Research, Inc., of New York for providing the raw data and instructions necessary for constructing the data set included here.

6. Age and presence of children (D6),
7. Race (D7),
8. Family income (D8),
9. Age of male head (D9),
10. Education of male head (D10).

The demographic data are in columns 4 through 14 of each family's first record. Table 1 indicates the exact location of data on each variable. Table 2 explains the numerical scheme used in coding the data on each variable. Table 3 contains the data set. All three tables are at the end of this appendix.

Purchase data

The purchase data for each of the four products span a period of 12 months: from July of one year to June of the next year. However, so that the data set's size is not too large, data pertaining to only the *first* and the *last* purchase during the 12-month period are reported. For each purchase within each product category, the purchase-related variables included in the data set are as follows:

1. Brand code.
2. Quantity purchased (number of units).
3. Total price paid (for the entire quantity purchased).
4. Regular purchase or special purchase (i.e., purchase made when a special promotion was in effect).
5. Month of purchase.

For the cereal product category, data are available on two additional variables: manufacturer's name and type of cereal.

The labels shown in Tables 1 and 2 for the purchase-related variables each consist of three characters. The first character represents the product category (T for toilet tissue, F for frosting, C for cereal, M for mayonnaise), the second character represents the purchase occasion (A for first purchase and B for last purchase), and the third character represents the variable itself (1 for brand code, 2 for quantity purchased, 3 for total price paid, 4 for regular purchase or special purchase, 5 for month of purchase, M for manufacturer's name, T for type of cereal; the last two symbols are relevant only to the cereal category).

The data set also includes the total number of purchases made by each family, within each product category, during the 12-month period. The variables denoting the total number of purchases are labeled in Tables 1 and 2 as TNP for toilet tissue, FNP for frosting, CNP for cereal, and MNP for mayonnaise.

AN ILLUSTRATION

To better understand the manner in which the data set (Table 3) is structured, let us infer from it the demographic characteristics and the purchase behavior of family 003. Specifically, let us interpret the fifth and sixth rows in the data set with the help of the coding guidelines presented in Tables 1 and 2.

Family 003 has the following demographic characteristics: The family's female head has had some college education; she is not employed. The family has no dog or cat, lives in a one-family house, owns the house, has children in all three age groups (under 6, 6–12, and 13–17), is white, and has an annual income of $10,000–$11,999. The family's male head is 55–64 years old; he has had some college education.

The family's first purchase of toilet tissue was brand 30. The family bought one unit of the brand, paid $0.49 for the unit, and made the purchase at a special price. This purchase occurred in month 02 (August of the first year). The family's last purchase of toilet tissue was brand 05. The family bought two units of this brand, paid a total of $1.76 for the two units, and made the purchase at a special price. This purchase occurred in month 12 (June of the second year). This family made a total of 10 toilet tissue purchases during the year.

Family 003 did not make any purchases of frosting during the year. (The rest of this family's first data record, beginning with column 43, is blank except for the zeros corresponding to FNP.)

The family's first purchase of cereal was brand 90, a private-label brand and a regular type. The family bought one unit of the brand, paid $1.10 for it, and made the purchase at regular price. This purchase occurred in month 02. The family's last purchase of cereal was brand 07, a Nabisco brand and a regular type. The family bought one unit of the brand, paid $0.93 for it, and made the purchase at a special price. This purchase occurred in month 12. This family made a total of 17 cereal purchases during the year.

The family's first purchase of mayonnaise was brand 003. The family bought one unit of the brand, paid $1.12 for it, and made the purchase at a special price. This purchase occurred in month 01. The family's last purchase of mayonnaise was brand 032. The family bought one unit of the brand, paid $0.69 for it, and made the purchase at a special price. This purchase occurred in month 12. The family made a total of two mayonnaise purchases during the year.

The next section of this appendix presents a number of exercises involving the NPD data set. These exercises require applying analysis concepts and techniques covered in Part Four of the text. The exercises are numbered sequentially but grouped according to the chapters to which they relate. Availability of the data set on computer and access to a standard statistical package such as SPSS or SAS are necessary for completing most of the exercises.

EXERCISES

Exercises for Chapter 16

1. Indicate the measurement level (i.e., nominal, ordinal, interval, or ratio scale) for each variable listed in Table 2.
2. Answer the following questions after creating the necessary transformed variables and analyzing the data on those variables.
   a. What proportion of the families who purchased toilet tissue at least twice during the year bought the *same* brand at the first and the last purchases?

b. What proportion of the families who purchased mayonnaise at least twice during the year bought the *same* brand at the first and last purchases?
c. What inference(s) can you make about the degree of brand loyalty for toilet tissue and mayonnaise? Explain your answer.

3. For each of the four product categories, set up the following transformed variables:

purchase duration = (month of last purchase) − (month of first purchase) + (1),
purchase intensity = (total number of purchases during the year) ÷ (purchase duration).

Compute the average purchase intensity (across all families) for each product category. What insights emerge from comparing these average purchase intensities?

4. In what proportion of the sample families having male and female heads do *both* heads have at least some college education?

5. Determine and interpret the appropriate measure of central tendency for each of the following variables: D3, D6, D8, TA2, TB2, FA4, FB4, CA4, CB4, TNP, FNP, CNP, and MNP.

6. Construct, compare, and interpret the one-way tables for variables in each of the following sets of variables:
a. D1 and D10.
b. TA4, TB4, MA4, and MB4.
c. TA5, FA5, CA5, and MA5.

7. Answer the following questions after constructing and examining the appropriate two-way tables.
a. Is there an association between whether the male family head has had at least some college education and whether the family income is at least $25,000?
b. Is there an association between whether a family has children under 18 years of age and whether the family owns a dog or a cat?
c. Is there an association between whether family income is at least $25,000 and whether a purchase is made at regular price for the first purchase of (i) toilet tissue, (ii) frosting, (iii) cereal, and (iv) mayonnaise? What inferences can you draw by comparing the results across the four product categories?

Exercises for Chapter 17

8. A firm manufacturing several brands of frosting is wondering whether to run a special advertising campaign to improve the frequency of purchase for the product. The firm wants to run the campaign only if it is reasonably sure (i.e., 95% confident) that the average family makes less than two frosting purchases during the year. On the basis of the NPD sample data on frosting purchases, should the firm run the campaign?

9. Considering only families that purchased a regular, presweetened, or nutritional cereal during the first purchase (i.e., the first three categories of variable CAT in the NPD data set), test the following null hypothesis at a significance level of .01: Family preferences for the three types of cereals are identical.

10. Assume that the income distribution of families in the United States is as follows:

Less than $10,000	15%
$10,000–$14,999	20%
$15,000–$24,999	25%
$25,000–$34,999	25%
$35,000 or more	15%
	100%

Can we be 95% confident that the NPD sample of families is representative of all United States families with respect to income?

11. Using the NPD data, test the null hypothesis that at least 30% of all families buy mayonnaise less than three times a year. (Assume an alpha value of .01.)

12. Is the mean number of cereal purchases per year for families with children under 18 significantly different from that for families with no children under 18? (Assume a significance level of .05.)

13. Is the mean number of units of toilet tissue bought during the first purchase significantly different from the mean number of units of toilet tissue bought during the last purchase, assuming a significance level of .05?

14. Are the proportions of families buying toilet tissue at regular price during the first purchase significantly different for families with an income of less than $25,000 and for those with an income of at least $25,000? (Assume a significance level of .1.)

Exercises for Chapter 18

15. Conduct a chi-square contingency test for each of the tables you set up under Exercise 7, assuming a significance level of .05.

16. Using a significance level of .1, repeat the chi-square contingency test corresponding to the first purchase of toilet tissue that you conducted under Exercise 15. Compare your inference from this test with that in Exercise 14. Are the two inferences alike? Explain your answer.

17. For which of the various chi-square contingency tests you conducted under Exercise 15 would computing the contingency coefficient and the Cramer's *V*-statistic be meaningful? Compute these values where appropriate and interpret them.

18. What is the nature and the degree of association between the education of the female head and that of the male head of families included in the NPD sample? Is this association statistically significant at the .05 significance level?

19. A firm's product line includes toilet tissue, frosting, cereal, and mayonnaise. This firm wants to ascertain the nature and the extent of association between the purchase frequency (i.e., total number of purchases per year) for each product and the purchase frequency for each of the other three products. To achieve the firm's information objective, perform appropriate analyses of the data on the TNP, FNP, CNP, and MNP variables in the NPD data set, and interpret the results.

20. Repeat Exercise 19 by analyzing data on *purchase intensity* (as defined in Exercise 3) rather than on purchase frequency. Do the results and inferences differ from those obtained in Exercise 19? Explain your answer.

21. For the first purchase of each product category in the NPD data set, perform the following simple regression analysis:

$$\text{quantity purchased} = a + b\ (\text{price per unit})$$

(Note that you first need to transform the "total price paid" variable in the NPD data set so as to obtain values for the independent variable in this equation.) What inferences stem from your analyses concerning the relative sensitivity of quantity purchased to price across the four product categories? How meaningful and trustworthy are those inferences? Why?

22. For each of the four product categories, conduct a multiple regression analysis with *purchase duration* (as defined in Exercise 3) as the dependent variable and with total number of purchases and family income as the independent variables. (Recode the 14 income categories as 1 through 14 and assume the resulting data are metric-scaled for illustrative purposes. Use the recoded income variable in the regression analysis.) Answer the following questions for each multiple regression equation:
   a. Is the regression equation trustworthy and useful? Explain.
   b. Are the regression coefficients statistically significant?
   c. Do the regression coefficients have meaningful interpretations? Is the problem of multicollinearity present? If so, is it serious? Explain your answers.

Exercises for Chapter 19

23. Create a transformed income variable with three categories as follows:

Low	$14,999 or less
Medium	$15,000 to $29,999
High	$30,000 or more

Considering the low, the medium, and the high categories as three treatments, conduct a one-way analysis of variance to ascertain whether differences exist across the three income groups in terms of the purchase frequency (i.e., total number of purchases during the year) for toilet tissue, frosting, cereal, and mayonnaise. Discuss the results.

24. Using the data pertaining to the first purchase of toilet tissue, perform an appropriate one-way analysis of variance to ascertain whether the quantity purchased (TA2) varies significantly depending on whether the purchase was made at regular price or at a special price (TA4).

25. Repeat Exercise 24 by treating TA4 as a dummy variable and conducting a simple regression analysis. Interpret the results and compare them with those in Exercise 24.

Table 1

Location of demographic and purchase data on each family's data records

COLUMN NUMBER	FIRST RECORD	SECOND RECORD
01–03	Family code number	Blank
	DEMOGRAPHIC DATA	
04	Education of female head (D1)	Blank
05	Employment status of female head (D2)	Blank
06	Pet ownership (D3)	Blank
07	Type of residence (D4)	Blank
08	Residence ownership (D5)	Blank
09	Age and presence of children (D6)	Blank
10	Race (D7)	Blank
11–12	Family income (D8)	Blank
13	Age of male head (D9)	Blank
14	Education of male head (D10)	Blank
	TOILET TISSUE PURCHASE DATA	**CEREAL PURCHASE DATA**
	First purchase of the year:	First purchase of the year:
15–16	Brand code (TA1)	Brand code (CA1)
17	Blank	Manufacturer's name (CAM)
18	Blank	Type of cereal (CAT)
19–20	Quantity purchased (TA2)	Quantity purchased (CA2)
21–24	Total price paid (TA3)	Total price paid (CA3)
25	Regular or special purchase (TA4)	Regular or special purchase (CA4)
26–27	Month of purchase (TA5)	Month of purchase (CA5)
	Last purchase of the year:	Last purchase of the year:
28–29	Brand code (TB1)	Brand code (CB1)
30	Blank	Manufacturer's name (CBM)
31	Blank	Type of cereal (CBT)
32–33	Quantity purchased (TB2)	Quantity purchased (CB2)
34–37	Total price paid (TB3)	Total price paid (CB3)
38	Regular or special purchase (TB4)	Regular or special purchase (CB4)
39–40	Month of purchase (TB5)	Month of purchase (CB5)
41–43	Total number of purchases during the year (TNP)	Total number of purchases during the year (CNP)
	FROSTING PURCHASE DATA	**MAYONNAISE PURCHASE DATA**
	First purchase of the year:	First purchase of the year:
44–46	Brand code (FA1)	Brand code (MA1)
47–48	Quantity purchased (FA2)	Quantity purchased (MA2)
49–52	Total price paid (FA3)	Total price paid (MA3)
53	Regular or special purchase (FA4)	Regular or special purchase (MA4)
54–55	Month of purchase (FA5)	Month of purchase (MA5)
	Last purchase of the year:	Last purchase of the year:
56–58	Brand code (FB1)	Brand code (MB1)
59–60	Quantity purchased (FB2)	Quantity purchased (MB2)
61–64	Total price paid (FB3)	Total price paid (MB3)
65	Regular or special purchase (FB4)	Regular or special purchase (MB4)
66–67	Month of purchase (FB5)	Month of purchase (MB5)
68–70	Total number of purchases during the year (FNP)	Total number of purchases during the year (MNP)

Table 2

Numerical coding scheme for data set

VARIABLE DESCRIPTION	VARIABLE LABEL(S)	DESCRIPTION OF NUMERICAL CODES REPRESENTING VARIABLE
Education of female head	D1	1 Grade school 2 Some high school 3 Graduated high school 4 Some college 5 Graduated college 6 Post graduate 0 No female head
Employment status female head	D2	1 Employed under 30 hours 2 Employed 30–34 hours 3 Employed 35 or more hours 8 Employed hours unknown 9 Not employed
Pet ownership	D3	0 No dog or cat 1 Dog only 2 Cat only 3 Both cat and dog
Type of residence	D4	1 One-family house 2 Building for two families 3 Building for three or more families 4 Mobile home or trailer 5 Other
Residence ownership	D5	1 Own 2 Rent or lease 3 Rent free
Age and presence of children	D6	1 Under 6 only 2 6–12 only 3 13–17 only 4 Under 6 & 6–12 5 Under 6 & 13–17 6 6–12 & 13–17 7 All three age-groups 9 No children under 18
Race	D7	1 White 2 Black 3 Oriental 4 Other

VARIABLE DESCRIPTION	VARIABLE LABEL(S)	DESCRIPTION OF NUMERICAL CODES REPRESENTING VARIABLE
Family income	D8	04 Under 8000 06 8000–9999 08 10,000–11,999 10 12,000–14,999 11 15,000–19,999 13 20,000–24,999 15 25,000–29,999 16 30,000–34,999 17 35,000–39,999 18 40,000–44,999 19 45,000–49,999 21 50,000–59,999 23 60,000–69,999 24 70,000 and over
Age of male head	D9	1 <25 2 25–29 3 30–34 4 35–39 5 40–44 6 45–49 7 50–54 8 55–64 9 65+ 0 No male head
Education of male head	D10	1 Grade school 2 Some high school 3 Graduated high school 4 Some college 5 Graduated college 6 Post graduate 0 No male head
Brand code	TA1, FA1, CA1, MA1, TB1, FB1, CB1, MB1	A two-digit code number for toilet tissue and cereal, and a three-digit code number for frosting and mayonnaise (brand names are confidential)
Quantity purchased	TA2, FA2, CA2, MA2, TB2, FB2, CB2, MB2	A two-digit number representing the actual number of units of the brand purchased
Total price paid	TA3, FA3, CA3, MA3, TB3, FB3, CB3, MB3	A four-digit number representing the actual price paid (in cents) for the total number of units of the brand purchased (e.g., a 0784 represents a total price of $7.84)

(*continued*)

Table 2 (Concluded)

VARIABLE DESCRIPTION	VARIABLE LABEL(S)	DESCRIPTION OF NUMERICAL CODES REPRESENTING VARIABLE
Regular or special purchase	TA4, FA4, CA4, MA4, TB4, FB4, CB4, MB4	1 Regular price 2 Special price 3 Free sample or gift
Month of purchase	TA5, FA5, CA5, MA5, TB5, FB5, CB5, MB5	A two-digit number from 01 to 12; 01 corresponds to July of one year and 12 corresponds to June of the next year
Manufacturer's name (relevant only for cereals)	CAM, CBM	1 Quaker 2 General Mills 3 Kellogg 4 Nabisco 5 Post 6 Ralston 7 Sunshine 8 Private label 9 All other
Type of cereal	CAT, CBT	1 Regular 2 Presweetened 3 Nutritional 4 Variety pack 5 Granola health food 6 Wheat germ
Total number of purchases during the year	TNP, FNP, CNP, MNP	A three-digit number representing the actual number of times the product category was purchased during the entire year

Note: For all variables, blank spaces in the data set represent missing values.

Table 3

NPD data set

RECORD COLUMNS													
01–05	06–10	11–15	16–20	21–25	26–30	31–35	36–40	41–45	46–50	51–55	56–60	61–65	66–70
00129	02191	04940	3 02	01781	0903	0201	78111	00200	10101	39110			001
		2	73101	01231	01153	10101	29111	00800	30100	78101	00301	01491	12005
00249	01191	16850	5 01	00692	0310	0504	00207	002					000
								00000	10101	59112			001
00349	01171	08843	0 01	00492	0205	0201	76212	010					000
		9	08101	01101	02074	10100	93212	01700	30101	12201	03201	00692	12002
00441	01191	24850	3 01	01151	0103	0202	14212	01001	20101	39110			001
		1	33101	01951	02133	10101	87111	00402	40101	69107	02901	01152	12002
00529	03291	10920	5 01	01291	0139	0100	90212	027					000
		1	53101	00942	01			001					000
00643	01192	13820	5 01	01792	0105	0101	59212	01400	30101	75106			001
		0	24101	01591	02195	10101	69212	00600	30100	86202	01301	01291	05003
00731	31191	11830	1 02	01001	0101	0401	96112	025					000
		3	03101	01181	08743	10101	91108	00300	60101	11112			001
00831	11161	13540	3 01	00992	0101	0101	26212	02600	30100	84201	00101	00842	12021
		8	28201	01591	01023	20101	73212	10600	30100	99202			001
00939	01191	11921	8 02	01242	0218	0101	39212	01409	30201	00201	00101	00792	12012
		1	93201	01351	09015	20101	84212	00500	30100	84201	00301	01272	09004
01041	31191	18844	3 02	01502	0104	0201	58211	011					000
		0	74101	01221	07214	10101	58112	01100	10101	39101	00101	01492	12012
01153	21191	21661	8 06	06542	0318	0607	14111	00558	50100	69101	58501	00621	09002
		1	52101	01242	01152	10101	01212	02100	10101	89101	00301	01842	12005
01239	01161	10430	5 02	01582	0154	0101	89112	01354	50201	98202	00101	01172	09007
		1	35201	01092	01282	10302	67112	05604	50100	85202	52902	01381	12003
01319	02291	04008	5 01	00791	0339	0101	03112	005					000
		9	29101	00431	01175	10100	99112	02506	50101	09101	55701	01291	12011
01429	31291	04430	1 01	01691	0239	0201	78112	01401	20101	19109			001
		0	92301	01791	01868	20101	09112	04600	30100	89102	00301	01091	12007
01539	01191	11830	1 02	00901	0101	0200	39212	02000	30101	19204			001
		1	62201	01991	11415	20101	79112	00300	50100	29201	00101	2	12009
01649	01391	10920	1 02	00961	0101	0101	97112	010					000
								00003	20100	89111			001
01763	14 91	13968	5 01	00691	0203	0100	77112	031					000
		3	03101	01201	01125	10101	70112	02100	30100	97202	00501	00772	12008
01852	01161	10450	1 01	00381	0101	0100	39110	01000	10101	39104	00301	01491	11005
		0	81301	01991	01081	30101	99111	03500	30101	49104	00301	01091	11004
01939	11131	11810	5 02	01422	0103	0203	06212	02600	10100	79210			001
		0	62201	01471	01074	10101	48112	01400	30100	89202	00301	01262	10008

(*continued*)

Table 3 (*Cont*)

RECORD COLUMNS													
01–05	06–10	11–15	16–20	21–25	26–30	31–35	36–40	41–45	46–50	51–55	56–60	61–65	66–70
02031	01191	10820	5 06	05342	0303	0201	96212	00800	10101	09204	00101	01191	10007
		4	72201	01731	01023	20101	48112	02301	30100	89201	00301	00992	12002
02143	01191	15820	5 02	01972	0105	01	312	014					000
		3	65101	01092	04115	10101	52212	01058	50100	85101	58502	01981	05002
02231	01191	06920	3 01	00892	0101	0200	98112	014					000
		1	71101	01011	01161	10100	96109	01000	10101	59101	02901	01191	11005
02333	01 31	19748	5 01	00691	0185	0100	65112	02601	20101	19202	00301	00792	09003
		3	69601	01281	02369	60101	69109	01758	50100	89101	00101	01542	12010
02429	01191	06920	3 01	01291	0103	0101	08112	02500	10101	29105			001
		2	82101	00742	01094	10101	24212	05900	90101	53203	00901	01362	06002
02549	21221	04312	7 01	01081	0127	0101	09211	01200	10101	49101			001
		2	14101	01631	03303	10101	22106	00200	30201	98202	00302	01982	08003
02639	01193	16665	6 01	00891	0105	0101	14104	004					
								00000	00100	99101	00001	01391	09003
02739	01191	24660	5 01	01291	0105	0101	39112	019					000
		0	74101	00952	01052	10100	89212	02200	50100	73104	00501	00731	10002
02852	11161	16445	4 01	01791	0154	0101	69112	02800	30101	09101	00301	01091	09006
		2	42201	01391	01236	20101	79112	05000	50101	57101	00501	02891	12005
02969	01131	19669	8 01	01191	0104	0101	29112	03101	201	202	01201	01531	12006
		1	62201	02042	01265	20203	17212	12600	30100	99103	00301	01251	12004
03049	11191	10930	1 01	01851	0101	0101	59209	006					000
		0	74101	01291	01			00100	50100	99202	00101	01452	12002
03133	31131	11620	3 01	01171	0103	0101	09111	01200	10101	05204			001
		5	92101	01312	01041	20101	92112	04600	30101	39101	00301	01691	12009
03239	11191	16830	5 02	01632	0139	0100	19212	01400	10100	49207			001
		1	53101	01291	01175	10100	35207	00400	30100	88201	18601	00372	12007
03369	01191	21960	5 01	01191	0143	0100	79212	011					000
		2	32301	01411	01115	10101	59112	05500	30100	79201	53401	00991	11004
03423	31131	15820	1 02	00781	0354	0100	99211	01400	30101	39109	00101	01191	09002
		1	62201	01642	01369	60101	89112	06500	10101	49102	00301	00651	11002
03531	21141	11539	8 02	00741	0198	0401	40112	01800	10100	40201	00101	00992	12014
		1	62201	01891	01162	20101	39112	02855	50101	09103	00101	2	12009
03653	21191	18910	5 01	00882	0105	0100	99211	007					000
		2	82101	01182	01036	10101	09212	03301	80100	99208			001
03749	01191	10922	7 02	01982	0127	0302	97212	002					000
		2	73101	01412	02195	10101	45212	00900	50101	49204	05101	01092	10003
03859	11141	16452	7 01	00981	0118	0100	83212	021					000
		2	61201	01311	01162	20101	54212	03400	50101	45101	00501	01751	12004
03943	11291	15552	7 01	01081	0103	0100	88112	01300	70100	39105			001
		5	43201	01791	01115	10101	00212	01300	30100	83201	00301	01162	10003

RECORD COLUMNS

01–05	06–10	11–15	16–20	21–25	26–30	31–35	36–40	41–45	46–50	51–55	56–60	61–65	66–70
04039	02232	04630	1 01	01591	0101	0100	49112	01100	10101	49112			001
		3	03101	01081	01303	10101	17112	00900	30101	49101	02701	00891	11014
04139	31131	16530	1 01	01292	0203	0201	98212	02601	201	202			001
		3	65101	01671	02203	20101	99112	02406	50100	95101	00501	01371	02002
04239	31191	17522	7 02	02181	0127	0201	48212	02400	10502	00203			001
		7	23202	04301	02			00100	30403	72203	57901	00931	08006
04352	01141	17250	1 03	00992	0101	0301	05112	021					000
		6	22201	02162	01282	10101	43212	04204	10100	99201	04101	01182	12013
04449	01291	15960	5 01	01091	0118	0101	29112	01100	30101	19101	00101	01581	11002
		1	73201	01091	01396	20101	79109	02006	50100	79101	00101	01591	12008
04539	12191	0674						00001	201	211			001
		0	52101	00392	01074	10100	67212	03256	50100	99204	00101	01172	11003
04639	01191	17940	3 01	00642	0127	0100	88212	03700	10101	49110			001
		0	74101	01191	01772	20101	77212	02600	30101	29202	18602	04332	12004
04729	01191	11830	3 01	01231	0105	0201	98212	02600	10101	19102			001
		1	83301	01721	02232	30102	66111	01556	90100	94111			001
04851	11191	17930	8 03	02372	0308	0602	62203	003					000
		0	74101	01491	05074	10101	59112	00803	70101	40109	00301	02822	09002
04939	04111	11240	4 01	00892	0118	0101	19212	02500	30100	69205	01201	00992	11002
		2	42201	01652	01772	20101	49212	03603	00100	87101	03001	01191	10006
05043	12132	16722	7 02	01582	0118	0201	71210	00901	20100	59201	01201	00442	09006
		7	03101	00792	01753	20101	59212	04300	30202	18201	00301	01791	12009
05153	31191	21253	9 01	00092	1239	0100	19212	00700	10100	95207			001
								00000	10100	89201	00101	01292	10004
05251	21113	18359	8 10	04902	0321	0100	79212	004					000
		9	49101	01591	03929	10100	50112	01006	20101	59104	06202	02982	12004
05333	02221	15555	4 01	01051	0143	0100	89212	02500	10101	29103			001
		0	52101	01131	01023	20101	79112	00702	50100	79103	00101	01191	12006
05449	21191	15730	3 02	02101	0103	0100	98212	012					000
		0	36101	01481	01868	20101	79112	00500	30101	27102	18601	01991	12012
05559	21141	13444	3 02	01981	0118	0201	98111	018					000
		2	32302	02781	01133	10101	80112	02000	50303	57203	00501	01011	12005
05651	31191	21850	5 01	00971	0105	0202	34112	022					000
		0	74101	01771	01074	10101	79112	03900	50101	49101	00501	01791	12009
05733	01111	11000	1 01	00391	0205	0100	49210	01100	10101	19102	00301	00692	07002
		1	53101	00792	03203	20101	74210	00700	30100	89103			001
05841	31311	17351	2 01	00991	0139	0100	88112	02200	10100	75201	58501	01031	07005
		0	52101	01581	01052	10101	55112	01200	30101	57101	00301	01292	11007
05939	31131	15730	5 01	00882	0103	0201	76209	00606	60201	46203	06602	01262	03002
		3	66201	01602	01152	10101	22112	04300	30100	79202	00301	00991	12009

(continued)

Table 3 (*Cont*)

RECORD COLUMNS													
01–05	06–10	11–15	16–20	21–25	26–30	31–35	36–40	41–45	46–50	51–55	56–60	61–65	66–70
06033	01191	16840	5 04	04362	0105	0303	27212	01601	20101	39106	00101	01292	11002
		1	15101	01391	01345	10101	82112	00804	10100	98202	00301	02391	12004
06139	01141	13330	1 01	01692	0201	0101	69211	01458	50100	69104			001
		6	82201	01532	01203	20102	23112	02700	30101	39201	00301	01481	10003
06259	03211	13368	5 02	00621	0185	0200	62112	027					000
		3	91201	01991	01592	10101	14212	02958	50100	79101	00701	01891	12013
06339	11191	13620	3 01	01191	0103	0201	94212	02300	10101	18203	00101	01312	11010
		1	53101	01122	01303	10100	54212	08900	30100	99201	00501	01482	12011
06459	11191	11931	8 02	02052	0105	0100	99211	00800	10101	28207			001
		3	03101	01291	02074	10101	27109	00500	30101	19103	00301	01291	08004
06539	13191	16925	6 01	01211	0108	0101	33112	013					000
		0	52101	01351	01365	10102	29112	02500	30102	72101	00601	02331	12019
06629	11191	06826	3 01	00591	0198	0100	59112	017					000
		1	08101	00651	01999	10100	94212	03806	50100	79101	02702	01382	12016
06729	11191	06940	3 01	00991	0105	0101	93112	01809	90100	24212			001
		0	66101	01991	03303	10100	52205	00300	10101	59103	50401	00991	07002
06829	11191	11002	7 01	01542	0227	0100	99211	00900	30101	59104			001
								00000	10101	49101	00301	01292	09007
06931	01191	17831	8 04	04362	0218	0303	57211	022					000
		2	05201	01451	01301	50101	49208	00800	50202	38208	00501	01392	11004
07049	03341	13550	1 02	00891	0185	0301	00112	05900	10101	19103	01201	00991	12011
		0	52101	01342	01622	20201	00212	07501	80100	99201	59201	01192	12007
07163	01131	23762	7 01	00892	0154	0100	69212	009					000
		1	23301	01891	01703	10101	39212	04700	50101	34201	00101	01492	12007
07239	03141	13233	9 01	00552	0130	0100	98112	01000	30100	99205			001
		3	32201	01841	04753	20102	09110	00700	31211	88201	02501	00992	12006
07369	01111	17452	7 02	01981	0327	01	312	010					000
		0	81301	01781	01052	10101	69212	10350	90100	95101	00301	01581	12006
07439	04191	08843	0 01	00492	0205	0201	76212	010					000
		9	08101	01101	02074	10100	93212	01700	30101	12201	03201	00692	12002
07539	01191	15830	5 10	06902	1105	0602	54212	00400	10101	26107			001
		0	36101	01751	06273	10101	58107	00400	30101	08112			001
07639	01191	15840	5 01	01151	0221	0100	79206	01000	30100	99202	00301	00742	11006
		2	32301	01402	01125	10101	48212	08100	30101	39101	00301	01542	07002

RECORD COLUMNS													
01–05	06–10	11–15	16–20	21–25	26–30	31–35	36–40	41–45	46–50	51–55	56–60	61–65	66–70
07739	31311	06135	4 01	00991	0154	0101	87112	02000	10101	49109			001
		2	26101	01211	01153	10101	82212	03306	50100	88101	06501	00991	12008
07829	14121	10326	3 01	00591	0163	0100	59112	01900	30101	29102	00301	01891	11008
		1	53101	02091	01052	10100	99112	03206	50100	69201	02701	00692	12010
07949	11121	17342	7 01	01642	0105	0101	66212	032					000
		1	33101	01391	01203	20204	78112	05204	10100	89201	04101	00992	10009
08031	31141	15240	5 02	01512	0143	0201	78211	00800	10100	77202	00101	00692	12005
		2	14101	00942	01396	20100	75212	05700	30201	58201	00301	00991	12007
08139	31211	13345	4 01	00892	0181	0200	78212	021					000
		7	03101	00792	01322	30102	49112	01600	60101	24201	02201	01492	12011
08249	11191	06944	3 01	00392	0443	0100	85210	002					000
								00000	10101	64210			001
08333	31291	11818	5 01	00791	0185	0100	79111	012					000
		6	22201	01291	01355	10101	69110	00300	50100	99102	02901	01291	09003
08431	01191	10830	5 01	00642	0139	0100	89212	01200	10100	68209			001
		0	52101	01171	01066	10100	92212	042					000
08551	31191	08912	7 02	01981	0218	0101	50211	01200	10101	28107	00101	01281	10003
		1	25101	01591	01125	10101	68111	04300	10101	12109	00301	01611	10002
08649	01191	18841	0 02	01762	0139	0201	98211	010					000
		2	26101	01092	01345	10101	94212	01702	90101	09202	00302	03132	10006
08739	01191	13930	5 01	01072	0103	0100	69212	012					000
		5	43201	01502	01622	20101	39109	01300	30101	19201	00301	01651	11007
08851	11111	08361	8 01	00992	0185	0100	68112	00800	10100	79205			001
		3	91201	01652	01592	10101	98112	02550	40101	67112			001
08949	04191	11930	3 02	01562	0203	0201	98210	008					000
		1	83301	01071	01183	30101	47212	00700	10100	37202	10001	00881	09004
09049	01191	10920	5 01	00792	0112	0100	49212	013					000
		7	03101	00792	01074	10101	83112	01104	10101	19103	00501	01751	12004
09119	11211	15630	5 02	01932	0212	0201	30212	013					000
		6	83201	00992	01415	20100	99212	04716	70201	72101	00101	01691	12006
09239	34111	13430	3 01	00892	1221	0100	79212	00600	10101	31104	56901	00891	11003
		3	03101	01011	01303	10100	99112	01900	30101	59101	54001	01351	11003
09323	11211	11130	5 01	01751	0114	0101	53111	010					000
		0	52101	01491	01543	20102	21112	03700	30100	83101	00301	02291	12015
09463	11131	19765	4 02	01981	0139	201	98112	022					000
		0	62201	01741	01342	20101	95112	03300	10101	70102	00101	01851	11004

(continued)

Table 3 (*Concluded*)

RECORD COLUMNS													
01–05	06–10	11–15	16–20	21–25	26–30	31–35	36–40	41–45	46–50	51–55	56–60	61–65	66–70
09529	11191	10821	8 02	02082	0118	0101	59212	004					000
		3	66201	01092	01763	10101	79112	02000	50101	13202	05101	01591	12009
09629	01191	04009	8 02	01581	0339	0100	99112	00700	30101	29102	00101	01141	05006
		1	23301	01591	04123	30101	69110	00500	50101	89112			001
09729	31191	06912	1 02	01582	0256	1209	96204	004					000
		0	52101	01351	01226	10101	59112	01455	00100	99202	55001	00991	11007
09853	02211	11000	5 01	00892	0405	0100	88211	012					000
		2	96101	01552	03282	10100	90211	01000	30100	77202	02901	01471	06003
09959	11241	15350	1 02	00841	0139	0100	49212	023					000
		3	91201	00832	01753	20101	45212	03600	50102	49201	00501	01791	10010
10049	11141	11320	3 02	01942	0103	0201	94211	00900	10100	89208	00101	01172	08002
		1	53101	01022	01052	10101	59212	03800	10101	49202	00302	02482	11014

Appendix B

Areas under the standard normal curve (areas to the left)

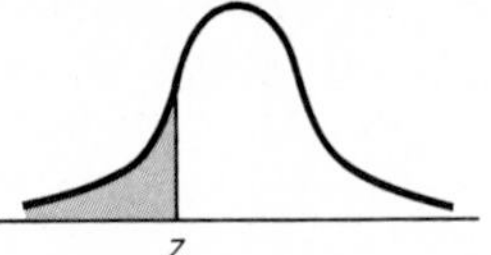

z	0	1	2	3	4	5	6	7	8	9
−3.0 *	.0013	.0013	.0013	.0012	.0012	.0011	.0011	.0011	.0010	.0010
−2.9	.0019	.0018	.0017	.0017	.0016	.0016	.0015	.0015	.0014	.0014
−2.8	.0026	.0025	.0024	.0023	.0023	.0022	.0021	.0021	.0020	.0019
−2.7	.0035	.0034	.0033	.0032	.0031	.0030	.0029	.0028	.0027	.0026
−2.6	.0047	.0045	.0044	.0043	.0041	.0040	.0039	.0038	.0037	.0036
−2.5	.0062	.0060	.0059	.0057	.0055	.0054	.0052	.0051	.0049	.0048
−2.4	.0082	.0080	.0078	.0075	.0073	.0071	.0069	.0068	.0066	.0064
−2.3	.0107	.0104	.0102	.0099	.0096	.0094	.0091	.0089	.0087	.0084
−2.2	.0139	.0136	.0132	.0129	.0125	.0122	.0119	.0116	.0113	.0110
−2.1	.0179	.0174	.0170	.0166	.0162	.0158	.0154	.0150	.0146	.0143
−2.0	.0228	.0222	.0217	.0212	.0207	.0202	.0197	.0192	.0188	.0183
−1.9	.0287	.0281	.0274	.0268	.0262	.0256	.0250	.0244	.0239	.0233
−1.8	.0359	.0351	.0344	.0336	.0329	.0322	.0314	.0307	.0301	.0294
−1.7	.0446	.0436	.0427	.0418	.0409	.0401	.0392	.0384	.0375	.0367
−1.6	.0548	.0537	.0526	.0516	.0505	.0495	.0485	.0475	.0465	.0455
−1.5	.0668	.0655	.0643	.0630	.0618	.0606	.0594	.0582	.0571	.0559
−1.4	.0808	.0793	.0778	.0764	.0749	.0735	.0721	.0708	.0694	.0681
−1.3	.0968	.0951	.0934	.0918	.0901	.0885	.0869	.0853	.0838	.0823
−1.2	.1151	.1131	.1112	.1093	.1075	.1056	.1038	.1020	.1003	.0985
−1.1	.1357	.1335	.1314	.1292	.1271	.1251	.1230	.1210	.1190	.1170
−1.0	.1587	.1562	.1539	.1515	.1492	.1469	.1446	.1423	.1401	.1379
− .9	.1841	.1814	.1788	.1762	.1736	.1711	.1685	.1660	.1635	.1611
− .8	.2119	.2090	.2061	.2033	.2005	.1977	.1949	.1922	.1894	.1867
− .7	.2420	.2389	.2358	.2327	.2296	.2266	.2236	.2206	.2177	.2148
− .6	.2743	.2709	.2676	.2643	.2611	.2578	.2546	.2514	.2483	.2451
− .5	.3085	.3050	.3015	.2981	.2946	.2912	.2877	.2843	.2810	.2776
− .4	.3446	.3409	.3372	.3336	.3300	.3264	.3228	.3192	.3516	.3121
− .3	.3821	.3783	.3745	.3707	.3669	.3632	.3594	.3557	.3520	.3483
− .2	.4207	.4168	.4129	.4090	.4052	.4013	.3974	.3936	.3897	.3859
− .1	.4602	.4562	.4522	.4483	.4443	.4404	.4364	.4325	.4286	.4247
− .0	.5000	.4960	.4920	.4880	.4840	.4801	.4761	.4721	.4681	.4641

(*continued*)

Appendix B *(Concluded)*

z	0	1	2	3	4	5	6	7	8	9
.0	.5000	.5040	.5080	.5120	.5160	.5199	.5239	.5279	.5319	.5359
.1	.5398	.5438	.5478	.5517	.5557	.5596	.5636	.5675	.5714	.5753
.2	.5793	.5832	.5871	.5910	.5948	.5987	.6026	.6064	.6103	.6141
.3	.6179	.6217	.6255	.6293	.6331	.6368	.6406	.6443	.6480	.6517
.4	.6554	.6591	.6628	.6664	.6700	.6736	.6772	.6808	.6844	.6879
.5	.6915	.6950	.6985	.7019	.7054	.7088	.7123	.7157	.7190	.7224
.6	.7257	.7291	.7324	.7357	.7389	.7422	.7454	.7486	.7517	.7549
.7	.7580	.7611	.7642	.7673	.7704	.7734	.7764	.7794	.7823	.7852
.8	.7881	.7910	.7939	.7967	.7995	.8023	.8051	.8078	.8106	.8133
.9	.8159	.8186	.8212	.8238	.8264	.8289	.8315	.8340	.8365	.8389
1.0	.8413	.8438	.8461	.8485	.8508	.8531	.8554	.8577	.8599	.8621
1.1	.8643	.8665	.8686	.8708	.8729	.8749	.8770	.8790	.8810	.8830
1.2	.8849	.8869	.8888	.8907	.8925	.8944	.8962	.8980	.8997	.9015
1.3	.9032	.9049	.9066	.9082	.9099	.9115	.9131	.9147	.9162	.9177
1.4	.9192	.9207	.9222	.9236	.9251	.9265	.9279	.9292	.9306	.9319
1.5	.9332	.9345	.9357	.9370	.9382	.9394	.9406	.9418	.9429	.9441
1.6	.9452	.9463	.9474	.9484	.9495	.9505	.9515	.9525	.9535	.9545
1.7	.9554	.9564	.9573	.9582	.9591	.9599	.9608	.9616	.9625	.9633
1.8	.9641	.9649	.9656	.9664	.9671	.9678	.9686	.9693	.9699	.9706
1.9	.9713	.9719	.9726	.9732	.9738	.9744	.9750	.9756	.9761	.9767
2.0	.9772	.9778	.9783	.9788	.9793	.9798	.9803	.9808	.9812	.9817
2.1	.9821	.9826	.9830	.9834	.9838	.9842	.9846	.9850	.9854	.9857
2.2	.9861	.9864	.9868	.9871	.9875	.9878	.9881	.9884	.9887	.9890
2.3	.9893	.9896	.9898	.9901	.9904	.9906	.9909	.9911	.9913	.9916
2.4	.9918	.9920	.9922	.9925	.9927	.9929	.9931	.9932	.9934	.9936
2.5	.9938	.9940	.9941	.9943	.9945	.9946	.9948	.9949	.9951	.9952
2.6	.9953	.9955	.9956	.9957	.9959	.9960	.9961	.9962	.9963	.9964
2.7	.9965	.9966	.9967	.9968	.9969	.9970	.9971	.9972	.9973	.9974
2.8	.9974	.9975	.9976	.9977	.9977	.9978	.9979	.9979	.9980	.9981
2.9	.9981	.9982	.9982	.9983	.9984	.9984	.9985	.9985	.9986	.9986
3.0†	.9987	.9987	.9987	.9988	.9988	.9989	.9989	.9989	.9990	.9990

* For $z \leq -4$ the areas are 0 to four decimal places.

† For $z \geq 4$ the areas are 1 to four decimal places.

Source: Neil Weiss, *Introductory Statistics,* © 1982, Addison-Wesley, Reading, Massachusetts. Pp. 576–577. Reprinted with permission.

Appendix C

Chi-square distribution (values of χ^2_α)

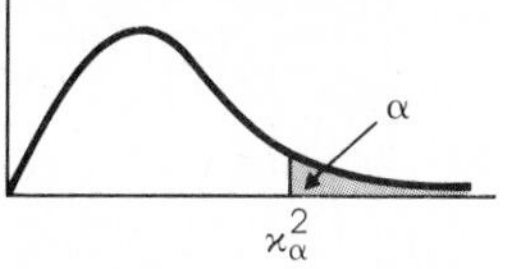

d.f. \ α	.995	.99	.975	.95	.90	.10	.05	.025	.01	.005
1	.00	.00	.00	.00	.02	2.71	3.84	5.02	6.63	7.88
2	.01	.02	.05	.10	.21	4.61	5.99	7.38	9.21	10.60
3	.07	.11	.22	.35	.58	6.25	7.81	9.35	11.34	12.84
4	.21	.30	.48	.71	1.06	7.78	9.49	11.14	13.28	14.86
5	.41	.55	.83	1.15	1.61	9.24	11.07	12.83	15.09	16.75
6	.68	.87	1.24	1.64	2.20	10.64	12.59	14.45	16.81	18.55
7	.99	1.24	1.69	2.17	2.83	12.02	14.07	16.01	18.48	20.28
8	1.34	1.65	2.18	2.73	3.49	13.36	15.51	17.54	20.09	21.96
9	1.73	2.09	2.70	3.33	4.17	14.68	16.92	19.02	21.67	23.59
10	2.16	2.56	3.25	3.94	4.87	15.99	18.31	20.48	23.21	25.19
11	2.60	3.05	3.82	4.57	5.58	17.28	19.68	21.92	24.72	26.76
12	3.07	3.57	4.40	5.23	6.30	18.55	21.03	23.34	26.22	28.30
13	3.57	4.11	5.01	5.89	7.04	19.81	22.36	24.74	27.69	29.82
14	4.07	4.66	5.63	6.57	7.79	21.06	23.68	26.12	29.14	31.32
15	4.60	5.23	6.26	7.26	8.55	22.31	25.00	27.49	30.58	32.80
16	5.14	5.81	6.91	7.96	9.31	23.54	26.30	28.85	32.00	34.27
17	5.70	6.41	7.56	8.67	10.09	24.77	27.59	30.19	33.41	35.72
18	6.26	7.01	8.23	9.39	10.86	25.99	28.87	31.53	34.81	37.16
19	6.84	7.63	8.91	10.12	11.65	27.20	30.14	32.85	36.19	38.58
20	7.43	8.26	9.59	10.85	12.44	28.41	31.41	34.17	37.57	40.00
21	8.03	8.90	10.28	11.59	13.24	29.62	32.67	35.48	38.93	41.40
22	8.64	9.54	10.98	12.34	14.04	30.81	33.92	36.78	40.29	42.80
23	9.26	10.20	11.69	13.09	14.85	32.01	35.17	38.08	41.64	44.18
24	9.89	10.86	12.40	13.85	15.66	33.20	36.42	39.36	42.98	45.56
25	10.52	11.52	13.12	14.61	16.47	34.38	37.65	40.65	44.31	46.93
26	11.16	12.20	13.84	15.38	17.29	35.56	38.89	41.92	45.64	48.29
27	11.81	12.88	14.57	16.15	18.11	36.74	40.11	43.19	46.96	49.65
28	12.46	13.56	15.31	16.93	18.94	37.92	41.34	44.46	48.28	50.99
29	13.12	14.26	16.05	17.71	19.77	39.09	42.56	45.72	49.59	52.34
30	13.79	14.95	16.79	18.49	20.60	40.26	43.77	46.98	50.89	53.67
50	27.99	29.71	32.36	34.76	37.69	63.17	67.50	71.42	76.15	79.49
100	67.33	70.06	74.22	77.93	82.36	118.5	124.3	129.6	135.8	140.2
500	422.3	429.4	439.9	449.1	459.9	540.9	553.1	563.9	576.5	585.2
1000	888.6	898.8	914.3	927.6	943.1	1058	1075	1090	1107	1119

Source: Neil Weiss, *Introductory Statistics*, © 1982, Addison-Wesley, Reading Massachusetts. P. 579. Reprinted with permission.

Appendix D
Student's t-distribution (values of t_α)

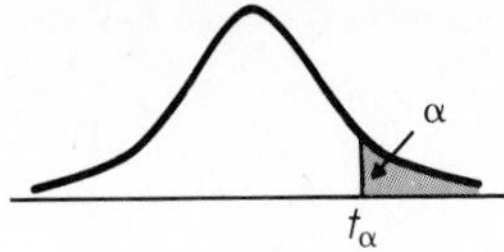

d.f.	$t_{.10}$	$t_{.05}$	$t_{.025}$	$t_{.01}$	$t_{.005}$
1	3.08	6.31	12.71	31.82	63.66
2	1.89	2.92	4.30	6.96	9.92
3	1.64	2.35	3.18	4.54	5.84
4	1.53	2.13	2.78	3.75	4.60
5	1.48	2.02	2.57	3.36	4.03
6	1.44	1.94	2.45	3.14	3.71
7	1.42	1.89	2.36	3.00	3.50
8	1.40	1.86	2.31	2.90	3.36
9	1.38	1.83	2.26	2.82	3.25
10	1.37	1.81	2.23	2.76	3.17
11	1.36	1.80	2.20	2.72	3.11
12	1.36	1.78	2.18	2.68	3.05
13	1.35	1.77	2.16	2.65	3.01
14	1.35	1.76	2.14	2.62	2.98
15	1.34	1.75	2.13	2.60	2.95
16	1.34	1.75	2.12	2.58	2.92
17	1.33	1.74	2.11	2.57	2.90
18	1.33	1.73	2.10	2.55	2.88
19	1.33	1.73	2.09	2.54	2.86
20	1.33	1.72	2.09	2.53	2.85
21	1.32	1.72	2.08	2.52	2.83
22	1.32	1.72	2.07	2.51	2.82
23	1.32	1.71	2.07	2.50	2.81
24	1.32	1.71	2.06	2.49	2.80
25	1.32	1.71	2.06	2.49	2.79
26	1.32	1.71	2.06	2.48	2.78
27	1.31	1.70	2.05	2.47	2.77
28	1.31	1.70	2.05	2.47	2.76
29	1.31	1.70	2.05	2.46	2.76
∞	1.28	1.64	1.96	2.33	2.58

Note: The last row of the table (d.f. = ∞) gives values for z_α. For example, the table shows that $z_{.10} = 1.28$ and $z_{.05} = 1.64$.

Source: Neil Weiss, *Introductory Statistics,* © 1982, Addison-Wesley, Reading, Massachusetts. P. 578. Reprinted with permission.

Appendix E

Critical values of the sample correlation coefficient *r*

d.f. \ α	.10	.05	.02	.01
1	.988	.997	.9995	.9999
2	.900	.950	.980	.990
3	.805	.878	.934	.959
4	.729	.811	.882	.917
5	.669	.754	.833	.874
6	.622	.707	.789	.834
7	.582	.666	.750	.798
8	.549	.632	.716	.765
9	.521	.602	.685	.735
10	.497	.576	.658	.708
11	.476	.553	.634	.684
12	.458	.532	.612	.661
13	.441	.514	.592	.641
14	.426	.497	.574	.623
15	.412	.482	.558	.606
16	.400	.468	.543	.590
17	.389	.456	.528	.575
18	.378	.444	.516	.561
19	.369	.433	.503	.549
20	.360	.423	492	.537
21	.352	.413	.482	.526
22	.344	.404	.472	.515
23	.337	.396	.462	.505
24	.330	.388	.453	.496
25	.323	.381	.445	.487
26	.317	.374	.437	.479
27	.311	.367	.430	.471
28	.306	.361	.423	.463
29	.301	.355	.416	.456
30	.296	.349	.409	.449
40	.257	.304	.358	.393
50	.231	.273	.322	.354
60	.211	.250	.295	.325
70	.195	.232	.274	.302
80	.183	.217	.257	.283
90	.173	.205	.242	.267
100	.164	.195	.230	.254

Note: A value given in the table is the *right-hand* critical value for a *two-tailed* test at the significance level indicated. The left-hand critical value is just the negative of the right-hand critical value.

Source: Neil Weiss, *Introductory Statistics*, © 1982, Addison-Wesley, Reading, Massachusetts. P. 586. Reprinted with permission.

Appendix F
Values of $F_{.05}$

d.f. FOR DENOMINATOR	d.f. FOR NUMERATOR								
	1	2	3	4	5	6	7	8	9
1	161.4	199.5	215.7	224.6	230.2	234.0	236.8	238.9	240.5
2	18.51	19.00	19.16	19.25	19.30	19.33	19.35	19.37	19.38
3	10.13	9.55	9.28	9.12	9.01	8.94	8.89	8.85	8.81
4	7.71	6.94	6.59	6.39	6.26	6.16	6.09	6.04	6.00
5	6.61	5.79	5.41	5.19	5.05	4.95	4.88	4.82	4.77
6	5.99	5.14	4.76	4.53	4.39	4.28	4.21	4.15	4.10
7	5.59	4.74	4.35	4.12	3.97	3.87	3.79	3.73	3.68
8	5.32	4.46	4.07	3.84	3.69	3.58	3.50	3.44	3.39
9	5.12	4.26	3.86	3.63	3.48	3.37	3.29	3.23	3.18
10	4.96	4.10	3.71	3.48	3.33	3.22	3.14	3.07	3.02
11	4.84	3.98	3.59	3.36	3.20	3.09	3.01	2.95	2.90
12	4.75	3.89	3.49	3.26	3.11	3.00	2.91	2.85	2.80
13	4.67	3.81	3.41	3.18	3.03	2.92	2.83	2.77	2.71
14	4.60	3.74	3.34	3.11	2.96	2.85	2.76	2.70	2.65
15	4.54	3.68	3.29	3.06	2.90	2.79	2.71	2.64	2.59
16	4.49	3.63	3.24	3.01	2.85	2.74	2.66	2.59	2.54
17	4.45	3.59	3.20	2.96	2.81	2.70	2.61	2.55	2.49
18	4.41	3.55	3.16	2.93	2.77	2.66	2.58	2.51	2.46
19	4.38	3.52	3.13	2.90	2.74	2.63	2.54	2.48	2.42
20	4.35	3.49	3.10	2.87	2.71	2.60	2.51	2.45	2.39
21	4.32	3.47	3.07	2.84	2.68	2.57	2.49	2.42	2.37
22	4.30	3.44	3.05	2.82	2.66	2.55	2.46	2.40	2.34
23	4.28	3.42	3.03	2.80	2.64	2.53	2.44	2.37	2.32
24	4.26	3.40	3.01	2.78	2.62	2.51	2.42	2.36	2.30
25	4.24	3.39	2.99	2.76	2.60	2.49	2.40	2.34	2.28
26	4.23	3.37	2.98	2.74	2.59	2.47	2.39	2.32	2.27
27	4.21	3.35	2.96	2.73	2.57	2.46	2.37	2.31	2.25
28	4.20	3.34	2.95	2.71	2.56	2.45	2.36	2.29	2.24
29	4.18	3.33	2.93	2.70	2.55	2.43	2.35	2.28	2.22
30	4.17	3.32	2.92	2.69	2.53	2.42	2.33	2.27	2.21
40	4.08	3.23	2.84	2.61	2.45	2.34	2.25	2.18	2.12
60	4.00	3.15	2.76	2.53	2.37	2.25	2.17	2.10	2.04
120	3.92	3.07	2.68	2.45	2.29	2.17	2.09	2.02	1.96
∞	3.84	3.00	2.60	2.37	2.21	2.10	2.01	1.94	1.88

d.f. FOR NUMERATOR									
10	12	15	20	24	30	40	60	120	∞
241.9	243.9	245.9	248.0	249.1	250.1	251.1	252.2	253.3	254.3
19.40	19.41	19.43	19.45	19.45	19.46	19.47	19.48	19.49	19.50
8.79	8.74	8.70	8.66	8.64	8.62	8.59	8.57	8.55	8.53
5.96	5.91	5.86	5.80	5.77	5.75	5.72	5.69	5.66	5.63
4.74	4.68	4.62	4.56	4.53	4.50	4.46	4.43	4.40	4.36
4.06	4.00	3.94	3.87	3.84	3.81	3.77	3.74	3.70	3.67
3.64	3.57	3.51	3.41	3.41	3.38	3.34	3.30	3.27	3.23
3.35	3.28	3.22	3.15	3.12	3.08	3.04	3.01	2.97	2.93
3.14	3.07	3.01	2.94	2.90	2.86	2.83	2.79	2.75	2.71
2.98	2.91	2.85	2.77	2.74	2.70	2.66	2.62	2.58	2.54
2.85	2.79	2.72	2.65	2.61	2.57	2.53	2.49	2.45	2.40
2.75	2.69	2.62	2.54	2.51	2.47	2.43	2.38	2.34	2.30
2.67	2.60	2.53	2.46	2.42	2.38	2.34	2.30	2.25	2.21
2.60	2.53	2.46	2.39	2.35	2.31	2.27	2.22	2.18	2.13
2.54	2.48	2.40	2.33	2.29	2.25	2.20	2.16	2.11	2.07
2.49	2.42	2.35	2.28	2.24	2.19	2.15	2.11	2.06	2.01
2.45	2.38	2.31	2.23	2.19	2.15	2.10	2.06	2.01	1.96
2.41	2.34	2.27	2.19	2.15	2.11	2.06	2.02	1.97	1.92
2.38	2.31	2.23	2.16	2.11	2.07	2.03	1.98	1.93	1.88
2.35	2.28	2.20	2.12	2.08	2.04	1.99	1.95	1.90	1.84
2.32	2.25	2.18	2.10	2.05	2.01	1.96	1.92	1.87	1.81
2.30	2.23	2.15	2.07	2.03	1.98	1.94	1.89	1.84	1.78
2.27	2.20	2.13	2.05	2.01	1.96	1.91	1.86	1.81	1.76
2.25	2.18	2.11	2.03	1.98	1.94	1.89	1.84	1.79	1.73
2.24	2.16	2.09	2.01	1.96	1.92	1.87	1.82	1.77	1.71
2.22	2.15	2.07	1.99	1.95	1.90	1.85	1.80	1.75	1.69
2.20	2.13	2.06	1.97	1.93	1.88	1.84	1.79	1.73	1.67
2.19	2.12	2.04	1.96	1.91	1.87	1.82	1.77	1.71	1.65
2.18	2.10	2.03	1.94	1.90	1.85	1.81	1.75	1.70	1.64
2.16	2.09	2.01	1.93	1.89	1.84	1.79	1.74	1.68	1.62
2.08	2.00	1.92	1.84	1.79	1.74	1.69	1.64	1.58	1.51
1.99	1.92	1.84	1.75	1.70	1.65	1.59	1.53	1.47	1.39
1.91	1.83	1.75	1.66	1.61	1.55	1.50	1.43	1.35	1.25
1.83	1.75	1.67	1.57	1.52	1.46	1.39	1.32	1.22	1.00

Source: Neil Weiss, *Introductory Statistics*, © 1982, Addison-Wesley, Reading, Massachusetts. Pp. 584–585. Reprinted with permission.

Glossary

Achieved Communality A term used in factor analysis; it represents the proportion of variance in an original variable accounted for by all the extracted factors. Each original variable will have an achieved-communality value in the factor analysis output.

Acquiescence Bias (Yea-Saying) A bias stemming from the tendency on the part of certain respondents to agree with whatever side is presented by one-sided questions.

Analysis of Covariance (ANCOVA) An advanced analysis of variance procedure in which the effects of one or more metric-scaled extraneous variables (called covariates) are removed from the dependent-variable data before one conducts the ANOVA.

Analysis of Variance (ANOVA) A technique for detecting relationships between a metric-scaled dependent variable and one or more categorical (nominal or ordinal) independent variables. ANOVA procedures are often used to analyze data from experimental studies.

Anchor Label A label used to define an extremity of a measurement scale.

Area Sampling A type of cluster-sampling procedure in which clusters are formed on the basis of the geographic location of the population units; that is, the clusters formed are subareas such as census tracts or counties.

Attitude A person's underlying mental state capable of influencing his or her choice of actions and maintaining consistency across those actions.

Automatic Interaction Detector (AID) A technique for identifying a set of key categorical (nominal or ordinal) independent variables that are most closely associated with a metric-scaled dependent variable. In identifying the key independent variables, AID uses an ANOVA procedure repeatedly.

Balanced Scale A scale that has an equal number of positive/favorable and negative/unfavorable response choices.

Bar Chart A chart consisting of a series of bars (of equal thickness) whose heights (or lengths, if the bars are drawn horizontally) represent values of items.

Bayesian Analysis (Decision Theory Approach) A mathematical procedure for estimating the monetary value of a marketing research project.

Bayes's Rule A principle used in deriving posterior probabilities from prior and conditional probabilities; it states that for any research outcome R_i and market state M_j,

$$P(M_j/R_i) = \frac{P(R_i/M_j) \times P(M_j)}{P(R_i)}.$$

Bivariate Analysis A special case of multivariate analysis involving just two variables.

Blocking Factor A relevant characteristic of study units that serves as the basis for forming matched sets of units (called blocks) in certain experimental studies.

Cartoon Test (Balloon Test) A nonstructured, disguised form of questioning in which respondents are shown one or more cartoon pictures with empty "balloons" and are asked to fill the balloons with words reflecting thoughts or verbal statements of the characters involved.

Case A sample unit for which data are available within a data set.

Case Study An in-depth examination, using a fairly flexible format, of a unit of interest such as a customer, store, salesperson, firm, or market area.

Census Study A study involving all units in a population.

Central Limit Theorem A theorem stating that for a sufficiently large sample size (in practice, a sample size of 30 or more), the sampling distribution curve for sample means associated with a sampling procedure will be centered on the population parameter value and will have all the properties of a normal probability distribution.

Chi-Square Contingency Test A nonparametric test for determining whether there is a statistically significant relationship between two categorical (nominal or ordinal) variables that have been cross-tabulated.

Chi-Square Goodness-of-Fit Test A nonparametric test to check whether the observed distribution of sample data on a nominal-scaled variable is consistent with an expected distribution, that is, a distribution that would be expected if the sample had come from a prespecified population.

Classification Data Data generated by questions dealing with respondents' personal or demographic characteristics.

Cluster Analysis A technique for segmenting objects (e.g., customers, market areas, products) into homogeneous groups, given data for the objects on a variety of characteristics.

Code of Ethics The standards governing the conduct of members of a profession.

Coding A term that broadly refers to the set of all tasks associated with transforming edited questionnaire responses into a form that is ready for analysis.

Coefficient of Determination (R^2) A global measure (varying between 0 and 1) of how good a regression equation is. It represents the proportion of variation in the dependent variable accounted for, or explained by, the independent variable(s) in the equation.

Comparative Rating Scale A scale that seeks respondents' feelings about an issue/object by explicitly asking them to compare the issue/object with a specified frame of reference.

Completely Nonstructured Question A question that is not necessarily presented in exactly the same wording to every respondent and does not have fixed responses.

Completely Randomized Design An experimental study design in which (1) the study units are randomly divided into as many groups as there are experimental treatments and (2) the treatments are randomly assigned to the groups.

Completely Structured Question A question that is presented verbatim to every respondent and has fixed response categories.

Complex Question A question that is difficult to answer because it contains terms unfamiliar to respondents and/or requires considerable respondent effort.

Computerized Interviewing A data collection procedure in which the questionnaire appears on a CRT terminal and the responses are directly entered into computer memory.

Computerized Search A computer-aided approach for quickly identifying potential sources of secondary data by simply specifying certain key words relating to the topic area on which data are desired.

Conclusive Research Research having clearly defined objectives and data requirements and capable of suggesting a specific course of action to be taken by decision makers.

Conditional Probability of a Research Outcome The probability that the research outcome would be observed if a particular market state or condition were to exist.

Confidence Interval A range of values (estimated from sample data) within which one can claim, with a prespecified degree of confidence, that a population parameter falls.

Confidence Level The minimum probability of not committing a Type I error when one is conducting a hypothesis test. The confidence level is 1 minus the specified significance level.

Confusion Matrix A table set up to evaluate the predictive accuracy of a discriminant function. It shows the degree of correspondence, or lack thereof, between the actual groupings of the sample units and the predicted groupings obtained by classifying the same units through the discriminant function.

Conjoint Analysis A technique for deriving the utility values that respondents presumably attach to various attributes of an object on the basis of respondents' overall preferences for different bundles of attributes or descriptive profiles of the object.

Consensor An electronic device used in certain focus groups. It consists of a set of hand-held terminals through which participants can express the nature and strength of their feelings about any issue raised by the moderator. The feelings of the group are instantly tabulated and displayed as a histogram on a video screen.

Constant-Sum Scale A scale that asks respondents to allocate a fixed number of points to various response categories in proportion to how the respondents feel about those categories (e.g., how important each category is or how much they like each category).

Constitutive Definition (Conceptual Definition) A definition that describes a construct in terms of other constructs.

Construct Validity A scale evaluation criterion that relates to the following question: "What is the nature of the underlying variable or construct measured by the scale?"

Content Validity (Face Validity) A scale evaluation criterion representing the extent to which the content of a measurement scale appears to tap all relevant facets of the construct it is attempting to measure.

Contingency Coefficient An index that measures the degree of association between two variables in a contingency table when the null hypothesis of independence between the variables is rejected.

Contingency Table A cross-tabulation set up for the purpose of conducting a chi-square contingency test.

Contrived Observation A data collection approach in which events and/or behaviors are observed in an environment artificially set up by the researcher.

Controlling (Control Function) Getting feedback from the marketplace and taking needed corrective action.

Convenience Sampling A nonprobability-sampling procedure in which a researcher's convenience forms the basis for selecting a sample of units.

Convergent Validity A form of construct validity that represents the extent of association between a measured construct and measures of other constructs with which the measured construct is expected to be related on theoretical grounds.

Cramer's *V*-Statistic An index (varying between 0 and 1) that measures the degree of association between two variables in a contingency table when the null hypothesis of independence between the variables is rejected. This index is a somewhat more useful measure than the contingency coefficient.

Cross-Sectional Sample A group of units selected specifically and solely for data collection at a single period of time.

Cross-Sectional Study A onetime study involving data collection at a single period of time.

Cross-Tabulation A process involving simultaneous tabulation of data on two or more variables.

Crowded One-On-One Interview A variation of the depth interview, conducted by a professional interviewer in the presence of up to three client personnel, who themselves can probe the respondent toward the end of the interview.

Data Accuracy The extent to which the collected data are error-free and trustworthy.

Data Error A form of nonsampling error that represents any systematic bias occurring during the process of data collection, analysis, or interpretation.

Data Record A series of spaces in a data storage medium capable of accommodating a prespecified number of numerical digits.

Data Set (Data File) An organized collection of data records in which one or more records are set aside for storing data obtained from each unit participating in a study.

Decision Making Under Certainty Choosing a course of action after observing the results of perfect, or error-free, marketing research conducted to reduce uncertainty in a situation.

Decision Making Under Uncertainty Choosing a course of action without conducting any marketing research to reduce uncertainty in a situation.

Decision Tree A diagram that lays out, in logical sequence, various available decision options, intervening events, and/or market states that can influence the monetary consequences of choosing each option.

Dependence Technique A multivariate analysis procedure in which one variable is designated as the dependent variable and the rest are treated as independent variables (e.g., regression analysis, ANOVA, AID, discriminant analysis).

Dependent Variable (Criterion Variable) A variable in multivariate analysis that is presumed to be influenced by one or more independent variables. It is conventionally plotted along the *Y*-axis in a scatter diagram.

Depth Interview (In-Depth Interview) A form of nonstructured, nondisguised questioning in which respondents are encouraged to provide as much information, in as unrestricted a fashion, as possible.

Descriptive Analysis Preliminary data analysis (e.g., computing measures of central tendency and dispersion) that helps summarize the general nature of variables included in a study and the interrelationships among them.

Descriptive Research A form of conclusive research that is intended to generate data describing the composition and characteristics of relevant groups of units such as customers, salespeople, organizations, or market areas.

Dichotomous Question A structured question that offers just two answer choices.

Direct Observation Observation that involves looking at a phenomenon rather than the phenomenon's consequences.

Discriminant Analysis A technique for generating a linear combination of independent variables (called a discriminant function) in such a way that values on it (called discriminant scores) are similar for sample units within prespecified subgroups and are maximally separated across the subgroups. The prespecified subgroup categories make up the categorical dependent variable in discriminant analysis.

Discriminant Validity A form of construct validity that represents the extent to which a measured construct is *not* associated with measures of other constructs with which the measured construct is not expected to be related on theoretical grounds.

Disguised Observation Observation in which respondents are unaware they are being observed.

Disguised Question An indirect question whose true purpose is not obvious to respondents.

Disproportionate Stratified Random Sampling A stratified-random-sampling procedure in which the number of units chosen from each stratum is based on the degree of variability within it. The more heterogeneous a stratum, the larger is the sample chosen from it.

Double-Barreled Question A question that raises several separate issues but only provides one set of responses.

Dual-Moderator Group A type of focus group in which there are two moderators, one responsible for ensuring the smooth flow of the session and the other responsible for ensuring that key issues get discussed.

Dueling-Moderator Group A variation of the dual-moderator focus group. The two moderators in a dueling-moderator group deliberately take opposite positions on the discussion topic so as to stimulate a lively and potentially revealing exchange of views among the participants.

Dummy Variable A variable that takes on a value of either 1 or 0. Categorical variables that normally would not be included in certain analysis procedures (e.g., regression analysis) can be included in such procedures after converting the variables into a set of dummy variables. A categorical variable with k categories will require $k - 1$ dummy variables to represent it.

Editing The process of examining completed questionnaires and taking whatever corrective action is needed to ensure that the data are of high quality.

Eigenvalue A term used in factor analysis; it represents the total standardized variance in the original data set accounted for by a factor. Each extracted factor will have an eigenvalue in the factor analysis output.

End Piling A phenomenon wherein most responses fall into just a few categories at one end of a measurement scale.

Expected Value of Decision Making With Imperfect Information The expected payoff to a decision maker who commissions a less-than-perfect research project, observes the research outcome, and chooses the best course of action corresponding to that outcome.

Expected Value of Imperfect Information The value obtained by subtracting the expected value under uncertainty from the expected value of decision making with imperfect information; this value represents the monetary worth of a proposed research project that is less than perfect.

Expected Value of Perfect Information The value obtained by subtracting the expected value under uncertainty from the expected value under certainty; this value represents the maximum amount a decision maker should be willing to pay for any research aimed at reducing uncertainty in a situation.

Expected Value Under Certainty The expected payoff to a decision maker who commissions a perfect research project, observes the research outcome, and chooses the best course of action corresponding to that outcome.

Expected Value Under Uncertainty The maximum expected payoff to a decision maker who chooses a course of action under uncertainty.

Experiment A procedure in which one (or sometimes more than one) causal variable is systematically manipulated and data on the effect variable are gathered, while controlling for other variables that may influence the effect variable.

Experimental Research (Causal Research) A form of conclusive research that is intended to generate the type of evidence necessary for confidently making causal inferences about relationships between variables.

Exploratory Research Research intended to develop initial hunches or insights and to provide direction for any further research needed.

External Marketing Research Research conducted by a firm with the aid of suppliers such as commercial marketing research firms and consultants.

External Secondary Data Data available from a source outside an organization for which a project is being conducted.

External Validity The extent to which results observed in an experiment are likely to hold beyond the experimental setting.

Eye-Tracking Equipment A device used in some mechanical-observation studies to ascertain which sections of a stimulus (e.g., an ad, product packaging, special display) respondents look at and how much time they spend looking at those sections.

Factor Analysis A technique that analyzes data on a relatively large set of variables and produces a smaller set of factors, which are linear combinations of the original variables, so that the set of factors captures as much information as possible from the original data set.

Factorial Design An experimental-study design in which two or more independent (causal) variables are manipulated simultaneously.

Factor Loading A term used in factor analysis; it represents the Pearson correlation coefficient between an original variable and a factor.

Factor Score A term used in factor analysis; it represents the value for a sample unit on a given factor and is obtained by substituting the sample unit's values on the original variables into the linear combination representing the factor.

Field Experiment A research study conducted in a natural setting in which one or more independent variables are manipulated by the experimenter under as carefully controlled conditions as the situation will permit.

Field Service Firm A data gathering firm that caters to research suppliers as well as in-house marketing research departments.

Filter Question A question meant to qualify respondents for a subsequent question or to ensure that the question is within their realm of experience.

Final Edit (Office Edit) A thorough examination of all completed questionnaires done in the office; it involves verifying response consistency and accuracy, making necessary corrections, and deciding whether some or all parts of a questionnaire should be discarded.

Focus Group Interview A setting in which respondents (typically about 8 to 12) discuss a given topic in a fairly informal fashion in the presence of a well-trained, objective moderator.

Forced-Choice Scale A scale that does not give respondents the option of expressing a neutral opinion.

Funnel Sequence An ordering of questions that begins with a very general question on a topic and gradually leads up to a narrowly focused question on the same topic.

Galvanic Skin Response (GSR) Meter A device for measuring changes in electrical resistance of the skin caused by changes in amount of perspiration.

Graphic Rating Scale A continuous scale, presented in the form of a straight line, along which a theoretically infinite number of response choices are possible.

Histogram A two-dimensional bar chart used for graphically displaying the absolute or relative frequency of occurrence of values pertaining to a variable. The variable values are plotted along the horizontal axis, and their frequencies of occurrence are plotted along the vertical axis.

History Effect A bias that occurs because of specific external events or occurrences during an experiment (e.g., changes in competitors' marketing mixes) that are likely to affect the dependent variable.

Ideal Population The collection of units most pertinent for the study; it is the population to which generalizations from the study should be desired.

Implied Population The collection of units to which any generalization from the actual sample obtained in a study is restricted.

Independent Variable (Explanatory or Predictor Variable) A variable in multivariate analysis that is presumed to influence a dependent variable. It is conventionally plotted along the *X*-axis in a scatter diagram.

Indirect Observation Observation that involves looking at the results or consequences of a phenomenon rather than directly observing the phenomenon itself.

Inferential Analysis Data analysis that goes beyond descriptive analysis; it involves verifying specific statements or hypotheses about the population(s).

Information The product of analysis and interpretation of data.

Information Consultant An individual with special skills pertaining to effective secondary-data management.

In-House Marketing Research Research conducted by a firm's own marketing research department or employee(s) in charge of marketing research.

Instrument Variation Effect A bias in experimental studies that relates to differences between pretest and posttest measurements owing to changes in the instruments (questionnaires) and/or procedures used to measure the dependent variable.

Interdependence Technique A multivariate analysis procedure in which there are no dependent- and independent-variable designations; all variables are treated equally in a search for underlying patterns of relationships (e.g., factor analysis, cluster analysis).

Internal Secondary Data Data available from a source within an organization for which a project is being conducted.

Internal Validity The extent to which results observed in an experiment are solely due to the experimental manipulation.

Interval Scale A set of numbers in which the differences (but not ratios) between numbers can be meaningfully interpreted.

Inverted-Funnel Sequence An ordering of questions that begins with very specific questions on a topic and moves on to more general questions on the same topic.

Itemized Rating Scale A scale that has a finite set of distinct response choices.

Judgment Sampling (Purposive Sampling) A nonprobability-sampling procedure in which a researcher exerts some effort in selecting a sample that he or she feels is most appropriate for a study.

Key-Informant Technique (Expert-Opinion Survey) Conducting exploratory research by seeking out and talking to individuals with expertise in areas related to the situation being investigated.

Kolmogorov-Smirnov Test A nonparametric test to check whether the observed distribution of sample data on an ordinal-scaled variable is consistent with an expected distribution. This test is similar to the chi-square goodness-of-fit test, except that it requires ordinal data.

Laboratory Experiment A research study conducted in a contrived setting in which the effect of all, or nearly all, possible influential independent variables not pertinent to the immediate problem is kept to a minimum.

Latin-Square Design An experimental-study design in which two blocking factors are employed simultaneously. In this design the number of levels of each blocking factor must be the same as the number of treatments.

Leading Question (Loaded Question) A question that tends to steer respondents toward a certain answer, irrespective of what their true answers are.

Least-Squares Approach An analysis procedure widely used in deriving a regression equation that is the best-fitting equation for a given set of data on dependent and independent variables.

Likert Scale A multiple-item scale consisting of a series of evaluative statements concerning an issue or object; responses to each statement are provided on a five-point, agree-disagree scale.

Line Chart A two-dimensional graph typically used to show movements in one or more items over time.

Longitudinal Study A repeated-measurement study involving data collection at several periods in time.

Mail Survey A questionnaire administration method in which there are no interviewers and no direct contact between the researcher and respondent.

Marketing Concept The philosophy of customer orientation urging firms to uncover customer needs first and then coordinate all their activities to satisfy those needs.

Marketing Decision Support System A marketing information system that permits managers to interact with it and request special types of data analyses or reports on an as-needed basis.

Marketing Information System A continuing and interacting structure of people, equipment, and procedures designed to gather, sort, analyze, evaluate, and distribute pertinent, timely, and accurate information to marketing decision makers.

Marketing Mix The set of product, promotion, price, and distribution (or place) decisions related to a firm's market offering.

Marketing Research A set of techniques and principles for systematically collecting, recording, analyzing, and interpreting data that can aid decision makers who are involved with marketing goods, services, or ideas.

Marketing Research Ethics Standards that govern the marketing research profession.

Matching A procedure used in certain experimental studies to form groups of units in such a way that the group compositions are similar with respect to some specific characteristic(s).

Maturation Effect A bias that occurs because of the impact on the dependent variable of physiological or physical changes in units participating in an experiment.

Mean A measure of central tendency that represents the simple average of a set of numbered responses.

Measurement The quantification of observations or responses by assigning numbers to them according to a given set of rules.

Mechanical Observation Observation in which mechanical or electronic devices (as opposed to human observers) are used to collect data.

Median A measure of central tendency that represents the category in which the 50th percentile response falls when all responses are arranged from lowest to highest (or vice versa).

Metric Data Data having interval- or ratio-scale properties.

Missing-Value Category A response category used to code questions for which answers should have been obtained but were not for some reason.

Mode A measure of central tendency that represents the most frequently occurring response category.

Mortality Effect A bias that occurs when certain participating units drop out of an experiment, and, as a result, the set of units completing the experiment significantly differs from the original set of units.

Motivation Research Research intended to uncover inner feelings and motives that people are unable or unwilling to reveal when questioned directly.

Multicollinearity A condition wherein two or more independent variables in a multiple regression equation are highly correlated.

Multidimensional Scaling A technique for inferring the number and the nature of dimensions underlying respondent evaluations/perceptions on the basis of similarity and/or preference judgments provided by respondents about objects (e.g., companies, products, brands).

Multiple-Category Question A structured question that offers more than two fixed-response choices.

Multiple Correlation Coefficient A measure of the overall degree of association between dependent and independent variables in a regression equation; it is simply the square root of the coefficient of determination (R^2).

Multiple-Item Scale A scale that consists of two or more questions pertaining to the construct it is intended to measure.

Multivariate Analysis Any procedure in which the focus is on analyzing data on two or more variables simultaneously.

Natural Observation A data collection approach in which events and/or behaviors are observed as they occur naturally.

Nominal Scale A set of numbers in which the numbers serve solely as identification labels.

Noncomparative Rating Scale A scale that seeks respondents' feelings about an issue/object without providing any frame of reference with which to compare the issue/object.

Nondisguised Observation Observation in which respondents are aware they are being observed.

Nonforced-Choice Scale A scale that gives respondents the option of expressing a neutral opinion.

Nonmetric Data Data having only nominal- or ordinal-scale properties.

Nonparametric Procedures Analysis techniques and hypothesis tests that are appropriate when the data are nonmetric (i.e., nominal or ordinal).

Nonprobability Sampling A subjective-sampling procedure in which the probability of selection for each population unit is unknown beforehand.

Nonrepresentative-Sample Bias A bias that occurs in

experimental studies when the participating units are not representative of the larger body of units to which the results are to be generalized.

Nonresponse Error A bias that occurs when the final sample differs in a systematic way from the planned sample; that is, when respondents and nonrespondents differ significantly on one or more critical characteristics.

Nonsampling Error Any error in a research study other than sampling error (which arises purely because a sample, rather than the entire population, is studied).

Nonstructured Observation Observation in which everything of relevance is observed and recorded in an open-ended fashion.

Not-at-Home Problem A potential source of nonresponse error; it is serious when respondents who are not at home when the interviewer makes contact differ significantly from those who are at home.

Observation A primary-data collection approach in which respondents play little or no active role in terms of interacting with the data gatherer.

Omnibus Panel A panel that serves as a ready source of samples for a variety of cross-sectional studies over time.

One-Sided Question A form of leading question that presents only one aspect of an issue for which respondents' reactions are being sought.

One-Stage Area Sampling A form of area sampling in which a few subareas are chosen at random and all the units in the chosen subareas are studied.

One-Tailed Test A hypothesis test in which values of the test statistic leading to rejection of the null hypothesis fall only in one tail of the sampling distribution curve.

One-Way Table A table showing the frequency distribution of data pertaining to categories of a single variable.

Open-Ended Question A question that respondents are free to answer in their own words.

Operational Definition A definition that describes a construct in terms of how it is to be measured.

Ordinal Scale A set of numbers in which the magnitudes of the numbers represent no more than a rank ordering.

Original Source A term used in the context of secondary data; it refers to the source that actually collects the data.

Paired-Comparison Rating Scale A scale that seeks comparative evaluations of two issues/objects at a time.

Panel A fixed group of units recruited to provide measurements over a period of time.

Panel Conditioning A bias that occurs when multiple-survey participation by panel members, over a period of time, induces them to alter their natural or usual behavior.

Parameter A summary measure based on data from all units in a given population.

Parametric Procedures Analysis techniques and hypothesis tests that are appropriate only when the data are metric (i.e., interval or ratio).

Payoff Table A table summarizing the net profits (or losses) under various possible combinations of decision alternatives and market states.

Pearson Correlation Coefficient (Pearson Product-Moment Correlation) An index (varying between -1 and $+1$) that measures the nature and the degree of association between two metric-scaled (interval or ratio) variables.

Periodicity Any cyclical pattern with respect to a relevant characteristic in a population list used in systematic sampling. The statistical efficiency of systematic sampling will be lowered when the periodicity coincides with the sampling interval, a multiple of the sampling interval, or an integral fraction of the sampling interval.

Personal Interview A questionnaire administration method in which the interviewer and respondent have face-to-face contact.

Pictogram A special type of bar chart that uses pictures of the items instead of the customary rectangular bars.

Pie Chart A circle divided into several slices whose areas are proportionate to the quantities to be represented on the chart.

Plus-One Dialing A method of reducing sampling frame error in telephone surveys; it involves adding a fixed integer (usually 1) to each telephone number chosen from a phone book so as to obtain a revised number to be dialed.

Point Estimate A dependent-variable value predicted by using a regression equation.

Population (Universe) The entire body of units of interest to decision makers in a situation.

Posterior Probabilities A set of revised probabilities for the various market states or conditions, contingent upon a particular research outcome being observed.

Power The probability that a hypothesis-testing procedure will lead to rejection of a null hypothesis that is false. Power is 1 minus the probability of committing a Type II error, which is represented by the symbol β; that is, power = $1 - \beta$.

Precision Level A measure of the degree of compactness of a confidence interval. The narrower the confidence interval, the higher the precision level is.

Prediction Error The difference between the actual value of a dependent variable and its estimated value obtained by using a regression equation.

Prediction Interval A confidence interval constructed around a point estimate (for the dependent variable) generated by a regression equation.

Predictive Validity A scale evaluation criterion representing how well a measured construct is able to predict some other variable or characteristic it is supposed to influence.

Preexperimental Design An experimental design that offers little or no control over the influence of extraneous factors and hence is not much better than a descriptive-research design when it comes to making causal inferences.

Preliminary Edit (Field Edit) A quick examination of completed questionnaires in the field, usually on the same day they are filled out.

Pretesting An important stage in the questionnaire refinement process, prior to finalizing the questionnaire; it involves administering the questionnaire to a limited number of potential respondents and other knowledgeable individuals in order to identify and correct design flaws.

Pretesting Effect A bias in experimental studies that occurs when responses given during a later measurement are influenced by those given during a previous measurement, regardless of what happens between the measurements.

Pretest-Manipulation Interaction Bias A bias that arises when the premeasurement increases or decreases respondents' sensitivity to the experimental manipulation.

Primary Data Data collected specifically for a project.

Prior Probability The probability that a particular market state or condition exists, based purely on the subjective feelings of a decision maker.

Probability-Proportional-to-Size Area Sampling A form of two-stage area sampling in which the probabilities of selection for the subareas in the first stage are adjusted to be proportional to the number of second-stage units in each.

Probability Sampling An objective-sampling procedure in which the probability of selection is known in advance for each population unit.

Projective Technique A nonstructured, disguised form of questioning in which a fairly ambiguous stimulus is presented to respondents, who are then asked to react to or describe the stimulus.

Proportionate Stratified Random Sampling A stratified-random-sampling procedure in which the number of units chosen from each stratum is proportional to its size; the more the number of units in a stratum, the larger is the sample chosen from it.

Pseudoresearch Research requested by managers for reasons other than aiding their decision making.

Pupillometer A device for measuring the extent of pupil dilation in response to a visual stimulus.

Qualitative Research A form of exploratory research involving small samples and nonstructured data collection procedures.

Quantitative Research A form of conclusive research involving large representative samples and fairly structured data collection procedures.

Quasi-Experimental Design An experimental design that does not offer as much control as a true experimental design but usually provides more measurements and more information than a typical preexperimental design.

Questioning (Communication) A primary-data collection approach in which respondents play an active role owing to their interaction with the data gatherer.

Questionnaire An instrument used for eliciting and recording responses in many, but not all, research projects employing the questioning approach.

Question with Implicit Assumptions A question that does not provide or imply the same frame of reference to all respondents.

Quota Sampling A nonprobability-sampling procedure in which (1) the population is divided into cells on the basis of relevant control characteristics, (2) a quota of sample units is established for each cell, and (3) interviewers are asked to fill the quotas assigned to the various cells.

Random Assignment A procedure used in experimental studies to form groups of units in such a way that the group compositions can be considered to be equivalent in all respects. This term also refers to assigning experimental treatments randomly to the various groups.

Random-Digit Dialing A method of reducing sampling frame error in telephone surveys; it involves randomly dialing the last four digits of telephone numbers within any exchange specified by a three-digit prefix.

Randomized-Block Design An experimental study design in which (1) the study units are divided into blocks, wherein each block is homogeneous (i.e., has units that are matched on some relevant characteristic) and contains as many units as there are treatments, and (2) the units within each block are randomly assigned to the treatments.

Random Sampling An objective procedure for selecting a representative sample of units for a study.

Ratio Scale A set of numbers in which the ratios between numbers can be meaningfully interpreted.

Raw Variable A variable that is directly measured by the data in a questionnaire.

Reactive Bias A bias that occurs in experimental studies when participants exhibit abnormal or unusual behavior simply because they are participating in an experiment.

Regression Analysis A technique that generates a mathematical function or equation linking one dependent variable with one or more independent variables.

Reliability A criterion for evaluating measurement scales; it represents how consistent or stable the ratings generated by a scale are.

Research Continuum A line or dimension along which conclusive research projects can be arrayed, with "purely descriptive with no control" at one extreme and "purely experimental with strict control and manipulation" at the other.

Research Subject (Respondent) An individual from and/or about whom data are gathered.

Research Supplier A commercial marketing research firm that provides information to a client firm.

Respondent Refusal Problem A potential source of nonresponse error; it is serious when respondents who refuse to participate in a study differ significantly from those who agree to participate.

Response Category Sequence Rotation The process of varying from respondent to respondent the order in which response choices to a multiple-category question are presented.

Response Latency The speed with which a respondent provides an answer.

Response Rate The percentage of units in the planned sample for a study that actually participated in the study.

Sampling The process of selecting a fraction of the total number of units of interest to decision makers for the ultimate purpose of being able to draw general conclusions about the entire body of units.

Sampling Distribution A representation of sample statistic values—obtained from every conceivable sample of a certain size chosen from a population by using a specified sampling procedure—along with the relative frequency of occurrence of those statistic values.

Sampling Error A measure of the difference between a statistic value that is generated through a sampling procedure and the parameter value, which can only be determined through a census study.

Sampling Frame A list or collection of population units from which the sample for a study is chosen.

Sampling Frame Error A bias that occurs when the population as implied by the sampling frame differs in a systematic fashion from the ideal population.

Sampling Interval The size of the gap between units chosen from a population list by using a systematic-sampling procedure.

Scatter Diagram A two-dimensional graph in which data on two metric-scaled (interval or ratio) variables are plotted.

Secondary Data Data collected for some purpose other than the research situation.

Secondary-Data Management Creating and operating a system for continuously monitoring various secondary-data sources and quickly retrieving needed data.

Secondhand Source A term used in the context of secondary data; it refers to a source that uses data collected by an original source to generate its own summaries, interpretations, and the like.

Selection Effect A bias that occurs when multiple groups participating in an experiment differ on characteristics that have a bearing on the dependent variable.

Semantic-Differential Scale A multiple-item scale consisting of a series of bipolar adjectival words or phrases pertaining to an issue or object; responses to each pair of opposite adjectives are provided on a seven-category scale separating the adjectives (with no intermediate numerical or verbal labels).

Sensitivity A criterion for evaluating measurement scales; it represents the extent to which ratings provided by a scale are able to discriminate between respondents who differ with respect to the construct being measured.

Sentence Completion Test A nonstructured, disguised form of questioning in which respondents are asked to finish a set of incomplete sentences. A typical sentence completion test is given to a group of respondents who are asked to finish the sentences in writing.

Shopper Study A study in which a professional interviewer plays the role of a customer and gathers relevant data (through questioning as well as observation) on issues of interest.

Shopping Mall Intercept Interview A form of personal interviewing in which respondents are intercepted in shopping malls and interviewed.

Significance Level Represented by the symbol α; it is the maximum probability of rejecting a true null hypothesis when one is conducting a hypothesis test; it is the maximum probability of committing a Type I error.

Simple Cluster Sampling A probability-sampling procedure in which (1) the population is divided into subpopulations, or clusters, (2) a simple random sample of clusters is selected, and (3) all units in the selected clusters are studied.

Simple Random Sampling A probability-sampling procedure in which every possible sample of a certain size within a population has a known and *equal* probability of being chosen as the study sample.

Simulated Test Market A hybrid experimental approach involving a laboratory setting that imitates real market conditions as much as possible.

Single-Item Scale A scale that consists of just one question pertaining to the construct it is intended to measure.

Skewed Response Distribution A one-way table in which a large proportion of responses are piled up toward one end of the range of data obtained.

Slope The regression coefficient (b-value) corresponding to an independent variable in a regression equation; it represents the change in the predicted value of the dependent variable per one-unit change in the independent variable, assuming all other variables likely to influence the dependent variable remain the same.

Spearman Correlation Coefficient An index (varying between -1 and $+1$) that measures the nature and the degree of association between two ordinal variables.

Split-Ballot Technique A procedure wherein (1) the study sample is split into two equivalent halves and (2) a different version of the same questionnaire (e.g., different sequencing of questions) is administered to each half.

Split-Half Reliability An indicator of the degree of consistency across ratings produced by items within a multiple-item scale.

Standard Deviation A measure of dispersion of a set of numbered responses from their mean.

Standard Error An indicator of the extent of sampling error; it represents the standard deviation of sample statistic values that will be obtained through repeated sampling from a population by using the same procedure.

Standard Error of the Regression An indicator of the dependent-variable variance left unexplained by the independent variable(s) in the equation; it can be viewed as a standard deviation of the prediction errors made by the regression equation.

Stapel Scale A multiple-item scale consisting of a series of words or phrases pertaining to an issue or object; responses to each item are provided on a 10-category scale containing numerical labels for the categories.

Statistic A summary measure based on data from a sample of units.

Statistical Design A term used to denote an experimental design that measures the relative effectiveness of multiple levels of one or more independent variables and requires somewhat complex data analysis procedures.

Statistical Efficiency A measure of how good a sampling procedure is in terms of the sampling error associated with it. One sampling procedure is statistically more efficient than another if for a given sample size it results in a smaller sampling error.

Stratified Random Sampling A probability-sampling procedure in which (1) the population is divided into homogeneous strata on the basis of some appropriate characteristic and (2) a random sample of units is chosen from each stratum to make up the total sample.

Stratum Chart A two-dimensional graph with time along the horizontal axis and containing a series of distinct strata, or layers, stacked in the vertical direction. Each stratum represents a particular item, and at any given time the width of the stratum indicates the relative magnitude of the item at that time.

Structured Observation Observation in which the data gathered pertain to discrete, clearly defined events or behaviors and are therefore recorded by merely making entries or checking off categories on an appropriate observation form.

Syndicated Data (Syndicated Services) Secondary data generated by research suppliers on a regular basis and sold to many clients.

Syndicated Source A firm that offers syndicated data or services.

Systematic Error Any error that is not random; that is, any error that results in a definite upward or downward bias in the estimates obtained from a study.

Systematic Sampling A probability-sampling procedure in which (1) a sampling interval *k* is determined as the ratio of population size to desired sample size, (2) one unit between the first and *k*th units in the population list is chosen randomly, and (3) every *k*th unit thereafter in the list is chosen.

Telephone Survey A questionnaire administration method in which there is only voice contact between the interviewer and respondent.

Test Marketing A form of field experiment for assessing a market's reactions to a new product and its associated marketing mix.

Test-Retest Reliability An indicator of the stability of ratings produced by a scale over time.

Test Statistic A term used in the context of hypothesis testing; it represents a standard variable whose value is computed from sample data and compared with a critical value (obtained from an appropriate probability table) to decide whether or not to reject the null hypothesis.

Thematic Apperception Test (TAT) A nonstructured, disguised form of questioning in which respondents are shown a series of pictures, one at a time, and are asked to write a story about each.

Total Error The combination of sampling and nonsampling errors in a study.

Transformed Variable A variable that is created by combining or modifying data on one or more raw variables.

True Experimental Design An experimental design that has built-in safeguards for controlling all, or almost all, threats to internal and external validity.

True Panel A panel participating in a longitudinal study involving measurement of the same sample units, with respect to the same variables, over time.

Two-Stage Area Sampling A form of area sampling that involves random selection at two stages: (1) in selecting a sample of subareas and (2) in selecting a sample of units from each chosen subarea.

Two-Tailed Test A hypothesis test in which values of the test statistic leading to rejection of the null hypothesis fall in both tails of the sampling distribution curve.

Two-Way Table A table showing the number of responses in each category of one variable falling into the categories of a second variable.

Type I Error A mistake that occurs in a hypothesis test when a true null hypothesis is rejected.

Type II Error A mistake that occurs in a hypothesis test when a false null hypothesis is not rejected.

Unbalanced Scale A scale in which a majority of the choices favor one side of the issue being probed.

Unbiased Estimate A sample statistic whose average value (over repeated samples) coincides with the population parameter it is intended to estimate.

Univariate Analysis Any procedure in which the focus is on analyzing data on just one variable.

Validity A criterion for evaluating measurement scales; it represents the extent to which a scale is a true reflection of the underlying variable or construct it is attempting to measure.

Voice Pitch Analysis (VOPAN): A technique for assessing how much emotional commitment is attached to a respondent's verbal answers; it involves measuring the voice pitch of verbal responses during an interview and comparing it with the respondent's normal voice pitch during routine conversation about neutral topics.

Word Association Test A nonstructured, disguised form of questioning in which respondents are asked to express the first word that comes to mind in response to each word on a list of words. In a typical word association test the words are read aloud, one at a time, to each respondent.

***Y*-Intercept** The constant a in a regression equation; it represents the predicted value of the dependent variable when all independent variables are set to zero.

Index